CIVIL LITIGATION

CIVIL LITIGATION

Kevin Browne LLB, Solicitor

Margaret J Catlow BA (Law), Solicitor

Published by

College of Law Publishing
Braboeuf Manor, Portsmouth Road, St Catherines, Guildford GU3 1HA

British Library Cataloguing-in-Publication Data
A catalogue record for this book is available from the British Library.

ISBN: 978 1 915469 05 2

Typeset by Style Photosetting Ltd, Mayfield, East Sussex
Tables and index by Moira Greenhalgh, Arnside, Cumbria

Preface

This book has been written as a tool for learning about civil procedure in England and Wales. In it we examine the practical issues that arise, from the start of a case until its ultimate conclusion, whether that is by settlement, court judgment or otherwise.

We have divided up the civil process into five stages. But it is important to remember that each stage cannot be learnt in isolation from the others. We urge anyone using this book to make frequent reference to the overview of the five stages at **1.3** and the flow diagram at **Appendix C(1)**. These will serve as a reminder of the various steps and how one part fits into the whole process.

In this edition we have incorporated developments in ADR orders, e-filing of documents, service of a claim form, time extensions, sanctions, costs management, the summary assessment of costs, summary judgment, repayment of an overpaid interim payment, security for costs orders, specific disclosure, the parties' disclosure obligations, witness statements, expert evidence and expert's fees, pre-action Part 36 offers, mistakes in Part 36 offers, cross-examination at trial and solicitors' guideline hourly rates.

New cases in this edition include *Benyatov v Credit Suisse Securities (Europe) Ltd* [2022] (costs), *LSREF 3 Tiger Falkirk Ltd I SARL v Paragon Building Consultancy Ltd* [2021] (service of claim form), *Jalla v Shell International Trading and Shipping Co Ltd* [2021] (time extensions), *Bailey v Barclays Bank UK Public Ltd Co* [2021] (Part 20), *Rapid Displays Inc v Ahkye* [2022] (sanctions), *Elias v Blemain Finance Ltd* [2021] (allocation), *Discovery Land Company, LLC v Axis Specialty Europe SE* [2021] (costs management), *Changing Climates Ltd v Warmaway Ltd* [2021] (summary assessment), *Brown v Fisk* [2021] and *Rolfe v Veale Wasbrough Vizards LLP* [2021] (summary judgment), *Wakefield v NJS* [2021] (interim payment), *Infinity Distribution Ltd (in administration) v Khan Partnership LLP* [2021], *Rowe v Ingenious Media Holdings plc* [2021] and *Tulip Trading Ltd v Bitcoin Association for BSV (a Swiss verein)* [2022] (security for costs), *Sheeran v Chokri* [2021] (specific disclosure), *Ayannuga v One Shot Products Ltd* [2021] (disclosure obligations), *Prime London Holdings 11 Ltd v Thurloe Lodge Ltd* [2022] and *Various Airfinance Leasing Companies v Saudi Arabian Airlines Corporation* [2021] (witness statements), *Radia v Marks* [2022], *Robinson v Liverpool University Hospital NHS Foundation Trust and Dr Mercier* [2021] and *Griffiths v Tui (UK) Ltd* [2021] (expert evidence), *Loggie v Loggie* [2022] (expert's fees), *The Huntsworth Wine Company Ltd v London City Bond Ltd* [2022] (pre-action Part 36 offers), *Reader v SPIE Ltd* [2021] (pre-trial Part 36 offers), *O'Grady v B15 Group Ltd* [2022] (mistakes in Part 36 offers), *Equitix Eeef Biomass 2 Ltd v Fox* [2021] (Part 36 enhanced interest) and *R (on the application of the Good Law Project) v Minister for the Cabinet Office* [2022] (cross-examination).

KEVIN BROWNE AND MARGARET J CATLOW
The University of Law
London

Contents

PREFACE   v

TABLE OF CASES   xiii

TABLE OF STATUTES   xxi

TABLE OF SECONDARY LEGISLATION   xxiii

TABLE OF ABBREVIATIONS   xxv

Chapter 1	INTRODUCTION TO CIVIL LITIGATION	1
	1.1 The Woolf and Jackson reforms	1
	1.2 The Rules	5
	1.3 An overview of a civil claim	5
	1.4 Case analysis	9
	1.5 Useful websites	11

Chapter 2	CONSIDERATIONS AT THE FIRST INTERVIEW INCLUDING FUNDING THE CLAIM	13
	2.1 Introduction	13
	2.2 Purpose of the first interview	14
	2.3 Professional conduct	14
	2.4 Funding	16
	2.5 Case analysis	24
	2.6 Viability and burden of proof	27
	2.7 Interest	29
	2.8 Foreign element and choice of forum	32
	2.9 Alternatives to litigation	33

Chapter 3	EARLY ACTION	37
	3.1 Writing to the client	38
	3.2 Interviewing witnesses	38
	3.3 Preserving documents	40
	3.4 Obtaining expert evidence	41
	3.5 Site visits	42
	3.6 Instructing counsel	43
	3.7 Pre-action protocols	44
	3.8 Pre-action correspondence	46
	3.9 Pre-action disclosure	49
	3.10 Settlement	50
	3.11 Researching the law	52
	3.12 Cost–benefit analysis	52
	3.13 Summary of pre-action steps	52
	3.14 Summary of Practice Direction on Pre-Action Conduct and Protocols	53

Chapter 4	ALTERNATIVE DISPUTE RESOLUTION	55
	4.1 The nature of ADR	55
	4.2 Advantages of ADR	56
	4.3 Disadvantages of ADR	57
	4.4 Types of ADR	59
	4.5 Organisations providing ADR	61
	4.6 Using ADR	62
	4.7 Choosing ADR	62

Chapter 5	COMMENCING PROCEEDINGS	65
	5.1 Choice of court	65

	5.2	Court personnel	68
	5.3	Issuing proceedings	68
	5.4	Parties to the proceedings	73
	5.5	Service of the claim form	77
	5.6	Extending time for service of the claim form	83
	5.7	Service of documents other than the claim form	84
	5.8	Service of particulars of claim	85
Chapter 6		RESPONDING TO PROCEEDINGS AND JUDGMENT IN DEFAULT	87
	6.1	Introduction	87
	6.2	Computation of time	88
	6.3	Acknowledgement of service (Part 10)	88
	6.4	The defence (Part 15)	90
	6.5	Admissions (Part 14)	91
	6.6	Default judgments (Part 12)	93
Chapter 7		STATEMENTS OF CASE	97
	7.1	Introduction	97
	7.2	Contents of the particulars of claim	102
	7.3	The defence	112
	7.4	Reply to defence	115
	7.5	The role of statements of case	115
	7.6	Amendments to statements of case (Part 17)	117
	7.7	Requests for further information (Part 18)	119
	7.8	Summary: how should you approach drafting particulars of claim?	121
	7.9	Summary: how should you approach drafting a defence?	122
Chapter 8		ADDITIONAL PROCEEDINGS AND PART 8 CLAIMS	125
	8.1	Introduction	125
	8.2	Procedure	126
	8.3	Drafting a counterclaim	129
	8.4	Part 8 claims	130
Chapter 9		CASE MANAGEMENT AND ALLOCATION OF CASES	133
	9.1	Introduction	133
	9.2	The court's powers	133
	9.3	Striking out a statement of case and other sanctions	134
	9.4	Relief from sanctions	137
	9.5	Allocation	138
	9.6	Allocation to a track	142
	9.7	Costs management	152
	9.8	Overview of multi-track case and costs management	157
Chapter 10		APPLICATIONS TO THE COURT	159
	10.1	Introduction	159
	10.2	Applications generally	159
	10.3	Interim costs	163
	10.4	Appeals against an interim order	166
	10.5	Particular types of application	167
	10.6	Interim remedies (Part 25)	174
	10.7	Interim payments	175
	10.8	Security for costs (r 25.12)	178
Chapter 11		DISCLOSURE AND INSPECTION OF DOCUMENTS – CPR 1998, PART 31	183
	11.1	Purpose of disclosure and inspection	183
	11.2	Definition of 'disclosure' (r 31.2) and 'documents' (r 31.4)	184
	11.3	Disclosure on each track	185
	11.4	Standard disclosure (r 31.6)	186
	11.5	Disclosure of copies (r 31.9)	188

	11.6	The duty to search (r 31.7)	188
	11.7	The right of inspection (r 31.3)	189
	11.8	Procedure for standard disclosure	189
	11.9	The disclosure statement	190
	11.10	Continuing obligation (r 31.11)	191
	11.11	Withholding inspection	191
	11.12	Disclosing the existence of documents: the list	197
	11.13	Failure to disclose (r 31.21)	198
	11.14	Subsequent use of disclosed documents (r 31.22)	198
	11.15	Applying for specific disclosure (r 31.12)	198
	11.16	Disclosure before proceedings start (r 31.16)	199
	11.17	Non-party disclosure (r 31.17)	199
	11.18	Disclosure obligations and solicitors' duties	200
	11.19	Inspection of standard disclosure documents	201
	11.20	Disclosure pilot scheme in the Business and Property Courts (PD 51U)	201
Chapter 12		EVIDENCE	205
	12.1	Introduction	205
	12.2	Witness evidence	207
	12.3	Form of witness statements	208
	12.4	Use of witness statements at trial	211
	12.5	Witness summaries (r 32.9)	211
	12.6	Sanctions for not serving a witness statement (r 32.10)	212
	12.7	Affidavits	213
	12.8	Opinion evidence	213
	12.9	Hearsay evidence	214
	12.10	Use of plans, photographs and models as evidence (r 33.6)	221
	12.11	Notice to admit facts (r 32.18)	222
	12.12	Notice to admit or prove documents (r 32.19)	222
	12.13	Expert evidence (Part 35)	222
	12.14	Professional negligence cases: the defendant's own evidence	231
	12.15	Assessors (r 35.15)	231
Chapter 13		SETTLEMENT	233
	13.1	Negotiations	233
	13.2	Pre-action settlements	234
	13.3	Settlements reached after the issue of proceedings	234
	13.4	Part 36	237
	13.5	Claims involving children and protected parties	255
	13.6	Discontinuance (Part 38)	256
Chapter 14		FINAL PREPARATIONS FOR TRIAL, TRIAL AND ASSESSMENT OF COSTS	257
	14.1	Final preparations for trial	257
	14.2	Trial	261
	14.3	Costs	266
Chapter 15		ENFORCEMENT OF MONEY JUDGMENTS	281
	15.1	Introduction	281
	15.2	Interest on judgment debts	282
	15.3	Tracing the other party	282
	15.4	Investigating the judgment debtor's means	283
	15.5	Methods of enforcement	284
	15.6	Summary of key points	291
Appendix A		COURT FORMS, PROTOCOLS AND GUIDELINES	293
	A(1)	Forms N1 and N1A – Claim Form and Notes for Claimant	295
	A(2)	Form N1C – Notes for Defendant on Replying to the Claim Form	301
	A(3)	Form N9, including Forms N9A–N9D – Response Pack	303
	A(4)	Form N215 – Certificate of Service	312

A(5)	Form N218 – Notice of Service on Partner	314
A(6)	Form N266 – Notice to Admit Facts	315
A(7)	Form N181 – Directions Questionnaire	316
A(8)	Appendix to Part 28	322
A(9)	Precedent H – Costs Budget and Guidance Notes	325
A(10)	Precedent R – Budget Discussion Report	336
A(11)	Form N263 – Disclosure Report	337
A(12)	Form N244 – Application Notice	338
A(13)	Form N260 – Statement of Costs for Summary Assessment	343
A(14)	Form N242A – Offer to Settle	348
A(15)	Form N170 – Pre-trial Checklist	353
A(16)	Form N252 – Notice of Commencement of Assessment of Bill of Costs	356
A(17)	Precedent S – Bill of Costs	357
A(18)	Precedent G – Points of Dispute	363
A(19)	Practice Direction – Pre-action Conduct and Protocols	365
A(20)	Professional Negligence Pre-action Protocol	368
A(21)	Guidance for the Instruction of Experts in Civil Claims 2014	373
A(22)	Guideline figures for the Summary Assessment of Costs	382
A(23)	Precedent T – Variation of Costs Budget	385
A(24)	Precedent Q – Model form of breakdown of the costs claimed for each phase of the proceedings	387
Appendix B	**TEMPLATES FOR DRAFTING KEY DOCUMENTS**	**389**
B(1)	Letter Before Claim under Practice Direction on Pre-action Conduct	391
B(2)	Letter of Claim under Professional Negligence Pre-action Protocol	393
B(3)	Particulars of Claim (Separate from Claim Form)	395
B(4)	Defence	396
B(5)	Defence and Counterclaim	397
B(6)	Case Summary for Use at a Multi-track Case Management Conference	398
B(7)	Directions Order: Drafting	399
B(8)	Directions Order: Key CPR Provisions	403
B(9)	Standard Disclosure List of Documents	408
B(10)	Witness Statement	410
B(11)	Hearsay Notice	411
B(12)	Expert's Report	412
B(13)	Part 36 Offer Letter	414
B(14)	Case Summary for Use at a Fast Track Trial	415
B(15)	Case Summary for Use at a Multi-track Trial ('Skeleton Argument')	416
Appendix C	**FLOW DIAGRAMS**	**419**
C(1)	Overview of the Five Stages of Litigation	421
C(2)	Steps under Practice Direction on Pre-action Conduct	422
C(3)	Steps under Professional Negligence Pre-action Protocol	423
C(4)	Interest	424
C(5)	Determining Jurisdiction under Regulation 1215/2012	425
C(6)	Possible Responses by Defendant to a Claim	426
C(7)	Table 1 – Admission of Claim in Whole but Request Time to Pay	427
C(8)	Table 2 – Admission of Part of Claim – Specified Amount	428
C(9)	Table 3 – File Acknowledgement of Service	429
C(10)	Table 4 – Default Judgment	430
C(11)	Possible Costs Orders on Setting Aside a Default Judgment	431
C(12)	Possible Costs Orders on Claimant's Application for Summary Judgment	432
C(13)	Consequences of Claimant Accepting Defendant's Part 36 Offer within Relevant Period	433
C(14)	Consequences of Defendant Accepting Claimant's Part 36 Offer within Relevant Period	434
C(15)	Consequences of Claimant Accepting Defendant's Part 36 Offer after Relevant Period has Expired	435
C(16)	Consequences of Defendant Accepting Claimant's Part 36 Offer after Relevant Period has Expired	436

C(17)   Consequences of Claimant Failing to Obtain Judgment More Advantageous than
Defendant's Part 36 Offer   437

C(18)   Consequences of Claimant Failing to Establish Liability at Trial and so not Obtaining
Judgment More Advantageous Than Defendant's Part 36 Offer   438

C(19)   Consequences of Claimant Obtaining Judgment at Least as Advantageous as Own
Part 36 Offer   439

C(20)   Consequences of Claimant Obtaining Judgment More Advantageous Than Defendant's
Part 36 Offer but not as Advantageous as Own Part 36 Offer   440

C(21)   The Standard Basis of Assessment of Costs   441

Appendix D   CASE STUDY DOCUMENTS   443

D(1)   Case Analysis   445
D(2)   Letter Before Claim   448
D(3)   Defendant's Letter of Response   450
D(4)   Particulars of Claim   453
D(5)   Defence and Counterclaim   455
D(6)   Reply and Defence to Counterclaim   457
D(7)   Defendant's Part 18 Request for Information   459
D(8)   Case Summary for Use at Case Management Conference   460
D(9)   Order for Directions   462
D(10)   Claimant's List of Documents   465
D(11)   Witness Statement of Marjorie Trudge   468
D(12)   Experts' Without Prejudice Meeting Statement   470
D(13)   Claimant's Part 36 Offer Letter   472
D(14)   Defendant's Brief to Counsel   473
D(15)   Consent Order   476

INDEX   477

Table of Cases

A

A v B [2019] EWHC 275 (Comm) — 231
Ablitt v Mills & Reeve (solicitors) and Norwich Union (1995) The Times, 25 October — 195
Ackerman v Ackerman [2012] 3 Costs LO 303 — 179
AF v BG [2009] EWCA Civ 757 — 255
Agents' Mutual Ltd v Gascoigne Halman Ltd [2019] EWHC 3104 (Ch) — 189
Agents' Mutual Ltd v Halman [2016] CAT 21 — 155
Akram v Adam [2004] EWCA Civ 1601, (2004) The Times, 29 December — 169
Alex Lawrie Factors Ltd v Morgan, Morgan and Turner (1999) The Times, 18 August — 209
Ali v Channel 5 Broadcast Ltd [2018] EWHC 840 (Ch) — 238, 255
Allen v Bloomsbury Publishing Ltd [2011] EWCA Civ 943 — 182
Anderson v Bank of British Columbia (1876) 2 Ch D 644 — 194
Aoun v Bahri [2002] EWHC 29 (Comm), [2002] CLC 776 — 179
Arena Property Services Ltd v Europa 2000 Ltd [2003] EWCA Civ 1943 — 99
Arkin v Borchard Lines Ltd [2005] EWCA Civ 655 — 22
Arrow Nominees Inc v Blackledge [2000] 1 BCLC 709 — 135
Arroyo v BP Exploration Co (Colombia) Ltd [2010] LTL, 4 June (QBD) — 192
Atos Consulting Ltd v Avis plc (No 2) [2007] EWHC 323 (TCC) — 195
AXA Insurance Co Ltd v Swire Fraser (2000) The Times, 19 January — 136
Ayannuga v One Shot Products Ltd [2021] EWHC 2930 (QB) — 200

B

Bailey v Barclays Bank UK Public Ltd Co [2021] EWHC 3698 (QB) — 127
Bailey v GlaxoSmithKline [2019] EWCA Civ 1924 — 206
Ball v Ball [2020] EWHC 1020 (Ch) — 131
Ballard v West Sussex Partnership NHS Foundation Trust [2018] EWHC 370 (QB) — 241
Bank of Scotland Plc v Watson [2013] EWCA Civ 6 — 119
Barclays Bank plc v O'Brien [1994] 1 AC 180 — 209
Barks v Instant Access Properties Ltd (In Liquidation) [2013] EWHC 114 — 170
Baron v Lovell [1999] CPLR 630 — 149
Barton v Wright Hassall LLP [2018] UKSC 12 — 80
Bates v Microstar Ltd [2000] LTL, 4 July — 173
Bayat Telephone Systems International Inc v Cecil [2011] EWCA Civ 135 — 84
BE v DE [2014] EWHC 2318 (Fam) — 51
Beathem v Carlisle Hospitals NHS Trust (1999) The Times, 20 May — 74
Benyatov v Credit Suisse Securities (Europe) Ltd [2022] WL 00509179 — 17
Bestford Developments LLP v Ras Al Khaimah Investment Authority [2016] EWCA Civ 1099 — 178
BGC Brokers LP v Tradition (UK) Ltd [2019] EWCA Civ 1937 — 196
Biguzzi v Rank Leisure plc [1999] 1 WLR 1926 — 135
Bim Kemi AB v Blackburn Chemicals Ltd [2003] EWCA Civ 889 — 267
Black v Arriva North East Ltd [2014] EWCA Civ 1115 — 165
Blankley v Central Manchester and Manchester Children's University Hospitals NHS Trust [2015] EWCA Civ 18 — 73
Bloomsbury Publishing Group Plc v News Group Newspapers Ltd [2003] 1 WLR 1633 — 76
Briggs v CEF Holdings Ltd [2018] Costs 123 — 243
Brit Inns Ltd v BDW Trading Ltd [2012] EWHC (TCC) — 268
British Airways v Spencer [2015] EWHC 2477 (Ch) — 222
British and Commonwealth Holdings plc v Quadrex Holdings Inc [1989] 3 WLR 723 — 177
British Gas Trading Ltd v Oak Cash & Carry Ltd [2016] EWCA Civ 153 — 137, 138
Brookes v Harris [1995] 1 WLR 918 — 285
Brown v AB [2018] EWHC 623 (QB) — 99
Brown v Fisk [2021] EWHC 2769 (QB) — 171
Brown v Mujibal [2017] 4 WLUK 42 — 219
Bulkhaul Ltd v Rhodia Organique Fine Ltd [2008] EWCA Civ 1452 — 26
Burrells Wharf Freeholders Ltd v Galliard Homes Ltd [1999] 2 EGLR 81 — 50
Business Finance Ltd v Bellagio Hospitality WB Ltd [2019] EWHC 1920 (QB) — 260

C

C v D [2011] EWCA Civ 646   238, 241
Cable & Wireless v IBM UK Ltd [2002] BLR 89   57
Callery v Gray [2001] EWCA Civ 1246   45
Calonne Construction Ltd v Dawnus Southern Ltd [2019] EWCA Civ 754   239
Cameron v Liverpool Victoria Insurance Co Ltd [2019] UKSC 6   75
Campbell v Ministry of Defence [2019] EWHC 2121 (QB)   243
Carrasco v Johnson [2018] EWCA Civ 87   32
Carver v BAA plc [2008] EWCA Civ 412   253
Cavendish Square Holdings BV v Tala El Makdessi [2013] LTL, 13 February   121
Celador Productions Limited v Melville [2004] EWHC 2362 (Ch), [2004] LTL, 26 October   171
Chandler v Brown [2001] CP Rep 103   179
Changing Climates Ltd v Warmaway Ltd [2021] EWHC 3117 (TCC)   164
Chapman v Tameside Hospital NHS Foundation Trust (Bolton County Court, 15 June 2016)   268
Childs v Vernon [2007] EWCA Civ 305, [2007] LTL, 16 March   230
Churchill v Boot [2016] EWHC 1322 (QB)   154
Civil Aviation Authority v R (on the application of Jet2.com Ltd) [2020] EWCA Civ 35   191
Cowan v Foreman [2019] EWCA Civ 1336   5
Cundall Johnson and Partners LLP v Whipps Cross University Hospital NHS Trust [2007] EWHC 2178   45
Cutts v Head [1984] Ch 290   51

D

Daniels v Walker [2000] 1 WLR 1382   230
Darbishire v Warran [1963] 1 WLR 1067   26
David Truex, Solicitor (a firm) v Kitchin [2007] EWCA Civ 618   23
Davies Solicitors LLP v Rajah [2015] EWHC 519 (QB)   138
Davies v Eli Lilly & Co [1987] 1 WLR 428   183
Denton v TH White Ltd [2014] EWCA Civ 906   137, 167
Depp v News Group Newspapers Ltd & Another [2020] EWHC 1689 (QB)   186
Digicel (St Lucia) Ltd v Cable and Wireless PLC [2010] EWHC 888 (Ch)   271
Director of the Serious Fraud Office v Eurasian Natural Resources Corporation (ENRC) Ltd [2018] EWCA Civ 2006   193
Diriye v Bojaj [2020] EWCA Civ 1400   78
Discovery Land Company, LLC v Axis Specialty Europe SE [2021] EWHC 2146 (Comm)   155
DN v London Borough of Greenwich [2004] EWCA Civ 1659   231
Douglas v Hello! Ltd [2004] EWHC 63 (Ch)   267
Downing v Peterborough & Stamford Hospitals NHS Foundation Trust [2014] EWHC 4216 (QB)   243
DSN v Blackpool Football Club Ltd [2020] EWHC 670 (QB)   273
Dubai Islamic Bank v PSI Energy Holding Co [2011] EWCA Civ 761   179
Dunhill (a protected party by her litigation friend Paul Tasker) v Burgin [2014] UKSC 18   74
Dunnett v Railtrack plc (in Railway Administration) [2002] EWCA Civ 303, [2002] 2 All ER 850   272
Durrant v Chief Constable of Avon and Somerset Constabulary [2013] EWCA Civ 1624   138

E

Earl of Malmesbury v Strutt & Parker [2008] EWHC 424   273
Earles v Barclays Bank Plc [2009] EWHC 2500   198
Elias v Blemain Finance Ltd [2021] EW Misc 15 (CC) per HHJ Keyser QC   143
EMI Records Ltd v Kudhail [1985] FSR 35   76
Ennis Property Finance Ltd v Thompson [2017] EWHC 3263 (Ch)   197
Equitix Eeef Biomass 2 Ltd v Fox [2021] EWHC 2781 (TCC)   250
Evans v Trebuchet Design Ltd [2020] EWHC 3037 (IPEC)   234
Excelsior Commercial and Industrial Holdings Ltd v Salisbury Hammer Aspden and Johnson [2002] EWCA Civ 879   245
EXP v Barker [2017] EWCA Civ 63   226

F

Factortame v Secretary of State [2002] EWCA Civ 22   254
Faidi v Elliott Corporation [2012] EWCA Civ 287   59
Farrar v Beswick (1836) 1 M & W 682   286
Farrington v Menzies-Haines [2019] EWHC 1297 (QB)   177
Favor Easy Management Ltd v Wu [2010] EWCA Civ 1630   187
Feltham v Bourskell [2013] EWHC 3086 (Ch)   254
Fernhill Mining Ltd v Kier Construction Ltd [2000] CPLR 23   180
Field v Leeds City Council [2000] 1 EGLR 54   223
Fifield v Denton Hall Legal Services [2006] EWCA Civ 169   219

Findcharm Ltd v Churchill Group Ltd [2017] EWHC 1108 (TCC)   153
Fiona Trust and Holding Corp v Privalov [2016] EWHC 2657 (Comm)   267
Ford v GKR Construction Ltd [2000] 1 WLR 1397   253
Forster v Outred & Co [1982] 2 All ER 753   25
Frost v Knight (1872) LR 7 Ex 111   26
FZO v Adams [2019] EWHC 1286 (QB)   251

G

G (a protected party by his litigation friend SX) v Hassan [2019] 6 WLUK 441   219
Gama Aviation (UK) Ltd v Taleveras Petroleum Trading DMCC [2019] EWCA Civ 119   173
Gardiner and Theobald LLP v Jackson (Valuation Officer) [2018] UKUT 253 (LC)   223
Garratt v Saxby [2004] LTL, 18 February   255
Gentry v Miller [2016] EWCA Civ 141   168
Gibbon v Manchester City Council [2010] EWCA Civ 726   240
Gibbons v Wall (1988) The Times, 24 February   177
Goldtrail Travel v Onur Air [2017] 1 WLR 3014   180
Goodwin v Avison [2021] EWHC 2754 (Ch)   272
Grant v Dawn Meats (UK) [2018] EWCA Civ 2212   95
Griffiths v Tui (UK) Ltd [2021] EWCA Civ 1442   226

H

Habib Bank Ltd v Abbeypearl Ltd [2001] EWCA Civ 62, [2001] 1 All ER 185   135
Hale v Watt, LTL 11 March 2016, CA   285
Halsey v Milton Keynes General NHS Trust [2004] EWCA Civ 576, [2004] 4 All ER 920   33, 272
Hammersmatch Properties (Welwyn) Ltd v Saint-Gobain Ceramics and Others [2013] EWHC 2227 (TCC)   267
Hannigan v Hannigan [2000] 2 FCR 650   3
Hardy Exploration & Production (India) Inc v Government of India [2018] EWHC 1916 (Comm)   288
Harlow v Aspect Contracts Ltd [2020] EWHC 1488 (TCC)   214
Harris v Wallis [2006] EWHC 630 (Ch)   179
Hegglin v Person(s) Unknown & Google Inc [2014] EWHC 3793   165
Hirschon v Evans [1938] 2 KB 801   288
Hochester v de la Tour (1853) 2 E & B 678   24
Hochtief (UK) Construction Ltd and another v Atkins Ltd [2019] EWHC 3028 (TCC)   254
Hoist UK Ltd v Reid Lifting Ltd [2010] EWHC 1922   256
Hotel Portfolio II UK Ltd (In Liquidation) v Ruhan [2020] 1 WLUK 232   180
Hughes v Alan Dick & Co Ltd [2008] EWHC 2695   169
Hunt v Caddick (Mill Harbour) Ltd [2019] EWHC 2933   50
Hunt v RM Douglas (Roofing) Ltd [1990] 1 AC 398   266
Huntley v Simmonds [2009] EWHC 406   253
Huscroft v P & O Ferries Ltd [2011] 2 All ER 762   182
Hussain v Woods and Another [2001] Lloyd's Rep PN 134   172
Hussein v Birmingham City Council [2005] EWCA Civ 1570   168

I

IBM Corporation v Phoenix International (Computers) Ltd [1995] 1 All ER 413   195
Icon SE LLC v SE Shipping Lines Pte Ltd [2012] EWCA Civ 1790   198
Intellimedia Systems Ltd v Richards (2017) LTL 3/2/2017   154
InterDigital Technology Corp v Nokia Corp [2008] EWHC 504   120
Inventors Friend Ltd v Leathes Prior (a firm) [2011] EWHC 711   17
Involnert Management Inc v Aprilgrange Ltd and others [2015] EWHC 2834 (Comm)   266

J

Jalla and another v Shell International Trading and Shipping Co Ltd and another [2021] EWCA Civ 1559   91
James v James [2018] EWHC 242 (Ch)   52
Jaura v Ahmed [2002] EWCA Civ 210   32
JD Wetherspoon plc v Harris (Practice Note) [2013] EWHC 1088 (Ch)   207, 225
JIH v News Group Newspapers Ltd [2011] EWCA Civ 42   265
Jirehouse Capital v Beller [2008] EWHC 725 (Ch)   179
JLE v Warrington & Halton Hospitals NHS Foundation Trust [2019] EWHC 1582 (QB)   254
Jones v Kaney [2011] UKSC 13   223
Jordan v MGN Ltd [2017] EWHC 1937 (Ch)   244
JSC Mezhdunarodniy Promyshlenniy Bank v Pugachev [2017] EWHC 1853 (Ch)   154

K

Kaines (UK) Ltd v Osterreichische [1993] 2 Lloyd's Rep 1   31
Kajala v Noble (1982) 75 Cr App R 15   220
Khader v Aziz [2010] EWCA Civ 716   260
Kiam v MGN Ltd [2002] 1 WLR 2810   245
Kimathi v The Foreign and Commonwealth Office [2018] EWHC 2066 (QB)   99
King v City of London Corporation [2019] EWCA Civ 2266   239
Kirschel & Others v Fladgate Fielder (a firm) [2000] LTL, 22 December   171
Kommalage v Sayanthakumar [2015] EWCA Civ 1832   75
Kooh Veisin Trading Co v Parsai [2013] LTL, 11 February   173
Kunaka v Barclays Bank Plc [2010] EWCA Civ 1035   243
Kuwait Airways Corporation v Kuwait Insurance Company SAK [2001] LTL, 16 June   31

L

L'Oreal and Others v eBay International AG and Others [2008] EWHC B13 (Ch)   236
Lederer v Kisby [2019] EWHC 554 (Ch)   180
Lejonvarn v Burgess [2020] EWCA Civ 114   246
Lewis v Denye [1939] 1 KB 540   29
Leyvand v Barasch (2000) The Times, 23 March   181
LG Blower Specialist Bricklayer Ltd v Reeves [2010] EWCA Civ 726   240
Lilleyman v Lilleyman (judgment on costs) [2012] EWHC 1056 (Ch)   254
Lindsay v Wood [2006] EWHC 2895 (QB)   73
Linklaters LLP v Mellish [2019] EWHC 177 (QB)   80
Little Olympian Each-Ways Ltd, Re [1994] 4 All ER 561   178
Liverpool Victoria Insurance Company Ltd v Zafar [2019] EWCA Civ 39   223
Locke v Camberwell Health Authority [1991] 2 Med LR 249   44
Loggie v Loggie [2022] EWFC 2   230
Lokhova v Longmuir [2017] EWHC 3152 (QB)   244
Lomax v Lomax [2019] EWCA Civ 1467   34, 60
Lonestar Communications Corp LLC v Kaye & Ors [2019] EWHC 3008 (Comm)   81
Loveridge v Healey [2004] EWCA Civ 173, (2004) The Times, 27 February   100
LSREF 3 Tiger Falkirk Ltd I SARL and another v Paragon Building Consultancy Ltd [2021] EWHC 2063 (TCC)   80
Lucas v Barking, Havering and Redbridge Hospitals NHS Trust [2003] EWCA Civ 1102   224
Lumb v Hampsey [2011] EWHC 2808   244

M

M A Lloyd & Sons Ltd (t/a KPM Marine) v PPC International Ltd (t/a Professional Powercraft) [2014] EWHC 41 (QB) 213
Maltez v Lewis (1999) The Times, 4 May   2
Marathon Asset Management LLP v Seddon [2017] EWHC 479 (Comm)   246
Marchment v Frederick Wise Ltd [2015] EWHC 1770 (QB)   138
Mars UK Ltd v Teknowledge Ltd (No 2) [1999] Masons CLR 322   268, 279
Masquerade Music Ltd v Springsteen [2001] EWCA Civ 563   220
Mastercigars Direct Ltd v Withers LLP [2009] EWHC 651   17
Matthews v Metal Improvements Co Inc [2007] EWCA Civ 215   254
Mayr and others v CMS Cameron McKenna Nabarro Olswang LLP [2018] EWHC 3669 (Comm)   227
McPhilemy v Times Newspapers Limited [1999] 3 All ER 775   98
McPhilemy v Times Newspapers Ltd (No 2) [2001] EWCA Civ 933, [2001] 4 All ER 861   250
Meadow v General Medical Council [2006] EWCA Civ 1390   223
Mealey Horgan plc v Horgan (1999) The Times, 6 July   182
Media Entertainment NV v Karyagdyev [2020] EWHC 1138 (QB)   103
MEF (A Protected Party, by his Mother and Litigation Friend, FEM) v St George's Healthcare NHS Trust
    [2020] EWHC 1300 (QB)   51
Meridian Global Funds Management Asia Limited v Securities Commission [1995] 2 AC 500 (PC)   113
Mid-East Sales v United Engineering and Trading Co (PVT) Ltd [2014] EWHC 1457   168
Miller v Sutton (Court of Appeal, 14 February 2013)   134
Mitchell v Precis 548 Ltd [2019] EWHC 3314 (QB)   259
Mohammed v Home Office [2017] EWHC 3051 (QB)   249
Momonakaya v Ministry of Defence [2019] EWHC 480 (QB)   244
Morgan v Spirit Group Ltd [2011] EWCA Civ 68   275
Morley t/a Morley Estates v Royal Bank of Scotland plc [2019] EWHC 2865 (Ch)   212
Morris v Wentworth-Stanley [1999] QB 1004   6
Moylett v Geldof [2018] EWHC 893 (Ch)   231
Muller v Linsley & Mortimer [1996] PNLR 74   196

Mumtaz Properties Ltd, The Matter of v Ahmed [2011] EWCA Civ 610   207
Murphy v Staples UK Limited [2003] 3 All ER 129   79
Murray v Neil Dowlman Architecture Ltd [2013] EWHC 872 (TCC)   153
Mustard v Flower [2019] EWHC 2623 (QB)   226
MV Yorke Motors v Edwards [1982] 1 All ER 1024   173
Myers v Elman [1940] AC 282   201

N

Nanglegan v Royal Free Hampstead NHS Trust [2001] EWCA Civ 127, [2001] 3 All ER 793   84
Nash v 4MA Ltd [2019] EWHC 3383 (TCC)   134
Necati v Commissioner of Police for the Metropolis [2001] LTL, 19 January   135
New Media Distribution Company Sezc Ltd v Kagalovsky [2018] EWHC 2742 (Ch)   214, 225
New York Laser Clinic Ltd v Naturastudios Ltd [2019] LTL 14 Feb (CA)   118
Nigel Witham Ltd v Smith [2008] EWHC 12   273
Noorani v Calver (No 2/Costs) [2009] EWHC 592   256
Northrop Grumman Missions Systems Europe Limited v BAE Systems (Al Diriyah C41) Ltd
    [2014] EWHC 3148 (TCC)   267, 273
Nugee LJ in Infinity Distribution Ltd (in administration) v Khan Partnership LLP [2021] EWCA Civ 565   180

O

O'Brien v Chief Constable of South Wales Police [2005] UKHL 26, (2005) The Times, 29 April   205
O'Grady v B15 Group Ltd [2022] EWHC 67 (QB)   242
Oceanbulk Shipping & Trading SA v TMT Asia Ltd [2010] UKSC 44   51
Ofulue v Bossert [2009] AC 990   51
Ohpen Operations UK Ltd v Invesco Fund Managers Ltd [2019] EWHC 2246 (TCC)   57
Olatawura v Abiloye [2003] 1 WLR 275   182
OMV Petrom SA v Glencore International AG [2017] EWCA Civ 195   250
Onassis v Vergottis [1968] 2 Lloyds Rep 403 at 431   207
Onay v Brown [2009] EWCA Civ 775   238
Otuo v Watch Tower Bible and Tract Society of Britain [2019] EWHC 346 (QB)   212
Owners of the Gravity Highway v Owners of the Maritime Maisie [2020] EWHC 1697 (Comm)   121

P

Pacific Biosciences of California, Inc v Oxford Nanopore Technologies Ltd [2018] EWHC 806 (Ch)   121
Pallet v MGN Ltd [2021] EWHC 76 (Ch)   243
Papa Johns (GB) Ltd v Doyley [2011] EWHC 2621   213
Peacock v MGN Ltd [2009] EWHC 769   165
Pearce v Ove Arup Partnership [2001] LTL, 8 November   223
Peet v Mid-Kent Healthcare Trust (Practice Note) [2001] EWCA Civ 1703, [2002] 3 All ER 688   230
Percy v Merriman White [2021] EWHC 22 (Ch)   44
Peskin v Anderson and Others [2001] 1 BCLC 372   172
PGF II SA v OMFS Company 1 Ltd [2013] EWCA Civ 1288   272
Phi Group Limited v Robert West Consulting Limited [2012] EWCA Civ 588   238
Piemonte v Dexia Crediop SpA [2014] EWCA Civ 1298   168
Porter Capital Corp v Zulifkar Masters & Others [2020] 7 WLUK 441   152
Portland Stone Firms Ltd v Barclays Bank Plc [2018] EWHC 2341 (QB)   99
Practice Statement (Alternative Dispute Resolution) (No 2) [1996] 1 WLR 1024   56
Premier Motorauctions Ltd v PWC LLP [2017] EWCA Civ 1872   180
Prime London Holdings 11 Ltd v Thurloe Lodge Ltd [2022] EWHC 79 (Ch)   209
Proton Energy Group SA v Orlen Lietuva [2013] EWHC 2872 (Comm)   223
Puharic v Silverbond Enterprises Ltd [2021] EWHC 351 (QB)   102

Q

Quah Su-Ling v Goldman Sachs International [2015] EWHC 759 (Comm)   118

R

R (on the application of Banks Renewables Ltd) v Secretary of State for Business, Energy & Industrial Strategy
    [2020] 2 WLUK 99   225
R (on the application of Network Rail Infrastructure Ltd) v Secretary of State for the Environment, Food and
    Rural Affairs [2017] EWHC 2259 (Admin)   260
R (on the application of Prudential Plc) v Special Commissioner of Income Tax [2013] UKSC 1   192
R (on the application of the Good Law Project) v Minister for the Cabinet Office [2022] EWCA Civ 21   264
R v London Borough of Barnet [1983] 2 AC 309   178

Radia v Marks [2022] EWHC 145 (QB)   223
Raiffeisen Bank International AG v Asia Coal Energy Ventures Ltd and Ashurst LLP [2020] EWCA Civ 11   192
Rajval Construction Ltd v Bestville Properties Ltd [2010] EWCA Civ 1621   169
Rapid Displays Inc v Ahkye [2022] EWHC 274 (Comm)   138
Rawbank SA v Travelex Banknotes Ltd [2020] EWHC 1619 (Ch)   255
Rea v Rea [2022] EWCA Civ 195   263
Reader v SPIE Ltd [2021] EWHC 1221 (QB)   240
Redbourn Group Ltd v Fairgate Development Ltd [2017] EWHC 1223 (TCC)   168
Reid Minty v Taylor [2002] WLR 2800   271
Reynolds v Stone Rowe Brewer [2008] EWHC 497   17
Robinson v Liverpool University Hospital NHS Foundation Trust and Dr Mercier (2021) Law Society Gazette,
    3 November   223
Rogers and Callery v Gray (No 2) [2001] EWCA Civ 1246   270
Rogers v Hoyle [2014] EWCA Civ 257   230
Rogers v Merthyr Tydfil CBC [2006] EWCA Civ 1134   20
Rolf v De Guerin [2011] EWCA Civ 78   272, 273
Rolfe v Veale Wasbrough Vizards LLP [2021] EWHC 2809 (QB)   172
Rowe v Ingenious Media Holdings plc [2021] EWCA Civ 29   182
Royal Brompton Hospital NHS Trust v Hammond & Others [2000] LTL, 4 December   97
Rush & Tomkins Ltd v Greater London Council [1989] 1 AC 1280   196

S

Sang Kook Suh v Mace (UK) Ltd [2016] EWCA Civ 4   51
Sarpd Oil International Limited v Addax Energy SA [2016] EWCA Civ 120   179
Sarwar v Alam [2001] EWCA Civ 1401, [2002] 1 WLR 125   18, 22
Satwinder Kaur v CTP Coil Ltd [2000] LTL, 10 July   83
Satyam Enterprises Ltd v Burton [2021] EWCA Civ 287   98
Scarlett v Grace [2014] EWHC 2307 (QB)   212
Scott Paper Co v Drayton Paper Works Ltd (1927) 44 RPC 151, 156   51
Secretary of State for Business Enterprise and Regulatory Reform v Aaron [2009] Bus LR 809   230
Secretary of State for Health v Norton Healthcare Ltd and Others [2004] LTL, 25 February   171
Secretary of State for Transport v Pell Frischmann Consultants Ltd [2006] EWHC 2756   199
Seekings v Moores [2019] EWHC 1476 (Comm)   154
Sempra Metals Ltd v Inland Revenue Commissioners [2007] UKHL 34   32
SG v Hewitt [2012] EWCA Civ 1053   244
Shah v Ul-Haq [2009] EWCA Civ 542   268
Sharp v Blank [2017] EWHC 3390 (Ch)   154
Sheeran v Chokri [2020] EWHC 2806 (Ch)   121
Sheeran v Chokri [2021] EWHC 3553 (Ch)   199
Sinclair v Chief Constable of West Yorkshire and Another [2000] LTL, 12 December   172
Skatteforvaltningen v Solo Capital Partners LLP (In Special Administration) [2020] EWHC 1624 (Comm)   209
Smith v Probyn (2000) The Times, 29 March   79
Smith v Trafford Housing Trust [2012] EWHC 3320 (Ch) at [13]   243, 254
Société Générale v Goldas Kuyumculuk Sanayi Ithalat Ihracat AS [2018] EWCA Civ 109   80, 84
SPI North Ltd v Swiss Post International (UK) Ltd [2019] EWCA Civ 7   113
St Helens Metropolitan BC v Barnes [2006] EWCA Civ 1372   24
Stallwood v David [2006] EWHC 2600   228
Standard Bank Plc v Agrinvest International Inc [2010] EWCA Civ 1400   167
Starbev GP Ltd v Interbrew Central European Holding BV [2013] EWHC 4038 (Comm)   192
Stephen Hawking and others v Secretary of State for Health & Social Care and National Health Service
    Commissioning Board [2018] EWHC 989 (Admin)   165
Sternberg Reed Solicitors v Andrew Paul Harrison [2019] EWHC 2065 (Ch)   51
Stevens v Gullis [1999] BLR 394   223
Straker v Tudor Rose (a firm) [2007] EWCA Civ 368   45
Stringman v McArdle [1994] 1 WLR 1653   177
Stroh v London Borough of Haringey [1999] LTL, 13 July   213
Swain Mason v Mills & Reeve [2012] EWCA Civ 498   58
Swain v Hillman [2001] 1 All ER 91   170
Sweetman v Shepherd (2000) The Times, 29 March   173

T

Tarajan Overseas Ltd v Kaye (2002) The Times, 22 January   150
Tate & Lyle Food and Distribution Ltd v Greater London Council [1982] 1 WLR 149   31

Taylor Wimpey UK Ltd v Harron Homes Ltd [2020] EWHC 1190 (TCC)   199
TBD (Owen Holland) Ltd v Andrew Simons & Others [2020] 2 WLUK 311   181
Tchenguiz v Grant Thornton UK LLP [2015] EWHC 405 (Comm)   98
Teasdale v HSBC Bank Plc [2010] EWHC 612   256
Tejani v Fitzroy Place Residential Ltd [2020] EWHC 1856 (TCC)   100
Telecom Centre (UK) Ltd v Thomas Sanderson Ltd [2020] EWHC 368 (QB)   60
Telefonica UK Ltd v The Office of Communications [2020] EWCA Civ 1374   252
Thakkar v Patel [2017] EWCA Civ 117   273
The Huntsworth Wine Company Ltd v London City Bond Ltd [2022] EWHC 98 (Comm)   238
Thimmaya v Lancashire NHS Foundation Trust (Manchester County Court, 30 January 2020)   223
Thomas v Home Office [2006] EWCA Civ 1355   84
Three Rivers DC v Governor and Company of the Bank of England [2005] EWCA Civ 889   261
Three Rivers DC v Governor of the Bank of England [2006] EWHC 816 (Comm)   271
Three Rivers District Council and Others v Governor and Company of the Bank of England (No 3 bis)
    [2001] 2 All ER 513, HL   171
Three Rivers District Council and Others v Governor and Company of the Bank of England [2004] UKHL 48,
    [2004] 3 WLR 1274   192
Tidal Energy Ltd v Bank of Scotland plc [2014] EWCA Civ 847   165
Tideland Ltd v Westminster City Council [2015] EWHC 2710 (TCC)   167
Tombstone Ltd v Raja [2008] EWCA Civ 1444   260
Toth v Jarman [2006] EWCA Civ 1028, [2006] 4 All ER 1276   226
Travis Perkins Trading Co Ltd v Caerphilly CBC [2014] EWHC 1498 (TCC)   69
Trebisol Sud Ouest SAS v Berkley Finance Ltd [2021] EWHC 2494 (QB)   236
Truscott v Truscott, Wraith v Sheffield Forgemasters [1998] 1 WLR 132   277
Tseitline v Mikhelson [2015] EWHC 3065 (Comm)   78
Tulip Trading Ltd v Bitcoin Association for BSV (a Swiss verein) [2022] EWHC 141 (Ch)   182

U

UCB Corporate Services Ltd v Halifax (SW) Ltd [1999] 1 Lloyd's Rep 154   136
UK Learning Academy Ltd v Secretary of State for Education [2020] EWCA Civ 370   97

V

Various Airfinance Leasing Companies v Saudi Arabian Airlines Corporation [2021] EWHC 3509 (Comm) 212
Verslot Dredging BV v HDI Gerling Vesicherung AG [2013] LTL   181
Vik v Deutsche Bank AG [2018] EWCA Civ 2011   284
Vinos v Marks & Spencer plc [2001] 3 All ER 784   83

W

W Nagel (a firm) v Pluczenik Diamond Company NV [2019] EWHC 3126 (QB)   283
Wakefield v NJS [2021] EWHC 3452 (QB)   178
Walayat v Berkeley Solicitors Ltd [2021] EWHC 227 (Ch)   127
Warner v Masefield [2008] EWHC 1129   77
Wates Construction Ltd v HGP Greentree Alchurch Evans Ltd [2006] BLR 45   246
Watts v Morrow [1991] 1 WLR 1421   31
Waugh v British Railways Board [1980] AC 521   193
Webb Resolutions Ltd v Waller Needham & Green (a firm) [2012] EWHC 3529 (Ch)   244
Webb v Liverpool Women's NHS Foundation Trust [2015] EWHC 449 (QB)   269
Weir v Hildson [2017] EWHC (Ch) 983   262
West v Stockport NHS Foundation Trust [2019] EWCA Civ 1220   270
WH Holding Ltd v E20 Stadium LLP (No 2) [2018] EWCA Civ 2652   193
Widlake v BAA Ltd [2009] EWCA Civ 1256   268
Williams v Jervis [2009] EWHC 1837 (QB)   271
Williams v Secretary of State for Business, Energy and Industrial Strategy [2018] EWCA Civ 852 268
Woods v Martin's Bank [1959] 1 QB 55   201
Woodward v Phoenix Healthcare Distribution Ltd [2018] EWHC 2152 (Ch)   3
Woodward v Phoenix Healthcare Distribution Ltd [2019] EWCA Civ 985   79
Woolley v Essex CC [2006] EWCA Civ 753   230
Wormald v Ahmed [2021] EWHC 973 (QB)   256

X

X v Y [2020] 11 WLUK 6   74
Xhosa Office Rentals Ltd v Multi High Tec PCB Ltd [2012] EWHC 3673   181
XXX v Camden London Borough Council [2020] EWCA Civ 1468   69

Z

Zenith Logistics Services (UK) Ltd & Others v Coury [2020] EWHC 774 (QB)   236
Zuberi v Lexlaw Ltd [2021] EWCA Civ 16   22

Table of Statutes

Arbitration Act 1996 33, 57, 60
  s 66 33, 58
  s 70(6) 179

Banking and Financial Dealings Act 1971 313

Children Act 1989
  s 96(2) 265
Civil Evidence Act 1972
  s 3(1) 42, 214, 223
  s 3(2) 213
Civil Evidence Act 1995 216, 259
  s 1 216
  s 1(2)(a) 214
  s 2 216
  s 2(1)(a) 216, 411
  s 2(4) 217, 218
  s 3 219
  s 4 217, 218, 219, 264
  s 5 219
  s 6 219–20
  s 8 220
  s 13 214
Civil Procedure Act 1997
  s 7 174
Companies Act 1985
  s 691 300
  s 744 300
Companies Act 2006
  s 1139(1) 79
Consumer Credit Act 1974 93, 284
County Courts Act 1984 356
  s 52 49, 174
  s 53 175
  s 69 29, 30, 31, 32, 93, 94, 99, 103, 234, 245, 266, 424
  s 74 282
Courts and Legal Services Act 1990
  s 58 18
  s 58(2)(a) 18
  s 58A 18
  s 58AA(3)(a) 20
  s 58AA(4) 20
  s 58B 22
Criminal Justice and Courts Act 2015
  s 88 165
  s 88(6) 165

Data Protection Act 2013
  s 169 172

Human Rights Act 1998 70, 105, 296
  s 4 77

Judgments Act 1838 282, 356
  s 17 250, 266

Late Payment of Commercial Debts (Interest) Act 1998 29, 30, 93, 99, 103, 105, 234, 266, 424
Limitation Act 1980 13, 24, 100
  s 2 24, 25
  s 5 24, 25
  s 14A 25
  s 14B 25

Mental Capacity Act 2005 25, 73
Mental Health Act 1983 300

Occupiers' Liability Act 1957 129, 474

Partnership Act 1890
  s 23 282

Road Traffic Act 1988 34
  s 151 171, 176

Sale of Goods Act 1979 99, 110
  s 14(2) 100
Senior Courts Act 1981
  s 33 49, 174
  s 34 175
  s 35A 29, 30, 31, 32, 93, 94, 99, 103, 109, 130, 234, 266, 424
  s 51 136
Social Security (Recovery of Benefits) Act 1997 350
Supply of Goods and Services Act 1982 99
  s 4(2) 10
  s 13 10

Torts (Interference with Goods) Act 1977
  s 4 174

Value Added Tax Act 1994 358

International legislation
European Convention on Human Rights 1950
  Art 6(1) 135, 180
  Art 8 194
Hague Convention 2005 81, 83, 178, 181
  Art 3 83

Table of Secondary Legislation

Civil Procedure Rules 1998 (SI 1998/3132) 1, 2, 4, 5, 11, 29,
    33, 38, 40, 42, 52, 56, 65, 70, 109–10, 133, 139
  Part 1
    r 1.1 1, 3, 206, 260
    r 1.1(1) 2, 3, 407
    r 1.1(2) 2, 3, 407
    r 1.1(2)(f) 168
    r 1.2 2, 3, 260
    r 1.3 2, 3, 4, 79, 138, 260, 268
    r 1.4 133
    r 1.4(1) 4
    r 1.4(2) 4
    r 1.4(2)(b) 149
    r 1.4(2)(e) 7, 56, 62
  PD 1A 4
  Part 2
    r 2.3 98
    r 2.3(1) 106, 297
    r 2.8 88
    r 2.11 84
  PD 2C 66
  Part 3 68, 133, 165, 170
    r 3.1 260
    r 3.1(2) 133–4
    r 3.1(2)(c) 150
    r 3.1(2)(m) 34, 60
    r 3.1(3) 182
    r 3.1(5) 134, 182
    r 3.1(6) 182
    r 3.1(6A) 134
    r 3.4(2) 133, 134
    r 3.4(2)(c) 182
    r 3.6 135
    r 3.8 137
    r 3.8(4) 137, 138
    r 3.9 80, 135, 137, 138, 168, 182, 213
    r 3.9(1) 137
    r 3.12(1) 152
    r 3.12(2) 152
    r 3.13 320
    r 3.14 154, 155, 255
    r 3.15(2) 407
    r 3.15A 153
    r 3.15A(1)–(6) 407
    r 3.18 156, 165
    r 3.18(b) 156
    r 3.19 165
  PD 3A 134
    para 1.9 136
  PD 3E
    para 2.2 155
    para B.3 154
    Precedent H 153, 325–35
    Precedent R 153, 336
    Precedent T 385–6
  PD 3F
    Section II 165

Civil Procedure Rules 1998 – continued
  Part 5
    r 5.4B 236
    r 5.4C 236
    r 5.4C(1) 56
  PD 5A 121, 122
    para 2.1 101, 111, 121, 122, 395, 396, 397
    para 2.2 100–1, 121, 122
    para 2.2(5) 395, 396
    para 2.2(6) 395, 396
  Part 6 77, 313, 351
    r 6.2(b) 82, 85
    r 6.3 77
    r 6.4(1) 82
    r 6.5(3)(a) 78
    r 6.5(3)(b) 78
    r 6.5(3)(c) 78
    r 6.7 79
    r 6.7(1)(b) 80
    r 6.9 80
    r 6.9(3) 81
    r 6.11 79
    r 6.12 79
    r 6.14 82, 301
    r 6.15 79, 80
    r 6.15(2) 79, 80
    r 6.16 80
    r 6.16(1) 81
    r 6.17(2) 82
    r 6.18 82
    rr 6.20–6.25 84
    r 6.26 84, 313
    rr 6.27–6.29 84
    r 6.35 303
    r 6.37(5) 303
    rr 6.40–6.44 83
  PD 6A
    para 2.1 78
    para 4 78–9
    para 4.2 79
    para 6.2 78
  PD 6B
    para 3.1 83
  Part 7 66, 275
    r 7.2 24
    r 7.4(3) 70
    r 7.5(1) 81, 313
    r 7.6(3) 83
  PD 7A
    para 2.1 65, 67
    para 2.4 66, 67
    para 2.4(1) 67
    para 3.1 3, 68
    para 3.6 69
    para 4.1 396, 397, 410
    para 4.1(1) 72
    para 4A.1 66

Civil Procedure Rules 1998 – *continued*
    para 5.1 24
    para 5A.3 75
    para 5B.2 78
    para 5C.2 75
    para 6.1 85
    Part 8 3, 66, 74, 93, 98, 130, 241, 256, 280
    r 8.2 3
    r 8.5(1)–(2) 3
    r 8.6(1)(b) 131
    PD 8 130
    Part 10 88
    r 10.2 88
    r 10.3 88, 90
    r 10.3(1) 88–9
    r 10.3(1)(a)–(b) 89
    r 10.5(3) 89
    r 10.5(4) 89
    r 10.5(5) 89
    Part 11 89
    Part 12 88, 93
    Part 13 167
    r 13.2 167
    r 13.3 167, 168
    r 13.3(1) 167
    r 13.3(2) 167, 168
    Part 14 88, 91
    r 14.7A 91
    PD 14
    para 6.1 93
    Part 15 88, 90
    r 15.4 90
    r 15.4(1) 90
    r 15.5 90
    Part 16 98
    r 16.2(1) 69
    r 16.2(1)(cc) 69
    r 16.3(2) 69
    r 16.4 93, 94
    r 16.4(1) 102
    r 16.4(1)(a) 395
    r 16.4(2) 102, 103, 122, 395
    r 16.5 135
    r 16.5(1) 112, 122, 396
    r 16.5(2) 112, 122, 396
    r 16.5(3) 112, 122–3
    r 16.5(4) 112, 123
    r 16.5(5) 112, 113, 123
    r 16.5(6)–(7) 112, 123
    r 16.5(8) 112, 123, 396, 397
    r 16.7(1) 115
    PD 16 98, 102, 122
    para 1.4 99
    para 2 68
    para 2.2 68, 72
    para 2.3 68
    para 2.4 68, 72
    para 2.5 68–9
    para 2.6 68–9
    para 2.6(a) 72
    para 3.4 122, 395, 396, 397
    para 3.7 122
    para 3.8(1)–(4) 395

Civil Procedure Rules 1998 – *continued*
    para 7.3 102, 122
    para 7.3(1) 395
    para 7.4 102, 122, 395
    paras 8.1–8.2 102
    para 10.6 113
    para 10.7 113, 396
    para 13.1 113, 396
    para 13.3(1)–(2) 100
    para 13.3(3) 99, 100
    Part 17 117–19
    r 17.1(2) 403
    r 17.2 119
    Part 18 119–21, 144, 159, 174, 459
    r 18.1 98
    r 18.1(1) 119, 403
    r 18.1(3) 403
    PD 18 174
    para 1 174
    para 5.5 121
    para 5.5(1) 174
    Part 19 77
    r 19.2 76
    r 19.2(2) 76–7
    r 19.2(3)–(4) 77
    r 19.4(2) 76
    r 19.5(2)–(3) 77
    Part 20 98, 125, 126, 143
    r 20.2(1)–(2) 125
    r 20.4 126
    r 20.4(2)(a) 129
    r 20.6 126–7, 128
    r 20.7 127
    r 20.8 128
    r 20.9(2) 127
    r 20.11 128
    r 20.13 128
    PD 20
    para 3 397
    para 5.3 128
    para 6.1 129, 397
    paras 7.1–7.2 128
    para 7.3 128, 397
    paras 7.4–7.6 128
    Part 21 73
    r 21.6 73
    r 21.7(1) 74
    r 21.10 241
    Part 22 70, 123
    r 22.1(1)(a) 73
    r 22.1(2) 119
    r 22.2 395, 396, 397
    r 22.3 210, 410
    PD 22
    para 2.1 71
    para 2.2 410
    para 2.5 71, 410
    para 3.1 70
    paras 3.4–3.7 71
    para 3.8 72
    para 3.8(3) 72
    para 3.10 71
    para 4 72

Civil Procedure Rules 1998 – *continued*
  PD 22
    para 2.1 395–7
  Part 23 159
    r 23.2 160
    r 23.6 160
  PD 23A 160, 401
    para 3 161
    para 6.2 161
    para 6.9–6.10 161
    para 9.1 160
  PD 23A 463
  Part 24 58, 170, 171, 172
    r 24.2 167, 170
    r 24.2(a) 170
    r 24.2(b) 170, 171
  PD 24
    para 1.3 170
    para 2.3 172
    para 4 173
    para 5.1 172
    para 5.2 173
  Part 25 174, 178, 181, 182
    r 25.1 174, 175
    r 25.1(1) 174–5
    r 25.1(1)(a)–(i) 174
    r 25.1(1)(j)–(m) 175
    r 25.1(1)(n)–(p) 175
    r 25.6 175
    r 25.7(1) 176
    r 25.12 178, 182
    r 25.12(1) 178
    r 25.13 178, 182
    r 25.13(1) 178
    r 25.14 178
  PD 25B (Interim Payments)
    para 2.1 176
  Part 26 138
    r 26.2 141
    r 26.2A 142
    r 26.3(6A) 139
    r 26.4(2) 139
    r 26.4A(5) 144
    r 26.5(2A) 144
    r 26.8(1) 142
    r 26.8(2) 143
  PD 26
    para 7.7 140, 143
    para 8.1(1)–(2) 143
    para 11 143
  Part 27 143, 144
    r 27.2(3) 144
    r 27.14 144
  PD 27 144
    Appendix B 144
  Part 28 145, 321
    r 28.2(1)–(4) 406
    r 28.4 145
    Appendix 322–4, 415
  PD 28 141, 145, 146
    para 3.7(1) 403
    para 3.9 229
    para 3.12 145

Civil Procedure Rules 1998 – *continued*
    para 4.2(1)–(2) 145
    para 4.5 146
    para 5 146
    paras 5.1–5.2 136
    para 5.4(1) 146
    para 6 146
    para 7 147
    para 7.2(4)(b) 146
    Appendix 145
  Part 29 147–52
    r 29.2(1)–(3) 406
    r 29.3(2) 149
    r 29.5 151
    r 29.6 151
  PD 29
    para 2.6 139
    para 4.8(1) 403
    para 4.10 148
    para 4.10(9) 62, 403
    para 4.11 406
    para 5.1 148
    para 5.2(2)–(3) 149
    para 5.5(1) 149, 406
    para 5.6 150
    para 5.7(1) 150
    para 5.7(1)(b) 151
    para 7 151
    paras 7.1–7.2 136
    para 8 151
  Part 30 67
  Part 31 144, 183–203, 222, 259, 318, 465
    r 31.2 184
    r 31.3 189
    r 31.3(1) 189
    r 31.4 184
    r 31.5 403
    r 31.5(1) 403
    r 31.5(3) 185
    r 31.5(6) 337
    r 31.5(7) 185, 337, 403
    r 31.5(8) 186
    r 31.6 186–7, 188, 191, 192, 196, 200, 203, 408, 465,
      466
    r 31.7 188
    r 31.8 187
    r 31.9 188
    r 31.10 408
    r 31.10(2) 408
    r 31.10(4)(b) 409
    r 31.10(5) 190, 408
    r 31.10(6)–(7) 408
    r 31.10(9) 190
    r 31.11 191
    r 31.12 198–9
    r 31.15 189, 404
    r 31.16 199
    r 31.16(3) 50
    r 31.16(3)(d)(iii) 162
    r 31.17 199–200
    r 31.19 194, 408, 465, 467
    r 31.19(3) 409
    r 31.20 404

Civil Procedure Rules 1998 – *continued*
    rr 31.21–31.22 198
  PD 31A
    para 2 189
    para 3.2 190, 408
    para 4.4 191
    para 4.7 190
  PD 31B 140, 188, 318, 399
    para 6 188
  PD 31C 201
  Part 32 144, 205, 208–10
    r 32.1(1)–(3) 206
    r 32.2(1) 99, 207
    r 32.2(3) 206, 404
    r 32.4(1) 208
    r 32.4(2) 207, 404
    r 32.5(1) 404
    r 32.5(2) 207, 404
    r 32.5(3) 211, 262
    r 32.5(5) 211
    r 32.9 211–12
    r 32.10 212–13, 404
    r 32.14 72
    rr 32.18–32.19 222
  PD 32 401, 463
    para 17 208
    paras 17.1–17.2 208, 410
    para 18 208
    para 18.1 208, 410
    para 18.1(1)–(5) 410
    para 18.2 209, 214, 410
    para 18.3 209, 410
    para 18.4 410
    para 18.6 209
    para 19 208
    para 19.1(5)–(6) 208, 410
    para 19.2 208, 410
    para 20 208
    para 20.1 410
    para 20.2 210, 410
    para 25.1 209
    para 27.5 259
    para 27.12 259
    para 27.15 259
  Part 33 205, 216
    r 33.2 259
    r 33.2(1) 216
    r 33.2(1)(b) 411
    r 33.2(2) 216, 411
    r 33.2(3)–(4) 216
    r 33.4 219
    r 33.5 219
    r 33.6 221–2, 259
  PD 34A 258
  Part 35 144, 222–31
    r 35.1 42, 222, 223
    rr 35.2–35.3 223
    r 35.4 223
    r 35.4(1)–(3) 404
    r 35.4(3A) 405
    r 35.5(1) 405
    r 35.5(2) 146
    r 35.6 229

Civil Procedure Rules 1998 – *continued*
  r 35.6(1)–(2) 405
  r 35.7 229
  r 35.7(1)–(2) 405
  r 35.8(1)–(4) 405
  r 35.10 225
  r 35.10(2)–(3) 413
  r 35.10(4) 224
  r 35.12 227, 400, 401, 463
  r 35.12(1)–(3) 405
  r 35.12(4) 227
  r 35.12(5) 227, 228
  r 35.13 406
  r 35.14 400, 401, 463
  r 35.15 231, 232
  PD 35
    para 3.1 225, 412
    para 3.2 225, 412
    para 3.2(1)–(9) 225
    para 3.2(6)(b) 226
    para 3.3 413
    para 5 224
    para 7 229
    para 9.2 227, 405, 406
    para 9.2(i)–(iv) 227
    para 9.3 227
    para 9.5 227
    para 9.6 406
    paras 9.7–9.8 227
    para 11 224
  Part 36 51–2, 53, 144, 155, 180, 187, 233, 237–55, 267, 268, 269, 279, 348, 414, 433–40, 472, 474
    r 36.2(3) 351
    r 36.2(3)(a) 255
    r 36.2(3)(b) 237
    r 36.3 238
    r 36.3(g)(ii) 240
    r 36.4 351
    r 36.5(1) 238, 240, 253
    r 36.5(1)(b)–(e) 414, 472
    r 36.5(2) 348
    r 36.5(4) 239, 240
    r 36.5(4)(b) 240
    r 36.5(5) 239
    r 36.6 239
    r 36.7(1) 237
    r 36.7(2) 240
    r 36.8 241
    r 36.9(4) 241
    r 36.10(3) 240
    r 36.11 352
    r 36.11(1) 241
    r 36.11(2) 240
    r 36.11(3)(d) 240
    r 36.13 238, 348
    r 36.13(2) 352
    r 36.13(5) 243
    r 36.13(5)(b) 243, 244
    r 36.15 352
    r 36.16 255
    r 36.16(1) 238, 240
    r 36.17 239, 241, 252
    r 36.17(1) 252–3, 437, 439

Civil Procedure Rules 1998 – *continued*
    r 36.17(1)(a) 252, 253, 437
    r 36.17(1)(b) 253, 439
    r 36.17(2) 253
    r 36.17(3) 240, 244, 245, 246–8, 253, 254, 255, 265, 267, 437
    r 36.17(3)(a) 245, 250, 255
    r 36.17(3)(b) 246, 438
    r 36.17(3)(c) 250
    r 36.17(4) 240, 248–52, 253, 254, 255, 265, 267, 272, 439
    r 36.17(4)(a) 248, 249, 250, 251, 254, 439, 474
    r 36.17(4)(b) 248, 249, 250, 252, 254, 255, 439, 474
    r 36.17(4)(c) 249, 254, 439, 474
    r 36.17(4)(d) 249, 250, 251, 252, 254, 439, 474
    r 36.17(4)(a)–(d) 474
    r 36.17(5) 253, 254
    r 36.17(5)(e) 255
    r 36.17(6) 249
    r 36.17(7) 241
    r 36.20.2 351
    r 36.20.3 351
    r 36.22 350
  PD 36A
    para 3.1 241
  Part 38 256
  Part 39
    r 39.2 162
    r 39.2(1)–(2) 162
    r 39.2(2A) 162
    r 39.2(3) 162
    r 39.2(4) 69
    r 39.5 401, 463
  PD 39A
    para 4.1 407
  Part 40
    r 40.6 235
    r 40.6(7) 235
  PD 40B
    para 3.5 235
  Part 44 267, 268, 269, 316
    r 44.1 267
    r 44.2 237, 268
    r 44.2(1) 267
    r 44.2(2)(a) 17, 265, 266, 267
    r 44.2(6)(d) 267
    r 44.2(6)(g) 267
    r 44.3 269
    r 44.3(2) 441
    r 44.3(5) 270, 272, 441
    r 44.3(8) 279
    r 44.4(1) 270, 441
    r 44.4(3) 270, 272, 275, 441
    r 44.6 284
    r 44.18 278
  PD 44
    para 3.2 156, 269
    para 3.3 269
    paras 3.6–3.7 269
    para 4.2 163
    para 9.5 343
  Part 45 70, 94, 164, 173, 274, 289
    r 45.6 289

Civil Procedure Rules 1998 – *continued*
    r 45.8 284, 288
  Part 46
    r 46.14 280
  Part 47
    r 47.9 276
    r 47.13 277
    r 47.20 351
    r 47.21 279
  PD 47 280
    para 5.A1–5.A4 275
    para 5.12 275–6
    para 5.19 276
    para 5.22 278
    para 5.22(1)–(6) 278
    para 8.3 279
    para 20 279
    Precedent Q 275, 387
    Precedent S 275
  Part 49 70
  PD 51R 66
  PD 51U 201–3
    para 2 202
    paras 2.3–2.4 202
    paras 2.7–2.8 202
    para 3 202
    para 4 202
    para 5 202
    para 6.4 202
    para 8 203
    para 12.1(1)–(3) 203
    para 12.3 203
  PD 51W 278
  Part 52 166, 279
    r 52.3(6) 166
    r 52.11 167
  Part 55
    r 55.3(4) 76
  Part 58 67, 70
  Parts 59–62 70
  PD 70
    para 6A.1 281
  Part 71 283
    rr 71.3–71.4 283
  PD 71 283
    para 1 283
    Appendix A, B 283
  Part 72 288
    r 72.6(2) 289
    r 72.8 289
  PD 72
    para 1 289
  Part 73 286, 288
    r 73.8 288
  PD 73
    para 1.2 287
  Part 81 190
  Part 83 284
  Part 89 289
  Practice Direction, Pre-action Conduct and Protocols 6, 7, 38, 44, 47, 52, 53–4, 90, 140, 165, 268, 365–7, 391–2, 422
    para 2 49

Civil Procedure Rules 1998 – *continued*
    para 3 45
    para 6(a) 46
    para 6(b) 48
    para 7 49
    para 8 45, 56
    paras 9–10 56
    para 11 56, 272
    para 12 49
    para 16 47, 48
   Pre-action Protocols 6, 44–6, 268
    Construction and Engineering 45
    Professional Negligence 44, 47, 368–72, 393–4, 423
Civil Proceedings Fees Order 2008 (SI 2008/1053)
   Sch 1
    para 1.1 127
Conditional Fee Agreements Order 2013 (SI 2013/689)
   reg 3 18
County Courts (Interest on Judgment Debts) Order 1991 (SI 1991/1184) 250, 266

Damages-Based Agreements Regulations 2013 (SI 2013/609) 21
   reg 4 21

Late Payment of Commercial Debt Regulations 2013 (SI 1013/395) 30
Late Payment of Commercial Debts (Amendment) Regulations 2015 (SI 2015/1336) 30

Taking Control of Goods Regulations 2013 (SI 2013/1894) 286

EU secondary legislation
Directive 2004/48
   Art 9 175
Regulation 1215/2012 425
   Art 4 425
   Art 7(1) 425
   Art 7(2) 425
   Art 7(5) 425
   Art 8(1)–(3) 425
   Art 10–26 425

Regulation 2016/679 (GDPR) 172

Code of Conduct
SRA Code of Conduct for Solicitors 16, 150
   para 1.2 19, 46
   para 1.4 15, 101, 200, 261
   para 2.4 101
   para 2.7 262
   para 6.2 14
   para 6.3 14, 101, 200, 261
   para 6.4 196
   para 8.7 19, 35
SRA Principles 196
   Principle 1 16, 150, 261, 262
   Principle 2 16, 19, 261
   Principle 3 16, 261
   Principle 4 16, 19, 261
   Principle 5 16, 19, 46, 261
   Principle 6 16, 19
   Principle 7 16, 150

Court Guides
Chancery Court Guide 229
Commercial Court Guide 67, 99, 101
   para A1.10 2
   para C1.4(e) 100
Queen's Bench Guide 229
   para 6.7.4 101
   para 6.7.4(1) 396
   para 6.7.4(3) 395
   para 6.7.4(4) 395, 396
   para 6.7.4(5) 396
   para 6.7.4(6) 395
   para 6.7.4(9) 396

Guidance
Guidance for the Instruction of Experts in Civil Claims 2014 223, 226, 373–81, 412
   paras 84–87 258
   para 88 41
Guidance for the Summary Assessment of Costs 382–4

Table of Abbreviations

ADR	alternative dispute resolution
AEI	after-the-event insurance
BEI	before-the-event insurance
CCA	County Courts Act 1984
CCMCC	County Court Money Claims Centre
CEDR	Centre for Effective Dispute Resolution
CFA	conditional fee agreement
CFA Regulations 2000	Conditional Fee Agreements Regulations 2000
CLSA 1990	Courts and Legal Services Act 1990
CPR 1998	Civil Procedure Rules 1998
DBA	damages-based agreement
ECHR	European Convention for the Protection of Human Rights and Fundamental Freedoms
ECtHR	European Court of Human Rights
EEA	European Economic Area
EU	European Union
FCA	Financial Conduct Authority
HCEO	High Court Enforcement Officer
LA	Limitation Act 1980
LAA	Legal Aid Agency
PD	Practice Direction
RCJ	Royal Courts of Justice
SCA	Senior Courts Act 1981
SRA	Solicitors Regulation Authority

CHAPTER 1

INTRODUCTION TO CIVIL LITIGATION

1.1	The Woolf and Jackson reforms	1
1.2	The Rules	5
1.3	An overview of a civil claim	5
1.4	Case analysis	9
1.5	Useful websites	11

LEARNING OUTCOMES

After reading this chapter you will have learned:

- why the Civil Procedure Rules were introduced
- the role of the Civil Procedure Rules
- how the overriding objective is applied
- the obligation on parties to further the overriding objective
- when the main steps in civil litigation are taken
- how to carry out and record case analysis.

1.1 THE WOOLF AND JACKSON REFORMS

The nature of civil litigation in England and Wales changed fundamentally on 26 April 1999, when the Civil Procedure Rules 1998 (CPR 1998) (SI 1998/3132) came into force. These Rules are the courts' attempt to implement the 'Woolf Reforms', as set out in Lord Woolf's report, *Access to Justice*, which was published in 1996. The philosophy behind this report was that the litigation system at the time was too expensive, too slow and incomprehensible to many litigants.

In April 2013, following a comprehensive review of the system by Lord Justice Jackson, further extensive changes were introduced aimed at enhancing the courts' powers to control the costs of litigation and permitting different methods of funding for civil cases.

1.1.1 The overriding objective

Lord Woolf hoped that his proposed reforms, now enshrined in the CPR 1998, would lead to a civil justice system that was just in the results it delivered, fair in the way it treated litigants, and easily understood by users of that legal system. It was hoped that the new system would also provide appropriate procedures at a reasonable cost which could be completed within a reasonable time-scale. In particular, he thought it necessary to transfer the control of litigation from the parties to the court. The court would then determine how each case should progress by making appropriate directions, setting strict timetables and ensuring that the parties complied with them, backed up by a system of sanctions which the court could impose itself without the need for an application by any party. The overriding objective of the reforms is set out in r 1.1 of CPR 1998:

(1)   These Rules are a procedural code with the overriding objective of enabling the court to deal with cases justly and at proportionate cost.

(2)   Dealing with a case justly and at proportionate cost includes, so far as is practicable—

    (a)   ensuring that the parties are on an equal footing and can participate fully in proceedings, and that parties and witnesses can give their best evidence;

    (b)   saving expense;

    (c)   dealing with the case in ways which are proportionate—

        (i)   to the amount of money involved;

        (ii)   to the importance of the case;

        (iii)   to the complexity of the issues; and

        (iv)   to the financial position of each party;

    (d)   ensuring that it is dealt with expeditiously and fairly;

    (e)   allotting to it an appropriate share of the court's resources, while taking into account the need to allot resources to other cases; and

    (f)   enforcing compliance with rules, practice directions and orders.

In *Maltez v Lewis* (1999) *The Times*, 4 May, the claimant's application was for a court order that the defendants should be prevented from instructing leading or senior counsel (barrister) for a copyright dispute between the parties as the claimant had only been in a position to instruct a junior counsel of seven years' experience. The court held that it was the fundamental right of citizens to be represented by counsel or solicitors of their own choice. The court did not have a power to require a party to change their solicitors, but the court was able to ensure compliance with the overriding objective. For example, if one party had instructed a big firm of expensive solicitors and the other party could only afford to instruct a small firm then the court could and should ensure that a level playing field was achieved. That might occur on disclosure (see **Chapter 11**) by allowing the smaller firm more time, or in the preparation of trial bundles (see **Chapter 14**) the court could direct that the larger firm prepared them. The court had a duty to ensure a fair trial and was used to dealing with one side being more expertly represented than the other. The court could ensure compliance with the overriding objective where the representatives could be said to be unequal. The court has power to prevent a party being unfairly required to pay excessive costs because the other party has instructed unreasonably expensive advisers (see generally **Chapter 14**).

In addition, note that in his *Final Report*, Lord Woolf suggested that:

> Where one of the parties is unable to afford a particular procedure, the court, if it decides that that procedure is to be followed, should be entitled to make its order conditional upon the other side meeting the difference in costs of the weaker party, whatever the outcome.

The overriding objective must be borne in mind at all times when conducting civil litigation, both by the court, because r 1.2 states:

> The court must seek to give effect to the overriding objective when it—
>
> (a)   exercises any power given to it by the Rules; or
>
> (b)   interprets any rule subject to rules 76.2, 79.2 and 80.2, 82.2 and 88.2.

and by the parties and their legal advisers, because r 1.3 states:

> The parties are required to help the court to further the overriding objective.

1.1.2 Parties' duty to further overriding objective

1.1.2.1 Parties' duty to the court

In a sense, all the other rules in the CPR 1998 are designed to try to achieve the overriding objective. It is important to note that solicitors and their clients have a positive duty, pursuant to r 1.3, to help the court to further the overriding objective. As the Commercial Court Guide (para A1.10) states, 'The Court expects a high level of co-operation and realism from the legal representatives of the parties. This applies to dealings (including correspondence) between legal representatives as well as dealings with the Court'.

Does the duty to assist the court to further the overriding objective mean that a party to litigation owes a duty to another party? The answer is, no. In *Woodward v Phoenix Healthcare Distribution Ltd* [2018] EWHC 2152 (Ch), it was said by HHJ Hodges:

> [170] In my judgment, the culture introduced by the CPR does not require a solicitor who has in no way contributed to a mistake on the part of his opponent, or his opponent's solicitors, to draw attention to that mistake. That is, in my judgment, not required by CPR 1.3; and it does not amount to 'technical game playing.
>
> [171] Looking first at CPR 1.3. It is headed 'Duty of the Parties' and requires the parties to help the court to further the overriding objective. CPR 1.2 provides that the court must seek to give effect to the overriding objective when it exercises any power given to it by the rules or interprets any rule. The content of the overriding objective is identified in CPR 1.1. By sub-rule (1), the CPR are said to be a new procedural code with the overriding objective of enabling the court to deal with cases justly and at proportionate cost. CPR 1.1 (2) contains a non-exhaustive elaboration of what is meant by dealing with a case justly and at proportionate cost ...
>
> [172] None of that, in my judgment, requires the court to impose on a party a duty to inform an opposing party of an error which has been made, even if there is still time for the opposing party to cure that error ...
>
> [180] In my judgment, 'technical game playing' is conduct such as taking arid procedural points which are, or may be, technically correct, but which are contrary to the spirit in which litigation should now be conducted, in terms of furthering the overriding objective. 'Technical game playing' is conduct such as resisting meritorious applications for relief from sanctions in circumstances where, in accordance with the criteria in *Denton v White*, such an application is bound to succeed.

1.1.2.2 Example

In the case of *Hannigan v Hannigan* [2000] 2 FCR 650, the Court of Appeal was faced with a claim that should have been started under Part 8 using Form N208, but in fact it was commenced on a pre-CPR form with the same number. The defendants sought to strike out the claim. The claimant conceded eight failings, namely:

(a)   the claim was issued on the wrong form;

(b)   the statement of case was not verified by a statement of truth;

(c)   there was a failure to include the Royal Coat of Arms;

(d)   the first defendant was incorrectly named;

(e)   Mrs Hannigan's witness statement was signed in the name of her firm rather than by her personally;

(f)   her witness statement did not have the requisite legend in the top right-hand corner;

(g)   her witness statement failed to have marginal notes or a 3.5cm margin; and

(h)   the exhibit to her witness statement failed to have the requisite legend in the top right-hand corner, or a front page setting out a list of the documents and the dates of all the exhibits. It also failed to have the documents paginated.

The district judge said that the proceedings were 'fundamentally flawed' and the circuit judge held that 'there is too much wrong with these proceedings to exercise a discretion in the appellants' favour'. However, the Court of Appeal refused to strike out the claim, Brooke LJ explaining:

> [32] ... It has not been suggested that the claimant's solicitors did not set out all the information required of a claimant using the Part 8 procedure (see CPR 8.2) or that the written evidence on which she intended to rely was not filed with the form which was used as a claim form or served on the defendant with that document (see CPR 8.5(1) and (2)). The problem was the technical one that her solicitors did not use CPR practice form N208 (the Part 8 claim form) to start the claim contrary to para 3.1 of the first Practice Direction supplementing CPR Part 7, and that they also made the other technical mistakes.

[33] I am in no doubt that the manner in which the judge exercised his discretion was seriously flawed, because he wholly failed to take into account the fact that in these proceedings, sealed by the county court within the relevant limitation period, the defendants were given all the information they required in order to be able to understand what order Mrs Hannigan was seeking from the court and why she was seeking it.

...

[36] ... The interests of the administration of justice would have been much better served if the defendants' solicitors had simply pointed out all the mistakes that had been made in these very early days of the new rules and Mrs Hannigan's solicitor had corrected them all quickly and agreed to indemnify both parties for all the expense unnecessarily caused by his incompetence. CPR 1.3 provides that the parties are required to help the court to further the overriding objective, and the overriding objective is not furthered by arid squabbles about technicalities such as have disfigured this litigation and eaten into the quite slender resources available to the parties.

1.1.2.3   Professional conduct

Each party, whether legally represented or not, is required to help the court to further the overriding objective. But a party has no duty or obligation to their opponent. A solicitor has a duty to act in their own client's best interests (see **2.3.6**), and that more often than not will be disadvantageous to the interests of their client's opponent.

A solicitor owes certain duties to the court and is bound by standards of professional conduct set by the Solicitors Regulation Authority (SRA – see **2.3**). This reflects the public interest in the proper administration of justice; the public interest, also covering the litigants themselves, being expressed in the overriding objective of the court dealing with each case justly.

1.1.3   Judicial case management

Before the introduction of the CPR 1998, the speed at which cases progressed was largely determined by the parties' solicitors. Under the CPR 1998, the court has a duty to manage cases and will therefore determine the pace of the litigation. Rule 1.4 states:

(1)   The court must further the overriding objective by actively managing cases.

(2)   Active case management includes—

   (a)   encouraging the parties to co-operate with each other in the conduct of the proceedings;

   (b)   identifying the issues at an early stage;

   (c)   deciding promptly which issues need full investigation and trial and accordingly disposing summarily of the others;

   (d)   deciding the order in which issues are to be resolved;

   (e)   encouraging the parties to use an alternative dispute resolution procedure if the court considers that appropriate and facilitating the use of such procedure;

   (f)   helping the parties to settle the whole or part of the case;

   (g)   fixing timetables or otherwise controlling the progress of the case;

   (h)   considering whether the likely benefits of taking a particular step justify the cost of taking it;

   (i)   dealing with as many aspects of the case as it can on the same occasion;

   (j)   dealing with the case without the parties needing to attend at court;

   (k)   making use of technology; and

   (l)   giving directions to ensure that the trial of a case proceeds quickly and efficiently.

Case management by the court is considered in further detail in **Chapter 9**.

1.1.4   Participation of vulnerable parties or witnesses

Practice Direction 1A makes provision for how the court is to give effect to the overriding objective in relation to vulnerable parties or witnesses. A person should be considered as vulnerable when a factor – which could be personal or situational, permanent or temporary – may adversely affect their participation in proceedings or the giving of evidence. The court, with the assistance of the parties, should try to identify vulnerability at the earliest possible stage of proceedings and consider whether a party's participation in the proceedings, or the quality of evidence given by a party or witness, is likely to be diminished by reason of vulnerability and, if so, whether it is necessary to make directions as a result in order to further the overriding objective. In particular, the court should consider ordering 'ground rules' before a vulnerable witness gives evidence, to determine what directions are necessary in relation to the nature and extent of that evidence, the conduct of the advocates and/or the parties in respect of the evidence of that person, and/or any necessary support to be put in place for that person.

1.2 THE RULES

1.2.1 Scope

The CPR 1998 apply to all proceedings in the County Court, High Court and the Civil Division of the Court of Appeal, except:

(a)   insolvency proceedings;

(b)   family proceedings;

(c)   adoption proceedings;

(d)   proceedings before the Court of Protection;

(e)   non-contentious probate proceedings;

(f)   proceedings where the High Court acts as a Prize Court (eg, Admiralty proceedings);

(g)   election petitions in the High Court.

Therefore, the CPR 1998 apply to virtually all types of civil litigation proceedings in England and Wales.

It is important to note that the CPR 1998 only apply as to how the relevant court proceedings are conducted and not to how the court should interpret and apply any relevant substantive law (see *Cowan v Foreman* [2019] EWCA Civ 1336).

1.2.2 Practice Directions

In order to understand and interpret the Rules correctly, it is necessary also to look at the Practice Directions which supplement the Rules.

In some cases, the Practice Direction (PD) for a particular Rule is more expansive than the Rule itself. In a sense, the Practice Direction puts flesh on the bare bones of the Rule.

Reference is made to the Rules and Practice Directions throughout this book. Sometimes a Rule or Practice Direction has been quoted in full; at other times it is paraphrased. When conducting civil litigation, it is essential always to check the wording of any relevant Rule or Practice Direction as there are frequent amendments. The Rules can also be accessed on the Internet, via the website of the Ministry of Justice and GOV.UK (see **1.5**), and HM Courts and Tribunals Service website (see **1.5**) provides access to court forms, explanatory leaflets and details of current court fees (amongst other things).

1.3 AN OVERVIEW OF A CIVIL CLAIM

Appendix C(1) sets out a flowchart showing the structure of a case that proceeds from the pre-action steps right through to a trial and the matters that may arise thereafter. We shall call these the five stages of litigation.

1.3.1 Stage 1: pre-commencement of proceedings

1.3.1.1 Client's objectives

With a new client it is vital to identify the client's objectives. Ask yourself: what is the client really seeking to achieve, legally or otherwise? Do they want compensation, an apology or their 'day in court'? Are all the suggested types of damage recoverable? Is it too late to claim a remedy, eg rejection of goods? In a commercial case, is a dispute damaging the client's business, and is maintaining a business relationship with the other side important?

1.3.1.2   Prospective parties

It is vital to ensure you consider who will constitute all the potential parties to any negotiations and court proceedings. Issues of professional conduct may arise (eg, a conflict of interest (see **2.3**)). Moreover, the general rule is that 'all persons to be sued should be sued at the same time and in the same action': see *Morris v Wentworth-Stanley* [1999] QB 1004. Once all potential defendants have been identified and located, consideration must be given as to whether each is worth pursuing (see **2.6**).

1.3.1.3   Evidence

At the end of the first interview summarise the steps you and the client will take and the reasons for these. The key task for a solicitor is to set about collecting relevant evidence. Never delay taking a statement, known as a proof of evidence, from the client and potential witnesses. Memories fade and evidence has a nasty habit of vanishing. So, if a person has a story to tell or documents that might help, get that information quickly.

1.3.1.4   Costs

Of course, the client will need to know from the outset how their legal costs are to be calculated and paid for. As to the important topic of funding, see **2.4**.

1.3.1.5   Limitation and jurisdiction

You also need to address the questions of limitation and jurisdiction. You must work out when the limitation period expires and ensure that a careful diary note is kept of this. If, for example, a client is involved in a commercial dispute, you should check to see if the contract provides for any litigation to be conducted in England and Wales or elsewhere (see further **2.8**) or for a shorter limitation period (see further **2.5.2.5**).

1.3.1.6   Dispute resolution

A client should not just launch into litigation. That is a last resort. A solicitor must always consider with the client what form of dispute resolution would be appropriate. The advantages and disadvantages of viable options should be discussed, and the client's expectations will have to be carefully managed. Therefore, a solicitor must ensure that the client receives a full and frank assessment of the merits of their case. The client will need to weigh up many factors, such as the costs involved, the time and resources that the client will have to commit to the matter, and the effect any particular dispute resolution process may have on the client's business.

1.3.1.7   Pre-action protocols

Pre-action protocols govern the steps parties should take before commencing a court case. The parties should establish what issues are in dispute, share information that is available to each of them concerning those issues and endeavour to resolve those matters. Failure to follow a protocol step or its spirit, without good reason, will usually incur a sanction for that party if litigation is commenced (eg, a successful claimant might be penalised by the award of less or no interest and/or costs).

A number of protocols have been approved by the Ministry of Justice, and these set out how parties should behave pre-action in particular types of cases, such as professional negligence claims (see **3.7**). Where no approved pre-action protocol applies, there is a Practice Direction on Pre-action Conduct and Protocols that the parties should follow (also see **3.7**). The main pre-action considerations for parties under either an approved protocol or the Practice Direction are set out at **1.3.1.8** to **1.3.1.10** below.

1.3.1.8 Alternative Dispute Resolution (ADR)

Parties and their legal representatives are encouraged to enter into discussions and/or negotiations prior to starting proceedings. Whilst the Practice Direction and approved protocols do not usually specify how or when this should be done, the parties must give serious consideration to using any suitable form of available ADR (see **Chapter 4**). If proceedings are commenced, the parties must remember that by r 1.4(2)(e), active case management by the court will include encouraging them to use an ADR procedure if the court considers that appropriate. See, for example, **9.5.1.1** and **14.3.3.6** (as to costs).

1.3.1.9 The standard letter before claim

Immediately after collecting sufficient evidence to substantiate a realistic claim, and before addressing issues of quantum in detail, the potential claimant should send to the proposed defendant a letter detailing the claim. Where the claim is one to which an approved protocol applies, such as professional negligence, the information to be included in the letter before claim will be specified in the protocol (see further **3.7** and **Appendix A(20)**). Where no approved protocol applies, see **Appendix A(19), Practice Direction – Pre-action Conduct and Protocols**. Enough information must be given so that the prospective defendant can commence investigations and at least put a broad valuation on the claim. The prospective claimant should set out any proposals they have for ADR.

1.3.1.10 The letter of response

The approved protocols and the Practice Direction on Pre-action Conduct and Protocols give guidance on the matters to be dealt with in the letter of response. (See **3.8** and **Appendices A(19)** and **(20)**.) The prospective defendant should acknowledge safe receipt of the letter of claim and, after investigating the matter, should state whether or not liability is admitted. Reasons should be given if liability is denied. Where primary liability is admitted but contributory negligence is alleged, details of that should be provided. Note that the potential claimant should also respond to any such allegation before issuing proceedings. The question of ADR should also be addressed.

1.3.2 Stage 2: commencement of the claim

Before starting a court case, the client should be fully aware of what will be involved. That is more than the chances of success and the pros and cons of litigation. The client should have a good idea of what will happen next, as well as how long that might take and the likely cost. In particular, the client should appreciate that the court will impose a strict timetable of steps that must be taken. Not only must the client keep relevant documentation safe, it must be clear to the client what documents, if any, that are harmful to their case will have to be shown to the other side (see **Chapter 11**). In addition, the client should be told that they might have to attend court, not only for the trial but for hearings before that. The client must be informed that if they want to stop the litigation at any time (see **13.6**), they will have to pay the opponent's costs, unless a more favourable settlement can be negotiated. At all times, the client's expectations must be carefully managed.

Proceedings are commenced by a claim form. A specimen can be seen at **7.2.1.6**. To activate the claim, this must be served on the defendant. Full details of the claim, called particulars, must also be served on the defendant. If the defendant wishes to contest the claim, they must file at the court and serve on the claimant a defence. This triggers in the County Court the allocation of the case to a particular 'track'. A claim of up to £10,000 will usually be allocated to the small claims track. Typically, these claims concern consumer disputes and the court does not expect parties to be legally represented.

Claims exceeding £10,000 and up to £25,000 are usually allocated to the fast track. Whilst parties will usually have legal representation on this track, the court will tightly control costs, as well as the type and amount of evidence each party can rely on. In particular, the expectation is that a single joint expert should be used by the parties where expert evidence is necessary, and the trial must be conducted within one day (effectively five hours). Claims exceeding £25,000 are usually allocated to the multi-track. As a claim cannot be started in the High Court unless it exceeds £100,000 (£50,000 for personal injury claims), all claims in that court are dealt with on the multi-track.

1.3.3 Stage 3: interim matters

Once on a track, the court carefully manages a case. Directions will be given to the parties as to the steps that must be taken to prepare for trial. A strict timetable will be imposed as to when each step must be taken. On the small claims track and fast track the expectation is that these directions can be given without any court hearing. In multi-track cases of any complexity it is usual for the parties to meet with a judge at a so-called case management conference in order clearly to define the issues in dispute and determine what steps need to be taken and when, in order to prepare for trial. The most common case management directions are for:

(a)   standard disclosure (ie, the parties list the documents in their possession that they intend to rely on, or which are adverse to their case, or support an opponent's case (see **Chapter 11**, in particular **11.20** as to the disclosure pilot scheme currently operating in the Business and Property Courts)); and

(b)   the exchange of evidence before trial that the parties intend to rely on (eg, experts' reports and statements, known as 'witness statements', of non-expert witnesses (see **Chapter 12**)).

Whatever the track, the parties will be working towards either a known trial date, or at least a period of time in the future when the trial will occur.

In addition to managing the procedural steps that the parties must take to prepare for trial, the court in most multi-track cases will also carry out costs management. This process allows the court to manage both the steps to be taken and the costs to be incurred by the parties to the proceedings so as to further the overriding objective (see **1.1.1**).

As to case and costs management generally, see **Chapter 9**.

In addition to case and costs management directions, parties may during this stage apply to the court for any specific orders that might be required (eg, to force an opponent who has neglected to take a required step in accordance with the timetable to do so on pain of having their case thrown out by the court). See further **Chapter 10**.

1.3.4 Stage 4: trial

A trial on the small claims track is informal and conducted at the discretion of the judge. The formal rules of evidence apply on the fast track and multi-track. At the end of a fast track trial, the judge will usually have resolved all issues (ie, liability, quantum (if relevant) and costs). As to costs, the judge will decide if any party should pay the other's costs and, if so, how much. This is known as a summary assessment of costs. The parties must provide each other and the court with a detailed breakdown of costs for this purpose. On the multi-track, the trial judge will decide who should pay costs. The general rule is the loser pays the winner's costs. If the parties cannot subsequently agree on the amount of those costs, they are determined post trial by a different judge, known as a costs judge, via a process called detailed assessment. See generally **1.3.5** and **14.3**.

1.3.5 Stage 5: post-trial

On all tracks a party may decide to appeal all or part of the trial judge's decision. As stated at **1.3.4** above, in a multi-track case, a detailed assessment of costs as awarded by the trial judge will take place if the parties cannot agree on the amount.

A party awarded damages and/or costs will expect to be paid by the date set by the court. What if that does not happen? The party will have to apply to the court to enforce the judgment. Most commonly, this involves instructing court officials to attend the debtor's premises and to take their belongings to be sold at public auction. The proceeds are then paid to the party. It is therefore vital, as indicated at **1.3.1** above, to ensure that at stage 1 steps are taken to check that any potential defendant is actually worth suing.

1.4   CASE ANALYSIS

1.4.1   Causes of action

A cause of action is the legal basis of a claim. Examples include breach of contract, negligence, negligent misstatement, misrepresentation and nuisance. To determine whether a client has a cause of action and their prospects of success, it is vital at the outset that a solicitor analyses all the known facts, whether given orally by the client and any witnesses, or contained in documentation. Lawyers call this evidence, and it is important to appreciate that the term is not limited to court proceedings.

1.4.2   Example: breach of contract

Take a claim for breach of contract as an example. The first thing to do is to assess the evidence that is available that will establish that there was a contract. Common law requires there to be an agreement with a promise, consideration, and intention to create legal relations. The last, certainly in any business context, will not be an issue. In practical terms, the solicitor will need to consider how and when the contract in dispute was formed, and whether it was written or oral. If it was written, then a copy should be obtained. If it was oral, the solicitor needs details of when and where it was made, who actually entered into the contract for each party, and the express terms agreed.

If the dispute concerns what express terms were agreed in a contract, the solicitor needs to assess the available evidence. If it is a written agreement, then the document will help; however, there may still be questions over the interpretation of those terms. In the case of an oral contract, this can be particularly tricky, as often the only evidence appears to come from the parties who made the contract. If they have different recollections of what was agreed, then the case can turn on their credibility. In such circumstances, it is important to look for other evidence, for example, someone else who was present when the contract was discussed, or notes of the meeting made by the client. In addition, where a contract is entered into during the course of a party's business, there may also be implied terms which apply to both written and oral contracts.

When the solicitor is satisfied that the existence of a contract can be established (or is not likely to be in dispute) and its terms, the solicitor will then need to consider how the client will prove that there was a breach which has resulted in recoverable losses. What does the client say the opponent did (or failed to do) that amounts to a breach of the contract? This is a question of fact, and the solicitor must assess the evidence the client has to prove the claim. Once a breach has been established, the factual consequences of that breach should be identified. Then each item of loss claimed will have to be similarly investigated. Finally, an assessment needs to be made of the overall strengths and weaknesses of the claim, and consideration given to what further evidence needs to be obtained.

1.4.3   Summary: breach of contract

A list of the basic facts that need to be established in order to succeed in making a claim for breach of contract includes the following:

(a)   contract (its formation – parties, date, written or oral, subject matter (goods, goods and services/materials and work, services), consideration);

(b)   terms relied on (express and/or implied);

(c)   breach of those terms;

(d)   factual consequences of the breach of those terms;

(e)   damage and loss.

Often, solicitors record their analysis in a grid chart. An example follows.

Client: Factory Goods (Mythshire) Limited ('FG')			
Opponent: Cool Systems (Mythshire) Limited ('CS')			
Cause of action: Breach of oral contract made on 29 November [last year] for CS to supply and install an air conditioning system at FG's factory.			
Implied terms relied on: The air conditioning system would be of satisfactory quality and installed exercising reasonable care and skill – s 4(2) and s 13 of the Supply of Goods and Services Act 1982.			
Elements to establish	**Facts to establish**	**Evidence available**	**Evidence to obtain**
Contract	CS, by its employee, Mr Wise, agreed on 29 November [last year], with Ms Riley, FG's employee, to supply FG with and install at FG's factory a new air conditioning system.	CS's estimate, invoice and receipted account. Proof of evidence of Ms Riley.	If necessary, proof of evidence from Mrs Clark who was present with Ms Riley on 29 November [last year].
Implied term	CS supplied the air conditioning system (goods) to FG and installed it (services) at FG's factory as part of CS's business.	N/a – not likely to be disputed as implied by statue.	N/a – not likely to be disputed.
Breach	The system is not of satisfactory quality and it was installed without reasonable care and skill being taken. The system does not start automatically and has to be set manually. The system failed to achieve the required setting of between 24 and 25 degrees Celsius in the summer and between 17 and 19 degrees Celsius in winter.	Report from the Head of FG's factory maintenance team identifying faults in the system and its installation. Daily record of dealings with the system kept by FG's factory maintenance team.	A report from an expert confirming FG's allegation.

Elements to establish	Facts to establish	Evidence available	Evidence to obtain
Factual consequences	Portable air conditioning units had to be hired. The factory had to close in excessively hot or cold weather and suffered a loss of profit. The system will have to be either upgraded or replaced.	Written complaints by FG's staff about extremes of temperatures since installation. Daily record of factory temperatures kept by Mrs Vaux, FG's employee responsible for health and safety.	Take a detailed proof of evidence from the individuals concerned. A report from an expert confirming the allegations.
Damage and loss	(1) Cost of upgrading system supplied or replacement of that system with a suitable system. (2) Loss of profit – time factory had to close due to excessively hot working conditions. (3) Client tried to mitigate loss – hired portable air conditioning units but these were insufficient.	(1) None. (2) Records of Mr Frame, FG's head of human resources, recording time factory closed. (3) Receipted invoices for portable units.	(1) A report from an expert. (2) FG's profit and loss accounts, production records, etc. (3) Expert needs to consider this point.

As a case develops, you should continually review which issues remain in dispute and how those are to be proved.

There are three key case analysis points: viability, liability, and quantum. **Chapters 2 and 3** will discuss the steps you will need to take in order to complete your case analysis.

1.5 USEFUL WEBSITES

The starting point for any exploration of the Web in this area should probably be the Ministry of Justice or GOV.UK websites that host the Civil Procedure Rules, at <http://www.justice.gov.uk/courts/procedure-rules/civil> or <https://www.gov.uk/guidance/the-civil-procedure-rules>. Court forms and guides are on the HM Courts and Tribunals Service site <http://www.gov.uk/government/organisations/hm-courts-and-tribunals-service>. For ease of reference, copies of commonly used court forms can be found in **Appendix A**. However, these forms are often subject to change and you should check on the website for the most recent version.

CHAPTER 2

CONSIDERATIONS AT THE FIRST INTERVIEW INCLUDING FUNDING THE CLAIM

2.1	Introduction	13
2.2	Purpose of the first interview	14
2.3	Professional conduct	14
2.4	Funding	16
2.5	Case analysis	24
2.6	Viability and burden of proof	27
2.7	Interest	29
2.8	Foreign element and choice of forum	32
2.9	Alternatives to litigation	33

LEARNING OUTCOMES

After reading this chapter you will have learned:

- what to consider when first interviewing a client
- how to advise a client about costs
- how to enter into a conditional fee agreement
- the different types of insurance cover
- the difference between a conditional fee agreement and a contingency fee
- the basics of Community Legal Service funding
- the effect of the Limitation Act 1980
- why it is essential to identify all possible defendants and check their solvency
- the remedies available in a typical claim
- how to claim interest
- the factors affecting any choice of forum
- when and why the client might use ADR methods.

2.1 INTRODUCTION

In **Chapter 1** we looked at the five stages of a civil claim (see **1.3**). Stage 1 – pre-commencement – is one of the key stages where you will be gathering evidence and establishing the facts in order to advise on viability. If any evidence or facts are overlooked, incorrect decisions could be made, and at worst this could result in the case being lost or costs being wasted.

In **Chapters 2** and **3** we discuss each step you will have to consider at Stage 1; not all will be necessary in every case, but you should always run through the checklist at **3.13** every time you open a new file.

In this chapter we consider the first interview and the issues you will need to discuss with the client before proceeding to the detailed fact and evidence gathering phase outlined in **Chapter 3.**

2.2 PURPOSE OF THE FIRST INTERVIEW

The first interview between the solicitor and client is very important from both parties' points of view. The client will be anxious that the solicitor appreciates their problem, and will want to be assured that there is a satisfactory solution to it. The client is likely to be concerned about the potential amount of legal costs and will want some idea of the timescale involved. At the same time, the solicitor needs to be able to extract relevant information from the client in order to give preliminary advice on such issues as liability and quantum.

A solicitor will need to:

(a) identify clearly the client's objectives in relation to the work to be done for the client;

(b) give the client a clear explanation of the issues involved and the options available to the client;

(c) agree with the client the next steps to be taken; and thereafter

(d) keep the client informed of progress.

As to (a), the scope of the work to be done for the client is formally known as the solicitor's 'retainer', namely the work for which the client has retained the services of the solicitor. It is usual to refer to a client 'instructing' their solicitor on a particular matter.

There is no comprehensive list of those matters that need to be dealt with at first interview because each case is different. However, the matters set out below should always be considered.

2.3 PROFESSIONAL CONDUCT

A detailed consideration of this area is contained in **Legal Foundations, Part II, Professional Conduct.**

The solicitor acting in civil proceedings must, in particular, have regard to the following rules of professional conduct.

2.3.1 Duty of confidentiality

By para 6.3 of the Solicitors Regulation Authority (SRA) Code of Conduct for Solicitors, a solicitor is under a duty to maintain the confidentiality of their client's affairs unless the client's prior authority is obtained to disclose particular information, or exceptionally the solicitor is required or permitted by law to do so. It is important to note that the duty of confidentiality continues after the end of the retainer.

If a solicitor holds confidential information in relation to a client or former client (A), they should not (unless appropriate safeguards can be put in place) risk breaching confidentiality by acting, or continuing to act, for another client (B) on a matter where that information might reasonably be expected to be material and client B has an interest adverse to client A. Ideally, therefore, before the first interview you should check that you do not have confidential information in respect of client A which you would be under a duty to disclose to the proposed new client B.

2.3.2 Conflict of interest

By para 6.2 of the SRA Code of Conduct, a solicitor generally should not act for two or more clients where this would cause a conflict of interests. A conflict of interests exists if the solicitor owes separate duties to act in the best interests of two or more clients in relation to the same or related matters, and those duties conflict or there is a significant risk that those duties may conflict.

> **EXAMPLES**
>
> 1.   A firm of solicitors already acts for a client in negotiating with publishers for the publication of the client's novel. The firm is now asked to act for a new client who alleges that the novel is plagiarised and breaches her copyright. As that is a related matter, there is a conflict of interest and the firm cannot act for the new client.
>
> 2.   A solicitor is instructed to act by two partners in a firm which has been sued for damages for fraudulent misrepresentation. However, the allegation is that only one of the partners made the fraudulent misrepresentation. The potential conflict arises because there is a significant risk that the 'innocent' partner may have a claim against the 'guilty' partner for the same matter, namely if the fraudulent misrepresentation is established.

2.3.3   Money laundering

Solicitors are subject to the money laundering legislation, and it is extremely important to ensure that adequate procedures are in place to check a new client's identity – see **Legal Foundations** for further information.

2.3.4   Who is my client and am I authorised to act?

A solicitor warrants their authority to take any positive step in court proceedings, eg to issue a claim form or serve a defence on behalf of the client (see further **5.4.6**). So a solicitor must always be able to answer the questions posed above.

> **EXAMPLE**
>
> Assume you attend a new client called Mrs Freeman. She wants to claim under a contract she entered into with Megawindows (Mythshire) Limited.
>
> First, we need to ask: in what capacity are we acting for Mrs Freeman? Is she an individual who entered into the contract on her own behalf? Was she acting as an agent for her principal? Is she a trustee acting on behalf of a trust? Is she, say, one of a hundred partners in a firm, and did she contract on behalf of the partnership such that the partnership is our client? Is she a director in a limited company, and did she contract on behalf of that company such that the company is our client?
>
> Secondly, if we are not acting for her as an individual in her own right, we need to consider whether she is the correct person to give us instructions on behalf of her principal, the trust, the partnership or limited company. Note that a solicitor may be ordered to personally pay the costs that are incurred where any steps are taken without authority, even if they do not know that they lack authority. For example, where the client gives instructions on behalf of a non-existent company, or is a person not properly authorised to give instructions on behalf of a company.

If a solicitor receives instructions from someone other than the client, or by only one client on behalf of others in a joint matter, the solicitor should not proceed without checking that all clients agree with the instructions given.

2.3.5   Solicitor's duty as an officer of the court

As well as owing duties to the client, the solicitor also has an overriding duty not to mislead the court (see para 1.4 of the SRA Code of Conduct). The duty to the court means that the solicitor must disclose all relevant legal authorities to the court, such as statutory provisions or case law, even if these are not favourable to their case (see para 2.7). The advocate is also under a duty to help the court achieve the overriding objective (see **1.1.2.3**).

2.3.6 Solicitor's core duties

The SRA Code of Conduct is based on certain mandatory Principles that are all-pervasive. So how might these affect a civil litigation practitioner? Table 2.1 flags up some possible examples.

Table 2.1   Code of Conduct Principles

Principle	Examples of potential problem areas
1 *Justice and the rule of law* You must uphold the constitutional principle of the rule of law, and the proper administration of justice.	Client asks you to act illegally or not within the spirit of the CPR. A court order or provision of the CPR conflicts with your duty to act in the client's best interest.
2 *Public confidence* You must act in a way that upholds public trust and confidence in the solicitors' profession and in legal services provided by authorised persons.	If you breach any of the other Principles.
3 *Independence* You must not allow your independence to be compromised.	Any arrangement for a third party to fund your client's civil claim which imposes constraints on how you conduct the case that are beyond the legitimate interests of the funder.
4 *Honesty* You must act with honesty.	You place yourself in contempt of court.
5 *Integrity* You must act with integrity.	You use your position to take unfair advantage of a client, an opponent or a third party. You use your position unfairly to advance your client's case.
6 *Equality, diversity and inclusion* You must act in a way that encourages equality, diversity and inclusion.	If you unfairly discriminate by allowing your personal views to affect your professional relationships and the way in which you provide your services.
7 *Best interests of clients* You must act in the best interests of each client.	A court order or provision of the CPR conflicts with this duty. Also see **2.3.2**.

PROFESSIONAL CONDUCT CHECKS TO MAKE BEFORE THE FIRST INTERVIEW
1.   Confidentiality and conflict of interest
   • Check name of client and opponent against existing and past clients.
2.   Money laundering
   • Check identity of client.

2.4 FUNDING

It is very important on taking instructions to discuss costs with the client. The solicitor should give their client the best information they can about the likely cost of the matter. This includes advising the client on the different types of funding available.

It is often impossible to tell at the outset of a case, particularly one involving prospective litigation, what the overall cost will be. So the solicitor should provide the client with as much information as possible at the start and keep the client regularly updated. Unless a fixed fee is agreed, where the client is paying privately the solicitor should explain the potential steps in the litigation and the potential costs and agree a ceiling figure or review dates. The client should be told how the solicitor's fee will be calculated, eg who is going to do the work and the hourly charging rate of that person. Often a payment on account will be required immediately, with interim bills delivered as the case progresses. The client should be advised of any foreseeable disbursements, such as court fees, barristers' fees and experts' fees.

Normally a solicitor will only agree a fixed fee to take some specific step in the litigation on behalf of a client, for example to draft a court document or attend a hearing. In these circumstances, it is vital that the solicitor obtains all the relevant information in order to set the fee at a reasonable but remunerative level. If the solicitor fixes the fee too low, they will still be 'obliged to complete the work, to the ordinary standard of care, even if it has become unremunerative' (per Cranston J in *Inventors Friend Ltd v Leathes Prior (a firm)* [2011] EWHC 711 [76]). In the case, the solicitors agreed a fixed fee to briefly review and comment on the terms of a document without seeing that document.

The consequences for a litigation solicitor who does not regularly give the client the best information then available about costs, can be seen in the case of *Reynolds v Stone Rowe Brewer* [2008] EWHC 497. There, a firm of solicitors was held to be bound by its original estimate of costs given to the client, because the firm failed to warn her that costs were increasing and that, as ultimately happened, the estimate would have to be revised upwards. See also *Mastercigars Direct Ltd v Withers LLP* [2009] EWHC 651.

The solicitor should also consider whether the client's liability for costs may be covered by existing legal expenses insurance cover (see **2.4.5**), and whether the likely outcome of the matter justifies the expense involved by conducting a costs–benefit analysis (see **3.12**).

In addition, the solicitor should advise the client of the risk that the client may be ordered to pay the opponent's costs if the case is lost.

2.4.1 Solicitor and client costs and costs between the parties

In litigation cases, the solicitor should explain to the client the distinction between solicitor and client costs (ie, the sum the client must pay to their own solicitor) and costs that may be awarded between the parties in litigation.

If the client loses the case, they will have to pay their own solicitor's costs and normally, in addition, their opponent's costs. Rule 44.2(2)(a) of the CPR 1998 provides that as a general rule the unsuccessful party in litigation will be ordered to pay the costs of the successful party. The opponent's costs are not necessarily all the costs incurred by the opponent. The court will assess what costs the client must pay towards the opponent's costs (unless there is agreement on this amount between the parties). The client will have to pay to their opponent only such costs as are ordered by the court or agreed between the parties.

If the client wins the case, they will still have to pay their own solicitor's costs. Indeed, if they are paying privately, they will usually already have paid these costs. The client will normally receive their costs from their opponent. Again, this will be an agreed amount or a sum assessed by the court. If the costs recovered are, as is usual, less than the costs paid, the client will have to bear the loss.

A client should always be warned that even if they win the case, they may not recover any costs if, for example, the opponent goes bankrupt or disappears. Furthermore, even if successful, the court has the power to reduce costs to reflect any unreasonable conduct on the part of the successful party (*Benyatov v Credit Suisse Securities (Europe) Ltd* [2022] WL 00509179) (see also **14.3.3.6**).

Traditionally, solicitors have charged their clients on a time basis where the client is billed for the time spent dealing with their case. Until recently, contingency fees were unlawful for litigation work. Under a contingency fee arrangement the client only pays a fee if they are successful – often called 'no win, no fee'. However, currently only two types of contingency fees are lawful. These are a conditional fee agreement (see **2.4.2**) and a damages-based agreement (see **2.4.4**).

2.4.2 Conditional fee agreements

A conditional fee agreement (CFA) is defined by s 58(2)(a) of the Courts and Legal Services Act 1990 (CLSA 1990) as 'an agreement with a person providing advocacy or litigation services which provides for his fees and expenses, or any part of them, to be payable only in specified circumstances'. Those circumstances are whether or not the client succeeds with a claim or, alternatively, successfully defends a claim.

A CFA is an agreement under which the solicitor receives no payment, or less than normal payment, if the case is lost, but receives normal, or higher than normal, payment if the client is successful. Many think of CFAs as 'no win, no fee' agreements. However, whilst a CFA may amount to 'no win, no fee', it can equally be 'no win, lesser fee', or 'win and pay usual fees' or 'win and pay increased usual fees'. The important point to grasp is that any fee payable is based on the solicitor's usual hourly charging rates, and a fee payable on success is a percentage increase in those usual hourly charging rates up to a maximum of 100%. The fee is not based on the solicitor receiving any proportion of money recovered by the client (as to such a contingency, see **2.4.4**).

A CFA is enforceable only if it meets the requirements of ss 58 and 58A of the Courts and Legal Services Act 1990. These provide that a CFA:

(a)   may be entered into in relation to any civil litigation matter, except family proceedings;

(b)   must be in writing; and

(c)   must state the percentage by which the amount of the fee that would be payable if it were not a CFA is to be increased (the success fee).

Where it is agreed that the solicitor should receive higher than normal payment if the case is won, the success fee cannot exceed 100% of the solicitor's normal charges. This limit is set by the CFA Order 2013 (SI 2013/689), reg 3 (although note that different provisions apply to personal injury claims).

EXAMPLE

A solicitor normally charges £200 an hour. A 10% success fee would mean an additional £20 per hour. A 50% success fee would mean an additional £100 per hour. The maximum 100% success fee would mean an additional £200 per hour.

Normal charge per hour	Success fee as percentage of normal charges	Amount of success fee	Total hourly charge to client if client wins
£200	10%	£20	£220
£200	50%	£100	£300
£200	100%	£200	£400

When advising a client about a CFA, the solicitor should explain the circumstances in which the client may be liable for their own legal costs (and when the solicitor would seek payment) and their right to an assessment of those costs. In addition, the duty to act in the best interests of the client means that a solicitor should always check to see if the client has the benefit of suitable before-the-event legal expenses insurance cover (see **2.4.5** and the case of *Sarwar v Alam*). If such exists, then there is no need for the client to enter into a CFA. Likewise, a solicitor must always be careful to ensure that any settlement achieved for a client under a CFA is in the client's best interests and not made with a view to obtaining the solicitor's fee.

Normally, a CFA will cover all work done by the solicitors' firm for the client over the five stages, apart from an appeal. This will include any charges incurred in enforcing a judgment (see **Chapter 15**). The CFA is usually worded so that the solicitors' firm has a right to take enforcement action in the client's name. An appeal will normally require its own risk assessment and so typically has its own CFA.

2.4.2.1 Drafting the CFA

It is of course essential that the CFA is drafted carefully. Consider, for example, the importance of a clear definition of the term 'win'. Does the client win if they succeed on all aspects of their claim, or is it enough that they recover some damages (even if they represent only a small percentage of the client's claim)? The Law Society provides assistance in the form of a model CFA for personal injury cases, which can be adapted for other types of work. Precedents are also available in practitioner works.

2.4.3 The success fee

If the client wins the case and their opponent is ordered to pay their costs, these cannot include the success fee. That will be payable by the client. It is therefore vital that the client is made fully aware of this before signing a CFA. The CFA itself should also be clear on this issue and so might read:

> If you win your claim, you pay our basic charges, our disbursements and the success fee. The amount of these is not based on or limited by the damages you recover. You can claim from your opponent part or all of our basic charges and disbursements. You cannot claim the success fee from your opponent. You are responsible for paying the success fee.

Obviously, the CFA needs to define all the terms in such a clause.

Whenever they enter into a CFA, the solicitor takes a financial risk. The solicitor who regularly acts on this basis will stay in business only if the success fees they recover on their 'wins' outweigh the fees sacrificed on their 'losses'. It is therefore essential that before entering into a CFA or agreeing the level of the success fee with a client, the solicitor performs a thorough risk assessment. Relevant factors would include:

(a)   the chances of the client succeeding on liability;

(b)   the likely amount of the damages;

(c)   the length of time it will take for the case to reach trial;

(d)   the number of hours the solicitor is likely to have to spend on the case.

The solicitor may need to spend some time gathering evidence and information about the client's case before the solicitor can perform a full risk assessment. For example, it may be appropriate to obtain an expert opinion and/or interview witnesses (see **Chapter 3**). It is, of course, essential to discuss with the client what work will have to be performed before a decision can be reached about whether the solicitor is prepared to enter into a CFA, and how that work is to be funded.

A solicitor should never arbitrarily set the level of a success fee. A proper risk assessment should always be carried out. But what if the client suggests a success fee well in excess of what the solicitor might set? Should the solicitor just accept that? The answer is no – and as you might expect, it is to be found in the SRA Code of Conduct. Principle 2 provides that a solicitor must act in a way that upholds public trust and confidence in the solicitors' profession and in legal services provided by authorised persons. Principles 4, 5 and 6 respectively provide that a solicitor must act with honesty, integrity and in the best interests of each client. By para 1.2, a solicitor must not abuse their position by taking unfair advantage of a client. In addition, para. 8.7 requires a solicitor to ensure that clients receive the best possible information about how their matter will be priced.

2.4.3.1 Funding disbursements and liability for the other side's costs

If a client with a CFA loses the case, they will not usually have to pay their own solicitor's fees but will nevertheless be liable for their opponent's costs including disbursements. In addition, the client will, during the course of the litigation, have to fund disbursements such as the fees of a barrister and expert witnesses, as well as items such as travelling expenses. Many CFA-funded clients are not in a position to pay these disbursements and/or may be concerned by the fact that they will not know until the end of the litigation whether they are liable to their opponent for costs and, if so, for how much.

In such circumstances, the client may benefit from purchasing after-the-event insurance (AEI). This type of legal expenses insurance policy provides cover for the other side's costs and the client's own disbursements in the event of losing the case. The premium payable depends on the strength of the client's case and the level of cover required. It may be possible to arrange a 'staged' premium, whereby additional instalments are paid if the case continues beyond certain defined stages. For example, in *Rogers v Merthyr Tydfil CBC* [2006] EWCA Civ 1134, the claimant had the benefit of AEI cover with a three-stage premium: namely, £450 was payable when the policy was taken out, a further £900 when proceedings were issued, and a final £3,510.60 just before the trial.

A solicitor should discuss with their client whether insurance is appropriate before the CFA is entered into. There are several sources available to solicitors either online or through journals, which can help them find an insurance policy at a competitive premium.

Of course, obtaining AEI insurance to cover the client's disbursements in the event that they lose does not solve the problem of how those disbursements are to be paid for during the course of the litigation. There are various solutions – for example, some banks offer loans to fund disbursements. As far as counsel's fees are concerned, counsel may be willing to enter into a CFA with the client. However, such an arrangement cannot be entered into with an expert witness. This is to avoid any possibility that the expert's evidence, which should be impartial, will be influenced if they are instructed on a 'no win, no fee' basis.

If necessary, many AEI insurers will arrange a loan to the client or the client's solicitors to fund both the disbursements and the cost of the AEI premium. The loan may even be on terms that it is not repayable if the client loses. If the client wins, the interest on the loan is usually deducted from the damages recovered.

2.4.4 Damages-based agreement

A damages-based agreement (DBA) is defined by s 58AA(3)(a) of the CLSA 1990 as:

> an agreement between a person providing advocacy services, litigation services or claims management services and the recipient of those services which provides that—
>
> (i)   the recipient is to make a payment to the person providing the services if the recipient obtains a specified financial benefit in connection with the matter in relation to which the services are provided, and
>
> (ii)   the amount of that payment is to be determined by reference to the amount of the financial benefit obtained.

What does that mean? Basically, if the client recovers damages, the solicitor's fee is an agreed percentage of those damages. So, if the client recovers £100,000 and the DBA is set at 10% then the client pays the solicitor a fee of £10,000.

A DBA is only enforceable if it meets the requirements of s 58AA(4) of the CLSA 1990. These are that the agreement:

(a)   must be in writing;

(b)   must not provide for a payment above a prescribed amount or for a payment above an amount calculated in a prescribed manner;

(c)   must comply with such other requirements as to its terms and conditions as are prescribed; and

(d)   must be made only after the person providing services under the agreement has provided prescribed information.

Requirement (a) is clear enough but the other three requirements can only be found elsewhere. Currently that is in the Damages-Based Agreements Regulations 2013 (SI 2013/609) which provide as set out below.

As to (b), the DBA must not provide for a payment above an amount which, including VAT, is equal to 50% of the sums ultimately recovered by the client.

Apart from VAT, note that this cap is inclusive of any counsel's fees but does not include disbursements for which the client remains responsible. The costs and disbursements may, of course, be recoverable from the opponent (subject to the indemnity principle and the usual rules of assessment: see **Chapter 14**).

It should be noted that the cap does not apply to any appeal proceedings.

So, what does this mean for the client? If damages are recovered, how much will the client actually receive? Regulation 4 provides that the client cannot be required to pay an amount other than the agreed fee net of the following:

(i)   any costs (including fixed costs: see **10.3.5**) and counsel's fees, that have been paid or are payable by another party to the proceedings by agreement or order; and

(ii)   any expenses incurred by the solicitor after accounting for any amount which has been paid or is payable by another party to the proceedings by agreement or order. Expenses in this context would include disbursements such as experts' fees and court fees.

EXAMPLE

A client enters into a DBA with their solicitor. The DBA is set at 20%. After proceedings are commenced, the claim is settled. The client recovers damages of £250,000 from the defendant. As part of the settlement, the defendant agrees to pay £40,000 towards the client's costs and expenses.

Counsel was instructed in the client's case and her fee was £5,000.

The expenses incurred by the solicitor on behalf of the client (court fees, etc) totalled £14,500.

In total, £290,000 is paid by the defendant. How will this be accounted for?

The defendant paid £40,000 towards the client's costs and expenses. So this will be used to meet the expenses incurred by the solicitor on behalf of the client totalling £14,500. That leaves £25,500.

Under the DBA, the solicitor is entitled to payment of a fee inclusive of VAT of £50,000 (that is, £250,000 x 20%). How will that be paid? First, with the remaining £25,500 paid by the defendant towards the client's costs. The balance of £24,500 will come out of the damages recovered by the client. The solicitor will, of course, be responsible for paying counsel's fee of £5,000.

From the damages award of £250,000, the client therefore has to pay £24,500 to the solicitor. So the client ends up with £225,500.

As to (c), the terms and conditions of a DBA must specify:

(i)   the claim or proceedings or parts of them to which the agreement relates;

(ii)   the circumstances in which the representative's payment, expenses and costs, or part of them, are payable; and

(iii)   the reason for setting the amount of the payment at the level agreed.

As to (d), the Regulations currently cover only employment matters.

The points made above (at **2.4.3**) in respect of combining a CFA with AEI cover apply equally to a DBA. Similar considerations to setting a CFA success fee will also apply to determining the amount of a DBA.

Is a DBA valid if it contains a clause which provides that the client must pay the solicitors' normal fees and disbursements if they terminate the retainer prematurely? Yes, see *Zuberi v Lexlaw Ltd* [2021] EWCA Civ 16. The case is also authority for the use of so-called 'hybrid DBAs'. For example, a law firm may receive concurrent funding via both a DBA and some other form of retainer; this might consist of the DBA in the event of the claim's success and discounted hourly rate fees in the event of the claim's failure. Alternatively, a DBA might comprise one or other of the methods of funding for different stages of the legal proceedings.

Note that slightly different provisions apply if the DBA concerns a personal injury claim or an employment matter.

2.4.5   Insurance

The solicitor should always check to see if the client has the benefit of an existing legal expenses insurance policy (often called before-the-event insurance, or 'BEI') that might fund the litigation. Such insurance is commonly purchased as part of household or motor insurance policies.

In the case of *Sarwar v Alam* [2001] EWCA Civ 1401, [2002] 1 WLR 125, the Court of Appeal laid down the following guidance:

> In our judgment, proper modern practice dictates that a solicitor should normally invite a client to bring to the first interview any relevant motor insurance policy, any household insurance policy and any stand alone before-the-event insurance policy belonging to the client and/or any spouse or partner living in the same household as the client.

A solicitor should discuss with the client (at the first interview and, as appropriate, thereafter) whether the client's liability for another party's costs is covered by existing insurance (BEI), or whether specially purchased insurance should now be obtained (AEI).

Where BEI cover is not available, the client may wish to consider purchasing AEI even if the client does not fund the litigation by way of a CFA or DBA. As discussed at **2.4.1**, one of the disadvantages of litigation is that if the case is lost, the loser will generally have to pay the winner's costs, and this liability cannot be quantified until the end of the proceedings. By purchasing AEI, the litigant removes this uncertainty (provided the cover bought is sufficient). Given these advantages, a solicitor who fails to discuss the possibility of such insurance with a client at the outset of litigation may well be negligent and in breach of professional conduct.

If a firm of solicitors advises a client on and/or arranges AEI cover for the client, the firm will be involved in the activity of insurance mediation, as to which see further **Legal Foundations** at **17.10**.

2.4.6   Third party funding

If a client is a member of a trade union or professional organisation, it may be possible to arrange for their union or organisation to be responsible for payment of their solicitor's costs.

Historically, the commercial funding of litigation has been unlawful. However, in recent years, private funding of large commercial claims has become accepted (see, for example, *Arkin v Borchard Lines Ltd* [2005] EWCA Civ 655). Section 58B of the CLSA 1990 makes provision for litigation funding agreements, but at the time of writing it is not in force.

2.4.7   Public funding

In very limited circumstances, clients may receive public funding (legal aid) for civil litigation, and the solicitor should always consider whether this might be available. Most civil litigation matters within the scope of this book will not, however, benefit from public funding and what follows is, therefore, no more than a broad outline.

Public funding for both civil and criminal matters is administered by the Legal Aid Agency (LAA).

Public funding will not usually be available for cases that could be financed by a CFA. With very limited exceptions, claims in negligence for personal injury, death or damage to property (including intellectual property) are excluded. Neither is funding available for matters arising out of the carrying on of a business, including claims brought or defended by sole traders.

In addition to these restrictions, public funding is only open to clients whose income and capital falls within financial eligibility limits. These limits vary, depending on whether the client is seeking full representation in proceedings or merely wants assistance from a solicitor to investigate a proposed claim.

Furthermore, where the client is financially eligible and the claim is of a type covered by public funding, it will be offered only if a merits test is also satisfied. This involves considering the client's prospects of success and applying cost–benefit criteria (ie, weighing the likely cost of the proceedings against their benefit to the client). Put simply, a client who has a strong claim that will not be expensive to pursue, but which would result in substantial damages, has a much better chance of securing funding than one whose prospects of winning are marginal or who wishes to pursue a claim that would involve costs that are disproportionate to its likely benefits.

Where a party is in receipt of public funding, they may be required to make a contribution from their disposable capital or their income towards the costs. Where a contribution is required from income, this is payable on a monthly basis for as long as the case is funded by the LAA. Any change in the client's circumstances must be notified to the LAA as it may affect the amount of the contribution or the client's entitlement to funding.

In *David Truex, Solicitor (a firm) v Kitchin* [2007] EWCA Civ 618, the Court of Appeal held that a solicitor must from the outset of a case consider whether a client might be eligible for legal aid. Why? First, it is quite wrong to incur substantial expenditure chargeable privately to the client if public funding is available. Secondly, a client will find it more difficult to change firms of solicitors if work has been done and a relationship built up before advice is given that a different firm could become involved. In this case, the Court observed that if the financial position of the defendant had been considered properly, and considered in the context of whether she might be eligible for public funding, the result would have been advice to go to a different firm offering legal aid at a very early stage. As a result, the claimant solicitors' firm was negligent and was denied its fees.

2.4.7.1   The statutory charge

Where a publicly-funded client recovers money as a result of the proceedings, they may have to repay some or all of their legal costs to the LAA out of the money recovered. This is known as the statutory charge, and it will apply only to the extent that the client does not succeed in recovering their costs from their opponent.

The same principle applies where the dispute involves property rather than money. Any property that is retained or transferred to the client is subject to the statutory charge.

The solicitor must ensure that the client has understood the statutory charge prior to accepting an offer of public funding.

2.5 CASE ANALYSIS

As was indicated at **1.4**, there are three key case analysis points – viability, liability, and quantum – which we would summarise in the following series of questions that need to be answered pre-action.

2.5.1 Liability

What is the cause of action? Is there more than one? If so, analyse each independently and identify the relevant law. Establish the legal elements which must be proved for the claim to succeed. Your objective will be to identify evidence already available or that can be obtained in respect of each of these elements. Does it support the case, or is it adverse? How strong is it?

2.5.2 Limitation

2.5.2.1 Solicitor's role

From the outset, a solicitor must ascertain when the limitation period began and when it will expire. The matter must be reviewed continually in the light of any new facts. Careful diary notes must be kept, reminding the solicitor that time is marching on and the expiration of the limitation period draws closer. Proceedings must be issued before the limitation period expires, otherwise the solicitor is likely to face a negligence claim.

Whilst it is always best practice to ensure that proceedings are started well before the limitation period expires, unfortunately some claim forms are sent, or delivered, to the court very close to the expiry date. In *St Helens Metropolitan BC v Barnes* [2006] EWCA Civ 1372, the Court of Appeal had to determine if proceedings had been 'brought' within the limitation period. The claimant's solicitors had delivered the claim form to the County Court on the day prior to the expiry of the limitation period and requested that the claim should be issued. However, the claim form was not issued by the court staff until four days later. The Court held that the matter was resolved in favour of the claimant by PD 7A, para 5.1, which provides that:

> Proceedings are started when the court issues a claim form at the request of the claimant (see rule 7.2) but where the claim form as issued was received in the court office on a date earlier than the date on which it was issued by the court, the claim is 'brought' for the purposes of the Limitation Act 1980 and any other relevant statute on that earlier date.

If a party is using the e-filing service under the Electronic Working Pilot Scheme, limitation is governed by PD 51O and the claim form will be deemed issued when the relevant court fee was paid on the CE-file.

The Limitation Act 1980 (LA 1980) (as amended) prescribes fixed periods of time for issuing various types of proceedings. This is important to a client because if this period of time elapses without proceedings being issued, the case becomes 'statute-barred'. The claimant can still commence their claim, but the defendant will have an impregnable defence. If the defendant wishes to rely on this, it must be stated specifically in their defence (see **Chapter 7**).

2.5.2.2 Claims founded on contract or tort (LA 1980, ss 2 and 5)

The basic rule is that the claimant has six years from the date when the cause of action accrued to commence their proceedings.

In contract, the cause of action accrues as soon as the breach of contract occurs. This will be a question of fact, and you will need to check to see if case law has established when the cause accrues. For example, with an anticipatory breach of contract, the cause of action accrues when the intention not to perform the contract is made clear, and not at the later date when performance was due to occur (*Hochester v de la Tour* (1853) 2 E & B 678).

In tort, the cause of action accrues when the tort is committed. In the tort of negligence, as damage is an essential element, the cause of action accrues only when some damage occurs.

This may be at a date considerably later than that when the breach of duty itself occurred. Like contract claims, it may be necessary to research any relevant case law. For example, in a negligent misstatement claim, the cause of action will accrue on the date the claimant sustains damage as a result of reliance on the advice (*Forster v Outred & Co* [1982] 2 All ER 753).

This basic rule is modified in the case of certain specific types of claim. As to personal injury cases, see **Personal Injury and Clinical Negligence Litigation.**

2.5.2.3 Latent damage

In a non-personal injury claim based on negligence, where the damage is latent at the date when the cause of action accrued, s 14A of the LA 1980 provides that the limitation period expires either:

(a)   six years from the date on which the cause of action accrued; or

(b)   three years from the date of knowledge of certain material facts about the damage, if this period expires after the period mentioned in (a).

In theory, these rules could mean that a defendant is indefinitely open to the risk of proceedings being issued in latent damage cases. In order to avoid this, there is a long-stop limitation period of 15 years from the date of the alleged breach of duty (LA 1980, s 14B). This long-stop may bar a cause of action at a date earlier than the claimant's knowledge; indeed, it may even bar a cause of action before it has accrued.

2.5.2.4 Persons under disability

A person under a disability is either a child (ie, someone who has not yet attained the age of 18), or a protected party (ie, a person of unsound mind within the meaning of the Mental Capacity Act 2005 and who is incapable of managing and administering their property and affairs).

Where the claimant is a person under a disability when a right of action accrues, the limitation period does not begin to run until the claimant ceases to be under that disability. See generally **5.4.1.**

2.5.2.5 Contractual limitation

In a contract case it is very important to check whether a contractual limitation period is specified in the contract. This is because any such provision is usually shorter than the statutory limitation periods referred to above, and the claim should therefore be commenced within the contractually specified period.

2.5.2.6 Summary

Type of claim	Statutory limitation period
Contract (excluding personal injury)	6 years (LA 1980, s 5)
Tort (excluding personal injury and latent damage)	6 years (LA 1980, s 2)
Latent damage	6 years or 3 years from date of knowledge (LA 1980, s 14A)

2.5.3 Remedies

There are a number of alternative remedies that a claimant can pursue against the defendant, assuming liability can be established. The most common remedy sought is damages. It is important to establish at an early stage what the client's objective is. If the client has unrealistic expectations or requires a remedy the court has no power to award, you should identify and discuss this at the earliest possible stage.

2.5.3.1 Damages

The rules as to quantum of damages in civil cases depend on the type of claim being pursued. As to claiming interest on damages, see **2.7** below.

2.5.3.2 Contract

A claim for damages arises when one party to the contract has failed to perform an obligation under the contract. The purpose of damages in such a situation is to place the injured party in the position they would have been in if the contract had been performed properly.

For example, damages can be recovered either for the repair of defective goods, or for repayment of the purchase price. In addition, there may be a claim for general damages in respect of physical discomfort and/or inconvenience. However, damages for injured feelings or mental distress are not generally recoverable. There is an exception where the subject matter of the contract was to provide enjoyment, peace of mind or freedom from distress, eg a contract for a holiday. In such cases, damages for mental distress and loss of enjoyment are recoverable.

The test for the recovery of damages for breach of contract is that they must not be too remote from the breach. In other words, did the loss flow naturally from the breach, or was the loss within the reasonable contemplation of the parties at the time the contract was made as being the probable result of the breach?

2.5.3.3 Tort

A claim for damages in tort arises where injury, loss or damage is caused to the claimant or the claimant's property. The aim of damages is, so far as possible, to place the claimant in the position they would have been in if the damage had not occurred. Damages are therefore compensatory in nature and, as a result, the claimant can seek compensation for any direct loss and consequential loss, provided the rules on remoteness are not broken. The rules on remoteness require that in order to be recoverable the loss must be a reasonably foreseeable consequence of the tort.

2.5.3.4 Reduction in damages – duty to mitigate

Any potential claim for damages for either breach of contract or tort may be reduced if it can be shown that the claimant has failed to mitigate their loss. In *Frost v Knight* (1872) LR 7 Ex 111 the court observed that this duty means looking at what the claimant 'has done, or has had the means of doing, and, as a prudent man, ought in reason to have done, whereby his loss has been, or would have been, diminished'. So a claimant cannot recover by way of damages 'any greater sum than that which he reasonably needs to expend for the purpose of making good the loss' (*Darbishire v Warran* [1963] 1 WLR 1067).

The duty arises only on the breach of contract or commission of the tort. If a defendant alleges that the claimant has failed to take all reasonable steps to mitigate the claimant's loss, the defendant should raise that in pre-action correspondence (see **Chapter 3**) and state it in their defence (see **7.3**). The burden of proof will be on the defendant at any trial. If, however, the claimant wishes to contest the issue properly, they should produce appropriate evidence: see *Bulkhaul Ltd v Rhodia Organique Fine Ltd* [2008] EWCA Civ 1452.

2.5.3.5 Debt

A debt action is a particular type of contract claim. Instead of claiming damages for breach of contract, the claimant is claiming a sum which the defendant promised to pay under the contract.

For example, in a sale of goods case, if the buyer wrongfully rejects the goods (and the seller accepts this as repudiation of the contract), the seller has a claim for damages for breach of contract. However, if the buyer takes delivery but then fails to pay then the action is for debt. The significance is that in the latter case the claimant has no duty to mitigate their loss.

2.5.4 Quantum

When you have determined the amount the client is claiming (quantum), you will need to think about the evidence you have to prove the loss. As with liability, the claimant must prove each item and what evidence is currently available or may be obtainable. Are any figures or estimates available? Do any issues of remoteness or mitigation of loss arise? Do you need to take any steps to preserve evidence? If you have evidence which cannot be preserved (eg perishable goods), make sure you carry out any necessary tests/expert examination before it is too late; and where possible, offer your opponent facilities for inspection so that they can carry out their own tests.

2.6 VIABILITY AND BURDEN OF PROOF

2.6.1 Viability

If your case analysis indicates that there is a legal basis for the claim and evidence to support the claim, there are a number of other issues affecting the overall viability of pursuing a claim against a potential defendant which need to be considered with the client at the earliest possible stage.

Viability involves a number of issues of which the claimant needs to be aware, including:

- Who is the prospective defendant?
- Is there more than one possible defendant?
- Where is the defendant?
- Is the defendant solvent?
- Where are the defendant's assets?
- What are those assets worth?
- Will the defendant be able to pay any judgment?
- What can the client afford to pay?
- Does the client have any suitable BEI?
- Is the case suitable for a CFA or DBA and/or AEI cover?
- Does the client qualify for public funding or require third-party funding?
- How much time and resources will the client have to commit to investigate and deal with the case?
- Does a cost–benefit analysis suggest the desirability of a quicker and cheaper solution than litigation can offer?

2.6.1.1 Identify all potential defendants and their status

As we saw at **1.3.1.2** above, the general rule is that all persons to be sued should be sued at the same time and in the same claim. Your case analysis must identify against whom each cause of action lies. Very often there is only one potential defendant, but, for example, where an employee or agent commits a tort when acting in the course of their employment, it is usual to sue both the employee or agent and the employer. This is because the latter is vicariously liable for the former. Likewise, a consumer may, in certain circumstances, have a cause of action against both the retailer and the manufacturer of a defective product.

Not only must you identify the prospective defendants, you must also ensure they are sued in their correct capacity. Broadly, you should consider if the potential defendant is an individual, a partnership or a limited company. Sometimes it is not as obvious as it seems.

> **EXAMPLE**
>
> Assume your client entered into a contract negotiated with a Mr Jones. We need to ask in what capacity Mr Jones acted. Did he act as an individual on his own behalf? Was he acting as an agent for someone else and, if so, did our client know that? Is he one of, say, 10 partners in a firm called Jones & Co, and did he contract on behalf of the partnership? Is he a director in a limited company called Jones Ltd, and did he contract on behalf of that company? Just exactly with whom did the client contract? Will he end up negotiating with, and potentially litigating against, Mr Jones, Mr Jones's principal, Jones & Co (a firm) or Jones Ltd? See further **5.4**.

2.6.1.2 Defendant's solvency

There is little point in suing a defendant who is on the verge of either bankruptcy or liquidation. Enforcement of any judgment obtained would be impossible. If there is doubt as to the liquidity of the prospective defendant then further enquiries should be made. For example, if the proposed defendant is a company, a company search should be carried out. For an individual, a bankruptcy search should be done. In any case an inquiry agent could be instructed, although the costs of doing this must be considered. It may also be possible to use various Internet search engines to see if there is any relevant information about the proposed defendant.

2.6.1.3 Defendant's whereabouts

Clearly, the defendant needs to be traceable and their whereabouts known in order to communicate the claim and, if necessary, serve proceedings. Again, an inquiry agent may be able to help.

2.6.1.4 The claim itself

This involves balancing the merits of the claim itself against the overall cost of pursuing it and the prospects of a successful outcome. The client may believe they have a good claim but will be concerned as to the costs of litigation. Finance has been discussed above (see **2.4**), but the client must be advised at this stage on the law, and any possible defences to the claim should be anticipated. The client must be told of the overriding objective and the requirement in r 1.3 that parties must help the court further the overriding objective. A commercial client will also need to take into account what damage, if any, may be caused to its market standing and/or product image by pursuing a claim.

2.6.1.5 Alternative remedies

The solicitor should consider whether there are any alternative remedies available to the client for resolving the problem and advise the client accordingly. For example, the client may wish to use one of the forms of alternative dispute resolution (see **Chapter 4**).

2.6.2 Burden of proof

There are two questions of proof that need to be considered.

2.6.2.1 Legal burden

The party asserting a fact must prove it unless it is admitted by their opponent. For example, a claimant who alleges negligence must prove all the elements of the tort (ie, a duty existed between the parties, the defendant breached that duty, and the claimant sustained damage as a result). Similarly, a claimant alleging breach of contract must prove that a contract existed between the parties, the defendant broke the relevant express and/or implied terms of the contract, and the claimant suffered loss as a result.

What about a defendant? Whilst they do not have to prove their defence, any allegation of failure to mitigate loss (see **2.5.3.4**) or contributory negligence will have to be proved. Note that as to contributory negligence, the defendant must also prove that the claimant's failure was a contributory cause of the defendant's damage: see *Lewis v Denye* [1939] 1 KB 540.

2.6.2.2 Balance of probabilities

In civil cases, the claimant is required to prove a fact on a balance of probabilities. This simply requires the judge to be persuaded that the claimant's version of events is more likely to be true than the defendant's version. Your case analysis should enable you to take a preliminary view on whether your client will be able to discharge the burden of proof and succeed on liability and quantum.

2.7 INTEREST

2.7.1 Specified and unspecified claims for money

The CPR 1998 provide no definition of a claim for a specified or unspecified sum of money. The N1A Notes for a claimant on completing the claim form (see **5.3.1** and the copy at **Appendix A(1)**) refer to a claim for a *fixed amount of money* as being a specified amount. On that basis, a specified claim is in the nature of a debt (ie, a fixed amount of money due and payable under and by virtue of a contract). The amount will be known already (from, say, an invoice), or it should be capable of being determined by mere mathematics (from, say, a contractual formula). Examples might include the price of goods sold, commission said to be due under express contractual terms or consideration said to have failed totally.

If the court will have to conduct an investigation to decide on the amount of money payable, the claim is best seen as being for an unspecified amount, even if the claimant puts some figures forward for the amount claimed. For example, in a damages claim for breach of contract, the claimant might have had to repair or replace goods. Whilst a figure can be given for the cost of that, it will be for the trial judge to determine if it is reasonable. Thus, damages claims should usually be regarded as unspecified.

What if a claim is a mixture of specified and unspecified amounts? For example, the recovery of consideration paid that has failed totally (a specified amount), plus damages for breach of contract (unspecified amounts). In these circumstances the entire claim is treated as an unspecified claim.

2.7.2 Entitlement to interest

Pre-action, a prospective claimant can demand interest on a claim only if entitled to it under any contractual provision (including any provision implied by the Late Payments of Commercial Debts (Interest) Act 1998: see further below).

Where the remedy sought by the claimant is either damages or the repayment of a debt, the court may award interest on the sum outstanding. The rules vary according to the type of claim. A claimant seeking interest must specifically claim interest in the particulars of claim.

2.7.2.1 Breach of contract including debt claims

In contract cases, there are three alternative claims to interest:

(a)   The contract itself may specify a rate of interest payable on any outstanding sum. This will be the rate negotiated between the parties. The court will usually apply this rate.

(b)   It may be possible to claim interest under the Late Payment of Commercial Debts (Interest) Act 1998 (see below).

(c)   In all other cases, the court has a discretion to award interest either under s 35A of the Senior Courts Act 1981 (SCA 1981) in respect of High Court cases, or under s 69 of the County Courts Act 1984 (CCA 1984) in respect of County Court cases. The current rate of interest payable under either statute is 8% pa in non-commercial cases and, generally, 1% or 2% pa over base rate in commercial cases (see further **2.7.2.3**).

Since a debt claim is for a specified amount of money, interest must be claimed precisely, giving as a lump sum the amount of interest which has accrued from breach of contract up to the date of issue of the proceedings and a daily rate thereafter. In a debt claim, where s 35A of the SCA 1981 or s 69 of the CCA 1984 applies, the convention is to claim interest from and including the day after the last day payment was due. In a damages claim, the request for interest is not set out in detail as the claim is for an unspecified amount of money.

EXAMPLE: SPECIFIED CLAIM

You act for Mr Tibbs, a local builder. He is in dispute with one of his customers, Mrs Little. He entered into a written contract to convert her basement into a bedroom last year. He finished the work on 12 September this year but, despite reminders, Mrs Little has not paid him the contract price of £13,000. The written contract between Mr Tibbs and Mrs Little provides that interest is payable on late payment. This is due at the rate of 20% per annum from and including the day of completion of the works. If a claim form is issued this year on 31 October, how much interest should be claimed?

Mr Tibbs is entitled to interest on £13,000 for 50 days (namely, 19 days in September and 31 days in October). For each day, he is entitled to interest of £7.12 (that is £13,000 × 20% ÷ 365; the answer of £7.1232876 is rounded down in the circumstances). So, on the claim form he should claim £356.00 by way of interest.

What if the contract did not provide for interest payable on late payment? Mr Tibbs would then claim interest in County Court (non-commercial) proceedings at 8% pa under s 69 of the CCA 1984. That would give him a daily rate of interest of £2.85 (£13,000 x 8% ÷ 365; the answer of £2.849315 is rounded up in the circumstances).

Late Payment of Commercial Debts (Interest) Act 1998

This Act (as amended by the Late Payment of Commercial Debt Regulations 2013 (SI 2013/ 395) and the Late Payment of Commercial Debts (Amendment) Regulations 2015 (SI 2015/ 1336)) gives a statutory right to interest on commercial debts that are paid late if the contract itself does not provide for interest in the event of late payment. The term 'commercial debt' includes debts arising from the supply of goods and services. As the Act is only concerned with commercial debt, it does not apply to unspecified claims or a specified amount owed by a consumer.

Interest under the Act can be claimed at a rate of 8% pa above the Bank of England's reference rate on the date the debt became due for payment. The reference rate is the base rate applicable on 31 December and 30 June each year and will apply for the following six months. For example, if the base rate is 0.5% pa on 30 June, this is the reference rate for the period 1 July to 31 December, and so interest of 8.5% pa in total can be claimed under the Act. The interest accrues from the expiry of any period of credit under the contract. If the contract does not provide for any such period, interest can be claimed from 30 days after the latest of:

(a)   delivery of the bill;

(b)   delivery of the goods;

(c)   performance of the service.

The parties may agree to extend the period from 30 days up to a maximum of 60 days. Any further extension must not be grossly unfair to the supplier. In addition to the debt and interest, the Act also provides for payment of a fixed sum of between £40 and £100 compensation for late payment, the amount varying according to the size of the debt. In addition, the supplier may also claim as compensation any 'reasonable' costs of recovering the debt that exceed the fixed sum.

An example appears in the claim form at **7.2.1.6.**

2.7.2.2   Tort

The court has a general discretion to award interest on damages in any negligence claim. This power is derived from SCA 1981, s 35A in respect of High Court claims, and from CCA 1984, s 69 in respect of County Court claims. Generally speaking, if interest has been claimed properly, the court will normally exercise its discretion to award interest for such period as it considers appropriate.

2.7.2.3   From what date is interest payable and for how much?

In a contract or tort claim for damages, from what date is the court likely to start an award of interest? In theory interest can be awarded from when the cause of action first arose (see **2.5.2.2**). However, in practice, the award is normally made from when the loss is sustained (if this is later). Consider the facts in the case of *Kaines (UK) Ltd v Osterreichische* [1993] 2 Lloyd's Rep 1. There, in June 1987 the defendants repudiated a contract to sell the claimants oil for lifting in September 1987 and payment in October 1987. As a result, the claimants contracted to buy the same quantity of oil at a higher price from another supplier but on exactly the same terms (lifting in September 1987 and payment in October 1987). In August 1987 the claimants issued proceedings. The Court of Appeal held that it was only in October 1987, when the claimants had paid the higher price, that the claimants had sustained any loss. Therefore, interest did not start to run on the damages until October 1987. So, the key is to work out carefully the date of loss.

EXAMPLE

In a negligent surveyor's case, liability is established, and quantum assessed by the court as the diminution in value of the property, ie the difference between what the claimant actually paid and the value of the property in its true condition. Assume the diminution in value is assessed at 10%. When is loss sustained by the claimant?

There are two dates to consider. First, when the claimant paid the deposit on exchange of contracts because he paid 10% too much and so was then out of pocket by that amount. (If a deposit of £25,000 was paid, the damages would be £2,500 plus interest from exchange.) Secondly, when the claimant paid the balance of the purchase price on completion, because again he had paid 10% too much and so was out of pocket. (If the balance paid was £225,000, the damages would be £22,500 plus interest from completion.) On both dates that money could have been in the claimant's bank earning interest. See *Watts v Morrow* [1991] 1 WLR 1421.

In a contract or tort claim for damages, how much interest is the court likely to award? Such an award is compensatory in nature. In *Kuwait Airways Corporation v Kuwait Insurance Company SAK* [2001] LTL, 16 June, Langley J stated that '[i]n principle interest is to be awarded to compensate the claimant for being kept out of the money from the date when it has been established that it was due to him'. In *Tate & Lyle Food and Distribution Ltd v Greater London Council* [1982] 1 WLR 149, Forbes J said:

> One looks, therefore, not at the profit which the defendant wrongly made out of the money he withheld – this would indeed involve a scrutiny of the defendant's financial position – but at the cost to the [claimant] of being deprived of the money which he should have had. I feel satisfied that in commercial cases the interest is intended to reflect the rate at which the [claimant] would have had to borrow money to supply the place of that which was withheld.

What is a commercial case? Generally, this is where all the parties are businesses and the claim is based on the transaction of trade and commerce, such as a business document or contract, the export or import of goods, banking and financial services, and the purchase and sale of commodities. Typically, non-commercial cases involve one party acting as a consumer, for example a prospective domestic house-buyer engaging the services of a surveyor.

In non-commercial cases, the courts award interest at their discretion under s 35A of the SCA 1981 or s 69 of the CCA 1984 at 8% pa. Traditionally, in commercial cases, the award of interest has been at 1% or 2% over base rate. However, in *Jaura v Ahmed* [2002] EWCA Civ 210, the Court of Appeal held that it is permissible for a judge to depart from this conventional rate if it is necessary to reflect the higher rate at which the claimant had to borrow, eg if the claimant was a small businessperson who could only borrow from a bank at 3% pa over base rate. In *Carrasco v Johnson* [2018] EWCA Civ 87 at [16], the Court of Appeal gave the following guidance:

(1)   Interest is awarded to compensate claimants for being kept out of money which ought to have been paid to them rather than as compensation for damage done or to deprive defendants of profit they may have made from the use of the money.

(2)   This is a question to be approached broadly. The court will consider the position of persons with the claimants' general attributes, but will not have regard to claimants' particular attributes or any special position in which they may have been.

(3)   In relation to commercial claimants the general presumption will be that they would have borrowed less and so the court will have regard to the rate at which persons with the general attributes of the claimant could have borrowed. This is likely to be a percentage over base rate and may be higher for small businesses than for first class borrowers.

(4)   Many claimants will not fall clearly into a category of those who would have borrowed or those who would have put money on deposit and a fair rate for them may often fall somewhere between those two rates.

As a general rule, unless a contractual term provides for it, an award of simple interest is made rather than an award of compound interest. In exceptional cases, such as a claim for restitution, compound interest may be awarded if that will achieve full justice for the claimant: see *Sempra Metals Ltd v Inland Revenue Commissioners* [2007] UKHL 34.

2.7.2.4   Key questions to be addressed

The flowchart at **Appendix C(4)** highlights the following key questions that you need to address:

(a)   *Pre-action* (to be demanded in the letter before claim): is the claim based on a written contract that provides for the payment of interest? Is the claim for the payment of a commercial debt?

(b)   *During proceedings* (to be demanded in the particulars of claim): is the claim based on a written contract that provides for the payment of interest? Is the claim for the payment of a commercial debt? Is the claim (contract and/or tort based) proceeding in the High Court or County Court?

Remember that a defendant might also be in a position to make a claim in contract and/or tort that includes interest. So, pre-action they might demand such in a letter of response (see **3.8.5**) and during proceedings in a counterclaim (see **8.2.1**).

2.8   FOREIGN ELEMENT AND CHOICE OF FORUM

If a solicitor is instructed by a client who is based abroad, or is instructed to take proceedings against a party based abroad, one of the first things which must be considered is the question of jurisdiction – in which country's courts can proceedings be commenced? This is usually determined by whether or not a claimant requires the court's permission to serve proceedings outside of England and Wales (see further **5.5.7**).

The English courts can hear any proceedings if the claim form was served on the defendant whilst they were present in England and Wales (no matter how briefly). The defendant could then, however, object to the proceedings continuing in England on the ground that the English courts are not the most appropriate ones for resolving the dispute.

So, if an English person has an accident in New York caused by the negligence of a local New Yorker, and then is able to serve the defendant with a claim form whilst the defendant is in England on holiday, the defendant could object to the proceedings continuing in England on the basis that New York state was a more convenient forum.

2.9   ALTERNATIVES TO LITIGATION

There are several alternatives to court proceedings that may produce the remedy the client wants, possibly at less cost. These alternative procedures should always be considered at first interview and reviewed regularly.

2.9.1   Arbitration

Arbitration is an adjudication operating outside the normal court process, by which a third party reaches a decision that is binding on the parties in dispute. Many business contracts contain an arbitration clause requiring the parties to refer their disputes to arbitration rather than litigation. In the absence of such a clause, the parties in dispute may agree to arbitration once the dispute has arisen, and may choose their own arbitrator with the relevant expertise. Arbitration itself is largely governed by statute, namely the Arbitration Act 1996 (provided the agreement to arbitrate is in writing).

The main advantages of the parties agreeing to arbitration instead of litigation are that:

(a)   arbitration may be quicker than litigation;

(b)   the procedures are less formal and occur in private;

(c)   the solutions reached are often more practical than those a court has power to order; and

(d)   at the same time those decisions are binding on the parties.

The winning party to an arbitration can apply to the High Court for permission to enforce the arbitration award as if it were a court judgment (Arbitration Act 1996, s 66).

On the other hand, the main disadvantages of using arbitration are that certain remedies, such as injunctions, are not available and, depending on the procedures adopted, the dispute may not receive the depth of investigation it would have done in the courts. Further, it is not always necessarily cheaper than litigation.

2.9.2   Alternative dispute resolution

Alternative dispute resolution (ADR) is a means of resolving disputes, normally by using an independent third party to help the parties to reach a solution. The third party will often suggest a solution to the parties but not impose one (known as 'non-determinative ADR'). But sometimes the third party will impose a solution (known as 'determinative ADR'). The decision to use ADR is voluntary; the parties choose the process and either of them can withdraw at any time before a settlement is reached.

There are various types of ADR, such as mediation, expert appraisal or expert determination.

Under the CPR 1998, the courts actively encourage parties to use some form of ADR. This is considered in more detail in **Chapter 4**.

Can a court order that parties must use an ADR method? No, held the Court of Appeal in *Halsey v Milton Keynes General NHS Trust* [2004] EWCA Civ 576, [2004] 4 All ER 920. As Dyson LJ stated:

> It is one thing to encourage the parties to agree to mediation, even to encourage them in the strongest terms. It is another to order them to do so. It seems to us that to oblige truly unwilling parties to refer their disputes to mediation would be to impose an unacceptable obstruction on their right of access to the court.

However, as to the costs consequences of unreasonably refusing to consider or use ADR, see **14.3.3.6**.

In *Lomax v Lomax* [2019] EWCA Civ 1467, the Court had to consider r 3.1(2)(m) of the CPR 1998, which gives the court power to '... make any other order for the purpose of managing the case and furthering the overriding objective, including hearing an Early Neutral Evaluation with the aim of helping the parties settle the case'. The defendant did not wish to engage in Early Neutral Evaluation (ENE), and at first instance the judge held that the court had no jurisdiction to order it without the consent of both parties. On appeal, the Court held that in the absence of any express reference to consent in r 3.1(2)(m), none was required and the court did have the power to order ENE. The Court distinguished the case from *Halsey* by virtue of the fact that ENE is itself a part of the court process, unlike mediation or other forms of ADR.

2.9.3 Trade schemes

Some professional bodies and trade associations operate schemes under which a potential claimant may be able to pursue a remedy outside the courts. This is often cheaper and quicker than court proceedings.

2.9.4 Negotiating settlements

A solicitor should always consider with the client whether it is possible to negotiate a settlement with the opponent. Negotiations should be commenced as soon as possible and a genuine attempt made to limit the areas of dispute between the parties. Once all reasonable attempts to settle have been exhausted, there may well be no alternative but to issue proceedings. However, the matter must always be kept under review, and the parties should make appropriate attempts to resolve the matter without issuing proceedings. Failure to do so may result in one or more of the parties being punished financially during litigation.

Negotiations are considered in more detail in **Chapter 13**.

2.9.5 Insurance

Many defendants to civil claims are insured. Drivers of motor vehicles are required by law to possess insurance that covers them for at least the minimum insurance (basically third party) under the Road Traffic Act 1988. Most professional bodies require their practising members to be insured against negligence claims by clients.

The existence of insurers does not in any way affect the conduct of the proceedings, and the insurers are not a party to the claim as there is no cause of action against them. However, the majority of insurance policies require the insured to notify the insurers of any potential claim in order that they can consider taking over the claim on behalf of the insured. Where an insurance company is involved, the company, or its solicitors, will usually deal with any negotiations or subsequent court proceedings.

In certain circumstances, a judgment against an insured defendant can be enforced against the insurers. Notice of the proceedings must be served on the insurers either before or within seven days of commencing proceedings to invoke these provisions.

2.9.6 Motor Insurers Bureau

The Motor Insurers Bureau (MIB) operates two schemes which allow the victims of either uninsured or untraced drivers to recover compensation for certain losses sustained. The MIB is a scheme set up by the insurance companies and is also financed by them.

2.9.7 Criminal Injuries Compensation Authority

The Criminal Injuries Compensation Authority (CICA) is a body set up by the Government to provide the victims of criminal acts with *ex gratia* compensation for any personal injuries sustained as a result of those acts.

2.9.8 Criminal compensation order

The criminal courts have powers to order compensation in respect of any personal injury, loss or damage resulting from a criminal offence when imposing sentence at the conclusion of criminal proceedings.

CASE STUDY: FIRST INTERVIEW CONSIDERATIONS FOR MR AND MRS SIMPSON

Professional Conduct

When Mr and Mrs Simpson made the appointment for the first interview with their solicitor, basic information, such as their full names, address, telephone number and Mr Templar's details, would have been taken. This would enable checks to be carried out to ascertain whether the solicitors' firm was acting or had acted in the past for Mr Templar. Obviously, if the firm already had instructions from Mr Templar to act for him in this matter, there would be a conflict of interest and the firm could not act for Mr and Mrs Simpson. But what if the firm had acted for Mr Templar in the past? Might the firm risk breaching the duty of confidentiality still owed to him? The answer might not be straightforward, as the confidential information held in respect of Mr Templar would have to be evaluated. If that information might reasonably be expected to be material to Mr and Mrs Simpson, such as Mr Templar's financial position or his attitude towards settling litigation then, given that the parties have opposing interests, the firm could not act for Mr and Mrs Simpson.

In our case study the checks reveal no problems. Moreover, Mr and Mrs Simpson provide satisfactory evidence of their identities so that the firm can complete its money laundering checks.

Funding

The solicitor must act in the best interests of Mr and Mrs Simpson, and that includes identifying the most cost-effective ways of achieving their objectives. They should be asked if they have any existing legal expenses insurance cover, and any policies should be checked. Enquiries should be made of any trade or professional organisations which might provide them with funding. Whether or not the firm acts under CFAs or DBAs or provides AEI, these options should be discussed. Eligibility for and availability of public funding should also be examined.

For the purposes of the case study, assume that Mr and Mrs Simpson decide to instruct their solicitors privately. The solicitors provide them with full details in accordance with para 8.7 of the SRA Code of Conduct.

Case Analysis

See **Appendix D(1)**. At this stage the facts as outlined by Mr and Mrs Simpson point to negligent driving by Mr Templar that has caused them loss. But will Mr Templar admit that? What evidence of quantum do they have? As the case progresses, we shall revisit the facts and evidence to see how the analysis develops.

Note that in order to keep this case study a straightforward claim against one defendant, the potential liability of the claimants' builders, if they did leave glass on the driveway, is ignored.

We have set out below a few key factors addressed in this chapter that form part of the analysis.

Limitation

The claim is in the tort of negligence and the limitation period will start from the date when the damage occurred. Here that is the date of the accident, namely 2 August 2021. As there is no claim for personal injuries, Mr and Mrs Simpson will have six years (ie until 2 August 2027) to start proceedings.

Viability

In this case we know the identity of the potential defendant, Mr Geoffrey Templar, and Mr and Mrs Simpson have contact details for him. These should be checked. If ultimately he cannot be located then he cannot be sent correspondence or later served with court documents.

Can he pay damages and costs if these become payable? As the damage occurred whilst he was driving his car, he can claim under his car insurance policy (assuming he is insured). This should be checked and his insurer's details obtained so that it can be notified of the claim.

Jurisdiction

As both parties are resident within England and Wales and the incident happened here, there are no jurisdiction issues in this case.

Alternatives to Litigation

The solicitor should consider with Mr and Mrs Simpson now and as the case develops whether any ADR method might be appropriate. Obviously, whether any method is viable will first depend upon Mr Templar also wishing to use it. See further **Chapters 3** and **4**.

CHAPTER 3

EARLY ACTION

3.1	Writing to the client	38
3.2	Interviewing witnesses	38
3.3	Preserving documents	40
3.4	Obtaining expert evidence	41
3.5	Site visits	42
3.6	Instructing counsel	43
3.7	Pre-action protocols	44
3.8	Pre-action correspondence	46
3.9	Pre-action disclosure	49
3.10	Settlement	50
3.11	Researching the law	52
3.12	Cost–benefit analysis	52
3.13	Summary of pre-action steps	52
3.14	Summary of Practice Direction on Pre-Action Conduct and Protocols	53

LEARNING OUTCOMES

After reading this chapter you will have learned:

- how to take a proof of evidence from a witness
- the role of experts at this stage
- when it may be appropriate to instruct a barrister
- how to comply with pre-action protocols
- what to include in a letter before claim
- how to conduct without prejudice negotiations
- why it may be necessary to research the law.

As we saw at **1.4** and **2.5**, case analysis is the key to representing a client effectively. So when you take the initial statement, otherwise known as a proof of evidence, from the client (or indeed any other witness), you should make a careful note of the main points and ask questions to obtain further information in order to develop that analysis. The key to obtaining a full and accurate set of instructions from the client is to probe but not prompt. Bear in mind that the statement should be in the client's own words. Let the client tell their story, and try to ensure that it develops logically and chronologically. Some clients will fail to do this, and you should make a note of any gaps and fill these in by questioning. If any part is ambiguous, get it clarified. You must end up with a clear picture of what the client's case is all about. You can then advise as to its strengths and weaknesses, and consider what further evidence needs to be obtained. You will not be in a position to negotiate effectively with the other side, or present your client's case in an ADR process or to a court, if you do not understand that case properly.

After the first interview with a potential claimant (or defendant), there are a number of practical preliminary steps the solicitor can take to advance the client's claim (or defence). The main requirements are to confirm the client's instructions and your advice in writing, and to obtain relevant evidence. The solicitor will also have to bear in mind at all times the pre-action protocols under the CPR 1998. Where no specific approved protocol applies to the claim, the solicitor must still comply with the 'spirit' of the protocols and the Practice Direction on Pre-action Conduct and Protocols which provides general guidance on the conduct of the case at this stage: see further **3.7** below.

3.1 WRITING TO THE CLIENT

You should set out your advice to the client in writing as soon as possible after the interview. By now you should have identified the cause of action, undertaken any necessary legal research and assessed the available evidence. If a proof of evidence has been taken from the client, this should be sent to the client for approval and signature. If there are any 'gaps' in the case – factual issues in respect of which there is no evidence or weak evidence – you must explain this to the client and outline the options.

The initial letter of advice to the client should include the following:

(a)   identify clearly the client's objectives in relation to the work to be done for the client;

(b)   give the client a clear explanation of the issues involved and the options available to the client; and

(c)   list the steps that are to be taken next.

Often, details of funding and costs are included in the initial letter of advice or a separate letter. The solicitor should give the client the best information possible about the likely overall cost of the matter. This should include:

(a)   advising the client of the basis and terms of the firm's charges;

(b)   advising the client of likely payments to third parties (eg court fees, barristers' fees, experts' fees);

(c)   setting out how the client has agreed to pay; and

(d)   advising the client of their potential liability for another party's costs.

Further, a solicitor should have discussed with the client whether the potential outcomes of any legal case would justify the expense or risk involved, including, if relevant, the risk of having to pay an opponent's costs. It is best practice to record this advice in writing and subsequently as the case develops.

Lastly, the letter should explain the next steps that are to be taken by the solicitor, and remind the client of any matters they have agreed to undertake.

3.2 INTERVIEWING WITNESSES

3.2.1 Proof of evidence

The solicitor should arrange to take a proof of evidence from any witnesses as soon as possible, while matters are still fresh in their minds. There is no 'property' in a witness, and the solicitor may request an interview with anyone who may have information about the case. However, there is nothing that can be done if a witness absolutely refuses to give a statement. A witness may do this, for example, because they do not wish to say anything against their employer, or simply because they do not wish to get involved.

3.2.2 Professional conduct

It is permissible for a solicitor to interview and take a proof of evidence (statement) from a prospective witness where that witness has already been interviewed by another party. However, there is a risk that the solicitor will be exposed to the allegation that they have improperly tampered with evidence. This can be overcome by offering to conduct the interview in the presence of a representative of the other party.

There is no objection to a client, through their solicitors, paying reasonable expenses to a witness and reasonable compensation for loss of time attending court.

3.2.3 The reluctant witness

At the eventual trial of the case, a person can be compelled to attend as a witness, but the solicitor will be reluctant to advise their client to call someone as a witness if they have not obtained a full statement from the witness beforehand, because, of course, the solicitor will have no guarantee that the witness is going to say anything relevant or favourable in the witness-box. Therefore, it is most important to persuade potential witnesses to give a statement if at all possible. If the witness refuses, the solicitor could use a witness summary (see **12.5**).

3.2.4 Taking a proof of evidence

The solicitor will normally write to the witnesses initially and arrange a convenient time for an interview to take place. This may be at the solicitor's office, or the solicitor may have to go out to the witness's home or place of work.

3.2.4.1 Personal details

Start an interview by taking down the basics, ie the witness's full name, address, date of birth, telephone contact numbers, e-mail address, etc. If you are not interviewing the client, make a note of any relationship the witness has with the client, eg relative or employee.

3.2.4.2 Open and closed questions

Obtaining facts from a witness can be a difficult task. Let the witness tell their own story by using open questions. This should give you a fair idea of what the witness can say. Then fill in any gaps in the detail by using closed questions. Clarify points that are unclear and ensure that you have the entire story. Pose probing questions but do not prompt a witness. Do not put words in the witness's mouth. Moreover, remember that it is the witness's words that you want to record and have in the proof of evidence, not your own version. Make suitable notes, or record the interview with the witness's consent.

3.2.4.3 Documents

Make sure that you obtain any relevant documents. You may have to think laterally about what relevant documents a witness can provide. Probe, as the witness may not volunteer a document (eg, ask if there was any written contract; pre-contract and/or post-contract correspondence; letters of complaint; in-house reports and memos; faxes; e-mails; documents held on a computer or laptop; documents in storage, etc).

3.2.4.4 'Picture painting'

Think of an interview as a 'picture painting' task. Ask yourself during the interview: do you understand what is being portrayed; can you picture in your mind what the witness is describing? It is best to take down the details in chronological order. Is the story clear? If it is not comprehensible to you then how are you going to communicate it effectively to the other side, or to an arbitrator or an ADR representative, or ultimately to a judge at trial? A site visit may also help, where appropriate. You can then observe the scene of any incident and will not have to imagine it. Equally, photographs and/or site plans may assist in some cases.

3.2.4.5 Structure

So that you can adapt a proof of evidence later for any court proceedings, it is best set out in numbered paragraphs. Each paragraph should deal with only one topic.

3.2.4.6 Credibility

'Picture painting' and the credibility of a witness are intrinsically linked. If a witness has already made a written statement, perhaps to the factory manager after an accident, make sure that you look out for any inconsistencies when you now interview that person. For example, in their statement to the manager the witness said that the injured person had 'put their hand on top of the machine'. Now, perhaps months later, the witness tells you that the injured person's hand was 'inside the machine'. If you fail to sort out this inconsistency, no doubt your opponent will use it to discredit the witness at trial.

Pursue any other lines of enquiry opened up by the interview. So if a witness tells you, 'I was advised by Mr Quinn who inspected my vehicle immediately after the incident that ...', do not rely on this witness repeating what Mr Quinn said. You should take a proof of evidence from Mr Quinn.

When interviewing witnesses, the solicitor should be wary of people who try too hard to be helpful, and they should try to ensure that the witness's story will stand up to cross-examination. It is better that any weakness in the case is identified at this stage rather than later on when a great deal of time and money has been spent on the case. The proof of evidence should be as comprehensive as possible, including background information which may not be directly relevant to the claim but which may assist in understanding the case. A formal statement (known as a witness statement) containing only the evidence that the witness will give at the hearing will be prepared at a later stage, and this later statement is the one that will be served on the other parties before the hearing (see **12.2**). At this stage, therefore, there is no need to worry unduly if the statement contains matters which will not be admissible in evidence at the trial, although, before proceedings are commenced, the solicitor must ensure that they have, or will have, enough admissible evidence to prove their client's case at trial.

At the end of an interview, summarise for the witness what you have grasped as the key parts of their story to ensure that there are no fundamental misunderstandings. Get the proof of evidence typed up while the interview is fresh in your mind. Further, send it out to the witness for correction and approval as quickly as possible.

PRACTICAL POINTS TO CONSIDER WHEN TAKING A PROOF OF EVIDENCE

1. How are you going to record the interview?
2. Start with the basics: full name, address, contact details.
3. Try to get the witness to tell the story in chronological order.
4. Use open questions to let the witness tell the story in their own words.
5. Use closed questions to fill any gaps in the facts.
6. Do not put words in the witness's mouth.
7. Collect any relevant documents from the witness.
8. At the end, summarise for the witness what you understand them to have said.

3.3 PRESERVING DOCUMENTS

The solicitor should ask the client to bring all relevant documents to them as soon as possible. A solicitor is under an obligation, both as a matter of professional conduct and under the CPR 1998, to ensure that the client understands the rules relating to disclosure of documents (see **Chapter 11**). A client who has little or no experience of the civil litigation process may be unaware, for example, that they are under an obligation during the course of the proceedings to disclose documents to the other side, even if those documents harm the client's case. Furthermore, if the solicitor reads the documents at an early stage, this should ensure that there is nothing to take them by surprise later on in the proceedings which may throw a different light on the case. In a case involving a contractual dispute, it is obviously imperative that the solicitor should see the contract as soon as possible to be able to advise the client properly. For example, the contract may include a provision imposing a limitation period for claims arising under the contract which may be considerably shorter than the statutory limitation period (see **2.5.2.5**).

The client should also be made aware that the term 'documents' includes any method of recording information, such as video tapes, DVDs, digital cameras, mobile telephones, memory sticks, laptops, desktop computers, back-up tapes and files, and is not merely limited to written documents. It is advisable to explain the disclosure obligations to the client from the outset and to confirm this in writing. In this initial letter you should explain that the duty extends to documents that the client might previously have had in their physical possession, even if they have now been, say, lost, destroyed or given to someone else.

It is also important to identify important documents in the possession of the opponent and to decide whether it is necessary to take any steps to ensure they are preserved.

3.4 OBTAINING EXPERT EVIDENCE

3.4.1 Instructing an expert

There are numerous instances when a solicitor may need to obtain expert evidence to advance a client's claim. For example, consulting engineers are regularly requested to report on accidents at the workplace and on road traffic accidents. Similarly, if expert evidence is required on building work, it is likely that the solicitors' firm already has contacts with suitable architects and surveyors. If counsel is involved at an early stage, they may be able to recommend suitable experts for the case. Alternatively, a suitable expert may be found through The Law Society (which maintains a register of experts), or from the Academy of Expert Witnesses or other similar organisations.

Specialist expertise is the vital quality required of an expert witness, but it is not the only quality. The ability to present a convincing report which can be easily understood, and to perform well as a witness, particularly under cross-examination, is equally important. There is no fixed test to qualify as an expert witness – anyone who has special expertise in an area can be considered as an expert. Expertise does not depend on qualifications alone, although frequently the expert will be highly qualified in their field. Expertise may have been acquired through years of practical experience. For example, an experienced carpenter with no formal qualifications could nevertheless be an expert on the proper seasoning of wood, and so assist in deciding whether, say, an oak dining table was of satisfactory quality.

The usual method of instructing an expert is by letter, the content of which will vary depending on what is required of the expert.

It will be necessary to provide an expert with all the relevant documents and statements from witnesses. It may also be necessary to arrange for an inspection of any relevant machinery or site. The solicitor may need to take urgent steps to ensure that material to be inspected is preserved, or, where this is not possible, to obtain the best alternative evidence, such as photographs or a video.

It is not only when acting for the prospective claimant that the solicitor will be obtaining expert evidence. The potential defendant is also entitled to have expert evidence available. Proper facilities for inspection and observation should be granted for this.

3.4.2 Payment of expert's fees

Where the client is to pay the expert's fees (eg, if they are not covered by insurance or public funding), the solicitor should obtain an estimate of the likely fees and then clear this with the client. In such cases, the solicitor will prefer to obtain money on account to cover the expert's fees. Where this is not done, the solicitor takes a risk, since they are responsible to the expert for payment of their charges.

Can an expert be instructed on a conditional or contingency fee basis? The answer should be no – see para 88 of the Guidance for the Instruction of Experts in Civil Claims (**Appendix A(21)**). The authors take the view that payment by a conditional or contingency fee is incompatible with an expert's duty of independence and impartiality.

It should be noted that the use of expert evidence during proceedings requires permission from the court (see **3.4.5**). Therefore, the client should be told that whilst the report is necessary to evaluate the strength of the claim, the fee paid to the expert may not be recoverable from the opponent even if the client is successful in litigation.

3.4.3 Experts' reports

When the expert's report is received, the solicitor should check it carefully. Mistakes can be made, even by an expert. The solicitor should send a copy to the client, so that they may also check it and inform the solicitor of any errors.

Whoever the expert is, never be afraid to return to them for clarification of the report. If the solicitor does not understand it, there is a good chance that no one else will, and that will defeat the object of obtaining the report.

3.4.4 Opinion

A significant advantage which the expert has over the ordinary witness (see **12.8**) is that the expert can give opinion evidence. For example, a surveyor may form the view that an earlier surveyor had been negligent in not observing certain defects in the structure of a building. This is a matter of opinion, but nevertheless the expert is permitted to state it. Section 3(1) of the Civil Evidence Act 1972 provides that

> where a person is called as a witness in any civil proceedings, his opinion on any relevant matter on which he is qualified to give expert evidence shall be admissible in evidence.

CASE STUDY

Would an expert help in this case? Mr and Mrs Simpson allege that Mr Templar was negligent, as he was driving too fast and so lost control of his vehicle. But they are assuming that. Are there other explanations? Tyre tracks on the drive, etc may be useful evidence, and so photographs should be taken to preserve that evidence. Consideration should be given to appointing an accident reconstruction expert, who can examine the scene and give his opinion as to the speed at which and path along which Mr Templar's car travelled, and what caused him to crash into Mr and Mrs Simpson's house.

3.4.5 Restrictions on the use of expert evidence

The CPR 1998 have introduced very significant restrictions on the use of expert evidence. Although a party to proceedings is free to obtain as much expert evidence as they wish, the extent to which such evidence may be used in court is strictly controlled. By r 35.1 of the CPR 1998, expert evidence is restricted to that which is reasonably required to resolve the proceedings. The court can therefore limit the number of expert witnesses who can give evidence, or order that a single joint expert be appointed, or restrict expert evidence to a written report rather than oral evidence in court. A solicitor advising a client on whether to obtain expert evidence should always bear in mind that the costs of doing so will usually be recoverable from the opponent (assuming the case is won) only if the court gives permission for the expert evidence to be used.

As a general rule, if the area of expertise is settled, such that any two or more experts are likely to give the same opinion, a single joint expert is appropriate. Where a range of views is likely then normally it serves the overriding objective for the court to allow each party to have its own expert so that the court has such a range of views.

The use of expert evidence in proceedings is considered further in **Chapter 12**.

3.5 SITE VISITS

Site visits may be needed for the purpose of taking photographs or making plans. Plans and photographs are unlikely to be disputed if they are accurate; but in the event of a dispute, the person who prepared the plan or took the photographs may have to give evidence, so they should be prepared by someone other than the solicitor who will be acting as an advocate at the hearing. If a formal plan is required (eg, in a boundary dispute) then this should normally be prepared by a surveyor. In some cases, a visit to the site of the incident, such as in a factory accident case, may be useful. On other occasions, it might help to visit the client's place of business to gain a better understanding of the nature of that business.

If the inspection will be expensive, the solicitor should obtain prior authorisation from the client.

3.6 INSTRUCTING COUNSEL

3.6.1 Use of counsel

It is not necessary to instruct a barrister (also known as counsel) in every case. As a highly trained lawyer, the solicitor should have confidence in their own knowledge and ability. The solicitor will be capable of forming an assessment of both the chance of success and the level of damages. Too frequent use of counsel may result in the costs being disallowed on an assessment of costs at the end of a case. Assessment of costs is discussed in more detail in **Chapter 14**.

Nevertheless, judicious use of counsel is sensible. If the issues are difficult, it is wise to instruct counsel to advise on liability.

Similarly, counsel's opinion on quantum may be needed at an early stage if the case is not straightforward. For example, if it appears that some element of the client's claim might arguably be too remote, it might be appropriate to check with counsel. Even in these cases, however, the solicitor should have formulated their own view, and counsel should be assisting with this. The solicitor should not be abrogating responsibility.

3.6.2 Method

Instructing counsel requires the preparation of a formal document (called 'Instructions to counsel'). It will bear the heading of the claim (or proposed claim) and should contain a list of the enclosures being forwarded to counsel. The enclosures will obviously vary with the case but will typically include copies of the client's statement, any other proofs of evidence, any existing statements of case, any experts' reports, and any relevant correspondence. It is not necessary to send counsel the whole file; some judgement should be exercised in deciding which papers counsel needs to have available.

The body of the instructions to counsel will identify the client and set out briefly both sides of the case. Counsel can refer to the enclosures for detail, but the instructions should contain sufficient information to enable the barrister to identify the major issues. The solicitor should indicate their own view of the case and draw counsel's attention to those areas on which particular advice is required.

The instructions will end with a formal request to counsel to carry out the required task.

The instructions must carry a back sheet endorsed with the title of the claim, what the instructions are (eg, 'Instructions to counsel to advise on quantum'), counsel's name and chambers, and the solicitor's firm's name, address and reference.

Sometimes, counsel may not be able to proceed without a conference (the name given to a meeting with counsel) with the solicitor and the client. This could occur, for example, because the facts of the case are too detailed and complicated to be able to cover all the aspects in the instructions. Alternatively, it may be that counsel's advice will, to some extent, depend on their assessment of the client as a potential witness, and this will have to be done face to face.

If a conference is needed, counsel is still instructed in the usual way, but arrangements are then made with counsel's clerk for the solicitor and the client to visit counsel in chambers (the name given to a barrister's office) to discuss the case. Counsel will not normally expect to provide a written opinion after the conference, so the solicitor must take comprehensive notes at the conference. If a written opinion is required, this should be made clear in the instructions, but the costs of both will not be recoverable from the other side unless the court thinks it was reasonable to seek a written opinion.

Traditionally, instructions to counsel are prepared using the third person ('Counsel is instructed to ...', and 'Instructing Solicitors seek Counsel's advice on ...'). Many firms now adopt a more modern approach, setting out the instructions as if writing a letter. Each firm can decide which approach it prefers. Nevertheless, the instructions should still be in a formal document, accompanied by a covering letter to counsel's clerk.

3.6.3   Professional conduct

How far can a solicitor rely on counsel's advice? In *Locke v Camberwell Health Authority* [1991] 2 Med LR 249, the Court of Appeal set out the following principles:

(a)   In general a solicitor is entitled to rely upon the advice of counsel properly instructed.

(b)   For a solicitor, without special experience in a particular field, to rely on counsel's advice is to make normal and proper use of the Bar.

(c)   However, the solicitor must not do so blindly but must exercise their independent judgement. If they think that counsel's advice is obviously or glaringly wrong, they are under a duty to reject it.

Where a solicitor relies on the advice of counsel and subsequently both are sued by the client in negligence, the solicitor is likely to seek an indemnity or a contribution from counsel (see, for example, *Percy v Merriman White* [2021] EWHC 22 (Ch) and **8.1**).

3.7   PRE-ACTION PROTOCOLS

Pre-action protocols are an important aspect of the CPR 1998. There are approved protocols for debt claims, personal injury, clinical disputes, construction and engineering, judicial review, media and communications, disease and illness, package travel claims, possession claims by social landlords, possession claims for mortgage arrears, housing condition cases (England); Housing Disrepair Cases (Wales), low value personal injury claims in road traffic accidents, personal injury claims below the small claims limit in road traffic accidents, dilapidations (commercial property), low value employers' and public liability claims, and professional negligence claims. The details of these protocols, save the last, are outside the scope of this book. It is vital to check to see whether any approved protocol applies to a client's case. Note, however, that there is also a Practice Direction on Pre-action Conduct and Protocols, which contains general guidance that should be followed in all cases unless any part of an approved protocol otherwise applies.

A copy of the Practice Direction on Pre-action Conduct and Protocols ('the Practice Direction') is set out at **Appendix A(19)**, and a copy of the Professional Negligence Protocol may be found at **Appendix A(20)**.

3.7.1   Aims

The aims of the Practice Direction and approved pre-action protocols are:

(a)   to initiate and increase pre-action contact between the parties;

(b)   to encourage better and earlier exchange of information;

(c)   to encourage better pre-action investigation by both sides;

(d)   to put the parties in a position where they may be able to settle cases fairly and early without litigation;

(e)   to enable proceedings to run to the court's timetable and efficiently, if litigation does become necessary.

3.7.2 Steps

The Practice Direction and protocols deal with matters such as notification to the defendant of a possible claim as soon as possible, the form of the letter before claim, disclosure of documents and the instruction of experts, where relevant.

Paragraph 3 of the Practice Direction makes it clear that, before commencing proceedings, the court will expect the parties to have exchanged sufficient information in order to:

(a) understand each other's position;

(b) make decisions about how to proceed;

(c) try to settle the issues without proceedings;

(d) consider a form of Alternative Dispute Resolution (ADR) to assist with settlement;

(e) support the efficient management of those proceedings; and

(f) reduce the costs of resolving the dispute.

Compliance with the Practice Direction or a relevant protocol should help the parties involved make an informed decision on the merits of the case and lead to a greater number of settlements without the need for court proceedings. In particular, the parties must give serious consideration to ADR. For example, para 8 of the Practice Direction states that the parties should consider whether some form of ADR procedure would enable them to settle their dispute without commencing proceedings. If proceedings occur, both the claimant and defendant will normally be required by the court to provide evidence that alternative means of resolving the dispute were considered. The courts take the view that litigation should be a last resort, and that claims should not be issued prematurely when a settlement is still actively being explored. Parties are warned that if this provision is not followed then the court must have regard to such conduct when determining costs (see **14.3.2.4**).

3.7.3 Sanctions for non-compliance

If proceedings are issued, the court will expect the parties to have complied with both the Practice Direction and the substance of any approved protocol that applies to their dispute. Where non-compliance has led to proceedings that might otherwise not have been commenced, or has led to unnecessary costs being incurred, the court may impose sanctions. These can include an order:

(a) that the party at fault pay some or all of their opponent's costs (perhaps on the penalty, indemnity basis – see **14.3.3**);

(b) depriving a claimant who is at fault of some or all of the interest they may subsequently be awarded on any damages they recover; or

(c) requiring a defendant who is at fault to pay interest on some or all of any damages that are subsequently awarded to the claimant at a rate of up to 10% pa above base rate.

In exercising these powers, the court should aim to place the innocent party in no worse a position than they would have been in had the Practice Direction or approved protocol been complied with (see *Straker v Tudor Rose (a firm)* [2007] EWCA Civ 368). As to sanctions, see **9.3**.

On the other side of the coin, if proceedings occur, the party awarded their costs should usually be able to recover their pre-action costs (see **14.3.2**), including those costs reasonably incurred in complying with the Practice Direction or approved pre-action protocol (see *Callery v Gray* [2001] EWCA Civ 1246).

In *Cundall Johnson and Partners LLP v Whipps Cross University Hospital NHS Trust* [2007] EWHC 2178, the court held that the claimant's failure to comply with the Pre-action Protocol for Construction and Engineering meant that the proceedings should be stayed in order to facilitate such compliance. Why? Because there was a real possibility of settlement if the parties went through the Protocol processes. It was therefore in their best interests. It might well save both parties from incurring unnecessary litigation costs and lead to an earlier resolution of the dispute between the parties. Also, it was unfair on the defendant to proceed immediately with litigation as it had not yet received a proper summary of the claim.

3.8 PRE-ACTION CORRESPONDENCE

3.8.1 The letter before claim

When the solicitor is satisfied that the client has a valid claim, they should advise the client and obtain instructions to send a letter to the prospective defendant setting out full details of the claim. This is called a 'letter before claim'. If the claim is of a type that is governed by a pre-action approved protocol, the letter should contain all the information required by the protocol.

Note that in the case of professional negligence, a preliminary notice of claim should be sent first, and the letter communicating the claim is known as the 'letter of claim' under the professional negligence pre-action protocol.

3.8.2 Professional conduct

The letter is normally addressed to the potential defendant in person, but if the solicitor is already aware that the defendant has solicitors acting for them, it should be addressed to the solicitors, as it is a breach of the SRA Code of Conduct (Principle 5 – to act with integrity – and para 1.2 – not to abuse the solicitor's position by taking unfair advantage of others) to write directly to a defendant in those circumstances. If the potential defendant is likely to be insured in respect of the claim, the solicitor should ask that the letter is passed on to the insurers and will usually enclose a copy for that purpose.

3.8.3 The letter before claim under the Practice Direction

3.8.3.1 Content

The Practice Direction provides at para 6(a) that the claimant's letter before claim should give concise details about the matter. This should normally enable the defendant to understand and investigate the issues without needing to request further information. We would suggest that the letter should:

(1) state the claimant's full name and address;

(2) state the basis on which the claim is made (ie why the claimant says the defendant is liable);

(3) provide a clear summary of the facts on which the claim is based;

(4) state what the claimant wants from the defendant;

(5) if financial loss is claimed, provide an explanation of how the amount has been calculated;

(6) list the essential documents on which the claimant intends to rely;

(7) set out the form of ADR (if any) that the claimant considers the most suitable and invite the defendant to agree to this;

(8) state the date by which the claimant considers it reasonable for a full response to be provided by the defendant; and

(9) identify and ask for copies of any relevant documents not in the claimant's possession and which the claimant wishes to see.

In a straightforward claim, for example an undisputed business debt, the claimant will usually demand that the letter before claim is acknowledged and/or a full response given within 14 days of the defendant's receiving it. However, if the case requires the involvement of the defendant's insurer or other third party, or where there are issues about evidence, then the claimant will usually demand that the letter before claim is acknowledged within 14 days of the defendant's receiving it and a full response given within 30 days. If the case is particularly complex, for example requiring specialist advice, then it may be appropriate for the claimant to allow up to three months for the defendant to respond in full.

Unless the defendant is known to be legally represented, we suggest that the letter should also:

(1)   refer the defendant to the Practice Direction and in particular draw attention to paragraph 16 concerning the court's powers to impose sanctions for failure to comply with the Practice Direction;

(2)   inform the defendant that ignoring the letter before claim may lead to the claimant starting proceedings and may increase the defendant's liability for costs;

(3)   warn the defendant of any claim for interest in proceedings that may be commenced; and

(4)   suggest that the defendant takes independent legal advice.

3.8.3.2   Templates

Note that **Appendices B(1) and B(2)** are templates to assist you to draft the letter before claim under the Practice Direction and the letter of claim under the Professional Negligence Pre-action Protocol.

3.8.3.3   Flow diagrams

Note that **Appendices C(2) and C(3)** are flow diagrams that set out the main steps to be taken under the Practice Direction and the Professional Negligence Pre-action Protocol.

CASE STUDY: THE LETTER BEFORE CLAIM

Assume that Mr and Mrs Simpson obtained a report from an accident reconstruction expert who states that the most likely cause of the accident was Mr Templar's speeding. The letter before claim is set out at **Appendix D(2)**. Let us consider how it was drafted.

1.   As Mr Templar has not instructed solicitors, the letter is sent to him. Formal notification has been given to his insurers and a copy of that letter is enclosed for his reference.

2.   The letter has a heading which is sufficient to enable Mr Templar to identify the claim being made against him. The full names and address of Mr and Mrs Simpson are then given, and Mr Templar can immediately see the purpose of the letter.

3.   Under a suitable heading the relevant background facts are briefly stated. You do not have to set out the evidence relied on here. In most cases the events leading up to the dispute will be largely undisputed.

4.   The legal basis of the claim is dealt with next. In a contractual dispute you would identify the express and/or implied terms of the contract alleged to have been broken. In a negligence claim, as here, the duty breached by the defendant should be stated.

5.   Having explained why the defendant is liable, full details of 'how' must be given, in other words, the factual basis of the claim. For a solicitor who has conducted a thorough case analysis, this will be a matter of translating the factual issues from the grid chart. As a general rule, it is best practice to summarise the facts on liability rather than attaching any expert's report at this stage. The question of expert evidence will usually be addressed by the parties later, following the defendant's response.

6.   Quantum must then be dealt with clearly and in sufficient detail, including an explanation of how the losses claimed flow from the breaches alleged. Where convenient, list each head of damage claimed separately, and give an estimate for any loss claimed where an actual figure is unavailable. As to documents relied on, it is usual to include those that support the amounts claimed, such as receipts, estimates, etc.

> 7.   The letter gives calendar dates for acknowledging and giving a full response, so Mr Templar can be in no doubt. Failing that, Mr Templar is subsequently warned of legal proceedings and their potential financial consequences for him.
>
> 8.   As no approved protocol applies here, a copy of the Practice Direction is enclosed and Mr Templar's attention is drawn to para 16.
>
> 9.   As Mr and Mrs Simpson are not aware that Mr Templar has any grounds to dispute their claim, it is rather premature in the circumstances to propose any ADR mechanism. Once any full written response is received, with any ADR proposal from Mr Templar, this can be reviewed.
>
> 10. Note how well described sub-headings make this letter clear and easy to read.

3.8.4   The letter of acknowledgement under the Practice Direction

We suggest that if the defendant is unable to provide a full written response within the deadline set by the letter before claim, the defendant should, instead, provide a written acknowledgement within the deadline. That acknowledgement should state whether an insurer is or may be involved and the date by which the defendant (or insurer) will provide a full written response, and it may request any further information needed by the defendant to provide a full response.

If a defendant is unable to provide a full response within the deadline set by the letter before claim because they intend to seek advice, the written acknowledgement should so state and include details of from whom the defendant is seeking advice and when the defendant expects to have received that advice and be in a position to provide a full response.

3.8.5   The letter of response under the Practice Direction

Paragraph 6(b) of the Practice Direction provides that the defendant's letter of response to the letter of claim should include:

(1)   confirmation as to whether the claim is accepted and, if it is not accepted, the reasons why;

(2)   an explanation as to which facts and parts of the claim are disputed; and

(3)   whether the defendant is making a counterclaim and, if so, its details.

In addition, we would suggest that the letter of response should also:

(1)   explain whether the defendant agrees to any proposal made by the claimant for ADR and, where appropriate, suggest an alternative form of ADR (or state why none is considered suitable);

(2)   list the essential documents on which the defendant intends to rely;

(3)   enclose copies of any documents requested by the claimant, or explain why they will not be provided; and

(4)   identify and ask for copies of any further relevant documents, not in the defendant's possession and which the defendant wishes to see.

CASE STUDY: THE LETTER OF RESPONSE

Assume that Mr Templar has instructed solicitors and obtained his own report from an accident reconstruction expert, who states that the most likely cause of the accident was shards of glass on the driveway which caused Mr Templar to lose control of his car. The letter of response is set out at **Appendix D(3)**. Let us briefly consider how it was drafted:

1.   Mr Templar's solicitors acknowledged receipt of the letter before claim within 14 days and agreed a new deadline for a full response.

> 2.   Under suitable headings the relevant details are given. First, why the claim is denied. Then details of the counterclaim. As an alternative to totally denying the claim, Mr Templar also makes an allegation of contributory negligence against Mr and Mrs Simpson.
>
> 3.   The quantum of the counterclaim is then detailed and documents in support of each item are enclosed.
>
> 4.   Given that each side has differing expert evidence on liability, Mr Templar suggests that ADR on that issue is inappropriate. He leaves open the question of whether ADR might be suitable to determine the quantum of the claim and/or counterclaim. As the case develops the parties should review the suitability of ADR for the issues that remain in dispute.

3.8.6 Claimant's reply

We suggest that the claimant should provide the documents requested by the defendant within as short a period of time as is practicable or explain in writing why the documents will not be provided.

If the defendant has made a counterclaim, the claimant should provide information equivalent to the defendant's response (see **3.8.5**).

3.8.7 Taking stock

After their initial exchange of correspondence, the parties should have a genuine opportunity to resolve the matter without needing to start proceedings. At the very least, it should be possible, as para 12 of the Practice Direction points out, to establish what issues remain outstanding so as to narrow the scope of any subsequent court proceedings, and therefore limit potential costs.

3.8.8 Instructing experts

Paragraph 7 of the Practice Direction reminds the parties that many matters can and should be resolved without the need for advice or evidence from an expert. If an expert is needed, the parties should consider how best to minimise the expense, for example by agreeing to instruct either a single joint expert (ie engaged and paid for jointly by the parties, whether instructed jointly or separately) or an agreed expert (ie the parties agree the identity of the expert but only one party instructs the expert and pays the expert's costs). As to a single joint expert, see **12.13.8**.

Where the parties go ahead and instruct their own expert or experts pre-action, it will be for the court to determine later if any party can rely on any particular expert's evidence and how expert evidence should be given at a trial (see further **12.13**).

3.8.9 False statements

Paragraph 2 of the Practice Direction reminds the parties that any person who knowingly makes a false statement in a pre-action protocol letter or other document prepared in anticipation of legal proceedings may be subject to proceedings for contempt of court. A client should be reminded of this regularly, particularly when asked to approve significant letters or documents.

3.9 PRE-ACTION DISCLOSURE

In a relatively small number of cases it may be necessary for a prospective claimant to see documents held by a potential defendant who is unwilling to show them voluntarily.

An application for disclosure of documents prior to the start of proceedings is permitted under s 33 of the SCA 1981, or s 52 of the CCA 1984. The application must be supported by evidence, and the procedure is dealt with in r 31.16(3) of the CPR 1998. The court may make an order for disclosure only where:

(a)   the respondent is likely to be a party to subsequent proceedings;

(b)   the applicant is also likely to be a party to the proceedings;

(c)   if proceedings had started, the respondent's duty by way of standard disclosure set out in rule 31.6, would extend to the documents or classes of documents of which the applicant seeks disclosure; and

(d)   disclosure before proceedings have started is desirable in order to–

(i)   dispose fairly of the anticipated proceedings;

(ii)   assist the dispute to be resolved without proceedings; or

(iii)   save costs.

An order under this rule must specify the documents or class of documents which the respondent must disclose, and require them, when making such disclosure, to specify any of those documents which they no longer have, or which they claim the right or duty to withhold from inspection. The order may also specify the time and place for disclosure and inspection to take place.

The most common examples of pre-action disclosure where the claimant is deciding whether or not to make a claim are to be found in personal injury litigation, for example where the other side holds the records of an accident. However, pre-action disclosure may also be ordered in significant commercial cases to try to resolve a dispute without proceedings or to save costs: see, for example, *Burrells Wharf Freeholders Ltd v Galliard Homes Ltd* [1999] 2 EGLR 81.

The court will not allow applications for pre-action disclosure where there is no sufficient evidence that a claim exists and the application is purely speculative (see *Hunt v Caddick (Mill Harbour) Ltd* [2019] EWHC 2933).

Disclosure and inspection of documents are dealt with fully in **Chapter 11**.

3.10   SETTLEMENT

3.10.1   'Without prejudice' negotiations

A solicitor may soon find that they are in a position to commence negotiations with their opposite number, or with the opponent directly (provided they are not represented) or with an insurance company (eg, in a professional negligence case). The opportunity to negotiate will continue throughout the pre-action stage, the proceedings, and even during the trial itself.

Any negotiations that take place as a part of a genuine attempt to settle a claim are impliedly 'without prejudice'. However, it is preferable to mark any correspondence accordingly, or to clarify at the start of a meeting/telephone negotiation that this is the basis on which you are proceeding. If 'without prejudice' negotiations take place, neither party may rely upon anything said or written in the course of the negotiations for the purpose of proving liability and/or quantum at trial.

EXAMPLE

A is suing B for damages of £150,000. A's solicitor writes to B's solicitor on a without prejudice basis, saying A will accept £120,000 if that sum is paid within 28 days. B does not accept that proposal.

Neither A nor B can refer to this letter at trial, and A can still try to obtain judgment for the full amount of the claim. Note that if A had marked the letter 'without prejudice save as to costs' then A could unilaterally show the letter to the judge when the judge was deciding the question of costs.

This rule exists to encourage litigants to reach a settlement, if possible, and to give effect to their implied agreement not to use information revealed on a 'without prejudice' basis in the proceedings (see *Ofulue v Bossert* [2009] AC 990). It means that all negotiations which are genuinely aimed at a settlement are excluded from being given in evidence. The rule applies whether the negotiations are oral or in writing, and thus applies to an attendance note of a without prejudice conversation as well as to correspondence. As Oliver LJ stated in *Cutts v Head* [1984] Ch 290:

> That the rule rests, at least in part, upon public policy is clear from many authorities, and the convenient starting point of the inquiry is the nature of the underlying policy. It is that parties should be encouraged so far as possible to settle their disputes without resort to litigation and should not be discouraged by the knowledge that anything that is said in the course of such negotiations (and that includes, of course, as much the failure to reply to an offer as an actual reply) may be used to their prejudice in the course of the proceedings. They should, as it was expressed by Clauson J in *Scott Paper Co v Drayton Paper Works Ltd* (1927) 44 RPC 151, 156, be encouraged fully and frankly to put their cards on the table ... The public policy justification, in truth, essentially rests on the desirability of preventing statements or offers made in the course of negotiations for settlement being brought before the court of trial as admissions on the question of liability ... The rule applies to exclude all negotiations genuinely aimed at settlement whether oral or in writing from being given in evidence.

Although as a matter of good practice the words 'without prejudice' should appear on this type of correspondence, the presence or absence of the words is not conclusive. What is important is that the letter is a genuine attempt to settle the case. If there is a dispute as to whether or not a communication is protected in this way, the court can examine the document (obviously in advance of the trial by someone other than the trial judge) to see whether or not its purpose was to settle the dispute. If it was, it cannot be used or referred to in evidence; if not then, even if it carries the words 'without prejudice', it can.

The court must consider the circumstances of the communications from an objective standpoint: *Sang Kook Suh v Mace (UK) Ltd* [2016] EWCA Civ 4. In addition, as Bodey J stated in *BE v DE* [2014] EWHC 2318 (Fam) at [24],

> [i]t must be necessary ... that both parties realised or must or should have realised [that the parties were seeking to compromise the dispute], not just the person now praying in aid the without prejudice protection.

Once a settlement is concluded, any 'without prejudice' correspondence can be produced in court to show the terms agreed between the parties. This might be necessary if, for example, a dispute arose as to enforcement of an agreed settlement or the true terms of the agreement reached (see *Oceanbulk Shipping & Trading SA v TMT Asia Ltd* [2010] UKSC 44).

As noted in the example above, if a party wishes to reserve the right to draw the trial judge's attention to a without prejudice offer to settle a case on the question of costs, they should mark the offer 'without prejudice save as to costs' (see *Cutts v Head* [1984] Ch 290, *Sternberg Reed Solicitors v Andrew Paul Harrison* [2019] EWHC 2065 (Ch) and also **3.10.2** below).

A without prejudice or without prejudice save as to costs offer of settlement that has no time limit for acceptance can be accepted even after the trial has started; such an offer does not lapse at the commencement of the hearing (see *MEF (A Protected Party, by his Mother and Litigation Friend, FEM) v St George's Healthcare NHS Trust* [2020] EWHC 1300 (QB)).

Details about the solicitor's authority to negotiate are to be found at **13.1**.

3.10.2 Pre-action offers under Part 36

As we have seen, before litigation starts the parties are encouraged to negotiate and settle the claim. It is open to the parties to make 'without prejudice' offers to settle (see **3.10.1**). Part 36 of the CPR 1998 formally recognises this and gives 'teeth' to such offers, which are made 'without prejudice save as to costs' (ie, once a trial judge has dealt with the issues of liability and quantum, they can be addressed on Part 36 offers when dealing with the question of costs). Any party can offer to settle a monetary claim for a specified sum, or on express terms for any non-monetary claim. So, if litigation occurs and the claimant fails to obtain a judgment more advantageous than a defendant's Part 36 offer, the claimant will usually suffer severe financial penalties (see **13.4.5**). Likewise, if a claimant makes a Part 36 offer and the judgment against the defendant is at least as advantageous to the claimant as the proposals contained in the claimant's Part 36 offer, the defendant will usually suffer severe financial penalties (see **13.4.6**).

Care should be taken when drafting the Part 36 offer to ensure that the stated terms are consistent with Part 36. If not, there is a risk that the court may not apply the financial penalties under Part 36, although the court may take the offer into account when exercising its general discretion with regard to costs (see *James v James* [2018] EWHC 242 (Ch)). See also **13.4.1.1**.

3.11   RESEARCHING THE LAW

Researching the law will often not be necessary. The solicitor will be familiar with the relevant law in the areas in which they practise. Nevertheless, from time to time, unfamiliar points arise which need to be researched.

On a point of law, reference should be made to the recognised practitioner works in the relevant subject; but as textbooks rapidly become out of date, it is essential to check a current authority.

If the point to be researched is procedural then the solicitor needs to refer to the CPR 1998 and Practice Directions themselves, together with any relevant case law on their interpretation and any recognised practitioners' works. For this purpose, it can be useful to look at one of the hard-copy versions of the CPR 1998 that are annotated and contain references to relevant cases and statutory instruments where appropriate.

3.12   COST–BENEFIT ANALYSIS

As we have seen, litigation is the last resort. A solicitor should discuss with the client whether the potential outcomes of any legal case will justify the expense or risk involved, including, if relevant, the risk of having to pay an opponent's costs. So, a form of cost–benefit analysis needs to be done at the beginning of a case, and this must be reviewed regularly.

The client will have already incurred legal costs at Stage 1. These will include the costs of investigating the case (whether a potential claim or a defence to such), taking the steps required by the appropriate pre-action protocol and possibly attempting some form of ADR. These costs may include barristers' and experts' fees. Hundreds or thousands of pounds may already have been spent. Once court proceedings start, legal costs will escalate. Have a quick look at the bill of costs at **Appendix A(17)**. If you just skim-read the description of work done, you can see that court fees will have to be paid, court documents prepared, and further time will be spent by the solicitor with the client and witnesses, etc.

You should now appreciate that a client runs up a solicitor's bill rather like a taxi fare – in other words, the longer a case goes on, the bigger the legal bill. This analogy is rather apt, as the professionals involved in a typical case – solicitors, barristers and experts – will all charge by the hour. Statistics from the Senior Courts Costs Office show that in recent years the average costs recovered by a successful party in a High Court case exceeded £39,000 in the Queen's Bench Division and £95,000 in the Chancery Division; whilst in the County Court the figure was £33,000. This gives you a very rough idea of the potential costs that may be incurred.

3.13   SUMMARY OF PRE-ACTION STEPS

(1)   Check any professional conduct points:
    – conflict of interests

         – confidentiality

         – identity of client for money laundering regulation purposes.

(2) Identify the client's objectives:

         – what does the client want?

         – what might realistically be achieved?

(3) Identify and locate, if necessary, all potential parties.

(4) Check the financial viability of the defendant:

         – will the defendant be able to pay any judgment and costs?

         – what assets are available?

(5) Check jurisdiction:

         – any relevant contractual clause?

         – are one or more parties outside the jurisdiction?

(6) Ascertain the limitation period:

         – any relevant contractual clause?

(7) Discuss and agree funding with the client:

         – explain all options

         – set out in a letter.

(8) Collect and preserve evidence:

         – where are relevant documents located?

         – what witnesses can proofs of evidence be taken from?

         – is an expert's report needed?

         – are photographs or a site visit needed?

(9) Carry out any necessary legal research.

(10) Do a case analysis:

         – have you identified all potential causes of action?

         – for each element, have you identified all the factual issues?

         – what is the likelihood of success?

         – what further evidence is needed?

(11) Write letter of advice to client summarising analysis and advising on options.

(12) Explore possible methods of ADR.

(13) Comply with any approved pre-action protocol requirements or the Practice Direction.

(14) Keep the client informed.

(15) Should the client make a Part 36 offer?

3.14 SUMMARY OF PRACTICE DIRECTION ON PRE-ACTION CONDUCT AND PROTOCOLS

(1) Litigation should be a last resort. The parties should consider whether negotiation or some other form of ADR might enable them to settle their dispute without commencing proceedings.

(2) The parties should exchange sufficient information in order to:

    (a) understand each other's position;

    (b) make decisions about how to proceed;

    (c) try to settle the issues without proceedings;

    (d) consider a form of ADR to assist with settlement;

    (e) support the efficient management of those proceedings; and

    (f) reduce the costs of resolving the dispute.

(3)   The steps taken under the Practice Direction should usually include:

    (a)   the claimant writing to the defendant with concise details of the claim;

    (b)   the defendant responding within a reasonable time; and

    (c)   the parties disclosing key documents relevant to the issues in dispute.

(4)   Only reasonable and proportionate steps should be taken by the parties to identify, narrow and resolve the legal, factual and/or expert issues.

(5)   Where a dispute has not been resolved after the parties have followed the Practice Direction, they should review their respective positions to see if proceedings can be avoided and at least seek to narrow the issues in dispute before the claimant issues proceedings.

(6)   If a dispute proceeds to litigation, the court will expect the parties to have complied with the Practice Direction. A party may be sanctioned for failing to do so.

CHAPTER 4

ALTERNATIVE DISPUTE RESOLUTION

4.1	The nature of ADR	55
4.2	Advantages of ADR	56
4.3	Disadvantages of ADR	57
4.4	Types of ADR	59
4.5	Organisations providing ADR	61
4.6	Using ADR	62
4.7	Choosing ADR	62

LEARNING OUTCOMES

This chapter develops further the concept that it may be possible to use less confrontational modes of dispute resolution to reach a quick, cheap and commercially realistic solution. It explains:

- how alternative dispute resolution differs from arbitration and litigation
- the advantages and disadvantages of alternative dispute resolution
- the various types of methods available to resolve disputes
- the organisations that may be able to help if the parties do choose to use some method of dispute resolution instead of arbitration or litigation.

4.1 THE NATURE OF ADR

Alternative dispute resolution (ADR) is a means of resolving disputes by using an independent third party, who may help the parties to reach their own solution but who either can ('determinative ADR') or cannot ('non-determinative ADR') impose a solution. It is voluntary and confidential. The parties choose the process and can withdraw at any time.

4.1.1 How ADR differs from other forms of dispute resolution

Litigation is not voluntary (save in the sense that the claimant chooses to issue a claim in the first place). Once the case is started, usually neither party can withdraw without paying the opponent's costs (see **13.6**). If the parties are unable to negotiate a settlement, the court will impose its own solution. The winner will enforce that solution.

Arbitration is voluntary in the sense that the parties voluntarily entered into an arbitration agreement. When a relevant dispute arises, however, one party can force the other to arbitrate against their will because of the original contractual agreement to do so, provided it is enforceable. The arbitrator will impose a solution which the winner can enforce. Of course, parties can always voluntarily take a dispute to arbitration. Strictly speaking, arbitration is a form of ADR. We have already dealt with it at **2.9.1** and shall not consider it further in any detail in this chapter.

Strictly speaking, negotiation is a form of ADR. It is both voluntary and non-binding. However, there is no independent third party and the negotiators will normally be identified with their respective 'sides'. We introduced the topic at **2.9.4** and consider it further at **13.1**. Negotiation is also dealt with in **Skills for Lawyers, Chapter 12**.

4.1.2   The independent third party

The independence of the third party is an essential feature of ADR, as is the fact that in non-determinative ADR they cannot impose a solution. As the parties know that the third party is independent and cannot do anything to harm them, they are more likely to trust and be open with the third party. They are less likely to be aggressive towards each other, and they will not want to be seen as an obstacle towards a settlement and are likely to be more accommodating, in the presence of the third party. The third party may therefore be able to defuse the dispute and make settlement more likely. A further advantage is that the independent third party not only will be trained to act as a neutral, but also should have any necessary industry knowledge required to understand the dispute.

The third party can help the parties to settle their dispute in another way. A commercially-minded neutral may come up with ideas that the parties might not have thought of, and which solve the problem without either side losing face.

4.1.3   What affects choice?

We will now go on in this chapter to consider the advantages and disadvantages of ADR. These will obviously be factors affecting a client's choice of dispute resolution process. As you consider each, reflect on how the following considerations may be relevant: the client's attitude to publicity; any difficult points of law that need resolving; any need to set a legal precedent; the type and amount of evidence involved; the remedy required; time and cost; and the possible effect on the parties' relationships.

4.2   ADVANTAGES OF ADR

The CPR 1998 specifically recognise the advantages of ADR. Rule 1.4(2)(e) provides that the court may further the overriding objective of dealing with cases justly by

> encouraging the parties to use an alternative dispute resolution procedure if the court considers that appropriate and facilitating the use of such procedure.

In *Practice Statement (Alternative Dispute Resolution) (No 2)* [1996] 1 WLR 1024, Waller J said:

> [T]he settlement of actions by means of ADR (i) significantly helps to save litigants the ever mounting cost of bringing their actions to trial; (ii) saves them the delay of litigation in reaching finality in their disputes; (iii) enables them to achieve settlement of their disputes while preserving their existing commercial relationships and market reputation; (iv) provides them with a wider range of settlement solutions than those offered by litigation; and (v) is likely to make a substantial contribution to the more efficient use of judicial resources ...

The Practice Direction on Pre-action Conduct and Protocols (see **3.7**) emphasises the importance of settlement and ADR in paras 8–11.

Arbitration and ADR procedures are confidential. Nothing said can be referred to in any later court proceedings unless all parties agree to waive confidentiality. However, court proceedings are usually conducted in open court. The media can attend and are able to report on most proceedings. As a general rule, anyone can obtain a copy of a statement of case, order or judgment that is on a court file (see CPR 1998, r 5.4C(1)).

Some of these points are amplified below.

4.2.1   Cheapness and speed

Apart from the fact that an independent third party may find it easier to lead the parties to a settlement, ADR has many other attractions. It can be significantly cheaper than both arbitration and litigation. This is because it is quicker. A skilled neutral can, in most cases that are suitable for ADR, help the parties to resolve their dispute in a relatively short period of time.

The parties do, of course, have to pay the third party for their services. The parties will usually instruct lawyers to help them on the day, and they will have to pay those lawyers. If ADR works, however, there will be a significant reduction in the amount of time the lawyers spend in preparing and presenting the case. This will save costs. Even more importantly, the client saves on the indirect costs involved in its employees and executives having to spend time reading court documents, consulting lawyers and attending court.

However, clients should not be given the impression that ADR comes at bargain basement prices. Any lawyer representing the client will want to be fully prepared, and that will take time (including the client's time in dealing with the lawyer's enquiries) and will cost money.

4.2.2 Flexibility

Speed and cheapness are the principal attractions of ADR, but it is also very flexible. The parties can choose one of several forms of ADR. They can choose the procedure to be followed in conjunction with their chosen neutral. They do not have to comply with any statutes or rules of court. There is not even any case law limiting what the parties or the neutral can do.

4.2.3 Preserving a business relationship

Arbitration and ADR share the virtue of privacy. Alternative dispute resolution is also ideal for cases where the parties to the dispute are going to have to continue to deal with each other. The fact that they have chosen a non-confrontational method of solving their problem makes it much easier for them to continue their relationship, since the solution is theirs and has not been imposed upon them.

4.2.4 Commercial reality

A third party unconnected with the dispute may be able to assist the parties to arrive at realistic and workable terms of settlement.

4.3 DISADVANTAGES OF ADR

4.3.1 It does not bind the parties to the procedure

As a general principle, no one can be forced to resolve a dispute by any form of ADR against their wishes. If one party suggests ADR, the other parties do not have to agree; and even if the parties have started to resolve a dispute by ADR, most ADR agreements allow any party to withdraw at any stage before a solution has been agreed. It will then be necessary to resort to litigation or, if there is an arbitration agreement, to arbitration.

The court can stay litigation that has been commenced in breach of an agreed method of resolving disputes. This is the case even if that method is not technically an arbitration agreement under the Arbitration Act 1996. Indeed, the courts have increasingly stayed proceedings for ADR to take place, whether or not pursuant to a contractual agreement. For example, in *Cable & Wireless v IBM UK Ltd* [2002] BLR 89, the parties were directed to pursue a previously agreed ADR method. The court held that there were strong case management grounds for allowing the reference to ADR to proceed. Any delay was not such that it would be unfair to impose the ADR procedure.

In *Ohpen Operations UK Ltd v Invesco Fund Managers Ltd* [2019] EWHC 2246 (TCC) the parties had included a tiered DR clause in an agreement. This provided for dispute resolution to be undertaken in stages starting with less formal negotiation and concluding with mediation by the Centre for Effective Dispute Resolution (CEDR). Only if mediation failed did the agreement permit the parties to commence court proceedings. Following an unsuccessful negotiation and without completing the staged DR process provided for by the agreement, the claimant issued proceedings and the defendant sought a declaration that the court would not exercise any jurisdiction to hear the claim and to stay the proceedings pending compliance with the tiered DR clause. O'Farrell J ordered that the proceedings should be stayed and stated the following principles:

i) The agreement must create an enforceable obligation requiring the parties to engage in alternative dispute resolution.

ii) The obligation must be expressed clearly as a condition precedent to court proceedings or arbitration.

iii) The dispute resolution process to be followed does not have to be formal but must be sufficiently clear and certain by reference to objective criteria, including machinery to appoint a mediator or determine any other necessary step in the procedure without the requirement for any further agreement by the parties.

iv) The court has a discretion to stay proceedings commenced in breach of an enforceable dispute resolution agreement. In exercising its discretion, the court will have regard to the public policy interest in upholding the parties' commercial agreement and furthering the overriding objective in assisting the parties to resolve their disputes.

4.3.2 The awards are not so easily enforceable

There is no equivalent of s 66 of the Arbitration Act 1996 (see **2.9.1**) enabling ADR awards to be enforced as if they were court judgments. However, if the parties do agree to terms suggested as a result of non-determinative ADR, they have entered into a contract. If one of the parties does not carry out that contract, they can be sued for breach of contract, and the claimant would usually expect to obtain summary judgment (see **10.5.2**) under Part 24 of the CPR 1998 without any difficulty.

It is standard practice in many forms of ADR to provide that no agreement will be binding upon the parties unless it is put in writing and signed by the parties.

A party who has commenced court proceedings but then resolved the dispute by ADR, can record the agreement reached in a consent order, which can be enforced by the usual methods.

4.3.3 The facts may not be fully disclosed

The speed of ADR has an associated disadvantage. Because there is no equivalent of disclosure, there is a risk that the parties may resolve the dispute without knowing all the facts. This may lead to the wrong decision. Many businesspersons, however, take the view that a quick decision, even if it is not completely accurate, is better than wasting time and money on a protracted dispute in order to get a more correct decision. They often feel that litigation is a lottery anyway.

4.3.4 ADR is not appropriate for all cases

Alternative dispute resolution is not appropriate in the following cases:

(a)   where the client needs an injunction or security for costs (though afterwards ADR may become appropriate);

(b)   where there is no dispute. If the case is a simple debt collection matter, the creditor should issue a claim form followed by a summary judgment application (see **10.5.2**), or consider insolvency proceedings (see **15.5.6**);

(c)   where the client needs a ruling on a point of law.

Whether or not ADR is appropriate in other cases can often be a moot point. What about the client with a very strong case, who fears that mediation means that some concessions will have to be made unnecessarily? If the client reasonably believes that they have a watertight case, that might well be sufficient justification for a refusal to mediate (see *Swain Mason v Mills & Reeve* [2012] EWCA Civ 498 and further at **14.3.3.6**).

Are cases concerning complex areas of law unsuitable for mediation? Not always. For example, disputes between neighbours might involve complex legal issues but the parties may be better advised to seek practical solutions through mediation (see *Faidi v Elliott Corporation* [2012] EWCA Civ 287). Parties should also consider using judicial appraisal (see **4.4.5**) to clarify legal issues.

The increasing importance that courts attach to the consideration of ADR is evidenced by a standard direction in proceedings, which requires a party who rejects a proposal for ADR to file a witness statement detailing their reasons for doing so (see **Appendix B(7)**). That witness statement will then be available to the trial judge when the issue of costs is considered (see **Chapter 14**).

4.4 TYPES OF ADR

4.4.1 Mediation and conciliation

Mediation and conciliation are usually interchangeable terms. For ease of reference, the term 'mediation' will be used to cover both processes in this chapter.

In a typical mediation, the third party who has been selected as mediator will have received written statements from both parties. Following that, the mediator will discuss the case with the parties. They will tell the mediator what they think about each party's case on a without prejudice basis. The mediator will not pass on to the other party information which is confidential, unless they are given permission to do so.

These discussions help the mediator to identify the real areas of disagreement and the points that are most important to the respective parties. They can then move the parties towards constructive solutions to the problem.

The method of mediation described above assumes that the mediator and the parties will meet in the same building. This enables things to be dealt with quickly because, if necessary, the parties can meet face to face to iron out their differences. There are, however, other forms of mediation. The parties do not have to meet. The matter can be dealt with by correspondence and telephone conversations.

It is vital that the parties are represented at the mediation by people who have authority to instruct their lawyers to reach agreement.

4.4.2 'Med-arb'

Under this form of ADR, the parties agree to submit their dispute to mediation and, if this does not work, that they will refer the matter to arbitration. They may, if they wish, use the person who has been acting as their mediator as their arbitrator. This will save costs, because the arbitrator will already know the facts of the case. There is a risk, however, that during the mediation, they will have become privy to confidential information belonging to one of the parties. This would compromise their position as arbitrator, so any agreement for 'med-arb' should give either party the right to object to the mediator's becoming the arbitrator.

4.4.3 'Mini-trial' or 'structured settlement procedure'

Under this procedure, the parties appoint a neutral who will sit as chair of a tribunal composed of the chair and a senior representative of each of the parties. These representatives may not be immediately connected with the dispute and should have authority to reach such compromise as they see fit. They will then hear and/or read the cases of the two parties (sometimes with an expert), after which they will negotiate with each other with the help of the independent arbiter.

4.4.4   Expert appraisal

The parties can refer all or part of their dispute to an expert in the disputed field for their opinion. Their opinion is not binding on the parties but could influence their approach to subsequent negotiations. It will be for the parties to choose the appropriate procedure, which could even involve a short trial before the expert makes their recommendation.

4.4.5   Judicial appraisal

The Centre for Effective Dispute Resolution (CEDR) has a scheme whereby former judges and senior counsel are available to give a quick preliminary view on the legal position, having heard representations from both parties. It is a matter for agreement between the parties as to whether this opinion is to be binding on them or not.

4.4.6   Expert determination

Expert determination is a halfway house between arbitration and ADR. As in arbitration, the parties select an expert to decide the case for them. They agree to accept the expert's decision, and if one fails to do so, the other can sue for breach of contract. The expert's decision cannot, however, be enforced as a court order, and they do not have the powers of an arbitrator under the Arbitration Act 1996. Also, unlike an arbitrator, they can be sued in negligence by a party who thinks their decision was wrong.

4.4.7   Final offer arbitration

The parties can instruct their chosen neutral that they will both make an offer of the terms on which they will settle, and that the neutral must choose one of those two offers and no other solution. Neither party can afford to make an unrealistic offer, because that will mean that the neutral will choose the opponent's offer. Thus, at least in theory, the offers are likely to be realistic.

4.4.8   Early neutral evaluation

As its name suggests, this method allows the parties to instruct their chosen neutral to make a preliminary assessment of the facts at an early stage in the dispute. Normally the parties submit written case summaries and supporting documents. The evaluator then makes a recommendation. This very often helps the parties to negotiate a settlement (or move to another ADR method), avoiding the expense of litigation.

Rule 3.1(2)(m) of the CPR 1998 provides that the court may take any step or make any order for the purpose of managing the case and furthering the overriding objective (see **1.1.1** and **2.9.2**), including hearing an early neutral evaluation (ENE) with the aim of helping the parties to settle the case. Can the court order that a judicial appraisal take place by way of ENE against the wishes of the parties? Yes, see *Lomax v Lomax* [2019] EWCA Civ 1467, because it is part of the court process which can assist with the fair and sensible resolution of a case. In addition, the parties may benefit from judicial ENE as Master McCloud summarised as follows in *Telecom Centre (UK) Ltd v Thomas Sanderson Ltd* [2020] EWHC 368 (QB):

> 6.   Early Neutral Evaluation is a procedure which involves, in this instance, an independent party expressing an opinion about a dispute or parts of it. The evaluative nature of ENE means that positive or negative views as to merits are expressed, perhaps robustly, by the judge. It is therefore different from many forms of 'mediation' where the focus is facilitative. The process to be adopted for Judicial (or any other form) of ENE is not stated in the Civil Procedure Rules and it is intended that the approach can be tailored to the needs of any given case. Thus one may for example proceed wholly on the basis of written evidence and submissions or by way of written evidence and written argument supplemented at an oral hearing.
>
> 7.   In the QBD, an ENE process may be useful for example where a view on merits is needed on the merits of points of law and construction... or whether alleged breaches if proved would likely amount to repudiatory breaches. Consideration may be given to ENE in respect of any or all

issues in a case and may also be especially useful where the resolution of some key issues would encourage settlement of others, or where the trial time estimate and use of resources and costs would be significantly reduced if parts of the case are resolved as a result of ENE.

8. ENE is a confidential process. The judge dealing with the ENE will thereafter not (absent agreement) try the case or deal with contentious applications. It will therefore be the case that in this instance once I have dealt with ENE I will release the case to another Master who will not be aware of the views expressed at the ENE appointment. That Master may then try the case if appropriate or release to some other judge or court in the usual way, perhaps on a much reduced trial time estimate if any issues have been resolved as a result of the ENE.

9. in the Chancery Division the Guide indicates that the opinion of the judge will be provided informally and that it may be necessary for a hearing of half a day to take place. In my judgment in the Queen's Bench Division given the vast range of types of case and complexity handled by Masters it is a matter for the judge to decide the form and degree of informality or formality of the opinion given, and to consider an appropriate time estimate which may well be more than half a day depending on complexity and substance in a QB case.

10. The outcome of Judicial ENE is normally 'without prejudice' unless privilege is mutually waived and is normally not binding unless the parties agree. It is possible that agreed terms of ENE may be that the decision is binding only upon the happening of certain events, or binding only for a defined period such as where an issue is dealt with on an interim basis.

11. Papers considered at the ENE will be returned to the parties at the end and not retained in the court file so as to ensure that subsequent judges or the public will not access them.

4.4.9 Ombudsman and similar schemes

The number of ombudsman schemes has grown over the years as the Government, as well as various public and private sector organisations, has sought to resolve complaints without litigation. Thus you can find schemes covering such diverse matters as financial services, pensions, police, telecommunications, local government, housing, estate agents, legal services, and the like. Full details can be found at the Ombudsman Schemes in the UK website, at <http://www.ombudsmanassociation.org/index.php>.

Some service and goods providers also offer similar schemes. Probably the best known is the travel industry ABTA arbitration scheme.

4.5 ORGANISATIONS PROVIDING ADR

Anyone can provide help in resolving disputes, but the job is not as easy as it sounds. It should be done by someone who has been trained. The two main organisations that have pioneered ADR in commercial matters in this country are the CEDR and ADR Group.

The CEDR is an independent, non-profit-making organisation promoting ADR, which runs training courses and maintains a panel of neutrals.

The ADR Group is a private company that undertakes mediation and training, and which has established a network of mediators in firms of solicitors throughout the country.

Two other organisations very active in the field of ADR, although their principal *raison d'être* arose from other functions, are the Chartered Institute of Arbitrators and the Academy of Experts.

Lastly, there is Mediation UK, whose general services include all forms of mediation.

Many professional bodies, like the Royal Institution of Chartered Surveyors (RICS), provide ADR services for disputes involving their members.

The judges of the commercial list in the High Court may be prepared to offer their services to help litigants to resolve their disputes without going to trial.

4.6   USING ADR

Parties to a dispute can always reach an ad hoc agreement, when the dispute arises, to use any form of ADR they see fit to solve their problems. It is more proactive, however, to agree in the original contract that, if any dispute does arise between the parties, they will resolve it by some specified form of ADR.

Such contracts may not be effective (see **4.3.1**), because a party cannot be forced to reach a consensual solution, but they do give the parties an opportunity to resolve their disputes peaceably. There is a very strong case for recommending that existing contracts which include an arbitration agreement should be amended, so that the agreement provides for mediation before the parties go to formal arbitration (which they would do only if mediation failed).

4.6.1   Disclosure obligations

An agreement to use ADR should include clauses dealing with some of the potential pitfalls associated with ADR. The parties should decide whether to have a clause requiring full disclosure. The drawback of such a clause is that the more information the parties have to provide to each other, the longer the proceedings may take and the more expensive they will be. Its advantage is that it would be possible to set aside any settlement reached, as a result of ADR, on discovering that one of the parties had concealed vital information. To prevent vexatious applications to set aside any settlement, it might be wise to stipulate in the disclosure clause that a settlement can be challenged only for fundamental non-disclosure of matters which would significantly have affected the result of the ADR process.

4.6.2   Confidentiality

A confidentiality clause in the agreement will encourage full disclosure. The mediator is always under a duty of confidentiality, but the parties will be more likely to disclose information to each other if they know that the other party has agreed not to divulge the information to anyone else. However, if the parties are commercial rivals, who need to keep their methods secret from each other, disclosure and confidentiality clauses are pointless.

4.6.3   Other matters

An ADR agreement should explain how the mediator or other arbiter will be appointed and specify the procedure they should follow. It should also specify that the representatives who attend any ADR process must have full authority to settle the dispute there and then.

4.7   CHOOSING ADR

A solicitor should discuss with the client the possible uses of ADR whenever a dispute arises in a commercial matter. If the client is willing (or has already agreed) to use ADR, it should be used unless it is obviously inappropriate, for example because an injunction is required, or the other party cannot be trusted to comply with an award or to cooperate in the process. There is no point, however, in proceeding with ADR if it looks like failing. In such cases, at the first sign of non-cooperation or lack of trust (eg, where the opponent will not help in the selection of the neutral), litigation or arbitration should be used. This does not mean abandoning ADR altogether – it may be appropriate to continue with ADR in conjunction with litigation, using the latter as a spur to cooperation with the former.

Not surprisingly, given r 1.4(2)(e) (see **4.2**), parties who do choose to litigate may well receive judicial encouragement (and sometimes a degree of pressure) at the case management conference (see **9.6.3.2**) and other hearings to attempt ADR.

The importance the court attaches to proposals for ADR is evidenced by para 4.10(9) of PD 29 (see **9.6.3.1**). Failure to respond to a reasonable proposal to attempt settlement by ADR may have a significant impact on any subsequent order for costs.

In an unreported case, a High Court master has made what is believed to be the first ever order for compulsory alternative dispute resolution. The order, made by consent, arose in the context of a claim made under the Civil Liability (Contribution) Act 1978 in a high-value case.

Master Davidson ordered a stay of proceedings until the end of February 2022 to enable the parties to attempt resolution of the proceedings via mediation. The parties were ordered to 'meaningfully engage in the mediation process in a genuine attempt to reach settlement of these proceedings'.

The order went on: 'The mediation shall be conducted on a without prejudice save as to costs basis and either party shall be at liberty to make an application relying on evidence as to the conduct of the parties at the mediation either with regards to the cost consequences of that conduct or with regards to the court deciding whether or not either party has failed to engage with the mediation process.'

CHAPTER 5

COMMENCING PROCEEDINGS

5.1	Choice of court	65
5.2	Court personnel	68
5.3	Issuing proceedings	68
5.4	Parties to the proceedings	73
5.5	Service of the claim form	77
5.6	Extending time for service of the claim form	83
5.7	Service of documents other than the claim form	84
5.8	Service of particulars of claim	85

LEARNING OUTCOMES

After reading this chapter you will have learned:

- when to commence proceedings in the High Court or County Court
- how to draft a claim form
- what a statement of value is
- the role of a statement of truth
- who can act as a litigation friend for a child
- how to obtain the court's approval of a settlement made on behalf of a child
- how to describe different parties in the title to proceedings
- the different types of methods of service of documents
- where to serve proceedings
- when deemed service takes place
- the basic rules for serving proceedings outside England and Wales
- the consequences of late service of the claim form or particulars of claim.

5.1 CHOICE OF COURT

5.1.1 Value of claim

Although the CPR 1998 apply to both the High Court and the County Court, in some cases a client will have a choice as to the court in which to start proceedings. The general rule is that the County Court has unlimited jurisdiction to hear all tort and contract cases. This is because PD 7A, para 2.1 provides that proceedings may not be started in the High Court unless the value of the claim is more than £100,000. So, if the value of the case is £100,000 or less, it must be started in the County Court. If the value of the case exceeds £100,000 then it can, if the client so wishes, be started in the High Court. In some cases, the High Court has exclusive jurisdiction, but those types of cases are beyond the scope of this book.

In this chapter we make extensive reference to specified and unspecified claims for money. Full details of these terms are to be found at **2.7.1**.

5.1.2 High Court or County Court

Where a claimant has the choice of issuing in the High Court or County Court then, by PD 7A, para 2.4,

> a claim should be started in the High Court if by reason of:
>
> (1)   the financial value of the claim and the amount in dispute, and/or
>
> (2)   the complexity of the facts, legal issues, remedies or procedures involved, and/or
>
> (3)   the importance of the outcome of the claim to the public in general,
>
> the claimant believes that the claim ought to be dealt with by a High Court judge.

A claim should therefore be commenced in the High Court only if that is where the case should be tried.

5.1.3 The County Court

5.1.3.1 Specified claims

Under PD 7A, para 4A.1, if a claim started in the County Court under Part 7 is a claim only for an amount of money, whether specified or unspecified, and no special procedures are required by the CPR 1998 or a practice direction, the claim form must be sent to the County Court Money Claims Centre, PO Box 527, M5 0BY.

If a hearing is required, the claim is sent to the defendant's home County Court (see **9.5**) or the claimant's preferred hearing centre specified in the claim form (see **5.1.5**).

Can any specified claims be issued online? Yes, individuals, businesses and government departments claiming a fixed amount of money of less than £100,000 can issue proceedings via the website Money Claim Online (MCOL). The claim must be for no more than one claimant and against no more than two defendants who have a service address within the jurisdiction of England and Wales. All MCOL claims are issued in the County Court Business Centre and proceed there unless they are sent to a County Court hearing centre.

In addition, PD 51R provides for a pilot scheme for litigants in person to issue claims online via the website Online Civil Money Claims for a specified amount not exceeding £10,000 including interest.

5.1.3.2 Unspecified claims

For all other County Court claims, including those under Part 8 (see **8.4**) or for an interim remedy (see **10.6**), the claimant can issue proceedings in any of the County Court hearing centres situated throughout England and Wales. In these circumstances most claimants will choose to start proceedings in the court closest to their home or business. See generally PD 2C.

5.1.4 The High Court

The High Court has three divisions, namely:

(a)   the Queen's Bench Division;

(b)   the Chancery Division; and

(c)   the Family Division.

If the claimant is claiming damages for breach of contract or tort, the claim should be commenced in the Queen's Bench Division. The Queen's Bench Division produces a *Guide to Litigation*, which is particularly aimed at those litigating in the Central Office.

On 2 October 2017, the Business and Property Courts (B&PCs) were established as a single umbrella for specialist civil jurisdictions in England and Wales. Within the B&PCs, there are specialist courts and lists, eg the Admiralty Court and Commercial Court will come under the Queen's Bench Division, and the Companies List and Intellectual Property List under the Chancery Division. In London, these specialist civil jurisdictions operate together in the Rolls

Building on Fetter Lane, forming the largest specialist centre for financial, business and property litigation in the world.

Business and Property Courts have also been established in the seven main centres outside London where specialist business similar to that in the Rolls Building is undertaken, namely Birmingham, Bristol, Cardiff, Leeds, Liverpool, Newcastle and Manchester. The main centre for the B&PCs in Wales is in Cardiff.

Cases that are likely to be suitable for hearing in the Commercial Court include complex cases arising out of business disputes, both national and international, encompassing all aspects of commercial disputes, in the fields of banking and finance, shipping, insurance and reinsurance and commodities. The Commercial Court produces a Commercial Court Guide, which gives guidance on the day-to-day practice in that court. See also CPR 1998, Part 58.

The Chancery Division of the High Court deals with such matters as trusts, contentious probate business, partnership claims, disputes about land, and landlord and tenant disputes. A claim should be commenced in the Chancery Division if the claimant is claiming an equitable remedy such as specific performance, or if it is an intellectual property claim, such as copyright or passing-off.

The Family Division deals with High Court family matters, which are outside the scope of this book.

A claimant commencing proceedings in the High Court normally has a choice of issuing in any of the District Registries of the High Court, which are usually situated in the same building as the regional County Court, or the Central Office of the High Court in London. Most claimants will choose to start proceedings in the court closest to their home or business.

5.1.5   Transfer between courts

Part 30 of the CPR 1998 deals with the powers of the High Court and County Court to send matters from one court to another.

There are provisions for the sending of claims to the preferred hearing centre specified by the claimant in their claim form (see **6.5.1, 6.6.2, 9.5** and **10.5.1.6**).

There are also provisions for sending to the defendant's home court in certain limited circumstances (see **9.5**).

CASE STUDY: CHOICE OF COURT

Negotiations between the parties' solicitors fail. Experts disagree over liability. Whilst some items of quantum are agreed, subject to liability, Mr Templar's expert does not agree that Mr and Mrs Simpson's extension needs demolishing and rebuilding. He is of the opinion that it can be repaired.

Court proceedings could be started by either party. Where would these be started, and why? We know from the receipts and estimates that Mr and Mrs Simpson's claim is in the region of £185,000. This is well in excess of the minimum amount of £100,000 required to commence a claim in the High Court (PD 7A, para 2.1), but are the criteria in PD 7A, para 2.4 satisfied? The case is not factually complicated, but there appear to be some complex expert issues. The case has no general importance to the public. Arguably the value of the claim is sufficient to satisfy para 2.4(1) and justify issuing the proceedings in the High Court. There is no good reason why the case should be tried in the Central Office and so proceedings should be started in the local District Registry where this will be more convenient for the parties and solicitors.

Mr Templar's documents reveal a claim of around £70,000. As this is below the minimum amount for High Court proceedings, he would have to commence any claim in the County Court at the County Court Money Claims Centre (see **5.1.3**).

5.2   COURT PERSONNEL

The great bulk of both County Court and High Court work is dealt with by district judges and, for matters proceeding in the Central Office in London, masters. These deal with the majority of interim applications (see **Chapter 10**) and also have jurisdiction to hear trials where the amount involved does not exceed £25,000. Trials for amounts in excess of that figure are heard by circuit judges in the County Court and by High Court judges in the High Court. Under Part 3 of the CPR 1998, the judges have extensive case and costs management powers (see **Chapter 9**).

5.3   ISSUING PROCEEDINGS

A party who wishes to start proceedings must complete a claim form in the prescribed way (PD 7A, para 3.1), which should either be handed in or sent to the appropriate court office (see **5.1**). Proceedings are commenced when the court 'issues' the claim form by sealing it with the court seal (although for limitation purposes, the relevant date is the date when the court receives the claim form: see **2.5.2**). A copy of a claim form appears at **Appendix A(1)**.

5.3.1   Completing the claim form

In addition to the points set out here, the Court Service provides detailed guidance notes on the completion of the claim form which appear at **Appendix A(1)**.

5.3.1.1   Claimant and defendant details

The person who makes the claim is described as the claimant, and the person against whom the claim is made is the defendant.

Practice Direction 16, para 2 provides as follows:

2.2   The claim form must include an address at which the claimant resides or carries on business. This paragraph applies even though the claimant's address for service is the business address of his solicitor.

2.3   Where the defendant is an individual, the claimant should (if he is able to do so) include in the claim form an address at which the defendant resides or carries on business. This paragraph applies even though the defendant's solicitors have agreed to accept service on the defendant's behalf.

2.4   Any address which is provided for the purpose of these provisions must include a postcode (or its equivalent in any EEA state, if applicable), unless the court orders otherwise.

2.5   If the claim form does not show a full address, including postcode, at which the claimant(s) and defendant(s) reside or carry on business, the claim form will be issued but will be retained by the court and will not be served until the claimant has supplied a full address, including postcode, or the court has dispensed with the requirement to do so. The court will notify the claimant.

2.6   The claim form must be headed with the title of the proceedings, including the full name of each party. The full name means, in each case where it is known:

    (a)   in the case of an individual, his full unabbreviated name and title by which he is known;

    (b)   in the case of an individual carrying on business in a name other than his own name, the full unabbreviated name of the individual, together with the title by which he is known, and the full trading name (for example, John Smith 'trading as' or 'T/as' 'JS Autos');

    (c)   in the case of a partnership (other than a limited liability partnership (LLP))—

        (i)   where partners are being sued in the name of the partnership, the full name by which the partnership is known, together with the words '(A Firm)'; or

        (ii)   where partners are being sued as individuals, the full unabbreviated name of each partner and the title by which he is known;

    (d)   in the case of a company or limited liability partnership registered in England and Wales, the full registered name, including suffix (plc, limited, LLP, etc), if any;

    (e)   in the case of any other company or corporation, the full name by which it is known, including suffix where appropriate.

It is important to note the effect of para 2.5 above. Whilst the court will issue a claim form that lacks service address details, it will not be served until the claimant has supplied a full address, including postcode, or the court has dispensed with the requirement to do so. If the claimant cannot supply full service address details, an application to dispense with such should be made when filing the claim form.

As to para 2.6 above, in what circumstances can a claimant seek anonymity? CPR 1998, r 39.2(4) provides that the court must order that the identity of any party (or witness) shall not be disclosed if, and only if, it considers non-disclosure necessary to secure the proper administration of justice and in order to protect the interests of that party (or witness). See further *XXX v Camden London Borough Council* [2020] EWCA Civ 1468.

Where one of the parties is not an individual over the age of 18, or is not suing or being sued in their personal capacity, special considerations may apply (see **5.4**). The Court Service guidance notes (see **5.3.1**) set out how these should be reflected in the claim form.

5.3.1.2   Brief details of claim

The claim form must contain a concise statement of the nature of the claim and specify the remedy that the claimant is seeking (see r 16.2(1) and the notes on completing the claim form).

In *Travis Perkins Trading Co Ltd v Caerphilly CBC* [2014] EWHC 1498 (TCC), Akenhead J stated at para 22:

(a) Only 'brief' details are required to describe 'the nature of the claim', although the remedy sought needs to be spelt out; a statement of value (not more than or more than £X) needs to be provided.

(b) Whilst it is open to a claimant to be specific and restrictive in what it, he or she seeks to claim by way of the 'Brief Details of Claim', it is not necessary.

(c) The Court should have regard to the wording overall to determine what is covered by the wording of the Brief Details to see whether and to what extent the rule has been fulfilled. The Court should not be prescriptive about what is required in terms of the words used by the claimant; all that is prescriptive is in the wording of the rule.

5.3.1.3   Value/the amount claimed

Rule 16.2(1)(cc) requires that where the claimant's only claim is for a specified sum, the claim form must contain a statement of the interest accrued on that sum (see also **2.7** and **7.2.1.5**).

Rule 16.3(2) requires that if the claim is for money, the claim form must either state the amount claimed or, if the claim is for an unspecified amount of money, whether or not the claimant expects to recover:

(a) not more than £10,000; or

(b) more than £10,000 but not more than £25,000; or

(c) more than £25,000; or

(d) that the claimant cannot say how much they expect to recover.

This information assists the County Court in allocating the claim to the multi-track, fast track or small claims track, as appropriate. Allocation of cases in the County Court is dealt with in detail in **Chapter 9**. The information will also form the basis on which the fee payable to issue the claim is calculated (see **5.3.1.5**).

5.3.1.4   High Court cases

Practice Direction 7A, para 3.6 provides that if a claim for an unspecified sum of money is started in the High Court, the claim form must:

(a) state that the claimant expects to recover more than £100,000; or

(b) state that some enactment provides that the claim may only be commenced in the High Court and specify that enactment; or

(c)   state that the claim is to be in one of the specialist High Court lists (see CPR 1998, Parts 49 and 58–62) and specify that list.

The Notes for Claimant on completing the claim form (see **Appendix A(1)**) suggest a form of words such as 'I wish my claim to issue in the High Court because', followed by one of the above grounds (eg, 'I expect to recover more than £100,000'). Arguably, the Notes are aimed at litigants in person, and most solicitors, when relying on the value exceeding £100,000 as giving the High Court jurisdiction, will simply put 'The Claimant expects to recover more than £100,000'.

5.3.1.5   The court fee

The claimant is obliged to pay a fee on issue of the claim form, based on the value of the claim. The amount of the fee should be stated on the front of the form. Details of court fees are contained in the leaflet EX50 – Civil and Family Court Fees, available at <http://www.gov.uk/government/publications/fees-for-civil-and-family-courts/court-fees-for-the-high-court-county-court-and-family-court>.

Note that where the claim is for a specified sum, the amount on which the issue fee is calculated is the total amount of the claim and the accrued interest. The figures for the specified sum and the accrued interest should be set out on the front page of the claim form under the heading 'Value' (see **5.3.1.3**).

5.3.1.6   Solicitor's costs

If the claim is for a specified amount of money, and was issued by a solicitor, the form should also include a figure for solicitor's costs. These are fixed costs payable by the defendant, in addition to the court fee, should the defendant admit the claim. Fixed costs are dealt with in Part 45 of the CPR 1998.

If the claim is for an unspecified amount of money, this box is usually completed 'to be assessed' (meaning that the court will in due course determine the amount of costs payable should the defendant have to pay the claimant's costs: see generally **14.3**).

5.3.1.7   Issues under the Human Rights Act 1998

The claimant is obliged to state whether the claim does or will include any issues under the Human Rights Act 1998.

5.3.1.8   The particulars of claim

The details of the claimant's claim, known as the particulars of claim, must be set out either in the claim form itself, or in a separate document that is served either with the claim form or within 14 days of service of the claim form. Care is needed in the drafting of the particulars of claim, and this issue is considered in **Chapter 7**.

By rule 7.4(3), if the claimant serves particulars of claim, then unless a copy of those particulars has already been filed at the court, the claimant must, within seven days of service on the defendant, file a copy of the particulars at the court.

5.3.2   The statement of truth

The CPR 1998 require that various documents, including the claim form, are verified by a statement of truth (see CPR 1998, Part 22). If the particulars of claim are served separately, they must also be so verified and the statement of truth in the claim form should be amended to read, 'the facts stated in this claim form are true'.

Who can sign the statement of truth? Practice Direction 22, para 3.1 gives this answer:

> In a statement of case, a response or an application notice, the statement of truth must be signed by:
>
> (1)   the party or his litigation friend [see **5.4.1**], or
>
> (2)   the legal representative of the party or litigation friend.

So how should you draft a statement of truth in a statement of case? Practice Direction 22, para 2.1 states as follows:

> [I believe] [The (*claimant or as may be*) believes] that the facts stated in this [*name document being verified*] are true. I understand that proceedings for contempt of court may be brought against anyone who makes, or causes to be made, a false statement in a document verified by a statement of truth without an honest belief in its truth.

By para 2.5 the statement of truth must be dated with the date on which it was signed.

5.3.2.1 Signed by the client

An individual signing as a party or on behalf of a party, eg a partner or company director, should express their own personal belief and sign, 'I believe ...'.

Who can sign on behalf of a partnership? Practice Direction 22, para 3.6 states:

> Where the document is to be verified on behalf of a partnership, those who may sign the statement of truth are:
> (1)   any of the partners, or
> (2)   a person having the control or management of the partnership business.

Who can sign on behalf of a company? Practice Direction 22, para 3.4 requires that it must be signed by a person holding a senior position in the company, and para 3.5 states that such a person may be a director, the treasurer, secretary, chief executive, manager or other officer of the company.

You should note that some practitioners draft a statement of truth for a company officer to sign as 'The [claimant or defendant etc] believes', rather than as 'I believe'. There is nothing in the CPR indicating that either version is right or wrong. Whatever way it is drafted, the individual signing on behalf of the company is assuming personal responsibility. If they do not have an honest belief in the truth of the contents of the document, they could be prosecuted for contempt of court.

Where an individual signs on behalf of a party, it is best practice and follows the model set out on various court forms to state that the person has authority to do so, ie by adding 'I am duly authorised by the [party] to sign this statement'.

5.3.2.2 Signed by a solicitor

Where a solicitor signs on behalf of the client, they should sign 'The [party] believes ...'.

Practice Direction 22, para 3.7 clarifies that the statement refers to the client's belief and not the solicitor's belief. In addition the solicitor must state the capacity in which they sign and the name of their firm, where appropriate. However, by PD 22, para 3.10, note that the solicitor must sign in their own name and not that of their firm.

EXAMPLE

The Claimant believes that the facts stated in these particulars of claim are true. The Claimant understands that proceedings for contempt of court may be brought against anyone who makes, or causes to be made, a false statement in a document verified by a statement of truth without an honest belief in its truth. I am duly authorised by the Claimant to sign this statement.

Signed:
LAWRENCE HODGES

Date:

Lawrence Hodges, Assistant Solicitor with Singleton Trumper & Co, solicitors acting for the Claimant in these proceedings

---

Where a legal representative signs a statement of truth, para 3.8 of PD 22 states that this will be taken as their statement:

(1)   that the client on whose behalf he has signed had authorised him to do so;

(2)   that before signing he had explained to the client that in signing the statement of truth he would be confirming the client's belief that the facts stated in the document were true; and

(3)   that before signing he had informed the client of the possible consequences to the client if it should subsequently appear that the client did not have an honest belief in the truth of those facts.

The consequences referred to in para 3.8(3) above are that proceedings for contempt of court may be brought against the client: see r 32.14.

5.3.2.3   What if the statement is omitted?

By PD 22, para 4, if a statement of case (which includes a claim form) is not verified by a statement of truth, it remains effective unless the court strikes it out, which the court may do on its own initiative or on the application of another party. If the statement of case is not struck out, the claimant will not, however, be allowed to rely on its contents as evidence (for example, on an interim application: see **Chapter 10**).

CASE STUDY: COMPLETING THE CLAIM FORM

Let us briefly consider how the claim form would be completed in the case study.

1.   Mr and Mrs Simpson start proceedings. Their solicitors have decided to issue the claim in the nearest District Registry of the High Court (see **5.1** above). The heading will therefore be as follows:

In the High Court of Justice
Queen's Bench Division
Weyford District Registry

The court will assign a claim number when the claim form is issued. This information must be included on the claim form and all subsequent statements of case (PD 7A, para 4.1(1)).

2.   The Parties need to be described accurately. Here there are two claimants, both of whom are individuals. Practice Direction 16, para 2.6(a) requires that their full names and title should be given as follows:

Mr William Ulysses Simpson (1)
Mrs Rupinder Simpson (2)

In addition their full address, including a postcode, should be stated (PD 16, paras 2.2 and 2.4).

The same information is required for the defendant. His name and full address will also appear in the box in the bottom left-hand corner of the claim form.

3.   Brief details of claim and remedy sought.

This might read: 'The Claimants claim damages arising out of the Defendant's negligent driving on 2 August 2021.'

4.   Value.

This information will help the court when managing the case. As the claim is for damages (an unspecified claim) exceeding £100,000, it should state: 'The Claimants expect to recover more than £100,000.'

5.   The court fee payable on issue is based on the value of the claim. There is no need for a figure to be inserted in the 'Solicitor's costs' box as this is an unspecified claim and any costs awarded will be assessed by the court.

> 6. Whilst particulars of claim could be inserted on the form, these will be prepared separately. If they are to be served with the claim form the words 'to follow' should be deleted.
>
> 7. A statement of truth will be required as the claim form is a statement of case and r 22.1(1)(a) requires that all statements of case should be verified by a statement of truth.
>
> 8. An address for service within the jurisdiction must be given. As solicitors act for Mr and Mrs Simpson and are instructed to accept service of court documents on their behalf, the name, address and reference details of the firm should be given.

5.4 PARTIES TO THE PROCEEDINGS

If the claimant and defendant are both individuals of full age, suing or being sued in their personal capacity, there are no special considerations. As much of the full, unabbreviated name of the individual party should be stated as possible (including first, middle and last names, and the title by which the party is known, eg Mr Thomas Patrick Clark, Dr Laurie Chris Brown, Professor Mary Banister, etc). In other cases, there may be special considerations because of the nature of the party concerned, for example in cases where the claimant or defendant is a child, a protected party, a sole trader, a partnership or a limited company. These special rules are considered below.

5.4.1 Children and protected parties

A child is a person aged under 18, and a protected party is a person who is incapable of managing and administering their own affairs (including court proceedings) because of a mental disorder, as defined by the Mental Capacity Act 2005. Part 21 of the CPR 1998 contains special provisions relating to these types of litigant.

5.4.1.1 The requirement for a 'litigation friend'

The Rules require a protected party to have a litigation friend to conduct proceedings, whether as claimant or defendant, on their behalf. A child must also have a litigation friend to conduct proceedings on their behalf, unless the court orders otherwise. In the case of protected parties, the litigation friend will usually be a person authorised under the 2005 Act to conduct legal proceedings in the name of a protected party; and in the case of a child, the litigation friend will normally be a parent or guardian.

If a solicitor is unsure whether or not their client falls within the definition of a protected party, the solicitor may seek an order of the court directing that the Official Solicitor consider the evidence, appoint a medical expert and appear at the hearing: see *Lindsay v Wood* [2006] EWHC 2895 (QB).

A solicitor's retainer will not necessarily automatically terminate where a client loses mental capacity: *Blankley v Central Manchester and Manchester Children's University Hospitals NHS Trust* [2015] EWCA Civ 18.

In relation to proceedings against a child or protected party, a person may not, without permission of the court, make an application against a child or protected party before proceedings have started, or take any step in the proceedings except:

(a) issuing and serving a claim form; or

(b) applying for the appointment of a litigation friend under r 21.6.

5.4.1.2 Steps to be taken by a litigation friend

A person authorised under the 2005 Act to act as a litigation friend on behalf of a protected party must file an official copy of the document which is their authority to act. Otherwise, a litigation friend acting on behalf of a protected party or child must file a certificate of suitability. If acting on behalf of a claimant, this must be done when making the claim; and if acting on behalf of a defendant, it must be done when first taking a step in the proceedings. The certificate of suitability must state that the proposed litigation friend:

(a) consents to act;

(b) believes the party to be a child or protected party (with reasons and medical evidence);

(c) can fairly and competently conduct proceedings on behalf of the party;

(d) has no adverse interest;

(e) if acting as a litigation friend for a claimant, undertakes to pay any costs which the claimant may be ordered to pay in the proceedings. Note that a counterclaim (see **Chapter 8**) is treated like a claim for the purposes of the costs undertakings.

The litigation friend must serve the certificate of suitability on every person on whom the claim form should be served and must then file a certificate of service when filing the certificate of suitability.

5.4.1.3 Cessation of appointment of a litigation friend

In relation to a child, the appointment of a litigation friend ceases when the child becomes 18. The appointment of a litigation friend for a protected party does not cease when the party ceases to be a protected party, but it continues until the appointment is ended by a court order sought by the former protected party, the litigation friend, or any party.

By CPR 1998, r 21.7(1), the court may direct that a person may not act as a litigation friend, terminate a litigation friend's appointment and appoint a new litigation friend in substitution for an existing one. See, for example, *X v Y* [2020] 11 WLUK 6.

5.4.1.4 Settlement of cases brought by or against a child or protected party

Special provisions apply where a case involving a child or protected party is settled. Such a settlement is not valid unless it has been approved by the court. Before the court approves a settlement, it will need to know:

(a) whether and to what extent the defendant admits liability;

(b) the age and occupation (if any) of the child or protected party;

(c) that the litigation friend approves of the proposed settlement.

The application to the court must, in most cases, be supported by a legal opinion on the merits of the settlement and the instructions on which it was based. Although the application will be heard in private, the formal approval of the settlement will usually be given publicly in open court – see *Beathem v Carlisle Hospitals NHS Trust* (1999) *The Times*, 20 May.

If a claim by or against a child or protected party is settled before proceedings are begun, and proceedings are issued solely to obtain the court's approval of the settlement, the claim must include a request to the court for approval of the settlement and must be made under Part 8 of the CPR 1998 (see **8.4**).

If money is recovered by or on behalf of or for the benefit of a child or protected party, the money should be dealt with in accordance with the directions of the court. The court will usually direct that the money be paid into the High Court for investment. In relation to a child, the money will be paid out when the child becomes 18.

A consent judgment involving a protected party that is reached without the appointment of a litigation friend and the approval of the court is invalid. Is that so even where the protected party's lack of capacity is unknown to everyone acting in the litigation at the time of the compromise? Yes – see *Dunhill (a protected party by her litigation friend Paul Tasker) v Burgin* [2014] UKSC 18.

5.4.2   Partnerships

5.4.2.1   Where a partnership is the claimant

Partnerships must normally sue in the name of the firm, rather than by naming individual partners. Pursuant to PD 7A, para 5A.3, it is usually easier and more convenient to use the name under which the partnership carried on business at the time the cause of action accrued, eg 'ABC & Co (a firm)'.

5.4.2.2   Where a partnership is the defendant

Partnerships must normally be sued in the name of the firm rather than in the names of the individual partners. Practice Direction 7A, para 5A.3 provides that where a partnership has a name, unless it is inappropriate to do so, claims must be brought against the name under which that partnership carried on business at the time the cause of action accrued. In practice, it is usually simpler and more efficient to sue a partnership in the name of the firm, especially as service on the firm can be effected by serving any one of the partners, or by serving the firm at its principal place of business (see **5.5**).

The advantage of suing partners in their firm's name is the ability to enforce the judgment against partnership property, but the disadvantage is the need to seek the court's permission to enforce a judgment against persons not identified in the proceedings as partners (see *Kommalage v Sayanthakumar* [2015] EWCA Civ 1832 and **15.1.1**).

5.4.3   Sole traders

5.4.3.1   Where a sole trader is the claimant

It is generally accepted practice that sole traders should sue in their own name and not in any trading or business name. However, there is no objection to adding any trading name, eg 'David Fadzanai Haruperi Kapaya trading as David's Dazzling Designs'.

5.4.3.2   Where a sole trader is the defendant

By PD 7A, para 5C.2, sole traders carrying on business within the jurisdiction and under a name other than their own can be sued in that name. If the trader is sued under their trade name, they will be referred to in the heading to the claim as, for example, 'Anthony Tucker T/A Marble Designs'. Note that T/A is an acceptable abbreviation of 'trading as'. If the claimant does not know the name of the sole trader, the claimant may sue naming the defendant under their business name, eg 'Welcome Homes (a trading name)'.

5.4.4   Limited companies

5.4.4.1   Where a limited company is the claimant

A company can sue under its corporate name.

5.4.4.2   Where a limited company is the defendant

A company can be sued under its corporate name.

Before commencing proceedings against a company, the claimant should carry out a company search to confirm the corporate status and continued existence of the proposed defendant company, to confirm the correct name of the company and to ascertain the registered address of the company if it is intended to serve the company at its registered office.

5.4.5   Unnamed parties

Are there any circumstances in which it is permissible to sue an unnamed defendant? Yes, but these are very limited held the Supreme Court in *Cameron v Liverpool Victoria Insurance Co Ltd* [2019] UKSC 6. Giving the unanimous ruling of the court, Lord Sumption said:

[9] The general rule remains that proceedings may not be brought against unnamed parties. ... The only express provision made for proceedings against an unnamed defendant, other than representative actions, is CPR 55.3(4), which permits a claim for possession of property to be brought against trespassers whose names are unknown.

[10] English judges have allowed some exceptions. They have permitted representative actions where the representative can be named but some or all of the class cannot. They have allowed actions and orders against unnamed wrongdoers where some of the wrongdoers were known so they could be sued both personally and as representing their unidentified associates. This technique has been used, for example, in actions against copyright pirates: see *EMI Records Ltd v Kudhail* [1985] FSR 35. But the possibility of a much wider jurisdiction was first opened up by the decision of Sir Andrew Morritt V-C in *Bloomsbury Publishing Group Plc v News Group Newspapers Ltd* [2003] 1 WLR 1633. The claimant in that case was the publisher of the Harry Potter novels. Copies of the latest book in the series had been stolen from the printers before publication and offered to the press by unnamed persons. An injunction was granted in proceedings against 'the person or persons who have offered the publishers of "The Sun", the "Daily Mail" and the "Daily Mirror" newspapers a copy of the book Harry Potter and the Order of the Phoenix by J K Rowling or any part thereof and the person or persons who has or have physical possession of a copy of the said book or any part thereof without the consent of the claimants.' The real object of the injunction was to deter newspapers minded to publish parts of the text, who would expose themselves to proceedings for contempt of court by dealing with the thieves with notice of the order ...

[12] The Civil Procedure Rules neither expressly authorise nor expressly prohibit exceptions to the general rule that actions against unnamed parties are permissible only against trespassers. ... The critical question is what, as a matter of law, is the basis of the court's jurisdiction over parties, and in what (if any) circumstances can jurisdiction be exercised on that basis against persons who cannot be named.

[13] In approaching this question, it is necessary to distinguish between two kinds of case in which the defendant cannot be named, to which different considerations apply. The first category comprises anonymous defendants who are identifiable but whose names are unknown. Squatters occupying a property are, for example, identifiable by their location, although they cannot be named. The second category comprises defendants, such as most hit and run drivers, who are not only anonymous but cannot even be identified. The distinction is that in the first category the defendant is described in a way that makes it possible in principle to locate or communicate with him and to know without further inquiry whether he is the same as the person described in the claim form, whereas in the second category it is not.

5.4.6   Addition and substitution of parties

On occasions, it will be necessary for another party to be added to a claim or for one party to be replaced by another. For example, A may take proceedings against B for damages for negligence, and subsequently may discover that C was also negligent. A may then want to add C to the proceedings as a second defendant. Or A may sue B (an individual) for a debt, but then discovers that A's contract was not with B trading on B's own account but with a company controlled by B. A will want to substitute the company for B as defendant.

As stated in r 19.4(2) of the CPR 1998, an application for permission to remove, add or substitute a party may be made by:

(a)   an existing party; or

(b)   a person who wishes to become a party.

The application may be made without notice and must be supported by evidence.

Nobody may be added or substituted as a claimant unless they have given their consent in writing and that consent has been filed with the court.

Rule 19.2 states:

(2)   The court may order a person to be added as a new party if—

(a)   it is desirable to add the new party so that the court can resolve all the matters in dispute in the proceedings; or

(b) there is an issue involving the new party and an existing party which is connected to the matters in dispute in the proceedings, and it is desirable to add the new party so that the court can resolve that issue.

(3) The court may order any person to cease to be a party if it is not desirable for that person to be a party to the proceedings.

(4) The court may order a new party to be substituted for an existing one if—

(a) the existing party's interest or liability has passed to the new party; and

(b) it is desirable to substitute the new party so that the court can resolve the matters in dispute in the proceedings.

Special provisions apply where parties are to be added or substituted after the end of the relevant limitation period. Rule 19.5 states:

(2) The court may add or substitute a party only if—

(a) the relevant limitation period was current when the proceedings were started; and

(b) the addition or substitution is necessary.

(3) The addition or substitution of a party is necessary only if the court is satisfied that—

(a) the new party is to be substituted for a party who was named in the claim form in mistake for the new party;

(b) the claim cannot properly be carried on by or against the original party unless the new party is added or substituted as claimant or defendant; or

(c) the original party has died or had a bankruptcy order made against him and his interest or liability has passed to the new party.

Part 19 also contains provisions enabling the Crown to be joined as a party to proceedings in which the court may wish to make a declaration of incompatibility in accordance with s 4 of the Human Rights Act 1998.

5.4.7 Professional conduct

A solicitor warrants their authority to take any positive step in court proceedings, for example to issue a claim form or serve a defence on behalf of the client. If a solicitor conducts proceedings without that authority, they will usually be personally liable for the costs incurred: see, for example, *Warner v Masefield* [2008] EWHC 1129.

Note that if a solicitor receives instructions from someone other than the client, or by only one client on behalf of others in a joint matter, the solicitor should not proceed without checking that all clients agree with the instructions given.

5.5 SERVICE OF THE CLAIM FORM

Once a claim form has been issued by the court, it must be served on the other parties if the claimant is to pursue the claim.

The rules governing service of court documents are set out in Part 6 of the CPR 1998.

5.5.1 How to serve a claim form

The following methods of service are permitted under r 6.3:

(a) personal service;

(b) first-class post, document exchange or other service which provides for delivery on the next business day;

(c) leaving the claim form at a specified place;

(d) fax or other means of electronic communication; or

(e) any other method authorised by the court.

5.5.1.1 Personal service

Rule 6.5(3)(a) provides that a claim form is served personally on an individual by leaving it with that individual. So personal service is carried out by handing the claim form to the individual party whilst they are in the jurisdiction (ie England or Wales). If they will not take the claim form, they should be told what the document contains, and it should be left with them or near them (see *Tseitline v Mikhelson* [2015] EWHC 3065 (Comm)).

What if the defendant is a partnership? According to r 6.5(3)(c), a document is served personally on a partnership (where partners are being sued in the name of their firm: see **5.4.2.2**) by leaving it either with a partner, or with a person who, at the time of service, has the control or management of the partnership business at its principal place of business. A notice in Form N218 must also be served (see **Appendix A(5)**). Note that the principal place of business of a partnership is its main office, not a branch office.

If you wish to serve a partner, PD 7A, para 5B.2 allows you to obtain from the partnership a written statement of the names and last-known places of residence of all the persons who were partners in the partnership at the time when the cause of action accrued.

By r 6.5(3)(b) and PD 6A, para 6.2, a document is served personally on a registered company (or other corporation) by leaving it with a person who holds a senior position within the company (or corporation), such as a director, the treasurer, secretary or chief executive.

5.5.1.2 First-class post or alternative 'next working day' delivery

First-class post, or an alternative service that provides for delivery on the next working day, is permitted, but note that the Rules do not allow for service by second-class post or any other postal method, such as recorded delivery, unless the alternative method provides for delivery on the next working day (for example, Royal Mail's 'Signed For 1st Class' service: see *Diriye v Bojaj* [2020] EWCA Civ 1400). See **5.5.3** for the address to be used where this method of service is adopted.

5.5.1.3 Leaving the claim form at a specified place

Here the claim form is delivered by hand. See **5.5.3** below for the address to be used for this method of service.

5.5.1.4 Through a document exchange (DX)

If a party has given a DX box number as its address for service then that can be used to serve the claim form (PD 6A, para 2.1). Alternatively, where a party or their solicitor's headed notepaper includes a DX box number, that may be used unless the party or their solicitors have indicated in writing that they are unwilling to be served by DX. If a solicitors' firm has a DX number but does not want to accept service by that method, it normally includes next to the DX number something like 'not for the purposes of service'.

5.5.1.5 By fax

To serve a claim form by fax transmission, the party to be served or their solicitors must have indicated in writing a willingness to accept service by fax and also stated the fax number to which the claim form should be sent (PD 6A, para 4). A fax number on the party's headed notepaper is not sufficient for this purpose. However, the fax number on a party's solicitors' headed notepaper is treated as agreement to service by this method on behalf of their client, unless the solicitors indicate otherwise in writing. If a solicitors' firm has a fax number and does not want to accept service by that method, it normally includes next to the fax number something like 'not for the purposes of service'.

5.5.1.6 By other electronic means such as e-mail

A party to be served by e-mail or similar electronic method must have expressly indicated in writing the e-mail address or electronic identification to which it should be sent (PD 6A, para

4). An e-mail address on a party's headed notepaper is not enough. If the party has instructed solicitors to accept service on its behalf, an e-mail address on the solicitors' notepaper is not enough unless it states that the e-mail address may be used for service purposes.

Note that in addition, PD 6A, para 4.2 requires the party who wishes to serve the claim form by e-mail or other electronic means (but not fax) to clarify with the intended recipient whether there are any limitations to the recipient's agreement to accept service by such means, including the format in which documents are to be sent and the maximum size of attachments that may be received.

5.5.1.7 Service on limited companies

Where the party to be served is a limited company, s 1139(1) of the Companies Act 2006 provides an alternative method of service in addition to the CPR (see *Murphy v Staples UK Limited* [2003] 3 All ER 129). The Act provides that documents may be left at or posted to the registered office of the company. Whilst second-class post may be used when serving under s 1139(1), it is not recommended.

5.5.2 Who should be served?

5.5.2.1 General rule: any solicitor authorised to accept service

Rule 6.7 provides that if a defendant has given in writing the business address of a solicitor within the United Kingdom or other European Economic Area (EEA) State as an address at which the defendant may be served with the claim form, or a solicitor acting for the defendant has notified the claimant in writing that the solicitor is instructed by the defendant to accept service of the claim form on behalf of the defendant at a business address within the United Kingdom or other EEA State, the claim form must be served at the business address of that solicitor.

If parties' solicitors have been in correspondence before litigation starts, it is usual for the claimant's solicitors to ask the defendant's solicitors if they are 'authorised to accept service of proceedings'. Rather uniquely, in *Smith v Probyn* (2000) *The Times*, 29 March, the parties' solicitors had corresponded prior to a claim form being issued but the defendant's solicitors were never asked if they were authorised to accept service. Equally, the defendant's solicitors had never intimated in any way that they were instructed to accept service. Just before the deadline to serve the claim form expired, the claimant's solicitors sent it in the DX to the defendant's solicitors. Morland J held that there had been no effective service of the claim form.

5.5.2.2 Other provisions

Where r 6.7 does not apply, the claimant must serve the defendant with the claim form by one of the permitted methods detailed at **5.5.1**, unless any special provision concerning service of the claim form applies: see r 6.11 for any contractually agreed method of service; r 6.12 for service on the agent of an overseas principal; and r 6.15 for service by an alternative method or at an alternative place in accordance with a court order. Under r 6.15(2), the court has power to order that an alternate method of service already taken is good service. In *Woodward v Phoenix Healthcare Distribution Ltd* [2019] EWCA Civ 985, the Court refused to validate service of the claim form retrospectively. The claim form, particulars and response pack had been sent to the defendant's solicitors shortly before the expiry of the deadline for service of the claim form. The defendant's solicitors did not have instructions to accept service and they waited until after expiry of the deadline for service to notify the claimant's solicitors that they were not authorised to accept service. The Court held that there was no duty requiring the solicitors to draw attention to the mistake made by the other party for which they were not responsible, nor were they in breach of r 1.3 in failing to warn of the defect in service before the validity of the claim form expired. (See also **1.1.2.1.**)

In *Barton v Wright Hassall LLP* [2018] UKSC 12, Mr Barton, a litigant in person, purported to serve the claim form on solicitors who had not indicated that they were instructed to accept service by email. By the time the error was discovered, and Mr Barton informed, the time for service of the claim form and the limitation period had expired. Mr Barton sought to rely on r 6.15(2), arguing that the claim had been brought to the attention of the defendant successfully. The court stated that whilst this was a necessary condition for an order under r 6.15, it was not sufficient to satisfy the 'good reason' test. The fact that Mr Barton was a litigant in person did not justify applying a lower standard of compliance with rules or orders of the court. See also *Linklaters LLP v Mellish* [2019] EWHC 177 (QB) and *Société Générale v Goldas Kuyumculuk Sanayi Ithalat Ihracat AS* [2018] EWCA Civ 109.

In *LSREF 3 Tiger Falkirk Ltd I SARL and another v Paragon Building Consultancy Ltd* [2021] EWHC 2063 (TCC), the court held that service of a £10 million claim was defective and refused to retrospectively validate service under CPR, r 6.15, dispense with service under r 6.16 or grant relief under r 3.9. The validity of the claim form had been extended three times by agreement. On the afternoon of the day on which validity expired, C's solicitors telephoned D's solicitors seeking a further extension. Having received no response from D's solicitors, C's solicitors emailed the proceedings to D's solicitors later that evening. It was held that service was defective because:

- C's solicitors had not asked D's solicitors whether they were instructed to accept service of the claim form, and D's solicitors had not notified C's solicitors that they were. Accordingly, service did not comply with r 6.7(1)(b).
- Nothing in the dealings between the parties' solicitors, their correspondence or the written extension agreement could be construed as amounting to D's solicitors having implied authority to accept service.

Fraser J refused to retrospectively validate service (r 6.15) or dispense with service (r 6.16). C had not taken reasonable steps to effect service in accordance with the Rules, and granting relief would substantially prejudice D through loss of a limitation defence. Consideration of r 3.9 was impermissible, because the relevant routes were r 6.15 and r 6.16.

5.5.3   Where to serve?

By r 6.9, where no solicitor is authorised to accept service and the defendant has not given any address for service, the claim form must be served on the defendant at the place shown in the following table:

Nature of defendant to be served	Place of service
1. Individual	Usual or last known residence.
2. Individual being sued in the name of a business	Usual or last known residence of the individual; or principal or last known place of business.
3. Individual being sued in the business name of a partnership	Usual or last known residence of the individual; or principal or last known place of business of the partnership.
4. Limited liability partnership	Principal office of the partnership; or any place of business of the partnership within the jurisdiction which has a real connection with the claim.
5. Corporation (other than a company) incorporated in England and Wales	Principal office of the corporation; or any place within the jurisdiction where the corporation carries on its activities and which has a real connection with the claim.

Nature of defendant to be served	Place of service
6. Company registered in England and Wales	Principal office of the company; or any place of business of the company within the jurisdiction which has a real connection with the claim.
7. Any other company or corporation	Any place within the jurisdiction where the corporation carries on its activities; or any place of business of the company within the jurisdiction.

What if a claimant has reason to believe that the address of the defendant referred to in entries 1, 2 or 3 in the above table is an address at which the defendant no longer resides or carries on business? Rule 6.9(3) provides that the claimant must take reasonable steps to ascertain the address of the defendant's current residence or place of business ('current address'). If the claimant ascertains the defendant's current address, the claim form must be served at that address; but if they are unable to do so, the claimant must consider whether there is an alternative place where or an alternative method by which service may be effected and make an application to the court accordingly.

In exceptional circumstances the court can dispense with service of the claim form under r 6.16(1). In *Lonestar Communications Corp LLC v Kaye & Ors* [2019] EWHC 3008 (Comm), there were five defendants. Three were served but attempts to serve the second defendant in Israel under the Hague Convention had not been successful. The claimant then made various attempts via social media and there was evidence that accounts to which messages had been sent had been closed. The court found that a proper attempt had been made to serve the second defendant under the Hague Convention and the defendant was aware of the proceedings and was taking active steps to evade service. It was fair, just and appropriate to make an order dispensing with service of the claim form.

5.5.4 When to serve?

By r 7.5(1), a claimant who wishes to serve a claim form in the jurisdiction must complete the step required by the following table in relation to the particular method of service chosen, before 12.00 midnight on the calendar day four months after the date of issue of the claim form.

Method of service	Step required
Personal service	Completing the relevant step required by the rules (see **5.5.1.1**)
First-class post, DX or other service which provides for delivery on the next business day	Posting, leaving with, delivering to or collection by the relevant service provider (see **5.5.1.2** and **5.5.1.4**)
Delivery of the document to or leaving it at the relevant place	Delivering to or leaving the document at the relevant place (see **5.5.1.3** and **5.5.3**)
Fax	Completing the transmission of the fax (see **5.5.1.5**)
Other electronic method	Sending the e-mail or other electronic transmission (see **5.5.1.6**).

5.5.5 When is the claim form deemed to be served?

The potential problem with any method of service, apart from personal service, is that the claimant cannot know precisely when the defendant receives the claim form. A claimant needs to know when service has occurred in order to take the next step in the proceedings. So, if the claim form was served marked 'particulars of claim to follow', the claimant must serve those next (see **5.8**). If particulars of claim have been served then the claimant must allow the defendant the requisite number of days to respond and can apply for default judgment if the defendant fails to respond (see **6.3** and **6.4**). Rule 6.14 introduces a simple, indisputable presumption that the claim form is deemed to have been served on the second business day after the step set out in **5.5.4** has occurred.

Note that by r 6.2(b) a 'business day' here means any day except Saturday, Sunday, a bank holiday, Good Friday or Christmas Day.

EXAMPLES

1. An individual defendant is personally served with a claim form on a Monday. It is deemed to be served on the Wednesday, provided Tuesday and Wednesday are business days.

2. A firm of solicitors authorised to accept service is served with the claim form by fax that is transmitted on a Saturday. Sunday will not count. Assume the Monday is a bank holiday and so does not count either. If Tuesday and Wednesday are business days, then deemed service of the claim form is on the Wednesday.

5.5.6   Service by the court or the claimant?

The claim form will usually be served by the court, and the court will choose the appropriate method of service, which will normally be by first-class post. The claimant must provide the court with enough copies for the court to serve the claim form on all other parties, together with a copy for the court's file.

Rule 6.4(1) provides that the court will not effect service where:

(a)   a rule or Practice Direction provides that the claimant must serve the claim form; or

(b)   the claimant notifies the court that they want to serve it; or

(c)   the court orders or directs otherwise.

Note that r 6.18 provides that where the court serves the claim form by post but the claim form is returned to the court, the court will send notification to the claimant that the claim form has been returned. However, the claim form will be deemed to be served unless the address for the defendant on the claim form is not the relevant address for the purpose of the Rules. This is rather an odd provision, but its purpose is to try to bring some certainty and finality to service of the claim form. So, if the address was that of a firm of solicitors authorised to accept service, the service is deemed to have occurred. However, it would obviously make sense to check that the correct address was used, and perhaps to telephone the solicitors for an explanation and agree a new method, such as fax or e-mail. Where service was to an address listed in the table at **5.5.3** the service is again deemed to have occurred. However, we take the view that the claimant should normally treat this as a situation where they have reason to believe that the address of the defendant referred to in entries 1, 2 or 3 in the table is an address at which the defendant no longer resides or carries on business. Therefore, the claimant should take reasonable steps to ascertain the current address of the defendant.

Where the claim form is served by the claimant, under r 6.17(2) they must file a certificate of service within 21 days of service of the particulars of claim (unless all the defendants have filed acknowledgements of service within that period), and may not obtain judgment in default (see **5.6**) unless they have filed the certificate of service. A copy is set out at **Appendix A(4)**.

5.5.7   Service out of the jurisdiction

5.5.7.1   Cases governed by the 2005 Hague Convention or contract

No special permission is required to serve proceedings outside of England and Wales, provided that for each claim made against the defendant to be served and included in the claim form:

(a)   the court has power to determine that claim under the 2005 Hague Convention and the defendant is a party to an exclusive choice of court agreement conferring jurisdiction on that court within the meaning of Article 3 of the 2005 Hague Convention; or

(b)   a contract contains a term to the effect that the court shall have jurisdiction to determine that claim.

As to (a), reference to the 2005 Hague Convention means the Convention on the service abroad of judicial and extrajudicial documents in civil or commercial matters signed at the Hague on 15 November 1965. It includes all European Union countries as well as Mexico, Singapore and Montenegro.

There are special provisions as to the methods of service that are acceptable where the claim form is to be served outside the jurisdiction (see rr 6.40–6.44).

5.5.7.2   All other cases

The claimant must otherwise obtain permission to serve proceedings out of the jurisdiction.

The grounds for obtaining permission are set out in PD 6B, para 3.1. Examples of the grounds set out in para 3.1 are where the claim is brought to enforce a contract that is governed by English law, or where the breach of contract occurred in England and Wales. In addition, the applicant must show that there is a serious issue to be tried in the proposed action and that England is clearly and distinctly the appropriate forum. The application must be supported by evidence and is made without notice.

If an order permitting service outside the jurisdiction is made, the time limit for responding to the claim will again be extended. Service is usually effected through the judicial authorities of the State in question or the British Consul.

5.6   EXTENDING TIME FOR SERVICE OF THE CLAIM FORM

What if a claimant is not able to serve the claim form before midnight on the calendar day four months after the date of issue (see **5.5.4**)? The court has a general discretion to extend this period. The application should always be made before the time limit expires. What if it is made after the limit has expired? The court still has a discretion to extend time retrospectively but, as you would expect, the test is much more difficult to meet, as r 7.6(3) provides that the court may extend time for service only if:

(a)   the court has been unable to serve the claim form; or

(b)   the claimant has taken all reasonable steps to serve the claim form but has been unable to do so; and

(c)   in either case, the claimant has acted promptly in making the application.

In *Vinos v Marks & Spencer plc* [2001] 3 All ER 784, the claim form was served nine days after the expiry of the four-month period. The claimant's solicitors had no explanation for this other than that it was an oversight, and their application for an extension was dismissed. The Court of Appeal upheld the decision, holding that the wording of r 7.6(3) was such that an extension could not be granted in these circumstances as neither ground (a) nor (b) applied.

This decision has been followed in other cases. For example, extensions have been refused where the claimant's solicitor was mistaken as to the date on which the claim form was issued or simply overlooked serving it (*Satwinder Kaur v CTP Coil Ltd* [2000] LTL, 10 July; *Hashtroodi v*

Hancock [2004] EWCA Civ 652, [2004] 3 All ER 530). Where the claimant's solicitors mistakenly served the defendant when they should have served the claim form on the defendant's solicitors who were nominated to accept service, an extension was also refused (*Nanglegan v Royal Free Hampstead NHS Trust* [2001] EWCA Civ 127, [2001] 3 All ER 793). In this context, it is, no doubt, right to say that negligent or incompetent advice is always a bad reason for granting an extension. That is because there is often a disciplinary factor in the decision to extend the validity of a claim form analogous to the disciplinary factor which is commonly found in decisions about relief from sanctions (*Société Générale v Goldas Kuyumculuk Sanayi Ithalat Ihracat AS* [2018] EWCA Civ 109).

Similarly, an extension was refused where the claimant did not serve in time only because it was not in a financial position to proceed immediately with the claim (*Bayat Telephone Systems International Inc v Cecil* [2011] EWCA Civ 135). As the Court stressed, the claimant should have served the claim form and then issued an application for a stay of proceedings.

Note that r 2.11 provides that 'Unless these Rules or a practice direction provide otherwise or the court orders otherwise, the time specified by a rule or by the court for a person to do any act may be varied by the written agreement of the parties.' So, the parties' solicitors can enter into a written agreement to extend the time for service of the claim form. The dangers of this for a claimant were highlighted In *Thomas v Home Office* [2006] EWCA Civ 1355, where the Court of Appeal held that a written agreement to extend the time for service of the claim form does not have to be in a single document but may consist of an exchange of letters or e-mails. An oral agreement that is then confirmed in writing by both sides is also a written agreement. However, an oral agreement between two solicitors that is subsequently recorded in a letter sent by one solicitor to the other, but not answered by the other, does not constitute a written agreement. Further, it is not enough for solicitors each to make an attendance note of an oral agreement, unless those notes are subsequently exchanged.

5.7   SERVICE OF DOCUMENTS OTHER THAN THE CLAIM FORM

5.7.1   How, who and where?

Rules 6.20 to 6.29 contain provisions relating to the service of all other court documents, such as statements of case. These are basically the same as for claim forms in respect of how to serve (see **5.5.1**), who to serve (see **5.5.2**) and where to serve (see **5.5.3**).

5.7.2   Deemed service of other documents

Rather surprisingly, a complex set of rules exist, which produce different deemed dates of service for other documents according to the method used. These are set out in r 6.26 and shown in the table below.

Method of service	Deemed date of service
Personal service	If the document is served personally before 4.30pm on a business day, on that day; or in any other case, on the next business day after that day.
First-class post (or other service which provides for delivery on the next business day)	The second day after it was posted, left with, delivered to or collected by the relevant service provider provided that day is a business day; or if not, the next business day after that day.
Delivering the document to or leaving it at a permitted address	If it is delivered to or left at the permitted address on a business day before 4.30pm, on that day; or in any other case, on the next business day after that day.

Method of service	Deemed date of service
Document exchange	The second day after it was left with, delivered to or collected by the relevant service provider provided that day is a business day; or if not, the next business day after that day.
Fax	If the transmission of the fax is completed on a business day before 4.30pm, on that day; or in any other case, on the next business day after the day on which it was transmitted.
Other electronic method	If the e-mail or other electronic transmission is sent on a business day before 4.30pm, on that day; or in any other case, on the next business day after the day on which it was sent.

Note that by r 6.2(b) a 'business day' here means any day except Saturday, Sunday, a bank holiday, Good Friday or Christmas Day.

EXAMPLES

1. A document is personally served at 3.30pm on a Monday. Provided that is a business day, service is deemed to occur that day as it has taken place before 4.30pm. If it was not a business day or had it been personally served after 4.30pm, deemed service would be on the next business day.

2. A document is posted first class on a Tuesday. The day of deemed service is the Thursday, the second day after it was posted, provided that is a business day. If the second day after posting first class (or its equivalent) is not a business day, the day of deemed service is the next business day.

3. A document is delivered to a permitted address at 5pm on a Thursday. Even though that is a business day, because it is after 4.30pm that is not the day of deemed service. Assume that the next day is Good Friday and so that does not count. Saturday and Sunday will not count. The following Bank Holiday Monday will not count. So, the day of deemed service is the next business day, namely Tuesday.

4. A document is left in a numbered box at the Document Exchange (DX) on a Friday. The day of deemed service is the second day after it is left, provided that is a business day. The second day will be Sunday. As that is not a business day, it does not count. The day of deemed service is the next day, Monday, provided that is a business day.

5. A document is sent by fax on a Saturday and the transmission of that fax is completed by 11.25am. Although that occurs before 4.30pm, it is not done on a business day and so does not count as the day of deemed service. Sunday also does not count. So, the day of deemed service is Monday, provided that is a business day.

5.8 SERVICE OF PARTICULARS OF CLAIM

What if a claim form is served marked 'particulars of claim to follow'. When must the particulars of claim be served? Practice Direction 7A, para 6.1 provides the following answer:

> Where the claimant does not include the particulars of claim in the claim form, they may be served separately:
>
> (1)   either at the same time as the claim form, or
>
> (2)   within 14 days after service of the claim form provided that the service of the particulars of claim is within 4 months after the date of issue of the claim form [see **5.5.4**].

EXAMPLE

A claim form marked 'particulars of claim to follow' is issued on 5 March 2021. The claim form must be served by 12 midnight on 5 July 2021.

If the claim form is served on, say, 9 April 2021, the claimant must serve the particulars of claim within 14 days, ie by 23 April 2021. However, if it is served later on, say, 25 June 2021, the claimant does not have 14 days after that to serve the particulars of claim, as that must be done by 5 July 2021.

CHAPTER 6

RESPONDING TO PROCEEDINGS AND JUDGMENT IN DEFAULT

6.1	Introduction	87
6.2	Computation of time	88
6.3	Acknowledgement of service (Part 10)	88
6.4	The defence (Part 15)	90
6.5	Admissions (Part 14)	91
6.6	Default judgments (Part 12)	93

LEARNING OUTCOMES

After reading this chapter you will have learned:

- how the time to take a particular step in litigation is calculated
- the different ways in which a defendant may respond to the service of proceedings
- what steps a claimant should take if the defendant admits the claim
- how to enter or apply for default judgment.

6.1 INTRODUCTION

What is the first step that a defendant should take in court proceedings? It is when served with the particulars of claim that a defendant must respond, otherwise the claimant will be able to 'win by default'. So where the defendant is served with a claim form marked 'particulars of claim to follow', there is nothing for the defendant to do but await service of the particulars of claim. The defendant will in these circumstances receive Form N1C (Notes for Defendants) explaining this. See the copy at **Appendix A(2)**.

When either the court or the claimant serves the particulars of claim on the defendant, the defendant must also be sent Form N9 (the response pack). A copy of this form appears at **Appendix A(3)**. The response pack explains to the defendant how they should respond to the claim and the time limits for doing so. There are three ways in which a defendant may respond, namely:

(a) by filing an acknowledgement of service;

(b) by filing a defence;

(c) by filing an admission.

See further the flowcharts in **Appendix C(6)–(10)**.

Before considering these steps in turn, it is important to be clear about the rules relating to the calculation of the time for doing any act, such as filing an acknowledgement of service and/or a defence. As we shall see at **6.6**, if the defendant does not respond within the appropriate time period, the claimant may enter judgment 'in default' of the defendant filing an acknowledgement of service and/or a defence. It is therefore essential that a party and their legal adviser are clear about the meaning of the various time periods prescribed in the rules.

6.2 COMPUTATION OF TIME

Rule 2.8 sets out how to calculate any period of time for doing an act which is specified in the Rules, a Practice Direction, or by a judgment or order of the court.

If the time for doing an act ends on a day when the court office is closed, the time does not actually expire until the end of the first day on which the court office is next open.

Any order imposing a time limit should, wherever practicable, give a calendar date, ie the day, month, year and deadline time for compliance, for example 'by [day], [date] [month] [year], by 4pm'.

Any period of time expressed as a number of days will be a period of 'clear days', as defined by r 2.8.

> **EXAMPLES**
> 1. On 5 October, the defendant is served with the particulars of claim.
>
>   The defendant has 14 days (not including the day of service of the particulars of claim) within which either to acknowledge service or file a defence.
>
>   The deadline for doing so is therefore 19 October.
> 2. An application to the court has been fixed for hearing on a Monday.
>
>   Generally, the notice of the application must be served on the other party at least three days prior to the hearing.
>
>   The notice must be served on the preceding Tuesday (ie, where notice of a hearing is being given, both the day on which notice is served and the day of the hearing are excluded in calculating the clear days.) However, it should be noted that in computing a period of five days or less, any weekend or bank holiday must be ignored.
> 3. Month means a calendar month.
>
>   So if a claim form for service within the jurisdiction is issued on 5 May, it must be served no later than four months later, namely by 5 September.

6.3 ACKNOWLEDGEMENT OF SERVICE (PART 10)

6.3.1 Time limits

When served with the particulars of claim, the defendant usually has a choice of what to do: they may either simply acknowledge service, or they may file a defence. The defendant may acknowledge service if they are unable to file a defence in time, or if they wish to contest the court's jurisdiction.

If the defendant fails to respond within a set time, the claimant can usually enter judgment. This is because r 10.2 provides that:

> If—
> (a) a defendant fails to file an acknowledgment of service within the period specified in rule 10.3; and
> (b) does not within that period file a defence in accordance with Part 15 [see **6.4**] or serve or file an admission in accordance with Part 14 [see **6.5**],
> the claimant may obtain default judgment if Part 12 allows it [see **6.6**].

The words 'within that period' in (b) indicate that judgment in default of both an acknowledgement of service and a defence is calculated by reference to the following time period prescribed by r 10.3:

> (1) The general rule is that the period for filing an acknowledgment of service is—

(a)   14 days after service of the particulars of claim where the defendant is served with a claim form which states that particulars of claim are to follow; and

(b)   in any other case, 14 days after service of the claim form.

We take the view that r 10.3(1)(a) applies to any situation where particulars of claim are served after the claim form has already been served. So, if a claim form states that particulars of claim are to follow but the particulars of claim are actually served with the claim form (for example, both documents are handed to the defendant at the same time or posted in the same envelope), r 10.3(1)(b) applies and the defendant has 14 days from the day of deemed service of the claim form to file an acknowledgement, defence or admission.

These rules may be summarised as follows:

	When default judgment can be entered
Claim form served with particulars of claim	15th day after (deemed) service of the claim form
Particulars of claim served after claim form served	15th day after (deemed) service of the particulars of claim

It can be seen from the above table why the defendant must be careful to calculate correctly the 14 days they have to respond; and equally why a claimant must accurately work out the first available date they can enter default judgment if the defendant fails to respond. This is because the date of deemed service of the claim form (see **5.5.5**) may be different from the date of deemed service of particulars of claim (see **5.7.2**).

6.3.2   Completing the acknowledgement form

The acknowledgement of service form is part of the response pack (Form N9). On the form, the defendant should set out their name in full; and if their name has been incorrectly set out in the claim form, it should be correctly set out on the acknowledgement of service form, followed by the words 'described as' and the incorrect name (eg, 'John Patrick Schiller described as Pat Schiller'). The defendant's address for service, including full postcode, which must be within England or Wales, must be stated. This will either be the defendant's residence or business address, or, if the acknowledgement of service form is signed by their solicitor, their solicitor's address. The defendant must state on the form whether they intend to defend all of the claim, part of the claim, or wish to contest jurisdiction. The form must be signed by the defendant or their solicitor. The defendant must file the completed acknowledgement of service form at the court where the claim was issued. The court will then notify the claimant in writing.

6.3.3   Defendant is a partnership

CPR, r 10.5(5) provides that where a claim is brought against a partnership, service must be acknowledged in the name of the partnership on behalf of all persons who were partners at the time when the cause of action accrued. The acknowledgement of service may be signed by any of those partners, or by any person authorised by any of those partners to sign it.

6.3.4   Defendant is a registered company

What if the defendant is a registered company? Pursuant to r 10.5(3) and (4), a person holding a senior position in the company, such as a director, the treasurer, secretary or chief executive, may sign the acknowledgement of service, provided they state the position that they hold.

6.3.5   Defendant disputes jurisdiction

By r 11, if a defendant wishes to dispute the jurisdiction of the court, they must indicate this on the acknowledgement of service. After filing the acknowledgement of service, they must then challenge the jurisdiction by making an application within 14 days or they will be treated as having submitted to the jurisdiction. The application to the court to dispute the court's jurisdiction must be supported by evidence as to why England and Wales is not the proper forum for the case. If the court grants the defendant's application and finds that the claim should not have been brought in England and Wales, service of the claim form will usually be set aside. In effect, that brings the proceedings to an end.

If the court refuses the defendant's application then the original acknowledgement of service ceases to have effect and the defendant must file a further acknowledgement within 14 days or such other period as the court may direct.

6.4 THE DEFENCE (PART 15)

6.4.1 Time limits

As we have seen, a defendant can respond to proceedings first by acknowledging service (see **6.3**) and then filing a defence, or by just filing their defence. What is the time limit, given the choice? That is laid down by r 15.4, as follows:

(1)   The general rule is that the period for filing a defence is—

(a)   14 days after service of the particulars of claim; or

(b)   if the defendant files an acknowledgment of service under Part 10, 28 days after service of the particulars of claim.

Arguably (a) above is inconsistent with the situation addressed at **6.3.1** where the claimant serves the claim form with particulars of claim. In those circumstances, r 10.3 suggests the defendant has 14 days after (deemed) service of the claim form to respond. We take the view that r 15.4 sets out the general position but r 10.3 applies in respect of default judgment. The point is not academic since the calculation of the day of deemed service of a claim form or particulars of claim (see **5.5.5.** and **5.7.2** respectively) will not always be the same.

However, (b) above is clear, and if the defendant files an acknowledgement of service then they have 28 days after (deemed) service of the particulars of claim within which to file a defence.

> **EXAMPLE**
>
> Assume a claim form with particulars of claim is deemed to have been served on Wednesday, 1 June (as to deemed service, see **5.7.2**). By what date must the defendant acknowledge service and indicate an intention to defend or file a defence? The defendant must do so within 14 days of service, not including the day of deemed service. So, they must act by Wednesday, 15 June (otherwise the claimant can enter default judgment on Thursday, 16 June: see **6.6**). If they choose to file an acknowledgement in time, they then have until Wednesday, 29 June to file their defence.

6.4.2 Extending the time limit

The time for filing a defence may be extended by agreement between the parties for a period of up to 28 days. If the parties do reach such an agreement, the defendant must give the court written notice of the agreement (see r 15.5).

Any further extension can only be authorised by the court. The court will usually grant an extension, but if the claimant has complied with the Practice Direction on Pre-action Conduct and Protocols or an approved pre-action protocol, such extension will probably be for a short period of time and will be granted at the defendant's expense. If, however, the claimant did not so comply, the court is likely to conclude that the defendant should be granted a significant extension of time. If the claimant has unreasonably refused to grant a voluntary extension of time and/or has opposed the defendant's application to the court unreasonably, the court may well order the claimant to pay the defendant's costs of seeking the extension.

The court will expect the party applying for an extension to have good reasons justifying the extension. In the case of *Jalla and another v Shell International Trading and Shipping Co Ltd and another* [2021] EWCA Civ 1559, the Court of Appeal upheld the lower court's decision to refuse the claimants a further extension of time for serving 'date of damage' pleadings and supporting evidence for limitation purposes. Although this was an 'in-time' application to extend time and did not involve an unless order, the court held that the *Denton* relief from sanctions principles applied by analogy. (See **9.3.1**.)

6.4.3 Drafting

There are forms the defendant can use that will have been served as part of the response pack. In the case of a claim for a specified amount, the appropriate form is Form N9B; and in the case of a claim for an unspecified amount or a non-money claim, the appropriate form is Form N9C. In practice, these forms will usually be used by defendants who are acting in person. Where solicitors are acting for a defendant, the defence is usually prepared as a separate document (see **Chapter 7**).

6.4.4 Filing and serving

When the defence is filed, a copy must be served on all other parties. The court will effect service, unless the defendant's solicitor has told the court that they will do so.

6.5 ADMISSIONS (PART 14)

If a defendant wishes to admit either the whole or part of the claim, they should complete the appropriate sections of the response pack. The way in which the defendant should complete the forms and the consequences of doing so vary depending on the nature of the claim and whether the admission is in full or only in part. See the flowcharts in **Appendix C(7) and C(8)**.

6.5.1 Admission in full of a claim for a specified amount

If a defendant admits the whole of a claim for a specified amount, they should serve the appropriate form of admission (Form N9A) on the claimant. This should be done within 14 days of service of the particulars of claim. On Form N9A, the defendant has to give certain personal details, together with details of their income and expenditure, and they should also make an offer of payment, which can be an offer to pay either in full by a certain date, or by monthly instalments.

Upon receipt of the form, the claimant may then file a request for judgment. If the claimant accepts the defendant's offer to pay either by a certain date or by monthly instalments, the claimant simply accepts the defendant's offer and files a request for judgment. See the flowchart in **Appendix C(7)**.

If the claimant rejects the defendant's offer to pay by a certain date or to pay by instalments then the court will decide the appropriate order. If the claim is for not more than £50,000, a court officer may decide the rate of payment without any court hearing; alternatively, the rate of payment will be decided by a judge. Where the rate of payment is to be decided by a judge, the proceedings must be automatically transferred to the 'defendant's home court', if the defendant is an individual. So where is the 'defendant's home court'? In the County Court, it is the County Court in which the defendant resides or carries on business. For a High Court claim, it is the District Registry for the district in which the defendant resides or carries on business, or, where there is no such District Registry, the Royal Courts of Justice. Note that, for claims issued in the County Court Money Claims Centre (CCMCC) (see **5.1.3**), if the defendant is not an individual the case will be transferred to the claimant's preferred hearing centre under r 14.7A.

The judge may make the decision without any hearing, but if there is to be a hearing, the parties must be given at least seven days' notice. In deciding the time and rate of payment, the court will take into account:

(a)   the defendant's statement of means;

(b)   the claimant's objections to the defendant's request; and

(c)   any other relevant factors.

6.5.2   Part admission of a claim for a specified amount

If a defendant admits only part of a claim for a specified amount, they must do so by filing Form N9A at the court within 14 days of service of the particulars of claim. The court will then give notice of the admission to the claimant, who must say whether they:

(a)   accept the offer in full satisfaction of their claim; or

(b)   accept the offer but not the defendant's proposals for payment; or

(c)   reject the offer and wish to proceed with their claim.

The claimant has 14 days in which to file their notice and serve it on the defendant. If they do not do so, the claim will be stayed until they do file their notice.

If the claimant accepts the offer, they will request judgment.

If the defendant has not requested time to pay, the claimant's request can stipulate the time for payment and the court will enter judgment accordingly.

If the defendant has requested time to pay, the procedure in **6.5.1** applies.

If the claimant rejects the offer, the case continues as a defended action.

See the flowchart in **Appendix C(8)**.

6.5.3   Admission of a claim for an unspecified amount (no offer made)

Where the defendant admits liability for a claim for an unspecified amount and makes no offer of payment, they must do so within the usual time for making an admission. The court will serve a copy of the admission on the claimant, who may then apply for judgment.

The court will then enter judgment for the damages to be assessed. The hearing at which the damages are assessed is often called a 'disposal hearing'. Where needed, the court will give directions to the parties as to the steps to be taken to prepare for the disposal hearing and may also allocate the case to a track if that is appropriate (see **Chapter 9**).

See the flowchart in **Appendix C(7)**.

6.5.4   Admission of a claim for an unspecified amount (offer made)

Where the defendant admits liability for a claim for an unspecified amount and offers a sum of money in satisfaction of the claim, they must do so in the usual time for making an admission.

The court will serve a notice on the claimant requiring them to return the notice stating whether or not they accept the amount in satisfaction of the claim. If the claimant does not file the notice within 14 days, their claim will be stayed until they do file the notice.

If the claimant does not accept the amount offered, they will enter judgment for damages to be assessed at a disposal hearing.

If the claimant accepts the offer and the defendant has not asked for time to pay, the claimant may enter judgment for the amount offered and will stipulate when payment should be made.

If the defendant has asked for time to pay the usual procedure applies (see **6.5.1**).

6.5.5   Challenging the court's decision

Where the court has decided the time and rate of payment, and the decision was made either:

(a)   by a court officer; or

(b)   by a judge without any hearing,

either party may apply for a re-determination by a judge. Such application must be made within 14 days of service of the determination on the applicant.

If the original decision was made by a court officer, the re-determination will be made by a judge without a hearing unless the application notice requests a hearing.

If the original decision was made by a judge, the re-determination must be at a hearing unless the parties agree otherwise.

6.5.6   Interest

Judgment where the defendant admits liability for the whole amount of a claim for a specified amount will include interest up to the date of judgment if:

(a)   the particulars of claim include the details required by r 16.4 (see **7.2.1**); and

(b)   where interest is claimed under s 35A of the SCA 1981 or s 69 of the CCA 1984 (see **2.7.2.1**), the rate is no higher than the rate of interest payable on judgment debts (currently 8% pa) at the date when the claim form was issued; and

(c)   the claimant's request for judgment includes a calculation of the interest claimed for the period from the date up to which interest was stated to be calculated in the claim form to the date of the request for judgment.

If the above conditions are not satisfied, the judgment will be for an amount of interest to be decided by the court, and the court will give directions as to how this should be achieved. For example, condition (b) will not be met if the claim was for a commercial debt and interest was claimed under the Late Payment of Commercial Debts (Interest) Act 1998 (see **2.7.2.1**).

6.5.7   Varying the rate of payment

By para 6.1 of PD 14, either party may apply to vary the time and rates of payment of a judgment on admissions if there has been a change of circumstances.

6.6   DEFAULT JUDGMENTS (PART 12)

6.6.1   Introduction

Once the proceedings have been served upon the defendant, it may be that the defendant takes no action. The defendant may fail to return the acknowledgement of service or file a defence. In those circumstances, the claimant can obtain judgment in default against the defendant. This means that the claimant obtains judgment without there being a trial of the issues involved in the case. See the flowchart in **Appendix C(10)**.

6.6.1.1   Cases where default judgment is not available

The claimant may not enter a default judgment in the following types of cases:

(a)   a claim for delivery of goods under an agreement regulated by the Consumer Credit Act 1974;

(b)   a Part 8 claim (see **Chapter 8**);

(c)   a mortgage claim;

(d)   a claim for provisional damages;

(e)   a claim in a specialist court.

6.6.2   Procedure

The claimant applies for default judgment by filing a request using the relevant form if they are claiming money (whether or not it is a claim for a specified amount) or goods (if the claim form gives the defendant the option of returning the goods). There are different forms, depending on whether the claim is for a specified or an unspecified amount. (See Forms N205A, N205B, N225 and N227.)

The claimant must satisfy the court that:

(a)   the particulars of claim have been served on the defendant;

(b)   the defendant has not acknowledged service or filed a defence (or any document intended to be a defence), at the date on which judgment is entered, and the relevant time period has expired;

(c)   the defendant has not satisfied the claim;

(d)   the defendant has not admitted liability for the full amount of the claim.

So, the filing of an acknowledgment of service or a defence, even late, will prevent the entry of judgment in default.

Where the amount of money is to be decided by the County Court, the proceedings will be sent to the claimant's preferred hearing centre.

6.6.3   Claims for specified amounts

A request for default judgment for a specified amount may indicate the date for full payment, or the times and rate at which it is to be paid by instalments. If it does not, the court will normally give judgment for immediate payment. Additional fixed costs are payable by the defendant (see CPR 1998, Part 45).

6.6.4   Claims for unspecified amounts

A request for default judgment for a claim for an unspecified amount is a request for the court to decide the amount of the claim and costs. This will involve a full hearing before a trial judge to decide the amount of the claim (again often called a disposal hearing), and it may, therefore, be necessary to allocate the claim to a track and give directions (see **Chapter 9**).

6.6.5   Interest

The default judgment may, in the case of a claim for a specified amount, include interest up to the date of judgment if:

(a)   the particulars of claim include the details required by r 16.4 (see **7.2.1.5**); and

(b)   where interest is claimed under s 35A of the SCA 1981 or s 69 of the CCA 1984 (see **2.7.2.1**), the rate is no higher than the rate of interest payable on judgment debts (currently 8% pa) at the date when the claim form was issued; and

(c)   the claimant's request for judgment includes a calculation of the interest claimed for the period from the date up to which interest was stated to be calculated in the claim form to the date of the request for judgment.

Otherwise the court will decide the amount of interest and will give directions for this.

EXAMPLE: SPECIFIED CLAIM

Assume County Court debt proceedings were issued on 1 June. Interest is claimed under s 69 of the CCA 1984 at 8% pa from when the debt was due to and including the day of issue. The daily rate of interest is £5.35. If default judgment is entered on 22 June, how much additional interest should be claimed? 21 days have passed since issue, so a further £112.35 (21 x £5.35) should now be claimed when entering default judgment.

6.6.6   Co-defendants

Where there are co-defendants, the claimant may enter a default judgment against one or more of the co-defendants while proceeding with their claim against the other defendants, provided the claim can be dealt with separately. Otherwise, the court will not deal with the default judgment until it deals with the claim against the other defendants.

6.6.7 Setting aside a default judgment

A defendant against whom a default judgment has been entered may apply to have it set aside. Such applications are considered in **Chapter 10.**

6.6.8 Effect of stay on time limits

Does the time for serving a statement of case still run if the court has imposed a stay? No, held the Court of Appeal in *Grant v Dawn Meats (UK)* [2018] EWCA Civ 2212:

> a stay operates to 'halt' or 'freeze' the proceedings. In general terms, no steps in the action, by either side, are required or permitted during the period of the stay. When the stay is lifted, or the stay expires, the position as between the parties should be the same as it was at the moment that the stay was imposed. The parties (and the court) pick up where they left off at the time of the imposition of the stay. (per Coulson LJ at [18])

6.6.9 Summary

A defendant might respond to a specified claim in any of the following ways:

(a)   admit the full amount and pay it. Alternatively, they can ask for time to pay, which, if rejected by the claimant, will be determined by the court; or

(b)   admit part of the claim and offer to pay it. Alternatively, they can ask for time to pay. If the claimant accepts the part admitted in full and final settlement but rejects the proposal as to payment, the court will determine the time for payment. However, if the claimant does not accept the part admitted in full and final settlement, the case will continue as a defended claim.

A defendant might respond to a claim for an unspecified amount of money in any of the following ways:

(a)   admit liability but make no offer of payment. The court will enter judgment for damages to be assessed at a disposal hearing; or

(b)   admit liability and make an offer to pay a sum of money. Additionally, they may ask for time to pay that amount. If the claimant accepts the offer but rejects any proposal as to payment, the court will determine the time for payment. However, if the claimant does not accept the offer, they will enter judgment for damages to be assessed at a disposal hearing.

Where a claimant enters default judgment on a specified claim, the judgment will be for a final sum of money as calculated by the claimant and they can immediately proceed to enforcement.

Where a claimant enters default judgment on a claim for an unspecified amount of money, the judgment will be for damages to be assessed by the court at a disposal hearing.

See further the flow diagrams in **Appendix C(6)–(10).**

CHAPTER 7

STATEMENTS OF CASE

7.1	Introduction	97
7.2	Contents of the particulars of claim	102
7.3	The defence	112
7.4	Reply to defence	115
7.5	The role of statements of case	115
7.6	Amendments to statements of case (Part 17)	117
7.7	Requests for further information (Part 18)	119
7.8	Summary: how should you approach drafting particulars of claim?	121
7.9	Summary: how should you approach drafting a defence?	122

LEARNING OUTCOMES

After reading this chapter you will have learned:

- the general principles of good drafting of statements of case
- what must be included in different particulars of claim
- how to draft a breach of contract claim
- what must be included in a defence
- the role of the reply to defence and defence to counterclaim
- how statements of case define the issues in dispute
- when and how to amend a statement of case
- when and how to make a request for further information.

7.1 INTRODUCTION

Statements of case are the formal documents in which the parties concisely and precisely set out their respective cases. Pre-CPR 1998, these documents were known as 'pleadings' and parties would 'plead' their case in them. Now we refer to 'statements of case' and parties 'stating' their case, but you will often still find reference to the old terminology in court judgments and textbooks.

Statements of case are served between the parties (as well as being filed at court) so that each party knows the case they will have to meet at the trial. They must therefore be drafted carefully and reviewed continually as the case develops as the trial court will not usually allow a party to pursue an issue which, on a fair reading of the statement of case, is not stated: see *Royal Brompton Hospital NHS Trust v Hammond & Others* [2000] LTL, 4 December. Nor will the trial court grant a party any relief not claimed in its statement of case (unless that is clearly addressed in subsequent documentation) (see *Whalley v PF Developments Ltd* [2013] LTL, 14 February).

In the case of *UK Learning Academy Ltd v Secretary of State for Education* [2020] EWCA Civ 370, Richards LJ said at [47]:

> Statements of case ought, at the very least, to identify the issues to be determined. In that way, the parties know the issues to which they should direct their evidence and their challenges to the evidence of the other party or parties and the issues to which they should direct their submissions on the law

and the evidence. Equally importantly, it enables the judge to keep the trial within manageable bounds, so that public resources as well as the parties' own resources are not wasted, and so that the judge knows the issues on which the proceedings, and the judgment, must concentrate. If, as [the trial judge] said, there was 'a prevailing view that parties should not be held to their pleaded cases', it is wrong. That is not to say that technical points may be used to prevent the just disposal of a case or that a trial judge may not permit a departure from a pleaded case where it is just to do so (although in such a case it is good practice to amend the pleading, even at trial), but the statements of case play a critical role in civil litigation which should not be diminished.

Where the parties' evidence and submissions at trial are based on their statements of case, the trial judge must not determine the issues on a totally different basis (*Satyam Enterprises Ltd v Burton* [2021] EWCA Civ 287).

By r 2.3 a 'statement of case':

(a)   means a claim form, particulars of claim where these are not included in a claim form, defence, Part 20 claim [see **Chapter 8**] or reply to defence; and

(b)   includes any further information given in relation to them voluntarily or by court order under r 18.1 [see 7.7].

We considered how to draft a claim form at **5.3.1**. In this chapter, at **7.2**, we shall examine in detail the contents of particulars of claim.

The defendant's statement of case is called a defence. Frequently, the only statements of case in a claim will be the claim form, separate particulars of claim and the defence. Sometimes, however, a claimant may wish to serve a reply to the defence, and in other cases a defendant may wish to make their own claim against the claimant by way of a counterclaim (see **Chapter 8**).

The rules relating to statements of case are contained in Part 16 of the CPR 1998 and the accompanying Practice Directions. Part 16 does not apply if the claimant has used the Part 8 procedure (see **Chapter 8**).

7.1.1   Setting parameters

In the case of *McPhilemy v Times Newspapers Limited* [1999] 3 All ER 775, Lord Woolf MR said:

[Statements of case] mark out the parameters of the case that is being advanced by each party [and] identify the issues and the extent of the dispute between the parties ... The need for extensive [statements of case] including particulars should be reduced by the requirement that witness statements are now exchanged. In the majority of proceedings identification of the documents upon which a party relies, together with copies of that party's witness statements, will make the detail of the nature of the case the other side has to meet obvious.

7.1.2   Where they fit into the five stages

When thinking about the five stages of litigation (see **1.3**), it can be seen that statements of case are dealt with at Stage 2. The detailed evidence is dealt with subsequently at Stage 3. So a statement of case should be thought of as putting together only the bare bones of the case. The 'flesh' will be put on by way of detailed evidence later.

In *Tchenguiz v Grant Thornton UK LLP* [2015] EWHC 405 (Comm), Leggatt J said at [1]:

Statements of case must be concise. They must plead only material facts, meaning those necessary for the purpose of formulating a cause of action or defence, and not background facts or evidence. Still less should they contain arguments, reasons or rhetoric. These basic rules were developed long ago and have stood the test of time because they serve the vital purpose of identifying the matters which each party will need to prove by evidence at trial.

For example, the particulars of claim in respect of a breach of contract claim should deal with the essential material facts that will establish the cause of action, namely:

(a) the status of the parties (eg, defendant's business when relying on sale during course of that business to establish terms implied by the Sale of Goods Act 1979 or the Supply of Goods and Services Act 1982);

(b) chronological story (eg, knowledge of certain facts that establish the damages claimed are not too remote, request for a sample; relevant pre-contract statements, etc);

(c) contract, ie date, type (written or oral), parties, subject matter, consideration;

(d) express terms relied on;

(e) implied terms relied on;

(f) chronological story (eg, delivery of goods, supply of services, payment of consideration, etc);

(g) breach alleged and particularised;

(h) factual consequences of breach;

(i) chronological story (eg, rejection, acceptance of repudiation, etc);

(j) damage and loss alleged and particularised;

(k) interest (contract; Late Payment of Commercial Debts (Interest) Act 1998; SCA 1981, s 35A, or CCA 1984, s 69 – see **2.7.2**).

It is important to bear in mind that the witness statements served later in the proceedings by the claimant and on which they intend to rely at trial will flesh out the detail as to the formation of the contract, etc. Any technical matters will, of course, be dealt with by expert evidence (see **12.13**).

The contents of statements of case are not, therefore, evidence in a trial (*Arena Property Services Ltd v Europa 2000 Ltd* [2003] EWCA Civ 1943 and *Kimathi v The Foreign and Commonwealth Office* [2018] EWHC 2066 (QB)). This is because statements of case are not supposed to contain evidence. Moreover, the general rule is that any fact which needs to be proved by the evidence of witnesses is to be proved at trial by their oral evidence given in public (see CPR 1998, r 32.2(1) at **12.12.1**).

That statements of case need to be concise is spelt out in PD 16, para 1.4, which provides that, if exceptionally a statement of case exceeds 25 pages (excluding schedules), an appropriate short summary must also be filed and served:

> While the Practice Direction does not say never, it is plainly intended to discourage parties from filing longer statements of case. One might think that the 25-page rule would be most often flouted in complex multi-million-pound commercial litigation. However, the Commercial Court Guide draws attention to the usual limit and requires parties to seek permission before filing a statement of case in excess of 25 pages in length. A good draftsman can, in my experience both judicially and as a commercial barrister, plead even a very complex and high-value claim in no more than 25 pages. (per Pepperall QC in *Brown v AB* [2018] EWHC 623 (QB) at [112])

[Note that the Commercial Court Guide now provides that whilst a statement of case should generally not exceed 25 pages, permission for a longer document is required only if it exceeds 40 pages.]

> There is one additional deficiency in the Particulars of Claim which requires mention because it contributed to making an over-long pleading even longer. Section C was entitled 'Background'. It included pages of background information of which the great majority was irrelevant and should not have appeared in a pleading. It may be of anecdotal interest to know that Sir Christopher Wren's specification for St Paul's Cathedral included the use of Portland stone, but it could not be relevant to a claim by a customer alleging fraudulent misrepresentation or breach of contract against its banker and a financial adviser in the 21st Century. (per Stuart-Smith J in *Portland Stone Firms Ltd v Barclays Bank Plc* [2018] EWHC 2341 (QB) at [138])

7.1.3 Referring to law, witnesses and attaching documents

In relation to either the particulars of claim or the defence, by para 13.3 of PD 16, a party may:

(1)   refer in his statement of case to any point of law on which his claim or defence, as the case may be, is based,

(2)   give in his statement of case the name of any witness he proposes to call, and

(3)   attach to or serve with this statement of case a copy of any document which he considers is necessary to his claim or defence, as the case may be (including any expert's report to be filed in accordance with Part 35).

As a general rule there is no need to state any law. Exceptionally the relevant law should be stated if the parties and the court would otherwise 'be left to speculate upon the relevance in law of a purely factual narrative' (per Buxton LJ in *Loveridge v Healey* [2004] EWCA Civ 173, (2004) *The Times*, 27 February). It will normally be a defendant, however, who will wish to raise a point of law, eg that the claim discloses no cause of action, such as a promise unsupported by consideration, or a defence under the LA 1980: see **7.3**.

The material facts should establish the relevant legal basis for a claim or defence. It is therefore normally unnecessary to state the statutory basis or legal principles on which the claim or defence is based. For example, where a seller sells goods in the course of a business and the buyer is also a business, there is an implied term that the goods supplied under the contract will be of satisfactory quality. This is implied by s 14(2) of the Sale of Goods Act 1979. So, where a claim is based on breach of that implied term, the claimant only needs to establish its factual basis; there is no need to cite the Act and the section number. See further **7.2.1.7** and **7.2.4**.

Whilst excessive factual details should not be given in a statement of case, a party can state 'the name of any witness he proposes to call'. So, a party can choose to indicate if they have any particular witness in mind who will prove a particular fact. There is little advantage in this unless, perhaps, the details have already been given to the other party pre-action, or it helps to particularise the party's case; for example, in an industrial accident claim, part of the defendant's case may be that the machinery in question was regularly checked, and so they should state by whom and when.

A party can attach to a statement of case any document they consider 'necessary' to their claim or defence. This provision ensures that the court has the fullest possible knowledge of relevant facts from the outset. So, if a party has voluntarily disclosed a document pre-action, or has received a document from the other side that assists their case, and it is admissible, then it may be appropriate to attach a copy. But this should only be done where the document is obviously of critical importance and necessary for a proper understanding of the statement of case.

Should an expert's report be attached? Only if the court has already given permission for the party to rely on that expert (which will be most unlikely at this stage) (see *Tejani v Fitzroy Place Residential Ltd* [2020] EWHC 1856 (TCC)). It therefore seems sensible to follow para C1.4(d) of the *Commercial Court Guide*, which states: 'An expert's report should not be attached to the statement of case and should not be filed with the statement of case'. This does not mean that material facts from an expert's report should not be included in a statement of case. Indeed, in many cases, issues of causation and breach can only be addressed by a suitable expert. But, just as the report should not be attached, equally the name of the expert and date of the report should not be included. Have a look at the claim illustrated at **7.2.1.7**, where the source of the material facts stated in paragraphs 6 (the particulars of breach) and 7 (the factual consequences of the breach) most likely derive from an expert's report.

7.1.4   Formalities

By PD 5A, para 2.2, every document prepared by a party for filing or use at the court must:

(1)   unless the nature of the document renders it impracticable, be on A4 paper of durable quality having a margin not less than 3.5cm wide;

(2)   be fully legible and should normally be typed;

(3)   where possible, be bound securely in a manner which would not hamper filing, or otherwise each page should be endorsed with the case number;

(4)   have the pages numbered consecutively;

(5)   be divided into numbered paragraphs;

(6)   have all numbers, including dates, expressed as figures; and

(7)   give in the margin the reference of every document mentioned that has already been filed.

Note that the requirement to express dates in figures and not words under (6) above refers to the day of the month and year only. For example, the correct way to express a date is 17 May 2021 and not 17/05/21.

The following principles (see the *Queen's Bench Guide*, para 6.7.4) should be followed:

(1)   a statement of case must be as brief and concise as possible and confined to setting out the bald facts and not the evidence of them,

(2)   a statement of case should be set out in separate consecutively numbered paragraphs and sub-paragraphs,

(3)   so far as possible each paragraph or sub-paragraph should contain no more than one allegation,

(4)   the facts and other matters alleged should be set out as far as reasonably possible in chronological order,

(5)   the statement of case should deal with the claim on a point-by-point basis, to allow a point-by-point response,

(6)   where a party is required to give reasons, the allegation should be stated first and then the reasons listed one by one in separate numbered sub-paragraphs,

(7)   a party wishing to advance a positive claim must identify that claim in the statement of case,

(8)   any matter which if not stated might take another party by surprise should be stated,

(9)   where they will assist, headings, abbreviations and definitions should be used and a glossary annexed; contentious headings, abbreviations, paraphrasing and definitions should not be used, and every effort should be made to ensure that they are in a form acceptable to the other parties,

(10)   particulars of primary allegations should be stated as particulars and not as primary allegations,

(11)   schedules or appendices should be used if this would be helpful, for example where lengthy particulars are necessary, and any response should also be stated in a schedule or appendix,

(12)   any lengthy extracts from documents should be placed in a schedule.

Further, as the *Commercial Court Guide* (Appendix 4) stresses, particular care should be taken to set out only those factual allegations which are necessary to support the case. Evidence should not be included.

By PD 5A, para 2.1, where a firm of solicitors prepares a statement of case, the document should be signed in the name of the firm.

7.1.5   Professional conduct

Pursuant to para. 1.4 of the SRA Code of Conduct for Solicitors, a solicitor must not mislead or attempt to mislead the court or allow or be complicit in the misleading acts of others. In respect of drafting a statement of case, this includes only making assertions and putting forward statements and representations which are properly arguable (para 2.4).

What if the client has filed a statement of case and subsequently tells their solicitor before the litigation ends that it contains a material error and the effect of that error is to mislead the court? In those circumstances, the solicitor should advise the client to amend the statement of case. If the client refuses to do so, the solicitor should cease to act for the client. In order to keep client confidentiality (see para 6.3), the solicitor should not inform the court or any other party of the reasons for ceasing to act.

7.2 CONTENTS OF THE PARTICULARS OF CLAIM

7.2.1 What must be included?

Rule 16.4(1) states that the particulars of claim must include:

(a)   a concise statement of the facts on which the claimant relies;

(b)   if the claimant is seeking interest, a statement to that effect and the details set out in paragraph (2) (see below).

7.2.1.1 Purpose

The primary function of the particulars of claim is to state concisely the facts upon which the claimant relies. The claimant should state all facts necessary for the purpose of showing that they have a complete cause of action. This might include, for example, a defendant's knowledge of a material fact that demonstrates a particular head of damage claimed is not too remote. This is often relevant where loss of a particular contract and/or profits is claimed.

Where the material facts stated in a claimant's particulars of claim conflict with those in the witness statements later filed in support of that case, that may prove fatal to the claim or, at the very least, will cast significant doubt on it: see *Puharic v Silverbond Enterprises Ltd* [2021] EWHC 351 (QB). If a party's factual (and indeed, expert) evidence changes the nature of the party's case, the party should apply to amend its statement of case accordingly (see **7.6**).

Practice Direction 16 goes into more detail as to what must be, or may be, included in the particulars of claim. There are particular requirements for certain types of cases, eg recovery of land and hire purchase claims.

7.2.1.2 Claim based on written contract

More generally, where a claim is based upon a written agreement, then by para 7.3 of PD 16:

(1)   a copy of the contract or documents constituting the agreement should be attached to or served with the particulars of claim and the original(s) should be available at the hearing, and

(2)   any general conditions of sale incorporated in the contract should also be attached (but where the contract is, or the documents constituting the agreement are bulky this practice direction is complied with by attaching or serving only the relevant parts of the contract or documents).

Therefore, where the claim arises out of a breach of a written contract, a copy of the relevant contract should be attached to, or served with, the particulars of claim.

7.2.1.3 Claim based on oral contract

By para 7.4 of PD 16:

Where a claim is based upon an oral agreement, the particulars of claim should set out the contractual words used and state by whom, to whom, when and where they were spoken.

See para 4 of the example at **7.2.1.7** below.

7.2.1.4 Other particular matters

Paragraphs 8.1–8.2 of PD 16 set out further matters that must be specifically included in the particulars of claim. For example, by para 8.2:

The claimant must specifically set out the following matters in his particulars of claim where he wishes to rely on them in support of his claim:

(1)   any allegation of fraud,

(2)   the fact of any illegality,

(3)   details of any misrepresentation,

(4)   details of all breaches of trust,

(5)   notice or knowledge of a fact,

(6)   details of unsoundness of mind or undue influence,

(7)   details of wilful default, and

(8)   any facts relating to a claim for mitigation expenditure.

As to (5) above, a claim for damages for the alleged misuse of confidential information requires the claimant to allege and particularise the essential fact that the defendant knew that the disclosures were unauthorised (*Media Entertainment NV v Karyagdyev* [2020] EWHC 1138 (QB)). Likewise, if a head of damage is alleged not to be too remote because the defendant had knowledge of relevant facts, the allegation and facts should be included.

As to (8) above, it is for the defendant to state in their defence and prove at trial any alleged failure of the claimant to mitigate loss (see **7.3.4**). There is no obligation on a claimant to state anything about the issue in their particulars of claim, unless the claimant is seeking damages for additional losses incurred in a reasonable attempt to mitigate their loss.

7.2.1.5   Interest

Rule 16.4(2) sets out the details that must be supplied where, as will usually be the case, the claimant is seeking interest. In such cases, the claimant must:

(a)   state whether he is doing so—

(i)   under the terms of a contract;

(ii)   under an enactment and if so which; or

(iii)   on some other basis and if so what that basis is; and

(b)   if the claim is for a specified amount of money, state—

(i)   the percentage rate at which interest is claimed;

(ii)   the date from which it is claimed;

(iii)   the date to which it is calculated, which must not be later than the date on which the claim form is issued;

(iv)   the total amount of interest claimed to the date of calculation; and

(v)   the daily rate at which interest accrues after that date.

A claimant may be entitled to claim interest pursuant to a particular clause in a contract. A claimant would normally seek to do this where the contractual interest rate is higher than the current statutory interest rate (ie usually 8% pa in non-commercial cases or 1% or 2% pa or more over base rate in commercial cases).

Where the contract does not provide for payment of interest, the claimant may nevertheless be entitled to claim a higher rate of interest than the statutory rate if the Late Payment of Commercial Debts (Interest) Act 1998 applies. A claimant who claims for interest under contract or the 1998 Act may well seek statutory interest under s 35A of the SCA 1981 or s 69 of the CCA 1984 in the alternative, just in case the court refuses to award interest under the contract or the 1998 Act.

In all cases a claimant can seek interest pursuant to statute. In the High Court this would be under s 35A of the SCA 1981, and in the County Court under s 69 of the CCA 1984.

For further details see **2.7.2** and the flowchart in **Appendix C(4)**.

There now follow two examples of particulars of claim, both concerning a breach of contract claim. In the first example the claim is for a specified amount of money. Interest is claimed under the Late Payment of Commercial Debts (Interest) Act 1998 where a reference rate of 0.5% pa has been assumed.

7.2.1.6   Example of particulars of claim in a County Court debt claim (particulars of claim set out on claim form)

Claim Form

You may be able to issue your claim online which may save time and money. Go to www.moneyclaim.gov.uk to find out more.

In the County Court Money Claims Centre	
Fee Account no.	ABCD12345
Help with Fees - Ref no. (if applicable)	H W F – ☐☐☐ – ☐☐☐

	For court use only
Claim no.	N185439
Issue date	5 August 2022

SEAL

Claimant(s) name(s) and address(es) including postcode
Brewsters Limited,
Unit 12, Brownside Industrial Estate,
Reading,
Berkshire
RG2 6DS

Defendant(s) name and address(es) including postcode
Gates Launderettes Limited,
73 Cider Street, Slough, Berkshire SL1 1PP
Tel: 01753 547790

Brief details of claim
The claim is for an unpaid debt of £63,450 in respect of 3 industrial drycleaners and 6 industrial washing machines supplied by the Claimant to the Defendant.

Value
The claim is for a specified sum of £63,450 plus accrued interest of £2,022.93 and compensation of £100.

You must indicate your preferred County Court Hearing Centre for hearings here (see notes for guidance)

Reading

Defendant's name and address for service including postcode	Gates Launderettes Limited, 73 Cider Street, Slough, Berkshire SL1 1PP		£
		Amount claimed	65,572.93
		Court fee	3,278.64
		Legal representative's costs	100.00
		Total amount	**£68,951.57**

For further details of the courts www.gov.uk/find-court-tribunal.
When corresponding with the Court, please address forms or letters to the Manager and always quote the claim number.

N1 Claim form (CPR Part 7) (10.21)   © Crown Copyright 2021

Claim No.	N185439

Does, or will, your claim include any issues under the Human Rights Act 1998? ☐ Yes ☑ No

Particulars of Claim ~~(attached)(to follow)~~

1. By clause 1 of a written agreement (the 'Agreement') dated 4 March 2022 the Claimant agreed to sell to the Defendant machinery, namely 3 Chloridal dry cleaning machines and 6 Isadal washing machines for an agreed price of £63,450.00. A copy of the Agreement is attached.

2. By clause 4 of the Agreement payment of the agreed price was due within 7 days of delivery.

3. In pursuance of clause 6 of the Agreement the machinery was delivered to the Defendant's premises at 6, Station Road, Reading on 18 March 2022.

4. In breach of the Agreement the Defendant has failed to pay the agreed price or any part thereof.

5. The Claimant claims the sum of £63,450.00.

6. The Claimant claims interest on the sum of £63,450.00 and compensation under The Late Payment of Commercial Debts (Interest) Act 1998.

AND THE CLAIMANT CLAIMS

1. The sum of £63,450.00

2. Interest pursuant to The Late Payment of Commercial Debts (Interest) Act 1998. For the purposes of the Act, both parties acted in the course of business. The statutory interest rate began to run from and including 26 March 2022 (the 8th day after delivery) at 8% over the reference rate of 0.75% then in force, totaling 8.75% per annum. Interest due to the date of issue is £2,022.93 (26 March 2022 to 5 August 2022 inclusive being 133 days) and is continuing until judgment or sooner payment at the daily rate of £15.21.

3. Compensation for late payment pursuant to The Late Payment of Commercial Debts (Interest) Act 1998 in the sum of £100.

DATED: 5 August 2022

Statement of Truth

I understand that proceedings for contempt of court may be brought against anyone who makes, or causes to be made, a false statement in a document verified by a statement of truth without an honest belief in its truth.

[✓] **I believe** that the facts stated in this particulars of claim are true.

[ ] **The Claimant** believes that the facts stated this particulars of claim are true. **I am authorised** by the claimant to sign this statement.

Signature

Brian Charlton

[✓] Claimant
[ ] Litigation friend (where judgment creditor is a child or a patient)
[ ] Claimant's legal representative (as defined by CPR 2.3(1))

Date

Day	Month	Year
05	08	2022

Full name

BRIAN CHARLTON

Name of claimant's legal representative's firm

Collaws

If signing on behalf of firm or company give position or office held

Claimant's or claimant's legal representative's address to which documents should be sent.

Building and street

14 Ship Street

Second line of address

Town or city

Weyford

County (optional)

Guildshire

Postcode

W E 1 8 H Q

If applicable

Phone number

01904876553

Fax phone number

01904876554

DX number

1599 Weyford

Your Ref.

BM/XYZ/Brewsters

Email

BM@Collaws.sol.net

Find out how HM Courts and Tribunals Service uses personal information you give them when you fill in a form:
https://www.gov.uk/government/organisations/hm-courts-and-tribunals-service/about/personal-information-charter

7.2.1.7   Example of particulars of claim in a High Court claim for breach of contract

IN THE HIGH COURT OF JUSTICE   2022 I No 876

QUEEN'S BENCH DIVISION

READING DISTRICT REGISTRY

BETWEEN

INDUSTRIAL MANUFACTURING LIMITED   Claimant

and

HEATECHS LIMITED   Defendant

PARTICULARS OF CLAIM

1. At all material times the Claimant was a manufacturer of small industrial machinery parts and the Defendant carried on business as a manufacturer and supplier of central heating boilers and systems.

2. By a written contract made on 25 April 2022 between the Claimant and Defendant, the Defendant agreed to sell to the Claimant a central heating gas boiler and integrated water pump described in clause 1 as a Heatechs Powerheat Unit Model 312K ('the Unit') for the sum of £70,000. A copy of the contract is attached.

3. The Claimant bought the Unit from the Defendant who sold it in the course of its business. It was an implied term of the contract that the Unit should be of satisfactory quality.

4. Further, during a telephone conversation at about 11.30 am on 20 April 2022, the Claimant by its contracts manager, Ian Jones, expressly or by implication made known to the Defendant (represented by their sales manager, Polly Rees) the particular purpose for which it required the Unit, namely for the purpose of installation in the Claimant's factory at 15 Normandale Lane, Reading 'as part of a heating system required to be in continuous use for 7 days per week'. It was an express and/or implied term of the contract that the Unit to be delivered by the Defendant should be reasonably fit for that particular purpose.

5. In purported performance of the contract the Defendant delivered the Unit on 24 June 2022 when the Claimant paid the Defendant the agreed sum of £70,000. The Unit was installed by the Claimant into its factory heating system on or about 6 July 2022.

6. In breach of the express and/or implied terms the Unit delivered by the Defendant was not of satisfactory quality and was not reasonably fit for its particular purpose.

PARTICULARS OF BREACH

The impeller retaining nut on the integrated water pump was insufficiently secure because the thread was 0.4cm wide whereas the maximum that it should have been was 0.2cm wide.

7. As a consequence of the breaches of terms the integrated water pump failed to operate and the boiler in the Unit became or had become drained of water on 8 August 2022 and overheated as a result. When the pump effectively re-engaged cold water flowed into the boiler causing it to explode and rupture on 8 August 2022 and the pipe connections to distort. As a result the boiler house had to be pumped out and repaired and a new boiler installed. During this time the Claimant lost 9 days of production.

8. By reason of the above the Claimant has suffered loss and damage.

PARTICULARS OF LOSS AND DAMAGE

8.1	Cost of new boiler	£72,500
8.2	Cost of installation of new boiler	£4,700
8.3	Cost of pumping out boiler house and repairing damaged premises	£17,625
8.4	Consequential losses as the result of production losses (estimated)	£25,000

9.   In respect of damages awarded the Claimant is entitled to interest pursuant to s 35A of the Senior Courts Act 1981 at such rates and for such period as the Court thinks just.

AND THE CLAIMANT CLAIMS:

(1)   Damages pursuant to paragraph 8 above;

(2)   Interest pursuant to paragraph 9 above.

Dated 9 December 2022.

Singleton Trumper & Co
SINGLETON TRUMPER & CO

STATEMENT OF TRUTH

I believe that the facts stated in these Particulars of Claim are true. I am duly authorised by the Claimant to sign this statement. I understand that proceedings for contempt of court may be brought against anyone who makes, or causes to be made, a false statement in a document verified by a statement of truth without an honest belief in its truth.

Signed: *D Smith*
DAVID SMITH
Director of Claimant company

Dated: 9 December 2022

The Claimant's Solicitors are Singleton Trumper & Co of Bank Chambers, Streatham, Reading RD62 5PA where they will accept service of proceedings on behalf of the Claimant.

To the Defendant

To the Court Manager.

7.2.2   Particulars of breach and damage

It is necessary to include detailed particulars of some aspects of the claim. For example, particulars of the breach of a contract or tortious duty must always be stated so that the defendant knows exactly the manner in which they are alleged to have been in breach. Similarly, the detail of the claim for damages is most conveniently set out in 'particulars of loss and damage' where each head of damage is itemised. See paras 6 and 8 in the example at **7.2.1.7.**

7.2.2.1   The summary for relief

The relief or remedy claimed must be specifically stated in the particulars of claim. Traditionally, although not a requirement of the CPR 1998, it is often repeated in summary form towards the end of the particulars of claim, immediately before the date, and will vary depending upon the subject matter of the claim. Pre-CPR 1998, it was known as the 'prayer for relief.'

In a debt claim, the summary will often include the claim for the amount of the debt, the exact amount of interest claimed up to the date of issue of the proceedings and the daily rate of interest claimed thereafter. In a damages claim, it will include the claim for damages plus interest.

7.2.3 The statement of truth

If the particulars of claim are not part of the claim form itself, they must be verified by a statement of truth (see **5.3.2** and the example at **7.2.1.7**).

7.2.4 Practical points

Whilst the CPR 1998 provide for the content and format of statements of case, practitioners will adopt their own style within that framework. For example, in the '*Industrial Manufacturing Limited v Heatechs Limited*' particulars of claim at **7.2.1.7**, para 3 states that the sale was in the course of the defendant's business. This is because the claimant wishes to rely upon the terms implied by the Sale of Goods Act 1979, which apply only where the sale was made in the course of the defendant's business. However, many practitioners do not consider it necessary to state this explicitly, as they rely upon the description of the defendant's business in the opening paragraph and the subsequent entry into the contract as satisfying this requirement. When looking at precedents, you will see that this additional paragraph appears in some but not others – neither is wrong, they are merely alternatives.

Another point to consider is the chronology of the material facts in the same example. We refer first (in para 2) to the contract that was made on 25 April 2022 and later (in para 4) to a conversation which took place on 20 April 2022. This is because the conversation became incorporated into the contract as a term. This is the traditional way of setting out such material. However, an alternative would be to deal with the conversation first, then with the contract and, thirdly, to refer back to the conversation when stating the relevant term of the contract.

A vital point to remember is that there must be a link or thread between the key parts of the particulars of claim. So, in a breach of contract claim:

(a) the express and/or implied terms relied on must be the same ones said to have been breached by the defendant;

(b) the factual consequences of the breach should be the same ones said to constitute the damage and loss.

You can see this in the *Industrial Manufacturing Limited v Heatechs Limited* example at **7.2.1.7**. Namely:

(a) the terms relied on are set out in paras 3 and 4, whilst exactly the same terms are said to have been broken in para 6;

(b) the factual consequences of the breach are set out in para 7 (boiler exploded, boiler house pumped out and repaired, new boiler installed and nine days of production lost), and these are then quantified and particularised in para 8.

7.2.5 Template

A template to help you draft particulars of claim is set out at **Appendix B(3)**.

CASE STUDY: DRAFTING THE PARTICULARS OF CLAIM

Let us now consider how the particulars of claim were drafted in the case study at **Appendix D(4)**.

In **Chapter 5** we demonstrated how the claim form would have been drafted. The heading of the particulars of claim will be identical, namely:

In the High Court of Justice   [Number]
Queen's Bench Division
Weyford District Registry

BETWEEN

MR WILLIAM ULYSSES SIMPSON (1)
MRS RUPINDER SIMPSON (2)

Claimants

-and-

MR GEOFFREY IAN TEMPLAR

Defendant

Then we should identify the document itself. Traditionally this is done in the centre of the page, and sometimes the title appears in capital letters in tramlines or underlined. However, the rules do not dictate how this is done.

PARTICULARS OF CLAIM

You will recall that in **Chapter 3** the parties set out their respective positions in the pre-action correspondence. Drafting the particulars of claim is like preparing the letter before claim but, as we have seen above, we have to do so according to a totally different set of rules.

Remember that the cause of action here is negligence. So, the initial material facts need to establish the duty of care situation, ie:

Paragraph 1 that the Claimants own the property, as defined, and

Paragraph 2 that on the material day and time the defendant drove his car onto that property.

Next in paragraph 3 the allegation of breach of that duty, namely negligence by the defendant, is made, followed by detailed particulars of that negligence. The purpose is to enable the defendant to understand exactly what he is alleged to have done wrong so that he can respond. In this case you will recall from **Chapter 3** that the claimants obtained a report from an accident reconstruction expert. From that report their solicitors will be able to identify the allegations showing the defendant fell below the required standard of care and so breached the duty of care that he owed to the claimants.

Note that the particulars of negligence are listed for ease of reference. The defendant will know that the claim against him is that he was driving too fast and lost control of the vehicle. This was apparent from his swerving on and off the driveway – an allegation based on the evidence of Mr Simpson, who was an eyewitness, and the conclusions drawn by the Simpsons' accident reconstruction expert from the tyre marks on the driveway. Note, however, that these sources of the allegation are not stated. Remember, the detailed evidence from witnesses and experts comes next, at Stage 3. Here, at Stage 2, only material facts should be stated, and these include the final particulars of negligence against the defendant of failing to use his brakes properly and manoeuvre the car so as to avoid the collision.

Next, in paragraph 4 it is stated that the defendant's negligence caused loss to the claimants. So that the defendant knows how much is being claimed, figures are stated where these are available, but otherwise estimates are given of each item claimed (otherwise known as the heads of damage).

What do the claimants want on any damages awarded? Interest – so this is stated at paragraph 5. The principles relating to the award of interest on damages were outlined at **7.2.1.5** but the detail can be found at **2.7**. As this is an unspecified claim, the claimants cannot calculate how much interest will be awarded, as they have to rely on the court's discretionary power to award interest at such rate and for such period as the court sees fit.

The particulars of claim are dated and signed by the claimants' solicitors in the name of the firm: see PD 5A, para 2.1.

A statement of truth is then included. Whilst a party's solicitor may sign the statement of truth, it is preferable, where possible, for the client to sign it. See **5.3.1.9** for a further discussion of the significance of the statement of truth and the options available. Here both claimants sign but expressing their own personal and individual belief in the truth of the contents of the document.

The document ends with the name and address of the claimants' solicitors and confirms that the address is the claimants' address for service. One copy of the particulars of claim will be filed at the court and another served on the defendant.

7.3 THE DEFENCE

7.3.1 Contents

As we saw in **Chapter 6**, the defendant has a limited amount of time in which to file a defence with the court, depending upon whether or not an acknowledgement of service has been filed.

Rule 16.5 sets out what must be contained in the defence:

(1)   In his defence, the defendant must state—

    (a)   which of the allegations in the particulars of claim he denies;

    (b)   which allegations he is unable to admit or deny, but which he requires the claimant to prove; and

    (c)   which allegations he admits.

(2)   Where the defendant denies an allegation—

    (a)   he must state his reasons for doing so; and

    (b)   if he intends to put forward a different version of events from that given by the claimant, he must state his own version.

(3)   A defendant who—

    (a)   fails to deal with an allegation; but

    (b)   has set out in his defence the nature of his case in relation to the issue to which that allegation is relevant,

shall be taken to require that allegation be proved.

(4)   Where the claim includes a money claim, a defendant shall be taken to require that any allegation relating to the amount of money claimed be proved unless he expressly admits the allegation.

(5)   Subject to paragraphs (3) and (4), a defendant who fails to deal with an allegation shall be taken to admit that allegation.

(6)   If the defendant disputes the claimant's statement of value under rule 16.3 he must—

    (a)   state why he disputes it; and

    (b)   if he is able, give his own statement of the value of the claim.

(7)   If the defendant is defending in a representative capacity, he must state what that capacity is.

(8)   If the defendant has not filed an acknowledgement of service under Part 10, he must give an address for service.

A party is required to verify that the facts stated in the defence are true by way of a statement of truth (see **5.3.1.9** and the example at **7.3.7**).

7.3.2 Admissions, non-admissions, denials and assertions

The defence must provide a comprehensive response to the particulars of claim, and therefore, in respect of each allegation in the particulars of claim, there should be an admission, a denial or, where the defendant has no knowledge of the matter stated, a requirement that the claimant prove the point, ie a non-admission. Any denial must be explicit, and a defendant must state their reasons for denying the allegation in the particulars of claim. If the defendant wishes to put forward a version of events different from that given by the claimant, the defendant must state their own version. A bare denial is not acceptable. Moreover, by the so-called 'rule of implied admissions', a defendant who fails to deal with an allegation is taken to admit it: see r 16.5(5) at **7.3.1** above.

7.3.3 Point-by-point response

In order to ensure that every allegation in the particulars of claim is dealt with and nothing is admitted through omission (see r 16.5(5)), the defence usually answers each paragraph of the claim in turn. If a paragraph contains more than one allegation, each should be answered point by point. This is the approach adopted in the defence to the breach of contract claim between *Industrial Manufacturing Limited and Heatechs Limited* in the example set out at **7.3.7** below.

As noted above, non-admissions are denials but the defendant is unable to give any version of their own because the facts alleged in the claim are not within their knowledge. Is there any obligation on a defendant to attempt to acquire knowledge in these circumstances? No, held the Court of Appeal in *SPI North Ltd v Swiss Post International (UK) Ltd* [2019] EWCA Civ 7:

> [3] Plainly, a defendant is able to admit or deny facts which are within his own actual knowledge, or which he is able to verify without undue delay, difficulty or inconvenience, by reference to records and other sources of information which are under his control or otherwise at his ready disposal. Furthermore, in the case of a corporate defendant, which can only act through human agents and has no mind of its own, its actual knowledge must clearly be understood as that of its individual officers, employees or other agents whose knowledge is for the purposes of applying rule 16.5 to be attributed to it, in accordance with the relevant rules of attribution: see the well-known observations of Lord Hoffmann in Meridian Global Funds Management Asia Limited v Securities Commission [1995] 2 AC 500 (PC) at 506-507. But does paragraph (1)(b), properly construed, go further, and require a defendant to make reasonable enquires of third parties before it can be said that he is 'unable' to admit or deny a particular allegation?
>
> [49] In my judgment, a number of factors point towards the conclusion that a defendant is 'unable to admit or deny' an allegation within the meaning of rule 16.5(1)(b) where the truth or falsity of the allegation is neither within his actual knowledge (including attributed knowledge in the case of a corporate defendant) nor capable of rapid ascertainment from documents or other sources of information at his ready disposal. In particular, there is no general obligation to make reasonable enquiries of third parties at this very early stage of the litigation. Instead, the purpose of the defence is to define and narrow the issues between the parties in general terms, on the basis of knowledge and information which the defendant has readily available to him during the short period afforded by the rules for filing his defence. (per Henderson LJ)

7.3.4 Causation and mitigation of loss

Very often, on the issue of causation, the defence will allege that the claimant caused the claimant's own loss. If known, the defendant should assert how. Also, it may be appropriate for the defendant to allege that the claimant failed to mitigate the claimant's loss. Details of the allegation should be given, for example an explanation of why the head of damage is said to be unreasonably large and an assertion as to what would have been a reasonable amount.

7.3.5 Defence of limitation

By PD 16, para 13.1, a defendant must give details of the expiry of any relevant limitation period that is relied on in their defence.

7.3.6 Address for service

When giving an address for service, the defendant must include a postcode. If the defendant is an individual, they must provide their date of birth in the defence (or acknowledgement of service, admission, defence, reply or other response). See PD 16, paras 10.6 and 10.7.

7.3.7   Example of a defence in a High Court claim for breach of contract

IN THE HIGH COURT OF JUSTICE   2022 I 876
QUEEN'S BENCH DIVISION
READING DISTRICT REGISTRY

BETWEEN

INDUSTRIAL MANUFACTURING LIMITED   Claimant

and

HEATECHS LIMITED   Defendant

DEFENCE

1. The Defendant admits paragraphs 1 to 4 of the Particulars of Claim.

2. The delivery of the Unit referred to in paragraph 5 of the Particulars of Claim was wholly in accordance with the terms of the contract and constituted full and complete performance thereof by the Defendant. Payment of the agreed sum of £70,000 by the Claimant is admitted. No admission is made as to the installation of the Unit by the Claimant as the Defendant has no knowledge of that matter.

3. The Defendant denies it was in breach of contract as alleged in paragraph 6 of the Particulars of Claim, or at all. The Defendant asserts that the Unit supplied was of satisfactory quality and fit for its purpose. In particular, the impeller retaining nut on the water pump was sufficiently secure by means of a 0.4cm thread.

4. The Defendant makes no admission as to the matters stated in paragraph 7 as the Defendant has no knowledge of these matters.

5. As to paragraph 8 it is not admitted that the Claimant has suffered the alleged or any loss and damage as the Defendant has no knowledge of these matters.

6. If, which is not admitted, the Claimant suffered the loss and damage alleged in paragraph 8, it is denied that this occurred as a result of the alleged or any breach of term by the Defendant. Any such loss or damage was caused by the Claimant's installation and/or subsequent use of the Unit.

7. If, which is not admitted, the Claimant suffered the loss and damage alleged in paragraph 8, the Claimant failed to mitigate that loss and damage. In particular, it was unreasonable to stop production for 9 days.

8. In all the circumstances it is denied that the Claimant is entitled to the relief claimed or any relief.

Dated 6 January 2023.

Haughton & Co

HAUGHTON & CO

STATEMENT OF TRUTH

I believe that the facts stated in this Defence are true. I am duly authorised by the Defendant to sign this statement. I understand that proceedings for contempt of court may be brought against anyone who makes, or causes to be made, a false statement in a document verified by a statement of truth without an honest belief in its truth.

Signed: *Darren Bennett*
Dated: 6 January 2023

DARREN BENNETT, Managing Director of the Defendant company

The Defendant's Solicitors are Haughton & Co, 19 High Pavement, Reading RD61 4UZ, where they will accept service of proceedings on behalf of the Defendant.

To the Court Manager and the Claimant.

7.3.8   Some points to note from the example

The consequence of making admissions in the defence is that the claimant does not have to prove the point at trial. Such admissions are most often made in respect of facts which came into existence prior to the alleged breach of contract or negligent act, such as the date, the parties and the terms of the contract. See para 1 of the example in **7.3.7** above.

When answering each paragraph of the claim, the defendant should clearly deny any allegations which are disputed and make clear admissions in respect of the factual issues which are not in dispute, eg para 1 in the above example. Any allegations of loss or damage which are disputed should be 'not admitted' in the defence, such as in para 4 of the example. The defendant should also include any additional facts in the defence which make their side of the story clearer (see paras 3, 6 and 7 of the example).

7.3.9   Counterclaim

If a defendant wishes to make their own claim against a claimant, they should do this by way of a counterclaim. The defence and counterclaim will form one document. Counterclaims are considered in more detail in **Chapter 8**.

7.3.10   Templates

A template to help you draft a defence can be found at **Appendix B(4)**, and a template for a defence and counterclaim at **Appendix B(5)**.

7.4   REPLY TO DEFENCE

A claimant may wish to file a reply to the defence but is under no obligation to do so. The claimant should do so if they need to allege facts in answer to the defence that were not included in the particulars of claim. By r 16.7(1), a claimant who does not file a reply to the defence is not taken to admit the matters raised in the defence. There is therefore no corresponding rule of implied admission like that we saw when looking at the defence itself (see **7.3.2**). In practice, replies to defences are most common where the defendant has made a counterclaim. Then a claimant must file a defence to the counterclaim to prevent default judgment being entered against them and will usually incorporate a reply to the defence as well.

7.5   THE ROLE OF STATEMENTS OF CASE

7.5.1   Defining the issues

How do the statements of case define the issues between the parties? If the particulars of claim have set out the factual allegations, and the defence answered each allegation by way of admission, non-admission or denial, then by comparing the two documents we can identify the issues in dispute (namely, those not admitted and denied). So, if we compare these documents in the *Industrial Manufacturing Limited v Heatechs Limited* example at **7.2.1.7** and **7.3.7**, we have the following agreed issues and issues in dispute:

EXAMPLE 1 – AGREED ISSUES

Particulars of claim	Defence	Issue
Paragraph 1	Paragraph 1	Defendant a manufacturer and supplier of central heating boilers and systems.
Paragraph 2	Paragraph 1	Written contract made on 25 April 2022 for the Unit.
Paragraph 3	Paragraph 1	Implied term that Unit to be of satisfactory quality.
Paragraph 4	Paragraph 1	Express or implied term that Unit to be reasonably fit to heat Claimant's factory continuously seven days a week.
Paragraph 5	Paragraph 2	Unit delivered to Claimant on 24 June 2022 when payment of £70,000 made.

EXAMPLE 2 – ISSUES IN DISPUTE

Particulars of claim	Defence	Issue
Paragraph 5	Paragraph 2	Claimant installed Unit on 6 July 2022.
Paragraph 6	Paragraph 3	Defendant breached contract as impeller retaining nut had insufficient thread.
Paragraph 7	Paragraph 4	On 8 August 2022 boiler overheated and exploded.
Paragraph 8	Paragraph 5	Claimant suffered loss due to Defendant's breach.
Paragraph 8	Paragraph 5	Claimant's loss consists of cost of new boiler and its installation, cost of pumping out and repairing boiler house and loss of profit.
Paragraph 8	Paragraph 6	Claimant caused own loss by way installed and/or subsequently used Unit.
Paragraph 8	Paragraph 7	Claimant failed to mitigate its loss.

CASE STUDY: THE DEFENCE

Let us consider how the defendant's solicitors set about drafting the defence at **Appendix D(5)**. Look again at the claimants' particulars of claim at **Appendix D(4)**. What facts is the defendant going to admit, not admit and dispute? For the disputed facts, what is the defendant's own version?

The defendant will admit that at the material time he was the driver of the car and that his vehicle collided with the extension of the claimants' property. The defendant does not strictly know that the Simpsons own the property and he could make a non-admission requiring the claimants to prove it. However, the defendant is prepared to admit it here. He will, of course, dispute that he drove negligently and that he is liable for any loss. At this stage he will not make any admissions about the amount of the claimants' loss as he has no knowledge of that.

So for the purposes of the defence the response to the particulars of claim in the case study will be:

Particulars of Claim	Issue	Response
Paragraph 1	Claimant is owner of Bliss Lodge	Admit – defendant does not dispute this
Paragraph 2	Date and time of accident, details of vehicle	Admit – these facts are agreed
Paragraph 3	Allegation of negligence resulting in collision with extension together with Particulars of Negligence.	Deny negligence and explain why. What about the collision? This is admitted. His car did collide with the extension but he denies it was his fault.
Paragraph 4	Allegation of loss caused by the negligence of the defendant and particulars of loss.	As above the defendant will admit the collision but will deny that the damage was caused by his negligence. He will make no admissions as to the losses claimed as he has no knowledge of these and will require the claimants to prove the amount of their losses.
Paragraph 5	Interest	There is no need to respond to the claim for interest. Interest can be awarded here only if the claimants are awarded damages, and the defendant will deny that the claimants are entitled to any damages.

In addition, the defendant can allege in the alternative that the claimants were contributory negligent. But does that deal with all the issues the defendant wants the court to decide? Look again at **Appendix D(3)**. From this letter we can see that the defendant has indicated an intention to defend the claim and make a claim of his own. He could start separate proceedings, but this would not be cost-effective and so his best course of action is to make his own claim by way of a counterclaim (**7.3.9** above). In **Chapter 8** we shall consider how to draft that part of the document.

7.6 AMENDMENTS TO STATEMENTS OF CASE (PART 17)

In a perfect world, nobody would ever have to amend their statements of case. However, sometimes mistakes are made, and on other occasions fresh information comes to light after the statement of case has been served. Part 17 of CPR 1998 provides the ways in which statements of case can be amended.

7.6.1 Amendments before service

A party may amend their statement of case at any time before it has been served.

7.6.2 Amendments with permission

After a party has served their statement of case, they can amend it only with either:

(a)   the written consent of all of the parties; or

(b)   the permission of the court.

On making an application for permission to amend the statement of case, the applicant should file a copy of the statement of case with the proposed amendments along with the application notice (see **Chapter 10**).

In deciding whether or not to exercise its discretion to grant the application, the court will consider the following:

(a)   The overriding objective is of the greatest importance. Applications always involve the court striking a balance between injustice to the applicant if the amendment is refused, and injustice to the opposing party and other litigants in general, if the amendment is permitted.

(b)   Where a very late application to amend is made, the correct approach is not that the amendments ought, in general, to be allowed so that the real dispute between the parties can be adjudicated upon. Rather, a heavy burden lies on a party seeking a very late amendment to show the strength of the new case and why justice to the party, their opponent and other court users requires the party to be able to pursue it. The risk to a trial date may mean that the lateness of the application to amend will of itself cause the balance to be loaded heavily against the grant of permission.

(c)   A very late amendment is one made when the trial date has been fixed and where permitting the amendments would cause the trial date to be lost. Parties and the court have a legitimate expectation that trial fixtures will be kept.

(d)   Lateness is not an absolute, but a relative concept. It depends on a review of the nature of the proposed amendment, the quality of the explanation for its timing, and a fair appreciation of the consequences in terms of work wasted and consequential work to be done.

(e)   Gone are the days when it was sufficient for the amending party to argue that no prejudice had been suffered, save as to costs. In the modern era it is more readily recognised that the payment of costs may not be adequate compensation.

(f)   It is incumbent on a party seeking the indulgence of the court to be allowed to raise a late claim to provide a good explanation for the delay.

(g)   A much stricter view is taken nowadays of non-compliance with the Civil Procedure Rules and directions of the Court. The achievement of justice means something different now. Parties can no longer expect indulgence if they fail to comply with their procedural obligations, because those obligations not only serve the purpose of ensuring that they conduct the litigation proportionately in order to ensure their own costs are kept within proportionate bounds but also the wider public interest of ensuring that other litigants can obtain justice efficiently and proportionately, and that the courts enable them to do so.

(See *New York Laser Clinic Ltd v Naturastudios Ltd* [2019] LTL 14 Feb (CA) and *Quah Su-Ling v Goldman Sachs International* [2015] EWHC 759 (Comm).)

If the court grants permission for the amendment, the applicant must file the amended statement of case and serve the order and the amended statement of case on all other parties.

The statement of case will be endorsed with the words:

Amended [describe the type of statement of case] by Order of [name of master/district judge] dated [   ].

The amended statement of case need not show the original text unless the court directs otherwise.

7.6.3   Directions following amendment

If the court gives permission to amend the statement of case, it may give directions regarding amendments to any other statement of case and service of the amended statements of case. It is common, for example, for a defendant to be allowed to amend their defence if the court has given the claimant permission to amend their particulars of claim.

7.6.4   Application to amend the statement of case outside the limitation period

If a claim is made after the relevant limitation period has expired, the defendant has an absolute defence (see **2.5.2.1**). So, if the amendment will add or substitute a new claim, the new claim must arise out of the same facts or substantially the same facts as the claim which the applicant has already made in the proceedings (see, eg, *Bank of Scotland Plc v Watson* [2013] EWCA Civ 6).

If the amendment is to correct a mistake as to the name of a party, the mistake must be genuine and one that would not have caused reasonable doubt as to the identity of the party in question.

If the amendment alters the capacity in which a party brings their claim, the new capacity must be one that party had when the proceedings commenced or has since acquired.

7.6.5   Statements of truth

By r 22.1(2), amendments to the statement of case have to be verified by a statement of truth (see **5.3.2**), unless the court orders otherwise.

7.6.6   Costs

A party applying for an amendment will usually be responsible for the costs of and caused by the amendment's being allowed (see **10.3**).

7.6.7   Amendments without permission

Where a party has amended their statement of case without requiring the court's permission (ie, in the case of an amendment by consent or before service), the court may disallow the amendment (r 17.2). A party may apply to the court asking it to exercise its discretion to disallow within 14 days of service of the amended statement of case.

7.7   REQUESTS FOR FURTHER INFORMATION (PART 18)

7.7.1   The request

A party to the proceedings, or the court itself, may wish another party to give further information about its case. By r 18.1(1), the court may at any time order a party to:

(a)   clarify any matter which is in dispute in the proceedings; or

(b)   give additional information in relation to any such matter,

whether or not the matter is contained or referred to in a statement of case.

If one of the parties requires further information then, before applying to the court for an order, that party should first serve a written request on the other party stating a date for the response, which must allow a reasonable time for the response.

A request should be concise and strictly confined to matters that are reasonably necessary and proportionate to enable the applicant to prepare their own case or to understand the case they have to meet. The most common request is by a defendant seeking further information from a claimant who has failed to give sufficient particulars of breach and/or damage (see **7.2.2**).

Requests must be made as far as possible in a single comprehensive document and not piecemeal.

If the text of the request is brief and the reply is likely to be brief, the request may be made by letter. If so, the letter must state that it contains a request made under Part 18 and must not deal with any other matter. Otherwise, the request should be made in a separate document.

Any request must:

(a)   be headed with the name of the court and the title and number of the claim;

(b)   state in its heading that it is a Part 18 request, identify the applicant and the respondent, and state the date on which it is made;

(c)   set out each request in a separate numbered paragraph;

(d)   identify any document and (if relevant) any paragraph or words in that document to which the request relates;

(e)   state the date for a response.

If the request is not in the form of a letter, the applicant may, if this is convenient, put the request on the left-hand side of the document so that the response may appear on the right-hand side. If so, the applicant should serve two copies of the request on the respondent.

7.7.2   Response to the request

The response must be in writing, dated and signed by the respondent or their solicitor. If the original request was made in a letter, the response can also be in the form of a letter or a formal reply. If in a letter, it should state that it is a response to the request and should not deal with any other matters. The response should set out the same information as the request and then give details of the response itself. The respondent must file at court and serve on all parties a copy of the request and the respondent's response.

The response must be verified by a statement of truth (see **5.3.2**).

EXAMPLE

In *InterDigital Technology Corp v Nokia Corp* [2008] EWHC 504, the parties were already involved in litigation known as UK2 and UK3. The defendant's defence to these proceedings included the following assertion:

> 9.1   This action is not brought for real commercial reasons but for tactical reasons relating to the ongoing litigation between InterDigital and Nokia . . .

The claimant asked for further information about para 9.1 as follows:

Request

Of paragraph 9.1 of the Defence.

Please specify each and all of the 'tactical reasons' for which it is alleged this action has been brought.

The defendant's answer included the following:

Response

InterDigital's full motives are known only to it. But without limitation to the scope of paragraph 9.1, InterDigital's reasons for commencing this litigation include the tactical reasons listed below:

(1)   in retaliation for and to punish Nokia for bringing the UK2 proceedings;

(2)   to deter Nokia from pursuing UK2 and/or from bringing further proceedings in respect of InterDigital 's claimed essential patents;

(3)   to force a more favourable settlement of UK2, in particular as a result of other matters referred to herein;

(4)   to trap Nokia into adopting inconsistent positions in UK2 and UK3;

(5)   to distract Nokia and in particular its external legal and expert advisers and from UK2 by imposing further burdensome work on them in the run-up to the UK2 trial.

CASE STUDY: PART 18 REQUEST

A further example of a Part 18 Request is in the case study at **Appendix D(7)**. There you will see that the Defendant has requested further information about certain aspects of the particulars of claim.

Also see *Cavendish Square Holdings BV v Tala El Makdessi* [2013] LTL, 13 February (where the claimant was ordered under Part 18 to give further information of an assertion made in the particulars of claim that it had during a stated period of time acted within the terms of the contract between the parties).

7.7.3 Cases where the respondent does not respond to the initial request

If the respondent objects to all or part of the request, or cannot comply with the request, they should inform the applicant, giving reasons and, where relevant, giving a date by which they will be able to comply with the request. They may do so by letter or by formal response. If the respondent considers that a response will involve disproportionate expense, they should explain briefly in their reply why they take this view.

7.7.4 Applications for court orders

If no response is received or the response is considered to be inadequate, the applicant can apply for an order from the court (see **Chapter 10**). The application can be made without notice where no response has been given, at least 14 days have passed since the request was served and the time stated in it for a response has expired (see PD 18, para 5.5 and *Sheeran v Chokri* [2020] EWHC 2806 (Ch)). The court will grant an order only if it is satisfied that the request is confined to matters that are reasonably necessary and proportionate to enable the applicant to prepare their case or understand the case they have to meet. As Norris J observed in *Pacific Biosciences of California, Inc v Oxford Nanopore Technologies Ltd* [2018] EWHC 806 (Ch):

> [19] A request for further information, under CPR 18, arises really as part of the responsibility of the court to manage cases and the parties to co-operate in the just and efficient disposal of the issues between them. The function of a request is to identify the material facts that are going to be relied upon at trial, but not to plead evidence that will be led to prove those facts. The identification of the material facts, ideally, ought to be with the same degree of particularity as will be relied on at the trial itself. That way, everyone knows where they stand.

> [20] A major objective of case management is to ensure that statements of case do set out the parties' cases, and define the dispute between them. As part of its responsibility for managing cases, the court must ensure that parties plainly state the factual ingredients of their case, so that the true nature and scope of the dispute can be identified.

If the court orders a response but none is given, the court may make an unless order (see **9.3.4**). How will the court determine whether or not a response given complies with the court's order? See *Owners of the Gravity Highway v Owners of the Maritime Maisie* [2020] EWHC 1697 (Comm) (Butcher J at para 33).

7.8 SUMMARY: HOW SHOULD YOU APPROACH DRAFTING PARTICULARS OF CLAIM?

7.8.1 Structure formalities: PD 5A

Examples include:

(1) Paragraph 2.1 provides that statements of case drafted by a legal representative as a member or an employee of a firm should be signed in the name of the firm.

(2) Paragraph 2.2 includes that the document should be divided into numbered paragraphs, with all numbers, including dates, expressed as figures.

7.8.2 Content: PD 16

Examples include:

(1)   If relying on written contract: PD 16, para 7.3 – a copy of the contract or documents constituting the agreement should be attached to or served with the particulars of claim.

(2)   If relying on oral contract: PD 16, para 7.4 – the particulars of claim should set out the contractual words used and state by whom, to whom, when and where they were spoken.

(3)   Stating a claim for interest: PD 16, para 3.7 (cross-referring to r 16.4(2)).

(4)   Statement of truth: PD 16, para 3.4.

7.8.3 General points

(1)   Be as brief and concise as possible. Include only material facts but ensure all material facts are stated.

(2)   State the case on a point-by-point basis in separate, consecutively numbered paragraphs and sub-paragraphs. So far as possible, each paragraph or sub-paragraph should contain no more than one allegation.

(3)   Put the facts in chronological order, unless it is inappropriate to do so.

(4)   Allege breach of terms and/or duty, or loss and damage, then follow that with particulars listed one by one in separately numbered sub-paragraphs.

(5)   Use definitions where appropriate.

(6)   Refer to evidence and law only where it is proportionate and necessary to help particularise the case.

(7)   Attach documents only where it is proportionate and necessary to help particularise the case.

7.9 SUMMARY: HOW SHOULD YOU APPROACH DRAFTING A DEFENCE?

7.9.1 Structure formalities: PD 5A

Examples include:

(1)   Paragraph 2.1 provides that statements of case drafted by a legal representative as a member or an employee of a firm should be signed in the name of the firm.

(2)   Paragraph 2.2 includes that the document should be divided into numbered paragraphs, with all numbers, including dates, expressed as figures.

7.9.2 Content: Rule 16.5

(1)   In their defence, the defendant must state—
    (a)   which of the allegations in the particulars of claim they deny;
    (b)   which allegations they are unable to admit or deny, but which they require the claimant to prove; and
    (c)   which allegations they admit.

(2)   Where the defendant denies an allegation—
    (a)   they must state their reasons for doing so; and
    (b)   if they intend to put forward a version of events different from that given by the claimant, they must state their own version.

(3)   A defendant who—
    (a)   fails to deal with an allegation; but
    (b)   has set out in their defence the nature of their case in relation to the issue to which that allegation is relevant,

shall be taken to require that allegation be proved.

(4)   Where the claim includes a money claim, a defendant shall be taken to require that any allegation relating to the amount of money claimed be proved unless they expressly admit the allegation.

(5)   Subject to paragraphs (3) and (4), a defendant who fails to deal with an allegation shall be taken to admit that allegation.

(6)   If the defendant disputes the claimant's statement of value under rule 16.3 they must—

(a)   state why they dispute it; and

(b)   if they are able, give their own statement of the value of the claim.

(7)   If the defendant is defending in a representative capacity, they must state what that capacity is.

(8)   If the defendant has not filed an acknowledgement of service under Part 10, they must give an address for service.

Part 22 requires a defence to be verified by a statement of truth.

7.9.3   General points

(1)   Be as brief and concise as possible. Include only material facts but ensure all material facts are stated in the defence.

(2)   Answer each allegation point-by-point by reference to the numbered paragraphs of the particulars of claim.

(3)   Assert own case by way of defence and any contributory negligence, eg allege breach of duty then follow that with particulars listed one by one in separately numbered sub-paragraphs.

(4)   Use same definitions as in particulars of claim and any additional ones, where appropriate.

(5)   Refer to evidence and law only where it is proportionate and necessary to help particularise the defence.

(6)   Attach documents only where it is proportionate and necessary to help particularise the defence.

CHAPTER 8

ADDITIONAL PROCEEDINGS AND PART 8 CLAIMS

8.1	Introduction	125
8.2	Procedure	126
8.3	Drafting a counterclaim	129
8.4	Part 8 claims	130

LEARNING OUTCOMES

After reading this chapter you will have learned:

- when to make a counterclaim
- the role of third party proceedings
- when to make a third party claim
- how to get the court's permission, if required, in order to make an additional claim
- how to draft a defence and counterclaim
- the basics of Part 8 claims.

8.1 INTRODUCTION

We have so far looked at the rules relating to a claimant bringing a claim against a defendant. Part 20 of the CPR 1998 deals with other types of 'additional claims' that may be brought in the proceedings as set out in r 20.2:

(1) This Part applies to—

    (a) a counterclaim by a defendant against the claimant or against the claimant and some other person;

    (b) an additional claim by a defendant against any person (whether or not already a party) for contribution or indemnity or some other remedy; and

    (c) where an additional claim has been made against a person who is not already a party, any additional claim made by that person against any other person (whether or not already a party).

(2) In these Rules—

    (a) 'additional claim' means any claim other than the claim by the claimant against the defendant; and

    (b) unless the context requires otherwise, references to a claimant or defendant include a party bringing or defending an additional claim.

Frequently, a defendant who has been sued by a claimant wants to make a claim against that person.

EXAMPLE

A supplies goods to B.

B has paid 50% of the price, but the other 50% is unpaid.

> B sues A for damages for breach of contract based on the allegation that the goods were not of satisfactory quality.
>
> A defends the claim (on the basis that the goods were of satisfactory quality) and also counterclaims for the balance of 50% of the price which is still outstanding.
>
> This counterclaim is governed by Part 20.

Another common scenario is where the defendant wishes to pass the blame, either in whole or in part, on to a third party. The defendant may be seeking a full indemnity from the third party, or a contribution towards any damages the defendant has to pay the claimant. A claim for an indemnity often arises where there is a contractual relationship between the defendant and the third party, and the defendant alleges that the third party is obliged by the terms of the contract to indemnify the defendant if they are found liable in respect of the claimant's claim against them. Sometimes a right to an indemnity may arise from statute or by implication of law. An example of a claim for an indemnity is where a consumer sues a retailer in respect of goods they allege are not of satisfactory quality, and the retailer alleges that there was an inherent defect in the goods and attempts to pass on liability to the manufacturer. The retailer will claim an indemnity from the manufacturer in respect of any sums that they are ordered to pay to the consumer.

A claim for a contribution often arises where there are joint wrong-doers, and the defendant claims that the third party is partly responsible for the harm that the claimant has suffered. An example of a claim for a contribution is where the claimant claims damages from the defendant as a result of a road traffic accident, and the defendant alleges that another driver was partly to blame for the accident. A defendant will then claim a contribution from the other driver towards the damages which the defendant is ordered to pay to the claimant.

These types of claims are further examples of additional claims.

8.2 PROCEDURE

8.2.1 Counterclaims (r 20.4)

If a defendant wishes to make a counterclaim against a claimant, they should file particulars of the counterclaim with their defence. This should form one document, with the counterclaim following on from the defence (see **Appendix D(5)**).

If a defendant does this, they do not need permission from the court to make the counterclaim. However, if a defendant decides to make a counterclaim after they have already filed their defence, they will need the court's permission. The application for permission should be made on notice.

If they wish to dispute the counterclaim, the claimant (who does not have the option of acknowledging service) has to file a defence to counterclaim within the usual 14-day period. This will usually be a reply (to the defence) and defence (to the counterclaim) (see **Appendix D(6)**). If the claimant fails to file a defence to the counterclaim, the defendant may enter judgment in default on the counterclaim. Therefore, if the claimant requires more time to file a defence to the counterclaim, they should request an extension of time from the defendant. As already seen (at **6.4**), the parties can agree an extension of up to 28 days in addition to the initial 14-day period.

8.2.2 Contribution or indemnity between parties (r 20.6)

If one defendant wishes to seek a contribution or an indemnity from another party, after filing their acknowledgement of service or defence, they may proceed with their claim against that party by:

(a)   filing a notice containing a statement of the nature and grounds of their additional claim; and

(b)   serving the notice on that party.

No permission is required if the defendant files and serves the notice with the defence or, if the party against whom the claim is made is added later, within 28 days of that party's filing their defence. Permission is required to file and serve the notice at all other times.

If a claim form is issued by a claimant against more than one defendant but not served on one of the defendants, and time for service of the claim expired without service on that defendant, a defendant who is served has to use CPR, r.20.7 if they wish to commence any Part 20 claim against the non-served defendant (*Bailey v Barclays Bank UK Public Ltd Co* [2021] EWHC 3698 (QB)).

8.2.3   Other additional claims (r 20.7)

In other additional claims, such as a claim against a third party, the defendant may make an additional claim without the court's permission by issuing an appropriate claim form before or at the same time as they file a defence. Particulars of the additional claim must be contained in or served with the additional claim.

If an additional claim is not issued at that time, the court's permission will be required. The application for permission can be made without notice, unless the court directs otherwise.

The court fee payable for making such as an additional claim is the usual 'starting proceedings' fee (see Civil Proceedings Fees Order 2008, Sch 1, para 1.1 and *Walayat v Berkeley Solicitors Ltd* [2021] EWHC 227 (Ch)).

8.2.4   Applications for permission to make an additional claim

When the court's permission is required, because the counterclaim or other type of additional claim was not made at the time of filing the defence, the application notice should be filed with a copy of the proposed additional claim. The application for permission must be supported by evidence stating:

(a)   the stage which the proceedings have reached;

(b)   the nature of the claim to be made by the additional claimant, or details of the question or issue which needs to be decided;

(c)   a summary of the facts on which the additional claim is based; and

(d)   the name and address of the proposed additional party.

If there has been any delay in making the application, the evidence must also explain the delay. Where possible, the applicant should provide a timetable of the proceedings to date.

Rule 20.9(2) sets out the matters the court takes into account in deciding whether to grant permission, and these include:

(a)   the connection between the additional claim and the claim made by the claimant against the defendant;

(b)   whether the additional claimant is seeking substantially the same remedy which some other party is claiming from him;

(c)   whether the additional claimant wants the court to decide any question connected with the subject matter of the proceedings—

(i)   not only between existing parties but also between existing parties and a person not already a party; or

(ii)   against an existing party not only in a capacity in which he is already a party but also in some further capacity.

The court may permit the additional claim to be made, dismiss it, or require it to be dealt with separately from the claim by the claimant against the defendant.

8.2.5   Service (r 20.8)

If the defendant did not need permission in order to make the additional claim then:

(a)   in the case of a counterclaim, they must serve it on every other party when they serve their defence;

(b)   except for claims for contributions or indemnities from another party, they must serve the additional claim on the new party within 14 days of issue.

If a defendant had to make an application for permission to issue an additional claim, the court will give directions as to service when granting permission to make the claim.

If a defendant serves an additional claim form on a person who is not already a party (such as a third party), they must also serve:

(a)   forms for defending or admitting or acknowledging service of the additional claim;

(b)   copies of every statement of case which has already been served; and

(c)   such other documents as the court may direct.

The defendant must also serve copies of the additional claim form on all existing parties to the proceedings.

8.2.6   Judgment in default on additional claims (r 20.11)

Special rules apply where the additional claim is not a counterclaim or a claim by a defendant for an indemnity or contribution against another defendant under r 20.6. In other cases, if the party against whom an additional claim is made fails to acknowledge service or file a defence in respect of an additional claim:

(a)   they are deemed to admit the additional claim and will be bound by any judgment or decision in the proceedings that affects the additional claim; and

(b)   if a default judgment is entered against the additional claimant, they may also enter judgment in respect of the additional claim by filing a request in the relevant practice forms. However, the additional claimant will need permission to enter default judgment (which can be obtained without notice unless the court directs otherwise) if they have not satisfied any default judgment obtained against them, or if they are seeking any remedy other than a contribution or an indemnity.

8.2.7   Directions (r 20.13)

If a defence is filed to an additional claim (other than a counterclaim), the court will arrange a hearing to give directions as to the future conduct of the case. In giving directions, the court must ensure that, as far as practicable, the additional claim and the main claim are managed together. At the directions hearing, the court may (see para 5.3 of PD 20):

(1)   treat the hearing as a summary judgment hearing,

(2)   order that the additional claim be dismissed,

(3)   give directions about the way any claim, question or issue set out in or arising from the additional claim should be dealt with,

(4)   give directions as to the part, if any, the additional defendant will take at the trial of the claim,

(5)   give directions about the extent to which the additional defendant is to be bound by any judgment or decision to be made in the claim.

8.2.8   Title of the proceedings

Paragraphs 7.1–7.6 of PD 20 give information as to how parties to additional claims should be described in the title of the proceedings. The title of every additional claim should include both the full name of each party and their status in the proceedings (ie, claimant, defendant, third party, fourth party).

8.3 DRAFTING A COUNTERCLAIM

8.3.1 Defence and counterclaim

A defence and counterclaim is essentially just what its title suggests: a defence and a (counter) claim, set out in a single document (see PD 20, para 6.1). The title to the action remains the same but the document should be entitled, 'DEFENCE AND COUNTERCLAIM'. The document itself is then sub-divided into two sections, normally by centred sub-headings of 'DEFENCE' (at the start) and then 'COUNTERCLAIM' (immediately after the defence ends).

8.3.2 Paragraph numbering

It is important to appreciate that, as this is one continuous document, the paragraph numbering therefore runs sequentially from the start of the defence through to the end of the counterclaim. The wording of any summary at the end should be, 'AND THE DEFENDANT COUNTERCLAIMS'.

8.3.3 Drafting skills

In drafting terms, the defence and counterclaim is essentially the same as a separate defence and particulars of claim. The counterclaim is a self-standing claim (akin to particulars of claim), and so it must deal with all the material facts and particulars that establish the claim. What if facts that are material to the counterclaim have already been set out in, or admitted in, the defence? Rather than stating these again in full in the counterclaim, all that is needed is to cross-refer to the relevant paragraph or paragraphs of the defence.

It is best practice, as indeed with all statements of case, to plan the structure and content of this document before attempting to draft it. Indeed, it is recommended that you plan the counterclaim first as normal particulars of claim. This will ensure that it is complete. You can then plan the defence and subsequently decide what matters in the counterclaim can be dealt with by simple cross-referencing to the defence, and those which need to be stated in full.

8.3.4 Template

A template to help you draft a defence and counterclaim may be found at **Appendix B(5)**.

CASE STUDY: DRAFTING THE DEFENCE AND COUNTERCLAIM

Let us briefly consider how the counterclaim was drafted as part of the statement of case at **Appendix D(5)**. In **Chapter 7** we saw how the defence was planned and drafted. As the defendant wants to bring a claim of his own against the claimants, a counterclaim needs to be added as part of the statement of case. The defendant will not need the permission of the court to bring his counterclaim as long as he files the counterclaim with the defence: see r 20.4(2)(a) at **8.2.1** above.

Practice Direction 20, para 6.1 requires that the defence and counterclaim should be contained in a single document. When planning the content of the counterclaim, the best approach is to start by considering it as a stand-alone claim. The defendant is basing his counterclaim on the duty owed to him by Mr and Mrs Simpson under the Occupiers' Liability Act 1957. So, let us first outline a case analysis for this, and then focus on the legal issues and the facts the defendant will be relying on for each element:

Duty of care	That the claimants were occupiers and the defendant a visitor to their property – this is, of course, part of the claimants' own claim (see paras 1 and 2 of the particulars of claim which have been admitted in paras 1 and 2 of the defence).

Breach	That the claimants left glass on the driveway which caused the defendant to lose control of the car resulting in the collision with the extension (see paras 3 and 4 of the defence).
Loss	That the defendant's car is written off, he has suffered property damage (computer and telephone) and consequential financial losses (accommodation, hire car, towing and storage).

So, how should Mr Templar's solicitors have approached drafting the counterclaim in light of this analysis? First, the basic formality of having a sub-heading for the title to this part of the statement of case. If you look at **Appendix D(5)** you will see that the defence is set out in paras 1 to 6, and that immediately following, in the centre of the page, is the sub-heading 'COUNTERCLAIM'. There is no rule that it needs to be in upper case characters – it just needs to stand out.

As the counterclaim is following the defence, there is no need to type out again the facts already stated in the defence that form part of the counterclaim. The first paragraph of the counterclaim simply states that the relevant paragraphs are repeated – see para 7. This establishes the duty of care situation and the allegation of breach. Also note that you do not restart numbering the paragraphs.

So, the rest of the counterclaim needs to make the allegations of loss resulting from the claimants' breach – see para 8.

The defendant should seek interest on any damages awarded, and so must include a claim for interest; here, as the claim is unspecified and in the High Court, it will be under s 35A of the SCA 1981 – see para 10.

The counterclaim is then dated and signed in the name of the solicitors' firm that drafted it.

A suitable statement of truth must then be added (see **5.3.2**) and the document completed with the usual closing formalities.

8.4 PART 8 CLAIMS

8.4.1 Introduction

The Part 8 claim procedure may be used by a claimant where they are seeking the court's decision on a question that is unlikely to involve a substantial dispute of fact, or if a Rule or Practice Direction requires or permits the use of the Part 8 procedure.

Practice Direction 8 lists various types of claim for which the procedure may be used, which include a claim by or against a child or patient that has been settled before the commencement of proceedings and where the sole purpose of the claim is to obtain the approval of the court to the settlement.

8.4.2 Procedure

The claimant issues a Part 8 claim form (Form N208), which must state:

(a) the question the court is to decide, or the remedy the claimant is seeking;

(b) any enactment under which the claim is being made;

(c) the representative capacity (eg, litigation friend) of any of the parties.

Instead of serving particulars of claim, the claimant must file and serve any written evidence, usually in the form of witness statements, with the claim form.

The defendant must then file and serve an acknowledgement of service not more than 14 days after service of the claim form. Again, instead of serving a defence, the defendant has to file and serve their written evidence with the acknowledgement of service.

If the defendant fails to file an acknowledgement of service, the claimant is unable to obtain a default judgment, and the defendant may still attend the hearing of the claim. However, the defendant may not take part in the hearing unless the court gives permission.

The court may give directions, including a hearing date, when the claim form is issued, or otherwise as soon as practicable after the defendant has acknowledged service or the time for acknowledging service has expired.

All Part 8 claims are allocated to the multi-track.

As noted above, the Part 8 regime requires the parties to provide all their written evidence at the outset:

> However, it is common for the court to permit further evidence to be relied on and disclosure is also ordered on occasions … CPR 8.6(1)(b) permits the court to give permission for further written evidence to be relied on if the court gives permission. The rule undoubtedly contains a sanction although I have to say that in my experience the court adopts a pragmatic approach and will generally permit further written evidence to be relied on without requiring an application for relief from sanctions. The Part 8 procedure is used in a wide range of cases and is compulsory in claims that are very likely to require additional evidence beyond that permitted by CPR rule 8.5 which sets a very strict framework with the evidence 'front-loaded'. It will usually be right to permit further evidence to be filed. (per Chief Master Marsh in *Ball v Ball* [2020] EWHC 1020 (Ch) at [13])

CHAPTER 9

CASE MANAGEMENT AND ALLOCATION OF CASES

9.1	Introduction	133
9.2	The court's powers	133
9.3	Striking out a statement of case and other sanctions	134
9.4	Relief from sanctions	137
9.5	Allocation	138
9.6	Allocation to a track	142
9.7	Costs management	152
9.8	Overview of multi-track case and costs management	157

LEARNING OUTCOMES

After reading this chapter you will have learned:

- the circumstances in which a statement of case may be struck out
- the different types of sanctions the court may impose on a party
- how to get relief from a sanction
- the role of the directions questionnaire
- what influences the allocation of a case to a particular track
- what claims are typically dealt with on the small claims track
- the type of directions given on the fast track
- the standard fast track timetable
- the role of a case management conference on the multi-track
- how to draft a case summary for use at a case management conference
- the role of costs budgets.

9.1 INTRODUCTION

One of the key elements of the CPR 1998 is the notion of case management. As we saw in **Chapter 1**, r 1.4 imposes a duty on the court to manage cases actively.

Part 3 of CPR 1998 gives the court a wide range of case management powers. We shall look first at the court's general powers in r 3.1(2) and then consider the specific power to strike out a party's statement of case in r 3.4(2).

9.2 THE COURT'S POWERS

Rule 3.1(2) sets out a non-exclusive list of the court's powers, which include instructions that the court can:

(a) extend or shorten the time for compliance with any Rule, Practice Direction or court order (even if an application for extension is made after the time for compliance has expired);

(b) adjourn or bring forward a hearing;

(bb) require that any proceedings in the High Court be heard by a Divisional Court of the High Court;

(c) require a party or a party's legal representative to attend the court;

(d)   hold a hearing and receive evidence by telephone, or by using any other method of direct oral communication;

(e)   direct that part of any proceedings (such as a counterclaim) be dealt with as separate proceedings;

(f)   stay the whole or part of any proceedings or judgment either generally or until a specified date or event;

(g)   consolidate proceedings;

(h)   try two or more claims on the same occasion;

(i)   direct a separate trial of any issue;

(j)   decide the order in which issues are to be tried;

(k)   exclude an issue from consideration;

(l)   dismiss or give judgment on a claim after a decision on a preliminary issue;

(ll)   order any party to file and exchange a costs budget;

(m)   take any other step or make any other order for the purpose of managing the case and furthering the overriding objective, including hearing an early neutral evaluation with the aim of helping the parties settle the case.

The court may make any order subject to conditions and can specify the consequence of non-compliance, for example that a party pay a sum of money into court pending the outcome of the proceedings. In particular, by r 3.1(5), the court may make such an order if that party has, without good reason, failed to comply with a Rule, Practice Direction or a relevant pre-action protocol. In exercising its power under r 3.1(5), however, the court must have regard to both the amount in dispute and the costs the parties have incurred or may incur. By r 3.1(6A), any money paid into court stands as security for any sum payable by that party to any other party in the proceedings.

9.3   STRIKING OUT A STATEMENT OF CASE AND OTHER SANCTIONS

Rule 3.4(2) gives the court a specific power to strike out all or part of a statement of case.

The court can exercise this power if it appears to the court:

(a)   that the statement of case discloses no reasonable grounds for bringing or defending the claim;

(b)   that the statement of case is an abuse of the court's process or is otherwise likely to obstruct the just disposal of the proceedings; or

(c)   that there has been a failure to comply with a rule, practice direction or court order.

9.3.1   Inadequate statements of case

Practice Direction 3A gives examples of the types of statement of case that may fall to be struck out within (a) above. These include particulars of claim that set out no facts indicating what the claim is about – for example, 'money owed £5,000' – and particulars of claim that contain a coherent set of facts, but where those facts, even if true, do not disclose any legally recognisable claim against the defendant (claims that are 'doomed to failure': see *Miller v Sutton* (Court of Appeal, 14 February 2013)). As far as defences are concerned, it gives examples of a defence that consists of a bare denial or otherwise sets out no coherent statement of facts, or a defence that, whilst coherent, would not, even if true, amount in law to a defence to the claim.

Where a statement of case is defective but can be cured by amendment (see **7.6**), rather than strike it out, the court may give the party concerned an opportunity to amend it (see, for example, *Nash v 4MA Ltd* [2019] EWHC 3383 (TCC)).

> **EXAMPLE**
>
> A claimant issues proceedings for the recovery of a debt. A defence is filed that simply consists of a bare denial that the money is due. The defendant has therefore failed to comply with r 16.5 of CPR 1998 (see **Chapter 7**). The judge, when looking at the case, may, as part of their case management powers under Part 3, make an order that unless the defendant files a full defence setting out their reasons for denying that the debt is owed within seven days of service of the order, the defence will be struck out.

Note that the court may, as in the example given, make such an order of its own volition; or, alternatively, the claimant in such a case may make an application to the court for an order in similar terms.

If, in the example given above, the defendant did not comply with the order then the claimant would be able to obtain judgment simply by filing a request for judgment. As this was a debt claim, the claimant would be able to obtain judgment for the amount of the debt, together with interest and costs. If it had been a claim for an unspecified sum, the judgment would be for an amount to be decided by the court at a disposal hearing. Note that the request must state that the right to enter judgment has arisen because the court's order has not been obeyed. See generally **6.6**.

Continuing with the above example, if judgment is entered in these circumstances against the defendant, the defendant can apply to the court under r 3.6 for the judgment to be set aside. Such an application must be made not more than 14 days after the judgment has been served. If the judgment had been entered incorrectly (eg, prematurely), the court must set aside the judgment. However, if the judgment was entered correctly, r 3.9 (relief from sanctions) applies (see **9.4**).

9.3.2　Non-compliance with a Rule, Practice Direction or court order

The striking-out sanction is not confined to cases where the statement of case is defective. As stated in **9.3**, the court can also strike out a party's statement of case and enter judgment against the party for 'failure to comply with a Rule, Practice Direction or court order'.

Striking out is, however, only one of a number of sanctions that the court can apply (see **9.3.3**). How does the court decide what is appropriate? The starting point for decisions on sanctions for default is *Biguzzi v Rank Leisure plc* [1999] 1 WLR 1926. This was an early post-CPR case where the Court of Appeal emphasised the importance of compliance with the CPR 1998 and court orders, but recognised that, whilst it would, on occasions, be appropriate to deal with non-compliance by striking out, there were less drastic but equally effective ways of dealing with default. In many cases, the use of these other powers would produce a more just result.

Given that there is a range of sanctions that the court can apply, when will it apply the ultimate sanction of striking out? In each case, the court will have to consider all the circumstances, and in particular the factors relevant to r 3.9 (relief from sanctions: see **9.4**). However, the case law emphasises that the overriding objective of dealing with cases justly and the duty to ensure fairness will be a central consideration in the exercise of the court's discretion (see, eg, *Necati v Commissioner of Police for the Metropolis* [2001] LTL, 19 January). The court should also bear in mind the observations of the Court of Appeal in *Arrow Nominees Inc v Blackledge* [2000] 1 BCLC 709, that striking out a case purely on the basis of a breach of the rules or an order of the court may infringe Article 6(1) of the ECHR unless the breach itself meant that it may no longer be possible to have a fair trial.

None of the above should, however, be read as a reluctance on the part of the courts to strike out a party's statement of case in appropriate circumstances. Where delay or non-compliance means that it is no longer possible to have a fair trial (see *Habib Bank Ltd v Abbeypearl Ltd* [2001]

EWCA Civ 62, [2001] 1 All ER 185), or where the default is so bad that it amounts to an abuse of the court (see *UCB Corporate Services Ltd v Halifax (SW) Ltd* [1999] 1 Lloyd's Rep 154), strike out may be the appropriate response.

9.3.3 Sanctions other than striking out

9.3.3.1 Costs

A common sanction is to require the party in default to pay the other party's costs occasioned by the delay on an indemnity basis. The court will make a summary assessment of those costs at the time of the hearing and may order those costs to be paid immediately. The solicitor handling the case would then have to explain to the client why they had been ordered to pay those costs. See generally **10.3** and **14.3.3.2**.

Where the court forms the view that the fault lies not with the party themselves but with their legal representative, the court may make a wasted costs order. This obliges the legal representative to pay costs incurred by a party as a result of any improper, unreasonable or negligent act or omission on the part of the legal representative (SCA 1981, s 51). Before making such an order, the court must allow the legal representative a reasonable opportunity to attend a hearing and give reasons why the order should not be granted.

9.3.3.2 Interest

Alternatively, the court may make orders affecting the interest payable on any damages subsequently awarded to the claimant. If the party at fault is the claimant, the court may reduce the amount of interest payable on their damages. If the party in default is the defendant, the interest payable on the claimant's damages at the end of the case may be increased.

9.3.3.3 Limiting the issues

The appropriate sanction may be to limit the issues that are allowed to proceed to trial. See, for example, *AXA Insurance Co Ltd v Swire Fraser* (2000) *The Times*, 19 January.

9.3.4 The unless order

If a party has not taken a step in the proceedings in accordance with a court order, what should the other party do? It will serve the overriding objective (see **1.1**) first to chase up the defaulting party promptly in correspondence. If that does not work, an application should be made to the court for an 'unless order'. This is reflected in fast track and multi-track proceedings, where, for example, a party fails to follow a case management direction. Practice Directions 28 (paras 5.1 and 5.2) and 29 (paras 7.1 and 7.2) both provide in these circumstances that

> [w]here a party has failed to comply with a direction given by the court any other party may apply for an order to enforce compliance or for a sanction to be imposed or both of these.

The party entitled to apply for such an order must do so without delay, but should first warn the other party of their intention to do so.

The unless order is not, strictly speaking, a sanction but rather a suspended sanction. The court makes an order that unless a party complies with a particular court order or rule within a specified time, their claim or defence will be struck out.

A party who is subject to an unless order but who cannot make the deadline set should apply to the court before that deadline expires to extend it. Why? Because the strike out takes effect without any further court order (see PD 3A, para 1.9).

> **EXAMPLE**
>
> Although an order of the court required the defendant, D, to serve their witness statements on their opponent, C, by a specific date, D did not do so despite reminders from C. In order to force D to comply, C applies for and obtains an unless order requiring D to serve the witness statements by a new deadline (usually seven or 14 days from the date of the unless order), failing which D's defence will be struck out.

9.4 RELIEF FROM SANCTIONS

A party's ability to obtain relief from the sanctions imposed by the court is dealt with by rr 3.8 and 3.9.

Where a party has failed to comply with a Rule, Practice Direction or court order, any sanction for failure to comply imposed by the Rule, Practice Direction or court order has effect unless the party in default applies for and obtains relief from the sanction. Note that where the sanction is the payment of costs, the party in default may obtain relief only by appealing against the order for costs.

Where a Rule, Practice Direction or court order requires a party to do something within a specified time, and specifies the consequence of failure to comply, can the time for doing the act in question be extended by agreement between the parties? Yes, unless the court has ordered otherwise or it would put at risk any hearing date, the parties may by prior written agreement agree an extension up to a maximum of 28 days (r 3.8(4)).

9.4.1 Relevant factors

By r 3.9(1), where a party applies for relief from any sanction for failure to comply with any rule, practice direction or court order, the court will consider all the circumstances of the case, so as to enable it to deal justly with the application, including the need:

(a)   for litigation to be conducted efficiently and at proportionate cost; and

(b)   to enforce compliance with rules, practice directions and orders.

It is clear from the wording of this provision that the court will take a robust view of any application.

How should the court approach the application? The test was established in *Denton v TH White Ltd* [2014] EWCA Civ 906 as follows:

(a)   The first stage is to identify and assess the seriousness or significance of the relevant failure. If a breach was not serious or significant, relief would usually be granted and there would be no need to spend much time on the second and third stages.

(b)   The second stage is to consider why the failure or default occurred.

(c)   The third stage is to evaluate 'all the circumstances of the case, so as to enable [the court] to deal justly with the application'.

In carrying out the first stage test, the court usually concentrates on an assessment of the seriousness and significance of the very breach in respect of which relief from sanctions is sought. The court normally considers as one of the relevant circumstances of the case the defaulter's previous conduct in the litigation, including any non-compliance with court orders. However, this approach was qualified in *British Gas Trading Ltd v Oak Cash & Carry Ltd* [2016] EWCA Civ 153. Where the breach consists of failure to comply with an unless order (see **9.3.4**) which was itself made as a result of a failure to comply with one or more previous orders, the assessment of seriousness should take account of the previous failure(s) as well as the failure to comply with the unless order itself.

If a judge concludes that a breach is not serious or significant, then relief from sanctions will usually be granted and it is normally unnecessary to spend much time on the second or third stages. If, however, the court decides that the breach is serious or significant, then the second and third stages assume greater importance.

The court also warned that a party might be penalised if they sought to take advantage of a mistake by an opponent where the failure was neither serious nor significant, a good reason could be demonstrated and it was obvious that relief from sanctions would be appropriate. Opposing an application for relief would be viewed as a breach of r 1.3, which requires parties to help the court to further the overriding objective. In such cases, the parties should be ready to agree reasonable extensions of up to 28 days under r 3.8(4).

In *Davies Solicitors LLP v Rajah* [2015] EWHC 519 (QB), it was stated that breaches which affect the effective timetabling of cases are likely to be considered significant. However, in *Marchment v Frederick Wise Ltd* [2015] EWHC 1770 (QB), relief was granted where the trial date had to be vacated when the claimant failed to serve a report on time. It was accepted that the breach was serious and there was no good reason. Failure to meet the trial date if relief was granted would be determinative in the majority of cases but, applying stage 3 of the *Denton* test and taking into account the facts that the trial was short and could be relisted within a reasonable time and other cases could be listed so there was no negative effect on public resources, the court granted relief.

Lack of promptness in applying for relief may often be a critical factor: see *Durrant v Chief Constable of Avon and Somerset Constabulary* [2013] EWCA Civ 1624 and *British Gas Trading Ltd v Oak Cash & Carry Ltd* [2016] EWCA Civ 153.

The factors considered by the court prior to April 2013 when considering applications for relief under r 3.9 are now subsidiary considerations to the overriding objective factors set out in the new r 3.9, but may be relevant to whether there was a 'good reason'. The witness statement accompanying the application might therefore explain matters such as:

(a)   why the failure occurred;

      A party who is seeking relief from sanction can be expected to come before the court with a full explanation of how the need for the application comes about. It is not for the parties' advocate to have to postulate matters that are not verified in evidence on a central issue, where the party is seeking the court's indulgence. (per HHJ Pearce in *Rapid Displays Inc v Ahkye* [2022] EWHC 274 (Comm) at [129])

(b)   the extent to which the party has otherwise complied with other rules, practice directions, court orders and any relevant pre-action protocol;

(c)   whether the failure to comply was caused by the party or their legal representative;

(d)   whether the trial date or the likely trial date can still be met if relief is granted;

(e)   the effect which the failure to comply has had on each party; and

(f)   the effect which the granting of relief will have on each party.

9.5 ALLOCATION

Part 26 of CPR 1998 deals with the preliminary stage of case management when cases are allocated to a particular track. This stage of case management arises where a defence has been filed.

Where the claim is defended then, on receipt of the defence, the court provisionally decides the appropriate track for the claim and serves on each party a notice of the proposed allocation (Form 149A: small claims; Form N149B: fast track; and Form N149C: multi-track). As to the factors affecting allocation, see **9.6**.

The notice of proposed allocation requires the parties to file and serve their answers to a questionnaire, known as the directions questionnaire. This is usually in Form N181, and a copy appears in **Appendix A(7)**. However, if the claim has provisionally been allocated to the small claims track, a slightly different form, N180, must be used. Note that the rest of this chapter will focus on the usual questionnaire Form N181.

Does the court send the directions questionnaire to each party? No, only if a party is unrepresented. Otherwise the parties' legal representatives should obtain the questionnaire themselves. It is available on HM Courts & Tribunals Service website (see **1.5**).

The notice of proposed allocation will state the date for return of the directions questionnaire and the address of the court or court office to which it should be sent.

Note that where a claim has been provisionally allocated to the multi-track, the following documents must also be prepared: a case summary, if a case management conference is to occur (see **9.6.3.2** and **9.6.3.4**), a disclosure report (see **11.3.3.1**), a costs budget and budget discussion report (see **9.7**). In all cases a draft order for directions should accompany the directions questionnaire (see **9.5.1.10**).

9.5.1 Completing the directions questionnaire

The directions questionnaire (Form N181) is a key document in the progress of a case and must be completed carefully by each party and filed by the set date. The parties should consult one another and cooperate in completing the questionnaire, although this must not delay its filing. Indeed, r 26.3(6A) provides that the date for filing cannot be varied by agreement between the parties. The form is divided into 10 parts, lettered A to J.

9.5.1.1 Part A Settlement

Part A deals with settlement. The parties are reminded that under the CPR 1998 every effort should be made to settle the case and that the court will enquire as to what steps have already been taken in that respect. To assist the court a solicitor must confirm (by ticking a box) that they have explained to the client the need to try to settle, the options available and the possibility of costs sanctions if the client refused to do so. Moreover, it is made clear to the parties that their answers to this part will be taken into account when the court decides who pays costs and the amount of those costs (see **14.3**). The parties must then indicate whether or not they want to attempt to settle at this stage. If a party answers yes, the next question asks the parties if they wish there to be a one-month stay of proceedings so that they can attempt to settle the case. If all the parties request a stay, the court will order a stay of one month (r 26.4(2)). Alternatively, the court, of its own initiative whether or not any party has requested it, may order a stay of any length if it considers it appropriate. If a stay is granted and the parties feel they require more time than the initial period granted to try to reach a settlement, any of the parties may, by letter to the court, request an extension of time. More than one extension of the stay may be granted. If a settlement is reached, the claimant must tell the court. If a settlement is not reached, the court will allocate the case and give directions in the usual way. Note that in Part A the parties can request the court to arrange a mediation appointment. If a party has indicated in Part A that they do not want to attempt to settle the case, they will have to set out their reasons why they consider it inappropriate at this stage.

9.5.1.2 Part B Court

Part B asks the parties whether there is any reason why the case needs to be heard at a particular court. If the claim has been issued in the Central Office of the Royal Courts of Justice (RCJ), each party should state whether they consider the claim should be managed and tried at the RCJ and, if so, why. As set out in para 2.6 of PD 29, claims suitable for trial in the RCJ include:

    (1)   professional negligence claims,

    (2)   Fatal Accident Act claims,

    (3)   fraud or undue influence claims,

    (4)   defamation claims,

(5)   claims for malicious prosecution or false imprisonment,

(6)   claims against the police,

(7)   contentious probate claims.

9.5.1.3   Part C Pre-action protocols

Part C of the questionnaire asks the parties to state whether they have complied with the Practice Direction on Pre-Action Conduct or any relevant pre-action protocol and, if not, to explain the reasons why.

9.5.1.4   Part D Case management information

Part D asks the parties if they have made an application to the court, including an application for summary judgment (see **Chapter 10**) or to join another party into the proceedings. Any such application should be made as soon as possible. If a party does not agree with the provisional allocation of the case, they should now set out their objections and reasons for allocating the claim to a different track.

The basic criteria for allocation to a particular track is the value of the claim which is in dispute, disregarding interest, costs and any question of contributory negligence. If there is a counterclaim or additional claim, in assessing the value the court will not usually aggregate the claims but generally will regard the largest of the claims as determining the financial value of the claim. So, for example, if the original claim was for £20,000, but there is a counterclaim valued at £35,000, the latter figure will usually be the relevant one for allocation purposes (PD 26, para 7.7).

If allocation to the multi-track is requested, the parties must state whether they have reached agreement about the disclosure of electronic documents (see **11.6.2**) either using the Electronic Disclosure Questionnaire in PD 31B or otherwise. If no agreement has been reached, they should state the issues to be decided and whether they can be dealt with at a case management conference (see **9.6.3.2**) or whether a separate hearing is required. The parties must then state what directions are proposed as to the disclosure of non-electronic documents, whether or not disclosure reports have been served and whether they have agreed a proposal in relation to disclosure that meets the overriding objective (see further **11.3**).

9.5.1.5   Part E Experts

The parties should indicate at Part E if they wish to rely on expert evidence at the trial, whether they have already provided any other party with a copy of an expert's report and whether they consider a single joint expert might be appointed. Any proposed expert must be named or their field of expertise identified. The likely cost of the expert's evidence must be stated. See further **12.13**.

9.5.1.6   Part F Witnesses

Part F asks the parties to name the witnesses of fact they intend to call at trial and identify the facts each witness will address. As the question concerns witnesses at trial, it may not be possible or desirable at this stage to put a name to all possible witnesses. A party may well not have interviewed all potential witnesses yet, or may be uncertain which witnesses to rely on in respect of particular facts in dispute. If a party does not wish to, or cannot, 'name names' at this stage, they can simply indicate the number of witnesses they may call on a particular fact. This practice is arguably consistent with the overriding objective and the court's duty to manage the case (see **1.1.1** and **1.1.3**). By the pre-trial stage, the court may well be in a position to direct which witnesses may be called or whose written evidence may be read (see **12.1.2**). But at this early point in the proceedings, the court is likely to consider only any necessary cap on the number of witnesses by a suitable direction such as 'Evidence of fact is limited to xx witnesses on behalf of each party.'

EXAMPLE – PART F: WITNESSES	
<u>Witness name</u>	<u>Witness to which facts</u>
Richard Williams	Telephone call placing order
1–2	Installation of system
Anne Freeman & 2 others	Defects in system
Janette Lee & 1 other	Damage and loss

9.5.1.7   Part G Trial

Here the parties must give a realistic estimate of how long the trial will last, including time for the judge to read the papers and give judgment.

9.5.1.8   Part H Costs

If a party is legally represented and the case is likely to be allocated to the multi-track, their legal advisers must normally file and serve a costs budget (see **9.7**). For the consequences of failing to file a costs budget by the required date, see **9.4.1** and also **9.7.1**.

9.5.1.9   Part I Other Information

If a party intends to make any application to the court in the immediate future, they must state its purpose.

Parties can then set out any other information they consider will help the judge to manage the claim.

9.5.1.10   Part J Directions

The parties should attempt to agree proposed directions, but whether agreed or not a draft order for directions must accompany the questionnaire.

All proposed directions for multi-track cases must be based on the specimen directions that appear on the Ministry of Justice's website. These appear as a menu of model paragraphs, grouped under the following categories:

*   A selection of headings
*   Allocation, docketing, Alternative dispute resolution
*   Before case management
*   Case management directions
*   Documents
*   Evidence of fact
*   Expert evidence
*   Paper Order Direction
*   Pre-trial
*   Restriction on Extension of Timetable
*   Schedules of loss
*   Trial

All proposed directions for fast track cases must be based on CPR, Part 28. See **Appendix A(8)**.

9.5.2   Transfer of money claims

Rule 26.2 provides for the automatic transfer of High Court proceedings where the claim is for a specified amount of money, the defendant is an individual and the claim was commenced in a court that is not the defendant's home court and the claim has not been transferred to another defendant's home court. When a defence is filed, the claim will be sent to the defendant's home court – this will be the hearing centre serving the address where the defendant resides or carries on business.

Rule 26.2A provides for transfer of money claims within the County Court. If the claim is referred to a judge for directions, a court officer may transfer the proceedings to the defendant's home court, the preferred hearing centre or another County Court hearing centre. If the defendant is an individual and the claim is for a specified sum of money, the claim must be sent to the defendant's home court when the parties have filed their directions questionnaires or any stay ordered by the court to attempt settlement has expired. If there are two or more defendants and one or more is an individual, the proceedings will be transferred to the home court of the defendant who filed their defence first.

Note that if proceedings are transferred, the court in which the proceedings commenced will serve the notice of proposed allocation before the proceedings are transferred and will not transfer the proceedings until all parties have complied with the notice or the time for doing so has expired.

A defendant to a money claim who is an individual may request that the proceedings are transferred to a County Court hearing centre that is not their home court.

9.5.3 Failure to file directions questionnaire

9.5.3.1 County Court Money Claim

If a claim is a claim to which r 26.2A applies and any party does not comply with the notice of proposed allocation (see **9.5.1**) by the date specified, the court will serve a further notice on that party, requiring them to comply within seven days. If that party fails to comply with the second notice, the party's statement of case is struck out automatically, without further order of the court.

9.5.3.2 All other claims

In all other cases, if a party does not comply with the notice of proposed allocation by the date specified, the court will make such order as it considers appropriate. This may include: (i) an order for directions; (ii) an order striking out the claim; (iii) an order striking out the defence and entering judgment; or (iv) listing the case for a case management conference.

9.5.4 Scrutinising your opponent's questionnaire

The parties must exchange questionnaires. What should you look for in your opponent's questionnaire? Pay particular attention to Part C and check that the answers are accurate. As to Part F, see how many witnesses of fact your opponent has and if any witnesses have been named. Should you consider interviewing any that are named? Then check your opponent's views on expert evidence. Is anything new revealed in Part E? Review what is said about electronic and other documents in Part D. Then check Part G and your opponent's costs in Part H (see **9.7**). Finally, see if your opponent supplied any additional information at Part I.

9.6 ALLOCATION TO A TRACK

How is a case allocated to one of the three tracks? Generally, the most important factor in allocation will be the financial value of the claim.

Claims not exceeding £10,000 will normally be allocated to the small claims track.

Claims between £10,000 and £25,000 will normally be allocated to the fast track.

Claims exceeding £25,000 will normally be allocated to the multi-track.

Rule 26.8(1) sets out the factors to which the court must have regard, including:

   (a)   the value, if any, of the claim;

(b) the nature of the remedy sought;

(c) the likely complexity of the facts, law or evidence;

(d) the number of parties or likely parties;

(e) the value of any counterclaim or other Part 20 claim and the complexity of any matters relating to it;

(f) the amount of oral evidence which may be required;

(g) the importance of the claim to persons who are not parties to the proceedings;

(h) the views expressed by the parties; and

(i) the circumstances of the parties.

By r 26.8(2), when the court calculates the value of a money claim, it will disregard:

(a) any amount not in dispute;

(b) any claim for interest;

(c) costs; and

(d) any contributory negligence.

The value of a claim is fundamental to the question of which is the normal track for allocation, although it is not necessarily determinative of the question of allocation in any particular case. Further, the question of what is proportionate necessarily involves consideration not only of complexity and trial-length but also of value. (*Elias v Blemain Finance Ltd* [2021] EW Misc 15 (CC) per HHJ Keyser QC at [16])

What if case involves more than one claim for money, eg a claim and counterclaim – should these be added together? No, states PD 26, para 7.7. The court will not generally aggregate the claims. Instead it will usually regard the largest of them as determining the value of the claims for allocation purposes.

Furthermore, the fast track is the normal track for claims with a value exceeding £10,000, but not £25,000, only if the trial is likely to last for no longer than one day; oral expert evidence at trial will be limited to no more than one expert per party in relation to any expert field and there will be expert evidence in no more than two expert fields. For example, if the court at the allocation stage considered that the trial was likely to last two days then the court will usually allocate it to the multi-track.

By PD 26, para 8.1(2), the court may allocate a claim to the small claims track even if it exceeds £10,000. The court will not normally allow more than one day for the hearing of such a claim.

Once all the parties have filed their completed directions questionnaires, a judge will allocate the case to a track and the court will serve notification on every party. The court may subsequently re-allocate a claim to a different track either on the application of any party, or on its own initiative.

If a party is dissatisfied with the allocation to a particular track, PD 26, para 11 provides that they may:

(a) appeal, if the order was made at a hearing at which they were present or represented, or of which they were given due notice; or

(b) in any other case (eg, the case was allocated without an allocation hearing), apply to the court to re-allocate the claim.

9.6.1 Allocation to the small claims track (Part 27)

Part 27 of CPR 1998 deals with allocation to the small claims track. The small claims track is designed to provide a procedure whereby claims of not more than £10,000 in value can be dealt with quickly and at minimal cost to the parties.

Note that PD 26, para 8.1(1) provides as follows:

(a)   The small claims track is intended to provide a proportionate procedure by which most straightforward claims with a financial value of not more than £10,000 can be decided, without the need for substantial pre-hearing preparation and the formalities of a traditional trial, and without incurring large legal costs.

(b)   The procedures laid down in Part 27 for the preparation of the case and the conduct of the hearing are designed to make it possible for a litigant to conduct their own case without legal representation if they wish.

(c)   Cases generally suitable for the small claims track will include consumer disputes, accident claims, disputes about the ownership of goods, and most disputes between a landlord and tenant other than those for possession.

(d)   A case involving a disputed allegation of dishonesty will not usually be suitable for the small claims track.

All claims other than road traffic accidents, personal injury or housing disrepair will be referred to the Small Claims Mediation Service if all parties consent to referral in their directions questionnaire. If the claim is settled following referral, the proceedings will be automatically stayed (r 26.4A(5)), but if the court has not been notified in writing that a settlement has been agreed within four weeks of the date on which the last directions questionnaire was filed, the claim will be allocated to a track (r 26.5(2A)).

In most small claims cases, the court will order standard directions and fix a date for the final hearing. The court does have the power to hold a preliminary hearing, but this will happen only in a very limited number of cases. Certain parts of the CPR 1998 do not apply to small claims, including Part 18 (Further Information), Part 31 (Disclosure and Inspection), Part 32 (Evidence), most of Part 35 (Experts and Assessors) and Part 36 (Offers to Settle), unless the court orders otherwise. But note that by r 27.2(3), the court may of its own initiative order a party to provide further information. The intention is to make the procedure as simple as possible because, in most cases, solicitors will not be involved. The reason for this is that, under r 27.14, the costs which can be recovered by a successful party are extremely limited, and therefore it is usually uneconomic for solicitors to represent the parties in a case proceeding on the small claims track.

The standard directions that the court gives in small claims cases are set out in various forms which are in the Appendices to PD 27 of CPR 1998. The directions vary depending on the type of case, so that there are particular directions for claims arising out of road accident cases, building disputes, goods sold, amongst others. The simplest forms of directions, as set out in Appendix B, are as follows:

1   Each party shall deliver to every other party and to the court office copies of all documents (including any expert's report) on which he intends to rely at the hearing no later than [   ] [14 days before the hearing].

2   The original documents shall be brought to the hearing.

3   [Notice of hearing date and time allowed.]

4   The court must be informed immediately if the case is settled by agreement before the hearing date.

5   No party may rely at the hearing on any report from an expert unless express permission has been granted by the court beforehand. Anyone wishing to rely on an expert must write to the court immediately on receipt of this Order and seek permission, giving an explanation why the assistance of an expert is necessary.

The hearing itself will be informal and, if all parties agree, the court can deal with the claim without a hearing at all. In other words, a court could make a decision based on the statements of case and documents submitted rather than by hearing oral evidence.

As mentioned earlier, the costs that can be recovered in a small claims case are limited by r 27.14. Generally speaking, the only costs recoverable are the fixed costs attributable to issuing the claim, any court fees paid and sums to represent travelling expenses and loss of earnings or leave. On those (rare) occasions where expert evidence is called, a limited amount may be recovered in respect of the expert's fees. The court does have power to award further costs if a party has behaved unreasonably.

9.6.2 Allocation to the fast track (Part 28)

When a case is allocated to the fast track, the court will give directions as to how the case is to proceed to trial. In most cases, the court will allocate the case to this track without a hearing and order standard directions.

9.6.2.1 Timetable of directions

Paragraph 3.12 of PD 28 (The Fast Track) sets out a typical timetable for case preparation of a case allocated to the fast track:

Disclosure	4 weeks
Exchange of witness statements	10 weeks
Exchange of experts' reports	14 weeks
Court sends pre-trial checklist, listing questionnaires	20 weeks
Parties file pre-trial checklists, listing questionnaires	22 weeks
Hearing	30 weeks

These periods will run from the date of allocation.

When the court gives directions, it will either fix the date of the trial or fix a period of up to three weeks within which the trial is to take place. Unless there are exceptional circumstances, the court will then give at least three weeks' notice of the trial date.

The parties may agree directions between themselves, but if they do so, the directions must be approved by the court (which will not necessarily accept them).

Fast track standard directions, dealing with disclosure, etc, are set out in the Appendix to PD 28. A copy appears at **Appendix A(8)**.

9.6.2.2 Varying directions (r 28.4)

Although the parties can vary certain directions by written agreement, for example for disclosure or exchange of witness statements, an application must be made to the court if a party wishes to vary the dates for:

(a)   the return of a pre-trial checklist;

(b)   the trial; or

(c)   the trial period.

Furthermore, the parties cannot agree to vary any matter if the change would lead to an alteration of any of those dates. For example, it would not be possible to agree to delay the exchange of witness statements until after the date for the return of the pre-trial checklist, since this would inevitably lead to the need to alter the trial date or period.

Practice Direction 28 states that any party who wishes to have a direction varied should take steps to do so as soon as possible (para 4.2(1)). There is an assumption that if an application to vary directions is not made within 14 days of the service of the order then the parties are content that the directions were correct in the circumstances then existing (para 4.2(2)).

A party dissatisfied with a direction or other order given by the court should either:

(a)   appeal, if the direction was given or the order was made at a hearing at which they were present or represented, or of which they had due notice; or

(b)   in any other case, apply to the court to reconsider its decision. Such an application would be heard by the same judge or same level of judge as gave the original decision.

9.6.2.3   Variation by consent (PD 28, para 4.5)

Where the agreement to vary relates to an act that does not need the court's consent, the parties need not file their written agreement to vary (which will usually be recorded in correspondence). In any other case, the party must apply to the court for an order by consent. The parties must file a draft of the order sought and an agreed statement of the reasons why the variation is sought. The court may make an order in the agreed terms, or in other terms, without a hearing, but it may well direct that a hearing is to occur.

9.6.2.4   Failure to comply with directions (PD 28, para 5)

If a party fails to comply with a direction, any other party may apply for an order enforcing compliance and/or for a sanction to be imposed (see **9.3.2**).

The application should be made without delay.

Practice Direction 28 is quite clear that a failure to comply with directions will not normally lead to a postponement of the trial date (see para 5.4(1)). This will not be allowed unless the circumstances of the case are exceptional.

If it is practical, the court will exercise its powers in a manner that enables the case to come up for trial on the date or within the period previously set. In particular, the court will assess what steps each party should take to prepare the case for trial, direct that those steps be taken in the shortest possible time and impose a sanction for non-compliance. Such a sanction may, for example, deprive a party of the right to raise or contest an issue, or to rely on evidence to which the direction relates.

Further, if the court is of the view that one or more issues can be made ready for trial within the time fixed, the court may direct that the trial will proceed on the issues which are, or will then be, ready. The court can also order that no costs will be allowed for any later trial of the remaining issues, or that those costs will be paid by the party in default. If the court has no option but to postpone the trial, it will do so for the shortest possible time and will give directions for the taking of all outstanding necessary steps as rapidly as possible.

It is clear, therefore, that the trial date is sacrosanct, and the parties should ensure that they are ready for trial on the due date.

9.6.2.5   Directions as to exchange of witness statements and exchange of expert reports

We shall look in detail at evidence in **Chapter 12**. However, the evidence of those witnesses on whom a party intends to rely at trial must be exchanged in the form of witness statements and experts' reports. The exchange should normally be simultaneous.

So far as expert evidence is concerned, the direction in relation to the evidence will say whether it gives permission for oral evidence, or written reports or both, and will usually name the experts concerned or the fields of expertise. The court will not make a direction giving permission for an expert to give oral evidence unless it believes that it is necessary in the interests of justice to do so (PD 28, para 7.2(4)(b) and r 35.5(2)). In fast track cases, therefore, the usual provision will be for expert evidence to be given by means of written reports, and experts will not be allowed to give oral evidence at the trial. Furthermore, the court may order that a single joint expert be appointed, rather than allowing each party to appoint its own.

9.6.2.6   The pre-trial checklist (PD 28, para 6)

The purpose of the pre-trial checklist is to check that directions have been complied with so that the court can fix a date for the trial (or confirm the date if one has already been fixed).

The directions order will specify a date by which the parties should return the pre-trial checklist. This date will be not later than eight weeks before the trial date or the start of the trial period. The pre-trial checklist will have been sent to the parties at least two weeks before it has to be filed at court. A copy of the pre-trial checklist (Form N170) appears at **Appendix A(15)**. Parties are encouraged to exchange copies of the pre-trial checklist before filing them with the court.

If no party files a pre-trial checklist, the court will direct that any claim, defence or counterclaim will be struck out unless a pre-trial checklist is filed within seven days. If some, but not all, parties have filed a pre-trial checklist, the court will give its normal listing directions or may hold a hearing (see **9.6.2.7** below).

9.6.2.7 Listing directions (PD 28, para 7)

The court will confirm or fix the date, length and place of the trial. The court will normally give the parties at least three weeks' notice of the trial.

The parties should try to agree directions. The agreed directions should deal with, among other things:

(a)   evidence;

(b)   a trial timetable and time estimate;

(c)   preparation of a trial bundle (see below).

The court may fix a listing hearing on three days' notice if either:

(a)   a party has failed to file the pre-trial checklist; or

(b)   a party has filed an incomplete pre-trial checklist; or

(c)   a hearing is needed to decide what directions for trial are appropriate.

Prior to the trial, the parties should try to agree the contents of the trial bundle (see **14.1.3**) which will contain all documents needed for use at the trial. The standard directions require that this bundle should be lodged with the court by the claimant not more than seven days and not less than three days before the start of the trial. Included in the bundle should be a case summary, not exceeding 250 words, outlining the matters still in issue, and referring, where appropriate, to the relevant documents. This is designed to assist the judge in reading the papers before the trial. The case summary should be agreed by the parties if possible.

9.6.3 Allocation to the multi-track (Part 29)

9.6.3.1 Directions

Cases which have a value of more than £25,000 will, as we have seen, usually be allocated to the multi-track. The multi-track therefore includes an enormously wide range of cases, from the fairly straightforward to the most complex and weighty matters involving claims for millions of pounds and multi-party claims. Case management on the multi-track has to reflect this wide diversity of claims. In straightforward cases, the standard directions, which we have already looked at in relation to the fast track, may be perfectly adequate, but in more complex cases the court will need to adapt the directions to the particular needs of the case.

When the matter is allocated to the multi-track, the court will either:

(a)   give directions for the management of the case and set a timetable for the steps to be taken between the giving of directions and the trial; or

(b)   fix a case management conference, or a pre-trial review or both and give such directions relating to the management of the case as it sees fit.

The court will fix the trial date or the week which the trial is to begin as soon as practicable. There is no deadline, however, of 30 weeks as we saw in the fast track (see **9.6.2.1**). The parties will be given confirmation by the court of the day or week in which the trial will begin following the filing of the pre-trial checklist, any listing hearing or any pre-trial review.

In a fairly straightforward case, the court may well give directions without holding a case management conference. If it does so, then, by para 4.10 of PD 29, its general approach will be:

(1)   to give directions for the filing and service of any further information required to clarify either party's case,

(2)   to direct standard disclosure between the parties,

(3)   to direct the disclosure of witness statements by way of simultaneous exchange,

(4)   to give directions for a single joint expert on any appropriate issue unless there is a good reason not to do so,

(5)   ... to direct disclosure of experts' reports by way of simultaneous exchange on those issues where a single joint expert is not directed,

(6)   if experts' reports are not agreed, to direct a discussion between experts ... and the preparation of a statement ...

(7)   to list a case management conference to take place after the date for compliance with the directions,

(8)   to specify a trial period; and

(9)   in such cases as the court thinks appropriate, the court may give directions requiring the parties to consider ADR. Such directions may be, for example, in the following terms:

'The parties shall by [date] consider whether the case is capable of resolution by ADR. If any party considers that the case is unsuitable for resolution by ADR, that party shall be prepared to justify that decision at the conclusion of the trial, should the judge consider that such means of resolution were appropriate, when he is considering the appropriate costs order to make.

The party considering the case unsuitable for ADR shall, not less than 28 days before the commencement of the trial, file with the court a witness statement without prejudice save as to costs, giving reasons upon which they rely for saying that the case was unsuitable.'

When drafting case management directions, the parties and the court will take as their starting point any relevant model directions and standard directions, which can be found online at <http://www.justice.gov.uk/courts/procedure-rules/civil/standard-directions>, and adapt them as appropriate to the circumstances of the particular case.

It is usual for the last direction to require the parties to 'inform the court immediately if the claim is settled whether or not it is then possible to file a draft consent order to give effect to their agreement'. This is in accordance with the overriding objective, and in particular the principles of saving expense and allotting to a case only an appropriate share of the court's resources (see **1.1.1**).

CASE STUDY: DIRECTIONS ORDER

A directions order made in the case study is provided at **Appendix D(9)**. You will note that this sets out a timetable of the steps the parties are required to take to prepare for the trial.

9.6.3.2   The case management conference

In many multi-track cases, the court will hold a case management conference where it feels that more of a 'hands on' approach is needed.

At any case management conference, the court will (by para 5.1 to PD 29):

(1)   review the steps which the parties have taken in the preparation of the case, and in particular their compliance with any directions that the court may have given,

(2)   decide and give directions about the steps which are to be taken to secure the progress of the claim in accordance with the overriding objective, and

(3)   ensure as far as it can that all agreements that can be reached between the parties about the matters in issue and the conduct of the claim are made and recorded.

What topics are the court likely to consider at the case management conference? These are likely to include:

(a)   Whether each party has clearly stated their case, for example has the claimant made clear the claim they are bringing and the amount they are claiming, so that the other party can understand the case they have to meet? As we saw in **Chapter 1**, r 1.4(2)(b) requires the court to identify the issues in dispute at an early stage.

(b)   Whether any amendments are required to the claim, a statement of case or any other document.

(c)   What disclosure of documents, if any, is necessary.

(d)   What expert evidence is reasonably required, and how and when that evidence should be obtained and disclosed. Note that PD 29, para 5.5(1) provides that the court will not at this stage give permission for any party to rely on expert evidence unless the court can in its order either name an expert or state the relevant field of expertise. The court will also consider whether expert evidence is to be given orally or by the use of a report only at trial.

(e)   What factual evidence should be disclosed.

(f)   What arrangements should be made about the giving or clarification of further information and the putting of questions to experts.

(g)   Whether it will be just and will save costs to order a split trial (eg, on liability and quantum) or the trial of one of more preliminary issues.

In all cases, the court will set a timetable for the steps it decides are necessary to be taken.

The parties must endeavour to agree appropriate directions for the management of the proceedings and submit agreed directions, or their respective proposals, to the court at least seven days before any case management conference. Where the court approves agreed directions, or issues its own directions, the parties will be so notified by the court and the case management conference will be vacated.

9.6.3.3   Who should attend the case management conference?

Rule 29.3(2) provides that where a party has a legal representative, a representative familiar with the case and with sufficient authority to deal with any issues that are likely to arise must attend the case management conference. Practice Direction 29, para 5.2(2) further adds that the representative should be someone who is personally involved in the conduct of the case, and who has both the authority and information available to deal with any matter that may reasonably be expected to be dealt with at the hearing, including the fixing of the timetable, the identification of issues and matters of evidence.

Practice Direction 29, para 5.2(3) warns that where the inadequacy of the person attending, or of their instructions, leads to the adjournment of a hearing, the court will expect to make a wasted costs order, ie the solicitor or their firm will be made personally responsible for paying the costs incurred by other parties in preparing for and attending at the hearing that is adjourned.

The consequences of failing to send a properly prepared legal representative to a directions hearing were considered by the Court of Appeal in *Baron v Lovell* [1999] CPLR 630. The court will usually make an order imposing a sanction (see **9.3.2**) where the inadequacy of the person attending or their instructions leads to the adjournment of the conference. In this case, the court made a wasted costs order against the solicitor concerned personally.

As well as giving rise to potential breaches of the CPR 1998, sending a representative to attend the case management conference who is not familiar with the case or who has insufficient authority to deal with issues arising may also be in breach of the SRA Code of Conduct. It would not be in the client's best interests (Principle 7) and arguably it may prevent the proper administration of justice (Principle 1).

In the case of *Tarajan Overseas Ltd v Kaye* (2002) *The Times*, 22 January, the Court of Appeal stressed that if a judge requires a party to attend a case management conference then the individual must know about the dispute and have authority to make decisions. The Court stressed that it would be 'objectionable ... to make an order that a party should attend with a view to putting pressure on the party concerned to drop the proceedings altogether'. The Court also considered what the judge should do if they had ADR in mind. Tuckey LJ said:

> There is no doubt that the court, in exercising its case management powers, can order the attendance of a party: CPR 1998, r 3.1(2)(c). One good reason why this may be appropriate is to facilitate settlement if the court takes the view that the case before it is one which the parties should strive to settle. There would be nothing wrong either in requiring the attendance of a party with a view to making an ADR order which, of course, is not coercive but simply suspends the proceedings to enable the parties to explore (if they agree) the prospect of settlement with the assistance of an experienced mediator. Such an order is one which could be made however, and usually is made, without the attendance of any party.

Practice Direction 29 sets out, at para 5.6, guidelines as to how parties should prepare for the case management conference. They should:

(1)   ensure that all documents that the court is likely to ask to see (including witness statements and experts' reports) are brought to the hearing,

(2)   consider whether the parties should attend,

(3)   consider whether a case summary will be useful, and

(4)   consider what orders each wishes to be made and give notice of them to the other parties.

Any party who wishes to apply for an order that is not usually made at a case management conference should issue and serve their application in plenty of time if they know that the application will be opposed; and they should warn the court if the time allowed for the case management conference is likely to be insufficient for their application to be heard.

9.6.3.4   Case summary

In most multi-track cases a case summary will be prepared for any case management conference. What are the formalities? These are set out in PD 29, para 5.7(1), as follows.

The case summary:

(a)   should be designed to assist the court to understand and deal with the questions before it;

(b)   should set out a brief chronology of the claim, the issues of fact which are agreed or in dispute and the evidence needed to decide them;

(c)   should not normally exceed 500 words in length; and

(d)   should be prepared by the claimant and agreed with the other parties if possible.

It can be seen that the function of the case summary is to assist the judge to identify the issues in dispute between the parties and so help the judge determine how the case should progress to trial, eg what issues require expert evidence, what issues might be suitable for ADR, etc.

Remember, that when completing Part F of the directions questionnaire (see **9.5.1.6**) a party can either give the names of its likely witnesses (expert and/or non-expert), or simply state the number of likely witnesses and any expert's field of expertise. Exactly the same principles apply to the case summary. It may be that some witnesses of fact have yet to be traced or provide a proof of evidence, or the client is uncertain whether to rely on their evidence. It may be that there are so many witnesses that listing all their names is pointless. All the court needs is an indication of their number so that it can consider whether it is reasonable, give appropriate directions and start to think about the length of the trial. Likewise, a suitable expert may not yet have been found. However, as a bare minimum the likely number of experts and their field or fields of expertise should be given.

A template to help you draft a case summary is set out at **Appendix B(6)**.

CASE STUDY: CASE SUMMARY

A case summary for use at a case management conference can be found in the case study at **Appendix D(8)**. You will note that this follows the structure required by PD 29, para 5.7(1)(b). How have the parties formulated the issues in dispute in respect of the claim and counterclaim? They have taken into account the denials and non-admissions made in the defence (**Appendix D(5)**) and defence to counterclaim (**Appendix D(6)**). This skill is analysed at **7.5.1**.

9.6.3.5 Variation of directions (r 29.5)

A party must apply to the court if they wish to vary the date which the court has fixed for:

(a)   a case management conference;

(b)   a pre-trial review;

(c)   the return of a pre-trial checklist under r 29.6;

(d)   the trial; or

(e)   the trial period.

Just like the fast track, any date set by the court or the rules for doing any act may not be changed by the parties if the change would make it necessary to vary any of the dates mentioned above.

A party who wishes to vary a direction (eg, because of a change of circumstances) must apply as soon as possible. There is an assumption that if an application to vary directions was not made within 14 days of service of the directions order, the parties were content that the directions ordered were correct in the circumstances then existing.

A party who is dissatisfied with the direction may appeal, but if they were not notified of the hearing or were not present when it was made, they must apply for the court to reconsider, and the court will give all parties three days' notice of the hearing.

9.6.3.6 Non-compliance with directions (PD 29, para 7)

If a party fails to comply with a direction, any other party may apply for an order for compliance and/or for the imposition of a sanction. Any delay in making the application will be taken into account by the court.

As we saw in the fast track, the trial date is sacrosanct. The court will not allow failure to comply with directions to lead to the postponement of the trial, unless the circumstances are exceptional.

9.6.3.7 The pre-trial checklist (PD 29, para 8)

The date for filing the completed pre-trial checklist will be not later than eight weeks before the trial date or the start of the trial period and the checklists will have been served on the parties at least 14 days before that date. The parties are encouraged to exchange copies of the checklists before they file them. If none of the parties files a checklist, the court will order that the claim, the defence and any counterclaim will be struck out unless any party files a checklist within seven days of service of the order.

If only some of the parties have filed a checklist, the court will usually fix a listing hearing and give directions.

On receipt of the pre-trial checklists, the court may decide that it is necessary to hold a pre-trial review (or may decide to cancel one already listed). The court must give the parties at least seven days' notice of its decision. A pre-trial review will usually occur in any heavy case, particularly when the trial is likely to last longer than 10 days.

As soon as practicable after:

(a)   each party has filed a completed pre-trial checklist;

(b)   the court has held a listing hearing; or

(c)   the court has held a pre-trial review,

the court will:

(a)   set a timetable for the trial, unless a timetable has already been fixed or the court considers that it will be inappropriate to do so;

(b)   confirm the date for trial or the week within which the trial is to begin; and

(c)   notify the parties of the trial timetable (where one is fixed under this rule) and the date or trial period.

As with the fast track, the court will also order, on listing, that a trial bundle of documents be prepared.

9.6.3.8   Templates

Templates to help you draft case management directions can be found at **Appendix B(7)** and **(8)**.

9.7   COSTS MANAGEMENT

9.7.1   Costs budgets

Costs management is an adjunct to case management, whereby the court, with input from the parties, actively attempts to control the future costs of the case. How is that done? Chiefly by the parties providing budgets in a prescribed form of their own future costs, with those budgets being updated from time to time and submitted for agreement to the other parties and, when not agreed, to the court for approval.

The purpose of costs management is that the court should manage both the steps to be taken and the costs to be incurred by the parties to any proceedings, so as to further the overriding objective (see r 3.12(2) and **1.1.1**). In effect, the court makes a costs management order with a view to ensuring that future costs are reasonable and do not become disproportionate by determining what steps should be taken in the proceedings and at what expense.

In *Porter Capital Corp v Zulifkar Masters & Others* [2020] 7 WLUK 441, the third defendant sought relief from sanctions following its failure to file a costs budget in time where the costs it sought to include in the budget had already been incurred. Applying *Denton* (see **9.4.1**) and refusing relief, the court confirmed that the regime was to control future costs and not to approve costs that had already been incurred.

9.7.1.1   Scope

As we have seen, cases on the small claims and fast tracks usually proceed to trial without interim hearings. As a result, r 3.12(1) limits costs management to all multi-track cases where the amount of money claimed is less than £10 million (or contains a statement of value valuing the claim at less than £10 million).

Does a litigant in person have to prepare a budget? No, but they must be provided with a copy of the budget of any other party. Litigants in person are also not required to file a budget discussion report (see **9.7.1.4**).

9.7.1.2 Timing

The court will set the date for filing the costs budget when it sends out the notice of proposed allocation – see **9.5**. For claims of less than £50,000, this will be when the directions questionnaire is filed; for all other claims, it will be 21 days prior to the first case management conference (see **9.6.3.2**).

9.7.1.3 Contents of budget

What must a budget contain? Unless the court otherwise orders, a budget must be in the form of Precedent H annexed to PD 3E (there is a copy at **Appendix A(9)**). As you will note from the form, the budget gives a detailed breakdown of the costs and disbursements already incurred (pre-action and issue/statements of case), plus an estimate of future costs and the assumptions on which those are based for the case management, disclosure, evidence, pre-trial review, trial preparation and trial stages, along with any ADR or settlement discussions and contingencies. These are known as phases.

A budget must be verified by a statement of truth signed by a senior legal representative of the party.

Note that where a party's budgeted costs do not exceed £25,000 or the value of the claim is less than £50,000, the parties must only use the first page of Precedent H.

9.7.1.4 Budget discussion report

After the costs budgets have been filed and served, the parties should complete a budget discussion report in the form of Precedent R (there is a copy at **Appendix A(10)**). This must be filed no later than seven days before the first case management conference.

A budget discussion report must set out:

(a)   those figures that are agreed for each phase;

(b)   those figures that are not agreed for each phase; and

(c)   a brief summary of the grounds of dispute.

> [T]he introduction of Precedent R, which requires each party to comment on the cost budget of the other, has led to a great saving of time, because it has obliged the parties to adopt a realistic attitude to the budget of the other side, and has assisted in the identification of the real disputes between the parties on costs. However, even now, some parties seem to treat cost budgeting as a form of game, in which they can seek to exploit the cost budgeting rules in the hope of obtaining a tactical advantage over the other side. In extreme cases, this can lead one side to offer very low figures in their Precedent R, in the hope that the court may be tempted to calculate its own amount, somewhere between the wildly different sets of figures put forward by the parties. [That] is an abuse of the cost budgeting process. [There is a] critical need to ensure that the Precedent R process is carefully and properly adhered to by the parties to civil litigation. (per Coulson J in *Findcharm Ltd v Churchill Group Ltd* [2017] EWHC 1108 (TCC) at [2], [3], [9] and [12])

Where a budget or only some of the phases of a budget are agreed between all parties, the court will record the extent of that agreement. It is only an entire budget or phases of a budget that are not agreed between all parties that the court will review (see **9.7.2**).

9.7.1.5 Subsequent changes in budget figures

What if a party's budget changes? Once a costs budget has been approved by the court, it will be extremely difficult to persuade a court that inadequacies or mistakes in the budget's preparation should be subsequently revised or rectified (*Murray v Neil Dowlman Architecture Ltd* [2013] EWHC 872 (TCC)).

A party must revise its budget in respect of future costs, upwards or downwards, if significant developments occur in the litigation (r 3.15A). What is a significant development?

> Significance must be understood in light of the claim – its size, complexity and the manner in which the litigation has unfolded – and also from the likely additional costs that have been, or are expected to

be, incurred. The amount of the additional expense is not determinative, but it is difficult to conceive that a development leading to modest additional legal expenditure, that is modest in proportion to the amount in the relevant budget phase or phases, is likely to be significant development. (per Chief Master Marsh in *Sharp v Blank* [2017] EWHC 3390 (Ch) at [33])

The starting point for the process of revision is the last approved or agreed budget. The court may be satisfied that the figures in that budget are reasonable and proportionate; for example, where the court has undertaken a thorough review and made adjustments to the budgets the parties had put forward before approving them. Or it may be that where the budgets have been agreed, it is apparent that the sums claimed and agreed are for relatively modest amounts which can be readily justified. But that may not be the case. Parties sometimes agree each other's budgets in sums which do not appear to be either reasonable or proportionate. When an application is made to revise a budget upwards, it is open to the court to look at the existing budget to see not only whether the 'significant developments' relied upon have already been catered for, but also to consider the sums already agreed for the relevant phase so that it may consider whether the 'significant developments' put forward warrant a revision (see *Seekings v Moores* [2019] EWHC 1476 (Comm)).

In *Churchill v Boot* [2016] EWHC 1322 (QB), the court considered that the adjournment of the trial might in certain circumstances (but not on the facts of the case itself) constitute a significant development. In *JSC Mezhdunarodniy Promyshlenniy Bank v Pugachev* [2017] EWHC 1853 (Ch), the lengthening of the trial from 8.5 days to 10 days was treated as a significant development and the court approved an increase in the claimant's budget by £84,000. As the court pointed out, this was proportionate given that the overall approved budget stood at £1.8 million.

Any amended budget must use Precedent T (there is a copy at **Appendix A(23)**) and be submitted to the other parties for agreement (PD 3E, para B.3). The budget must then be submitted to the court with an explanation (if not agreed) of the points of difference. The court may approve, vary or disallow the proposed variations, having regard to any significant developments that have occurred since the date when the previous budget was approved or agreed.

9.7.1.6   What if a party fails to comply with the direction to file its budget?

What are the consequences of not filing a budget by the set deadline or at all? Rule 3.14 provides that unless the court orders otherwise, any party who fails to file a budget despite being required to do so, will be treated as having filed a budget comprising only the applicable court fees: in effect, only the court fees incurred by the defaulting party may potentially be recoverable under a costs order in the future.

See further **9.4.1** as to obtaining relief from this sanction. A formal application should be made to be heard at the case management conference.

EXAMPLE

In *Intellimedia Systems Ltd v Richards* (2017) LTL 3/2/2017, during the proceedings, a date had been fixed for a case management conference. The defendants filed their costs budget. The claimant e-mailed the defendants to inform them that the solicitor with conduct of the case was ill and that there would be a delay filing the claimant's costs budget. When it was filed, it was late. Relief from the sanction was granted. Why? The breach was not trivial, as it had risked disrupting the case management conference and the conduct of the litigation, and had caused additional work for the defendants. The solicitor's illness could not excuse him from acting professionally, as he should either have delegated the responsibility or sent the client elsewhere. But the application had been made promptly, and in all the circumstances it was appropriate to grant relief. Although the claimant had been inefficient, the sanction was not a proportionate one in the case.

The sanction imposed by r 3.14 may subsequently be eased if the party subject to it later becomes entitled to costs under a relevant provision of CPR, Part 36 (see **13.4.12**).

9.7.1.7   What about the costs of preparing a budget?

Is the cost of preparing a budget potentially recoverable? Paragraph 2.2 of PD 3E makes it clear that, apart from exceptional circumstances, the recoverable costs of initially completing Precedent H cannot exceed the higher of £1,000 or 1% of the approved budget, and all other recoverable costs of the budgeting and costs management process cannot exceed 2% of the approved budget.

9.7.1.8   Relationship with costs capping

Note that a party can in very limited circumstances supplement costs management by applying for a costs capping order: see **10.3.6**.

9.7.2   Judicial approach

As we have seen, parties are encouraged to agree budgets where this is possible, and the court will record the extent of any agreement.

The court is only concerned with a budget that is not agreed in whole or part, since the court will then review what is not agreed and, after making any appropriate revisions, record its approval. Note that the court's approval relates only to the total figures for each phase of the proceedings, although in the course of its review the court may consider the constituent elements of each total figure. When reviewing budgets, the court is not carrying out a detailed assessment (see **Chapter 14**) in advance but rather considering whether the budgeted costs fall within the range of reasonable and proportionate costs.

> Certainly in the context of costs management, the Court should allow some flexibility to the parties to ensure that their conduct of the action is not unnecessarily and potentially unfairly hampered by an unrealistically low assessment or by only the lowest assessment of what would constitute reasonable and proportionate expenditure. Expenditure which is within a reasonable and proportionate range is still reasonable and proportionate even if it is not at the lower end. (*Discovery Land Company, LLC v Axis Specialty Europe SE* [2021] EWHC 2146 (Comm))

As part of the costs management process, the court may not approve costs incurred before the date of any budget. The court may, however, record its comments on those costs, and will take those costs into account when considering the reasonableness and proportionality of all subsequent costs.

EXAMPLE

In *Agents' Mutual Ltd v Halman* [2016] CAT 21, none of the phases in the defendant's budget for future work were agreed by the claimant. Set out below are the amounts claimed in the budget, the amounts approved by the court and, by way of example, an extract from the judgment explaining the approved figure for witness statements.

Phase	Costs already incurred £	Estimate of future costs £	Approved future costs £
Witness statements	53,194	246,625	146,806
Expert reports	153,933	163,200	86,067
PTR		105,725	40,000
Trial preparation		98,175	80,000
Trial		842,195	550,000
ADR	237	19,525	19,525

Witness Statements

13. The total estimated under this head is £299,819. That is based on the assumption that Gascoigne Halman will have 6–7 witnesses and also the task of reviewing the Claimant's 4 witness statements and the evidence of Moginie James in the related action. The Claimant's budget under this head is £147,650 and it is perhaps relevant to note that its budget is £19,575 for witness statements in the Moginie James action.

14. I recognise that preparation of witness statements is time-consuming and that in this case the costs for Gascoigne Halman are likely to exceed those of the Claimant because it has more witnesses. Nonetheless, I regard the total of close to £300,000 as unreasonable and disproportionate. The explanation may be that a significant share of the work in the legal team at Gascoigne Halman's solicitors is being undertaken by two partners: between them, it is proposed that they will spend 150 hours on witness statements, whereas the associate on the case (who herself is being billed at £395 per hour) is expected to spend 215 hours. I think it is reasonable to expect that a much greater share of the work would be undertaken by more junior lawyers, subject only to review by the partners. Taking a broad view, I consider a reasonable and proportionate sum under this head is £200,000.

15. As £53,194 has already been incurred, I would revise the budget for estimated future costs to £146,806. In adopting that approach, I recognise that there is the possibility that on a detailed assessment the recoverable amount in respect of costs already incurred might be reduced to below £53,194. But I have set out what I consider should be the total and how the budget for future costs is therefore derived, and in that eventuality this should provide a basis to depart from the costs budget under CPR rule 3.18(b).

9.7.3 Practical points

9.7.3.1 Re-filing and re-serving an approved or agreed budget

After a party's budget has been approved or agreed, that party must re-file and re-serve the budget in the form approved or agreed with re-cast figures. The budget should be annexed to the order approving it or recording its agreement. Typically that order reads, 'The court approves the costs budgets of the parties as shown in the Table annexed hereto and initialled by the Master/District Judge.' See further **Appendix B(7) and B(8)**.

9.7.3.2 Effect of court making a costs management order

What is the practical significance of budgets and costs management? Rule 3.18 has the answer. If, during the proceedings, a costs management order is made, that will affect the party who secures a standard basis costs order in the litigation. Why? Because when the court decides how much is payable on the standard basis (see **14.3.3.2**), it must have regard to that party's last approved or agreed budget for each phase of the proceedings, and it cannot depart from that unless satisfied that there is good reason to do so.

Note that this provision does not apply where the assessment of any costs included in an agreed or approved budget is on the indemnity basis (see **14.3.3.3**).

Further note that the provision does not apply to costs falling outside the phases addressed in an agreed or approved budget. Those costs will be subject to a detailed assessment (save any agreement reached between the parties) in the usual way (see **14.3.6.1**).

9.7.3.3 Effect of court not making a costs management order

What if no costs management order has been made? Practice Direction 44, para 3.2 then applies. This provides that if there is a difference of 20% or more between the costs claimed by a receiving party on a detailed assessment and the costs shown in a budget filed by that party, the receiving party must provide a statement of the reasons for the difference with the bill of costs. What if the court does not accept the explanation? The court may regard the difference between the costs claimed and the costs shown in the budget as evidence that the costs claimed are unreasonable or disproportionate.

Further, if a paying party claims to have reasonably relied on a budget filed by a receiving party or wishes to rely on the costs shown in the budget in order to dispute the reasonableness or proportionality of the costs claimed, the paying party must serve a statement setting out the case in this regard in that party's points of dispute. Where it appears to the court that the paying party reasonably relied on the budget, the court may restrict the recoverable costs to such sum as is reasonable for the paying party to pay in the light of that reliance, notwithstanding that such sum is less than the amount of costs reasonably and proportionately incurred by the receiving party.

9.8   OVERVIEW OF MULTI-TRACK CASE AND COSTS MANAGEMENT

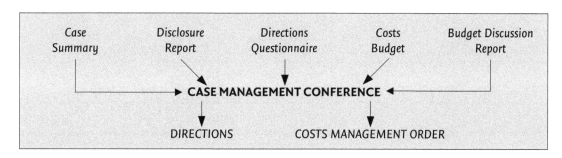

CHAPTER 10

Applications to the Court

10.1	Introduction	159
10.2	Applications generally	159
10.3	Interim costs	163
10.4	Appeals against an interim order	166
10.5	Particular types of application	167
10.6	Interim remedies (Part 25)	174
10.7	Interim payments	175
10.8	Security for costs (r 25.12)	178

LEARNING OUTCOMES

After reading this chapter you will have learned:

- how to make an interim application
- the different type and effect of interim costs orders
- when and how to set aside a default judgment
- the purpose of summary judgment proceedings
- the procedure for applying for summary judgment
- the basic remedies available under Part 25
- when and how to apply for an interim payment
- when the court may make a security for costs order.

10.1 INTRODUCTION

In this chapter, we shall consider the way in which a party to the case can make an application to the court. We are considering applications made after the issue of proceedings and before the trial. These are known as interim applications.

Part 23 of CPR 1998 sets out the general rules governing applications to the court. These rules are subject to any express provisions which may apply to specific types of application.

We have already considered some possibilities, for example pre-action disclosure (see **3.9**); permission to serve a claim form out of the jurisdiction (see **5.5.7.2**); challenging the court's jurisdiction (see **6.3**); extension of time to serve a claim form or defence (see **5.6** and **6.4** respectively); permission to amend a statement of case (see **7.6.2**); requiring a reply to a Part 18 request (see **7.7.4**); permission to make an additional claim (see **8.2.4**); and relief from a sanction (see **9.4**).

10.2 APPLICATIONS GENERALLY

An application to the court is made by an application notice. Form N244 (see **Appendix A(12)**) should be used.

The party who is making the application is known as the applicant, and the party against whom the order is sought is known as the respondent.

10.2.1 Where to make the application

By r 23.2, the application must be made to the court where the claim has been started, or the court to where the claim has been sent. If the claim has already been listed for trial, it must be made to the court where the trial is to take place. Most applications will be heard by a master in the RCJ, or a district judge in either the County Court or a High Court District Registry.

Any application made before a claim form has been issued should normally be made to the court where the proceedings will be started, but in the County Court can be made to any County Court hearing centre unless any enactment, rule or practice direction provides otherwise.

10.2.2 Content of the application notice

By r 23.6, an application notice must state what order the applicant is seeking and, briefly, why the applicant is seeking the order.

If the applicant wishes to rely on matters set out in the application notice as evidence at the hearing, then it must be verified by a statement of truth. This appears on the second page of Form N244.

10.2.3 Draft order

Practice Direction 23A states that, except in the most simple application, the applicant should attach a draft of the order sought. If the case is proceeding in the RCJ and the order is unusually long or complex, it should also be supplied on disk for use by the court office.

10.2.4 Evidence in support of the application

As we shall see at **10.2.9** and **10.6**, certain of the rules set out a specific requirement for evidence in support of a particular application. Apart from that, PD 23A states, at para 9.1, that where there is no specific requirement to provide evidence, it should be borne in mind that, as a practical matter, the court will often need to be satisfied by evidence of the facts that are relied on in support of, or for opposing, the application. The evidence will usually take the form of a witness statement, although a party may also rely on the contents of a statement of case or the application notice itself as evidence, provided it is verified by a statement of truth.

Affidavits (see **10.7**) may be used, but the extra cost of preparing an affidavit over and above that of a witness statement may be disallowed since affidavits are no longer required, except for a limited number of specific applications.

Any evidence relied upon must be filed at the court as well as served on the parties with the application notice. Any evidence in response must be served as soon as possible.

10.2.5 Service of the application notice

Unless the rules relating to a particular type of application specify another time-limit, the application notice must be served at least three clear days before the court is to deal with the application. The court may allow a shorter period of notice if this is appropriate in the circumstances. When served, the application notice must be accompanied by a copy of any supporting written evidence and a copy of any draft order.

10.2.6 Consent orders

If the parties have reached agreement on the order they wish the court to make, they can apply for an order to be made by consent without the need for attendance by the parties. The parties must ensure that they provide the court with any material it needs to be satisfied that it is appropriate to make the order, and usually a letter will suffice.

10.2.7 Orders made without notice

Most applications have to be made on notice (ie, served on the other party so that they can respond and object to the application if they wish to do so). However, in certain cases it is possible for an application to be made without notice being given to the other side. Paragraph 3 of PD 23A indicates that this may be done in the following circumstances:

(a) where there is exceptional urgency;

(b) where the overriding objective is best furthered by doing so;

(c) by consent of all parties;

(d) with the permission of court;

(e) where a date for a hearing has been fixed and the party wishes to make an application at that hearing but does not have sufficient time to serve an application notice, they should inform the other party and the court (if possible in writing) as soon as they can of the nature of the application and the reason for it. They should then make the application orally at the hearing;

(f) where a court order, Rule or Practice Direction permits.

The most common examples are freezing injunctions and search orders (see **10.6**).

When an order is made on an application without notice to the respondent, a copy of the order must be served on the respondent, together with a copy of the application notice and the supporting evidence. The order must contain a statement of the right of the respondent to make an application to set aside or vary the order. The respondent may then apply to set aside or vary the order within seven days of service of the order on them.

10.2.8 Telephone hearings and video conferencing

Many district registries of the High Court and County Court have facilities to deal with interim applications by telephone conferencing. These are known as 'telephone conference enabled courts'. By PD 23A, para 6.2, the general rule is that at a telephone conference enabled court, all allocation hearings (see **9.6**), listing hearings (see **9.6.2.7** and **9.6.3.7**), interim applications, case management conferences (see **9.6.3.2**) and pre-trial reviews (see **9.6.3.7**) with a time estimate of less than one hour will be conducted by telephone. The exceptions are any hearing of an application made without notice to the other party, or where all the parties are unrepresented, or where more than four parties wish to make representations at the hearing (for this purpose, where two or more parties are represented by the same person, they are treated as one party).

Can a party, or a party's legal representative, to an application being heard by telephone attend the judge in person while the application is being heard? No, not unless every other party to the application has agreed. As to the mechanics of how the telephone conference call takes place, see PD 23A, paras 6.9 and 6.10.

Note that the applicant's legal representative (or failing that a legal representative nominated by the court) must file and serve a case summary and draft order no later than 4 pm at least two days before the telephone hearing if the claim has been allocated to the multi-track or, in any other case, if the court so directs.

Where the parties wish to use video conferencing facilities, and those facilities are available in the relevant court, they should apply to the master or district judge for directions.

10.2.9 Preparing supporting evidence

Most solicitors will prepare a witness statement in support of, or in opposition to, an interim application. Whilst the Rule under which the application is made may dictate some of the content of that statement, the following general questions must always be answered:

(a)   Who should make the statement? It should be the person best able to address the relevant points from personal knowledge. For example, on an application for pre-action disclosure that relies on ground (d)(iii) of r 31.16(3), the person who can quantify and justify the savings in costs (see **3.9**) will probably be best placed to make the witness statement.

(b)   What needs to be included? List the important points to be brought to the court's attention. Include all the relevant detailed evidence relied on and anticipate your opponent's case, where appropriate.

(c)   How should the statement appear? Divide up the important points into numbered paragraphs. Set out the relevant information in chronological order.

(d)   What about hearsay evidence (see **12.9**)? When relying on this, state the source of the information. A witness statement must indicate which of the contents derive from the maker's own knowledge and which are either matters of information they have received from a third party or form the basis of their own belief. The source of any matters of information or belief must also be given. For example, a witness may state, 'I am advised by Laura Smith who inspected the machinery immediately after it broke down that ...'.

(e)   What is the key to possible success? Focus on detail and exhibit any relevant supporting documents. A witness statement containing highly relevant details and made by a person with first-hand knowledge of the facts will be very persuasive indeed. If any of the facts arise from or are supported by documents, these should be exhibited.

Should points of law be included? No. Legal arguments should be left to the advocates at the hearing. But all the relevant facts should be included so that it is possible to make the legal arguments. However, your client may have to express a legal opinion. For example, when applying for summary judgment (see **10.5.2**), there must be a statement of belief that on the evidence the respondent has no real prospect of succeeding and there is no other compelling reason for a trial.

10.2.10   Hearings in public or private

CPR 1998, r 39.2 provides as follows:

(1)   The general rule is that a hearing is to be in public. A hearing may not be held in private, irrespective of the parties' consent, unless and to the extent that the court decides that it must be held in private, applying the provisions of paragraph (3).

(2)   In deciding whether to hold a hearing in private, the court must consider any duty to protect or have regard to a right to freedom of expression which may be affected.

(2A)   The court shall take reasonable steps to ensure that all hearings are of an open and public character, save when a hearing is held in private.

(3)   A hearing, or any part of it, must be held in private if, and only to the extent that, the court is satisfied of one or more of the matters set out in sub-paragraphs (a) to (g) and that it is necessary to sit in private to secure the proper administration of justice –

    (a)   publicity would defeat the object of the hearing;

    (b)   it involves matters relating to national security;

    (c)   it involves confidential information (including information relating to personal financial matters) and publicity would damage that confidentiality;

    (d)   a private hearing is necessary to protect the interests of any child or protected party;

    (e)   it is a hearing of an application made without notice and it would be unjust to any respondent for there to be a public hearing;

    (f)   it involves uncontentious matters arising in the administration of trusts or in the administration of a deceased person's estate; or

    (g)   the court for any other reason considers this to be necessary to secure the proper administration of justice.

10.3 INTERIM COSTS

10.3.1 Costs of applying for or opposing an application

Any interim application will involve the parties in expense. A party may be involved in collecting evidence, interviewing witnesses, conducting a site visit, negotiating, etc. The applicant will prepare the notice of application (see **10.2**) and supporting witness statement (see **10.2.4**). A court fee is payable for making the application. The respondent will usually prepare a witness statement in response. The more complex the application, the greater the costs involved. Moreover, the cost of travelling to and from the court, and the advocate dealing with the application, must also be taken into account.

10.3.2 'Pay as you go' litigation

At the end of any interim application, the judge may decide that one party should pay the other party's costs. This is often called 'pay as you go' litigation. The general costs rule applies, namely, the loser pays the winner's costs. So if the application is granted, it is normal to order the respondent to pay the applicant's costs. But the type of costs order will depend on the nature of the application, and interim costs orders usually reflect to a large extent the conduct of the parties. For example, a party who wants permission to amend their statement of case (see **7.6**) starts from a weak position, as they want the court to allow them to do something. Hence, the normal order is that such an applicant pays the respondent's costs of the application, which may include additional costs, eg, if the respondent has to amend, file and serve their own statement of case as a result of the amendment. Such a costs order would be expressed as 'costs of and caused by' (see the table below).

10.3.3 Possible orders

Different costs orders may be made at the end of an interim hearing. The most common orders are set out in PD 44, para 4.2 and include the following:

Term	Effect
[Named party's] costs ([Named party's] costs in any event)	The party named in the order and thereby in whose favour the order is made (eg, claimant's costs) is entitled to the costs in respect of the part of the proceedings to which the order relates, whatever other costs orders are made in the proceedings. These costs are normally summarily assessed and ordered to be paid within 14 days.
Costs in the case (Costs in the application)	In this order, no party is named. At this interim stage no party is able to recover their costs of the interim hearing. The outcome at the end of the proceedings will determine which party recovers these interim costs. The party in whose favour the court makes an order for costs at the end of the proceedings is entitled to their costs of the part of the proceedings to which the order relates.
[Named party's] costs in case	If the named party is awarded costs at the end of the proceedings, that party is entitled to their costs of the part of the proceedings to which the order relates. So the party not named in the order is never entitled to recover their interim costs of the application. The named party recovers their interim costs of the application only if they are ultimately awarded costs at the conclusion of the proceedings.

Term	Effect
[Named party's] costs thrown away	Where, for example, a judgment or order is set aside, the party in whose favour the costs order is made is entitled to the costs which have been incurred as a consequence. This includes the costs of: (a) preparing for and attending any hearing at which the judgment or order which has been set aside was made; (b) preparing for and attending any hearing to set aside the judgment or order in question; (c) preparing for and attending any hearing at which the court orders the proceedings or the part in question to be adjourned; (d) any steps taken to enforce a judgment or order which has subsequently been set aside.
[Named party's] costs of and caused by	Where, for example, the court makes this order on an application to amend a statement of case, the party in whose favour the costs order is made is entitled to the costs of preparing for and attending the application and the costs of any consequential amendment to their own statement of case.
No order as to costs (Each party to pay their own costs)	Each party is to bear their own costs of the part of the proceedings to which the order relates whatever costs order the court makes at the end of the proceedings.

If the order made at the hearing makes no mention of costs, the general rule is none are payable in respect of that application. So it is always vital to ensure that the judge makes some sort of costs order.

10.3.4 Summary assessment

If the court makes an order for costs in favour of one of the parties to the application (eg, 'claimant's costs', or 'claimant's costs thrown away' or 'defendant's costs of and caused by') then the court will make a summary assessment of costs there and then. Any such costs are payable within 14 days, unless the court orders otherwise. In order for the court to be able to assess the costs at the end of the application, the parties are required, not less than 24 hours prior to the hearing, to file and serve a statement of costs. This provides a breakdown of the costs incurred in relation to the application. A model form of the statement of costs (Form N260) appears at **Appendix A(13)**. If a party fails to comply with this requirement without reasonable excuse, this will be taken into account by the court in deciding what costs order to make (see, for example, *Changing Climates Ltd v Warmaway Ltd* [2021] EWHC 3117 (TCC)). To help the judge carry out a summary assessment, they will take into account the guideline rates for solicitors and counsel: see **Appendix A(22)** and **14.3.4.2**.

The parties may well agree the amount of costs at an interim hearing. The judge is likely to reject an agreed figure only if they consider it to be disproportionate.

10.3.5 Fixed costs

On a few occasions, the court may award fixed costs rather than making one of the orders set out above (see, eg, **6.6.3** and **10.5.2.5**). Part 45 sets out the occasions on which fixed costs may be granted and specifies the amount awarded to the receiving party. Where fixed costs are granted there is, of course, no need for a summary assessment.

10.3.6 Costs-capping order (r 3.19)

10.3.6.1 The problem to be addressed

In heavy, complex litigation, costs can build up quickly. If one or more of the parties does not strictly follow the Practice Direction on Pre-action Conduct and Protocols or any approved pre-action protocol that applies (see **3.7**), a large amount of unnecessary costs may be incurred. In these exceptional circumstances the court may make an order capping the amount of costs recoverable by a party that are incurred after the date of the order. An order does not act retrospectively.

What is the difference between costs capping and the court making a costs management order (see **9.7**)?

> [A] costs management order ... is not a costs cap by another route, because the status of any such order is defined by CPR 3.18. It does not limit the costs recoverable unless varied. It is, instead, a matter to which the court on the detailed assessment will have regard and from which it will not depart unless satisfied that there is good reason to do so. (*Hegglin v Person(s) Unknown & Google Inc* [2014] EWHC 3793, per Edis J at [22])

That a court will make a costs capping order only in exceptional circumstances is demonstrated by the fact that most reported applications have failed (see, for example, *Tidal Energy Ltd v Bank of Scotland plc* [2014] EWCA Civ 847 and *Black v Arriva North East Ltd* [2014] EWCA Civ 1115).

Costs capping may well remain important only for applications concerning a limited amount of money, such as trust funds (see PD 3F, Section II). There is specific provision for costs capping orders in judicial review proceedings. This is governed by s 88 of the Criminal Justice and Courts Act 2015. The provisions apply where an application for leave to bring judicial review proceedings has been granted, and the test is set out in s 88(6). The proceedings must be public interest proceedings, and it must be established that without a costs capping order the applicant would be very likely to withdraw the application. The test was considered in *Stephen Hawking and others v Secretary of State for Health & Social Care and National Health Service Commissioning Board* [2018] EWHC 989 (Admin).

10.3.6.2 Making the application

Any party may apply for a costs-capping order, but normally it is a defendant seeking to cap what the claimant might recover in costs. The application should be made as soon as possible, preferably before or at the first case management conference (see **9.6.3.2**). The evidence in support should set out whether the costs-capping order is in respect of the whole of the litigation or a particular issue which is ordered to be tried separately, and why a costs-capping order should be made. It should be accompanied by a budget, setting out the costs and disbursements incurred by the applicant to date and those the applicant is likely to incur in the future conduct of the proceedings. The court will normally direct that all other parties file a similar budget.

10.3.6.3 Grounds for making an order

By r 3.19, the court can make a costs-capping order against all or any of the parties, if:

(a)   it is in the interests of justice to do so;

(b)   there is a substantial risk that without such an order costs will be disproportionately incurred; and

(c)   it is not satisfied that the risk in sub-para (b) can be adequately controlled by –

    (i)   case management directions or orders made under Part 3, and

    (ii)   detailed assessment of costs. So where the concerns are that the other side's hourly charges and use of leading counsel are excessive, as in *Peacock v MGN Ltd*

[2009] EWHC 769, the order will be refused on the basis that a costs judge can deal with these issues on a detailed assessment (see **14.3**).

In considering whether to exercise its discretion under the rule, the court will consider all the circumstances of the case, including:

(a)   whether there is a substantial imbalance between the financial position of the parties;

(b)   whether the costs of determining the amount of the cap are likely to be proportionate to the overall costs of the litigation;

(c)   the stage which the proceedings have reached; and

(d)   the costs incurred to date and the future costs.

10.3.6.4   Effect of order

A costs-capping order, once made, limits the costs recoverable by the party subject to the order unless that party successfully applies to vary it. However, no such variation will be made by the court unless there has been a material and substantial change of circumstances since the date the order was made, or there is some other compelling reason why a variation should be made.

10.3.7   Conditional fee agreements and the summary assessment of interim application costs

The fact that one (or even both) of the parties has entered into a conditional fee agreement (a CFA) will not prevent the costs of the interim application from being summarily assessed if the court has awarded costs in favour of a party.

10.3.7.1   Receiving party CFA funded

Where the receiving party (the party whose costs are to be paid) is CFA funded, the court cannot order payment to be made unless satisfied that the receiving party is immediately liable to their solicitor for the costs of the application under the terms of the CFA. To order otherwise would be contrary to the indemnity principle (see **14.3**). Accordingly, the form of agreement recommended by The Law Society entitles solicitors to payment of costs on all successful interim applications, whatever the outcome of the proceedings at trial.

It should be noted that where the receiving party is on a CFA, the court's summary assessment can deal only with the base costs.

10.3.7.2   Paying party CFA funded

A party who is CFA funded may not be in a position to pay interim costs if ordered to do so. Although many CFA clients have the benefit of AEI, it is common for such policies not to cover the payment of interim costs awarded to the other side. The court may therefore decide to defer the payment of the interim costs until the end of the proceedings. In considering whether to do so, the court should take into account the unfairness of this on the receiving party.

The topic of CFAs is dealt with at **2.4.2**.

10.4   APPEALS AGAINST AN INTERIM ORDER

The procedure for appeals is set out in Part 52. An appeal from a decision of a district judge in the County Court is made to a circuit judge, and from a master or district judge in the High Court to a High Court judge.

Permission to appeal is required and will be granted only if the appeal has a real prospect of success, or there is some other compelling reason for the appeal to be heard (r 52.3(6)). Permission may be sought either at the original hearing, or from the appeal court within 21 days of the original decision. If permission is sought at the original hearing but refused, a further application for permission may be made to the appeal judge.

The appeal hearing will usually be limited to a review of the district judge's or master's original decision, and no new evidence will be admitted unless the court orders otherwise (r 52.11). The appeal will be allowed if the original decision was either wrong or unjust because of a serious procedural or other irregularity. If the appeal is allowed, the appeal judge may make a variety of orders (eg, setting aside or varying the original order and ordering a re-hearing).

10.5 PARTICULAR TYPES OF APPLICATION

10.5.1 Applications to set aside a default judgment (Part 13)

10.5.1.1 The mandatory grounds

Under r 13.2, the court is obliged to set aside a default judgment that was wrongly entered before the defendant's deadline for filing an acknowledgement of service or a defence (whichever is applicable) expired. The court is also obliged to set aside a default judgment entered after the claim was paid in full.

10.5.1.2 The discretionary grounds

Rule 13.3(1) gives the court the power to set aside or vary a default judgment where:

    (a)   the defendant has a real prospect of successfully defending the claim; or

    (b)   it appears to the court that there is some other good reason why—

        (i)   the judgment should be set aside or varied; or

        (ii)   the defendant should be allowed to defend the claim.

The court will take account of the promptness of the defendant's application to set aside, and it is therefore essential that the defendant should issue the application as soon as they become aware of the default judgment. This is because the overriding objective expressly recognises the importance of ensuring that cases are dealt with expeditiously and fairly (see **1.1.1**), and r 13.3(2) makes it an explicit requirement for the court to have regard to whether the application was made promptly. No other factor is specifically identified for consideration, which suggests that promptness carries a great deal of weight. But it is not a condition that must be satisfied before the court can grant relief, because other factors may carry sufficient weight to persuade the court that relief should be granted even though the application was not made promptly. The strength of the defence may well be one. However, promptness will always be a factor of considerable significance, and if there has been a marked failure to make the application promptly, the court may well be justified in refusing relief, notwithstanding the possibility that the defendant might succeed at trial: see *Standard Bank Plc v Agrinvest International Inc* [2010] EWCA Civ 1400.

In *Tideland Ltd v Westminster City Council* [2015] EWHC 2710 (TCC) the court set aside a judgment, the application having been made two months after the judgment. During that time the defendant had sought a stay and disclosure of documentation. In giving judgment, the court stated that it was not necessary to act with the utmost speed possible, just with all reasonable speed.

As to ground (a), that the defendant has a real prospect of successfully defending the claim, see the same test (albeit with a different burden of proof) in r 24.2 at **10.5.2.1**.

What other factors will the court take into account when adjudicating on grounds (a) and/or (b)? The court will apply the three-stage approach set out in the case of *Denton* (see **9.4.1**):

> CPR 13.3 requires an applicant to show that he has real prospects of a successful defence or some other good reason to set the judgement aside. If he does, the court's discretion is to be exercised in the light of all the circumstances and the overriding objective. The Court must have regard to all the factors it considers relevant of which promptness is both a mandatory and an important consideration. Since

the overriding objective of the Rules is to enable the court to deal with cases justly and at proportionate cost, and since under the new CPR 1.1 (2) (f) the latter includes enforcing compliance with rules, practice directions and orders, the considerations set out in CPR 3.9 are to be taken into account: see *Hussein v Birmingham City Council* [2005] EWCA Civ 1570 per Chadwick LJ at [30]; *Mid-East Sales v United Engineering and Trading Co (PVT) Ltd* [2014] EWHC 1457 at [85]. So also is the approach to CPR 3.9 in *Mitchell/Denton* ...

Denton makes clear that any application for relief against sanctions involves considering (i) the seriousness and significance of the default (ii) the reason for it and (iii) all the circumstances of the case. At the third stage factors (a) and (b) in CPR 3.9 are of particular, but not paramount, importance. (*per* Christopher Clarke LJ in *Piemonte v Dexia Crediop SpA* [2014] EWCA Civ 1298 at [40] and [41])

The first questions that arise, however, in dealing with an application to set aside a judgment under CPR Part 13.3 are the express requirements of that rule, namely whether the defendant has a real prospect of successfully defending the claim or whether there is some other reason why the judgment should be set aside, taking into account whether the person seeking to set aside the judgment made an application to do so promptly. Since the application is one for relief from sanctions, the *Denton* tests then come into play. The first test as to whether there was a serious or significant breach applies, not to the delay after the judgment was entered, but to the default in serving an acknowledgement that gave rise to the sanction of a default judgment in the first place. The second and third tests then follow, but the question of promptness in making the application arises both in considering the requirements of CPR Part 13.3(2) and in considering all the circumstances under the third *Denton* stage. (per Vos LJ in *Gentry v Miller* [2016] EWCA Civ 141 at [24])

The application to the court must be on notice and must be supported by evidence. Although the rule states that only one of the grounds needs to be satisfied, in practice the defendant will usually have to show a defence with a real prospect of success at trial in order to persuade the court to exercise its discretion.

EXAMPLE 1

A issues a claim form (with particulars of claim) against B, claiming the price of goods sold and delivered to B. B receives the claim form but forgets to deal with it and A is able to enter default judgment.

B then instructs solicitors. They immediately apply to set the default judgment aside. The evidence in support of the application is a witness statement from B in which he seeks to show that the goods were not of satisfactory quality.

If B can show that he has a real prospect of successfully defending the claim, the default judgment will be set aside. Although the court must be careful not to embark on a detailed 'mini-trial', it ought to test the assertions being made by B to see if they have any real substance, and/or whether they are contradicted by contemporaneous documents. It is also necessary to see whether giving B a further opportunity to put in further evidence and/ or documents would or could make any difference (*Redbourn Group Ltd v Fairgate Development Ltd* [2017] EWHC 1223 (TCC)). B may, however, have to pay the costs of the application, which will be summarily assessed, as he was to blame for the default judgment being entered.

EXAMPLE 2

Mr and Mrs X buy a dining room table and chairs from Y Ltd. There is a dispute about the quality of the wood used in the construction of the furniture. Mr and Mrs X refuse to pay Y Ltd. Whilst they are away on holiday, Y Ltd issue proceedings for the price of the furniture, serve the proceedings and enter default judgment when no acknowledgement or defence is filed within the prescribed time. On their return from holiday, Mr and Mrs X open their post and discover the proceedings and default judgment.

Mr and Mrs X have a good reason for asking the court to set aside the default judgment as they were away on holiday when the proceedings were served and default judgment entered. Hence they were unable to respond to the proceedings through no fault of their own. They should immediately ask Y Ltd to agree to the default judgment's being set aside, or otherwise make an application to the court. Any application should be supported by evidence to show that they were away on holiday at the material times and that they have acted promptly in making the application once they became aware of the default judgment. Any delay should be explained. They should also state the basis of the defence to the claim and the evidence they have to support that to show that there is a defence with a real prospect of success at trial.

EXAMPLE 3

What if the claimant posts the proceedings to the defendant's last known residence (see **5.5.3**) and the proceedings are not returned undelivered, but the defendant does not receive the proceedings because they have moved to a new address? These are the facts of *Akram v Adam* [2004] EWCA Civ 1601, (2004) *The Times*, 29 December. In these circumstances the defendant has a good reason for asking the court to set aside the default judgment as they were unable to respond to the proceedings through no fault of their own. The defendant should immediately ask the claimant to agree to the default judgment's being set aside, or otherwise make an application to the court. Any application should be supported by evidence to show that the defendant had moved from and had no connection with the address to which the proceedings were sent, and that the defendant acted promptly in making the application once they became aware of the default judgment. Any delay should be explained. The defendant should also state the basis of the defence to the claim and the evidence they have to support that to show that there is a defence with a real prospect of success at trial.

EXAMPLE 4

What if the claimant serves the claim form but without a response pack? If that leaves the defendant unsure of what to do and by when, the court may find that a good reason to set aside the default judgment: see *Hughes v Alan Dick & Co Ltd* [2008] EWHC 2695 and *Rajval Construction Ltd v Bestville Properties Ltd* [2010] EWCA Civ 1621.

What about the interim costs (see **10.3**) in Examples 2, 3 and 4? If the court accepts that there is a good reason then, as neither party can be said to be at fault in those circumstances, it is likely that the court will set aside the default judgment and make an order for costs in the case. The court may, or may not, summarily assess these. If, however, the reason is rejected and the default judgment set aside on the ground of a defence with a real prospect of succeeding at trial, the court is likely to order the defendant to pay the claimant's (summarily assessed) costs within 14 days.

If the original claim was for a specified amount of money and the defendant is an individual then, if the judgment was not entered in the defendant's home court, the application to set aside the default judgment will be transferred to the defendant's home court and the case proceeds there (see **9.5**).

10.5.1.3 Orders the court may make

The court may set aside the default judgment, refuse the application or make a conditional order. Where the judgment is set aside, the court usually gives directions for the future management of the case. In respect of a conditional order, the normal condition is that the defendant pays into court the amount of the claim or such amount as they can reasonably afford (within a set time period, otherwise the default judgment stands). The court will usually impose such a condition only if the application was made very late.

10.5.1.4 Costs

The costs order made at the conclusion of the application will depend on the outcome. If the application is granted on a mandatory ground, the claimant will have been at fault for entering judgment when they should not have done so, and therefore normally the claimant is ordered to pay the defendant's costs. Where the defendant establishes the discretionary ground of a good reason for the default then, as neither side is at fault, costs are usually in the case. Where the defendant only establishes the discretionary ground of a defence with a real prospect of success at trial, the defendant is at fault in failing to deal with the proceedings and normally has to pay the claimant's costs. If a conditional order is made due to a very late application then the defendant is normally penalised by being ordered to pay the claimant's costs.

10.5.1.5 Practical point: prepare for all possible outcomes

As the judge will invariably make some sort of costs order at the end of the interim application, it is vital that an advocate is able to deal with it. An advocate needs to prepare for all potential outcomes. These are summarised in the flowchart in **Appendix C(11)**.

10.5.2 Summary judgment (Part 24)

We saw at **9.3** that the court has the power, under its case management powers contained in Part 3 of CPR 1998, to strike out a statement of case if it discloses no reasonable grounds for bringing or defending the claim. The court has similar powers under Part 24 of CPR 1998, which deals with applications for summary judgment. The aim behind the Part 24 procedure is to enable a claimant or defendant to obtain judgment at an early stage without the time and expense involved in proceeding to a full trial.

10.5.2.1 Grounds for the application

Rule 24.2 states that:

> The court may give summary judgment against a claimant or defendant on the whole of the claim or on a particular issue if—
>
> (a)   it considers that—
>
>   (i)   that claimant has no real prospect of succeeding on the claim or issue; or
>
>   (ii)   that defendant has no real prospect of successfully defending the claim or issue; and
>
> (b)   there is no other compelling reason why the case or issue should be disposed of at trial.

Therefore, either party can make an application for summary judgment (or indeed the court could list the case for a Part 24 hearing on its own initiative). According to para 1.3 of PD 24, the application may be based on:

> (1)   a point of law (including a question of construction of a document),
>
> (2)   the evidence which can reasonably be expected to be available at trial or the lack of it, or
>
> (3)   a combination of these.

The focus is on the 'claim', the 'case' and the 'issue' in accordance with r 24.2(a) and (b). That means the court must scrutinise how the parties have stated their respective cases and examine the essence of the way in which the case or issue is put at the hearing, but no more than that (*Barks v Instant Access Properties Ltd (In Liquidation)* [2013] EWHC 114).

The court can give summary judgment against a claimant in any type of proceedings and against the defendant in most types of proceedings, with some exceptions which are beyond the scope of this book.

What cases are not suitable for summary judgment? In *Swain v Hillman* [2001] 1 All ER 91, Lord Woolf MR said:

> Useful though the power is under Part 24, it is important that it is kept to its proper role. It is not meant to dispense with the need for a trial where there are issues which should be investigated at the trial ... the proper disposal of an issue under Part 24 does not involve the judge conducting a mini trial, that is not the object of the provisions; it is to enable cases, where there is no real prospect of success either way, to be disposed of summarily.

What is a compelling reason for the purposes of r 24.2(b)? In *Secretary of State for Health v Norton Healthcare Ltd and Others* [2004] LTL, 25 February, the claimants alleged that the defendants had operated an unlawful price-fixing cartel or under an anti-competition arrangement in supplying a particular drug. The seventh defendant applied for summary judgment on the basis that the claim against it was legally and factually flawed. The application was dismissed. The court held that the public interest in controlling pharmaceutical costs and the investigation of a possible cartel was a compelling reason for a trial. In addition, the claim involved allegations of conspiracy between the parties, and those accusations could only be properly examined at trial.

In *Kirschel & Others v Fladgate Fielder (a firm)* [2000] LTL, 22 December, the court refused applications for summary judgment by both parties for the compelling reason that their contrary submissions raised difficult questions of law, two of which did not appear to be covered by authority and so ought to be tried. However, in *Brown v Fisk* [2021] EWHC 2769 (QB), summary judgment was granted to the defendant as the court found that the claimant had no real prospect of establishing that a yard owned by a club was a public place for the purposes of s 151 of the Road Traffic Act 1988.

A compelling reason for a trial may be to allow the respondent more time to investigate the matter, particularly if they have a good reason for being unable so far to get in touch with a material witness. Alternatively, the respondent may argue that the claim or defence is of such a highly complicated and/or technical nature that it can only be properly understood if the usual procedural steps are taken and the evidence then given at a full trial subject to cross-examination (see *Three Rivers District Council and Others v Governor and Company of the Bank of England (No 3 bis)* [2001] 2 All ER 513, HL). For example, in *Celador Productions Limited v Melville* [2004] EWHC 2362 (Ch), [2004] LTL, 26 October, the case concerned infringement of a TV game show format. The application for summary judgment was refused. The court held that in order to determine whether similarities between the formats were the result of copying, it was necessary both for standard disclosure (see **Chapter 11**) to be given and for witnesses to be cross-examined at trial (see **14.2.3.2**). Those were compelling reasons for refusing the application.

10.5.2.2 Procedure

The claimant may not apply for summary judgment until the defendant has filed an acknowledgement of service or a defence unless the court gives permission. The reason for this is that if the defendant fails to file an acknowledgement of service or defence, the claimant can enter a default judgment without having to make an application for summary judgment. If the claimant applies for summary judgment before the defendant has filed a defence, the defendant need not file a defence until after the application for summary judgment has been heard.

The defendant may apply for summary judgment at any time. Irrespective of who makes the application, it should be made without delay and usually prior to, or at the time of, filing of directions questionnaires (see **9.5.1**).

The respondent to the application must be given at least 14 days' notice of the date fixed for the hearing. A respondent who wishes to rely on written evidence must file and serve this at least seven days before the hearing. An applicant who wishes to rely on written evidence in reply to the respondent's submissions must file and serve it at least three days before the hearing.

The application notice itself must state that it is an application for summary judgment and the application notice or the evidence contained or referred to in it, or served with it, must, as stated in para 2(3) of PD 24:

(a)   identify concisely any point of law or provision in a document on which the applicant relies, and/or

(b)   state that it is made because the applicant believes that on the evidence the respondent has no real prospect of succeeding on the claim or issue, or (as the case may be) of successfully defending the claim or issue to which the application relates,

and in either case state that the applicant knows of no other reason why the disposal of the claim or issue should await trial.

If the application notice does not contain all the applicant's evidence, it should identify the written evidence (such as a witness statement or statement of case) the applicant intends to rely on. The application notice should also inform the respondent of their right to file and serve written evidence in reply.

10.5.2.3 Orders the court may make on an application for summary judgment

On a Part 24 application the court may order:

(1)   judgment on the claim,

(2)   the striking out or dismissal of the claim,

(3)   the dismissal of the application,

(4)   a conditional order.

(See para 5.1 of PD 24.)

To grant summary judgment, the court will have to come to the conclusion that the claim or defence has no real prospects of succeeding at trial (and there is no other compelling reason for a trial). For example, in the Court of Appeal case of *Peskin v Anderson and Others* [2001] 1 BCLC 372, Mummery LJ described the claimant's case as a 'flight of fancy [that] does not, on the pleaded facts, even make it to the take off point and should be grounded immediately under CPR Part 24'. Simon Brown LJ added that the claim was 'worthless and must fail'. So, summary judgment should be granted where the claim, etc is 'merely fanciful, imaginary, unreal or intrinsically unrealistic' (*per* Otton LJ in *Sinclair v Chief Constable of West Yorkshire and Another* [2000] LTL, 12 December).

> The claim is for damages for misuse of confidential information, breach of confidence, negligence, damages under s82 of the GDPR and s169 Data Protection Act 2013 ... There is no credible case that distress or damage over a de minimis threshold will be proved. In the modern world it is not appropriate for a party to claim, (especially in the High Court) for breaches of this sort which are, frankly, trivial. The case law referred to above provides ample authority that whatever cause of action is relied on the law will not supply a remedy in cases where effectively no harm has credibly been shown or be likely to be shown. (*Rolfe v Veale Wasbrough Vizards LLP* [2021] EWHC 2809 (QB))

Note that the court will grant judgment on the claim under Part 24 only if the claimant makes an application. It will strike out the claim only on a defendant's application. Therefore a defendant who wishes to oppose an application for summary judgment and also to apply for an order striking out the claim must make their own application for summary judgment.

When should the application be dismissed? Pill LJ in *Hussain v Woods and Another* [2001] Lloyd's Rep PN 134 suggested this was appropriate where 'an apparently credible witness says one thing and another apparently credible witness says the opposite, and there is not conclusive circumstantial evidence pointing one way or the other'.

A conditional order is an order which requires a party:

(1)   to pay a sum of money into court, or

(2)   to take a specified step in relation to his claim or defence, as the case may be,

and provides that that party's claim will be dismissed or his statement of case will be struck out if he does not comply. (para 5.2 of PD 24)

The court is likely to make a conditional order where it appears to the court possible that a claim or defence may succeed but improbable that it will do so. See PD 24, para 4. This is a situation where the statement of case might be described as 'shadowy and unsatisfactory' (*per* Sir Richard Scott V-C in *Bates v Microstar Ltd* [2000] LTL, 4 July). For example, where a claimant applies for summary judgment in a debt or damages case, if the court is not satisfied that the defence has a 'real prospect' of success, but none the less considers that success is possible (although improbable), the court may allow the defendant to continue to defend the claim on the condition that they pay the amount of the claim into court or such amount as they can reasonably afford (see *Gama Aviation (UK) Ltd v Taleveras Petroleum Trading DMCC* [2019] EWCA Civ 119 and *MV Yorke Motors v Edwards* [1982] 1 All ER 1024). Such a condition may also be appropriate if the defendant's claim is weak and the defendant has behaved dishonestly in the litigation, for example by tampering with the evidence (see *Kooh Veisin Trading Co v Parsai* [2013] LTL, 11 February). The money would remain in court pending the final outcome of the case. If the defendant fails to make the payment into court then the defence would be dismissed and judgment entered for the claimant.

But what financial condition will the judge impose on a claimant where the claim may possibly succeed, although it probably will not do so at trial? In the case of *Sweetman v Shepherd* (2000) *The Times*, 29 March, the Court of Appeal indicated that in the absence of financial constraints, it would expect a claimant to pay into court a sum of about 75% to 80% of those costs the defendant could reasonably expect to recover at the end of the claim if it were fully contested. The defendant should produce an estimate of those costs (see **9.7**).

10.5.2.4 Directions

When the court determines a summary judgment application it may:

(a) give directions as to the filing and serving of a defence, if one has not already been filed; and

(b) give further directions.

So, where the court dismisses the application or makes an order that does not completely dispose of the claim, the court may well give case management directions as to the future conduct of the case.

10.5.2.5 Costs

The costs order made at the conclusion of the hearing will depend on the type of claim and the outcome of the application. Where a claimant is successful in obtaining summary judgment for a specified sum, the court may award fixed costs (see Part 45). The fixed costs are £175 if the judgment exceeds £25 but does not exceed £5,000, and £210 if the judgment exceeds £5,000. In fairly straightforward cases, it is likely that the court will award fixed costs. However, it is open to the successful claimant to ask for costs to be summarily assessed, as often these are going to be far more than the fixed costs. See **10.3**.

What is the effect if a claimant of an unspecified sum is awarded summary judgment? The claimant will have established liability but a later assessment of the quantum of damages will be necessary. The court will normally award the claimant their costs of making the application (claimant's costs) and summarily assess these (see **10.3**). The court will then usually fix a date to assess quantum and deal with the costs of the entire claim ('a disposal hearing'), and may allocate the matter to a track and give case management directions.

What if the defendant secures summary judgment (ie, the claim is struck out)? The court will normally award the defendant their costs of the claim (including pre-action costs) and, unless agreed, these will be subject to a summary assessment.

If a conditional order is made the claimant's application has not been granted, but equally the defendant has not got the application dismissed. Neither side can be said to have won and so the usual order is costs in the case.

10.5.2.6 Practical point: prepare for all possible outcomes

As the judge will invariably make some sort of costs order at the end of the interim application, it is vital that an advocate is able to deal with it. An advocate needs to prepare for all potential outcomes. These are summarised in the flowchart at **Appendix C(12)**.

10.5.3 Application for further information (Part 18)

As we saw in **Chapter 7**, a party may request further information from another party to clarify any matter in dispute, or give additional information in relation to any such matter.

If the request is not met, the party can apply for an order from the court.

Provided that the request made complied with para 1 of PD 18 (see **Chapter 7**), and at least 14 days have elapsed and the time stated for a response has expired, the application notice need not be served on the other party and the court may deal with the application without a hearing (PD 18, para 5.5(1)). Otherwise, the application notice must be served on the other party.

10.6   INTERIM REMEDIES (PART 25)

The court has wide powers to grant parties to a claim, or to a proposed claim, various interim remedies. These are set out in r 25.1:

(1)   The court may grant the following interim remedies—

   (a)   an interim injunction;

   (b)   an interim declaration;

   (c)   an order—

    (i)   for the detention, custody or preservation of relevant property;

    (ii)   for the inspection of relevant property;

    (iii)   for the taking of a sample of relevant property;

    (iv)   for the carrying out of an experiment on or with relevant property;

    (v)   for the sale of relevant property which is of a perishable nature or which for any other good reason it is desirable to sell quickly; and

    (vi)   for the payment of income from relevant property until a claim is decided;

   (d)   an order authorising a person to enter any land or building in the possession of a party to the proceedings for the purposes of carrying out an order under sub-paragraph (c);

   (e)   an order under section 4 of the Torts (Interference with Goods) Act 1977 to deliver up goods;

   (f)   an order (referred to as a 'freezing injunction')—

    (i)   restraining a party from removing from the jurisdiction assets located there; or

    (ii)   restraining a party from dealing with any assets whether located within the jurisdiction or not;

   (g)   an order directing a party to provide information about the location of relevant property or assets or to provide information about relevant property or assets which are or may be the subject of an application for a freezing injunction;

   (h)   an order (referred to as a 'search order') under section 7 of the Civil Procedure Act 1997 (order requiring a party to admit another party to premises for the purpose of preserving evidence etc);

   (i)   an order under section 33 of the Supreme Court Act 1981 or section 52 of the County Courts Act 1984 (order for disclosure of documents or inspection of property before a claim has been made);

(j)   an order under section 34 of the Supreme Court Act 1981 or section 53 of the County Courts Act 1984 (order in certain proceedings for disclosure of documents or inspection of property against a non-party);

(k)   an order (referred to as an order for interim payment) under rule 25.6 for payment by a defendant on account of any damages, debt or other sum(except costs) which the court may hold the defendant liable to pay;

(l)   an order for a specified fund to be paid into court or otherwise secured, where there is a dispute over a party's right to the fund;

(m)   an order permitting a party seeking to recover personal property to pay money into court pending the outcome of the proceedings and directing that, if he does so, the property shall be given up to him;

(n)   an order directing a party to prepare and file accounts relating to the dispute;

(o)   an order directing any account to be taken or inquiry to be made by the court; and

(p)   an order under Article 9 of Council Directive (EC) 2004/48 on the enforcement of intellectual property rights (order in intellectual property proceedings making the continuation of an alleged infringement subject to the lodging of guarantees).

An interim remedy may be obtained before proceedings are issued (eg, for pre-action disclosure of documents – see **11.16**), during proceedings or even after judgment has been given. A court may grant a remedy before a claim is issued only if the matter is urgent, or it is otherwise desirable to do so in the interests of justice. Unless the court orders otherwise, a defendant may not apply for one of the orders listed in r 25.1 until they have filed an acknowledgement of service or defence.

A court may grant an interim remedy on an application made without notice if it appears to the court that there are good reasons for not giving notice. Examples of applications that will, by their very nature, be made without notice are freezing injunctions and search orders. A freezing injunction restrains a party from removing their assets from the jurisdiction (ie, England and Wales). If notice was given to the respondent of such an application, the respondent could simply transfer their assets prior to the hearing of the application.

A search order is an order compelling the respondent to allow their premises to be searched by the applicant. It is obtained where the applicant believes that the respondent has documents that, it is usually alleged, belong to the applicant. Again, if notice was given to the respondent in advance, it would be a simple matter for the respondent to hide the documents somewhere else. Because freezing injunctions and search orders can be quite draconian in their impact upon the respondent, such applications must be made to a High Court judge and the evidence in support of these applications must be by way of affidavit. Evidence in support of other applications for interim remedies is by the usual methods:

(a)   witness statements;

(b)   the application notice;

(c)   the statement(s) of case.

The contents of (b) and (c) may be relied on as evidence only where they contain a statement of truth. By their very nature, (a) must contain a statement of truth (see **12.3**).

10.7 INTERIM PAYMENTS

One particular type of interim remedy is an interim payment (see r 25.1(1)(k) at **10.6** above). An interim payment is an advance payment on account of any damages, debt or other sum (excluding costs) which a defendant may be held liable to pay. The interim payment procedure enables a claimant who has a strong case on liability to avoid the financial hardship and/or inconvenience that might otherwise be suffered because of any delay during the period between the start of the claim and its final determination.

Before making an application to the court, the claimant should try to negotiate with the defendant or the defendant's insurance company to obtain a voluntary interim payment. If one is not forthcoming, and if the claimant feels they have good grounds for making the application, then the application should be made as soon as possible.

A claimant may not seek an interim payment until after the time for acknowledging service has expired. The claimant may make more than one application.

10.7.1 Procedure

An application notice for an interim payment must be supported by evidence and be served at least 14 days before the hearing date.

The evidence required in support of an interim payment application is set out in para 2.1 of PD 25B – Interim Payments. The evidence must, amongst other matters, deal with:

(a)   the amount of the interim payment being sought;

(b)   the items or matters in respect of which the interim payment is sought;

(c)   the likely amount of the final judgment;

(d)   the reasons for believing that the conditions for an interim payment are satisfied (see **10.7.2** below);

(e)   any other relevant matters.

Any documents in support of the application should be exhibited.

If the respondent wishes to rely on evidence then this should be served at least seven days before the hearing. If the applicant wishes to use evidence in reply to the respondent's evidence, this should be served at least three days before the hearing.

10.7.2 Grounds for making the order

By r 25.7(1), the grounds for the court making an interim payment are as follows:

(a)   the defendant against whom the order is sought has admitted liability to pay damages or some other sum of money to the claimant;

(b)   the claimant has obtained judgment against that defendant for damages to be assessed or for a sum of money (other than costs) to be assessed;

(c)   it is satisfied that if the claim went to trial the claimant would obtain judgment for a substantial amount of money (other than costs) against the defendant from whom he is seeking an order for an interim payment, whether or not that defendant is the only defendant or one of a number of defendants to the claim;

(d)   the following conditions are satisfied—

    (i)   the claimant is seeking an order for possession of land (whether or not any other order is also sought), and

    (ii)   the court is satisfied that, if the case went to trial, the defendant would be held liable (even if the claim for possession fails) to pay the claimant a sum of money for the defendant's occupation and use of the land while the claim for possession was pending; or

(e)   in a claim in which there are two or more defendants and the order is sought against any one or more of those defendants, the following conditions are satisfied—

    (i)   the court is satisfied that, if the claim went to trial, the claimant would obtain judgment for a substantial amount of money (other than costs) against at least one of the defendants (but the court cannot determine which), and

    (ii)   all the defendants are either—

        (a)   a defendant that is insured in respect of the claim;

        (b)   a defendant whose liability will be met by an insurer under s 151 of the Road Traffic Act 1988, or an insurer acting under the Motor Insurers Bureau Agreement, or the Motor Insurers Bureau where it is acting itself, or

        (c)   a defendant that is a public body.

The rules do not require the applicant to show any need for the interim payment, or that they will suffer prejudice if they do not receive it: see *Stringman v McArdle* [1994] 1 WLR 1653. However, if the delay in assessment of damages is unlikely to be substantial, the court may be reluctant to exercise its discretion to make an order unless the claimant has some special reason for requiring it.

A respondent cannot contest the application on the grounds of poverty. However, the respondent will know from the claimant's evidence how much the claimant is seeking. If the respondent wishes the court to take into account their ability to pay that sum (or indeed any sum) when deciding whether or not to exercise its discretion, sufficient details of the respondent's financial position should be disclosed in their evidence in reply to the application.

The applicant must prove the grounds of application relied upon up to the civil standard of the balance of probabilities. There are degrees of probability within the civil standard, and ground (c) has been interpreted as meaning that

> the burden is a high one within that standard if only because litigation of its nature involves uncertainties. A [claimant] with what may on paper appear to be a strong case may find it fails at trial. If he does then he will have to repay the whole or, to the extent that he fails, part of the interim payment. But ... the [claimant] may spend it ... If he does it may be difficult ... to recover ... Clearly the burden resting on the applicant in those circumstances is towards the top of the flexible scale. (*per* May LJ in *Gibbons v Wall* (1988) The Times, 24 February).

As the burden is so high, it is not surprising that the court has interpreted ground (c) as meaning that the applicant *will* succeed. It is not enough that the court thinks it likely that the claimant will succeed at trial: see *British and Commonwealth Holdings plc v Quadrex Holdings Inc* [1989] 3 WLR 723.

An application for an interim payment is often combined with an application for summary judgment (see **10.5.2**). Where the respondent satisfies the court only that it is possible that their claim or defence may succeed but improbable that it will do so, the court might be persuaded to order an interim payment rather than make a conditional order.

If the applicant can establish an entitlement to an interim payment, the court then has a discretion as to two questions:

(a)   whether to make an order; and

(b)   if so, the amount.

As to question (a), an interim payment may be inappropriate if the issues are complicated, or if difficult questions of law arise that may take many hours and the citation of many authorities to resolve: see *British and Commonwealth Holding plc v Quadrex Holdings Inc*, above. Likewise, the court will not make an order where significant issues of causation remain at large. The court cannot assume, for example, that the claimant will obtain judgment for a substantial amount of money if, because causation is disputed, the defendant is contending that the amount which will be recovered is not substantial at all (see *Farrington v Menzies-Haines* [2019] EWHC 1297 (QB)).

In respect of question (b), the court must not make an interim payment of more than a 'reasonable proportion of the likely amount of the final judgment' after taking into account contributory negligence and any relevant set-off or counterclaim that would reduce any judgment. In other words, the court will seek to calculate what sum is indisputably due to the claimant and then finally consider what sum the defendant is able to pay. For example, in *British and Commonwealth Holding plc v Quadrex Holdings Inc*, the claim was for over £100 million and the judge made an order for an interim payment of £75 million. The Court of Appeal found that such a payment would have a severe adverse impact on the business of the defendant which would be irremediable. In particular, the repayment of that sum if the defendant's defence succeeded at trial would not remedy the damage caused to it by making an interim payment of that size. In the circumstances the court reduced the amount to £5 million.

10.7.3 Consequences of an interim payment order

If a defendant has made an interim payment that exceeds their total liability under the final judgment, the court will invariably order repayment of the excess (*Wakefield v NJS* [2021] EWHC 3452 (QB)) and may award interest on the overpaid amount from the date of the interim payment.

The trial judge will not be told about any interim payment until after they have decided all issues of liability and quantum, unless the defendant consents.

10.8   SECURITY FOR COSTS (r 25.12)

10.8.1   Purpose

We have seen at **3.12** that the time and expense involved in dealing with prospective and actual litigation, including defending a claim, are often considerable. Even if the claim is defeated and the defendant obtains an order for their costs, the full amount spent on the litigation will never be recovered. Even worse, the claimant may be unable or unwilling to pay the costs order, leaving the defendant with the unenviable choice between bearing their own costs or investing further time and money in trying to enforce the order. The provisions in CPR 1998, Part 25 about security for costs may be of assistance, as the defendant can ask the court to exercise its discretion to order the claimant to provide security for the costs that the defendant is likely to be awarded if they defeat the claim.

Rule 25.12(1) provides that a defendant to any claim may apply for security for their costs of the proceedings. So a defendant here will include a claimant defending a counterclaim.

10.8.2   Discretionary power

By r 25.13(1) the court may make an order for security for costs if:

(a)   it is satisfied, having regard to all the circumstances of the case, that it is just to make such an order; and

(b)   one or more of the conditions in Part 25 applies.

10.8.3   The conditions on which the defendant may apply

The defendant can obtain an order for security only if they are able to show that one or more of the conditions set out in rr 25.13 and 25.14 applies. The conditions set out below are the most common relied upon.

10.8.3.1   Claimant resident outside a 2005 Hague Convention State

The defendant may apply where the claimant (whether an individual, a company or other incorporated body) is resident out of the jurisdiction (namely, England and Wales) and is not resident in a State bound by the 2005 Hague Convention on Choice of Court Agreements. Those States are Denmark, the European Union (excluding Denmark), Mexico, Montenegro, Singapore and the United Kingdom.

If the claimant is an individual, where do they reside? It is the place where they normally and habitually live (*R v London Borough of Barnet* [1983] 2 AC 309). Companies reside where their central control and management are located (*Re Little Olympian Each-Ways Ltd* [1994] 4 All ER 561).

This condition recognises the difficulties that the defendant may have in enforcing a costs order outside the EU States and other States bound by the 2005 Hague Convention. For example, in *Bestford Developments LLP v Ras Al Khaimah Investment Authority* [2016] EWCA Civ

1099, the Court of Appeal confirmed that it was quite proper to make an order under this ground where the claimants resided in Georgia and there was a real risk that any eventual award of costs could not be enforced there.

10.8.3.2   Claimant an impecunious company

The defendant may apply where the claimant is a company or other body (whether incorporated inside or outside Great Britain) and there is reason to believe that it will be unable to pay the defendant's costs if ordered to do so. It is therefore essential that evidence is given of the company's assets and the likely total costs of the litigation.

How can the belief in the claimant company's inability to pay be established? The defendant will often produce evidence of the company's accounts, poor credit ratings, any outstanding insolvency petitions, etc. In the case of *Sarpd Oil International Limited v Addax Energy SA* [2016] EWCA Civ 120, the claimant company was an overseas company that was not required to file accounts. In making an order for security for costs, the Court stated that it is wholly appropriate for a court to make presumptions against a company that does not disclose its assets when there is no publicly available evidence as to its solvency.

This condition applies not only to limited companies, but also to unlimited companies: see *Jirehouse Capital v Beller* [2008] EWHC 725 (Ch).

10.8.3.3   The claimant has taken steps to make enforcement difficult

Security may be applied for against a claimant who has taken steps in relation to their assets that would make it difficult to enforce an order for costs against them. This is analogous to the claimant's right to apply for a freezing injunction (see **10.6**) against a defendant. The general principles that govern the making of an order under this condition were summarised by Roth J in *Ackerman v Ackerman* [2012] 3 Costs LO 303, at para 16, as follows:

  i)   The requirement is that the claimant has taken in relation to his assets steps which, if he loses the case and a costs order is made against him, will make that order difficult to enforce. It is not sufficient that the claimant has engaged in other conduct that may be dishonest or reprehensible: *Chandler v Brown* [2001] CP Rep 103 at paras 19–20;

  ii) The test in that regard is objective: it is not concerned with the claimant's motivation but with the effect of steps which he has taken in relation to his assets: *Aoun v Bahri* [2002] EWHC 29 (Comm), [2002] CLC 776, at paras 25–26;

  iii) If it is reasonable to infer on all the evidence that a claimant has undisclosed assets, then his failure to disclose them could itself, although it might not necessarily, lead to the inference that he had put them out of reach of his creditors, including a potential creditor for costs: *Dubai Islamic Bank v PSI Energy Holding Co* [2011] EWCA Civ 761 at para 26;

  iv) There is no temporal limitation as to when the steps were taken: they may have been taken before proceedings had been commenced or were in contemplation: *Harris v Wallis* [2006] EWHC 630 (Ch) at paras 24–25;

  v)   However, motive, intention and the time when steps were taken are all relevant to the exercise of the court's discretion: *Aoun v Bahri, ibid; Harris v Wallis, ibid.*

10.8.3.4   Statutory provisions

There are a number of other statutory provisions that permit the court to require security to be given. For example, s 70(6) of the Arbitration Act 1996 enables the court to grant security in relation to various applications to challenge an arbitration award or appeal on a point of law.

10.8.4   Factors relevant to the court's exercise of its discretion

In considering whether it is just to make an order, the following matters are likely to be considered important.

10.8.4.1   The strength of the claim and the defence

The less likely the defendant is to win at trial, the less justified they are in seeking security. The court will therefore consider whether the claim has a reasonably good prospect of success. Any open admission or offer of settlement and any Part 36 offer (see **Chapter 13**) made by the defendant will tend to undermine the application. However, the true strength of each party's case may not be easy to assess and a detailed consideration of the merits is discouraged (*Fernhill Mining Ltd v Kier Construction Ltd* [2000] CPLR 23).

10.8.4.2   The claimant's ability to provide security

Where the claimant can show a reasonable prospect of success, the courts will be reluctant to make an order for security with which the claimant cannot comply, since the effect is to stifle the claim. The court must strike a balance between the right of the claimant to pursue a genuine claim and the unfairness to the defendant of allowing the claimant to do so without providing security. It is possible that to make an order which the claimant cannot meet would amount to a breach of their right to a fair trial under Article 6(1) of the ECHR. The burden of proving that an order for security will stifle the claim lies on the claimant on a balance of probabilities (see *Lederer v Kisby* [2019] EWHC 554 (Ch) and *Goldtrail Travel v Onur Air* [2017] 1 WLR 3014).

The cost of providing different sorts of security may be relevant:

> The only candidates put forward by the parties were either the proposed deed of indemnity or a payment into court. Which of these was ordered would potentially make a very substantial difference to TKP if it lost at trial: see paragraphs 24 and 25 above, which show that the potential cost to TKP of losing might well be an extra £195,000 if security were provided by way of deed of indemnity. That is a significant extra disadvantage to TKP, especially when compared with the amount in issue on the substantive claim, namely £337,525 and interest. In those circumstances I would have thought it manifest that this was a material and relevant consideration when the Court was considering the manner in which security was to be ordered. That does not mean that such a consideration would always or necessarily be decisive, as what is fair and just depends on the potential consequences for the claimant as well as the defendant ... (per Nugee LJ in *Infinity Distribution Ltd (in administration) v Khan Partnership LLP* [2021] EWCA Civ 565 at [36] and [37])

An increasing problem for defendants is likely to be the difficulty of persuading the court to order security when the claimant is funding the litigation by a CFA (see **2.4.2**). Where, however, the claimant has purchased AEI (see **2.4.5**), which will cover payment of the defendant's costs if the claim fails, no order for security is likely to be sought (*Premier Motorauctions Ltd v PWC LLP* [2017] EWCA Civ 1872). Note that the Court indicated that a defendant is entitled to some assurance as to the scope of the ATE cover and that it was not liable to be avoided for misrepresentation or non-disclosure. For an example of an inadequate ATE policy, see *Hotel Portfolio II UK Ltd (In Liquidation) v Ruhan* [2020] 1 WLUK 232.

10.8.4.3   The causes of the claimant's impecuniosity

The claimant may be able to persuade the court that their shortage of money has been caused by or contributed to by the defendant's behaviour.

EXAMPLE

C Ltd's business is dependent on a few major contracts, including one with D Ltd. As a result of a disagreement, D Ltd breaks off the relationship. C Ltd sues, alleging that D Ltd was not entitled to terminate the contract. D Ltd applies for security, on the basis that C Ltd will be unable to pay its costs if it wins at trial. C Ltd admits it is in financial difficulties but opposes the application, contending that these difficulties are the result of D Ltd's wrongful termination.

10.8.4.4   Property within the jurisdiction

Where the application is made against a claimant ordinarily resident outside the EU and other States bound by the 2005 Hague Convention (see **10.8.3.1**), the court is unlikely to grant security if the claimant has substantial property of a permanent or fixed nature within the jurisdiction that would be available to meet the defendant's costs.

The court will not necessarily order security if the claimant does not have property within the jurisdiction. The single criterion is what is just in all the circumstances (*Leyvand v Barasch* (2000) *The Times*, 23 March).

10.8.4.5   The timing of the application

The application should be made as soon as practicable. Where the defendant has delayed for no good reason, the court may be less willing to order security, particularly for costs already incurred. Where the claimant would find it difficult to provide security, a delay in applying that has prejudiced the claimant's ability to raise the necessary funds would be a relevant consideration.

10.8.5   Procedure

An application for security may be made at any time, but, as mentioned at **10.8.4.5**, the defendant would be wise to apply as soon as the facts justifying the application are known. As with other interim applications, the defendant is encouraged, where practicable, to indicate that they intend to apply on the directions questionnaire (see **9.5.1**), so that the application can be dealt with at any case management conference (see **9.6.3.2**).

Before applying, the defendant should (except in exceptional circumstances, such as the evasive removal of assets) write to the claimant and ask that security be provided voluntarily.

Where an application to the court is necessary, it must be supported by written evidence. This is often provided in the form of a witness statement. The CPR 1998, Part 25 does not prescribe the content of the evidence, but there are three objectives, namely, to:

(a)   establish that a condition exists;

(b)   persuade the court that it is just to exercise its discretion in favour of the defendant; and

(c)   justify the amount sought.

The defendant will usually apply both in relation to costs already incurred and estimated future costs, giving details of these in a costs budget (see **9.7.1**). On a first application, the court may well refuse to grant security to cover the defendant's estimated costs up to and including trial, preferring to order an amount estimated to cover the costs up to a particular stage in the litigation and leaving the defendant to reapply as the claim progresses. In special or unusual circumstances, the court can order the defendant to provide a cross-undertaking in damages; see *TBD (Owen Holland) Ltd v Andrew Simons & Others* [2020] 2 WLUK 311.

10.8.6   The form and effect of the order

If the court grants the application, it will specify in the order:

(a)   the amount of the security;

(b)   the date by which the claimant must provide it; and

(c)   the form it is to take.

Most commonly, the claimant is required to make a payment into court. Alternatively, the security may be held by the defendant's solicitor, and will sometimes take the form of a banker's draft or a guarantee (eg, an order to provide £500,000 security by way of a bank guarantee from a first-class London bank: see *Verslot Dredging BV v HDI Gerling Vesicherung AG* [2013] LTL, 5 February; or a charge on the claimant's property: see *Xhosa Office Rentals Ltd v Multi High Tec PCB Ltd* [2012] EWHC 3673). On other occasions, the requirement for security is satisfied by the claimant giving a suitable undertaking to the court. It is only in a rare and exceptional case that the court should require a cross-undertaking in favour of a claimant as a condition of ordering security for costs, and only in even rarer and more exceptional cases that it should do so in favour of commercial litigation funders (see *Rowe v Ingenious Media Holdings plc* [2021] EWCA Civ 29).

Note that in *Tulip Trading Ltd v Bitcoin Association for BSV (a Swiss verein)* [2022] EWHC 141 (Ch), the court rejected an application that security for costs be given by Bitcoin on the basis that the fluctuating values of Bitcoin would not provide the defendants with adequate security.

What happens if the claimant fails to provide the security by the date ordered? Part 25 is silent on this point, but in practice the court will frequently order that the claim is to be struck out and the defendant entitled to apply without further order for judgment to be entered with costs to be assessed. Even if this penalty is not set out in the order, the defendant will be entitled to apply for a strike out for non-compliance with a court order under the power in r 3.4(2)(c): see **9.3**.

10.8.7　Security under r 3.1(5)

In addition to the powers in Part 25, the court has the power under r 3.1(5) to order a party to make a payment into court if that party has, without good reason, failed to comply with a rule, Practice Direction or pre-action protocol. The money paid in provides security for any sum ordered to be paid to another party in the proceedings.

This power broadens the court's discretion to grant security, since a payment in may be required against a defendant as well as a claimant, and there is no requirement to establish that one of the conditions in r 25.13 applies.

In considering whether to make such an order the court must have regard to the amount in dispute and the costs the parties have incurred or may incur in the future (r 3.1(6)). The court will doubtless also have in mind the ability of the party against whom the order is made to apply for relief under r 3.9, and will take into account the factors identified in that rule (see **9.4**).

The circumstances in which the courts choose to exercise their power under r 3.1(5) are limited and tend to be occasions where the court considers that the other side needs protection, either because there is a history of repeated breaches of the timetable or court orders, or because of a suspicion that a party is not acting in good faith: see *Mealey Horgan plc v Horgan* (1999) *The Times*, 6 July, cited with approval in *Olatawura v Abiloye* [2003] 1 WLR 275.

Note further that in *Huscroft v P & O Ferries Ltd* [2011] 2 All ER 762, Moore-Bick LJ warned (at [14]):

> It would be wrong, in my view, to encourage litigants to regard rule 3.1(3) as providing a convenient means of circumventing the requirements of Part 25 and thereby of providing a less demanding route to obtaining security for costs. In my view, when the court is asked to consider making an order under rule 3.1(3) or 3.1(5) which is, or amounts to, an order for security for costs, or when it considers doing so of its own motion, it should bear in mind the principles underlying rules 25.12 and 25.13. These include the principle that a personal Claimant who is resident within the jurisdiction or in one of the other member states of the European Union cannot be required to provide security for costs just because he is impecunious, even though his conduct of the proceedings may be open to criticism. Although it might be argued that the Defendant in such a case should be entitled to obtain protection against the risk of being unable to enforce a judgment for costs, a policy decision has been taken to the contrary. This suggests that an order of that kind should not be made in the exercise of the power under rule 3.1(3) unless one or more additional factors are present which make it appropriate to impose a burden of that kind on one party and a corresponding benefit on the other.

See also *Allen v Bloomsbury Publishing Ltd* [2011] EWCA Civ 943, where the relevant law is reviewed at [7].

CHAPTER 11

DISCLOSURE AND INSPECTION OF DOCUMENTS – CPR 1998, PART 31

11.1	Purpose of disclosure and inspection	183
11.2	Definition of 'disclosure' (r 31.2) and 'documents' (r 31.4)	184
11.3	Disclosure on each track	185
11.4	Standard disclosure (r 31.6)	186
11.5	Disclosure of copies (r 31.9)	188
11.6	The duty to search (r 31.7)	188
11.7	The right of inspection (r 31.3)	189
11.8	Procedure for standard disclosure	189
11.9	The disclosure statement	190
11.10	Continuing obligation (r 31.11)	191
11.11	Withholding inspection	191
11.12	Disclosing the existence of documents: the list	197
11.13	Failure to disclose (r 31.21)	198
11.14	Subsequent use of disclosed documents (r 31.22)	198
11.15	Applying for specific disclosure (r 31.12)	198
11.16	Disclosure before proceedings start (r 31.16)	199
11.17	Non-party disclosure (r 31.17)	199
11.18	Disclosure obligations and solicitors' duties	200
11.19	Inspection of standard disclosure documents	201
11.20	Disclosure pilot scheme in the Business and Property Courts (PD 51U)	201

LEARNING OUTCOMES

After reading this chapter you will have learned:

- the role of disclosure and inspection
- how to carry out a search for documents
- what constitutes a claim for legal professional privilege
- the effect of inadvertent disclosure
- how to complete the prescribed form for giving standard disclosure
- what applications might be made for disclosure.

11.1 PURPOSE OF DISCLOSURE AND INSPECTION

In plain language, litigation in this country is conducted 'cards face up on the table'. Some people from other lands regard this as incomprehensible. 'Why', they ask, 'should I be expected to provide my opponent with the means of defeating me?' The answer, of course, is that litigation is not a war or even a game. It is designed to do real justice between opposing parties and, if the court does not have all the relevant information, it cannot achieve this object. (*per* Sir John Donaldson MR in *Davies v Eli Lilly & Co* [1987] 1 WLR 428)

As we saw in **Chapter 3**, the pre-action protocols require the parties to prospective litigation to share information. However, there is no general obligation on a party to show their opponent the contents of documents, and in particular no requirement to show documents that are adverse to the party's own position. A party may request that an opponent disclose documents that they would normally show during court proceedings, but the only way to compel that disclosure is by way of court order (see **3.9** and **11.16**). Therefore, prior to a claim form being issued, the parties may to a large extent select those documents they wish to show and keep all the others hidden.

The main purpose of disclosure and inspection is to enable the parties better to evaluate the strength of their opponent's case in advance of the trial. The parties have to reveal to each other the documents which have a bearing on the case. This is the disclosure stage. It is usually done by each party providing the other with a list of their documents. The parties may then inspect, that is read, some of the other side's documents. The process is intended to promote settlements and therefore a saving in costs. It ensures that the parties are not taken by surprise at the trial and that the court has all relevant information in order to do justice between the parties. However, inspection is subject to restrictions, and some documents may not have to be shown to the opponent (see **11.11**).

Disclosure is governed by Part 31 of CPR 1998, which applies to all claims save those allocated to the small claims track (see **9.6.1**).

11.2 DEFINITION OF 'DISCLOSURE' (r 31.2) AND 'DOCUMENTS' (r 31.4)

11.2.1 The meaning of 'disclosure'

'Disclosure' is defined in r 31.2, which states:

> A party discloses a document by stating that the document exists or has existed.

This is done by preparing and serving a list of documents on every other party (see **11.8**). But before we consider how disclosure is given in civil litigation, let us briefly consider how a document can be described. This will then help you understand disclosure. There are two ways. Consider the book that you are now reading. I can describe the actual document to you, namely it is the 'the Civil Litigation Textbook published by CLP'. Alternatively, I can just describe it generally as 'a textbook'. However, either way, I have disclosed to you the existence of a document. In the first example you know precisely what document I am referring to; whilst in the second example you only know that it is some sort of textbook. Bear this in mind as you read the rest of this chapter.

11.2.2 What is a 'document'

'Documents' are defined in r 31.4 as being anything in which information of any description is recorded. 'Documents' therefore include written documents, audiotapes, videotapes and photographs.

11.2.2.1 Electronic documents

Electronic documents, such as texts, e-mails, apps and the messages on them, word-processed documents and databases, are also documents. In addition to documents that are readily accessible from computer systems and other electronic devices and media, the definition includes those documents that are stored on servers and back-up systems, and electronic documents that have been 'deleted'. See further **11.6.2**.

11.2.2.2 Information recorded in a document

Whilst it is important to appreciate how wide the definition of a document is under the CPR 1998, it is crucial to your understanding of how to give disclosure that you spend some time with this definition. You should focus on three words, namely 'information ... is recorded'. It is the information recorded in a document that will determine whether or not it forms part of disclosure. The procedure has nothing to do with whether or not the document itself is admissible at trial. It is also irrelevant whether or not a party would wish to rely on the document itself at trial. Remember, it is what a document records that governs whether or not it will form part of disclosure.

11.3 DISCLOSURE ON EACH TRACK

11.3.1 Small claims track

The provisions for disclosure and inspection in Part 31 do not apply on the small claims track. The usual direction on that track is that each party shall, at least 14 days before the date fixed for the final hearing, file and serve on every other party copies of all documents (including any expert's report) on which they intend to rely at the hearing.

11.3.2 Fast track

The norm is for the parties to give standard disclosure (see **11.4**).

11.3.3 Multi-track

For all multi-track claims (save for proceedings in the Business and Property Courts which are subject to a pilot scheme from 1 January 2019 – see **11.20**) which include a claim for personal injuries, the norm is for the parties to give standard disclosure (see **11.4**).

11.3.3.1 Disclosure report

For all multi-track claims which do not include a claim for personal injuries, r 31.5(3) requires the parties to file and serve a disclosure report not less than 14 days before the first case management conference. The report should be in Form N263 (a copy is at **Appendix A(11)**). The report should:

(a) describe what documents exist or may exist that are or may be relevant to the matters in issue in the case;

(b) describe where and with whom those documents are or may be located;

(c) describe how any electronic documents are stored;

(d) include an estimate of the broad range of costs that could be involved in giving standard disclosure in the case, including the costs of searching for and disclosing any electronically stored documents. The basis on which the estimate is given should be set out;

(e) state what disclosure directions are sought (see **11.3.3.2**); and

(f) be verified by a statement of truth. On the form this reads: 'I believe that the facts stated in this Disclosure Report are true.' The form provides that it can be signed by the party or their legal representative.

11.3.3.2 Meeting the overriding objective

Not less than seven days before the first case management conference, and on any other occasion as the court may direct, the parties must, at a meeting or by telephone, discuss and seek to agree a proposal in relation to disclosure that meets the overriding objective. The court will seek to tailor the order for disclosure to the requirements of the particular case. The financial position and views of the parties, the importance of the case and the complexity of the issues will be taken into account when considering what order to make.

11.3.3.3 Disclosure directions

As to (e), what directions might be sought? Rule 31.5(7) gives the following 'menu' of options:

(a)   an order dispensing with disclosure;

(b)   an order that a party disclose the documents on which they rely, and at the same time request any specific disclosure they require from any other party;

(c)   an order that directs, where practicable, the disclosure to be given by each party on an issue by issue basis;

(d)   an order that each party disclose any documents which it is reasonable to suppose may contain information which enables that party to advance their own case or to damage that of any other party, or which leads to an enquiry which has either of those consequences;

(e)   an order that a party give standard disclosure (see **11.4**);

(f)   any other order in relation to disclosure that the court considers appropriate.

How might the court assist the parties or impose disclosure obligations? Rule 31.5(8) provides that the court may at any point give directions as to how disclosure is to be given, and in particular:

(a)   what searches are to be undertaken, of where, for what, in respect of which time periods and by whom and the extent of any search for electronically stored documents;

(b)   whether lists of documents are required;

(c)   how and when the disclosure statement is to be given;

(d)   in what format documents are to be disclosed (and whether any identification is required);

(e)   what is required in relation to documents that once existed but no longer exist; and

(f)   whether disclosure should take place in stages.

11.4   STANDARD DISCLOSURE (r 31.6)

Standard disclosure is defined in r 31.6 and requires a party to disclose only:

(a)   the documents on which he relies; and

(b)   the documents which—

(i)   adversely affect his own case;

(ii)   adversely affect another party's case; or

(iii)   support another party's case; and

(c)   the documents which he is required to disclose by a relevant practice direction. [At the time of writing, there are none.]

It should not be difficult to identify information in a document on which the client relies, as most clients provide their solicitors with favourable documents from the outset of a case. But that is not always true, and a thorough search for documents – both favourable and unfavourable (wholly or in part) – should be made at Stage 1 (see **Chapters 1** to **3**).

11.4.1   Identify the issues in dispute

As we have just seen, standard disclosure obligations require the parties to disclose the existence of documents that record information on which they intend to rely on, or which adversely affect or support another party's 'case'.

So what is the 'case'? Remember that we have just reached Stage 3 of Civil Litigation and are dealing with what is normally the first procedural step. At Stage 2 the 'case' should have been set out and defined by the statements of case (see **7.5.1**). So the parties should focus on the issues in dispute and search for documents dealing with those issues and which affect the case 'to a material extent'. See *Depp v News Group Newspapers Ltd & Another* [2020] EWHC 1689 (QB). Consider Example 2 at **7.5.1**. The claimant should search for documents concerning the issues identified as being in dispute. There is no need to search for and disclose documents that record only information relating to agreed issues (see Example 1). For instance, there is no need to search for documents dealing with delivery of the Unit in June 2021 as this is not disputed. But as it is not admitted that the claimant installed the Unit in July 2021, documents that record information concerning that matter should be searched for and disclosed.

In many cases both liability and quantum will be the legal issues in dispute. But costs will also normally be a live issue at trial, and so documents that record information concerning costs (such as Part 36 or other offers of settlement: see **Chapter 13**) should be included as part of standard disclosure.

Do documents that *only* call into question the reliability or credit of a party or one of their witnesses adversely affect that party's own case or otherwise support their opponent's case? No – there is no obligation to disclose documents on matters that record information that would be used *solely* in cross-examination as to credit: *Favor Easy Management Ltd v Wu* [2010] EWCA Civ 1630.

11.4.2 Control of documents

The duty of disclosure is limited to documents that are or have been in a party's control (see r 31.8). This means that:

(a)   the document is or was in their physical possession; or

(b)   they have or have had a right to possession of it; or

(c)   they have or have had a right to inspect or take copies of it.

Documents held by a party's agent would therefore be within that party's control.

Note that it is open to the parties to agree in writing to dispense with or limit standard disclosure, but this is not common. Any difficulties in giving disclosure, etc, should be raised at the first opportunity, eg at a case management conference (see **9.6.3.2**).

11.4.3 Practical point

Remember that a document is anything in which *information is recorded* (see **11.2**). You are not concerned at this stage about what use, if any, your client or opponent might make of any particular document at trial. Your task is to scrutinise the contents of documents to see if any fall within the r 31.6 definition.

CASE STUDY: RULE 31.6 DOCUMENTS

Consider the case study in **Appendix D**. Assume that you act for the claimants. Is the letter before claim (**Appendix D(2)**) a r 31.6 document? By comparing para 3 of the particulars of claim with para 3 of the defence and counterclaim, we know that the defendant denies the legal issue of liability and the factual basis of the claim, ie the allegation in the letter that he 'drove up the drive at excessive speed and without properly controlling the Car.' So the letter before claim records information on which your clients rely. It is therefore a r 31.6 document.

What about the particulars of claim and the defence and counterclaim (**Appendix D(4)** and **(5)**)? Are these r 31.6 documents? The answer is yes. The particulars of claim record information on which your clients rely, ie the legal issues of liability and quantum and their factual bases in paras 3 and 4 respectively. The defence and counterclaim record information adverse to your clients' case and supporting the defendant's case; for example, as to liability, that the collision was caused or contributed to by your clients (para 4). Your clients have denied this in para 2 of the reply and defence to counterclaim (**Appendix D(6)**). So the reply and defence to counterclaim is also a r 31.6 document.

11.5 DISCLOSURE OF COPIES (r 31.9)

A party need not disclose more than one copy of a document unless the copy contains 'a modification, obliteration or other marking or feature' on which the party intends to rely, or which supports another party's case, or which could adversely affect their own or another party's case. In that case, the copy document is treated as a separate document.

The most common example in practice of a document that has been modified, so creating another copy, is one where handwritten notes have been made on the original.

EXAMPLE

A managing director of a company receives a letter before action. She forwards it to a colleague to get out any records that might still exist, having written on the letter, 'I remember this person's accident. It was the company's fault but after all this time he probably can't prove it.' What this copy of the letter now records is adverse to the company's case if it does go on to defend the claim. The handwritten notes are a form of admission. So this will meet the r 31.6 definition (see **11.4**) and that copy will be subject to standard disclosure.

11.6 THE DUTY TO SEARCH (r 31.7)

11.6.1 A reasonable search

In order to give standard disclosure, a party must make a reasonable search for all documents that could adversely affect their own or another party's case, or which support another party's case.

What is reasonable depends on:

(a)   the number of documents involved;

(b)   the nature and complexity of the proceedings;

(c)   the ease and expense of retrieval of any particular document; and

(d)   the significance of the document.

11.6.2 Electronic documents

Practice Direction 31B sets out detailed provisions for the disclosure of electronic documents where the case has been or is likely to be allocated to the multi-track. The following general principles are prescribed by para 6:

(1)   Electronic Documents should be managed efficiently in order to minimise the cost incurred;

(2)   technology should be used in order to ensure that document management activities are undertaken efficiently and effectively;

(3)   disclosure should be given in a manner which gives effect to the overriding objective;

(4)   Electronic Documents should generally be made available for inspection in a form which allows the party receiving the documents the same ability to access, search, review and display the documents as the party giving disclosure; and

(5)   disclosure of Electronic Documents which are of no relevance to the proceedings may place an excessive burden in time and cost on the party to whom disclosure is given.

Before directions are given or any case management conference occurs, the parties should discuss and, if possible, agree such matters as the categories of electronic documents and where these are held; keywords; preservation of documents; exchange of data and the format for inspection. It is crucial that the parties try to agree any limitations they intend to place on their reasonable search for electronic documents. For example, a party identifies that 20 people were involved in the disputed issues in a case, but decides that only five played any significant role and might hold relevant data. The opposing party may well object to some or all of the other 15 people being excluded. Similarly, where one party proposes to conduct a search by certain keywords, the other side may wish to suggest additional keywords. A simple example is the spelling of the keyword itself. If relevant documents might have been created using both the American and English spelling of a keyword, both should be used.

Keyword searches can be conducted with a high degree of sophistication, including use of 'wildcards' and 'boolean operators'. Wildcards enable searches of words containing a variant of a keyword: thus "cat*" may bring up documents referring to 'cats', 'category' and 'catechism'. Boolean operators enable the use of conjunctions ('and', 'or', 'not', etc) to combine or exclude keywords in a search (as observed by Smith J in *Agents' Mutual Ltd v Gascoigne Halman Ltd* [2019] EWHC 3104 (Ch) at [4]).

The Practice Direction includes an Electronic Disclosure Questionnaire that the parties can use, although this is not mandatory. When preparing for any case management conference, the parties must file a summary of the matters on which the parties agree and disagree in relation to the disclosure of electronic documents. The court will either give written directions or order a separate hearing in relation to electronic disclosure and may direct the parties to complete and exchange the Questionnaire if they have not already done so.

11.6.3 Putting limits on a search

If a party has limited the search for certain documents, they must state this in their disclosure statement (see **11.9**). Practice Direction 31A suggests, at para 2, for example, that it may be reasonable to decide not to search for documents coming into existence before some particular date, or to limit the search to documents in some particular place or places, or to documents falling into particular categories.

11.6.4 Practical point: anticipate any potential problems or disputes

Before case management directions are given (see **Chapter 9**), and particularly prior to the first case management conference in a multi-track case (see **9.6.3.2**), the parties should discuss any issues that may arise regarding searches for, and the preservation of, documents.

11.7 THE RIGHT OF INSPECTION (r 31.3)

Rule 31.3(1) gives a party a right of inspection of a disclosed document, except where:

(a)   the document is no longer in the control of the party who disclosed it (see **11.4**);

(b)   the party disclosing the document has a right or a duty to withhold inspection of it (see **11.11**); or

(c)   a party considers it would be disproportionate to the issues in the case to permit inspection of documents within a category and states in their disclosure statement (see **11.9**) that inspection of those documents will not be permitted on the grounds that to do so would be disproportionate.

By r 31.15, where a party has a right to inspect a document, that party wishing to inspect must give written notice of their wish to inspect, and the party who disclosed the document must permit inspection not more than seven days after the date on which they received the notice. Rather than going to inspect the documents personally, a party may also request a copy of the document, provided the party also undertakes to pay reasonable copying costs. In this case, the party who disclosed the document must supply a copy not more than seven days after the date on which they received the request.

11.8 PROCEDURE FOR STANDARD DISCLOSURE

Where an order for standard disclosure has been made, each party must make and serve a list of documents using Practice Form N265 (a copy of which appears in the case study at **Appendix D(10)**), which must identify the documents in a convenient order and manner and as concisely as possible. Practice Direction 31A, at para 3.2, states that it will normally be necessary to list the documents in date order, to number them consecutively and to give each a concise description (eg, letter, claimant to defendant). It also suggests that where there is a large number of documents all falling into a particular category, the disclosing party may list those documents as a category rather than individually.

The list is in three parts on the final page. The first part of the list sets out the documents within the party's control and which they do not object to the other party inspecting. The second part of the list sets out other documents of which the party has control but where the party objects to the other party inspecting them. The most common reason for objection is that the party claims privilege from inspection in relation to those documents (see **11.11**).

The third part of the list consists of documents which are not privileged from inspection but are no longer in the party's control. The list must state what has happened to these documents.

See further **11.12**.

11.9   THE DISCLOSURE STATEMENT

11.9.1   An individual must sign

It will have been seen from the definition of standard disclosure at **11.4** that a party is under an obligation to disclose documents that might adversely affect their own case or support another party's case. A party is therefore under an obligation to disclose documents that could be very detrimental to that party's chances of success, but which the other party does not know exist until disclosure. It is, therefore, essential that parties comply fully and honestly with the requirements of disclosure. Partly for that reason, the list of documents contains a disclosure statement (see r 31.10(5)). This is a statement made by the party disclosing the documents:

(a)   setting out the extent of the search that has been made to locate documents of which disclosure is required;

(b)   certifying that they understand the duty to disclose documents;

(c)   certifying that, to the best of their knowledge, they have carried out that duty.

Where the party making the disclosure statement is a company, firm, association or other organisation, the statement must also identify the person making the statement, the office or position they hold, and explain why they are considered the appropriate person to make the statement.

In what circumstances can (and should) a solicitor sign a disclosure statement? Obviously if a firm of solicitors is itself a party to proceedings then, as a party, the solicitor in the firm who deals with disclosure should sign. Otherwise, by r 31.10(9), a disclosure statement may be made by a person who is not a party only where this is permitted by a relevant Practice Direction. The only provision in PD 31A is at para 4.7, which provides that 'an insurer or the Motor Insurers' Bureau may sign a disclosure statement on behalf of a party where the insurer or the Motor Insurers' Bureau has a financial interest in the result of proceedings brought wholly or partially by or against that party'. However, remember that the different divisions of the High Court produce their own *Court Guides* (see **5.1**), and these should be consulted for any variation of this general rule.

11.9.2   Contempt of court

Proceedings for contempt of court may be brought against a person if they make, or cause to be made, a false disclosure statement without an honest belief in its truth. The proceedings require the permission of the court unless they are brought by the Attorney-General (see Part 81).

11.9.3 Solicitors' duties

Practice Direction 31A, at para 4.4, also states that if the disclosing party has a legal representative acting for them, the legal representative must endeavour to ensure that the person making the disclosure statement understands the duty of disclosure (see further at **11.18**).

A solicitor therefore is under a clear duty to advise their client as to the requirements of disclosure. The solicitor must ensure as far as possible that all documents which have to be disclosed are preserved and made available for inspection. (See **11.18**.) This is obviously something a solicitor must explain to the client on receiving instructions. It is best practice to confirm that advice in writing.

11.10 CONTINUING OBLIGATION (r 31.11)

Disclosure is an obligation that continues until the proceedings are concluded. If documents to which the duty of disclosure extends come to a party's notice at any time during the proceedings, even though the party has already supplied a list of documents, they must immediately notify every other party.

If a document is found after a party's list of documents has been served and it satisfies the test in r 31.6 (see **11.4**), notice should be given by way of letter or a supplemental list. If the party wishes to rely on the document at trial, either the opponent will have to agree or a successful application made to the court for permission to do so (see **11.13**). Even if permission is given, the opponent may still argue at trial that little weight should be attached to the evidence (see **12.9.3**). Late disclosure of an important document can be highly damaging to a case.

11.11 WITHHOLDING INSPECTION

As we have already seen, a party can withhold the right to inspect a document that has been disclosed. The usual reason for this is that a party claims that the documents are privileged from inspection. These privileged documents fall into three classes:

(a) documents protected by legal professional privilege;

(b) documents tending to incriminate the party producing them;

(c) documents privileged on the grounds of public policy.

11.11.1 Legal professional privilege

11.11.1.1 Communications passing between a party and their legal advisers or between a party's legal advisers ('advice privilege')

Letters and other communications passing between a party and their solicitor are privileged from inspection provided they are written by or to the solicitor in their professional capacity and for the sole or dominant purpose of obtaining legal advice or assistance for the client (the so-called 'dominant purpose test' might otherwise be described as 'mainly or predominantly': see *Civil Aviation Authority v R (on the application of Jet2.com Ltd)* [2020] EWCA Civ 35, and also the case of *Waugh* at **11.11.1.3**). 'Legal advice' is not confined to telling the client the law; it includes information passed by solicitor to client, or vice versa, so that advice may be sought and given, and it includes advice about what should prudently and sensibly be done in the relevant legal context.

Let us briefly consider an example. In a conveyancing transaction the buyer's solicitor sends a short letter, asking the client to make an appointment to see the solicitor to discuss the contract. The letter contains no legal advice. At that meeting, when legal advice is given, the client makes notes of what their solicitor says and the solicitor subsequently makes an attendance note of the legal advice given. Is the letter to the client, asking them to make an appointment, privileged from inspection? No, as legal advice is not given. However, unless the document meets the test in r 31.6 (see **11.4**) it would not be disclosable. What about the client's and the solicitor's notes of the meeting? As these record legal advice given, they are privileged from inspection.

Privilege, however, does not extend without limit to all solicitor/client communications. The range of assistance given by solicitors to their clients has greatly broadened in recent times; for example, many solicitors now provide investment advice to clients. The scope of legal professional privilege has to be kept within reasonable bounds. See further *Three Rivers District Council and Others v Governor and Company of the Bank of England* [2004] UKHL 48, [2004] 3 WLR 1274.

The privilege extends to communications between a party and their solicitor's employee or agent, and also to communications between a party and a solicitor in their service, for example a solicitor to a government department or in a legal department of a commercial enterprise. It also applies to communications from a solicitor to a third party containing information provided by the client to the solicitor which is covered by legal advice privilege and which the client has given the lawyer authority to disclose (*Raiffeisen Bank International AG v Asia Coal Energy Ventures Ltd and Ashurst LLP* [2020] EWCA Civ 11).

The underlying purpose of legal professional advice privilege is to allow free access to the legal profession (see **11.11.1.4**) So, in this context, solicitors, in-house solicitors, barristers and foreign lawyers are included. The privilege therefore also covers instructions and briefs to counsel, counsel's opinions, and counsel's drafts and notes. However, the privilege does not apply to an accountant who gives legal advice (*R (on the application of Prudential Plc) v Special Commissioner of Income Tax* [2013] UKSC 1).

11.11.1.2 Communications passing between the solicitor and a third party ('litigation privilege')

Communications passing between the solicitor and a third party are privileged from inspection only if:

(a)   they come into existence after litigation is contemplated or commenced; and

(b)   they are made with a view to the litigation, either for the sole or dominant purpose of obtaining or giving advice in regard to it, or for obtaining evidence to be used in it.

Examples of documents that may come within this head of privilege are a report from an expert obtained by a solicitor with a view to advising the solicitor's client about existing or contemplated litigation, or witness statements obtained by a solicitor for the purpose of existing or contemplated litigation. Does an AEI policy attract this privilege? Yes, the communications in the negotiation and drafting of the policy, as well as the final agreed policy, would have been brought into existence for the dominant purpose of conducting litigation and would reflect the legal advice given as to the prospects of success (see *Arroyo v BP Exploration Co (Colombia) Ltd* [2010] LTL, 4 June (QBD)).

11.11.1.3 Communications between the client and a third party ('litigation privilege')

Documents that have passed between the client and a third party are privileged if the sole or dominant purpose for which they were produced was to obtain legal advice in respect of existing or contemplated litigation, or to conduct, or aid in the conduct of, such litigation, usually to have as evidence. It must be the case that litigation was reasonably in prospect at the time when the document was created, and that the sole or dominant reason for obtaining the document was either to enable solicitors to advise as to whether a claim should be made or resisted, or to have as evidence.

In *Starbev GP Ltd v Interbrew Central European Holding BV* [2013] EWHC 4038 (Comm), the court stated (per Hamblen J at [11]):

> It is not enough for a party to show that proceedings were reasonably anticipated or in contemplation; the party must also show that the relevant communications were for the dominant purpose of either (i)

enabling legal advice to be sought or given, and/or (ii) seeking or obtaining evidence or information to be used in or in connection with such anticipated or contemplated proceedings. Where communications may have taken place for a number of purposes, it is incumbent on the party claiming privilege to establish that the dominant purpose was litigation.

In order to determine whether the document is privileged, one must look at the dominant purpose at the time when it came into existence. So if a client asks an expert to prepare a report, it is the client's intention that is relevant. If the document is subsequently used by solicitors for the purposes of litigation, that will not mean that it is privileged if the original purpose of the document was something different.

CASE EXAMPLE

In *Waugh v British Railways Board* [1980] AC 521, the claimant's husband, an employee of the defendant Board, was killed in an accident while working on the railways. In accordance with the defendant's usual practice, a report on the accident was prepared by two of its officers very shortly after the accident. Although the report was headed 'For the information of the Board's solicitor', the defendant accepted that it had been prepared for two purposes. First, to establish the cause of the accident so that appropriate safety measures could be taken. Secondly, to enable the defendant's solicitor to advise in the litigation that was almost certain to follow. Whilst the first purpose was more immediate than the second, the defendant stated that both were of equal importance. The House of Lords held that as preparing the report for use in anticipated litigation was merely one of the purposes and not the dominant purpose for which it was prepared, the report was not privileged from inspection.

Where a client is not an individual, this form of privilege is also applied to communications between individuals within that organisation. Thus, a memorandum sent by one partner of a firm to another would be privileged if it was prepared for the dominant purpose of obtaining legal advice in respect of existing or contemplated litigation, or to aid the conduct of such litigation.

Two recent cases have illustrated the importance of ensuring that no documents are created internally by a company which could fall outside the scope of litigation privilege and thus be disclosable. In *Director of the Serious Fraud Office v Eurasian Natural Resources Corporation (ENRC) Ltd* [2018] EWCA Civ 2006, the Court of Appeal overturned the High Court decision concerning the extent to which litigation privilege could apply in internal investigations. ENRC successfully argued that documents prepared during internal investigations, both by its lawyers and a firm of forensic accountants, were protected by litigation privilege. The test for litigation privilege is whether, at the time a communication is made:

(a)   litigation, in the form of adversarial proceedings, is reasonably in contemplation; and

(b)   the communication is made for the dominant purpose of conducting that litigation.

In the second case, *WH Holding Ltd v E20 Stadium LLP (No 2)* [2018] EWCA Civ 2652, the Court of Appeal considered whether privilege can be claimed over internal client communications that discussed a commercial proposal for settlement of the dispute. In its judgment at para 27, the Court provided the following guidance:

i)   Litigation privilege is engaged when litigation is in reasonable contemplation.

ii)   Once litigation privilege is engaged it covers communications between parties or their solicitors and third parties for the sole or dominant purpose of obtaining information or advice in connection with the conduct of the litigation ...

iii)   Conducting the litigation includes deciding whether to litigate and also includes whether to settle the dispute giving rise to the litigation.

iv)   Documents in which such information or advice cannot be disentangled or which would otherwise reveal such information or advice are covered by the privilege.

v)   There is no separate head of privilege which covers internal communications falling outside the ambit of litigation privilege as described above.

11.11.1.4   Purpose of legal professional privilege

Legal professional advice privilege is concerned with the fundamental human right to respect for private life guaranteed by Article 8 ECHR. In this context it means that a client should be able to consult their lawyer in confidence, knowing that whatever is said will not be revealed without the client's agreement. So documents which record confidential communications between a client and their lawyer are privileged from inspection if the purpose of the communication was to give or receive legal advice.

The same principle applies to legal professional litigation privilege. Its objective was described in the classic statement of Jessel MR in *Anderson v Bank of British Columbia* (1876) 2 Ch D 644 at 649:

> The object and meaning of the rule is this: that as, by reason of the complexity and difficulty of our law, litigation can only be properly conducted by professional men, it is absolutely necessary that a man, in order to prosecute his rights or to defend himself from an improper claim, should have recourse to the assistance of professional lawyers, and it being so absolutely necessary, it is equally necessary, to use a vulgar phrase, that he should be able to make a clean breast of it to the gentleman whom he consults with a view to the prosecution of his claim, or the substantiating his defence against the claim of others; that he should be able to place unrestricted and unbounded confidence in the professional agent, and that the communications he so makes to him should be kept secret, unless with his consent (for it is his privilege, and not the privilege of the confidential agent), that he should be enabled properly to conduct his litigation. That is the meaning of the rule.

11.11.1.5   Waiver of privilege

The privilege is the client's and not the solicitor's, and therefore it may be waived by the client. Once a copy of a privileged document is served on the other side, the privilege is waived.

Note that subsequent to disclosure and inspection, each party is required by the court to serve on the other(s) copies of the witness statements and expert reports upon which they intend to rely at trial (see further **Chapter 12**). This waives the privilege in these documents unless it had been waived earlier.

Special considerations apply to the written instructions given by a solicitor to an expert whose report is relied upon at trial (see **12.13.3**).

11.11.2   Documents tending to incriminate the party who would produce them

A party is entitled to claim privilege for documents that will tend to incriminate either themselves, their spouse or civil partner. This rule applies to criminal liability or penal proceedings under the law of any part of the UK. The details are beyond the scope of this book.

11.11.3   Documents privileged on the ground of public policy

If producing a copy of a document would be injurious to the public interest, it may be withheld on the ground of public policy.

The judge has to consider whether the withholding of the documents is necessary for the proper functioning of the public service. Examples of documents which have been withheld from production on this ground are documents dealing with matters of national defence, information as to ill-treatment of children given to the NSPCC, local authority social work records, probation service records, and evidence which might reveal the identity of a police informant.

11.11.4   Challenging a claim to privilege (r 31.19)

A party who wishes to challenge their opponent's claim to privilege can apply for the court to decide whether the claim to privilege should be upheld. In any case where there is a claim to privilege, the court may require the party claiming privilege to produce the document to the court and may invite any person, even if not a party, to make representations. See, for example, *Atos Consulting Ltd v Avis plc (No 2)* [2007] EWHC 323 (TCC).

11.11.5 Inadvertent disclosure of privileged documents

11.11.5.1 An obvious mistake

If privileged documents are mistakenly listed in part 1 of a party's list (instead of part 2), no harm is done if the error is spotted before the other side inspects the document since the list may be amended and re-served.

But what if inspection of privileged material is allowed inadvertently, for example where copies of privileged documents have been sent in error to the other side's solicitor? In *IBM Corporation v Phoenix International (Computers) Ltd* [1995] 1 All ER 413, it was held:

(a)   If it is obvious to the solicitor receiving the privileged document that a mistake has been made, the solicitor should return the document. There is no question of asking the client what should be done. Any breach of this obligation may see the court order that the solicitor can no longer act in the litigation.

  In *Ablitt v Mills & Reeve (solicitors) and Norwich Union* (1995) *The Times*, 25 October, the claimant was suing Norwich Union, which had instructed the firm of solicitors, Mills & Reeve. During the course of the litigation, seven lever-arch files in two large cardboard boxes were sent in error by a clerk in the claimant's barrister's chambers to the defendant firm of solicitors. The papers contained a great many documents attracting legal professional privilege, the contents of which were highly confidential to the claimant. They included, for example, advice from counsel in relation to the merits of the claimant's claim, a 20-page advice on evidence, draft statements from over 20 possible witnesses – including expert witnesses – and a substantial quantity of privileged correspondence passing between solicitor and client and between solicitor and counsel. Whilst the defendant firm of solicitors recognised this was an obvious error, it still read the papers on its client's instructions to do so. The claimant's application for an injunction restraining the solicitors' firm from acting for Norwich Union in the proceedings was granted.

  > To my mind it offends elementary notions of fairness and justice if, by knowingly taking advantage of the mistaken delivery of [the claimant's barrister's papers], Norwich Union, although not itself told what those papers contained, can nevertheless continue to have the services in the action of those who, on its instructions, have read all of those papers and who, as a result, have a very accurate perception of just how those who act for the [claimant] view the merits of the [claimant's] claim and of the steps, tactically and otherwise, which they are advising the [claimant] to take in the pursuit of his claim. (*per* Blackburne J)

(b)   If it is not obvious to the solicitor receiving the privileged document that a mistake has been made, the receiving party may make use of the document in the litigation, but the disclosing party may obtain an injunction to prevent its use if it can persuade the court that it would have been obvious to a hypothetical reasonable solicitor that disclosure had occurred as the result of a mistake. In addition, the court may also order that the receiving party's solicitors can no longer act in the litigation. Relevant factors to consider when deciding whether or not an obvious mistake has been made include the nature of the document and the date it was created.

11.11.5.2 Practical point

As we have just seen (at **11.11.5.1**), if it is obvious to a solicitor receiving a document that it is privileged from inspection and that the disclosing party has made a mistake, the solicitor should return the document. Why? Surely it will be in the best interests of the solicitor's client to read the document if it appears to undermine the disclosing party's case? Surely in those circumstances the solicitor will have a duty to pass that information on to their client as it may assist their client in the litigation? The answer is that in order to comply with the SRA Principles to uphold the proper administration of justice and to act with integrity, the solicitor should stop reading the document once they realise it is privileged from inspection and an obvious mistake has been made. Further, whilst the solicitor has a duty of disclosure of relevant information to their client regardless of its source, that duty is subject to exceptions, and this is one of those exceptional circumstances (see SRA Code of Conduct, para 6.4).

Where it is not obvious to a solicitor receiving a document that it is privileged from inspection but the solicitor has any doubt, it is best practice to point out to the other side if and when reliance will be placed on the document in the litigation.

11.11.6 Without prejudice correspondence

As we saw at **3.10.1,** without prejudice correspondence will record information as part of a party's genuine attempt to settle a case. The correspondence will probably therefore satisfy the r 31.6 definition, as it is likely to set out the strengths of a party's case, and indeed may contain concessions that are adverse to that case and support the opponent. You should remember that it is irrelevant to standard disclosure that the recipient of a document has already seen it. So without prejudice correspondence, just like the other common correspondence between parties that meets the r 31.6 test, should be disclosed and no privilege from inspection claimed. This is because when the letters were being drafted by a solicitor and before being sent to the other party, the letters were privileged from inspection; but the privilege was waived by sending them to the other side.

We do accept that many practitioners claim privilege from inspection for any without prejudice correspondence written to, or received from, another party. Indeed, some textbooks encourage this on the basis that there is some sort of general without prejudice privilege. With respect, we disagree with this approach. It confuses the step required by standard disclosure to allow inspection of all non-privileged r 31.6 documents with the issue of admissibility of without prejudice correspondence at trial. The fact that a party does not claim privilege from inspection of without prejudice correspondence does not make it admissible. As explained at **3.10.1,** all negotiations genuinely aimed at a settlement are excluded from being given in evidence.

The only time privilege from inspection is relevant to without prejudice correspondence is in multi-party litigation where not all the parties are involved in that correspondence. So what does that mean if, for example, C sues D1 and D2, but C has without prejudice correspondence only with D1? As between C and D1, that correspondence will go in the first part of their respective list of documents as not being privileged from inspection. However, as between C and D2, that correspondence will go in the second part of C's list of documents as it is privileged from inspection by D2. The correspondence will not, of course, appear in D2's list of documents as D2 never received it.

In *BGC Brokers LP v Tradition (UK) Ltd* [2019] EWCA Civ 1937, the Court summarised the key principles as follows (at [11]–[13]):

> Written or oral communications which are made for the purpose of a genuine attempt to compromise a dispute between the parties may generally not be admitted in evidence ....
>
> In disputes between the parties to the without prejudice communication ('two-party' cases), an additional basis for the rule may be an express or implied agreement between the parties. In situations involving a third party who was not a party to the negotiations ('three-party' cases), however, the documents are protected as against the third party purely by reason of the public policy justification: see *Muller v Linsley & Mortimer* [1996] PNLR 74 at 77 (Hoffmann LJ).
>
> Where communications are inadmissible on the basis of without prejudice privilege, they are also protected from inspection by other parties in the same litigation, whether or not a settlement was concluded: see *Rush & Tomkins Ltd v Greater London Council* [1989] 1 AC 1280 at 1300, 1305 (Lord Griffiths).

11.12   DISCLOSING THE EXISTENCE OF DOCUMENTS: THE LIST

A party discloses a document by stating that the document exists or has existed. As we saw at **11.2**, there are two possible ways of disclosing the existence of a document, namely by identifying either:

(a)   the actual document itself; or

(b)   the type of document.

11.12.1   Part 1 of the list

In the first part of the list of documents, the actual documents are identified so that the other parties can decide whether or not they wish to inspect them. Remember that these are documents in the party's control which they do not object to being inspected.

What if a Part 1 document contains material that is confidential and irrelevant to any issues in the claim? When giving inspection, that part of the document can be redacted, that is to say blanked out. The description of such a document in Part 1 of the list should make it clear that the document disclosed is redacted (*Ennis Property Finance Ltd v Thompson* [2017] EWHC 3263 (Ch)). For example, 'Minutes of board meeting of [date] save the confidential and irrelevant entries that are blanked out.'

11.12.2   Part 2 of the list

In the second part of the list of documents the party should disclose the type of documents for which they are claiming privilege from inspection, for example 'confidential correspondence between the claimant and their solicitors'; 'various experts' reports and witness statements', etc. It is quite proper to do this. The existence of the document has been disclosed and so the duty to give disclosure is thereby discharged. However, the general description as to the type of document ensures that the contents are not indirectly revealed. The objections to inspection must then be stated. A legitimate ground must be claimed. It is *not* a ground of objection that the document is adverse to the party's case or is confidential. For examples of different possible grounds, see **11.11**.

In practice, the most common objection is based on legal professional privilege. For advice privilege, the objection to inspection is that the documents are communications between the party and their solicitor that were created for the purpose of obtaining legal advice. For litigation privilege, there are two key matters to include: (i) when the document was created, and (ii) why it was created. An example might be: 'Expert's report obtained by the Claimant's solicitors when this litigation was pending for the sole purpose of having as evidence to be used in this litigation.'

If different grounds are relied on for different documents, they should be arranged and listed separately.

11.12.3   Part 3 of the list

In the third part of the list of documents the party must state the actual (non-privileged) documents that they once had, but no longer have, in their control. This often comprises little more than the original letters, written by or on behalf of the party, copies of which have already been detailed in the first part of the list. In respect of each document it is necessary to state when it was last in the party's control and where it is now. The purpose is to enable the parties receiving the list to continue their investigations elsewhere. If they can locate the present whereabouts of the documents they may be able to obtain copies on an application for disclosure by a non-party (see **11.17**).

> **CASE STUDY: CLAIMANTS' LIST OF DOCUMENTS**
>
> The claimants' list of documents can be found by way of example in the case study at **Appendix D(10)**. You will note that this is on the prescribed form, N265. The first two pages are taken up mostly with the disclosure statement. Did you spot how the claimants limited their search? Then the final page contains the three parts of the list. Note how each document in the first part is explicitly described so that the defendant can identify it and decide whether or not to inspect it. Contrast that with the second part of the list. Here, the documents are identified only generally but, most importantly, the claim to privilege from inspection is described in full. Look closely at the wording used. Lastly, the third part records the fact that the claimants once had in their possession the originals of the copy documents listed in the first part of their list.

11.12.4 Template

A template to help you draft a list of documents may be found at **Appendix B(9)**.

11.13 FAILURE TO DISCLOSE (r 31.21)

A party who fails to disclose a document or fails to allow inspection of a document may not rely on that document at trial unless the court permits. Note importantly, however, that a party who fails to disclose a document that harms their case may find that their case is struck out as a result of failure to comply with an order for specific disclosure (see **11.15**).

A party who fails to give disclosure properly may be penalised financially. For example, in *Earles v Barclays Bank Plc* [2009] EWHC 2500, the court held that the successful defendant should recover only one half of its costs because of its failure to conduct disclosure adequately.

11.14 SUBSEQUENT USE OF DISCLOSED DOCUMENTS (r 31.22)

Where a document has been disclosed to a party, they may use that document only for the purposes of the case in which it has been disclosed unless:

(a)   the document has been read or referred to during a public hearing (eg, at trial); or

(b)   the court grants permission; or

(c)   the party who disclosed the document and the person to whom the document belongs consent.

Where (a) applies, the court may make an order restricting or prohibiting the use of the document.

11.15 APPLYING FOR SPECIFIC DISCLOSURE (r 31.12)

If a party is dissatisfied with disclosure provided by the other party and believes it is inadequate, they may make an application for an order for specific disclosure. The application notice must specify the order the applicant wants the court to make, and the grounds of the application must be set out in the application notice or in the supporting evidence. For example, in a claim arising out of the supply of allegedly defective goods sold by the defendant to the claimant, the claimant may suspect that the defendant should have quality control records. If these have not been disclosed then an application for specific disclosure may be justified. Also see *Icon SE LLC v SE Shipping Lines Pte Ltd* [2012] EWCA Civ 1790 (the issue in the case was whether the defendant had acted in anticipatory breach of contract by refusing to pay a commitment fee; the court ordered specific disclosure by the defendant of its documents in relation to the commitment fee).

Before making such an application, a party should write to the other side explaining why they believe the documents are disclosable and asking the other party to comply properly with the order for disclosure. If a satisfactory response is not forthcoming then it would be appropriate to issue the application.

An application will require a witness statement in support. This should detail the date of the order for standard disclosure and the document or documents that the applicant believes should have been included in the list. If it is not obvious, the witness statement should explain how these documents satisfy the definition of standard disclosure and why the applicant believes they exist. A reference to the request for the documents and the respondent's response should be made to show that the applicant has complied with the overriding objective by trying to avoid making an application.

An order for specific disclosure may require a party to:

(a)   disclose specified documents or classes of documents;

(b)   carry out a search as specified by the order and disclose any documents located as a result of that search.

When deciding whether to make an order for specific disclosure, the court will take into account all the circumstances of the case:

> [W]here a detailed disclosure exercise has already been undertaken, it is not sufficient that the party seeking disclosure simply speculates that further documents may or should exist or that it is implausible that they do not. Something more is needed to show that there is a likelihood (as opposed to a possibility) of further relevant documents existing. (per Mr Robin Vos in *Sheeran v Chokri* [2021] EWHC 3553 (Ch) at [65])

If the court is satisfied that the respondent has failed adequately to comply with the obligations imposed by the order for disclosure, will usually make such order as is necessary to make sure those obligations are adequately complied with. For example, the order will often be made in the form of an 'unless' order (see **9.3.4**). The applicant would also seek an order that the respondent pay the applicant's costs.

A party can also apply for an order for specific inspection, which would require a party to permit inspection of documents which they omitted from their disclosure statement on the grounds that inspection would be disproportionate (see **11.7**).

11.16   DISCLOSURE BEFORE PROCEEDINGS START (r 31.16)

As we saw at **3.9**, a party may make an application for pre-action disclosure.

This procedure will normally be used where a party is unsure whether they have a good case against another party, and therefore does not know whether to issue proceedings. The party could apply for pre-action disclosure against the intended defendant so that they can then make an informed decision as to whether or not to issue proceedings against that person.

In the case of *Taylor Wimpey UK Ltd v Harron Homes Ltd* [2020] EWHC 1190 (TCC), the agreement between the parties contained a dispute resolution (DR) clause. An application for pre-action disclosure pursuant to r 31.16 by the potential defendant was refused. To allow the application would have undermined or frustrated the DR clause. As to enforceability of DR clauses, see **4.3.1**.

11.17   NON-PARTY DISCLOSURE (r 31.17)

Where proceedings have commenced, a party to the proceedings can apply for disclosure against a non-party. For an example, see *Secretary of State for Transport v Pell Frischmann Consultants Ltd* [2006] EWHC 2756.

This procedure enables a party to proceedings that are already in existence to obtain disclosure of documents from a non-party if it is going to help resolve the issues in the case.

The most common application of this procedure would be where a party indicates in their list of documents that they no longer have a document in their possession. The party also indicates that X now has possession of that document. The other party may then write to X asking for a copy of the document. If X refuses to supply that copy voluntarily, the other party could then apply for an order for non-party disclosure against X.

The application must be supported by evidence.

The court may order non-party disclosure only if:

(a)   the documents in question are likely to support the applicant's case or adversely affect the case of another party; and

(b)   disclosure is necessary to dispose fairly of the case or to save costs.

The order must:

(a)   specify the documents or classes of documents to be disclosed; and

(b)   require the non-party to specify which documents are no longer in their control and which are privileged.

The order may specify a time and place for disclosure and inspection, and may require the non-party to indicate what has happened to the documents no longer in their control.

11.18   DISCLOSURE OBLIGATIONS AND SOLICITORS' DUTIES

The SRA Code of Conduct, para 1.4, provides that a solicitor must never mislead the court. This duty might be broken if a solicitor does not promptly disclose a document that they become aware of during the course of a case, which should have been, but was not, disclosed. Obviously, this situation may arise after the client's list of documents has been served. The solicitor needs to advise the client to disclose it and determine how the document should be disclosed. A supplemental list is probably appropriate (see **11.10**). If the document is privileged from inspection, it should be listed in the second part of the list. If it is not privileged from inspection, it should be listed in the first part, and, of course, the opponent may then wish to inspect it. If a client refuses to allow disclosure, the solicitor should withdraw from the case. In order to keep client confidentiality (see para 6.3), the solicitor should not inform any other party (or the court) of the reasons for ceasing to act.

A solicitor must ensure that their client understands the duties to conduct a reasonable and proper search and then give full and frank disclosure. The client must also appreciate that disclosure is an ongoing obligation. As an officer of the court, a solicitor has a duty to ensure disclosure is properly given and that the court is not misled. Moreover, the client should sign the disclosure statement only after receiving legal advice. Remember, that statement includes the following:

> I certify that I understand the duty of disclosure and that to the best of my knowledge I have carried out that duty. I further certify that the list of documents set out in or attached to this form, is a complete list of all documents which are or have been in my control and which I am obliged under the order to disclose. I understand that I must inform the court and the other parties immediately if any further document required to be disclosed by Rule 31.6 comes into my control at any time before conclusion of the case.

So during the first three Stages of Civil Litigation the client must be made aware of the extent of their disclosure obligations and the importance of not destroying documents that might have to be disclosed. A client should start to preserve documents when first notified of the claim (*Ayannuga v One Shot Products Ltd* [2021] EWHC 2930 (QB)). A solicitor should advise a client that if the client destroys disclosable documents deliberately and contumaciously, or such that a fair trial is rendered impossible, the client's statement of case is likely to be struck out.

Woods v Martin's Bank [1959] 1 QB 55 imposes a duty on a solicitor to the court to examine their client's documents themselves in order to ensure that proper disclosure is made. *Myers v Elman* [1940] AC 282 provides that if the client will not permit this, or insists on giving imperfect disclosure, the solicitor must withdraw from the case, as otherwise they will be participating in a deception of the court.

11.19 INSPECTION OF STANDARD DISCLOSURE DOCUMENTS

11.19.1 Scrutinise the opponent's list

What checks should you make when you receive an opponent's list of standard disclosure documents?

Start with the disclosure statement. None of this should come as a surprise if both parties have fully cooperated in setting the parameters of the reasonable search, especially for electronic documents. But always double-check the limitations imposed and ensure they are in line with any agreement reached or what you consider to be reasonable.

Before you look at Part 1 of your opponent's list, ask yourself, the client and any expert instructed on a disputed issue what you should expect to see in it. That way you may be able to spot any documents omitted from the list. Also, see if there are any unexpected documents. If your opponent has included a document and you do not know why, you will need to inspect it. Likewise, any document not already seen needs to be inspected.

Part 2 of your opponent's list is likely to be uncontroversial. Just check that each privilege has been properly claimed.

Part 3 will usually only refer to the originals of any copy documents listed in Part 1. But it is always worth checking just in case your opponent has listed something else here or omitted to include a document.

11.19.2 Inspection

When requesting inspection of Part 1 documents, consider carefully whether photocopies of paper documents will suffice or if the originals need to be seen. Disclosure of electronic documents should normally be given in the format in which the document was created and stored.

A key point to bear in mind is that a photocopy of a paper document will not necessarily reveal if another document was once attached to it by something like a paperclip or staple. Also, handwritten notes in the margins or on the back of a document can easily be overlooked in the photocopying process. Equally, when you do inspect, check that all relevant documents have been sent. For example, an e-mail may refer to an attachment, but have you received a copy of the attachment?

11.20 DISCLOSURE PILOT SCHEME IN THE BUSINESS AND PROPERTY COURTS (PD 51U)

From 1 January 2019, all new and existing proceedings in the Business and Property Courts of England and Wales and the Business and Property Courts in Birmingham, Bristol, Cardiff, Leeds, Liverpool, Manchester and Newcastle are subject to a disclosure pilot scheme. The pilot does not affect any disclosure order that was made prior to 1 January 2019 unless that order is varied or set aside. Further the pilot shall not, unless otherwise ordered, apply to proceedings which are:

(a)   a competition claim as defined in PD 31C;

(b)   a public procurement claim;

(c)   within the Intellectual Property and Enterprise Court;

(d)   within the Admiralty Court;

(e)   within the Shorter and Flexible Trials Schemes; or

(f)   within a fixed costs regime or a capped costs regime.

Practice Direction 51U, paras 2–4 deal with the principles and duties in relation to disclosure and the preservation of documents.

Paragraph 2.3 specifically refers to the obligation of the parties to cooperate with each other and assist the court to ensure that the scope of disclosure is agreed or determined in the most efficient way possible. Paragraph 2.4 states that the scope of disclosure should be no wider than is reasonable and proportionate to determine the issues. Disclosure includes adverse documents as defined in para 2.7, and 'known adverse documents' are those of which a party is aware without undertaking any further search and which are or have been in that party's control. The factors to be considered when determining what is reasonable and proportionate are set out in para 6.4.

For the purposes of establishing what documents exist which may be subject to disclosure, companies and organisations will need to identify persons with accountability, including those who may have left the company or organisation. Any documents of which a person with accountability is aware and which have been within the party's control will be within the definition in para 2.8 and subject to the disclosure duties set out in para 3.

11.20.1   Initial Disclosure (para 5)

Unless either:

(a)   the parties agree to dispense with Initial Disclosure, or

(b)   the court orders otherwise, or

(c)   a party files a statement that initial disclosure would exceed 1,000 pages or 200 documents,

each party must file with their statement of case an Initial Disclosure List of Documents that lists and is accompanied by copies of—

(i)   the key documents on which it has relied (expressly or otherwise) in support of the claims or defences advanced in its statement of case (and including the documents referred to in that statement of case); and

(ii)   the key documents that are necessary to enable the other parties to understand the claim or defence they have to meet.

Copies of documents not already supplied to or seen by other parties should be supplied in electronic form. The List, but not the documents, should also be filed with the court.

11.20.2   Extended Disclosure

Within 28 days of the final statement of case, each party should state, in writing, whether or not it is likely to request Extended Disclosure on one or more issues in the case. Practice Direction 51U contains various models but it is not necessary to specify a model at this stage.

Where one or more of the parties has indicated that it is likely to request Extended Disclosure, the claimant must, within 42 days of the final statement of case, prepare and serve on the other parties a draft List of Issues for Disclosure unless the equivalent of such a list has already been agreed between the parties (for example, as part of a fuller list of issues).

'Issues for Disclosure' means, for the purposes of disclosure only, those key issues in dispute, which the parties consider will need to be determined by the court with some reference to contemporaneous documents in order for there to be a fair resolution of the proceedings. It does not extend to every issue which is disputed in the statements of case by denial or non-admission. In the event of any dispute or disagreement, the parties should attempt to agree the List of Issues prior to the first case management conference.

Practice Direction 51U, para 8 sets out the Extended Disclosure Models the court can order and defines what is covered by each model. The Models are:

- Model A: Disclosure confined to known adverse documents
- Model B: Limited Disclosure
- Model C: Request-led search-based disclosure
- Model D: Narrow search-based disclosure, with or without Narrative Documents
- Model E: Wide search-based disclosure

There is no entitlement to Extended Disclosure, and Models D and E are likely to be used in limited circumstances. Model D is similar to standard disclosure under r 31.6 but this is not to be regarded as the default model. The court will have wide-ranging powers and may limit Extended Disclosure to particular issues, to some parties and not others and may combine the Models.

Where Models C, D or E are sought, the parties will have to complete a Disclosure Review Document. The parties must identify, discuss and seek to agree the scope of any Extended Disclosure sought and provide that information in due course to the court. A finalised single joint Disclosure Review Document should be filed by the claimant not later than five days before the case management conference. The parties must each file a signed Certificate of Compliance substantially in the form set out in Appendix 3 as soon as reasonably practicable after the claimant has filed the finalised single joint Disclosure Review Document but in any event in advance of the case management conference. The Disclosure Review Document should also contain an estimate of the likely costs of giving disclosure and the likely volume of documents involved.

11.20.3   Disclosure Guidance Hearing

The parties may seek guidance from the court by way of a discussion with the court in advance of or after a case management conference, concerning the scope of Extended Disclosure or the implementation of an order for Extended Disclosure, where—

(a)   the parties have made real efforts to resolve disputes between them; and

(b)   the absence of guidance from the court before a case management conference is likely to have a material effect on the court's ability to hold an effective case management conference, or the absence of guidance from the court after a case management conference is likely to have a material effect on the parties' ability to carry out the court's case management directions effectively.

11.20.4   Compliance with an Extended Disclosure Order

By para 12.1, an order for Extended Disclosure is complied with by undertaking the following steps:

(1)   service of a Disclosure Certificate substantially in the form set out in [PD 51U] Appendix 4 signed by the party giving disclosure, to include a statement supported by a statement of truth signed by the party or an appropriate person at the party that all known adverse documents have been disclosed;

(2)   service of an Extended Disclosure List of Documents (unless dispensed with, by agreement or order); and

(3)   production of the documents which are disclosed over which no claim is made to withhold production or (if the party cannot produce a particular document) compliance with paragraph 12.3.

CHAPTER 12

EVIDENCE

12.1	Introduction	205
12.2	Witness evidence	207
12.3	Form of witness statements	208
12.4	Use of witness statements at trial	211
12.5	Witness summaries (r 32.9)	211
12.6	Sanctions for not serving a witness statement (r 32.10)	212
12.7	Affidavits	213
12.8	Opinion evidence	213
12.9	Hearsay evidence	214
12.10	Use of plans, photographs and models as evidence (r 33.6)	221
12.11	Notice to admit facts (r 32.18)	222
12.12	Notice to admit or prove documents (r 32.19)	222
12.13	Expert evidence (Part 35)	222
12.14	Professional negligence cases: the defendant's own evidence	231
12.15	Assessors (r 35.15)	231

LEARNING OUTCOMES

After reading this chapter you will have learned:

- how the courts control evidence
- the role of witness statements
- how to draft a witness statement for use at trial
- when opinion evidence from a non-expert witness is admissible
- the definition of hearsay evidence
- how to use hearsay evidence
- how a judge will assess hearsay evidence
- possible responses to the service of hearsay evidence
- the role of expert evidence
- how to use expert evidence.

12.1 INTRODUCTION

12.1.1 Relevance

Any evidence, to be admissible, must be relevant. Contested trials last long enough as it is without spending time on evidence which is irrelevant and cannot affect the outcome. Relevance must, and can only, be judged by reference to the issue which the court is called upon to decide. (per Lord Bingham of Cornhill in *O'Brien v Chief Constable of South Wales Police* [2005] UKHL 26, (2005) *The Times*, 29 April)

12.1.2 Judicial control

The rules on evidence are contained primarily within Parts 32 and 33 of the CPR 1998. These rules do not change the law on the admissibility of evidence, save for the fact that the court, as might be expected through its court management powers, can control the evidence brought before the court.

Rule 32.1 states:

(1)   The court may control the evidence by giving directions as to—

   (a)   the issues on which it requires evidence;

   (b)   the nature of the evidence which it requires to decide those issues; and

   (c)   the way in which the evidence is to be placed before the court.

(2)   The court may use its power under this rule to exclude evidence that would otherwise be admissible.

(3)   The court may limit cross-examination.

In addition, under r 32.2(3):

(3)   The court may give directions—

   (a)   identifying or limiting the issues to which factual evidence may be directed;

   (b)   identifying the witnesses who may be called or whose evidence may be read; or

   (c)   limiting the length or format of witness statements.

In exercising its powers under this Rule, the court will bear in mind the overriding objective in r 1.1 and will attempt to define and identify the issues between the parties. For example, the court may decide, prior to the trial, that a particular issue that has been raised is no longer important, and may make an order excluding any evidence the parties intended to use in relation to that particular issue. Or the court may prescribe by list what issues should proceed to trial. Any party dissatisfied by such an order must appeal it or otherwise follow the order (*Bailey v GlaxoSmithKline* [2019] EWCA Civ 1924).

12.1.3   Judicial approach

How does a trial judge decide whether a claimant has established the claim 'on the balance of probabilities'? The judge will have to assess what weight should be given to the admissible evidence, and in particular should answer the following questions:

(a)   Does the evidence address a disputed issue in the case?

(b)   If so, how important is that issue in the case?

(c)   What other evidence is available on the same issue?

(d)   Is the evidence more probative than any other evidence?

A trial judge is likely to have to weigh up many different types of evidence, such as oral evidence from expert and non-expert witness, as well as documents produced by the parties. The credibility of a witness is often said to be a key point. But what is meant by this?

> 'Credibility' involves wider problems than mere 'demeanour' which is mostly concerned with whether the witness appears to be telling the truth as he now believes it to be. Credibility covers the following problems. First, is the witness a truthful or untruthful person? Secondly, is he, though a truthful person telling something less than the truth on this issue, or though an untruthful person, telling the truth on this issue? Thirdly, though he is a truthful person telling the truth as he sees it, did he register the intentions of the conversation correctly and, if so has his memory correctly retained them? Also, has his recollection been subsequently altered by unconscious bias or wishful thinking or by over much discussion of it with others? Witnesses, especially those who are emotional, who think that they are morally in the right, tend very easily and unconsciously to conjure up a legal right that did not exist. It is a truism, often used in accident cases, that with every day that passes the memory becomes fainter and the imagination becomes more active. For that reason a witness, however honest, rarely persuades a Judge that his present recollection is preferable to that which was taken down in writing immediately after the accident occurred. Therefore, contemporary documents are always of the utmost importance. And lastly, although the honest witness believes he heard or saw this or that, is it so improbable that it is on balance more likely that he was mistaken? On this point it is essential that the balance of probability is put correctly into the scales in weighing the credibility of a witness. And motive is one aspect of probability. All these problems compendiously are entailed when a Judge assesses the credibility of a witness; they are all part of one judicial process. And in the process contemporary

documents and admitted or incontrovertible facts and probabilities must play their proper part. (*per* Lord Pearce in *Onassis v Vergottis* [1968] 2 Lloyds Rep 403 at 431)

There are many situations in which the court is asked to assess the credibility of witnesses from their oral evidence, that is to say, to weigh up their evidence to see whether it is reliable. Witness choice is an essential part of the function of a trial judge and he or she has to decide whose evidence, and how much evidence, to accept. This task is not to be carried out merely by reference to the impression that a witness made giving evidence in the witness box. It is not solely a matter of body language or the tone of voice or other factors that might generally be called the 'demeanour' of a witness. The judge should consider what other independent evidence would be available to support the witness. Such evidence would generally be documentary but it could be other oral evidence, for example, if the issue was whether a defendant was an employee, the judge would naturally consider whether there were any PAYE records or evidence, such as evidence in texts or e-mails, in which the defendant seeks or is given instructions as to how he should carry out work.

In my judgment, contemporaneous written documentation is of the very greatest importance in assessing credibility. Moreover, it can be significant not only where it is present and the oral evidence can then be checked against it. It can also be significant if written documentation is absent. For instance, if the judge is satisfied that certain contemporaneous documentation is likely to have existed were the oral evidence correct, and that the party adducing oral evidence is responsible for its non-production, then the documentation may be conspicuous by its absence and the judge may be able to draw inferences from its absence. (*per* Arden LJ in *The Matter of Mumtaz Properties Ltd v Ahmed* [2011] EWCA Civ 610 at [12] and [14])

12.1.4 Factual and expert evidence

Evidence falls into two broad types. First, factual evidence from a witness (see **12.2** to **12.9**). Secondly, expert evidence from a suitably qualified expert (see **12.13**).

12.2 WITNESS EVIDENCE

12.2.1 General rule

Under r 32.2(1), the general rule is that any fact that needs to be proved is to be proved at trial by oral evidence given in public, and at any other hearing by evidence in writing. The Rules also provide that the court may allow a witness to give evidence by any means, including a video link.

We have just seen that the general rule is that any fact which needs to be proved by the evidence of witnesses is to be proved at trial by their oral evidence given in public. In addition, r 32.5(2) provides another general rule, that where a witness is called to give oral evidence, their witness statement will stand as their evidence in chief. As a result, no party should include in any witness statement evidence which the maker of the statement could not give orally (see *JD Wetherspoon plc v Harris (Practice Note)* [2013] EWHC 1088 (Ch)). The evidence should meet the test of relevance (see **12.1.1**) and, where appropriate, satisfy the requirements for admissibility as opinion (see **12.8**) and hearsay (see **12.9**) evidence.

12.2.2 Pre-trial exchange

As already seen in **Chapter 9**, when giving directions for trial, the court will usually order witness statements to be exchanged. Rule 32.4(2) states that the court will order a party to serve on the other parties any witness statement of the oral evidence upon which the party serving the statement intends to rely in relation to any issue of fact to be decided at the trial. As outlined at **12.6**, where a witness statement is not served, the witness will be allowed to give evidence at trial only with the court's permission.

The court may give directions as to the order in which witness statements are to be served. Usually the court will order simultaneous exchange, but exceptionally it may order one party (usually the claimant) to serve first (sequential exchange). Once a witness statement is served, it ceases to be privileged (see further **11.11.1.4**).

12.2.3 Objections to contents

By r 32.4(1), a witness statement is a written statement signed by a person that contains the evidence which that person would be allowed to give orally. So what should you do if, after exchanging witness statements, you object to the relevance or admissibility of material contained in your opponent's statements? Best practice is to notify the other party of your objection immediately and seek to resolve the dispute. Failing that, raise the matter at any pre-trial review or at the beginning of the trial itself.

12.2.4 Additional evidence

What if, after the exchange of witness statements, a party wants a witness to give additional evidence? It may well be that a witness needs to deal with events occurring, or matters discovered, after the exchange, or in response to matters dealt with by another party's witness. The answer is to prepare and serve a supplemental witness statement dealing with these points as soon as possible. The other party should be asked to agree to the evidence being adduced at trial. Failing that, an application for permission to rely on the evidence should be made at any pre-trial review or at the beginning of the trial itself.

12.3 FORM OF WITNESS STATEMENTS

12.3.1 Structure and contents

Rules relating to the form of witness statements are set out in paras 17–20 of PD 32.

By para 17.1, the witness statement should be headed with the title of the proceedings, and by para 17.2 the top right-hand corner should state:

(a)   the party on whose behalf the statement is filed (eg Claimant);

(b)   the initials and surname of the witness (eg ML Banister);

(c)   the number of the statement in relation to that witness (eg 1st);

(d)   the identifying initials and number of each exhibit referred to (eg MLB1-3);

(e)   the date the statement was made (eg 16/05/19); and

(f)   the date of any translation.

Other key formality requirements in PD 32 are:

(a)   the witness statement should be divided into numbered paragraphs (para 19.1(5));

(b)   all numbers, including dates, should be expressed in figures and not words (para 19.1(6) and see also **7.1.4**);

(c)   the witness statement should normally follow the chronological sequence of the events or matters dealt with. Each paragraph of a witness statement should as far as possible be confined to a distinct portion of the subject (para 19.2); and

(d)   the witness statement should be drafted in the witness's own language. What if that is a foreign language? Then, the party wishing to rely on it must have it translated; the translator must sign the original statement and must certify that the translation is accurate. In addition, the foreign language witness statement must be filed with the court.

By PD 32, para 18.1, the statement should be in the witness's own words as far as practicable and must in any event be drafted in their own language. It should be in the first person and state:

(a)   the full name of the witness;

(b)   where he lives or, if the statement is made as part of their employment or business, the address at which they work, position in the business and the name of the business;

(c)   their occupation or description;

(d)   (if so) that they are a party or an employee of a party; and

(e)   the process by which it has been prepared, for example, face-to-face, over the telephone, and/or through an interpreter.

PD 32, para 25.1 provides that if there is any defect in the witness statement, the court may refuse to admit it as evidence in the case, and may refuse to allow the costs arising from its preparation. So, how should you respond if your opponent serves a witness statement that fails to meet one or more of the above formalities? The sensible course of action is to raise that concern with the other side and attempt to reach agreement on the issue. Where that is not possible, seek the assistance of the court, by application for a determination on the documents or at a hearing. However, this should be done at a time and in a manner that does not cause disruption to trial preparation or unnecessary costs. Obviously, the more serious the defect, the greater the sanction that should be requested from the court (see *Prime London Holdings 11 Ltd v Thurloe Lodge Ltd* [2022] EWHC 79 (Ch)).

12.3.2   Witness's own words

In the case of *Alex Lawrie Factors Ltd v Morgan, Morgan and Turner* (1999) *The Times*, 18 August, the Court of Appeal held that the purpose of a witness statement was for the witness to say, in their own words, what the relevant evidence was. It was not to be used by the lawyer who prepared it as a vehicle for complex legal argument to which the witness would not be readily able to speak if cross-examined on the document. In this case, the second defendant, Mrs Morgan, was seeking to avoid liability to the claimant under a deed of indemnity. She had claimed that the reason why her signature appeared on the deed was due to her former husband's fraudulent actions and misrepresentations. The claimant applied for summary judgment (see **10.5.2**) and, in her evidence in reply, Mrs Morgan stated that she had had the opportunity of studying the decision of the House of Lords in *Barclays Bank plc v O'Brien* [1994] 1 AC 180 in some detail. She made a number of points in reliance on that decision. The judge said that Mrs Morgan was clearly, from her evidence, an intelligent woman. He concluded that her evidence as to how she came to sign the deed of indemnity was simply not credible and he awarded summary judgment.

On the appeal, Mrs Morgan's counsel sought permission to put in new evidence going to her intelligence. The court allowed this because the situation was susceptible of injustice if the matter proceeded on the basis on which the judge had considered it, which would derive from the judge's interpretation of the kind of woman Mrs Morgan must be from a perusal of her evidence. The court said that the case was a very good warning of the grave dangers that could occur when lawyers put into witnesses' mouths a sophisticated legal argument which, in effect, represented the lawyers' arguments in the case, to which the witnesses themselves would not be able to speak if cross-examined. Having had the benefit of further evidence, the court did not consider that this was a case in which it was appropriate to disregard Mrs Morgan's evidence as incredible and it allowed the appeal.

In the case of *Skatteforvaltningen v Solo Capital Partners LLP (In Special Administration)* [2020] EWHC 1624 (Comm), the judge criticised the content and length of seven factual witness statements and ordered further copies of the statements highlighting which passages were to be relied on as factual evidence, rather than legal argument.

12.3.3   Sources of information and belief (PD 32, para 18.2)

The statement must indicate which of the statements are based on the witness's own knowledge and which are matters of information or belief, and the source of the witness's information and belief.

12.3.4   Exhibits (PD 32, paras 18.3 and 18.6)

Any exhibit used in connection with a witness statement should be verified and identified by the witness and remain separate from the statement. Exhibits should be numbered and, where a witness makes more than one statement in which there are exhibits in the same proceedings, the numbering of the exhibits should run consecutively throughout and not start again with each witness statement.

12.3.5 Statement of truth (PD 32, para 20.2)

The witness statement must contain a statement of truth in the witness's own language in the following words:

> I believe that the facts stated in this witness statement are true. I understand that proceedings for contempt of court may be brought against anyone who makes, or causes to be made, a false statement in a document verified by a statement of truth without an honest belief in its truth.

The statement of truth must be signed by the witness themselves. Proceedings for contempt of court may be brought against a person who makes a false statement in a witness statement or in a document, prepared in anticipation of or during proceedings and verified by a statement of truth, without an honest belief in its truth.

Rule 22.3 provides that if the maker of a witness statement fails to verify the witness statement by a statement of truth, the court may direct that it shall not be admissible as evidence.

12.3.6 Template

A template to help you draft a witness statement is set out at **Appendix B(10)**.

CASE STUDY: WITNESS STATEMENT

An example of a witness statement to be used at trial may be found in the case study at **Appendix D(11)**. This witness statement, filed on behalf of the Defendant, would have been exchanged by the Defendant's solicitors in accordance with the directions order (see **9.6.3.1** and **Appendix D(9)**).

12.3.7 Key points in drafting a witness statement

- A witness statement is a written statement signed by the deponent with a statement of truth which contains the evidence which the deponent would be allowed to give orally. Inadmissible material should therefore not be included. Irrelevant material should likewise not be included.
- A witness statement must comply with the formalities required by PD 32.
- The function of a witness statement is to set out in writing the evidence-in-chief of the deponent. Accordingly witness statements should, so far as possible, be expressed in the witness's own words.
- A witness statement should only include evidence relating to those issues which the party serving the statement wishes that witness to give as evidence-in-chief. Any facts included should be relevant and admissible. It should not deal with other matters merely because they may arise in the course of the trial.
- A witness statement should be as concise as the circumstances of the case allow without omitting any relevant matters. It should be no longer than is essential to convey the first hand evidence of the witness.
- It is not the function of a witness statement to engage in matters of argument, expressions of opinion or submissions about the issues, nor to make observations about the evidence of other witnesses. There should not be recitation of the content of documents or commentary on the issues in the claim.
- A witness statement should be written in:
  - consecutively numbered paragraphs;

    – in an orderly and readily comprehensible manner (usually in chronological order).

- It must be signed by the deponent, and contain a statement that they believe that the facts stated in their witness statement are true. In addition, that statement must confirm the deponent's understanding that proceedings for contempt of court may be brought against anyone who makes, or causes to be made, a false statement in a document verified by a statement of truth without an honest belief in its truth.

- A witness statement must indicate which of the statements made are made from the deponent's own knowledge and which are made on information and belief, giving the source of the information or basis for the belief.

- A witness statement must comply with any direction of the court about its length or the issues referred to.

12.4   USE OF WITNESS STATEMENTS AT TRIAL

Having served a witness statement on the other side, the witness will usually be called to give oral evidence at trial, unless the court orders otherwise or the party uses the statement as hearsay evidence (see **12.9**).

As the witness statement will usually stand as the evidence-in-chief, the witness will normally simply be asked to confirm that it is true, and will then be subject to cross-examination by the other side. It is because it is subject to cross-examination that oral evidence from witnesses is considered to be the 'best' form of evidence as it has been tested in court.

Because a witness statement normally stands as the witness's evidence-in-chief, the trial judge will have read it before the trial starts, and all witnesses are expected to have re-read their witness statements shortly before they are called to give evidence.

12.4.1   Additional examination-in-chief

The witness statement will stand as the evidence-in-chief of the witness (see **14.2.3.2**) unless the court orders otherwise. When preparing a witness statement to be used at trial, it is, therefore, essential to ensure that the statement is comprehensive. By r 32.5(3), a witness may amplify their statement or give evidence of matters that have arisen since they served their witness statement, or in response to matters dealt with by another party's witness, but only if the court gives permission. The court will not do so unless it considers that there is good reason why the evidence was not dealt with by the witness in their witness statement. Pursuant to the overriding objective, a court will usually allow amplification or additional examination-in-chief where admitting that evidence will not cause any other party injustice. For example, additional expense to a party caused by a late, unjustified change of tack by their opponent may see an application under r 32.5(3) refused.

12.4.2   Use by opponent

If a party who has served a witness statement does not call the witness or use the statement as hearsay evidence, any other party may use the witness statement as hearsay evidence (r 32.5(5)).

12.5   WITNESS SUMMARIES (r 32.9)

Sometimes it will be very difficult to persuade a witness to give a witness statement. As we shall see at **14.1.2**, the means exist to compel a witness to come to court, but it is obviously risky to do that if you do not know what the witness is going to say and, of course, as no witness statement will have been exchanged, permission of the court will be necessary anyway before the witness can give oral evidence.

> **EXAMPLE**
>
> Fred is suing his former employers for damages arising out of an accident he suffered at work. Fred believes that his former colleague, Mark, could give evidence about poor safety practices within the firm, but Mark has refused to give a witness statement to Fred's solicitors as he is worried that if he does he might be dismissed.

Rule 32.9 provides that Fred's solicitors can apply to court without notice for an order to serve a 'witness summary'. The witness summary must contain:

(a)   the evidence that would otherwise go in a witness statement; or

(b)   if the party serving the summary does not know what evidence will be given, the areas about which they propose to question the witness; and

(c)   the witness's name and address.

An application for permission to rely on a witness summary under r 32.9 raises four issues:

(a)   whether the applicant has shown an inability to obtain a witness statement;

(b)   the extent to which the proposed witness is likely to be able to give relevant evidence;

(c)   whether allowing the summary is compatible with the overriding objective (see **1.1.1**); and

(d)   the adequacy of the summary's content (see *Otuo v Watch Tower Bible and Tract Society of Britain* [2019] EWHC 346 (QB) and *Morley t/a Morley Estates v Royal Bank of Scotland plc* [2019] EWHC 2865 (Ch)).

As to (a), the test that a witness summary will only be permitted when a party is unable to obtain a witness statement has to be applied with a degree of rigour (see *Scarlett v Grace* [2014] EWHC 2307 (QB)). However, the test may nevertheless be met if the court is satisfied that, had such a request been made, it would have been turned down.

Unless the court orders otherwise, the summary must be served on the other side by the deadline set for the exchange of witness statements.

12.6   SANCTIONS FOR NOT SERVING A WITNESS STATEMENT (r 32.10)

If a party does not serve a witness statement or witness summary within the proper time-limit, the witness cannot give oral evidence unless the court gives permission.

What if a party knows that they will not make the deadline to exchange? As soon as that becomes clear, they should contact all other parties and seek an agreement to an extension. They must try to ascertain when the witness's signed statement is going to be available. Any agreement reached must be recorded in writing, but it must be remembered that the parties cannot alter the key case management dates set in fast track or multi-track cases (see **9.6.2.2** and **9.6.3.5**). If no agreement is reached, or if a key case management date will not be met, an immediate application to the court should be made with supporting evidence providing an explanation for the need for the extension (*Various Airfinance Leasing Companies v Saudi Arabian Airlines Corporation* [2021] EWHC 3509 (Comm)).

What if a party is ready to exchange within the deadline but their opponent is not? If a good reason is given for an extension it should be agreed, subject to the above comments. But what if there has been no request or application for an extension? If the party complies with the direction and serves the statements on the opponent then that party potentially gains an advantage in that they will see the evidence first and could tailor their own evidence accordingly. The usual practice in these circumstances is for the party to file the statements with the court and explain the situation in a covering letter. Subsequently, an application might be made to strike out the opponent's case for failing to complying with the court order (see **9.3**).

Will the court allow an application to serve a witness statement late or to rely on a witness at trial without having previously served a statement? All will turn on the circumstances of the case and the application of the overriding objective. What if a party discovers a new, favourable witness after witness statements have already been exchanged? At an interim application before trial, will the court's permission be given to serve the statement in order that the party can rely on the evidence at trial? The court will scrutinise why the discovery was made so late in the day, and only in exceptional cases is it likely that the party will be successful: see *Stroh v London Borough of Haringey* [1999] LTL, 13 July, where the Court of Appeal upheld the refusal of permission as it was clear that the judge had had in mind the overriding objective and he was entitled to conclude that the prejudice to the respondent outweighed the prejudice to the applicant.

Note that in *Papa Johns (GB) Ltd v Doyley* [2011] EWHC 2621, it was held that r 32.10 imposes a sanction on the party seeking the court's permission and so the court should apply r 3.9 (see **9.4.1**) when deciding the application. Time limits for service of documents are likely to be strictly enforced. In *M A Lloyd & Sons Ltd (t/a KPM Marine) v PPC International Ltd (t/a Professional Powercraft)* [2014] EWHC 41 (QB), the claimant failed to comply with an order for the sequential exchange of witness statements on a particular issue. The court held that the claimant's delay was substantial and there had been no good reason for it, and so the claimant was debarred from producing evidence about that issue at trial.

12.7 AFFIDAVITS

Affidavits are sworn statements of evidence (ie, the maker of the affidavit has to swear before a solicitor (not their own), or other authorised person, that the contents of the affidavit are true). Prior to the CPR 1998 coming into force, affidavits were the usual means of submitting evidence at interim applications. As we have seen, however, evidence at such applications is now given by witness statements, the statement of case itself or the application notice provided it contains a statement of truth.

In the great majority of cases, therefore, there is no need to go to the extra expense (an oath fee) of using sworn affidavits as evidence. Indeed, if you do, it is very unlikely that the court would allow you to recoup the extra cost from the other side.

On some occasions, however, it is still necessary to use affidavits. The Rules provide that if you are applying for a freezing injunction or search order (see **10.6**), the evidence in support of such an application must be by way of affidavit rather than a witness statement.

12.8 OPINION EVIDENCE

12.8.1 Relevant facts personally perceived

The general rule is that opinion evidence is not admissible. The function of a witness is to relate the facts to the court so that the court can draw its own conclusions. However, there are some situations in which it may be difficult for a witness to separate fact and opinion. A typical example is speed. If a witness gives evidence that a vehicle was being driven at 'about 60 mph', that is only the witness's opinion. Nevertheless, it is difficult to see how else the witness could express what they saw unless they restricted themselves to describing the speed as 'fast'. Accordingly, whilst the accuracy of the witness's assessment of the speed might be challenged, it would usually be admissible. Similarly, a witness may be permitted to express a view that 'John was drunk'. Properly, the witness should relate the physical characteristics they observed which led to that conclusion (eg, slurred speech, glazed eyes, an unsteadiness of gait, breath smelling of alcohol, etc). However, the witness's opinion, whilst it might be challenged, will be admissible. This is confirmed by s 3(2) of the Civil Evidence Act 1972, which states that where a person is called as a witness in any civil proceedings, a statement of opinion by him on any relevant matter on which he is not qualified to give expert evidence, if made as a way of conveying relevant facts personally perceived by him, is admissible as evidence of what he perceived.

12.8.2 Practical point

When a solicitor prepares a witness statement, it is vital that any relevant opinions expressed are based firmly on what the witness personally perceived. Assume that you act for a claimant in negligence proceedings against the defendant, Mr X. When you interview a former personal assistant of Mr X, they tell you, 'Mr X was always very disorganised'. That is a conclusion the witness has drawn. What you want to know is what did the witness see or hear that led them to that conclusion. Was it that Mr X's office was untidy, with the files on the floor and not in the cabinet? That Mr X did not keep his diary up to date and missed appointments? That Mr X told the witness at least once a week that he had been late for a meeting?

12.8.3 Expert evidence

As indicated in s 3(1) of the Civil Evidence Act 1972, the other main exception to the inadmissibility of opinion evidence concerns expert evidence (see **12.13**).

In *Harlow v Aspect Contracts Ltd* [2020] EWHC 1488 (TCC), the claimants objected to the production of a witness statement which included comments on an expert's findings and which did not comply with PD 32, para 18.2. The judge in refusing to allow the statement to go into evidence held that the witness was 'clearly carrying out an exercise of expressing his opinion'. This case clearly demonstrates the need for care when drafting witness statements.

12.9   HEARSAY EVIDENCE

Special considerations apply where hearsay evidence is to be used. Before looking at these, it is necessary to understand what is meant by 'hearsay'.

12.9.1 Definition

Hearsay evidence is defined in s 1(2)(a) of the Civil Evidence Act 1995 as 'a statement made otherwise than by a person while giving oral evidence in the proceedings which is tendered as evidence of the matters stated'.

Hearsay evidence may be an oral or a written statement made outside the courtroom, which is repeated to the court in order to prove the truth of the matter stated out of court.

Note that s 13 of the 1995 Act defines a 'statement' as 'any representation of fact or opinion'.

The statement that constitutes the hearsay evidence must itself constitute admissible evidence. So any fact must be relevant (see **12.1**). Likewise, any opinion must be that of a non-expert based on that person's perception (see **12.8.1**). Equally, the hearsay provisions cannot be used to adduce expert evidence either by way of inclusion in the witness statement or as an exhibit to it (see *New Media Distribution Company Sezc Ltd v Kagalovsky* [2018] EWHC 2742 (Ch)).

Therefore, in considering whether evidence is admissible hearsay, the following three questions must be answered in the affirmative:

(a)   Does the evidence consist of an oral or written statement made outside the courtroom?

(b)   Is that statement being presented to the court in order to prove that it is true? If the previous statement is being related, for example, to show a person's state of mind or simply to show that the statement was made, it will not be hearsay.

(c)   Is the statement an admissible statement of fact or opinion?

EXAMPLE 1

Richard is giving evidence. He says in his evidence, 'Dave told me that Peter had stolen a car'. Richard is repeating what someone else said outside the courtroom, so the first part of the definition of hearsay is satisfied. But consider why Richard is giving this evidence. If it is as part of a case against Peter where it is relevant to show that Peter did, indeed, steal a car, then it will be hearsay. On the other hand, if Richard is giving evidence in a defamation claim brought by Peter against Dave then it will not be hearsay, as Richard is not giving the evidence to show that Peter stole a car. Indeed, this would be exactly what Peter does not want to show! Richard is relating the evidence simply to show that the statement was made.

EXAMPLE 2

Michael booked a holiday with Fancy Tours Ltd. When booking, the agent assured him that the hotel would be quiet and peaceful, close to the beach and with its own swimming pool. However, the hotel was noisy, some distance away from the beach, and did not have a swimming pool. Michael is now suing for misrepresentation and wishes to repeat in evidence the oral statements made to him by the agent. This will be relevant evidence on the issue of liability but it will not be hearsay because it is not being related to show the truth of those statements. It is being related to show the effect that the statements had on his state of mind, namely that he relied on them and was misled by the misrepresentations.

EXAMPLE 3

Clive arrives at the scene of an accident shortly after the claimant, Anna, a pedestrian, was knocked over by a motorbike ridden by the defendant, Matthew. The accident takes place in a 30 miles per hour zone. The defendant denies liability, alleging that he was not speeding and that Anna ran out in front of him. Clive's evidence is, 'When I arrived at the accident a woman I know only as Liz came up to me and said, "That pedestrian was knocked over by the motorbike that was going at at least 45 miles per hour. It was the bike rider's fault"'. Assume Clive is called as a witness by Anna. Her solicitor's attempts to trace Liz fail. Clive can repeat what Liz told him about the pedestrian being knocked over by the motorbike and that in Liz's opinion the motorbike was travelling at at least 45 miles per hour. That would be admissible evidence if given by Liz in court. It is relevant to the issue of liability and based on what Liz perceived. But Clive cannot repeat Liz's opinion that the accident was the defendant's fault. Liz would be a witness of fact in court. A witness of fact cannot give evidence beyond relevant facts and perceptions. This would be inadmissible opinion evidence from Liz. So it cannot be admissible as hearsay evidence for Clive to repeat it.

Hearsay evidence may be either first-hand or multiple.

EXAMPLE 1

Sara gives evidence of something that she was told by John (in order to prove the truth of John's statement). Sara's evidence is first-hand hearsay.

EXAMPLE 2

Sara also gives evidence of something that John was told by Michelle (in order to prove the truth of what Michelle said). This evidence is multiple hearsay.

> **EXAMPLE 3**
>
> Sara keeps a diary. She records what she saw one day. Sara's diary is used at a trial to prove the truth of its contents. That evidence is first-hand hearsay.

> **EXAMPLE 4**
>
> Sara keeps a diary. She records what she was told by John one day. Sara's diary is used at a trial to prove the truth of what John said. That evidence is multiple hearsay.

12.9.2 Using hearsay evidence

12.9.2.1 Notice requirements

Section 1 of the Civil Evidence Act 1995 provides that, in civil proceedings, evidence shall not be excluded on the ground that it is hearsay. Therefore, hearsay evidence is admissible in civil proceedings. Section 2 of the Act provides that a party proposing to bring hearsay evidence must notify any other party of that fact and, on request, give particulars of, or relating to, the evidence. This must be read in conjunction with Part 33 of the CPR 1998 which sets out the rules relating to how hearsay evidence may be used.

Rule 33.2 states:

(1)   Where a party intends to rely on hearsay evidence at trial and either—

    (a)   that evidence is to be given by a witness giving oral evidence; or

    (b)   that evidence is contained in a witness statement of a person who is not being called to give oral evidence;

that party complies with section 2(1)(a) of the Civil Evidence Act 1995 by serving a witness statement on the other parties in accordance with the court's order.

(2)   Where paragraph (1)(b) applies, the party intending to rely on the hearsay evidence must, when he serves the witness statement—

    (a)   inform the other parties that the witness is not being called to give oral evidence; and

    (b)   give the reason why the witness will not be called.

(3)   In all other cases where a party intends to rely on hearsay evidence at trial, that party complies with section 2(1)(a) of the Civil Evidence Act 1995 by serving a notice on the other parties which—

    (a)   identifies the hearsay evidence;

    (b)   states that the party serving the notice proposes to rely on the hearsay evidence at trial; and

    (c)   gives the reason why the witness will not be called.

(4)   The party proposing to rely on the hearsay evidence must—

    (a)   serve the notice no later than the latest date for serving witness statements; and

    (b)   if the hearsay evidence is to be in a document, supply a copy to any party who requests him to do so.

12.9.2.2 Practical points

Therefore, if a party serves a witness statement that contains hearsay evidence, but intends to call the person who made the witness statement to give evidence at trial, simply serving the statement on the other party complies with the notice requirements of the Civil Evidence Act 1995. However, if a party does not intend to call a witness but instead intends to rely on the statement itself as hearsay evidence, that party must inform the other side by way of a hearsay notice when they serve the witness statement that they are not calling the witness to give oral evidence and give the reason why, if any, the witness will not be called.

> **EXAMPLE 1**
>
> The witness statement of Mr X is exchanged by the claimant. The statement contains hearsay, namely (a) Mr X repeats what Mrs Y told him outside a courtroom; (b) the claimant will be asking the court to accept that the statement of Mrs Y is true; and (c) her statement is an admissible statement of fact or opinion (see **12.9.1**). When exchanging witness statements (including Mr X's), the claimant does not serve any hearsay notice in respect of Mr X's evidence and does not serve a witness statement made by Mrs Y on the defendant. From this, the defendant will know that the claimant intends to (a) call Mr X to give oral evidence at trial; and (b) rely on the hearsay evidence of Mrs Y at trial.

> **EXAMPLE 2**
>
> The witness statement of Miss Z is exchanged by the defendant. With it, the defendant serves a hearsay notice explaining that Miss Z will not be called to give oral evidence at trial as she is too ill. Those parts of the witness statement that the defendant will be asking the court to accept as true and are admissible facts or opinions expressed by Miss Z (or indeed anyone else to her) will be admissible as hearsay evidence at the trial.

Note that by s 2(4), a party's failure to comply with the notice requirement does not affect the admissibility of the evidence, but it may be taken into account by the court as a matter adversely affecting the weight to be given to the evidence in accordance with s 4 (see **12.9.3.3**) and/or when the court makes a costs order at the end of the trial (see **14.3**).

Notice of intention to rely on hearsay evidence is only required for evidence to be used at a trial.

A template to help you draft a hearsay notice is set out at **Appendix B(11)**.

12.9.3   Weight to be attached to hearsay evidence

12.9.3.1   'Second best' evidence

Whilst hearsay evidence is admissible, it is important to remember that it is not normally the best evidence of a fact. Out-of-court statements are not made on oath or with any form of affirmation. It is not uncommon for a person to lie, or to make ill-considered statements that are inaccurate. The greater the number of times a statement is repeated, the more likely there is to be an error in the transmission process. Therefore hearsay statements may be less likely to be true or accurate.

The memory or power of observation of the maker of a hearsay statement may be defective, but such weaknesses cannot be directly revealed by cross-examination. The trial judge cannot assess the reliability of the statement by observing the witness's demeanour as the witness is not giving evidence. But are there any safeguards? If X tells the court what Y said, then even though Y cannot be cross-examined as to their means of knowledge and reliability, X can be cross-examined both about X's own reliability and about their view of Y's reliability. As to the latter, that depends on how well X knows Y, if at all, and how accurately and honestly X is prepared to give their views about Y. Although this is undoubtedly inferior to cross-examination of Y, Y's reliability can be tested to some degree. But if X tells the court what Y told them Z said, there is not even this indirect check on Z's reliability (when neither Y nor Z is called to give evidence).

12.9.3.2   Judicial approach

A trial judge will normally start to assess the probative value of any hearsay evidence by answering these questions:

(a)   What issue, if any, does the hearsay evidence address?

(b)   How important is that issue in the case?

(c)   What other evidence is available on the same issue?

(d)   Is the hearsay evidence more probative than any other evidence which the proponent could procure through reasonable efforts?

12.9.3.3   Statutory guidelines

Section 4 of the Civil Evidence Act 1995 provides guidelines for the courts to assist them in assessing the weight they should attach to hearsay evidence. It provides that the court is to have regard to any circumstances from which any inference can reasonably be drawn as to the reliability or otherwise of the evidence, and, in particular, to the following:

(a)   Whether it would have been reasonable and practicable for the party adducing the evidence to have called the person who made the original statement as a witness. How credible is any reason? Is the maker of the statement dead, or abroad and unwilling or unable to return, or unfit to attend trial, or untraceable, or unlikely to remember the details of their statement? What if the maker of the statement is the opponent or the opponent's spouse?

So where a party chooses to rely on hearsay evidence on a key issue when the maker of the statement is readily available to give oral evidence, you can expect the other side to comment adversely on this in its closing speech, and the trial judge may well decide to give it little or no weight. The inference is that such evidence, if called, would have been unfavourable to the party and so it has relied on hearsay instead.

(b)   Whether the original statement was made contemporaneously with the events in question. Was the statement made at a time when the facts referred to in it were fresh in the memory of the person making it? Since the accuracy and completeness of recollection decrease rapidly as time passes, an out-of-court statement made soon after an event is likely to be more reliable than the testimony of the maker of the statement given days, weeks, months, or even years later. What is likely to be more reliable: a note a witness makes of a car registration number immediately after the car drives off, or such a note made by the witness the next day?

(c)   Whether the evidence involves multiple hearsay. For example, Anne says to Brian, 'I saw an accident in Bow Street today involving a lorry and a red taxi'. The next day Brian says to Chris, 'Anne said to me yesterday that she saw an accident in Bow Road where a red lorry hit a taxi'. For Chris to repeat in court what Brian informed him Anne had said about the accident would be multiple hearsay. The danger with multiple hearsay is that it may become less and less reliable. Note that Brian tells Chris something slightly different from what Anne told him. Chris's version could become even less like what Anne originally said. There is always the danger of mishearing, exaggeration, unclear reporting and general inaccuracy through repetition.

(d)   Whether any person involved had any motive to conceal or misrepresent matters. Was the maker of the statement employed by the party who now relies on it? Did the employee make the statement with a view to pleasing their employer?

(e)   Whether the original statement was edited, or was made in collaboration with someone else or for a particular purpose. Is a statement made by a person who is trained to make it or record it more or less reliable than a statement made by, or to, someone not so trained?

(f)   Whether the circumstances suggest an attempt to prevent proper evaluation of the weight of the evidence. Was notice given of the intention to adduce the hearsay evidence and, if so, was that notice given sufficiently in advance of the trial to permit the party affected by it a fair opportunity to respond to it? If notice was given, did the other side object? Note that by s 2(4) of the 1995 Act, this guideline includes any failure to comply with the notice requirements (see **12.9.2**)

12.9.4 Right of the opposing party to cross-examine the person who originally made the statement

Section 3 of the Civil Evidence Act 1995 provides that where a party adduces hearsay evidence from a person whom they do not call as a witness, any other party may, with the permission of the court, call that person as a witness and cross-examine them. An application for such permission must be made not later than 14 days after service of the hearsay notice (CPR 1998, r 33.4).

What is the scope of this provision? It applies to any hearsay evidence upon which a party relies, whether that hearsay statement is contained in a witness statement made by the author of the hearsay statement or in some other witness statement or expert report (see *Brown v Mujibal* [2017] 4 WLUK 42).

So, if a party to an action chooses not to give oral evidence and rely on hearsay, can the other party use this provision to compel the opponent to attend the trial and be cross-examined? In *Brown*, this was answered in the affirmative. But that decision was distinguished and doubted in *G (a protected party by his litigation friend SX) v Hassan* [2019] 6 WLUK 441. The decision in *Brown* was distinguishable on its facts because the claimant's capacity had been in dispute in that case. That was an important distinction with the instant case where the experts agreed that the claimant lacked capacity. Furthermore, the legal analysis in *Brown* had been incomplete in that there had been no consideration of the question of the compellability of witnesses. If the defendant was correct, then one party in civil litigation could become a compellable witness at the suit of the other party in the litigation. That proposition could not be accepted as a matter of law, nor was there any binding authority for it. Similarly, the judge in *Brown* had not considered the Civil Evidence Act 1995, s 4 (see **12.9.3.3**) on the weight to be given to hearsay evidence. That section adequately protected a defendant in that the trial judge could attach little or no weight to such evidence to the claimant's detriment.

12.9.5 Competence (Civil Evidence Act 1995, s 5)

Hearsay evidence is not admissible if the original statement was made by a person who was not competent as a witness because of their mental or physical infirmity or lack of understanding.

12.9.6 Credibility (Civil Evidence Act 1995, s 5)

Where hearsay evidence is adduced and the person who made the original statement is not called as a witness, evidence is still admissible to attack or support their credibility, or to show that they have made another, inconsistent statement. The party wishing to call such evidence must give notice to the other party not later than 14 days after service of the hearsay evidence (CPR 1998, r 33.5).

Although notice may have been given under s 5, how will the party actually adduce the discrediting evidence (such as an allegation of bias, previous convictions or a previous inconsistent statement) at trial? It is now too late to include such allegations in any witness statements as they have already been served pursuant to the directions order. The opponent's agreement, or otherwise the court's permission, should be sought to rely on the evidence. An application to the court should be made at any pre-trial review or trial. If done at a pre-trial review then permission should be requested to serve a supplemental witness statement dealing with the evidence.

12.9.7 Previous inconsistent statements (Civil Evidence Act 1995, s 6)

The effect of this provision is that, where a party calls a witness to give evidence at the trial, the opposing party may cross-examine the witness about a previous inconsistent statement provided that they have complied with the requirements of the Civil Evidence Act 1995 concerning the use of hearsay evidence. For example, in *Fifield v Denton Hall Legal Services* [2006]

EWCA Civ 169, the claimant's doctor, during a consultation, wrote down certain facts that the claimant told him about how she sustained her injuries. The defendants contended that the facts in the doctor's record were inconsistent with the facts advanced by the claimant in her own evidence. So in the circumstances the doctor's record was hearsay evidence and notice should have been given by the defendants to the claimant. If the court concludes that the inconsistent statement was made, it is unclear whether the earlier inconsistent statement itself can be treated as evidence of its contents, or if it only affects the credibility of the witness.

This provision does not prevent a person's witness statement that has been exchanged in accordance with a case management order from being treated as their evidence-in-chief. Indeed, the judge at the trial can, and usually will, order that a witness statement which was served before the trial shall stand as the evidence-in-chief of that witness. The witness will, of course, be present at the trial, and will be subject to cross-examination. In these circumstances, their witness statement is not treated as hearsay evidence.

12.9.8   Statements contained in documents (Civil Evidence Act 1995, s 8)

This provision provides that where a statement contained in a document is admissible as evidence in civil proceedings, it may be proved (a) by the production of that document, or (b) whether or not that document is still in existence, by the production of a copy of that document or of the material part of it, authenticated in such manner as the court may approve. Whilst it is immaterial for this purpose how many removes there are between a copy and the original, how much weight should a court give to secondary evidence when the original document is not produced? In *Masquerade Music Ltd v Springsteen* [2001] EWCA Civ 563, Parker LJ stated at [85]:

> In every case where a party seeks to adduce secondary evidence of the contents of a document, it is a matter for the court to decide, in the light of all the circumstances of the case, what (if any) weight to attach to that evidence. Where the party seeking to adduce the secondary evidence could readily produce the document, it may be expected that (absent some special circumstances) the court will decline to admit the secondary evidence on the ground that it is worthless. At the other extreme, where the party seeking to adduce the secondary evidence genuinely cannot produce the document, it may be expected that (absent some special circumstances) the court will admit the secondary evidence and attach such weight to it as it considers appropriate in all the circumstances. In cases falling between those two extremes, it is for the court to make a judgment as to whether in all the circumstances any weight should be attached to the secondary evidence. Thus, the 'admissibility' of secondary evidence of the contents of documents is, in my judgment, entirely dependent upon whether or not any weight is to be attached to that evidence. And whether or not any weight is to be attached to such secondary evidence is a matter for the court to decide, taking into account all the circumstances of the particular case.

Recognising that the factors relevant to the question of the admissibility or weight of secondary evidence will vary from case to case and that the list of relevant factors will not be a closed one, Smith J in *Promontoria (Oak) Ltd v Emanuel* [2020] EWHC 104 (Ch) at [46] considered that the following are factors of particular importance that a judge needs to bear in mind:

> (1)   *The probative difference between the 'primary' and the 'secondary' evidence.* The probative difference between primary and secondary evidence (or 'best' and 'second best' evidence) varies from case to case:
>
>   (a)   Were the evidence in question to be an electronic document, it is meaningless to seek to differentiate between the identical saved document on different persons' computers. In *Kajala v Noble* (1982) 75 Cr App R 15 the Divisional Court held that justices had been entitled to rely on a copy of a video recording made from an original shown on BBC television news bulletins. The original was in the possession of the BBC and the copy was produced and identified by an employee of that organisation. The justices had been satisfied that it was an authentic copy. They accepted that the BBC policy of refusing to

allow the original to leave their premises was reasonable and that the film crew who took the original was overseas.

(b) Equally, there will be many cases were a photocopy will be as good, or nearly as good, as the original.

(c) On the other hand, there will be cases where primary evidence will be clearly and distinctly preferable to the secondary evidence. Were a court to be presented with a choice between the written agreement between A and B, and B's effort to reconstruct the terms of that agreements some months after signing it, it is clear that (all other things being equal) the court would wish to see the written agreement, and that B's reconstruction (no matter how careful and well-intentioned) would be a poor substitute for the primary evidence, namely the written agreement itself.

(2) *The point at issue between the parties.* The extent to which a court will wish to have primary as opposed to secondary evidence before it will be affected by the point at issue between the parties:

(a) Thus, for example, if the allegation is that a document has been forged, the court will wish to have the original before it in order to explore and resolve this question. If, on the other hand, the point at issue between the parties is the construction of a particular contractual provision, it is difficult to see why a court needs to see the original contract, as opposed to a photocopy or image of the original.

(b) It is worth noting that this sort of question may arise independently of the 'best evidence' rule. Suppose the dispute between the parties is that emails between certain persons have been tampered with. A court would not wish to see the 'original' emails – it is likely that no such thing could even be defined – but rather would wish to have evidence going to the integrity of the IT infrastructure whereby the emails were sent, in order to satisfy itself as to whether the products of that system, the emails, were or were not capable of being altered.

(3) *The reason for a party's inability to produce the original.* The point has been made in most of the cases articulating the 'best evidence' rule, that a court's reaction to the non-production of primary evidence is significantly informed by the reason for the non-production of that evidence. If there is a good reason why the document cannot be produced – for instance, months before litigation commenced, the office storing a party's original documents burned down – then the extent to which the court will be inclined to draw adverse inferences from the failure to produce the original will be limited. If, on the other hand, the original is readily available, and the party who holds it can provide no coherent explanation for the failure to produce the original, adverse inferences of some sort are likely to be drawn. Why, the court will ask itself, is a party producing secondary evidence when better evidence – the primary evidence – is readily available? The natural inference, in such a case, is that the primary evidence does not tell the same story as the secondary evidence, and that the primary evidence is not being adduced for that reason.

(4) *The procedural history.* A trial is a culmination of a process. That process involves identifying and framing the issues between the parties, and then ensuring that proper disclosure of documentary evidence appropriate to the resolution of those issues takes place. Generally speaking, the issue of a party's failure to produce an original ought to be raised and resolved well before trial. The English courts have established procedures, taking place well before trial, to flush out the points parties are taking in relation to documents. Thus, for instance, the fact that a party is contending that a certain document is a forgery will not (absent wholly exceptional circumstances) be raised for the first time at the trial itself. There will have been anterior debate about the precise allegation being made, and the mechanism (for instance, the use of handwriting experts) whereby the allegation of forgery is to be resolved. When considering the best evidence rule, a trial judge will, plainly, take into account the interlocutory steps that have, or have not, been taken by the parties in bringing their dispute to trial.

12.10 USE OF PLANS, PHOTOGRAPHS AND MODELS AS EVIDENCE (r 33.6)

Where evidence such as a plan, photograph, model or the records of a business or public authority is to be given in evidence and it is not:

(a) contained in a witness statement, affidavit, or expert's report;

(b)   to be given orally at the trial; or

(c)   the subject of a hearsay notice;

the evidence will not be admissible unless the party intending to use it has disclosed their intention to use such evidence within the deadline for serving witness statements.

They must disclose their intention at least 21 days before the hearing, if:

(a)   there are not to be witness statements; or

(b)   they intend to use the evidence solely to disprove an allegation made in a witness statement.

If the evidence forms part of an expert's report, they must disclose their intention when they serve their expert's report.

Where a party has given notice of their intention to put in the evidence, they must give every other party an opportunity to inspect it and to agree to its admission without further proof.

12.11   NOTICE TO ADMIT FACTS (r 32.18)

In order to try to avoid the expense of proving a particular fact at trial, a party may serve on another party a notice requiring that party to admit certain facts or a certain part of their case, as specified in the notice. Form N266 should be used. A copy is set out at **Appendix A(6)**.

Such a notice must be served no later than 21 days before the trial.

If the party upon whom the notice is served refuses to admit the relevant fact(s), the other party will still be required to prove the fact(s) at trial. Where, however, they do so, the court may take this into account when considering the issue of costs. Effectively, this means that the party who served the notice will usually recover the cost of proving the facts in question (even if they lose the case).

12.12   NOTICE TO ADMIT OR PROVE DOCUMENTS (r 32.19)

A party is deemed to admit that any document disclosed in a list of documents served under Part 31 (see **Chapter 11**) is genuine unless they serve notice that they want the document to be proved at trial.

A notice to prove a document must be served by the later of the following:

(a)   the latest date for serving witness statements; or

(b)   within seven days of disclosure of the document.

12.13   EXPERT EVIDENCE (PART 35)

As we saw at **3.4**, in many cases a party may wish to instruct an expert and rely upon expert evidence. However, parties do not have an unfettered right to use expert evidence and, as part of its case management powers, the court will restrict expert evidence to that which is reasonably required to resolve the proceedings, bearing in mind the overriding objective and particularly the issue of proportionality.

Judicial guidance on applying the test in r 35.1 was provided in *British Airways v Spencer* [2015] EWHC 2477 (Ch). In that case, Warren J held that the following questions should be asked by a court when determining whether expert evidence should be permitted:

(a)   Is it necessary for there to be expert evidence before the issue can be resolved? If it is necessary, rather than merely helpful, then it must be admitted.

(b)   If the evidence is not necessary then would it be of assistance to the court in resolving that issue? If it would be of assistance, but not necessary, then the court would be able to determine the issue without it.

(c) Since, under (b) above, the court will be able to resolve the issue without the evidence, the third question is whether, in the context of the proceedings as a whole, expert evidence on that issue is reasonably required to resolve the proceedings.

By s 3(1) of the Civil Evidence Act 1972, subject to the rules of court, 'where a person is called as a witness in any civil proceedings, his opinion on any relevant matter on which he is qualified to give expert evidence shall be admissible in evidence.'

See the Guidance for the Instruction of Experts (**Appendix A(21)**) for a detailed consideration of the duties of experts, their appointment, etc.

Part 35 of the CPR governs the use of experts by parties only during court proceedings. This is because an expert is defined by r 35.2 as a person who has been instructed to give or prepare expert evidence for the purpose of the proceedings.

12.13.1 The duty of an expert

Although in many cases an expert is instructed by one particular party, r 35.3 makes it clear that the duty of an expert is to help the court on the matters within their expertise, and this duty overrides any obligation to the person from whom they have received instructions or by whom they are paid. If the expert is unsure of the nature of these obligations, they may file a request for directions from the court. Experts should, therefore, be completely objective and unbiased in the way in which they provide their opinion for the benefit of the court (see *Stevens v Gullis* [1999] BLR 394). Likewise, it is not for an expert to comment on issues concerning the credibility of a party or the reliability of a party's evidence (see *Radia v Marks* [2022] EWHC 145 (QB)).

We saw at **3.4.2** that payment of the expert's fee on a conditional or contingency fee basis might call into question the independence and impartiality of the expert. In *Gardiner and Theobald LLP v Jackson (Valuation Officer)* [2018] UKUT 253 (LC), a case concerning rating valuations, the expert was not paid on a conditional fee basis but their firm was entitled to a 'success-related fee' if the firm secured a reduction in liability for rates on the properties. This gave rise to concerns about independence, as in the judge's view it gave the expert a 'direct financial interest' in the assessment of rateable value.

An expert is not disqualified by the fact of being employed by one of the parties, although the court will need to be satisfied that the expert was sufficiently aware of their responsibilities to the court (*Field v Leeds City Council* [2000] 1 EGLR 54). Given the risk of the appearance of bias, parties will generally prefer to instruct an expert who is independent. See also *Proton Energy Group SA v Orlen Lietuva* [2013] EWHC 2872 (Comm).

An expert who behaves improperly is likely to be reported to their governing body by the trial judge at the end of the hearing, as suggested in *Pearce v Ove Arup Partnership* [2001] LTL, 8 November and *Meadow v General Medical Council* [2006] EWCA Civ 1390. If an expert's improper behaviour wastes the costs of the opposing party, the expert may be ordered to contribute towards payment of those costs (see *Thimmaya v Lancashire NHS Foundation Trust* (Manchester County Court, 30 January 2020) and *Robinson v Liverpool University Hospital NHS Foundation Trust and Dr Mercier* (2021) *Law Society Gazette*, 3 November). An expert who deliberately or recklessly makes a false statement in their report is likely receive a custodial sentence for being in contempt of court (*Liverpool Victoria Insurance Company Ltd v Zafar* [2019] EWCA Civ 39). Note also that a party may sue their own expert in negligence: see *Jones v Kaney* [2011] UKSC 13.

12.13.2 The court's power to restrict expert evidence

Rule 35.1 provides that expert evidence must be restricted to that which is reasonably required to resolve the proceedings, and r 35.4 provides that no party may call an expert or put in evidence an expert's report without the court's permission. Permission is usually granted at the directions stage, and the party applying for permission must identify both the field in which they wish to rely on expert evidence and, where practicable, the name of the expert in that field on whose evidence they wish to rely, the issues the expert evidence will address and an estimate of the costs of the proposed expert evidence. As we saw in **Chapter 9**, this information should normally be provided in the directions questionnaire.

The options available to the court in giving directions on expert evidence include:

(a)   directing that no expert evidence is to be adduced at all, or no expert evidence of a particular type or relating to a particular issue;

(b)   limiting the number of expert witnesses which each party may call, either generally or in a given speciality;

(c)   directing that evidence is to be given by one or more experts chosen by agreement between the parties or, where they cannot agree, chosen by such other manner as the court may direct;

(d)   directing that some or all of the experts from like disciplines shall give their evidence concurrently (PD 35, para 11).

The court will also decide whether it is necessary for experts to give oral evidence at trial. This is probably going to be the case in multi-track proceedings, but in fast track proceedings the normal position is that expert evidence will be given in the form of a written report or reports rather than by way of oral evidence (see **9.6.2.5**).

The court also has the power to limit the amount of the expert's fees and expenses that the party who wishes to rely on the expert may recover from any other party.

12.13.3   Instructions to an expert witness

You would normally expect the instructions from a solicitor to an expert witness to be privileged from inspection by other parties (see **11.11**). However, r 35.10(4) states:

> The instructions referred to in paragraph (3) [the substance of all material instructions, written or oral, on which the report is based] shall not be privileged against disclosure but the court will not, in relation to those instructions—
>
> (a)   order disclosure of any specific document; or
>
> (b)   permit any questioning in court other than by the party who instructed the expert,
>
> unless it is satisfied that there are reasonable grounds to consider the statement of instructions given under paragraph (3) to be inaccurate or incomplete.

As we shall see at **12.13.5**, the report itself must contain the substance of all material instructions received.

So has legal professional privilege in relation to instructions to an expert gone? The answer appears to be that it has not. Rule 35.10(4) is qualified by PD 35, para 5, which provides that such cross-examination will be permitted only where it is in the 'interests of justice'. Arguably the instructions remain privileged from inspection unless and until the court makes an order under the Rule. Such an order will be made only if there are reasonable grounds for believing that the expert's statement of instructions is inaccurate or incomplete: *Lucas v Barking, Havering and Redbridge Hospitals NHS Trust* [2003] EWCA Civ 1102.

Of course, a party can always waive privilege if they wish to do so. Indeed, there are many occasions when solicitors might use a standard format for instructions to an expert, especially where recommended by a pre-action protocol. In such a case there should be no objection to the expert exhibiting those to their report. However, there is no question of confidential information concerning the merits of the case having to be disclosed. The court will not readily entertain any applications for disclosure or cross-examination in this context. After reports have been exchanged it should be routine for a party to send a copy of the other side's report to their own expert for comment. Obviously one point that can be looked for is whether any report is based on inaccurate or incomplete instructions. If there are doubts the matter should be raised in correspondence and/or an interim application made for directions concerning the 'suspicious' report.

12.13.4 Form of expert evidence

Expert evidence is to be given in a written report unless the court directs otherwise, and, if the party wishes to rely on the expert evidence at trial, the report must be disclosed to the other party in accordance with the directions given by the court. The usual order is for simultaneous mutual exchange on or before a set date.

When first obtained, an expert's report that has been prepared for the sole or dominant purpose of the litigation is a privileged document. A copy must be given to the other party only if the party who commissioned it wishes to rely on it at trial. If they decide not to rely on the report (perhaps because it is unfavourable), they do not have to allow the other side to inspect it. It is, however, disclosable in part 2 of the list of documents. See further **Chapter 11**.

A party cannot use a witness statement (see **12.3**) to adduce evidence which that witness could not give orally (*JD Wetherspoon plc v Harris (Practice Note)* [2013] EWHC 1088 (Ch)) and therefore cannot include evidence that could only be given by way of an expert (*New Media Distribution Company Sezc Ltd v Kagalovsky* [2018] EWHC 2742 (Ch):

> It is not right for a factual statement ... to be used to adduce expert, when there are clear procedural rules of this court that no party may call an expert or put in evidence an expert's report without the court's permission. It is not right for these provisions in CPR 35 to be circumvented simply by attaching the expert statements to a statement of fact'. (per Smith J at [10])

The position was confirmed in R *(on the application of Banks Renewables Ltd) v Secretary of State for Business, Energy & Industrial Strategy* [2020] 2 WLUK 99. Where a party does not have permission to rely on an expert's report, neither the party nor any of its witnesses should exhibit the report to their witness statement. It is important to ensure that the CPR 1998 and the refusal of permission to adduce an expert's report are not circumvented by it being exhibited to a witness statement.

12.13.5 Contents of the report

Rule 35.10 and PD 35, paras 3.1 and 3.2 give the following detailed instructions on the contents of an expert's report:

3.1   An expert's report should be addressed to the court and not to the party from whom the expert has received his instructions.

3.2   An expert's report must:

    (1)   give details of the expert's qualifications;

    (2)   give details of any literature or other material which the expert has relied on in making the report;

    (3)   contain a statement setting out the substance of all facts and instructions given to the expert which are material to the opinions expressed in the report or upon which those opinions are based;

    (4)   make clear which of the facts stated in the report are within the expert's own knowledge;

    (5)   say who carried out any examination, measurement, test or experiment which the expert has used for the report, give the qualifications of that person, and say whether or not the test or experiment has been carried out under the expert's supervision;

    (6)   where there is a range of opinion on the matters dealt with in the report—

        (a)   summarise the range of opinion, and

        (b)   give reasons for the expert's own opinion;

    (7)   contain a summary of the conclusions reached;

    (8)   if the expert is not able to give his opinion without qualification, state the qualification; and

    (9)   contain a statement that the expert:

(a)   understands their duty to the court, and has complied with that duty; and

(b)   is aware of the requirements of Part 35, this practice direction and the Guidance for the Instruction of Experts in Civil Claims 2014.

The report must also be verified by a statement of truth that states:

> I confirm that I have made clear which facts and matters referred to in this report are within my own knowledge and which are not. Those that are within my own knowledge I confirm to be true. The opinions I have expressed represent my true and complete professional opinions on the matters to which they refer. I understand that proceedings for contempt of court may be brought against anyone who makes, or causes to be made, a false statement in a document verified by a statement of truth without an honest belief in its truth.

As to para 3.2(6)(b), even if there is not a range of opinions, some reasoning is necessary in order to support an expert's conclusion:

> If the expert is to fulfil his overriding duty to assist the court, it is inevitable that a report must contain a basis for the expert's conclusions. This is reflected in paragraph 62 of the Civil Justice Council 'Guidance for the instruction of experts in civil claims' (2014) which, amongst other things, provides that the summary should be at the end of a report 'after the reasoning' and that the judge may be 'assisted in the comprehension of the facts and analysis if the report explains at the outset the basis of the reasoning'. Obviously, the extent of the reasoning required will depend upon what is necessary in the circumstances. (per Asplin LJ in *Griffiths v Tui (UK) Ltd* [2021] EWCA Civ 1442 at [76])

These formalities do not address the question of any potential or actual conflict of interest. In *Toth v Jarman* [2006] EWCA Civ 1028, [2006] 4 All ER 1276, the Court of Appeal held that, whilst the presence of a conflict of interest does not automatically disqualify an expert, the key question is whether the expert's opinion is independent. So, where an expert has a material or significant conflict of interest, the court is likely to refuse the party permission to rely on that evidence, or otherwise the trial judge may well decline to accept it. It is therefore important that a party who wishes to call an expert with a potential conflict of interest should disclose details of that conflict at as early a stage in the proceedings as possible. In any event, an expert should produce their *curriculum vitae* when they provide their report, and this should give details of any employment or activity that raises a possible conflict of interest:

> Our adversarial system depends heavily on the independence of expert witnesses, on the primacy of their duty to the Court over any other loyalty or obligation, and on the rigour with which experts make known any associations or loyalties which might give rise to a conflict. (per Irwin LJ in *EXP v Barker* [2017] EWCA Civ 63 at [51])

A template to help you check the contents of an expert's report may be found at **Appendix B(12)**.

12.13.6   Questions to the expert

After an expert's report has been disclosed, the party who did not instruct the expert may put written questions to the expert about their report. Where a party sends a written question or questions direct to an expert, a copy of the question(s) should, at the same time, be sent to the other party or parties.

Such written questions:

(a)   may be put once only;

(b)   must be put within 28 days of service of the report;

(c)   must be to clarify the report, unless the court permits or the other party agrees to allow questions for a different purpose.

Questions that are wholly disproportionate, overwhelmingly not for the purposes of clarification and amount to cross-examination will be disallowed (*Mustard v Flower* [2019] EWHC 2623 (QB)).

The answers will be treated as part of the expert's report.

12.13.7 Discussion between experts (r 35.12)

12.13.7.1 Court direction

The court will often direct that the parties' experts should meet and have a without prejudice discussion. Rule 35.12(4) confirms that the content of the discussion between the experts shall not be referred to at the trial unless the parties agree.

The purpose of the discussion is not for the experts to settle the case but to agree and narrow the issues. Practice Direction 35, para 9.2 states that the experts should identify:

(i)   the extent of the agreement between them;

(ii)   the points of and short reasons for any disagreement;

(iii)   action, if any, which may be taken to resolve any outstanding points of disagreement; and

(iv)   any further material issues not raised and the extent to which these issues are agreed.

Before the experts meet, the parties must discuss and if possible agree whether an agenda is necessary, and if so attempt to agree one that helps the experts to focus on the issues which need to be discussed. The agenda must not be in the form of leading questions or hostile in tone (PD 35, para 9.3).

Should the parties and/or their legal representatives attend an experts' discussion? No – unless all the parties and the experts agree or the court allows that. Practice Direction 35, para 9.5 provides that if legal representatives do attend, they should not normally intervene in the discussion except to answer questions put to them by the experts or to advise on the law; and the experts may if they so wish hold part of their discussions in the absence of the legal representatives.

12.13.7.2 Written joint statement

Following the discussion, a statement must be prepared by the experts dealing with the points raised in PD 35, para 9.2(i)–(iv) above. Individual copies of the statements must be signed by the experts at the conclusion of the discussion, or as soon thereafter as practicable, and in any event within seven days. Copies of the statements must be provided to the parties no later than 14 days after signing.

Practice Direction 35, para 9.7 makes it clear that the experts must give their own opinions to assist the court and do not require the authority of the parties to sign a joint statement.

What if an expert significantly alters an opinion as a result of the discussion? The joint statement must include a note or an addendum by that expert, explaining the change of opinion (PD 35, para 9.8).

Note that r 35.12(5) makes it clear that where the experts reach agreement on an issue during their discussions, the agreement does not bind the parties unless the parties expressly agree to be bound by the agreement.

> **CASE STUDY: EXPERTS' WITHOUT PREJUDICE MEETING STATEMENT**
> The experts' without prejudice meeting statement in the case study is at **Appendix D(12)**. You will note that this sets out the issues that are agreed and those that remain in dispute. The parties are likely to adopt this position, and so the disputed issues will be taken forward to trial.

12.13.7.3 Failure of expert to comply with directions

In *Mayr and others v CMS Cameron McKenna Nabarro Olswang LLP* [2018] EWHC 3669 (Comm), the claimants' expert was instructed in two separate matters – the 'LMM issue' and the 'Turkish issue'. The order for directions in both claims provided for simultaneous exchange of initial reports followed by a joint meeting. The outcome of that joint meeting was to be recorded in a joint memorandum setting out any areas on which they were able to reach agreement and those where they could not, with reasons for the inability to agree.

The initial reports for the LMM issue were prepared and exchanged and a joint meeting took place. The joint memorandum of that meeting stated that no further agreement had been reached but that the situation may change when the claimants' expert completed their supplemental report. For each issue under discussion, the memorandum stated that the claimants' expert had not finalised their thinking but anticipated that they would have done so by the date fixed for filing a supplemental report. The same sequence of events occurred in the case involving the Turkish issue. The case came before the court on 14 December 2018, with opening written submissions due on 16 January 2019.

Mr Justice Males stated:

> Nobody involved in litigation in this court, whether as client, lawyer or expert, can be in any doubt that the court expects and requires the experts at the joint meeting to take a constructive approach, discussing the contents of their report and the issues on which they are required to express their opinions, reaching agreement where they can and setting out concisely where they cannot reach agreement and why they cannot.
>
> … It seems to me that the position is that the claimants have failed to comply with the terms on which they were given permission to adduce evidence of the Turkish pharmaceutical industry in this case. The burden is on them to provide a workable solution which they have not done. It is for them too to apply for relief from sanctions. Again, they have not done so …
>
> … The order which I make therefore is that as matters stand the claimants do not have permission to adduce evidence of the Turkish pharmaceutical industry at the trial. The burden will be on them to come forward, as I have said, with a proper and acceptable procedure which will include a proper joint meeting and will meet the criteria of relief from sanctions if they wish to pursue this evidence. If they have simply left it too late to do so in an acceptable way then that is something for which they must take the consequences.
>
> … that the effect of my ruling is to strike out a significant part of the claim without there having been an unless order, a party is not entitled to disregard the rules, secure in the knowledge that until an unless order is made it will always get a second chance. Be that as it may, however, the ruling which I made was not a final striking out of the claim. It put the ball firmly in the claimants' court to come back to court with proposals which will put the situation right and will do so without causing serious prejudice to the trial. Although not expressed as an unless order, that is broadly similar in its effect.

12.13.7.4 Changing experts

If a party has permission to rely on an expert but that expert changes their opinion on certain issues following the without prejudice meeting, can that party now obtain the court's permission to rely upon additional expert evidence? This was the question in *Stallwood v David* [2006] EWHC 2600. Teare J observed that as an agreement between experts does not bind the parties unless they expressly agree to be bound by it (see r 35.12(5)), so a modification of an expert's opinion also cannot bind the party who instructed them. But at trial, when the experts' evidence is given, it will be rare that a party will have any prospect of persuading the court not to follow the agreed opinion of the experts. The party will have to demonstrate a good reason to rely upon additional expert evidence. This might include that their expert's change of mind was based on unsound reasons or a mistaken view of the facts, or that their expert acted outside their area of expertise or instructions. As Teare J stressed in the case, the starting point is normally for the party to ask their expert why they changed their mind, if this is not clear from the joint statement.

12.13.8 The single joint expert (r 35.7)

12.13.8.1 When appropriate?

Whether it is appropriate for each party to call its own expert evidence depends on the issues raised in each particular case. However, in a fast track case the general approach of the court is to order a single joint expert unless there is good reason not to do so (see para 3.9 of PD 28). A joint expert is less likely to be ordered in a multi-track case. Even where the court is willing to allow the parties to call their own expert evidence on the issue of liability, it may order a joint expert on any quantum issues that require expert evidence.

Note that PD 35, para 7 provides as follows:

When considering whether to give permission for the parties to rely on expert evidence and whether that evidence should be from a single joint expert the court will take into account all the circumstances in particular, whether:

(a)   it is proportionate to have separate experts for each party on a particular issue with reference to—

    (i)   the amount in dispute;

    (ii)   the importance to the parties; and

    (iii)   the complexity of the issue;

(b)   the instruction of a single joint expert is likely to assist the parties and the court to resolve the issue more speedily and in a more cost-effective way than separately instructed experts;

(c)   expert evidence is to be given on the issue of liability, causation or quantum;

(d)   the expert evidence falls within a substantially established area of knowledge which is unlikely to be in dispute or there is likely to be a range of expert opinion;

(e)   a party has already instructed an expert on the issue in question and whether or not that was done in compliance with any practice direction or relevant pre-action protocol;

(f)   questions put in accordance with rule 35.6 are likely to remove the need for the other party to instruct an expert if one party has already instructed an expert;

(g)   questions put to a single joint expert may not conclusively deal with all issues that may require testing prior to trial;

(h)   a conference may be required with the legal representatives, experts and other witnesses which may make instruction of a single joint expert impractical; and

(i)   a claim to privilege makes the instruction of any expert as a single joint expert inappropriate.

Both the Queen's Bench Division and the Chancery Court Guides provide that:

In many cases it is possible for the question of expert evidence ... to be dealt with by a single expert. Single experts are, for example, often appropriate to deal with questions of quantum in cases where the primary issues are as to liability. Likewise, where expert evidence is required in order to acquaint the court with matters of fact, as opposed to opinion, a single expert will usually be appropriate. There remain however, a body of cases where liability will turn upon expert opinion evidence and where it will be appropriate for the parties to instruct their own experts. For example, in cases where the issue for determination is as to whether a party acted in accordance with proper professional standards, it will usually be of value to the court to hear the opinions of more than one expert as to the proper standard in order that the court becomes acquainted with the range of views existing upon the question and in order that the evidence can be tested in cross-examination.

12.13.8.2 Court direction

Where the court orders a single joint expert it will usually direct that:

(a)   the parties should prepare joint instructions for the expert;

(b)   the expert's fees should be paid jointly by the parties; and

(c)   if the parties have been unable by a set date to agree on the identity of the expert, further directions should be obtained from the court.

As to (b), the court may limit the amount that can be paid by way of fees and expenses to the expert. From the parties' point of view, it is sensible to place a financial cap on the expert's costs (see *Loggie v Loggie* [2022] EWFC 2). Should it become necessary to exceed the cap, any party or the expert can apply to the court to vary the direction.

It is less likely in the case of a single joint expert that the court will think it appropriate to allow oral evidence at trial.

Where there is an order for a single joint expert there is, of course, no need for a direction that reports be exchanged.

12.13.8.3   Practical points

Note that the parties have a duty to assist the court to further the overriding objective (see **1.1.1**) by spotting any manifest ambiguities or errors in the report of a single joint expert and resolving these by asking one or more suitable questions: see *Woolley v Essex CC* [2006] EWCA Civ 753. By analogy, there is a corresponding duty to point out such errors in a report prepared by an opponent's expert.

There is useful guidance from the Court of Appeal in relation to dealing with problems with a single joint expert in the case of *Daniels v Walker* [2000] 1 WLR 1382:

(a) where the parties cannot agree joint instructions for the expert, it is perfectly proper for one party to give separate or supplemental instructions;

(b) where a party is dissatisfied with the expert's report, they should first submit questions to the expert;

(c) if this does not resolve the problem, the dissatisfied party can apply to the court for permission to call another expert. This application will be granted if the court is satisfied that it would be unjust, having regard to the overriding objective, to refuse to allow the further evidence to be called;

(d) where the dissatisfied party has already obtained its own expert's report, the court should not grant permission for that evidence to be used at trial until the experts have met to resolve their differences. Permission for oral evidence to be given at trial is a last resort.

Further, where a single joint expert is appointed by the parties pursuant to a court order, neither party should meet that expert without the other party's being present. See *Peet v Mid-Kent Healthcare Trust (Practice Note)* [2001] EWCA Civ 1703, [2002] 3 All ER 688. Likewise, it is wholly improper for one party to have any discussion with a joint expert without the other party's being present. It might be possible if the absent party gives fully-informed consent: see *Childs v Vernon* [2007] EWCA Civ 305, [2007] LTL, 16 March.

12.13.9   Challenging the admissibility of expert evidence

Should an application to exclude all or part of an opponent's expert's report be made pre-trial or at trial itself? The norm is the latter.

In *Rogers v Hoyle* [2014] EWCA Civ 257, Clarke LJ stated the following:

> 53. In so far as an expert's report does no more than opine on facts which require no expertise of his to evaluate, it is inadmissible and should be given no weight on that account. But, as the judge also observed, there is nothing to be gained, except in very clear cases, from excluding or excising opinions in this category. I agree with what he said in para 117 of his judgment:
>
>> Such an exercise is unnecessary and disproportionate especially when such statements are intertwined with others which reflect genuine expertise and there is no clear dividing line between them. In such circumstances, the proper course is for the whole document to be before the court and for the judge at trial to take account of the report only to the extent that it reflects expertise and to disregard it in so far as it does not. As Thomas LJ trenchantly observed in *Secretary of State for Business Enterprise and Regulatory Reform v Aaron* [2009] Bus LR 809, para 39: 'It is

> my experience that many experts report views on matters on which it is for the court to make its decision and not for an expert to express a view. No modern or sensible management of a case requires putting the parties to the expense of excision; a judge simply ignores that which is inadmissible.'

54. The judge concluded that the whole of the report was admissible, it being a matter for the trial judge to make use of the report as he or she thought fit. Even if he had concluded that it contained some inadmissible material, he would not have thought it sensible to engage in an editing exercise. The trial judge should see the whole report and leave out of account any part of it that was inadmissible.

In *Moylett v Geldof* [2018] EWHC 893 (Ch), Carr J was asked to consider the admissibility of parts of the claimant's expert report and the objection that the report went beyond what was permissible for an expert by expressing an opinion on the ultimate question in the proceedings. He answered this saying:

> ... it is much preferable for the court, rather than picking through expert reports, seeking to excise individual sentences and engaging in an editing exercise, to allow the trial judge to consider the report in its entirety, assuming that it is genuine expert evidence, and to attach such weight as it sees fit at the trial to those passages in the report. (at 4)

The presumption that the issue is a matter for the trial judge may be rebutted if an applicant for exclusion can establish that they will suffer a real prejudice if the report is submitted in its entirety to the trial judge (A v B [2019] EWHC 275 (Comm)).

12.13.10 Summary: the admissibility of expert evidence at trial

To be admissible at trial, an expert's evidence must be:

(a) relevant and within the expertise of the expert (see **12.13**);

(b) in the correct format by way of a report that complies with Part 35 (see **12.13.5**); and

(c) permitted by the court which has given a direction allowing either a named expert or an expert in a specified field of expertise to give evidence.

That evidence, as directed by the court, may be given orally or in the form of a written report (see **12.13.2**).

12.14 PROFESSIONAL NEGLIGENCE CASES: THE DEFENDANT'S OWN EVIDENCE

Rather uniquely, in professional negligence claims a defendant is allowed to give their own expert opinion on what they did or did not do that is said to amount to negligence. There is no need for this to be in the format of a Part 35 report. The defendant's witness statement will suffice. Why? In *DN v London Borough of Greenwich* [2004] EWCA Civ 1659, the Court of Appeal explained this exception to the general rule as follows.

> It very often happens in professional negligence cases that a defendant will give evidence to a judge which constitutes the reason why he considers that his conduct did not fall below the standard of care reasonably to be expected of him. He may do this by reference to the professional literature that was reasonably available to him as a busy practitioner or by reference to the reasonable limits of his professional experience; or he may seek to rebut, as one professional man against another, the criticisms made of him by the claimant's expert(s). Such evidence is common, and it is certainly admissible ...

> Of course a defendant's evidence on matters of this kind may lack the objectivity to be accorded to the evidence of an independent expert, but this consideration goes to the cogency of the evidence, not to its admissibility. (*per* Brooke LJ at [25] and [26])

12.15 ASSESSORS (r 35.15)

In some cases of a technical nature, the court may seek the assistance of someone with technical knowledge in the relevant field. Such a person is known as an assessor, and they have a judicial role in that they are instructed to assist the court. They are not an expert witness and cannot be cross-examined by any of the parties. Their function is to 'educate' the judge and to enable the judge to reach a properly-informed decision.

By r 35.15, the assessor shall take such part in the proceedings as the court may direct. The court may direct the assessor to prepare a report and/or direct the assessor to attend the trial. Any report prepared by an assessor will be sent to the parties.

The use of assessors is rare.

CHAPTER 13

SETTLEMENT

13.1	Negotiations	233
13.2	Pre-action settlements	234
13.3	Settlements reached after the issue of proceedings	234
13.4	Part 36	237
13.5	Claims involving children and protected parties	255
13.6	Discontinuance (Part 38)	256

LEARNING OUTCOMES

After reading this chapter you will have learned:

- the role of negotiations
- how to record a settlement
- the role of pre-action Part 36 offers
- how to make a Part 36 offer
- the consequences of acceptance or non-acceptance of a claimant's Part 36 offer
- the consequences of acceptance or non-acceptance of a defendant's Part 36 offer
- the financial consequences of a r 36.17(3) order
- how much should be awarded under r 36.17(4)
- the restrictions on disclosure of a Part 36 offer
- the effect of a claimant discontinuing the proceedings.

Most disputes are resolved not by a judgment of the court but by the parties reaching a settlement. This may happen at any stage, from before the issue of proceedings to during the trial. Settlement may be achieved as a result of negotiations, which will often involve the use of the procedures set out in Part 36, or (less commonly) the use of alternative dispute resolution (ADR).

In this chapter we start by considering how the parties' solicitors might negotiate a settlement and then safeguard their clients' respective positions by formally recording that agreement. The main part of this chapter looks at the CPR 1998, Part 36. This is often described as a negotiation tool, as it gives the parties the ability to make offers of settlement that may have financial penalties for the opponent if rejected. The chapter ends with the procedure known as discontinuance. This is where a claimant abandons their claim. Unless this is negotiated on terms that are favourable to the claimant, discontinuance will mean the claimant having to pay the defendant's costs of the proceedings.

13.1 NEGOTIATIONS

13.1.1 Solicitor's authority

The scope of the solicitor's authority to negotiate on their client's behalf depends on whether or not proceedings have been issued. Prior to issue, the solicitor has no implied authority to settle the client's claim. Acceptance of any offer can therefore only be subject to the client's approval. Where the client wishes to accept, it is advisable for the solicitor to obtain written confirmation of this.

Once proceedings have been issued, the solicitor has implied authority to compromise a claim. However, in practice it is, of course, essential to seek the client's express instructions.

13.1.2 Basis on which to conduct negotiations

Negotiations may be conducted either orally or in writing. Whichever method is adopted, care should be taken to ensure that the negotiations proceed on a 'without prejudice' basis. This ensures that the negotiations cannot be referred to in court at a later date except to prove the terms of any settlement reached (see further **3.10.1**) or unless all parties to the negotiations agree.

Negotiation is dealt with further in *Skills for Lawyers*, **Chapter 12**.

13.2 PRE-ACTION SETTLEMENTS

13.2.1 Costs and interest

Where a settlement is reached prior to the issue of proceedings, the prospective claimant will not be entitled to recover their legal costs unless this has been agreed. Neither will they be entitled to interest on any sum agreed under s 69 of the CCA 1984, or s 35A of the SCA 1981. There may, however, be an entitlement to interest under contract or the Late Payment of Commercial Debts (Interest) Act 1998, and such should be taken into account during any negotiations and as part of any settlement. The topic of interest is dealt with at **2.7**. Whatever the position, it is important that the parties are clear whether any amount for costs and/or interest is included in the terms being proposed.

13.2.2 Recording a pre-action settlement

It is equally important that once settlement terms have been agreed, they are clearly and accurately recorded in writing, so that the agreement can be enforced if one of the parties defaults.

It may be sufficient for a settlement reached before the issue of proceedings to be recorded in an exchange of correspondence. Commonly, there will be a letter from the potential defendant setting out the terms being offered 'in full and final settlement' of all claims which the prospective claimant may have, and a reply accepting these terms. More complicated settlements should normally be recorded in a formal settlement agreement.

Care should be taken to ensure that all necessary terms are included in any offer to settle. In *Evans v Trebuchet Design Ltd* [2020] EWHC 3037 (IPEC), a letter sent to a litigant in person and marked 'Without Prejudice Save as to Costs' included an offer to settle the claim in full and final settlement. The claimant sent an email accepting the offer followed by an invoice for the agreed amount. The defendant's solicitor then sent a standard form settlement agreement which included a non-disclosure clause. Neither party signed the agreement and the court held that there was a binding agreement to settle when the offer was accepted by the claimant. The standard form settlement agreement was an attempt to modify that agreement, but it was ineffective because it was never signed.

13.3 SETTLEMENTS REACHED AFTER THE ISSUE OF PROCEEDINGS

It is preferable for the settlement to be recorded in a court order or judgment, since this will make enforcement easier if the agreement is not honoured. In particular, enforcement proceedings (see **Chapter 15**) may be commenced to recover any money due under the settlement (including costs). The date by which payment of any debt or damages is due must, however, be specified in the judgment or order.

Unless the settlement provides otherwise, interest is not payable on costs until judgment is entered (see **15.2**).

13.3.1   Consent orders or judgments

Where none of the parties is a litigant in person, it will often be possible to avoid an application to the court by drawing up a consent order or judgment for sealing by a court officer under r 40.6. Although in theory the court retains the power not to approve the proposed order, it will in practice be referred to a judge only if it appears to be incorrect or unclear.

The formalities for a consent order are set out in r 40.6(7) as follows:

(a)   the order agreed by the parties must be drawn up in the terms agreed;

(b)   it must be expressed as being 'By Consent';

(c)   it must be signed by the legal representative acting for each of the parties to whom the order relates.

> **CASE STUDY**
>
> An example of a consent order appears in the case study at **Appendix D(15)**. The claimants have agreed to accept £150,000 in settlement of their claim. Provided that is paid in accordance with para 1, then under para 2 both the claim and counterclaim will come to an end. What if it is not paid? Interest will run (see **15.2**) and the claimants can take enforcement proceedings (see generally **Chapter 15**). What about costs? You will see that by para 3, each side has agreed to pay its own costs.

It is important to note two things. First, the terms of a consent order will be open to public inspection. Secondly, the terms agreed must be within the powers of a court to order, eg the payment of a sum of money, specific performance of a contract and the dismissal of a claim. If the parties want any terms to be confidential and/or beyond the powers of a court to order, they should use a special form of consent order known as the *Tomlin* order (see **13.3.2** below).

13.3.2   *Tomlin* orders

A *Tomlin* order stays the claim on agreed terms that are set out in a schedule to the order, an agreement annexed to the order or a separate document. The basic formalities are in r 40.6(7) (see **13.3.1**). But the key to drafting a *Tomlin* order correctly is to appreciate that certain terms must appear in the order itself, whilst others can be put in the schedule, agreement or separate document. This is because PD 40B, para 3.5 provides as follows:

> Where the parties draw up a consent order in the form of a stay of proceedings on agreed terms, disposing of the proceedings, and where the terms are recorded in a schedule to the order, any direction for:
>
> (1)   payment of money out of court, or
>
> (2)   payment and assessment of costs
>
> should be contained in the body of the order and not in the schedule.

A direction for the payment of money held by the court will be rare. It is most likely to occur where a party has had to pay a sum into court under a previous order, eg a conditional order made on a summary judgment application (see **10.5.2.3**). Where one party is to pay another party's costs and/or the parties want the amount of those costs assessed by the court (known as a detailed assessment: see **14.3**), that direction must go in the order. When addressing the payment of costs, there are four key questions to be answered. Who pays? For what? How much? By when? For example, where there has been a claim and a counterclaim, is the defendant to pay the claimant's costs of making the claim and defending the counterclaim, or is the claimant to pay the defendant's costs of defending the claim and making the counterclaim? Will the paying party pay all or only some of the receiving party's costs? If only some, is that to be a fixed amount or a percentage of what is found to be due? Is any assessment of costs by the court to be done on the standard or indemnity basis (see **14.3.3**)? Finally, when are the costs to be paid?

Moreover, because there is a possibility that a party may not perform its part of the agreement, the order should include a provision that any party is at liberty to apply for the stay to be lifted so that the court can enforce the settlement. This means that it is not necessary to start new proceedings to enforce the terms (*Trebisol Sud Ouest SAS v Berkley Finance Ltd* [2021] EWHC 2494 (QB)).

Whether the terms of the settlement are recorded in a schedule to the *Tomlin* order, an agreement annexed to the document or a separate document depends largely on the degree of confidentiality required. Under r 5.4B and r 5.4C, parties and non-parties can apply for permission to obtain copies of documents filed with the court. In *L'Oreal and Others v eBay International AG and Others* [2008] EWHC B13 (Ch), disclosure of the schedule to a *Tomlin* order was permitted under r 5.4B. Therefore the only way to ensure complete confidentiality is to record the settlement in a separate document which is referred to in the schedule and clearly identifiable but not filed with the court. In *Zenith Logistics Services (UK) Ltd & Others v Coury* [2020] EWHC 774 (QB), the court confirmed that the fact the terms were referred to but not set out in the schedule was entirely unobjectionable. The reason was to preserve confidentiality so that the terms were not accessible to third parties. And there was no breach of the 'open justice' principle.

The schedule, annexed agreement or separate document may contain any agreed term. Often this will be for the payment of a sum of money. When this is not in the order, a provision should be made for interest to run on any late payment. The schedule, annexed agreement or separate document must also record any agreed terms that the court cannot impose, eg that the parties enter into a particular contract, or that in future dealings one party gives the other a discount.

The following table summarises the main points to consider when drafting the order and schedule.

Order	Schedule/Annexed Agreement/Separate Document
'By Consent'	Include any agreed term that court could not order
Stay of proceedings	Any payment of money should include provision for interest on late payment
Liberty to apply	
Payment of money out of court	
Payment of costs	
Detailed assessment of costs	
Signed by the parties' solicitors	

An example of a *Tomlin* order follows. You will see that the order is made 'By Consent', the proceedings are stayed, there is liberty to apply and the defendant has agreed to pay £10,000 of the claimant's costs. Then the schedule records at paragraph 1 the settlement payment, at paragraph 2 the provision for interest on any late payment, and at paragraph 3 that the parties will enter into a particular contract as part of the settlement.

EXAMPLE

IN THE HIGH COURT OF JUSTICE   20XX L 164

QUEEN'S BENCH DIVISION

WEYFORD DISTRICT REGISTRY

BETWEEN

LA BOULE PLC   Claimant

and

CHRISTALINE LIMITED   Defendant

ORDER BY CONSENT

UPON the parties having agreed terms of settlement

BY CONSENT IT IS ORDERED THAT:

1. All further proceedings in this action shall be stayed upon the terms set out in the attached schedule, except for the purpose of carrying such terms into effect.

2. Each party shall have liberty to apply to the court if the other party does not give effect to the terms set out in the schedule.

3. The Defendant do pay the Claimant within 28 days the sum of £50,000 in respect of the Claimant's costs.

Dated: ....

We consent to the making of an order in the above terms.

....

Swallows & Co., Solicitors for the Claimant

....

Singleton Trumper & Co., Solicitors for the Defendant

SCHEDULE

1. The Defendant shall pay or cause to be paid to the Claimant the sum of £500,000 within 28 days of the Order in full and final satisfaction of all claims and counterclaims arising in this action.

2. In the event of late payment, the Defendant will pay interest on the sum of £500,000 or any part remaining due at a daily rate equal to 10% above the Bank of England base rate as at 1 January 20XX.

3. The Claimant and the Defendant will on the making of the Order enter into a distribution agreement on terms agreed between the parties and held by the Claimant's solicitors as part of the compromise of this action.

13.4 PART 36

As we saw in **Chapter 3**, before litigation starts the parties are encouraged to negotiate and settle the claim. It is open to the parties to make 'without prejudice' offers to settle (see generally **3.10.1**). If proceedings are issued, the parties should continually review the case and consider making offers to settle it. By r 36.7(1), a Part 36 offer may be made both before and during proceedings (including, by r 36.2(3)(b), appeal proceedings).

A party may make an offer to settle in whatever way they choose. By r 44.2, the court will take into account when deciding the issue of costs any admissible offer to settle that has been made. So what are the advantages of making an offer to settle in accordance with the formalities required by Part 36? First, by r 36.16(1), a Part 36 offer will be treated as 'without prejudice except as to costs'. So the fact that a Part 36 offer has been made must not normally be communicated to the trial judge (or to any judge allocated in advance to conduct the trial) until the case has been decided, ie the issues of liability and quantum have been adjudicated on. Secondly, if a defendant makes a Part 36 offer and the claimant fails to obtain a judgment more advantageous than that offer, the claimant will usually suffer severe financial penalties (see **13.4.5**). Likewise, if a claimant makes a Part 36 offer and the judgment against the defendant is at least as advantageous to the claimant as the proposals contained in the claimant's Part 36 offer, the defendant will usually suffer severe financial penalties (see **13.4.6**).

If a Part 36 offer is made before proceedings commence, there may be an argument during subsequent proceedings as to whether that offer constituted a claimant's or defendant's Part 36 offer. As to resolving that issue, see *The Huntsworth Wine Company Ltd v London City Bond Ltd* [2022] EWHC 98 (Comm).

13.4.1   Form and content of a Part 36 offer

For clarity (and consistent with the definition in r 36.3), in the rest of this chapter we shall refer to a party who makes a Part 36 offer as 'the offeror' and to the party to whom the offer is made as 'the offeree'.

13.4.1.1   Formalities

Pursuant to r 36.5(1), to be a valid Part 36 offer, the offer must:

(a)   be in writing;

(b)   make clear that it is made pursuant to Part 36;

(c)   specify a period of not less than 21 days during which, if the offeree accepts the offer, the defendant will pay the claimant's costs under r 36.13 (see **13.4.4.3**) (known as 'the relevant period');

(d)   state whether it relates to the whole of the claim or to part of it, or to an issue that arises in it, and if so to which part or issue; and

(e)   state whether it takes into account any counterclaim.

It is vital to comply with requirement (c) above. See *Phi Group Limited v Robert West Consulting Limited* [2012] EWCA Civ 588, where the offer did not specify a period of not less than 21 days; that was fatal. It is sufficient to state a period of 21 days as 'the relevant acceptance period' (see *Onay v Brown* [2009] EWCA Civ 775), or that 'this offer will be open for 21 days from the date of this letter' and identify that period as 'the relevant period' (see *C v D* [2011] EWCA Civ 646). But it is not part of this mandatory requirement, once the period has been specified, to state expressly that this is the period 'within which the defendant will be liable for the claimant's costs in accordance with rule 36.13 if the offer is accepted'. However, it is arguably best practice to include this information.

In *James v James* [2018] EWHC 242 (Ch), an offer expressed to be a defendant's Part 36 offer contained a provision that the claimant pay the defendant's costs of the claim and counterclaim. This was inconsistent with the costs provisions in r 36.13 and the court held that it was not a valid Part 36 offer. The claimant subsequently failed to obtain a judgment more advantageous that the defendant's offer, but the defendant was not able to benefit from the costs consequences of Part 36 due to the defect in the offer.

If an offeree receives a Part 36 offer and they wish to challenge the validity of the offer, they should do so without delay. In *Ali v Channel 5 Broadcast Ltd* [2018] EWHC 840 (Ch), the claimants failed to beat a defendant's Part 36 offer which included the following wording: 'If you think that this offer is defective or non-compliant with Part 36, you must let us know promptly.' It was held that the failure to challenge the validity of the offer at the time meant that the claimants were estopped from challenging its validity later on.

The offer can be made using Form N242A (see **Appendix A(14)**). However, many practitioners set out the terms in a letter. A template to help you draft a Part 36 offer letter is set out at **Appendix B(13)**.

Most commonly, Part 36 offers are made by a claimant and/or a defendant in a monetary claim to settle the claim on payment of a lump sum. However, in a non-monetary claim, such as an injunction, an offeror may set out the terms that they would accept.

Note that by r 36.6, a Part 36 offer by a defendant to pay a sum of money in settlement of a claim must be an offer to pay a single sum of money. Moreover, the defendant must be prepared to pay that sum to the claimant within 14 days of the claimant's accepting the defendant's offer (see further **13.4.4.2**).

Does an offeror have to set out separately in their Part 36 offer (i) the sum that they are willing to pay or accept, and (ii) the amount of interest to be paid on that sum? The answer is no. By r 36.5(4), a Part 36 offer that offers to pay, or offers to accept, a sum of money is treated as inclusive of all interest until the relevant period expires. Does this mean that a Part 36 offer that is made exclusive of interest will not be a valid Part 36 offer? Yes – see *King v City of London Corporation* [2019] EWCA Civ 2266:

> Part 36 proceeds on the basis that interest is ancillary to a claim, not a severable part of it. Just as a party cannot make a Part 36 offer providing for costs consequences other than those prescribed by Part 36, so a Part 36 offer must, if it offers to pay or accept a sum of money, be inclusive of all interest, as CPR 36.5(4) says. Interest cannot be hived off. True it is that, on occasion, there may be room for substantial dispute as regards interest and that the amount at stake could be large, but the same could be said about costs. (per Newey LJ at [40])

Can a valid Part 36 offer be made that includes provision for the payment of interest after the relevant period expires? Yes, under r 36.5(5), 'a Part 36 offer to accept a sum of money may make provision for accrual of interest on such sum after the date specified in paragraph (4). If such an offer does not make any such provision, it shall be treated as inclusive of all interest up to the date of acceptance if it is later accepted.' For example, in *Calonne Construction Ltd v Dawnus Southern Ltd* [2019] EWCA Civ 754, the claimant's Part 36 offer was to settle for a lump sum payment that was 'inclusive of interest until the relevant period has expired. Thereafter, interest at a rate of 8% per annum will be added.'

13.4.1.2   Making more than one offer

An offeror can make more than one Part 36 offer. For example, a claimant making a monetary claim might start with a Part 36 offer to the defendant of, say, £100,000, and subsequently be prepared to reduce that to £95,000 and later £90,000. Of course, the lower the claimant goes, the more chance there is that the defendant might accept one of the offers and put an end to the case. But if none is accepted, the financial consequences of r 36.17 (see **13.4.6**) will be imposed on the defendant should the claimant secure a judgment that is at least as advantageous to them as the proposals contained in one of their Part 36 offers. Equally, a defendant facing a monetary claim might start with a Part 36 offer to the claimant of, say, £65,000, and subsequently be prepared to increase that to £70,000 and later £75,000. Of course, the higher the defendant goes, the more chance there is that the claimant might accept one of the offers and put an end to the case. But if none is accepted, the financial consequences of r 36.17 (see **13.4.5**) will be imposed on the claimant should the claimant fail to obtain a judgment more advantageous than one of the defendant's offers. Here we have considered a change in the terms of an offer that are more favourable to the offeree. If the terms become less advantageous, see **13.4.2**.

A Part 36 offer is not like an offer in the ordinary law of contract where an offer which is rejected, either expressly or by the making of a counter-offer, cannot subsequently be accepted. That is not true of a Part 36 offer, which may be accepted even after the offeree has put forward a different proposal:

Basic concepts of offer and acceptance clearly underpin Part 36, but that is inevitable given that it contains a voluntary procedure under which either party may take the initiative to bring about a consensual resolution of the dispute. Such concepts are part of the landscape in which everyone conducts their daily life. It does not follow, however, that Part 36 should be understood as incorporating all the rules of law governing the formation of contracts, some of which are quite technical in nature. Indeed, it is not desirable that it should do so. (per Moore-Bick LJ in *Gibbon v Manchester City Council* [2010] EWCA Civ 726 at [6])

13.4.1.3   Offers made close to trial

As the relevant period is a minimum of 21 days, can an offer be made less than 21 days before the start of a trial? The answer is yes. By r 36.3(g)(ii), in those circumstances the relevant period is the period up to the end of the trial (or such longer period as the parties agree). Note that by r 36.5(4)(b), such an offer is deemed inclusive of interest up to a date 21 days after the offer was made. If the trial starts then, by r 36.11(3)(d), the offeree will need the court's permission to accept the Part 36 offer. Generally no party should leave making a Part 36 offer so late. This is especially so as the financial benefits under r 36.17(3) or (4) (see **13.4.5** and **13.4.6**) will not apply to a Part 36 offer made less than 21 days before trial unless the court has abridged the relevant period (*Reader v SPIE Ltd* [2021] EWHC 1221 (QB)).

13.4.1.4   Offer made when served

Rule 36.7(2) provides that a Part 36 offer is made when it is *served* on the offeree. If the offeree is legally represented, the offer must be served on their solicitors. As the offer has to be served, it appears the usual rules on deemed service of documents other than a claim form (see **5.7.2**) apply. So, for example, if the offer is posted, first class, to the offeree on Monday, 7 October, it will be deemed to have been served on Wednesday, 9 October (ie the second day after it was posted as that is a business day). If the offer has the usual minimum 21 days limit to accept, the last day of the relevant period (day 21) will be Wednesday, 30 October.

CASE STUDY: CLAIMANT'S PART 36 OFFER

The claimant's Part 36 offer in the case study is at **Appendix D(13)**. You will note that this sets out the offer, and in particular how it complies with the formalities at **13.4.1.1**. Whilst it is not necessary to refer to the provisions of the CPR 1998, r 36.5(1) in the offer letter, we take the view that it should help to prevent any ambiguity and so the need for the offeree to ask for any clarification. In addition, whilst the offer is deemed by r 36.5(4) to be inclusive of interest, confirmation that that is what the offeror is proposing should again ensure there is no uncertainty. Why is the letter headed up 'without prejudice save as to costs' when that is the effect of a Part 36 offer under the CPR 1998, r 36.16(1)? Again, it is simply to make it clear to the offeree that a Part 36 offer is being made.

13.4.2   Withdrawal of a Part 36 offer or change in its terms

Can an offeror either withdraw their offer, or change its terms so that the offer is less advantageous to the offeree, during the relevant period? By r 36.10(3), that will be possible only if the court gives its permission. However, after expiry of the relevant period, either step can be taken without the court's permission, provided, of course, that the offeree has not previously served notice of acceptance of that offer. The offeror must serve written notice of the withdrawal or change of terms on the offeree. This can be done by letter. There is no prescribed form.

Where a claimant reduces the amount they are prepared to accept, or a defendant increases the amount they are willing to pay, the offeror will not bother to withdraw the earlier offer. But a Part 36 offer may be accepted at any time (see **13.4.4**), whether or not the offeree has subsequently made a different offer, *unless* the offeror has served notice of withdrawal of that offer on the offeree: r 36.11(2) (see *LG Blower Specialist Bricklayer Ltd v Reeves* [2010] EWCA Civ

726). So what should a claimant who wishes to increase the sum they were previously prepared to accept, or a defendant who wishes to decrease the amount they previously offered, do? The answer is to serve notice of variation of the original offer under r 36.9(4). This has the advantage of preserving the relevant period of the original offer for the purpose of costs where the offeree fails to beat the less advantageous offer. In *Ballard v West Sussex Partnership NHS Foundation Trust* [2018] EWHC 370 (QB), the defendant made two Part 36 offers, the second a year after the first and shortly before the trial of the case. The claimant established liability but failed to beat either offer. As the defendant had served notice withdrawing the first offer at the same time as the second offer was served, the court held it was only entitled to its costs from the expiry of the relevant period of the second offer.

It is vital that an offeror understands the effect of withdrawing or reducing the terms of their offer. By r 36.17(7), where a Part 36 offer is withdrawn or its terms made less advantageous to the offeree, and the offeree has beaten the less advantageous offer, the financial consequences of r 36.17 (see **13.4.5** and **13.4.6**) will not apply to it.

13.4.3 Clarification of a Part 36 offer

In most cases the terms of a Part 36 offer should not be ambiguous, particularly where the only claim or claims concern a sum or sums of money. But where monetary and/or non-monetary remedies are sought, it is possible that an offeree may not be clear about the terms proposed. By r 36.8, an offeree may, within seven days of receiving a Part 36 offer, request clarification from the offeror. Although the rule is silent on the point, best practice is to make the request in writing. If the offeror does not give the clarification requested, the offeree can (unless the trial has already started) apply to the court for an order that they do so.

Remember that 21 days minimum is given to an offeree to accept a Part 36 offer (the relevant period: see **13.4.1**). After that the offeree may accept the offer but suffer a costs penalty (see **13.4.4.3**), or proceed to trial where they are at risk of suffering the financial consequences of r 36.17 (see **13.4.5** and **13.4.6**). So when making any clarification order, the court will also specify the date when the relevant period is treated as having started.

13.4.4 Acceptance of a Part 36 offer

A Part 36 offer may be accepted at any time, whether or not the offeree has subsequently made a different offer, unless the offeror has served notice of withdrawal of that offer on the offeree (see *C v D* [2011] EWCA Civ 646 and **13.4.2** as to withdrawing an offer).

So whilst a Part 36 offer must specify a period of not less than 21 days within which the offeree may decide to accept it (the relevant period: see **13.4.1**), the offeree can still accept that offer even after the relevant period has expired. However, there may be adverse costs consequences of such late acceptance (see **13.4.4.3**).

13.4.4.1 How to accept

By r 36.11(1), an offeree can accept a Part 36 offer by serving written notice of the acceptance on the offeror. This can be done by letter. There is no prescribed form. If proceedings have started, PD 36, para 3.1 provides that the notice of acceptance must also be filed with the court where the case is proceeding.

Note that r 21.10 provides that acceptance on behalf of a child or protected party is not valid unless the court has approved the settlement (see **5.4.1.4**). If the matter concerns a pre-action Part 36 offer, the application for approval should be made under CPR Part 8 (see **8.3** and **13.5**).

13.4.4.2 Practical consequences of acceptance

When a Part 36 offer is accepted, the claim is stayed. However, that does not affect the power of the court to enforce the terms of a Part 36 offer and to deal with any question of costs (including interest on costs) relating to the proceedings.

Is an agreement reached by the acceptance of a Part 36 offer void if that Part 36 offer was a clear and obvious mistake that was appreciated by the Part 36 offeree at the point of acceptance? Yes, and to that extent the doctrine of common law mistake can apply to a Part 36 offer: see *O'Grady v B15 Group Ltd* [2022] EWHC 67 (QB). In that case, the sequence of events was as follows.

> 20 April 2020: the Defendant's solicitors put forward a Part 36 offer whereby they offered to apportion liability on the basis of a 60/40 split in favour of the Claimant. At that stage the Defendant had not made any formal admission in relation to primary liability. The Claimant did not accept this offer, but neither was it withdrawn;
>
> 10 February 2021: the Defendant formally conceded primary liability but made clear that contributory negligence remained live;
>
> 11 February 2021: Claim Form issued by the Claimant in respect of claims under the 'Law Reform (Miscellaneous Provisions) Act 1934 and the Fatal Accidents Act 1976';
>
> 23 February 2021: the Claimant's solicitor put forward a Part 36 on the issue of liability. The offer (literally) read: *'The Claimant offers to resolve the issue of liability of on 80/20 basis. For the avoidance of doubt if the Defendant accepts this offer it will only be required to pay 20% of the Claimant's damages.'*
>
> 24 February 2021: Having received the Claimant's offer by e-mail at 15.51 on 23 February, the Defendant's solicitor accepted it by e-mail at 10.02 on 24 February.
>
> 24 February 2021: The Claimant's [solicitor] replied by e-mail at 10.12 to make clear that the offer that he intended to make on behalf of the Claimant was 80/20 in the Claimant's favour.
>
> The Claimant says it was surely always obvious that the 23 February 2021 communication was not that intended. Read literally, the assertion in the 'clarification clause' of the offer that the Defendant would only be required to pay '20%' of the Claimant's damages made no sense and plainly invited clarification. Further, any mention of an 80:20 ratio in an offer from a claimant would ordinarily indicate an expectation for an 80% apportionment in their favour, yet this phrase, insofar as it meant anything, oddly suggested the opposite. The implausibility of the Claimant truly intending to compromise her claim for only 20% of its value becomes even more striking given the Defendant had made an offer many months previously of 60:40 in her favour as well as subsequently admitting primary liability. [at 6]

Where a claimant accepts a defendant's Part 36 offer that is, or includes, an offer to pay a single sum of money, that sum must be paid to the claimant within 14 days of the date of acceptance (unless the parties agree otherwise in writing). If the accepted sum is not paid within 14 days (or such other period as has been agreed), the claimant may enter judgment for the unpaid sum. In respect of any other kind of Part 36 offer, any party who has accepted it, but considers that the other party has not honoured its terms, may apply to the court in any existing proceedings to enforce the terms of the offer.

13.4.4.3   Costs consequences of acceptance

Acceptance within relevant period

Where a defendant's Part 36 offer is accepted by the claimant within the relevant period, the claimant is entitled to their costs of the proceedings up to the date on which notice of acceptance is served on the defendant. Those costs should be agreed by the parties or otherwise will be assessed by the court on the standard basis (see **14.3.3.1**). This is summarised in the flowchart at **Appendix C(13)**.

Where a claimant's Part 36 offer is accepted by the defendant within the relevant period, the claimant is entitled to their costs of the proceedings up to the date on which notice of acceptance is served on the claimant. Those costs should be agreed by the parties, or otherwise will be assessed by the court on the standard basis (see **14.3.3.1**). This is summarised in the flowchart at **Appendix C(14)**.

'Late' acceptance

What is the outcome if the claimant accepts 'late' a defendant's offer, ie after the relevant period as specified in the offer has expired? If the parties cannot agree who pays costs, the court will make an order. What costs order will the court make? By r 36.13(5), unless the court considers it unjust to do so:

(a) the defendant will be ordered to pay the claimant's costs of the proceedings up to the date on which the relevant period expired; and

(b) the claimant will be ordered to pay the defendant's costs for the period from the date of expiry of the relevant period to the date of acceptance.

This is summarised in the flowchart at **Appendix C(15)**.

As you would expect, where a claimant's Part 36 offer is accepted late by the defendant, if the parties cannot agree on costs, the court will usually order that the defendant pay the claimant's costs of the proceedings up to the date of acceptance unless the defendant can satisfy the court that it would be unjust to do so. This is the effect of r 36.13(5) and it is summarised in the flowchart at **Appendix C(16)**.

In *Pallet v MGN Ltd* [2021] EWHC 76 (Ch), the defendant had made both pre- and post-action Part 36 offers, neither of which were accepted by the claimant. There was some disclosure, but the claimant declined to negotiate further until full disclosure had been given. Following full disclosure, the claimant made a Part 36 offer. The defendant accepted the offer on day 22 and asked the court to consider its liability for costs under r 36.13(5), arguing that the claimant's failure to negotiate justified disallowing costs from the date when the claimant had received early disclosure. The judge said:

> For the defendant to succeed, it had to establish that the claimant had failed to engage, falling so far short of the standards which the courts expected of litigants in terms of willingness to negotiate that it could discharge the burden of showing that it would be unjust to apply the normal Part 36 consequences ... Although it could be said that the claimant had not engaged in negotiation before October 2020, it could not be said that in the circumstances she should have been negotiating, or that the absence of negotiation was culpable so as to make it unjust to allow the normal consequences of the late acceptance of a Part 36 offer. The claimant would have all the costs of the proceedings.

For these purposes the claimant's costs include any costs incurred in dealing with a defendant's counterclaim if the Part 36 offer states that it takes that into account.

If the parties cannot agree costs when late acceptance occurs, the court will assess costs on the standard basis (see **14.3.3.1**).

So, the presumption is that the price of late acceptance for a claimant is to pay the defendant's costs on the standard basis from when the relevant period expired until the date of acceptance. The court must guard against making an exception from the norm on the grounds that the regime itself is harsh or unjust but must find something about the particular circumstances of the case which takes it out of the norm (see *Downing v Peterborough & Stamford Hospitals NHS Foundation Trust* [2014] EWHC 4216 (QB) at [61]) and keep in mind the salutary purpose of the Part 36 regime which is to promote compromise and avoid unnecessary expenditure of costs and court time (see *Smith v Trafford Housing Trust* [2012] EWHC 3320 (Ch) at [13]). Finally, the burden is on the claimant to show injustice: uncertainties in the litigation and the usual contingencies of litigation do not render it unjust for the normal costs order to operate (see *Briggs v CEF Holdings Ltd* [2018] Costs 123). Subject to this guidance, the court exercises a broad discretion as to the appropriate costs order (*Campbell v Ministry of Defence* [2019] EWHC 2121 (QB)).

Only in 'exceptional circumstances' will the court not require the claimant to make the payment of costs under r 36.13(5)(b). For example, in *Kunaka v Barclays Bank Plc* [2010] EWCA Civ 1035, the Court of Appeal emphasised that particular care should be taken when making a

Part 36 offer to a litigant in person. There, the defendant bank made the claimant, who was acting in person, a Part 36 offer. He did not accept it. About three months after the relevant period had expired, the bank wrote to the claimant reminding him that its Part 36 offer 'remains open for you to accept'. Why did the court hold that it was unjust to apply r 36.13(5)(b) when the claimant subsequently accepted that offer? It so held because the bank had failed to draw his attention to that provision. See also *Lumb v Hampsey* [2011] EWHC 2808; *SG v Hewitt* [2012] EWCA Civ 1053, *Webb Resolutions Ltd v Waller Needham & Green (a firm)* [2012] EWHC 3529 (Ch) and *Momonakaya v Ministry of Defence* [2019] EWHC 480 (QB).

Should a claimant ever be ordered to pay the defendant's costs incurred between expiry of the relevant period and acceptance on the indemnity basis? Yes, if in that period the claimant behaved in a way that went outside the norm (*Lokhova v Longmuir* [2017] EWHC 3152 (QB)). Case law demonstrates that a failure by the claimant to offer any explanation for the belated acceptance of a Part 36 offer can be a proper basis for inferring such unreasonable conduct, at least if the failure is itself inadequately explained: see *Jordan v MGN Ltd* [2017] EWHC 1937 (Ch).

13.4.5 Part 36 consequences at trial of a defendant's offer

If the claimant at trial (or earlier by way of summary judgment) obtains a judgment that is more advantageous than a defendant's Part 36 offer, the claimant can be seen to have been justified in not accepting the offer. In those circumstances, the defendant will have to pay the amount of the judgment (damages plus interest in a monetary claim) and will normally be ordered to pay the claimant's costs on the standard basis (see **14.3.3.1**). Note that interest is payable on those costs only from the date of judgment (see **15.2**).

But what if a claimant fails to obtain a judgment that is more advantageous than the defendant's Part 36 offer? The court will, unless it considers it unjust to do so (see **13.4.8**), make what is commonly called a 'split costs' order under r 36.17(3). This penalises the claimant financially for proceeding with the claim but failing to secure a judgment that is any better for the claimant than the defendant's Part 36 offer.

13.4.5.1 The 'like with like' comparison

Before we look at r 36.17(3), we need to answer this question: how can the court tell if the claimant has been awarded a judgment that is not more advantageous to them than the earlier defendant's Part 36 offer? Where the claimant has made a money claim, the judgment will be for a capital sum plus interest awarded at the trial judge's discretion, usually from when the loss was sustained up to judgment given at the end of the trial, or subsequently if judgment is reserved (see **2.7.2.3**). If the judge has made an award of interest, it is necessary for them to be provided with a calculation of the amount of interest they would have awarded had the judgment been given at the date the relevant period for the Part 36 offer expired.

To make a 'like with like' comparison you should:

(a)   calculate the interest that would have accrued on the sum awarded by the judge from the date interest becomes payable (see **2.7.2.3**) up to and including the end of the relevant period (normally day 21); and

(b)   add the figure in (a) to the amount of the judgment.

If the figure in (b) is less than or the same as the amount offered by D, C has failed to obtain a judgment more advantageous than D's Part 36 offer and r 36.17(3) should apply. See also **13.4.7**.

EXAMPLE

C instructs solicitors in April 2017. A letter of claim is sent in May 2017 seeking £70,000 damages plus interest from July 2015 (when the loss was sustained by D's alleged negligence).

> In July 2017, C commences County Court proceedings that include a claim for interest under s 69 of the CCA 1984. C is served with a Part 36 offer from D in the sum of £50,000 (inclusive of interest) on 5 January 2018. The relevant period expires on 26 January 2018. C does not accept the sum.
>
> At trial in July 2021 C is awarded £38,000 plus interest up to that date of approximately £15,200 (five years at 8% per annum). C has been awarded £53,200 in total. But has C secured a judgment more advantageous than D's Part 36 offer made back in January 2018? To decide that we must compare like with like, and so calculate the amount of interest that would be awarded on £38,000 from July 2015 to 26 January 2018. That is approximately two and a half years, totalling £7,600 in interest. Hence, at January 2018 C would have been awarded a total of approximately £45,600 and so has not secured a judgment more advantageous than D's Part 36 offer. Hindsight has shown that C should have accepted the offer in January 2018, and in effect C has wasted the time and money of D and the court ever since.

13.4.5.2   What is a split costs order?

So what is a r 36.17(3) 'split costs' order? The rule provides that

> the court must, unless it considers it unjust to do so, order that the defendant is entitled to—
>
> (a)   costs (including any recoverable pre-action costs) from the date on which the relevant period expired; and
>
> (b)   interest on those costs.

Remember, the usual costs order is that the losing party should pay the winning party's costs and that interest on costs is normally only payable from the date of judgment. The claimant is the 'winner' of the proceedings, having secured a judgment for the defendant to pay the claimant a sum of money, but the claimant has in these circumstances not been awarded more than the defendant's Part 36 offer. In hindsight the claimant should have accepted that offer. By failing to do so the claimant has, since the relevant period expired, wasted the time and money of both the defendant and court.

The effect of r 36.17(3) is as follows:

(a)   the defendant pays the claimant's costs from when those costs were first incurred until the relevant period expired (usually day 21). The defendant will not normally be ordered to pay the claimant any interest on those costs (see **14.3.2.2** and **15.2**). Those costs should be agreed by the parties, or otherwise will be assessed by the court on the standard basis (see **14.3.3.1**); and

(b)   the claimant pays the defendant's costs from expiry of the relevant period (usually day 22) until judgment. Those costs should be agreed by the parties, or otherwise will be assessed by the court on the standard basis (see **14.3.3.1**). But in addition the claimant pays interest on those costs from when each item was incurred. Why is the starting point for the payment of costs by the claimant to the defendant under r 36.17(3)(a) on the standard and not the indemnity basis? This is because the relevant principles governing indemnity costs are generally as follows:

   (i)   Indemnity costs are appropriate only where the conduct of a paying party is unreasonable 'to a high degree. "Unreasonable" in this context does not mean merely wrong or misguided in hindsight': see *Kiam v MGN Ltd* [2002] 1 WLR 2810.

   (ii)   The court must therefore decide whether there is something in the conduct of the action, or the circumstances of the case in general, which takes it out of the norm in a way which justifies an order for indemnity costs: see *Excelsior Commercial and Industrial Holdings Ltd v Salisbury Hammer Aspden and Johnson* [2002] EWCA Civ 879 (and where the Court confirmed that it is wrong to award indemnity costs solely on the basis that a claimant fails to obtain a judgment more advantageous than a defendant's Part 36 offer).

The question to be answered is whether at any stage from the date of the offer to the date of the outcome there was a point when the reasonable claimant would have concluded that the offer represented a better outcome than the likely outcome at trial (see *Lejonvarn v Burgess* [2020] EWCA Civ 114 at [80]).

(iii)   The pursuit of a weak claim will not usually, on its own, justify an order for indemnity costs, provided that the claim was at least arguable. But the pursuit of a hopeless claim (or a claim which the party pursuing it should have realised was hopeless) may well lead to such an order: see, for example, *Wates Construction Ltd v HGP Greentree Alchurch Evans Ltd* [2006] BLR 45. It has long been the position that a defendant's eventual defeat of speculative, weak, opportunistic or thin claims can give rise to an order for indemnity costs (*Lejonvarn v Burgess* [2020] EWCA Civ 114 at [44]).

As a general rule, interest is not payable on costs until after judgment (see **14.3.2.2** and **15.2**). So, what is the interest rate for the payment of costs by the claimant to the defendant under r 36.17(3)(b)? The rule is silent. However, in *Marathon Asset Management LLP v Seddon* [2017] EWHC 479 (Comm), it was held that the award of interest should be at the normal commercial rate (see **2.7**).

The effect of r 36.17(3) is summarised in the flowchart at **Appendix C(17)**.

Trial outcomes summary – defendant's Part 36 offer

In the example in **13.4.5.1**, there are three possible trial outcomes. The table that follows considers each.

Result at trial	Likely costs order (subject to the court's discretion)
Judgment **more** advantageous than D's offer.	C awarded their costs of the claim to be paid by D on the standard basis.
Judgment the same as or less advantageous than D's offer.	The court will make a split costs order: D ordered to pay C's costs on the standard basis from April 2017 up to and including 26 January 2018. C ordered to pay D's costs on the standard basis from and including 27 January 2018 until judgment in July 2021 plus interest on those costs.
C **loses** at trial.	C pays D's costs of defending the claim from when first incurred to judgment in July 2021. C pays interest on D's costs from and including 27 January 2018 until judgment in July 2021.

13.4.5.3   Financial consequences of r 36.17(3) order

Let us consider a very simple example to show the potential financial effect on the parties of a r 36.17(3) 'split costs' order. The first step is to ascertain the end of the relevant period. In the example we call this the 'split date'.

EXAMPLE

Assume that C is awarded £45,000 damages (inclusive of interest) at trial. Before the split date C's costs are in the region of £10,000 and D's approximately £8,500. After the split date C's costs are in the region of £15,500 and D's approximately £13,250. Who pays what?

D will pay C:

(a)   the £45,000 damages; and

(b)   C's costs of £10,000 up to the split date.

After the split date C pays:

(a)   D's costs of £13,250 plus interest on those costs; and

(b)   C's own costs of £15,500 to their solicitors.

What is the overall effect on C?

	C receives: £	C pays out: £
Damages	45,000	
Costs before split date	10,000	
TOTAL	55,000	
Own legal costs		25,500
D's costs from split date		13,250 (plus interest)
TOTAL		38,750
BALANCE	**16,250**	

C recovers £45,000 damages and £10,000 costs, a total of £55,000.

C pays out their own costs totalling £25,500 and D's costs of £13,250 (exclusive of interest), a total of £38,750 (plus the interest on D's costs).

C receives the balance of £16,250.

What is the overall effect on D?

	D receives: £	D pays out: £
Damages		45,000
C's costs before split date		10,000
Own legal costs		21,750
TOTAL		76,750
Costs from split date	13,250 (plus interest)	
TOTAL	13,250 (plus interest)	
BALANCE		63,500

D pays C £45,000 damages and £10,000 costs and D pays their own costs of £21,750, a total of £76,750.

D receives from C costs of £13,250 plus interest on those costs.

D is out of pocket by £63,500 (less the interest recovered on costs from the split date).

> **Conclusion**
>
> If D had not made a Part 36 offer then D would have paid the £45,000 damages, C's costs totalling £25,500 and D's own costs of £21,750 – a total of £92,250. By making what is seen at the conclusion of the trial to have been a reasonable offer to C to settle the case, C's refusal to accept that offer has cost C (and saved D) in excess of £28,750.

As to the assessment of the amount of costs payable under a court order, see **14.3**.

13.4.5.4   Rule 36.17(3) and a claimant who loses at trial

What if at trial the claimant fails to establish liability and so is awarded no sum of money whatsoever? This may seem an unlikely outcome where a defendant has made a Part 36 offer, but it has occurred in practice and no doubt will do so again, albeit very occasionally. The normal court order would be for the claimant as the loser to pay the defendant's costs from when those were first incurred by the defendant to judgment. Interest would normally be payable on those costs only from the date of judgment (see **14.3.3.2** and **15.2**). However, in these circumstances, a defendant should argue that r 36.17(3) applies. After all, the claimant has failed to obtain a judgment more advantageous than the defendant's Part 36 offer. If the court agrees then the claimant should start paying interest on the defendant's costs (arguably at the normal commercial rate (see **2.7**)) from when the relevant period for acceptance of that offer expired. This is summarised in the flowchart at **Appendix C(18)**.

13.4.5.5   Tactical considerations

From the point of view of a defendant who considers themselves at risk on liability, a Part 36 offer can provide a useful mechanism for pressurising the claimant to accept a reasonable settlement and will often be used tactically as part of settlement discussions. Of course, the defendant has to make a careful assessment of how much to offer. An over-generous offer will be snapped up by a claimant eager to receive more than the true value of the claim. An unrealistically low offer will impose no real pressure since the claimant will feel confident of beating it at trial. The wise defendant will aim to pitch their offer at a level that is just high enough for the claimant to feel that it would be unsafe not to accept.

Also important is the stage in the litigation at which a Part 36 offer is made. The earlier this is done, the greater the potential costs protection for the defendant and the greater the pressure placed on the claimant. Thus, the vulnerable defendant should make an offer as soon as they have enough information to judge its amount accurately.

13.4.6   Part 36 consequences at trial of a claimant offer

13.4.6.1   Claimant's failure to beat their Part 36 offer

No specific penalty is imposed on the claimant if they fail at trial (or earlier summary judgment) to do better than the proposals in their Part 36 offer, although the making of the offer may be taken into account by the court in exercising its general discretion as to costs, especially if the claimant has exaggerated their claim.

13.4.6.2   Judgment is at least as advantageous to the claimant as their Part 36 offer

If the judgment against the defendant is at least as advantageous to the claimant as the proposals contained in the claimant's Part 36 offer, r 36.17(4) provides that the court must, unless it considers it unjust to do so, order that the claimant is entitled to:

(a)   interest on the whole or part of any sum of money (excluding interest) awarded at a rate not exceeding 10% above base rate for some or all of the period starting with the date on which the relevant period expired;

(b)   costs (including any recoverable pre-action costs) on the indemnity basis [see **14.3.3**] from the date on which the relevant period expired;

(c)   interest on those costs at a rate not exceeding 10% above base rate; and

(d)   an additional amount, which shall not exceed £75,000, calculated by applying the prescribed percentage set out below to an amount which is—

(i)   where the claim is or includes a money claim, the sum awarded to the claimant by the court; or

(ii)   where the claim is only a non-monetary claim, the sum awarded to the claimant by the court in respect of costs—

Amount awarded by the court	Prescribed percentage
up to £500,000	10% of the amount awarded;
above £500,000 up to £1,000,000	10% of the first £500,000 and 5% of any amount above that figure

Did you spot the difference in wording between (a) and (b) as to when interest on damages and indemnity costs start to be payable? Do not worry if you did not, as it appears the point is not taken in practice. Technically, under (a), the interest on damages at up to 10% pa above base rate can start *on* the date the relevant period expires, ie usually day 21. Under (b), the entitlement to indemnity costs starts *from* when the relevant period expires, ie usually day 22. We take the view that a commonsense reading and interpretation of this provision is that under both (a) and (b) the payment is from and including the day after the relevant period expires, ie usually day 22. After all, the defendant had up until the very last day of the relevant period to accept the offer, ie usually day 21. So any financial penalty should start to be paid only from the next day.

Why is an order under r 36.17(4)(a), (b), (c) and (d) a financial penalty for the defendant? Remember that the usual order would be that the defendant pays the claimant interest on damages awarded at around 1% or 2% pa above base rate in a commercial case, or 8% pa in a non-commercial case (see **2.7.2.3**). Under (a), that rate can be increased up to 10% over base rate for the period from day 22 to judgment. Then the usual costs order would be for the defendant to pay the claimant's costs on the standard basis. Interest is not normally payable on those costs before judgment. However, under (b), the defendant has to pay the costs incurred by the claimant from day 22 to judgment at a penalty rate, the indemnity basis, under (c) interest on those indemnity costs from when each was incurred until judgment at up to 10% pa above base rate, plus under (d) an additional amount representing up to 10% of damages or costs up to a maximum of £75,000. In calculating the additional amount on an award of damages, should interest awarded be included or excluded? It should be included, whether the interest arises under a contract or the court's discretionary power (see **2.7**), but any enhanced interest awarded under r 36.17(4)(a) must not be included: see *Mohammed v Home Office* [2017] EWHC 3051 (QB). See the flowchart at **Appendix C(19)**.

13.4.6.3   The 'like with like' comparison

Before we look at r 36.17(4), we need to answer this question: how can the court tell if the judgment is at least as advantageous to the claimant as the claimant's Part 36 offer? Where the claimant has made a money claim, the judgment will be for a capital sum plus interest awarded at the trial judge's discretion, usually from when the loss was sustained up to trial. If the judge has made an award of interest, it is necessary for them to be provided with a calculation of the amount of interest they would have awarded had the judgment been given at the date the relevant period of the claimant's Part 36 offer expired. So the process is similar to that described at **13.4.5.1**.

13.4.6.4   Calculating the financial penalties

Enhanced interest on damages

There is a cap on the amount of interest that can be awarded on damages by the trial judge generally and under r 36.17(4). This is set out in r 36.17(6), which provides that 'where the court awards interest under [r 36.17(4)] and also awards interest on the same sum and for the same period under any other power, the total rate of interest may not exceed 10% above base rate'.

This award of interest on damages under r 36.17(4) is often called 'enhanced interest'. But how much should the court award? The words of the rule provide for enhanced interest to be awarded 'at a rate not exceeding 10% above base rate'. That does not make the figure of 10% a starting point. It makes it the maximum possible enhancement. The level of interest awarded must be proportionate to the circumstances of the case which may include, for example: (a) the length of time that elapsed between the deadline for accepting the offer and judgment; (b) whether the defendant took entirely bad points or whether it had behaved reasonably in continuing the litigation, despite the offer, to pursue its defence; and (c) what general level of disruption can be seen, without a detailed inquiry, to have been caused to the claimant as a result of the refusal to negotiate or to accept the Part 36 offer (OMV Petrom SA v Glencore International AG [2017] EWCA Civ 195, where the maximum was awarded to reflect the 'deplorable, if not outrageous' conduct of the defendant in calling witnesses who had lied to the court, refusing to engage in any negotiating or mediation process, and using its vast asset base to seek to frustrate the claimant's attempts to reach a compromise solution).

The enhanced interest is awarded on the amount of damages awarded, not on the amount offered by the claimant (Equitix Eeef Biomass 2 Ltd v Fox [2021] EWHC 2781 (TCC)).

Interest on indemnity costs

If indemnity costs are awarded, how much interest should be awarded on those indemnity costs? In OMV Petrom SA v Glencore International AG [2017] EWCA Civ 195, the Court of Appeal established the following principles:

(a)   The specified rate of 10% is not the starting point. Why? Because the words of the rule provide for enhanced interest to be awarded 'at a rate not exceeding 10% above base rate'. That makes it the maximum possible finishing point.

(b)   If it were right to say that the provision for additional interest were entirely compensatory, the 10% cap would only rarely be engaged and then probably only in unusual cases where, for example, the period of the enhanced interest award was very short. The provision, along with the others in r 36.17(4)(a), (b) and (d), provides for a scheme of penalties and rewards in order to encourage the making of reasonable settlement offers and the acceptance of such offers.

(c)   Different factors may affect the calculation of interest here under r 36.17(3)(c) as opposed to under r 36.17(3)(a) above. This is because account may need to be taken of how the costs, on which an enhanced rate of interest is claimed, were incurred. It could be, for example, that despite the fact that it was unreasonable to refuse the Part 36 offer, the conduct of the litigation was itself reasonable, so that the costs on which enhanced interest is sought are not incurred in contesting bad points or dishonesty by the defendants.

In the OMV Petrom SA case, the court found that the factors which led to the maximum award under r 36.17(3)(a) also justified the maximum award under r 37.17(3)(c).

How do you calculate interest on the indemnity costs? According to the Court of Appeal in McPhilemy v Times Newspapers Ltd (No 2) [2001] EWCA Civ 933, [2001] 4 All ER 861, interest runs on the indemnity costs from the date upon which the work was done or liability for the disbursement was incurred.

Note that according to the McPhilemy case, both enhanced interest on damages and interest on indemnity costs runs under r 36.17(4) only until judgment. Thereafter interest is payable on damages and costs ordered to be paid under a judgment pursuant to either s 17 of the Judgments Act 1838 or the County Courts (Interest on Judgment Debts) Order 1991 (see **14.2.8.2**).

Additional amount

In most cases where r 36.17(4)(d) takes effect, the claimant will have been awarded damages. So the size of the additional amount will depend on the size of those damages inclusive of interest awarded by the court under any contract or discretionary power (see **2.7**) but not including any enhanced interest awarded under r 36.17(4)(a) (see further **13.4.6.2**).

Note that interest is not payable on the additional sum (see *FZO v Adams* [2019] EWHC 1286 (QB)).

EXAMPLES		
Amount of damages	**Additional amount calculation**	**Additional amount**
£100,000	£100,000 x 10%	£10,000
£600,000	£500,000 x 10% plus £100,000 x 5%	£55,000
£1,500,000	£500,000 x 10% plus £500,000 x 5%	Maximum of £75,000

EXAMPLE

In order to understand in full the implications of r 36.17(4) in a particular case, you need to identify these key dates:

(a) The date interest on damages starts to be payable: this is normally when the damage was suffered (see **2.7.2.3**).

(b) The date the claimant first incurred costs: this is often the first time the claimant instructs solicitors.

(c) The relevant period (see **13.4.1.1**): see **13.4.1.4** for how to calculate the date of service of a Part 36 offer. The relevant period usually expires 21 days after service of the offer. It is from the 22nd day that the financial penalties under r 36.17(4) can be imposed.

Assume C alleges a breach of contract by D, which occurred on 16 March 2016 when C sustained loss. C first instructs solicitors on 1 August 2017.

C issues proceedings in December 2017, claiming damages estimated at £750,000 plus interest. In March 2018, C serves a Part 36 offer of £600,000. The relevant period expires on 27 March 2018. D does not accept, the case proceeds to trial and judgment is given on 21 September 2021.

(i) *If C wins but fails to obtain a judgment at least as advantageous as C's own Part 36 offer*

Here Part 36 will have no effect and the court will usually award C their costs of the claim on the standard basis. C will not usually be penalised for having made a Part 36 offer, albeit unsuccessful, neither will C gain any advantage. C first instructed solicitors on 1 August 2017, so C may receive their costs incurred from that date until judgment on 21 September 2021. Do not forget that C will receive the damages plus any interest awarded on those by the court (see **2.7**). The interest will usually start to run from the date loss was suffered on 16 March 2016 and will continue until judgment on 21 September 2021.

(ii) *If C wins and obtains a judgment at least as advantageous as C's own Part 36 offer*

Here, the court will, unless it considers it unjust, impose the financial penalties under r 36.17(4). So D will pay C:

> - interest on the damages awarded from 16 March 2016 (when loss suffered) until and including 27 March 2018 (when relevant period expired), plus
> - enhanced interest on the damages awarded from and including 28 March 2018 (day 22) to judgment on 21 September 2021 at no more than 10% pa above the base rate, plus
> - the costs incurred by C from 1 August 2017 (first incurred) up to and including 27 March 2018 on the standard basis, plus
> - the costs incurred by C from and including 28 March 2018 to judgment on 21 September 2021 on the indemnity basis, plus
> - interest on those indemnity basis costs from when each item was incurred until judgment on 21 September 2021 at a maximum of 10% pa above base rate, plus
> - an additional amount up to a maximum of £75,000.
>
> (iii)   *If D wins*
>
> C will usually be ordered to pay D's costs of defending the claim on the standard basis from when first incurred until judgment.

13.4.6.5   Tactical considerations

Where the defendant does not accept a claimant's Part 36 offer and the claimant obtains a judgment that is at least as advantageous as the claimant's own Part 36 offer, the defendant is likely to pay a heavy price. In contrast, we have seen that a claimant who fails to achieve such a judgment is usually in no worse position than if their offer had not been made. The result is that, while there is no downside for the claimant in making such an offer, a reasonable proposal will place the defendant under considerable pressure.

Since the penalties in r 36.17(4) are imposed as from the expiry of the relevant period, the earlier the claimant makes their offer, the greater the pressure on the defendant. It is tactically sensible for a claimant to make an offer as soon as there is enough information to judge its amount, and prior to issuing proceedings where practicable.

If a claimant's Part 36 offer is too high and/or a defendant's Part 36 offer too low, Part 36 has no effect (see the flowchart in **Appendix C(20)**).

13.4.7   Can the court award some but not all of the penalties under r 36.17(4)?

In *Telefonica UK Ltd v The Office of Communications* [2020] EWCA Civ 1374, the claimant was successful at trial and was awarded approximately 8% and 9% more than in two Part 36 offers made prior to trial. The trial judge awarded indemnity costs under r 36.17(4)(b) and an additional sum of £75,000 under r 36.17(4)(d) but refused enhanced interest on the sum awarded or the costs. The Court of Appeal, in allowing the appeal, stated that the decision as to whether or not it was just to award costs consequences should apply to all four costs consequences collectively. The Court also stated that the margin of difference between the offer and the sum awarded is not relevant where the offer is a genuine offer to settle – the court should apply the costs consequences, but it retains the discretion to determine the rate to be awarded.

13.4.8   What does 'advantageous' mean in r 36.17?

Rule 36.17(1) states that:

> (1)   This rule applies where upon judgment being entered—
>
>   (a)   a claimant fails to obtain a judgment more advantageous than a defendant's Part 36 offer; or

(b)   judgment against the defendant is at least as advantageous to the claimant as the proposals contained in a claimant's Part 36 offer.

In a money claim, do (a) and (b) require just a mathematical comparison of the figures, or can the court look at all the circumstances of the case in deciding where the balance of advantage lies? In *Carver v BAA plc* [2008] EWCA Civ 412, Ward LJ posed this question: if a claimant beats a defendant's Part 36 offer in a money claim by a modest amount, even £1, have they obtained a judgment more advantageous than the defendant's Part 36 offer so that (a) does not apply? The Court held that the only way to answer that question was to look at all the circumstances of the case. This decision led to much satellite litigation and uncertainty about the interpretation and application of r 36.17(1). As a result, the case has been overturned by r 36.17(2), which provides as follows:

> For the purposes of paragraph (1), in relation to any money claim or money element of a claim, 'more advantageous' means better in money terms by any amount, however small, and 'at least as advantageous' shall be construed accordingly.

So, r 36.17(1)(a) applies where a claimant is awarded a money judgment that is exactly the same as or less than the amount stated in a defendant's Part 36 offer. To answer Ward LJ's question, (a) will not apply if a claimant beats a defendant's Part 36 offer in a money claim by a modest amount, even £1, because in those circumstances they have obtained a judgment more advantageous than the defendant's Part 36 offer.

Likewise, r 36.17(1)(b) applies where a claimant is awarded a money judgment that is exactly the same as or more than the amount stated in that claimant's own Part 36 offer. So (b) will not apply if a claimant's award is less than their own Part 36 offer in a money claim, even if it is only £1 less, because in those circumstances they have not obtained a judgment that is at least as advantageous as their own Part 36 offer.

13.4.9 When an order under r 36.17(3) or (4) might be unjust

As we have seen, a well-judged offer that is not accepted will lead to an order under r 36.17(3) or (4), unless it would be unjust for the court to make that order.

In considering whether it would be unjust to make the orders referred to in r 36.17(3) or (4) (see **13.4.5** and **13.4.6**), the court will, by r 36.17(5), take into account all the circumstances of the case including:

(a)   the terms of the Part 36 offer;

(b)   the stage in the proceedings when the Part 36 offer was made, including in particular how long before the trial started the offer was made;

(c)   the information available to the parties at the time when the Part 36 offer was made; and

(d)   the conduct of the parties with regard to the giving of or refusal to give information for the purposes of enabling the offer to be made or evaluated;

(e)   whether the offer was a genuine attempt to settle the proceedings.

In *Ford v GKR Construction Ltd* [2000] 1 WLR 1397, the Court of Appeal indicated that the court should take into account such matters as late disclosure, late service of evidence or the development of unanticipated contentions, and the stage in the litigation when these events occur, as well as their nature and effect on the outcome of the litigation. Lord Woolf observed:

> If a party has not enabled another party to properly assess whether or not to make an offer, or whether or not to accept an offer which is made, because of non-disclosure to the other party of material matters, or if a party comes to a decision which is different from that which would have been reached if there had been proper disclosure, that is a material matter for a court to take into account in considering what orders it should make.

In *Huntley v Simmonds* [2009] EWHC 406, Underhill J indicated that when looking at the terms of the offer, technical errors under r 36.5(1) as to form and content (see **13.4.1**) that cause no real uncertainty or other prejudice to the offeree are unlikely to make the order unjust.

However, a significant error, such as failing to state on the face of an offer letter that it was made pursuant to Part 36, might make it unjust.

In *Smith v Trafford Housing Trust* [2012] EWHC 3320 (Ch) at [13], Briggs J summarised the position as follows:

(a)   The question is not whether it was reasonable for the claimant to refuse the offer. Rather, the question is whether, having regard to all the circumstances and looking at the matter as it affects both parties, an order that the claimant should pay the costs would be unjust: see *Matthews v Metal Improvements Co Inc* [2007] EWCA Civ 215, *per* Stanley Burnton J (sitting as an additional judge of the Court of Appeal) at paragraph 32.

(b)   Each case will turn on its own circumstances, but the court should be trying to assess 'who in reality is the unsuccessful party and who has been responsible for the fact that costs have been incurred which should not have been': see *Factortame v Secretary of State* [2002] EWCA Civ 22, *per* Walker LJ at paragraph 27.

(c)   The court is not constrained by the list of potentially relevant factors in Part [36.17(5)] to have regard only to the circumstances of the making of the offer or the provision or otherwise of relevant information in relation to it. There is no limit to the types of circumstances which may, in a particular case, make it unjust that the ordinary consequences set out in Part [36.17] should follow: see *Lilleyman v Lilleyman (judgment on costs)* [2012] EWHC 1056 (Ch) at paragraph 16.

(d)   Nonetheless, the court does not have an unfettered discretion to depart from the ordinary cost consequences set out in Part [36.17]. The burden on a claimant who has failed to beat the defendant's Part 36 offer to show injustice is a formidable obstacle to the obtaining of a different costs order. If that were not so, then the salutary purpose of Part 36, in promoting compromise and the avoidance of unnecessary expenditure of costs and court time, would be undermined.

In the case of *Feltham v Bourskell* [2013] EWHC 3086 (Ch), the court had to decide whether it would be unjust to award a claimant who had obtained a judgment more advantageous than her Part 36 offer, an additional amount under r 36.17(4)(d) totalling just under £75,000. The Part 36 offer had expired two working days before the trial commenced, and crucial allegations that had not been pleaded were raised during the opening of the case. In those circumstances the trial judge exercised their discretion that it would be unjust to make an order for an additional amount under r 36.17(4)(d).

In determining whether or not it is unjust to make the r 36.17(3) or (4) orders, will it ever be relevant to consider by how much the claimant failed to obtain a judgment more advantageous than a defendant's Part 36 offer or by how much the judgment against the defendant was more advantageous to the claimant as the proposals contained in the claimant's Part 36 offer? The answer is no. Why? As we saw at **13.4.7**, 'more advantageous' means better in money terms by any amount, *however small* (see also *JLE v Warrington & Halton Hospitals NHS Foundation Trust* [2019] EWHC 1582 (QB)).

In *Hochtief (UK) Construction Ltd and another v Atkins Ltd* [2019] EWHC 3028 (TCC), the claimants made a Part 36 offer covering two claims against the defendant. The claimants succeeded at trial on one claim, failed on the other but secured a judgment against the defendant that was at least as advantageous to the claimants as the proposals contained in their Part 36 offer. The court held that it was not unjust to award the claimants the prescribed benefits under r 36.17(4)(a)–(d). However, it was appropriate to make a proportional costs order under (b) in order to reflect the parties' relative successes and failures in the proceedings. So, the court required the defendant to pay 85% of the claimants' costs on the indemnity basis.

Is there a single test of unjustness so that all or none of the normal consequences in r 36.17(4) apply or should the test be applied separately to each of the four consequences? It is the latter according to Stewart J in *JLE v Warrington & Halton Hospitals NHS Foundation Trust* [2019] EWHC 1582 (QB). So, is the award of an additional sum under r 36.17(4)(d) all or nothing? Yes, again according to Stewart J in *JLE*. If it is just to award it, then payment should be ordered of the full amount. Likewise, if it is unjust to award it, nothing should be payable.

In *Rawbank SA v Travelex Banknotes Ltd* [2020] EWHC 1619 (Ch), the claimant made a Part 36 offer to accept 0.3% less than the full sum claimed. On the facts there was no dispute over quantum and no defence, so the fact that the claimant was giving up part of the claim with a near certain prospect of success was enough to satisfy the requirement in r 36.17(5)(e) that the offer was a genuine attempt to settle the proceedings.

13.4.10   Rule 36.17(3) and a CFA

What if a claimant who has entered into a CFA (see **2.4.2**) with their solicitors establishes liability but is awarded damages that only equal or are less than a defendant's Part 36 offer? In those circumstances, how will an order under r 36.17(3) affect the CFA success fee? The answer will have to be found in the wording of the CFA. The usual provisions are as follows. If the claimant rejected the offer on the basis of advice from the solicitors or counsel, the success fee is not payable by the client on charges incurred after the date the relevant period expired (day 22). The firm's normal charges and disbursements will remain payable. However, if the client rejected the offer against the advice of the solicitors or counsel, the success fee remains payable (as well as the firm's normal charges and disbursements).

13.4.11   Secrecy

Except in very limited circumstances, a Part 36 offer should not be revealed to the trial judge until all questions of liability and quantum have been decided (see r 36.16).

What if a Part 36 offer is made known to the trial judge? In *Garratt v Saxby* [2004] LTL, 18 February, the Court of Appeal indicated that the judge had to determine whether the disclosure of the offer made a fair trial possible, or whether justice required the judge to withdraw from the case. The judge in exercising that discretion was entitled to take into account the additional time, cost and difficulty involved for all concerned if the hearing were to be aborted.

13.4.12   Part 36 offer in respect of a counterclaim

If a defendant makes a Part 36 offer in respect of their counterclaim and at trial obtains a judgment on that counterclaim that is at least as advantageous as their Part 36 offer, can the court impose financial penalties on the claimant under r 36.17(4)? Yes, held the Court of Appeal in *AF v BG* [2009] EWCA Civ 757. It should be noted that r 36.2(3)(a) expressly provides that a Part 36 offer may be made in respect of the whole, or part of, or any issue that arises in a counterclaim.

13.4.13   Part 36 and Rule 3.14 sanction

We saw at **9.7.1.6** that any party who fails to file a costs budget at all or late is treated as having filed a budget comprising only the applicable court fees unless the court gives relief from that sanction.

Where the sanction applies, its effect may subsequently be reduced if the party subject to it becomes entitled to costs under any of the following provisions of CPR, Part 36:

(a)   late acceptance of an offer (see **13.4.4.3**); or

(b)   an order under r 36.17(3)(a) (see **13.4.5.2**) or r 36.17(4)(b) (see **13.4.6.2**).

In these circumstances, the party is entitled to 50% of its agreed or assessed costs falling within the relevant provision, together with any other recoverable costs. (See *Ali v Channel 5 Broadcast Ltd* [2018] EWHC 840 (Ch).)

13.5   CLAIMS INVOLVING CHILDREN AND PROTECTED PARTIES

Where a claim is made by or on behalf of a child or protected party, or against a child or protected party, no settlement of that claim is binding without the approval of the court.

Thus, a Part 36 offer even if accepted can be withdrawn prior to obtaining the court's approval (see *Wormald v Ahmed* [2021] EWHC 973 (QB)).

Approval is required even if a compromise is reached before the issue of proceedings. In such a case the application for approval should be made under Part 8 (see **8.3**).

13.6 DISCONTINUANCE (PART 38)

13.6.1 General provisions

A claimant may decide not to pursue their claim, even though no settlement has been reached. For example, they may conclude that their chances of succeeding at trial or of recovering any money from the defendant are so slim that they would be better to discontinue. A claimant may discontinue a claim at any time and, if there are co-defendants, the claimant may do so against all or any of them. The claimant will need the court's permission to discontinue a claim where:

(a)   the court has granted an interim injunction; or

(b)   any party has given an undertaking to the court.

If an interim payment has been made, the claimant may discontinue only if:

(a)   the defendant who made the payment consents in writing; or

(b)   the court gives permission.

Where there are two or more claimants, a claimant may discontinue only if:

(a)   all the other claimants consent in writing; or

(b)   the court gives permission.

13.6.2 Procedure

The claimant must file and serve a notice of discontinuance on all other parties. If the claimant needs the consent of another party in order to discontinue, a copy of that consent must be attached to the notice.

If the claimant discontinues in a case where consent or the court's permission was not required, any defendant may apply to set aside the notice of discontinuance. The application must be made within 28 days.

13.6.3 Liability for costs

A claimant who discontinues is liable for the defendant's costs on the standard basis (see **14.3.3.1**) unless the court orders otherwise. It is therefore vital that a solicitor acting for a potential claimant explains this to the client. How can a claimant client avoid paying costs when discontinuing? Either by negotiating a settlement that includes such a term, or otherwise by convincing the court. As to the latter, the application should be made either at the same time as serving notice of discontinuance, or promptly after doing so (see *Hoist UK Ltd v Reid Lifting Ltd* [2010] EWHC 1922). As to when a claimant's application might succeed, see the review of the law in *Teasdale v HSBC Bank Plc* [2010] EWHC 612.

Note that in the case of *Noorani v Calver (No 2/Costs)* [2009] EWHC 592, the discontinuing claimant was ordered to pay the defendant's costs on the penalty, indemnity basis (see **14.3.3.2**) because of the claimant's unreasonable conduct both before and during the litigation.

If proceedings are only partly discontinued, the claimant is liable only for the costs of the part of the claim they are discontinuing, and those costs must not be assessed until the rest of the case is over unless the court orders otherwise.

CHAPTER 14

FINAL PREPARATIONS FOR TRIAL, TRIAL AND ASSESSMENT OF COSTS

14.1	Final preparations for trial	257
14.2	Trial	261
14.3	Costs	266

LEARNING OUTCOMES

After reading this chapter you will have learned:

- how to brief counsel to conduct a trial
- the use of a witness summons
- what goes into the trial bundle
- the role of the trial timetable
- trial procedure
- what factors influence a judge's decision on costs
- the difference between the standard basis and indemnity basis of assessment of costs
- the role of a summary assessment of costs
- what costs are payable on the fast track
- how to conduct a detailed assessment of costs on the multi-track
- how to challenge your opponent's bill.

14.1 FINAL PREPARATIONS FOR TRIAL

14.1.1 Briefing counsel

If the solicitor intends to brief counsel to deal with the trial, counsel should be instructed well in advance of the trial date. Very often, of course, counsel will already have been instructed in a case to advise, draft a statement of case or appear at a case management conference. Moreover, the trial date or period will have been known since allocation. The brief to counsel should contain copies of all relevant documents which will be required at the trial.

The content of the brief should deal in detail with the facts still in issue and how they are to be proved. Even though the barrister may be familiar with the case, the solicitor should nevertheless take the time to set matters out fully in the brief in case it is passed on to another barrister at a later stage. Occasionally, the barrister originally instructed may be unable to attend the trial, in which case the brief will be handed over to another barrister at short notice.

Practice varies as to whether there will be a conference with counsel before the hearing. This will depend on the extent to which there have already been conferences, and the value, importance and complexity of the case.

When acting for a private or commercial client, it is for the solicitor to negotiate the brief fee with counsel's clerk following delivery of the brief. In a fast track case, you should try to restrict the brief fee to the maximum amount allowed for the advocacy in a fast track case (see **14.3.6**).

In a multi-track case, the fee covers only one day unless agreed otherwise. If the case takes more than one day, counsel will be entitled to charge a 'refresher fee' for each subsequent day. For example, the brief fee (to cover preparation for trial and the first day) might be £15,000 for a fairly complex High Court case, with a refresher fee of £4,500.

A brief to counsel may be found in the multi-track case study at **Appendix D(14)**.

14.1.2 Attendance of witnesses

14.1.2.1 Witnesses in general

All witnesses should be kept fully informed of the expected trial date and, once the date has been fixed, should be told of that date without delay. It is essential that, at an early stage, witnesses are asked whether any particular periods would be inconvenient for them to attend the trial. Details of a witness's availability have to be given to the court on the directions questionnaire and pre-trial checklists, listing questionnaires (see **Chapter 9**).

Even where witnesses have been kept fully informed and involved, it is unwise to rely on the assumption that they will attend court voluntarily. Instead, their attendance should be encouraged by serving them with a witness summons. This is a document issued by the court requiring a witness to:

(a) attend court to give evidence; and/or

(b) produce documents to the court.

A witness summons should be served at least seven days before the date on which the witness is required to attend court. It will then be binding upon the witness, and if the witness fails to attend court, they will be liable to be fined and, in High Court proceedings, to imprisonment for contempt. If a party wishes to issue a summons less than seven days before the date of the trial, permission from the court must be obtained.

The witness summons will normally be served by the court, unless the party on whose behalf it is issued indicates that they wish to serve it themselves.

At the time of service of a witness summons the witness must be offered or paid:

(a) a sum reasonably sufficient to cover their expenses in travelling to and from the court; and

(b) such sum by way of compensation for loss of time as may be specified in PD 34A.

The danger in not serving a witness with a witness summons is that if they fail to attend the trial, the first question the judge will ask the solicitor or barrister conducting the case is why a witness summons was not served. If a witness summons had been served, there is a greater possibility that the court will be sympathetic enough to grant an adjournment of the trial if that is required because of the crucial nature of the missing witness's evidence.

Police officers must always be served with a witness summons, because they will not give evidence in a civil matter on behalf of either party unless they are under a legal obligation to do so.

14.1.2.2 Expert witnesses

Paragraphs 84–87 of the Guidance for the Instruction of Experts (see **Appendix A(21)**) deal with the attendance of experts at court. Experts are expected to keep those instructing them informed of their availability and make every effort to ensure that they are available to attend court if required. A witness summons to require the attendance of an expert at trial should be used only if required by the expert.

Failure to inform an expert of the trial date being fixed and failure to act promptly when informed by an expert that they are unable to attend trial are likely to see any application to vacate the trial date being dismissed (*Mitchell v Precis 548 Ltd* [2019] EWHC 3314 (QB)).

14.1.3 Preparing trial bundles

14.1.3.1 What to include

Unless the court orders otherwise, the claimant must file the trial bundle not more than seven days and not less than three days before the start of the trial. By para 27.5 of PD 32 – Miscellaneous Provisions Relating to Hearings, unless the court orders otherwise, the trial bundle should include a copy of:

(1) the claim form and all statements of case,

(2) a case summary and/or chronology where appropriate,

(3) requests for further information and responses to the requests,

(4) all witness statements to be relied on as evidence,

(5) any witness summaries,

(6) any notices of intention to rely on hearsay evidence under rule 33.2,

(7) any notices of intention to rely on evidence (such as a plan, photograph etc) under rule 33.6 which is not—

    (a) contained in a witness statement, affidavit or expert's report,

    (b) being given orally at trial,

    (c) hearsay evidence under rule 33.2,

(8) any medical reports and responses to them,

(9) any expert's reports and responses to them,

(10) any order giving directions as to the conduct of the trial, and

(11) any other necessary documents.

Paragraph 27.12 of PD 32 provides that the contents of the trial bundle should be agreed where possible. The parties should also agree where possible that the documents contained in the bundle are authentic even if not disclosed under Part 31, and that documents in the bundle may be treated as evidence of the facts stated in them even if a notice under the Civil Evidence Act 1995 has not been served. Where it is not possible to agree the contents of the bundle, a summary of the points on which the parties are unable to agree should be included. Unless the court otherwise directs, the documents in the trial bundle should be copied double-sided (PD 32, para 27.15).

The party filing the trial bundle should supply identical bundles to all the parties to the proceedings and for the use of the witnesses.

14.1.3.2 Case summary (skeleton argument)

Each party should prepare a case summary (often called a 'skeleton argument') to use at trial. This is designed to assist both the court and the parties by indicating what points are or are not in issue, and the nature of the argument about the disputed matters. It should also assist the court in its advance reading. As a general rule a case summary should therefore:

(a) concisely review the party's submissions of fact in relation to each of the issues with reference to the evidence;

(b) concisely set out the propositions of law advanced with reference to the main authorities relied on (as to citing those authorities, see the Lord Chief Justice's *Practice Direction: Citation of Authorities* (2012));

(c) be divided into numbered paragraphs and paginated consecutively; and

(d) identify any key documents which the trial judge should, if possible, read before the trial starts.

Templates to help you draft case summaries for use at a fast track or multi-track trial are set out at **Appendices B(14)** and **B(15)**.

In *Tombstone Ltd v Raja* [2008] EWCA Civ 1444, the Court of Appeal stressed that the case summary or skeleton argument should assist the court, as well as the parties, by improving preparations for, and the efficiency of, adversarial oral hearings. The Court here (and subsequently in *Khader v Aziz* [2010] EWCA Civ 716) reminded practitioners that

> skeleton arguments should not be prepared as verbatim scripts to be read out in public or as footnoted theses to be read in private. Good skeleton arguments are tools with practical uses: an agenda for the hearing, a summary of the main points, propositions and arguments to be developed orally, a useful way of noting citations and references, a convenient place for making cross references, a time-saving means of avoiding unnecessary dictation to the court and laborious and pointless note-taking by the court. Skeleton arguments are aids to oral advocacy. (*per* Mummery LJ, at paras 126 and 127)

In *R (on the application of Network Rail Infrastructure Ltd) v Secretary of State for the Environment, Food and Rural Affairs* [2017] EWHC 2259 (Admin), Holgate J stated (at [11] and [12]):

> Prolix or diffuse ... skeletons, along with excessively long bundles, impede the efficient handling of business in the ... Court ... Where the fault lies at the door of a claimant, other parties may incur increased costs in having to deal with such a welter of material before they can respond to the Court in a hopefully more incisive manner. Whichever party is at fault, such practices are likely to result in more time needing to be spent by the judge in pre-reading material so as to penetrate or decode the arguments being presented, the hearing may take longer, and the time needed to prepare a judgment may become extended. Consequently, a disproportionate amount of the Court's finite resources may have to be given to a case prepared in this way and diverted from other litigants waiting for their matters to be dealt with. Such practices do not comply with the overriding objective and the duties of the parties (CPR 1.1 to 1.3). They are unacceptable.

> The Court has wide case management powers to deal with such problems (see for example CPR 3.1). For example, it may consider refusing to accept excessively long skeletons or bundles, or skeletons without proper cross-referencing. It may direct the production of a core bundle or limit the length of a skeleton, so that the arguments are set out incisively and without 'forensic chaff'. It is the responsibility of the parties to help the Court to understand in an efficient manner those issues which truly need to be decided and the precise points upon which each such issue turns. The principles in the CPR for dealing with the costs of litigation provide further tools by which the Court may deal with the inappropriate conduct of litigation, so that a party who incurs costs in that manner has to bear them.

Further, an advocate's oral submissions should follow their skeleton argument:

> The matter came before me on 21 March 2019 and things got off to an unpromising start. Counsel for the applicant referred to what he described as a 'road-map' through which he intended to guide me in the course of his oral submissions. Unhappily the road-map followed a markedly different path than that which had been laid out in the written skeleton argument which had preceded it and, although the intended destination was the same, the new route now included a number of unheralded scenic diversions through an unfamiliar landscape.

> Of course, oral submissions are important but they should be seen primarily as the means by which arguments already articulated in outline in the skeleton arguments are to be fleshed out, refined and tested. Perhaps my experience is unrepresentative but there appears to me to be a growing trend for advocates to present cases orally in a way which bears only a passing resemblance to the structure earlier laid out in their written submissions. (*per* Turner J at [16] and [17] in *365 Business Finance Ltd v Bellagio Hospitality WB Ltd* [2019] EWHC 1920 (QB))

14.1.3.3 Time estimates and core bundles

The trial bundle should be accompanied by an estimated length of reading time and an agreed estimate of the likely length of the hearing. If the trial bundle is very large, a 'core' bundle of key documents, to be read by the trial judge, should be prepared.

14.2   TRIAL

14.2.1   Venue

The County Court has hearing centres throughout England and Wales. The trial of the case, whether fast track or multi-track, will take place at a hearing centre, which may not be the same location that managed the case.

The High Court is based at the Royal Courts of Justice in London, and has District Registries in many cities in England and Wales that also act as trial centres.

14.2.2   Timetable

In most cases, in both the fast track and multi-track, a trial timetable will have been fixed after filing the pre-trial checklists (listing questionnaires). The timetable may, for example, limit the time for cross-examination and re-examination of each particular witness. For example, in *Three Rivers DC v Governor and Company of the Bank of England* [2005] EWCA Civ 889, the trial judge (upheld by the Court of Appeal) limited the cross-examination of a key witness which was projected to last 12 weeks to seven weeks instead. In a complex and long multi-track case, the timetable is usually set at the pre-trial review.

14.2.2.1   Trial timetable

At the trial, the judge may confirm or vary any timetable given previously, or, if none has been given, set their own.

The judge will generally have read the papers in the trial bundle (which, as we saw at **14.1.3**, will have been filed with the court prior to the hearing).

A fast track trial should usually be completed within one day. However, if it lasts more than one day, the judge will normally sit on the next court day to complete the trial. A typical fast track timetable for a day's trial is as follows:

Opening speeches:	20 minutes
Cross-examination and re-examination of claimant's witnesses:	90 minutes
Cross-examination and re-examination of defendant's witnesses:	90 minutes
Defendant's closing submissions:	15 minutes
Claimant's closing submissions:	15 minutes
Judge preparing and delivering judgment:	30 minutes
Summary assessment of costs:	30 minutes

In multi-track cases, the judge will normally sit on consecutive court days until the trial has been completed.

14.2.2.2   Professional conduct

The SRA Code of Conduct, para 1.4, provides that a solicitor must never mislead the court. A solicitor might fall foul of this rule at a trial by, for example:

(a)   submitting inaccurate information or allowing a witness to do so;

(b)   indicating agreement with information that a witness has put forward which the solicitor knows is false;

(c)   calling a witness whose evidence the solicitor knows is untrue.

Where a client admits to their solicitor that they have committed perjury or misled the court in any material matter relating to the proceedings, the solicitor must not act further in those proceedings unless the client agrees to disclose the truth to the court (see Principles 1 to 5). If the client refuses to do so, the solicitor should cease to act for the client. In order to keep client confidentiality (see para 6.3), the solicitor should not inform the court or any other party of the reasons for ceasing to act.

There are some types of information that a solicitor is obliged to disclose to the court, whether or not it is in the best interests of the client to do so. Failure to disclose this information could amount to a failure to meet Principle 1. For example, the advocates on both sides must advise the court of relevant cases and statutory provisions. If one of them omits a case or provision, or makes an incorrect reference to a case or provision, it is the duty of the other to draw attention to it even if that assists the opponent's case (see para 2.7). Just how far does this duty extend? 'It plainly does not require [the advocate] to cite every authority which might conceivably be useful to their opponent, especially as almost every decision is now reported in one form or another. In essence I think it is an aspect of [the advocate's] obligation not to mislead the court: if [the advocate] submitted that the law was X and suppressed an authority that established that the law was not X but Y, that would be misleading.' (per Nugee J in *Weir v Hildson* [2017] EWHC (Ch) 983 at [114]).

What if a solicitor knows of facts that, or of a witness who, would assist the opponent? Is the solicitor under any duty to inform the opponent, or indeed the court, of this to the prejudice of their own client? The answer is no.

A solicitor has particular duties when acting as an advocate. These include that a solicitor should:

(a)   not say anything that is merely scandalous or intended only to insult a witness or any other person;

(b)   avoid naming in open court any third party whose character would thereby be called into question, unless it is necessary for the proper conduct of the case;

(c)   not call into question the character of a witness they have cross-examined unless the witness has had the opportunity to answer the allegations during cross-examination; and

(d)   not suggest that any person is guilty of a crime, fraud or misconduct, unless such allegations go to a matter in issue which is material to the client's case and appear to be supported by reasonable grounds.

14.2.2.3   Use of live text from court

What if the client, a member of their family or a business colleague in the public gallery, or indeed anyone else, wishes to use Twitter or the like to report on the progress of the proceedings? *Practice Guidance: the use of live text-based forms of communication (including Twitter) from court for the purposes of fair and accurate reporting* [2011] 1 WLR 61 states that permission of the judge is needed unless the person is a member of the press.

14.2.3   Order of proceedings

14.2.3.1   Preliminary issues

Before the case formally commences, a party may wish to raise a preliminary issue with the trial judge. These will normally concern procedural matters. But bear in mind that most of these issues should have been dealt with if a pre-trial review occurred.

Possible preliminary issues include:

(a)   Permission to amend a statement of case (see **7.6**). This would be a very late application liable to fail, and prior notice to the other side would be essential.

(b)   Permission to adduce more evidence by way of examination-in-chief from a witness under r 32.5(3) (see **12.4**). However, the trial judge may prefer to deal with this application immediately after the witness in question has been sworn.

(c)   An application to strike out part of an opponent's witness statement (see **12.2**).

(d)   Variation of any timetable made at an earlier hearing.

14.2.3.2 The claimant

If allowed by the judge, the claimant may make an opening speech setting out the background to the case and the facts which remain in issue. If this is allowed by the timetable set by the court, it must be very concise. The claimant's advocate will use the case summary (or skeleton argument) filed with the trial bundle (see **14.1.3**).

THE EVIDENCE

Examination-in-chief

The claimant and their witnesses will then give evidence. In most cases, the witness statements will stand as the evidence-in-chief. If that is the case then, after being sworn, the witness may simply be asked to confirm that their statement is correct. They will be able to amplify what is in their witness statement only if allowed to do so by the judge (see **12.4.1**). If some form of limited examination-in-chief is allowed by the judge then the usual rule is that a witness cannot be asked leading questions by their own advocate to encourage them to relate the story. It is difficult to define a leading question. Basically, it is one which suggests the answer or assumes a fact that has not yet been proved. For example, a question to the claimant in a breach of contract case, 'did the defendant supply your firm with goods that did not match the sample?' suggests that the goods did not match the sample. It is therefore an objectionable leading question. Instead, the claimant should be asked in general terms, 'describe to the court the condition of the goods when they arrived as compared to the sample provided earlier'.

Cross-examination

The next stage is the cross-examination of the witness. There is no bar on leading questions. The purpose of cross-examination is to extract favourable evidence and to discredit the person being cross-examined in order to make their evidence appear less believable either on the case overall, or in relation to a specific element of it. There are many ways in which this may be done. It may involve highlighting inconsistencies in the evidence given by the witness, or the improbability of the witness's version of events. It may involve alleging that the witness is biased in some way. If the witness has previous convictions, it is even possible for the advocate to cross-examine on these to show the witness's character generally in a bad light.

As all the evidence to be used at trial has been seen by the parties before the trial starts, you can prepare your line of cross-examination questions in advance. Think about the submissions you will wish to make in your closing speech about the evidence of any particular witness. Ensure that you cover all those points with that witness. The trial judge cannot make any particular finding of fact based on the evidence of a witness if that point did not come out in the examination of the witness.

Sometimes, the witness's evidence will be inconsistent with an earlier statement. This will then give the advocate scope to cross-examine on the previous inconsistent statement to show the court how the witness has given different versions of events at different times and therefore should not be believed. See further **12.9.7**.

However, cross-examination does not always involve an aggressive attack on the witness and their credibility. Cross-examination can be conducted in a more subtle fashion, and often the best results are achieved by a less confrontational approach.

In addition to the above, however, there is one mandatory rule concerning cross-examination. This is that the cross-examining advocate must put their own party's case to the witness they are cross-examining (*Rea v Rea* [2022] EWCA Civ 195). Thus, the claimant's advocate must put the claimant's case to the defendant in cross-examination. For example, perhaps the claimant has given evidence that they made known to the defendant a particular purpose for the goods they have bought. The defendant denies this in their witness statement/examination-in-chief.

It must be put to the defendant in cross-examination that the defendant did know of this particular purpose.

It is highly unlikely that the witness being cross-examined in this way will change their story as a result of the allegation being put to them. Nevertheless, it is essential that the cross-examining advocate puts their own client's case to the witness in this way, as failure to challenge the opponent's evidence implies acceptance of that evidence.

> The general rule is that the evidence of a witness is accepted unless given the opportunity to rebut the allegation made against them, or there is undisputed objective evidence inconsistent with that of the witness that cannot sensibly be explained away so that the witness's testimony is manifestly wrong. (R (on the application of the Good Law Project) v Minister for the Cabinet Office [2022] EWCA Civ 21 at [86])

Re-examination

Following cross-examination, the advocate is given the opportunity to ask further questions of their own witness. However, re-examination is strictly limited to matters arising out of the cross-examination. It is not possible to introduce new issues at this stage. Accordingly, if some ambiguity has been left as a result of the cross-examination, this might be an opportunity to resolve it and try to restore the witness's credibility on that point. For example, perhaps cross-examination has established that the witness normally wears glasses but that they were not wearing them on the day of the incident in question. In so far as this detracts from their credibility in implying that perhaps they did not see what they thought they saw, re-examination would be an opportunity to clarify the fact that the witness wears glasses only for reading. As with examination-in-chief, the advocate cannot ask a leading question.

Problem witnesses

One problem that can arise with the evidence of a witness is the possibility of the witness unexpectedly being unfavourable to the party who has called them. For example, a witness might change their story during cross-examination. If they do this, there is little that the advocate who called the witness can do to remedy the situation. It is not possible for a party's advocate to cross-examine a witness they have themselves called.

However, sometimes matters proceed further than this, and the witness proves not merely to be unfavourable to the party who called them, but actually to be hostile in giving their evidence. It is difficult to be precise as to when a witness can be said to have passed from merely being unfavourable to being hostile, but it would probably be apparent from the witness's demeanour and lack of cooperation that they have no desire either to see justice done, or to give their evidence fairly. One indicator would be the extent to which the witness's evidence is inconsistent with the statement previously given to the party calling them. It is then for that party to make an application to the court for the witness to be declared hostile; if they are, the party who called them can then (contrary to the usual rule) cross-examine that witness on the facts of the case and on the previous inconsistent statements. The witness's general character cannot, however, be attacked by the party who called them, neither can the witness be cross-examined about any previous convictions. Having a witness declared hostile should be regarded as a damage limitation exercise. Whilst it may allow the advocate to retain some control over the case, they are clearly not going to win it unless the damage done can be repaired by evidence from another witness. Strictly, by virtue of s 4 of the Civil Evidence Act 1995 (see **12.9.3.3**), it would be open to the court to attach weight to the previous inconsistent statement as evidence. In practice, however, the court is more likely to take the view that this witness is not someone who can be relied upon.

14.2.3.3   The defendant

The defendant will present their evidence in exactly the same way as the claimant.

14.2.4   Children as witnesses

A child who understands the nature of an oath will give sworn evidence. Otherwise, s 96(2) of the Children Act 1989 provides that:

> The child's evidence may be heard by the court if, in its opinion—
>
> (a)   he understands that it is his duty to speak the truth; and
>
> (b)   he has sufficient understanding to justify his evidence being heard.

A child for these purposes is a person under the age of 18.

It is for the judge to decide whether the child can give evidence and, if so, whether it will be given on oath. As a general rule, it will be assumed that children over the age of 14 can give sworn evidence, and the judge will make enquiries of children under that age in order to form an opinion.

The judge will speak to the child to discover whether they appreciate the solemnity of the occasion and the added responsibility to tell the truth that is involved in taking an oath, over and above the ordinary social duty to be truthful. If so, the child can give sworn evidence. If not, but nevertheless the conditions in s 96(2) are satisfied, the child can give unsworn evidence.

14.2.5   Closing speeches

After the evidence has been given, usually the defence advocate will make a closing speech followed by the claimant's advocate.

14.2.6   The judgment

The judge will either deliver their judgment immediately, perhaps after a short adjournment if they require time to collect their thoughts, or (if the case is complex) judgment may be reserved to be delivered at a later date. If the court gives judgment on both the claim and counterclaim then, if there is a balance in favour of one of the parties, the court will order the party whose judgment is for the lesser amount to pay the balance.

A judgment will normally address the following matters:

(a)   *Liability.* Has the claimant established a cause of action? The judge will review the evidence and should give reasons.

(b)   *Quantum.* In a claim for a specified amount of money, the judge will deal with the figure work, eg any counterclaim established may be set off against the claim. With an unspecified claim the judge will deal with the heads of damage.

(c)   *Interest.* This topic is dealt with in detail at **2.7** (and also see **7.2.1** above and **14.2.8** below). Once the trial judge has indicated that they will award interest, the rate of such and the period, it is for the advocates to work out the figures.

(d)   *Costs.* By r 44.2(2)(a), the general rule is that the unsuccessful party will be ordered to pay the costs of the successful party, but the court may make a different order. See **14.3**. At the end of a fast track trial, the trial judge will not only make a costs order but will also assess the amount payable (see **14.3.6**). However, at the end of a multi-track trial, the trial judge will only determine who should pay costs. A different judge (known as a costs judge) will determine the amount (failing any agreement of the parties) at a later ('detailed assessment') hearing (see **14.3.7**).

The judgment will name the parties unless an anonymity order is justified: see *JIH v News Group Newspapers Ltd* [2011] EWCA Civ 42, particularly at [21].

14.2.7   Part 36

A claimant should now apply for an order under r 36.17(4) and a defendant pursuant to r 36.17(3), if appropriate (see **13.4**).

14.2.8 Interest

14.2.8.1 Interest up to the date of judgment

Interest will normally be awarded, provided it has been claimed in the particulars of claim. In the absence of any contractual provision to the contrary, or entitlement to interest under the Late Payment of Commercial Debts (Interest) Act 1998, interest on the damages will usually be awarded by the judge in their discretion (under SCA 1981, s 35A or CCA 1984, s 69) from the date the loss was sustained until the date of judgment. See further **2.7.2.3**.

Interest is a discretionary matter and the judge might choose to award at a different rate or for a different period. For example, if the claimant has been very slow about pursuing the claim then the judge may disallow interest for a period, even if the claimant eventually succeeds in their claim.

14.2.8.2 Interest after judgment

Once judgment has been given, different rules apply. In the High Court, interest is payable under s 17 of the Judgments Act 1838 at a rate of 8% pa (unless there is a contractual right to more). In the County Court, interest is payable at 8% pa under the County Courts (Interest on Judgment Debts) Order 1991 (SI 1991/1184), provided the judgment was for at least £5,000 (or, if less, that the Late Payment of Commercial Debts (Interest) Act 1998 applies). In neither case is the interest discretionary, and it accrues on both the judgment and on costs.

It should be noted that whilst judgment interest cannot accrue on damages until they have been quantified, interest is payable on costs from the date of judgment even if the amount to be paid has yet to be assessed (*Hunt v RM Douglas (Roofing) Ltd* [1990] 1 AC 398). As a result, it is in the interests of the party paying costs to make a payment on account as soon as possible, even if an interim order requiring such a payment is not made by the court (see **14.3.6.13**).

The court has a discretion when deciding what rate of interest to apply and when the judgment rate takes effect. In *Involnert Management Inc v Aprilgrange Ltd and others* [2015] EWHC 2834 (Comm), the court ordered a payment on account of costs but limited interest payable on the outstanding costs to 2% over base rate until three months after the date the costs order was made, after which the judgment rate took effect.

14.2.9 Register of Judgments Orders and Fines

Judgments of the High Court and County Court are officially recorded on the Register of Judgments Orders and Fines. Usually the registration lasts for six years and may affect a judgment debtor's creditworthiness. Normally a judgment may be removed only if it is set aside or paid in full within a month. Any later payment in full will be marked as 'satisfied'.

14.3 COSTS

14.3.1 The indemnity principle

Although the court has a wide discretion, the general rule is that the loser in litigation will be ordered to pay the winner's costs (r 44.2(2)(a)). Note that the winner (the receiving party) is entitled to an 'indemnity' in respect of the costs they have incurred. In other words, they cannot make a profit out of the paying party by seeking more than their solicitor and client costs. This is known as the indemnity principle (not to be confused with the indemnity basis: see **14.3.3**).

The word 'indemnity' is misleading. In reality, the receiving party will not receive a full indemnity in respect of their costs. The paying party will invariably challenge particular items (see **14.3.7.6**).

14.3.2 General provisions about costs (Part 44)

At the end of the trial, under r 44.2(1) the court has a discretion as to:

(a)   whether the costs are payable by one party to another;

(b)   the amount of those costs; and

(c)   when they are to be paid.

14.3.2.1 What are costs?

By r 44.1, 'costs' include fees, charges, disbursements, expenses and remuneration. These therefore include the charges of solicitors, barristers, experts, etc. Are pre-action costs included? Yes – see r 44.2(6)(d).

14.3.2.2 Interest on costs

Is interest payable on costs before judgment? The general rule is that it is not. We have already seen that an exception is when r 36.17(3) or (4) applies: see **13.4.6**. Also note that by r 44.2(6)(g), the court has a discretion when awarding costs to award interest on such from any date it sees fit, including before judgment. Over recent years, the court has increasingly acceded to requests to award interest before judgment on costs to the receiving party who has 'had to put up money paying its solicitors and been out of the use of that money in the meanwhile' (per Waller LJ at [18] in *Bim Kemi AB v Blackburn Chemicals Ltd* [2003] EWCA Civ 889). When seeking to measure the extent to which the receiving party has been out of pocket, the appropriate dates from which interest should run are the dates on which the invoices for costs were actually paid by that party, rather than from the dates on which they were rendered, and that rate of interest will run until judgment (see *Douglas v Hello! Ltd* [2004] EWHC 63 (Ch)). The rate of interest is the normal commercial rate (see *Fiona Trust and Holding Corp v Privalov* [2016] EWHC 2657 (Comm) and **2.7**).

14.3.2.3 Factors

Whilst the general rule is that the court will order the unsuccessful party to pay the costs of the successful party, this is only a starting point, and the court can make a different order for costs if it thinks it appropriate to do so.

All the circumstances will be considered, including:

(a)   the conduct of all the parties;

(b)   whether a party has succeeded on part of their case, even if they have not been wholly successful; and

(c)   any admissible offer to settle made by a party that is drawn to the court's attention (and which is not an offer to which costs consequences under Part 36 apply).

With regard to (c), the court should only depart from the general rule where there is an open offer made for more than is recovered, or an offer purportedly under Part 36 for a sum in excess of the sum recovered but where, for some reason, it does not have the Part 36 costs consequences (*Hammersmatch Properties (Welwyn) Ltd v Saint-Gobain Ceramics and Others* [2013] EWHC 2227 (TCC)).

In *Northrop Grumman Missions Systems Europe Limited v BAE Systems (Al Diriyah C41) Ltd* [2014] EWHC 3148 (TCC), the losing claimant argued that the defendant's costs should be reduced by 50% as it had unreasonably refused to mediate the dispute. The defendant had previously offered, without prejudice save as to costs, to settle on the basis of no payment and each party bearing its own costs. This would have put the claimant in a better position than it found itself at the conclusion of the litigation, and the court concluded that the fair and just outcome was that neither party's conduct should be taken into account in order to modify what would otherwise be the general rule that the loser pays the winner's costs.

14.3.2.4 Conduct of the parties

Note that the conduct of the parties includes:

(a) conduct before, as well as during, the proceedings, and in particular the extent to which the parties followed the Practice Direction on Pre-action Conduct and Protocols or any relevant pre-action protocol. In *Chapman v Tameside Hospital NHS Foundation Trust* (Bolton County Court, 15 June 2016), the defendant informed the claimant in pre-action correspondence that it had no documents to disclose. Proceedings were issued and the defendant subsequently disclosed documents that led to the claimant withdrawing her claim. In awarding the claimant the costs she had incurred in pursuing her claim from the date when the defendant should have disclosed those documents pursuant to the relevant Pre-Action Protocol, the judge commented:

> The Defendant's behaviour in the conduct of this litigation was entirely unacceptable. It's exactly the type of conduct which Part 44.2 is designed to address ... [I]t always has to be borne in mind the provisions of CPR 1.3, that the parties to litigation have an obligation to assist the Court to further the overriding objective. The overriding objective firstly being to try and avoid costs and the issue of proceedings if at all possible, which is the whole purpose of the pre-action protocol ...

(b) whether it was reasonable for a party to raise, pursue or contest a particular allegation or issue;

(c) the manner in which a party has pursued or defended their case or a particular allegation or issue; and

(d) whether a claimant who has succeeded in their claim, in whole or in part, exaggerated their claim.

An example of conduct being taken into account in making a decision on costs is the decision of Jacob J in *Mars UK Ltd v Teknowledge Ltd (No 2)* [1999] Masons CLR 322, ChD. In that case, he indicated that the successful claimant would be likely to receive only 40% of the costs because of the heavy-handed way in which it had rushed into court proceedings against a smaller opponent who had been genuinely attempting to achieve a negotiated settlement. Likewise, parties who make fraudulent claims (see *Shah v Ul-Haq* [2009] EWCA Civ 542) or exaggerated claims (see *Widlake v BAA Ltd* [2009] EWCA Civ 1256) can expect that conduct to be taken into account.

In *Brit Inns Ltd v BDW Trading Ltd* [2012] EWHC (TCC), the court penalised a claimant who had adopted an unrealistic approach to the litigation, and used its discretion under Part 44 to make a costs order in favour of the defendant despite the claimant's obtaining a judgment more advantageous than the defendant's Part 36 offer. However, it will be rare for a party to be awarded costs in these circumstances.

Where the CPR 1998 provides for a specific sanction for failure to follow the required procedure and the criteria are not met to apply that sanction, the court can use the general powers under r 44 to limit costs to those which would have been payable had the sanction applied (see *Williams v Secretary of State for Business, Energy and Industrial Strategy* [2018] EWCA Civ 852).

14.3.2.5 Costs budgets and Costs Management Orders

If a Costs Management Order (CMO) has been made, when assessing costs on the standard basis, the court will not depart from the last approved or agreed budget unless there is a good reason to do so. Note that this provision does not apply where the assessment of any costs included in an agreed or approved budget is on the indemnity basis (see **14.3.3.3**). Further note that the provision does not apply to costs falling outside the phases addressed in an agreed or approved budget. Those costs will be subject to a detailed assessment (save any agreement reached between the parties) in the usual way (see **14.3.6.1**).

If no CMO was made, the court will have regard to any costs budgets when assessing costs. Whether or not the court makes a CMO, it may record on the face of any case management order any comments it has about the incurred costs that are to be taken into account in any subsequent assessment proceedings. If there is a difference of more than 20% between the figure claimed by the receiving party and the last costs budget filed, the receiving party must file a statement setting out the reasons for the difference (PD 44, para 3.2).

If the paying party:

(a) claims to have reasonably relied on a budget filed by a receiving party; or

(b) wishes to rely upon the costs shown in the budget in order to dispute the reasonableness or proportionality of the costs claimed,

the paying party must serve a statement setting out the case in this regard in that party's points of dispute (PD 44, para 3.3).

If the court accepts that the paying party reasonably relied on the budget, the court may restrict the recoverable costs to such sum as is reasonable for the paying party to pay in the light of that reliance, even if it is less than the amount of costs reasonably and proportionately incurred by the receiving party (PD 44, para 3.6).

Further, if any explanation provided by the receiving party is deemed unsatisfactory, the court may regard the difference between the amount claimed and the budget figure as evidence that the costs claimed are unreasonable or disproportionate (PD 44, para 3.7).

See further **9.7.3.**

14.3.2.6 Different types of orders

The order may reflect the decision on particular issues by providing for payment of, for example:

(a) a proportion of a party's costs;

(b) a stated amount of a party's costs;

(c) costs from or until a certain date only;

(d) costs incurred before the proceedings began;

(e) costs of a particular step;

(f) costs of a distinct part of the proceedings;

(g) interest on costs from or until a certain date, including a date before judgment.

Orders whereby the winner receives only part of their costs are becoming increasingly common, and a party who raises a number of issues but who succeeds on only some of them can no longer expect to recover the whole of their costs. For example, where both claim and counterclaim succeed, the court may well set off the costs payable on each and direct only payment of the balance.

In *Webb v Liverpool Women's NHS Foundation Trust* [2015] EWHC 449 (QB), the claimant raised two separate issues. The claimant succeeded on the first but not the second. A Part 36 offer had been made by the claimant to settle both issues and it was not disputed that the judgment was more advantageous to the claimant than the Part 36 offer. The defendants argued that a proportionate costs order should be made and the court, in ordering payment of the claimant's costs on the successful issue with Part 36 enhancements, rejected the argument that Part 36 is a self-contained costs regime which prevents application of the provisions in Part 44.

14.3.3 The basis of assessment (r 44.3)

When the court assesses costs, it will assess those costs either on the standard basis or on the indemnity basis, but in either case the court will not allow costs that have been unreasonably incurred or which are unreasonable in amount.

14.3.3.1   Relevant factors in assessing the amount of costs (r 44.4(3))

The court must first take into account on an item by item basis the following factors in deciding the amount of costs the receiving party is entitled to:

(a)   the conduct of all the parties, including conduct before as well as during the proceedings and the efforts made, if any, before and during the proceedings in order to try to resolve the dispute;

(b)   the amount or value of any money or property involved;

(c)   the importance of the matter to all the parties;

(d)   the particular complexity of the matter or the difficulty or novelty of the questions raised;

(e)   the skill, effort, specialised knowledge and responsibility involved;

(f)   the time spent on the case;

(g)   the place where and the circumstances in which work or any part of it was done;

(h)   the receiving party's last approved or agreed budget.

14.3.3.2   The standard basis

The standard basis will apply unless the court orders otherwise. Costs on this basis must be proportionate to the matters in issue. Costs that are disproportionate may be disallowed or reduced even if they were reasonably or necessarily incurred. No costs that were unreasonably incurred or are unreasonable in amount are allowable. Rule 44.3(5) sets out the test for determining proportionality as follows:

> Costs incurred are proportionate if they bear a reasonable relationship to—
>
> (a)   the sums in issue in the proceedings;
>
> (b)   the value of any non-monetary relief in issue in the proceedings;
>
> (c)   the complexity of the litigation;
>
> (d)   any additional work generated by the conduct of the paying party;
>
> (e)   any wider factors involved in the proceedings, such as reputation or public importance; and
>
> (f)   any additional work undertaken or expense incurred due to the vulnerability of a party or any witness. [see **1.1.4**]

If there is any doubt, it will be resolved in favour of the paying party.

Guidance as to how the court should set about assessing costs on the standard basis by applying the test of proportionately was given in the following terms by the Court of Appeal in *West v Stockport NHS Foundation Trust* [2019] EWCA Civ 1220:

> 88   First, the judge should go through the bill line-by-line, assessing the reasonableness of each item of cost. If the judge considers it possible, appropriate and convenient when undertaking that exercise, he or she may also address the proportionality of any particular item at the same time. That is because, although reasonableness and proportionality are conceptually distinct, there can be an overlap between them, not least because reasonableness may be a necessary condition of proportionality: see *Rogers and Callery v Gray (No 2)* [2001] EWCA Civ 1246 at paragraph 104. This will be a matter for the judge. It will apply, for example, when the judge considers an item to be clearly disproportionate, irrespective of the final figures.
>
> 89   At the conclusion of the line-by-line exercise, there will be a total figure which the judge considers to be reasonable (and which may, as indicated, also take into account at least some aspects of proportionality). That total figure will have involved an assessment of every item of cost, including court fees, the ATE premium and the like.
>
> 90   The proportionality of that total figure must be assessed by reference to both r.44.3(5) and r.44.4(1). If that total figure is found to be proportionate, then no further assessment is required. If the judge regards the overall figure as disproportionate, then a further assessment is required. That should not be line-by-line, but should instead consider various categories of cost,

such as disclosure or expert's reports, or specific periods where particular costs were incurred, or particular parts of the profit costs.

91   At that stage, however, any reductions for proportionality should exclude those elements of costs which are properly regarded as unavoidable, such as court fees, the reasonable element of the ATE premium in clinical negligence cases, and the like. Specifically, therefore, if the ATE premium is assessed as reasonable, it will not fall to be reduced by any further assessment of proportionality.

92   The judge will undertake the proportionality assessment by looking at the different categories of costs (excluding the unavoidable items noted above) and considering, in respect of each such category, whether the costs incurred were disproportionate. If yes, then the judge will make such reduction as is appropriate. In that way, reductions for proportionality will be clear and transparent for both sides.

93   Once any further reductions have been made, the resulting figure will be the final amount of the costs assessment. There would be no further stage of standing back and, if necessary, undertaking a yet further review by reference to proportionality. That would introduce the risk of double-counting.

14.3.3.3   The indemnity basis

Costs on the indemnity basis are awarded as a penalty, usually to reflect the court's displeasure with the manner in which a party has behaved either pre-action and/or during proceedings. Costs on this basis must be:

(a)   reasonably incurred; and

(b)   reasonable in amount.

Any benefit of the doubt is given to the party receiving the costs.

The principles relating to an award of indemnity costs are summarised at **13.4.5.2(b)**.

To this can be added a number of other specific and general points:

(i)   The discretion to award indemnity costs is a wide one and must be exercised taking into account all the circumstances and considering the matters complained of in the context of the overall litigation (see *Three Rivers DC v Governor of the Bank of England* [2006] EWHC 816 (Comm) and *Digicel* (above)).

(ii)   Dishonesty or moral blame does not have to be established to justify indemnity costs (*Reid Minty v Taylor* [2002] WLR 2800).

(iii)   The conduct of experts can justify an order for indemnity costs in respect of costs generated by them (see *Williams v Jervis* [2009] EWHC 1837 (QB)).

(iv)   A failure to comply with Pre-Action Protocol requirements could result in indemnity costs being awarded.

(v)   A refusal to mediate or engage in mediation or some other alternative dispute resolution process could justify an award of indemnity costs.

(vi)   If a claimant casts its claim disproportionately wide, and requires the defendant to meet such a claim, there is no injustice in denying the claimant the benefit of an assessment on a proportionate basis given that, in such circumstances, the claimant had forfeited its rights to the benefit of the doubt on reasonableness: see *Digicel (St Lucia) Ltd v Cable and Wireless PLC* [2010] EWHC 888 (Ch).

14.3.3.4   The difference between the two bases

Where there is no doubt over the reasonableness of costs, the difference between the two bases is that in assessing costs on the standard basis the court will allow only those costs that are proportionate to the matters in issue (see **14.3.3.2**).

I have considered and reminded myself carefully of the differences between the standard basis of assessment and the indemnity basis. The chief differences are that the latter basis of assessment is not hedged by any considerations of proportionality and that the burden of proof on the question of reasonableness of costs (in terms of their being incurred and their quantum) switches from the receiving party (on the standard basis) to the paying party (on the indemnity basis). (per HHJ Davis-White QC in *Goodwin v Avison* [2021] EWHC 2754 (Ch) at [13])

The great majority of costs orders are awarded on the standard basis. An award on the indemnity basis is usually reserved for occasions where there has been culpable behaviour on the part of the paying party (for example, pursuing an unjustified claim or defence, or where there has been non-compliance with court orders). We also saw it applied at **13.4.6** in respect of r 36.17(4). Where the court does not specify in its order which basis is to apply, the standard basis is used.

14.3.3.5 Summary of the standard basis

Follow the steps in order to identify and apply the correct tests on a standard basis assessment:

Step 1. Apply factors listed in r 44.4(3) to each item of cost.

Step 2. Are the costs claimed by the receiving party proportionate applying r 44.3(5)?

• If no, costs may be disallowed or reduced, even if reasonably or necessarily incurred.

Step 3. Resolve any doubt in favour of the paying party.

See also the flowchart in **Appendix C(21)**.

14.3.3.6 Conduct and ADR

As to factor (a) in **14.3.3.1** above, parties must seriously consider ADR proposals made by the other side. In *Dunnett v Railtrack plc (in Railway Administration)* [2002] EWCA Civ 303, [2002] 2 All ER 850, the Court of Appeal deprived the successful party of its costs because it unreasonably refused to mediate before the appeal was heard. The Court of Appeal in *Halsey v Milton Keynes General NHS Trust* [2004] EWCA Civ 576, [2004] 4 All ER 920, laid down guidelines in this area. It held that there is no presumption in favour of mediation. The question whether a party has acted unreasonably in refusing ADR must be determined having regard to all the circumstances of the particular case, including:

(i)   the nature of the dispute;

(ii)   the merits of the case;

(iii) the extent to which other settlement methods have been attempted;

(iv)   whether the costs of the ADR would be disproportionately high;

(v)   whether any delay in setting up and attending the ADR would have been prejudicial; and

(vi)   whether the ADR had a reasonable prospect of success.

As to (vi), Rix LJ in *Rolf v De Guerin* [2011] EWCA Civ 78 stated (at [48]):

> It is possible of course that settlement discussions, or even mediation, would not have produced a solution; or would have produced one satisfactory enough to the parties to have enabled them to reach agreement but which [the Defendant] might now, with his hindsight of the judge's judgment, have been able to say did him less than justice. Nevertheless, in my judgment, the facts of this case disclose that negotiation and/or mediation would have had reasonable prospects of success. The spurned offers to enter into settlement negotiations or mediation were unreasonable ...

The *Halsey* principles were endorsed in *PGF II SA v OMFS Company 1 Ltd* [2013] EWCA Civ 1288. The Court made it clear that any refusal of a proposal for ADR by a party should be based on the *Halsey* principles and clearly communicated to the proposing party. In the instant case, the defendant made no response to two requests by the claimant to engage in mediation. That failure to respond was deemed to be a refusal that amounted to unreasonable conduct justifying costs sanctions. See also the Practice Direction on Pre-action Conduct, para 11.

Moreover, if a party agrees to mediate but frustrates the process by delaying and dragging its feet for no good reason, such that the other party loses confidence in the process which then does not go ahead, that conduct will merit a costs sanction (*Thakkar v Patel* [2017] EWCA Civ 117).

In the case of *Northrop Grumman Missions Systems Europe Limited v BAE Systems (Al Diriyah C41) Ltd* [2014] EWHC 3148 (TCC), the successful party, who had rejected an offer to mediate but who had made a without prejudice offer to settle, was not held to have acted unreasonably.

It is not always easy to decide when mediation should occur. This was recognised in *Nigel Witham Ltd v Smith* [2008] EWHC 12. The court accepted that a premature mediation simply wastes time. It can also sometimes lead to a hardening of positions on both sides, which makes any subsequent attempt at settlement doomed to fail. Conversely, a delay in any mediation until after full particulars and documents have been exchanged can mean that the costs incurred become the principal obstacle to a successful mediation. The solution is to identify the point when the detail of the claim and the response are known to both sides, but before the costs that are incurred in reaching that stage become so great that a settlement is no longer possible. Note that in an exceptional case where mediation occurs very late and its chances of success are very poor, if the successful party in the litigation unreasonably delayed in consenting to the mediation then this may lead to an adverse costs order. See further **3.7**.

Is a party who agrees to mediation but then causes the mediation to fail by taking an unreasonable position to be treated the same as a party who unreasonably refuses to mediate? Yes, held Jack J in *Earl of Malmesbury v Strutt & Parker* [2008] EWHC 424. See also *Rolf v De Guerin* above ('a sad case about lost opportunities for mediation'). But remember that ADR procedures are confidential unless all parties agree to waive confidentiality (see **Chapter 4**).

The increasing importance the court attaches to the consideration of ADR is evidenced by the standard directions that require a party who rejects a proposal for ADR to file a witness statement detailing that party's reasons for rejecting the proposal (see **Appendix B(7)**). That witness statement will be available to the trial judge when the issue of costs is considered. In *DSN v Blackpool Football Club Ltd* [2020] EWHC 670 (QB), the successful claimant argued that the defendant should pay its costs on an indemnity basis because it had failed to engage in settlement discussions. Pursuant to the case management directions, the defendant filed a statement indicating that it had refused to engage in ADR because, after considering all of the evidence in the case, it continued to believe that it had 'a strong defence to this claim and stands by the content of its defence'. The defendant also rejected the claimant's various Part 36 offers. The judge found that the reasons given by the defendant for refusing to engage with ADR were inadequate and that 'no defence, however strong, by itself justifies a failure to engage in any kind of alternative dispute resolution'. Although the judge refused to make an indemnity order for the whole of the proceedings, he ordered that the defendant pay the claimant's costs on an indemnity basis from one month after the date of the master's case management order.

14.3.3.7   Time is money

As to factor (f) at **14.3.3.1** above, regional hourly guideline figures (for a summary assessment) are set by the Master of the Rolls, most recently in 2021. Examples appear at **Appendix A(22)**. See also **14.3.6.8**.

Judges bring a vast experience to an assessment of costs. A judge will be familiar with the typical charges imposed by local solicitors, counsel, experts, etc. Even on a detailed assessment, the examples given at **Appendix A(22)** are a useful starting point. The complete guidance (to be found on the Court Service website – see **1.5**) has some specific examples that give a flavour of how a judge would assess the reasonableness of certain costs.

> On appeals where both counsel and solicitors have been instructed, the reasonable fees of counsel are likely to exceed the reasonable fees of the solicitor. In many cases the largest element in the solicitors'

reasonable fees for work on an appeal concerns instructing counsel and preparing the appeal bundles. Time spent by the solicitor in the development of legal submissions should only be allowed where it does not duplicate work done by counsel and is claimed at a rate the same or lower than the rate counsel would have claimed.

14.3.4 Procedure for assessing costs

Where the court orders one party to pay costs to another, the court will either make a summary assessment of costs there and then, or order detailed assessment of the costs by the costs officer. (The costs officer is the district judge or, in London, the costs judge.)

The general rule is that the court should, unless there is good reason not to do so (eg, where the paying party shows substantial grounds for disputing the sum claimed for costs that cannot be dealt with summarily, or there is insufficient time to carry out a summary assessment), make a summary assessment of the costs:

(a)   at the conclusion of the trial of a case which has been dealt with on the fast track, in which case the order will deal with the costs of the whole claim; and

(b)   at the conclusion of any other hearing, which has lasted not more than one day, in which case the order will deal with the costs of the application or matter to which the hearing related. If this hearing disposes of the claim, the order may deal with the costs of the whole claim;

(c)   in certain hearings in the Court of Appeal.

To assist the court to make a summary assessment, the parties must file and serve at least 24 hours before an interim hearing a breakdown of their costs – see Costs Form N260 Statement of Costs for Summary Assessment at **Appendix A(13)**.

14.3.5 Fast track costs (Part 45)

14.3.5.1 Trial costs

In fast track cases, there is a specified figure for the advocate for preparing for and appearing at the trial.

Value of the claim	Amount of fast track trial costs which the court may award
Up to £3,000	£485
More than £3,000 but not more than £10,000	£690
More than £10,000 but not more than £15,000	£1,035
More than £15,000	£1,650

The court may not award more or less than the amount shown except in limited circumstances. For example, an additional £345 may be awarded where it is necessary for a legal representative to attend to assist the advocate. Therefore, if a barrister is instructed to conduct the fast track trial and a representative from the solicitor's office attends court with the barrister, £345 may be awarded for that attendance, provided the court thinks that it was necessary.

14.3.5.2 Valuing the claim

If the claimant succeeds then the value of the claim is based on the amount awarded, excluding any interest or reduction for contributory negligence.

If the defendant was successful then the value of the claim is based on the amount claimed by the claimant.

Improper or unreasonable behaviour by one of the parties may lead to a departure from the specified figure.

If there is more than one claimant or defendant but the successful parties used only one advocate, there will be only one award. If the successful parties used separate advocates, there will be a separate award for each party.

14.3.5.3 Summary assessment of other fast track costs

The fast track trial costs are in addition to the rest of the costs in bringing the claim. The usual practice on fast track cases is for these to be summarily assessed at the end of the case. The trial judge should carry out any standard basis assessment by first applying the test of proportionality and then go on to consider the individual elements of the receiving party's bill, item by item (see *Morgan v Spirit Group Ltd* [2011] EWCA Civ 68), applying the factors listed in r 44.4(3). In fast track cases, therefore, the party should always file and serve a statement of costs (see **10.3.4**) at least 48 hours prior to the hearing.

14.3.6 Multi-track cases

14.3.6.1 Procedure

In multi-track cases there are no specified trial costs. Although the judge does have the power to make a summary assessment of costs, in multi-track cases the court will usually order detailed assessment.

Detailed assessment proceedings are commenced by the receiving party serving on the paying party:

(a)   notice of commencement in Form N252 (see **Appendix A(16)**);

(b)   a copy of the bill of costs;

(c)   copies of the fee notes of counsel and of any other expert in respect of fees claimed in the bill;

(d)   written evidence as to any other disbursement which is claimed and which exceeds £500;

(e)   a statement giving the name and address for service of any person upon whom the receiving party intends to serve the notice of commencement;

(f)   if a costs management order has been made, a breakdown of the costs claimed for each phase of the proceedings.

Where a case management order has been made, Precedent Q (a model form of breakdown of the costs claimed for each phase of the proceedings) (see **Appendix A(24)**)must also be filed.

This action must be taken within three months of the date of the judgment or order.

14.3.6.2 Bill of costs

Bills of costs for detailed assessment in most Part 7 claims must be in a prescribed electronic spreadsheet format and compliant with CPR, PD 47, paras 5.A1 to 5.A4. A model electronic bill in pdf format is annexed to the PD as Precedent S, and a link to an electronic spreadsheet version of the same model bill is provided in para 5.A2 of the PD. A copy of a completed Precedent S appears at **Appendix A(17)**.

14.3.6.3 Categories of work

The main body of the bill comprises a breakdown of the work performed, divided into different categories of work as set out in PD 47, para 5.12:

(1)   attendances at court and upon counsel;

(2)   attendances on and communications with the receiving party;

(3)   attendances on and communications with witnesses including any expert witness;

(4)   attendances to inspect any property or place for the purposes of the proceedings;

(5)   attendances on and communications with other persons;

(6)   communications with the court and with counsel;

(7)   work done on documents: preparing and considering documentation, including documentation relating to pre-action protocols where appropriate, work done in connection with arithmetical calculations of compensation and/or interest and time spent collating documents;

(8)   work done in connection with negotiations with a view to settlement (if not already covered under another head);

(9)   attendances on and communications with agents and work done by them;

(10)   other work done which was of or incidental to the proceedings and which is not already covered above.

The work done within each of these heads is set out chronologically in numbered items. As can be seen from the electronic bill at **Appendix A(17)**, the information is presented in columns, with the amount claimed for profit costs, disbursements and VAT being shown separately.

'Communications', in the context of para 5.12, means letters out, e-mails out and telephone calls. Most will be classed as routine and charged at a standard rate of six minutes (thus a routine letter drafted by an assistant solicitor charging a rate of £140 per hour would be charged at £14). Where letters out, e-mails out or telephone calls are sufficiently complex and/or lengthy not to be classed as routine, they may be charged according to the time actually spent on them. Letters in and e-mails received are not charged for separately.

Local travelling expenses (generally train or taxi fares, petrol costs, etc, within a 10-mile radius of the court) cannot be claimed, but the solicitor is entitled to claim at up to the hourly rate for time spent travelling and waiting (depending on the amount they charged their client). See further **14.3.6.8**.

The cost of postage, couriers, out-going telephone calls, fax and telex messages will in general not be allowed, but the court may exceptionally in its discretion allow such expenses in unusual circumstances or where the cost is unusually heavy. See further **14.3.6.8**.

14.3.6.4   Costs associated with detailed assessment

Note that the bill of costs must not contain any claims in respect of costs or court fees that relate solely to the detailed assessment proceedings. A claim may only be made for the reasonable costs of preparing and checking the bill of costs (see PD 47, para 5.19). The award of costs at a detailed assessment is made at its conclusion.

14.3.6.5   Late commencement of the assessment process

Permission is not required to commence detailed assessment proceedings out of time, but if the receiving party does not commence the process within three months, the court may disallow all or part of any interest accruing on the costs.

It is open to the paying party to apply for an order that the receiving party lose their right to costs unless detailed assessment proceedings are commenced by a certain date.

14.3.6.6   Challenging the bill

The paying party has 21 days from service of the notice of commencement to serve points of dispute on the receiving party (r 47.9). A specimen can be found at **Appendix A(18)**. If they do not do so, the receiving party can apply for a default costs certificate, which will include an order to pay the costs. The default costs certificate will be set aside only if good reason is shown by the paying party. If the paying party serves the points of dispute late (but before the default certificate is issued), the paying party may not be heard further unless the court gives permission.

On service of the points of dispute, the receiving party may serve a reply within 21 days (r 47.13). The receiving party must file a request for an assessment hearing within three months of the expiry of the period for commencing detailed assessment proceedings.

There will then be a detailed assessment hearing, at which the court will decide what costs are to be paid. The receiving party must, within 14 days of the hearing, file a completed bill showing the amount of costs finally due.

The receiving party will normally be entitled to the costs of the detailed assessment proceedings, but the court may take into account:

(a)   the conduct of the parties;

(b)   the amount of any reduction from the original amount claimed;

(c)   the reasonableness of claiming or challenging any particular item.

The court must also take into account any written offer expressed to be 'without prejudice save as to the costs of the detailed assessment proceedings' (see **14.3.7.10**).

No time is specified for service of such an offer, but any offer made more than 14 days after:

(a)   service of the notice of commencement (paying party);

(b)   service of the points of dispute (receiving party),

will be given less weight unless good reason is shown.

14.3.6.7   Provisional assessment

This procedure applies to all proceedings for detailed assessment in the High Court or County Court where the amount of costs claimed is less than a prescribed limit, currently £75,000. On filing the request for assessment in Form N258 there will be an application for a provisional assessment. On receipt of the request the court will endeavour to complete the provisional assessment within six weeks. The points of dispute will be returned with a note of the court's decision. The parties then have 14 days to agree the sum due to the receiving party on the basis of the court's provisional assessment. If the parties cannot agree, they can make written submissions to the court. Written submissions can also be made in respect of the costs of the provisional assessment.

If any party is unhappy with the provisional assessment, they can request an oral hearing within 21 days. However should that party fail to achieve an adjustment in their favour of at least 20% of the sum provisionally assessed, unless the court orders otherwise, they will pay the costs of the oral hearing.

14.3.6.8   At the assessment

Typically at an assessment, the following areas of costs are targeted by a paying party.

The hourly charging rate

A paying party will often argue for a reduction in the receiving party's solicitors' hourly charges if these exceed the guideline figures – see **Appendix A(22)**. Whilst the guideline rates are general approximations rather than scale figures, they are often the starting and finish points.

If the receiving party's solicitors are from an area that has higher hourly charging rates than the court where the case is proceeding, the paying party will argue for a reduction. The receiving party will have to show that it was reasonable to use those solicitors rather than a local, cheaper firm (see *Truscott v Truscott, Wraith v Sheffield Forgemasters* [1998] 1 WLR 132).

The status of the fee earner who did the work

A paying party will often accept that it was necessary or reasonable (as appropriate) for work to have been done, but will argue that the lawyer used was too senior, eg a partner should not prepare a simple list of documents, that could have been done by an assistant solicitor.

So the grade of fee earner used has to be justified as being reasonable. The grades are set out in the guideline charges (see above). Therefore, in a straightforward case the paying party may well argue that a Grade A or B fee earner can be justified only for a small amount of time to supervise and oversee the case, and that most of the work should have been done by a Grade C or D fee earner.

The length of time it took to do the work

A paying party will often argue that the time it took for a piece of work to be completed was excessive, eg in a very simple case with only a small number of documents, you would not expect preparation of a list of documents to take more than one hour.

No entitlement under CPR

Note that other, somewhat technical points can sometimes be made. Often this will be a challenge to an item that the paying party argues is not allowed under PD 47, para 5.22, which provides as follows:

(1) Routine letters out, routine e-mails out and routine telephone calls will in general be allowed on a unit basis of 6 minutes each, the charge being calculated by reference to the appropriate hourly rate. The unit charge for letters out and e-mails out in will include perusing and considering the relevant letters in or e-mails in and accordingly no separate charge is to be made for in-coming letters.

(2) The court may, in its discretion, allow an actual time charge for preparation of electronic communications other than e-mails sent by legal representatives, which properly amount to attendances provided that the time taken has been recorded.

(3) Local travelling expenses incurred by legal representatives will not be allowed. The definition of 'local' is a matter for the discretion of the court. While no absolute rule can be laid down, as a matter of guidance, 'local' will, in general, be taken to mean within a radius of 10 miles from the court dealing with the case at the relevant time. Where travelling and waiting time is claimed, this should be allowed at the rate agreed with the client unless this is more than the hourly rate on the assessment.

(4) The cost of postage, couriers, out-going telephone calls, fax and telex messages will in general not be allowed but the court may exceptionally in its discretion allow such expenses in unusual circumstances or where the cost is unusually heavy.

(5) The cost of making copies of documents will not in general be allowed but the court may exceptionally in its discretion make an allowance for copying in unusual circumstances or where the documents copied are unusually numerous in relation to the nature of the case. Where this discretion is invoked the number of copies made, their purpose and the costs claimed for them must be set out in the bill.

(6) Agency charges as between principal legal representatives and their agents will be dealt with on the principle that such charges, where appropriate, form part of the principal solicitor's charges.

14.3.6.9 Damages-based agreements

If a party has entered into a damages-based agreement, the costs recoverable cannot exceed the amount payable by that party under the agreement (r 44.18).

14.3.6.10 Capped Costs Pilot Scheme

In 2019, a Capped Costs Pilot Scheme started in selected Business and Property Courts throughout the country. The specific rules and procedure are set out in PD 51W. It is principally designed for claims of up to £250,000 and where the trial is estimated not to exceed two days. The stated aims are:

... to improve access to the Business and Property Courts, primarily through—

(1) streamlining the procedures of the pilot courts;

(2) lowering the costs of litigation;

    (3)   increasing the certainty of costs exposure; and

    (4)   speeding up the resolution of claims.

The scheme is voluntary, but once a case is allocated to the Capped Costs List, there are restrictions on the length of the statements of case and a requirement to serve a bundle of core documents with the particulars of claim. A case management conference should be applied for and fixed to take place between 10 and 12 weeks after filing of an acknowledgement of service. The normal rules for costs budgeting do not apply. The general rule is that no further disclosure will be ordered and disclosure will be limited to those documents contained in the core bundle. The court will make case management orders about witnesses and experts reports at the case management conference. The Practice Direction makes provision for the maximum amount of costs allowable at each stage of the proceedings subject to an overall maximum of £80,000.

14.3.6.11 Appeals

Where the assessment was by a judge, the appeals process is governed by Part 52. An appeal from a detailed or summary assessment by a district judge is made to a circuit judge. An appeal from an assessment by a circuit judge is made to a High Court judge. Permission to appeal is required either from the original court, or from the appeal court. If permission is not sought at the original assessment, it must be sought from the appeal court within 21 days. The appeal takes the form of a review of the original decision, rather than a re-hearing.

Part 52 does not apply where the detailed assessment was performed by an officer of the court. In this case, r 47.21 applies (as supplemented by para 20 of PD 47). Permission to appeal is not required and the appeal takes the form of a rehearing, either by a costs judge or a district judge of the High Court.

14.3.6.12 Agreeing costs

Rather than go through the detailed assessment procedure, it is always open to the parties to agree the figure for costs payable by one side to another. Very often, the parties will attempt to agree a figure for costs, and proceed to a detailed assessment only if they are unable to reach agreement.

14.3.6.13 Offers to settle a detailed assessment

Costs of a detailed assessment can be significant. Pursuant to PD 47, para 8.3, the paying party must state in an open letter accompanying the points of dispute what sum, if any, that party offers to pay in settlement of the total costs claimed. The paying party can also make an offer under Part 36. Similarly the receiving party can make an offer without prejudice save as to the costs of the detailed assessment proceedings.

14.3.6.14 Interim orders

The detailed assessment of costs procedure initially means that there will be some delay in the successful party receiving their costs from the unsuccessful party. Rule 44.3(8) of CPR 1998 allows the court at trial or on a later application to order an interim payment of part of these costs, and in *Mars UK Ltd v Teknowledge Ltd (No 2)* [1999] Masons CLR 322, Jacob J indicated that the court should make an order for the interim payment of costs in most cases.

14.3.7 Costs only proceedings

What if the parties to a dispute:

(a)   have reached an agreement on all issues (including which party is to pay the costs);

(b)   made or confirmed that agreement in writing;

(c)   but have failed to agree the amount of those costs; and

(d)   no proceedings have been started?

The answer is provided by r 46.14. Either party to the agreement may start proceedings by issuing a claim form in accordance with Part 8 (see **8.3**). The claim form must contain or be accompanied by the agreement or confirmation.

14.3.8 As a paying party, what should you look for in the opponent's bill of costs?

When scrutinising an opponent's bill of costs, consider the following:

(1) Check the scope of the costs order – are there any limits (see **14.3.2.6**)?

(2) What is the basis of assessment – standard or indemnity (see **14.3.3**)? Where standard, consider overall proportionality first and identify the correct tests (see **14.3.3.4**).

(3) What is the effect, if any, of any interim costs orders (see **10.3**)?

(4) Check the costs budgets/CMOs. Is there a 20% or more difference (see **14.3.2.5**)?

(5) As a rough guide, compare solicitors' hourly rates and counsels' fees with the summary assessment rates (see **14.3.3.7** and **Appendix A(22)**).

(6) Check compliance with PD 47 as to content. Are all items claimed allowable (see **14.3.7**)?

CHAPTER 15

ENFORCEMENT OF MONEY JUDGMENTS

15.1	Introduction	281
15.2	Interest on judgment debts	282
15.3	Tracing the other party	282
15.4	Investigating the judgment debtor's means	283
15.5	Methods of enforcement	284
15.6	Summary of key points	291

> **LEARNING OUTCOMES**
>
> After reading this chapter you will have learned:
>
> - when interest is payable on a judgment debt
> - how to investigate a judgment debtor's means
> - when different types of enforcement methods should be used
> - how to conduct each type of enforcement
> - how to enforce a judgment outside England and Wales.

15.1 INTRODUCTION

Once a party has obtained a judgment against their opponent, the opponent will usually pay the amount they have been ordered to pay without any further action being necessary. If, however, the losing party fails to pay the amount they have been ordered to pay, the winning party will have to take steps to enforce the judgment debt. The judgment will not be enforced by the court automatically – unless the winning party takes enforcement action, they will not receive the money that they were awarded. The winning party will have to consider with their solicitor the best method of enforcing payment.

Where the opponent is not insured, the question of enforcement is one which should be considered before proceedings are ever commenced, because it is obviously not worth obtaining a judgment against a party who does not have the means to pay. The solicitor should be satisfied that the defendant's whereabouts are known, that prima facie they have the means to pay the amount in issue, and that they have assets which can be taken from them to enforce payment if necessary.

It is often overlooked, but a client may be able to claim under the terms of their own household insurance for an unsatisfied judgment in respect of personal injury, damage to property or a fatal accident claim. The precise terms of the client's policy will have to be closely examined.

15.1.1 Enforcing a judgment against partnership property

Practice Direction 70, para 6A.1 provides that a judgment made against a partnership may be enforced against any property of the partnership within the jurisdiction.

A judgment against a partnership may also be enforced against any person who is not a limited partner and who either:

(a)   acknowledged service of the claim form as a partner; or

(b)   having been served as a partner with the claim form, failed to acknowledge service of it;

(c)   admitted in their statement of case that they are or were a partner at a material time; or

(d)   was found by the court to have been a partner at a material time.

Can proceedings be taken against partnership property for a partner's separate judgment debt? Yes – see s 23 of the Partnership Act 1890.

15.2   INTEREST ON JUDGMENT DEBTS

15.2.1   High Court judgments

Under the Judgments Act 1838, interest accrues on all High Court judgments from the date judgment is pronounced. The current rate of interest is 8% pa. Where judgment is entered for damages to be assessed, interest begins to run from the date when damages are finally assessed or agreed (ie, the date of the final judgment). Interest on an order for the payment of costs runs from the date of the judgment, not from the date of the final costs certificate following a detailed assessment (see **14.2.8.2**). Therefore, interest is accruing on the costs before the paying party knows how much they have to pay in costs. They can alleviate the situation by making a payment on account of costs.

15.2.2   County Court judgments

Under s 74 of the CCA 1984, interest accrues on County Court judgments of £5,000 or more. The current rate of interest is 8% pa.

Where, under the terms of the judgment, payment is deferred, or to be in instalments, interest will not accrue until that date, or until an instalment falls due.

Where enforcement proceedings are taken, the judgment debt ceases to carry interest unless the enforcement proceedings fail to produce any payment, in which case interest will continue to accrue on the judgment debt as if the enforcement proceedings had never been issued. 'Enforcement proceedings' do not include an application for an order to obtain information from the judgment debtor (see **15.4.2**). If an attachment of earnings order is in force, interest does not accrue.

Care needs to be taken as regards interest in the County Court. If enforcement proceedings are taken and anything at all is recovered, the balance of the debt will become interest free.

When applying to enforce a judgment in the County Court, a party must supply a certificate setting out the amount of interest claimed, the sum on which it is claimed, the dates from and to which interest has accrued, and the rate of interest applied.

15.3   TRACING THE OTHER PARTY

There are a number of methods of enforcement available, but before commencing enforcement proceedings the other party's whereabouts need to be established. If the other party's whereabouts are not known, consideration should be given to employing an enquiry agent to trace them. If this is to be done, the enquiry agent should be given as much information as possible to assist their enquiries (eg, the other party's last known address, their last known employer, details of any known relatives). A limit should be placed on the costs that may be incurred by the enquiry agent, so that a disproportionate amount of money is not wasted in attempts to trace the defendant, which might be unsuccessful in the end. In practice, these enquiries are likely to have been made at the outset of the case, since there is little point in suing a defendant you cannot trace (see **15.1** above).

15.4   INVESTIGATING THE JUDGMENT DEBTOR'S MEANS

The next thing to consider is what assets the judgment debtor has, since the method of enforcement chosen will depend upon what type of assets are available to pay the judgment debt. The winning party may already have enough information about their opponent for a decision to be taken, otherwise further enquiries will have to be made.

There are two main ways to investigate the judgment debtor's assets: the winning party can either instruct an enquiry agent to make investigations; or they can apply to the court for an order to obtain information from the judgment debtor. However, do not forget that pre-action it is usual to make a bankruptcy search against an individual and a company search against a company (see **2.6.1.2**). Those should be updated now.

Can a person be compelled for examination as a judgment debtor if the only outstanding parts of the judgment against them are costs orders for sums which have yet to be agreed or determined by assessment, payment of those sums not yet having fallen due? Yes – see *W Nagel (a firm) v Pluczenik Diamond Company NV* [2019] EWHC 3126 (QB).

15.4.1   Instructing an enquiry agent

The enquiry agent should be given as much information as possible to assist their enquiries, and a limit should be placed on the amount of costs to be incurred, to avoid spending a disproportionate amount on these preliminary enquiries. Even so, this method of carrying out the investigations is likely to be more expensive than applying to the court for an order to obtain information from the judgment debtor. However, the enquiry agent may be able to discover assets which are not disclosed at the hearing, and may produce results more quickly, depending on the speed with which the hearing can take place at the court.

15.4.2   Obtaining information from judgment debtor (Part 71)

An order to obtain information from a judgment debtor is a court order requiring the judgment debtor to attend before an officer of the court to be examined on oath as to their means. The judgment creditor obtains the order by making an application without notice. The purpose of the order is to assist the judgment creditor in deciding on the most appropriate method for enforcing the judgment.

15.4.2.1   How to make the application – PD 71

(a)   The judgment creditor must complete and file an application notice in Form N316 if the debtor is an individual, and N316A if an officer of a company or other corporation is to be questioned. The application notice must contain a statement of truth.

(b)   Practice Direction 71, para 1 sets out the matters to be contained in the application notice. These include the name and address of the judgment debtor, the judgment or order the creditor is seeking to enforce and the amount presently owed. If the creditor wishes the examination to be conducted by a judge, this must be stated in the application notice, together with reasons. If the creditor wishes the debtor to bring any specific documents to court, these must be identified.

(c)   Rules 71.3 and 71.4 set out the procedure for service of the order and for payment of the judgment debtor's travelling expenses to court.

15.4.2.2   The hearing

(a)   The hearing will usually take place in the County Court hearing centre for the area where the debtor resides or carries on business.

(b)   The examination will be conducted by an officer of the court, or a judge if considered appropriate or if requested by the judgment creditor.

(c)   Where the examination is conducted by a court officer, standard questions to be asked are set out in Appendices A and B to PD 71. The judgment creditor may attend the hearing and ask questions themselves. Alternatively they can ask the officer of the court to ask additional questions, provided these were set out in the application notice. The officer will make a written record of the responses given by the debtor, who will be invited to read and sign it at the end of the hearing. If a solicitor attends the hearing, fixed costs may be awarded (r 45.8).

(d)   Where the hearing is to be conducted before a judge, the standard questions are not used. The questions will be asked by the judgment creditor and the hearing will be tape-recorded. The judge may make a summary assessment of costs at the end of the hearing (r 44.6).

(e)   If the debtor fails to attend court, or having attended court refuses to take an oath or affirm or answer questions, a committal order may be made against them (see *Vik v Deutsche Bank AG* [2018] EWCA Civ 2011).

15.5   METHODS OF ENFORCEMENT

There are four common methods of enforcement to choose from:

(a)   taking control of goods (ie, seizure and sale of the debtor's goods);

(b)   charging order (ie, a charge on the debtor's land or securities);

(c)   third party debt order (ie, an order requiring a third party who owes money to the debtor to pay it directly to the creditor);

(d)   attachment of earnings order (ie, an order requiring the debtor's employer to make deductions from their earnings and pay them to the creditor).

The solicitor must decide, in the light of the information they have obtained about the judgment debtor, which method of enforcement is most suitable.

Each method of enforcement mentioned is now considered in more detail.

15.5.1   Taking control of goods (Part 83)

This process allows an enforcement agent, for simplicity referred to as a High Court Enforcement Officer (HCEO) or enforcement officer (County Court), to seize and sell the debtor's personal goods to pay the judgment debt and costs, and the costs of enforcement. The items seized are sold by public auction. After deducting the expenses of sale, the judgment debt and costs are paid, and any surplus proceeds are returned to the debtor.

As a general rule the HCEO or enforcement officer cannot force entry to a debtor's home, although they may be able to break into business premises if there is no living accommodation attached and they believe the debtor's goods are inside. Second-hand furniture and electrical items are normally taken only if they are likely to sell well at auction. In addition to the usual contents of a home or business premises (although note certain items are exempt: see **15.5.1.4**), any money, banknotes, bills of exchange, promissory notes, bonds, specialties or securities for money belonging to the debtor can be taken.

15.5.1.1   Choice of court

High Court

A party who has obtained a judgment in the High Court may issue a writ of control in that court, regardless of the amount to be enforced.

County Court

Where a party has obtained judgment in the County Court, and the amount to be enforced is £5,000 or more, it must be enforced in the High Court unless the proceedings originated under the Consumer Credit Act 1974.

Where the sum to be enforced is less than £600, it must be enforced in a County Court.

In the case of County Court judgments of £600 or more but less than £5,000, the judgment creditor can choose whether to issue in the High Court or the County Court. If they choose to use the High Court, the County Court judgment must first be transferred to the High Court. The advantage of this is that interest then accrues on the judgment debt.

A party with a County Court judgment for £5,000 or more will be able to issue a part warrant in that court, for example where an instalment order or the final balance is less than £5,000.

To enforce in the County Court, the party must apply for a warrant of control.

15.5.1.2   Procedure in the High Court

(a)   The judgment creditor completes two copies of a writ of control and a praecipe for a writ of control.

(b)   The judgment creditor delivers these documents to the court office, together with the judgment and the costs officer's certificate where the enforcement relates to costs.

(c)   The court seals the writ and returns one copy of it to the judgment creditor.

(d)   The judgment creditor forwards the sealed copy writ to the HCEO for the county where the debtor resides or carries on business, to be executed.

15.5.1.3   Procedure in the County Court

(a)   The judgment creditor completes the form of request for a warrant of control.

(b)   The judgment creditor files this at the County Court hearing centre which serves the address where the goods are to be seized, together with the fee.

(c)   The warrant is executed by the enforcement officer of the County Court for the district where the debtor resides or carries on business.

15.5.1.4   Items exempt from seizure

Certain items cannot be seized. These are:

(a)   goods on hire or hire-purchase;

(b)   tools, books, telephones, computer equipment, vehicles and other items of equipment that are necessary to the debtor for use personally in their job, trade, profession, study or business, subject to a maximum aggregate value of £1,350;

(c)   clothing, bedding, furniture, household equipment and provisions that are reasonably required for satisfying the basic domestic needs of the debtor and their family.

'Necessary items' are items so essential to the debtor that, without them, they could not continue their existing job or business. This is not always clear-cut. For example, in *Brookes v Harris* [1995] 1 WLR 918, the defendant had a substantial collection of records, tapes and compact discs. The defendant was the presenter of musical programmes on radio and television, and it was held that their collection constituted tools of their trade and was therefore exempt from seizure.

Note that the necessary items exemption only applies to individuals and not to a judgment debtor that is a partnership, limited company, etc.

Further note that in *Hale v Watt*, LTL 11 March 2016, CA, it was held that a houseboat, even if used as a house, was not exempt from seizure under the regulations. Why? Because a vessel is a chattel and does not change its essential nature as a chattel once occupied. It is not exempt because the words 'necessary for basic domestic needs' in the regulations are qualified by the former words 'domestic appliances'.

Motor vehicles

It should be the exception rather than the rule that a debtor is allowed to retain a motor vehicle as a necessary item. It is for the debtor to satisfy the HCEO or enforcement officer that the vehicle is necessary to allow them to continue their job or business. The fact that a debtor claims to need a vehicle to get to and from their place of work should not by itself be considered grounds to exempt the vehicle. The HCEO or enforcement officer must be satisfied that no reasonable alternative is available.

Household items

Items such as stereo equipment, televisions, videos and DVD players are not considered to be necessary for satisfying the basic domestic needs of the debtor and their family.

Control may be taken of goods owned by the judgment debtor jointly with another person(s). This power is derived from the common law (see *Farrar v Beswick* (1836) 1 M & W 682), and in these circumstances the HCEO or enforcement officer will account to any joint owner(s) for their share of the proceeds of sale.

It is always helpful to inform the HCEO or enforcement officer of specific items that could be seized, for example tell them the make, type and registration number of the debtor's car.

See further the Taking Control of Goods Regulations 2013 (SI 2013/1894).

15.5.1.5   Controlled goods agreement

In practice, the debtor's goods are not usually removed immediately. The debtor and the HCEO or enforcement officer will enter into an agreement whereby the HCEO or enforcement officer agrees not to remove the goods at once and, in return, the debtor agrees not to dispose of them or permit them to be moved. This gives the debtor a further opportunity to pay the sum due, and they may apply for suspension of the writ or warrant. If this is granted, it means that the writ of control/warrant of control is suspended on condition that the debtor pays the sum due by specified instalments.

The HCEO or enforcement officer must not effect a forcible entry to any residential premises without a court warrant.

15.5.2   Charging order on land (Part 73)

A judgment creditor may apply to the court for an order charging the judgment debtor's land with the amount due under a judgment. A charging order can also be made in respect of land the debtor owns jointly with another person, in which case the order is a charge upon the debtor's beneficial interest, rather than upon the land itself.

15.5.2.1   Restrictions on making a charging order

Where a judgment debtor is required by the County Court or High Court order to pay a sum by instalments, can a charging order be made even though there has been no default in payment? Yes, but the court must take the lack of default into account in deciding whether or not to make the order. Note that an order for sale to enforce the charging order (see **15.5.2.4**) may not be made where there has been no default in the payment of instalments under a court order.

15.5.2.2   Registration of the charging order

Once a charging order has been made, it should be registered if possible.

If the judgment debtor is the sole owner of the land, the charging order can be registered at the Land Charges Department as an order affecting land if the title is unregistered, or at Land Registry as a notice if the land is registered.

Where the land is jointly owned, the debtor technically has an interest only in the proceeds of sale under the trust for sale, rather than an interest in the land itself. Therefore, in the case of unregistered land, the charging order is not registrable because it is not an order relating to land. In the case of registered land, the charging order can be protected by entry of a restriction on the register.

If the creditor does not know whether the land is registered, they should make an Index Map Search before applying for a charging order. If the creditor does not know whether the land is jointly owned, they should make a search of the title in the case of registered land, again before applying for a charging order.

15.5.2.3 Notice

Whether or not the charging order is registered, written notice of it should be given to any prior chargee(s) to prevent any tacking of later advances. A search may be necessary at Land Registry (registered land) or the Land Charges Department (unregistered land) to discover the existence of prior incumbrances.

Once this has been done, the creditor has security for the debt, but they still have not obtained the sum due.

15.5.2.4 Order for sale

In order to obtain the money, the creditor can apply to the court for an order for sale of the land charged. The judgment will then be satisfied out of the proceeds of sale.

15.5.2.5 Choice of court

Where an application for a charging order is to be made to the County Court, it must be made to the County Court Money Claims Centre, unless the application is for a charging order over an interest in a fund in court.

15.5.2.6 Procedure

(a) The judgment creditor must file an application notice in the prescribed form (N379) containing the information specified in PD 73, para 1.2. This includes details of the judgment debt, the land over which the charging order is sought, and the names and addresses of any other person on whom the interim order will be served. This will include parties with a prior charge over the property. The application notice must be verified by a statement of truth.

(b) The judgment creditor must also file a draft interim charging order.

(c) In most cases the application will be dealt with without a hearing by a court officer who will either make the interim order or refer the application to a judge, who can either make the interim order or refer the application to the debtor's home court for a hearing to determine if a final order should be made.

(d) Copies of the interim charging order, the application notice and any documents filed in support of it must be served by the judgment creditor within 21 days of the date of the interim charging order. The judgment creditor must file a certificate of service within 28 days of the date of the interim order. If the application has been transferred out of the County Court Money Claims Centre, service must be effected not less than 21 days before the date of the hearing.

(e) A request for a review of the court officer's decision by a District Judge can be made within 14 days of service of the decision.

(f) The interim charging order should be registered either at the Land Charges Department, or at HM Land Registry if registration is possible.

(g) If any person objects to the making of a final charging order, they must file and serve written evidence stating the grounds of objection within 28 days of service of the interim charging order.

(h) If an objection is received or at the expiry of the period allowed for serving notice of objection, the court will transfer the application to the judgment debtor's home court, which will then fix a hearing date and serve notice of the hearing on the judgment creditor and debtor.

(i)   At the hearing the court can make a final charging order confirming the interim charging order, discharge the interim order, deal with issues in dispute between the parties or direct a trial of any such issues – r 73.8. Fixed costs are payable on the making of the final order – r 45.8.

(j)   The creditor now has a charge on the debtor's land which can be enforced by an order for sale of the property.

(k)   In order to enforce the charging order by sale of the property charged, fresh proceedings would have to be commenced, normally in the same court that made the final charging order.

15.5.3   Charging order on securities (Part 73)

A judgment creditor may also obtain a charging order on a judgment debtor's beneficial interest in certain specified securities. These include UK government stock; stock of any body, other than a building society, incorporated within England and Wales; stock of any body incorporated outside England and Wales or of any State or territory outside the UK, being stock registered in a register kept at any place within England and Wales; and units of any unit trust in respect of which a register of the unit holders is kept at any place within England and Wales. In this context, 'stock' includes shares, debentures and any securities of the body concerned, whether or not constituting a charge on the assets of that body.

Note that the court may order that the charge extends to any dividend that is payable.

The procedure is similar to the procedure for obtaining a charging order on land. An application notice in the prescribed form (N380) must be completed.

15.5.4   Third party debt orders (Part 72)

Where a third party owes money to the judgment debtor, the court can make an order requiring that third party to pay the judgment creditor the whole of that debt, or such part of it as is sufficient to satisfy the judgment debt and costs. This is known as a third party debt order. A bank account or building society account is often the target of such an order. Judgment debtors who are self-employed often have trade debts due to them. It is possible to find out at the hearing of an order to obtain information from a judgment debtor what these debts are and then to take these proceedings accordingly.

The debt must belong to the judgment debtor solely and beneficially. An order cannot be made against joint debts unless all the people owed the debt are joint judgment debtors. This means, for example, that the judgment creditor cannot get an order over the husband and wife's joint bank account if the husband alone is the judgment debtor (*Hirschon v Evans* [1938] 2 KB 801).

Also note that the third party must be within the jurisdiction. Likewise, the court normally has no jurisdiction to make a third party debt order if the relevant debt to be attached is situated outside England and Wales (see *Hardy Exploration & Production (India) Inc v Government of India* [2018] EWHC 1916 (Comm)).

15.5.4.1   Choice of court

The application should be issued in the County Court hearing centre that made the order being enforced or, if the proceedings have been transferred to a different court, in that court.

If the judgment was made at the County Court Money Claims Centre and the proceedings have not been sent or transferred to a County Court hearing centre, the application should be filed at the County Court hearing centre for the district in which the judgment debtor resides or carries on business.

15.5.4.2 Procedure

(a) The application is made without notice on the prescribed form (N349). The contents of the application notice are set out in para 1 of PD 72.

(b) The hearing will be before a judge. If successful, the judge will make an interim third party debt order. They will also fix a hearing for the final third party debt order, which will be not less than 28 days after the interim order is made.

(c) The interim order is served on the third party not less than 21 days before the hearing date for the final order, and on the judgment debtor within seven days of service on the third party. In practice the interim order will be served as soon as possible as it will not be effective and binding on the third party until served.

(d) Once the third party has been served with the interim order the third party is required to disclose certain information to the judgment creditor pursuant to r 72.6(2).

(e) Before the third party debt order is made final the court will consider any objections made by either the third party, or the judgment debtor or anyone else claiming to have a prior interest in the money: see r 72.8.

(f) Once a final order is made the third party is required to pay the money held to the judgment creditor. Fixed enforcement costs are also payable – r 45.6.

(g) The rules enable the judgment debtor to apply for the order to be discharged in cases of hardship.

15.5.4.3 Third party debt proceedings against a deposit taking institution

A bank or building society account, provided it is in credit, is an ideal target for third party debt proceedings. Once the interim third party debt order is served, the account is frozen (up to the amount outstanding under the judgment or order) and, upon the making of the final order, the money in the account (or amount required to discharge the judgment) must be paid over to the judgment creditor.

There are some special points to bear in mind when third party debt proceedings are taken against a deposit taking institution, namely:

(a) The application notice must state (if known) the name and address of the branch at which the account is believed to be held and the account number.

(b) An order against a building society or credit union cannot require payment which would reduce the balance in the account to a sum less than £1.

(c) Before paying the judgment creditor, the deposit taking institution is entitled to deduct a prescribed sum in respect of administration expenses.

15.5.4.4 Costs

The costs of a successful application are fixed (see Part 45) and may be retained by the judgment creditor out of the money recovered from the third party in priority to the judgment debt. If the application is unsuccessful the court will exercise its discretion in deciding what, if any, costs order to make.

15.5.5 Attachment of earnings (Part 89)

An attachment of earnings order is an order which compels the judgment debtor's employer to make regular deductions from the debtor's earnings and pay them into court. The High Court has no power to make an attachment of earnings order. If the judgment has been obtained in the High Court, the proceedings will have to be transferred to the County Court before this method of enforcement can be used. The amount remaining due under the judgment must be at least £50 for an attachment of earnings application to be made. Also, the debtor must be employed; an order cannot be made if the debtor is unemployed or self-employed. The judgment debtor must be an individual. An order cannot be made against a partnership or corporate judgment debtor.

15.5.5.1 Procedure

(a)   The judgment creditor completes the prescribed application form and files it at the County Court Money Claims Centre.

(b)   The court informs the debtor of the application and requires them either to pay the sum due, or to file a statement of means in the prescribed form. The court will make a diary entry for return of the form.

(c)   If the debtor returns the form, the court staff will make an attachment of earnings order. The court staff will fix the repayment rate by applying certain guidelines which they are given to the debtor's statement of means. If necessary, the application will be referred to the district judge. The order will specify the 'normal deduction rate' and the 'protected earnings rate'. The latter is the amount which the debtor is allowed to retain out of their earnings in any event. If their earnings for a particular week are equal to or less than the 'protected earnings rate', the creditor will receive nothing that week.

(d)   The order will be sent to the parties, and to the debtor's employer, with instructions to deduct the amount ordered from the debtor's pay and forward it to the court. The employer is entitled to deduct a small additional sum in respect of their administrative costs for each deduction which they make in accordance with the order.

(e)   If either party objects to the order that has been made, he can apply for the matter to be reconsidered by the district judge. If such an application is made, there will be a hearing before the district judge. In the meantime, the employer will be required to make deductions as ordered unless and until the order is varied.

(f)   If the debtor informs the court that they are unemployed or self-employed, the application will be dismissed.

(g)   If the debtor does not respond to the initial notice sent to them by the court, an order to produce a statement of means will be served on them personally by the court bailiff. This order is automatically issued by the court. If the creditor has provided the name and address of the debtor's employer, the employer will also be contacted at this stage for a statement of earnings.

(h)   If the debtor still does not respond when the order is served on them by the court bailiff, the court will automatically issue a notice to show cause. This will be served on the debtor by the court bailiff, and it will give notice of a hearing before the district judge which the debtor is required to attend. Failure to attend will lead to their committal to prison.

15.5.6 Insolvency

15.5.6.1 Bankruptcy

Where the judgment debt is for £5,000 or more, the judgment creditor may decide to petition for bankruptcy of the judgment debtor. However, they will not be able to do this if they have already registered a charging order because they are then in the position of a secured creditor, and a secured creditor cannot petition for bankruptcy unless they give up their security.

Bankruptcy procedure is not dealt with in detail here (for more detail, please refer to **Business Law and Practice**). Briefly, the first step is for the judgment creditor to serve on the judgment debtor a statutory demand in the prescribed form, unless execution has been levied and remains unsatisfied, in whole or in part, in which case there is no need for a statutory demand. Three weeks after service of the statutory demand, the petitioner may file the bankruptcy petition. In addition, an affidavit is required to verify the truth of the petition. The court will issue the petition indorsed with the date and place of hearing. The petition must be served on the debtor at least 14 days before the hearing. At the hearing, the judgment creditor must prove that the debt is still outstanding, and the court will usually then make a bankruptcy order, although the petition may be dismissed, stayed or adjourned. If a bankruptcy order is made, all the debtor's property vests in the trustee in bankruptcy.

15.5.6.2 Winding up

If the judgment debtor is a company, the judgment creditor may consider winding up the company if the debt is £750 or more. The procedure for this is very similar to the bankruptcy procedure for individuals.

15.6 SUMMARY OF KEY POINTS

When considering enforcement proceedings, take the following points into account:

(1) What is the most cost-efficient way of investigating the judgment debtor's means and enforcing the judgment?

(2) Taking control of the judgment debtor's goods. Where are the goods? What goods are exempt? Remember that goods owned with another person can be seized.

(3) A charging order may be made over any beneficial interest the judgment debtor has in land or certain specified securities.

(4) A third party debt order may only be made against a bank account or building society account in the sole name of the judgment debtor, or against a joint account where it is in the names of all the co-judgment debtors but no one else.

(5) A third party debt order may only be made against a trade debt owed solely to the judgment debtor, or against a joint debt where it is owed to all the co-judgment debtors but no one else.

(6) Is the judgment debtor employed so that an attachment of earnings order might be made?

Court Forms, Protocols and Guidelines

A(1)   Forms N1 and N1A – Claim Form and Notes for Claimant

A(2)   Form N1C – Notes for Defendant on Replying to the Claim Form

A(3)   Form N9, including Forms N9A–N9D – Response Pack

A(4)   Form N215 – Certificate of Service

A(5)   Form N218 – Notice of Service on Partner

A(6)   Form N266 – Notice to Admit Facts

A(7)   Form N181 – Directions Questionnaire

A(8)   Appendix to Part 28

A(9)   Precedent H – Costs Budget and Guidance Notes

A(10)   Precedent R – Budget Discussion Report

A(11)   Form N263 – Disclosure Report

A(12)   Form N244 – Application Notice

A(13)   Form N260 – Statement of Costs for Summary Assessment

A(14)   Form N242A – Offer to Settle

A(15)   Form N170 – Pre-trial Checklist

A(16)   Form N252 – Notice of Commencement of Assessment of Bill of Costs

A(17)   Precedent S – Bill of Costs

A(18)   Precedent G – Points of Dispute

A(19)   Practice Direction – Pre-action Conduct and Protocols

A(20)   Professional Negligence Pre-action Protocol

A(21)   Guidance for the Instruction of Experts in Civil Claims 2014

A(22)   Guideline figures for the Summary Assessment of Costs

A(23)   Precedent T – Variation of Costs Budget

A(24)   Precedent Q – Model Form of Breakdown of the Costs

A(1)   Forms N1 and N1A – Claim Form and Notes for Claimant

Claim Form

In the

Fee Account no.	
Help with Fees - **Ref no.** (if applicable)	H W F – ☐☐☐ – ☐☐

For court use only

Claim no.	
Issue date	

You may be able to issue your claim online which may save time and money. Go to www.moneyclaim.gov.uk to find out more.

SEAL

Claimant(s) name(s) and address(es) including postcode

Defendant(s) name and address(es) including postcode

Brief details of claim

Value

You must indicate your preferred County Court Hearing Centre for hearings here *(see notes for guidance)*

Defendant's name and address for service including postcode

	£
Amount claimed	
Court fee	
Legal representative's costs	
Total amount	

For further details of the courts www.gov.uk/find-court-tribunal.
When corresponding with the Court, please address forms or letters to the Manager and always quote the claim number.

N1 Claim form (CPR Part 7) (10.21)   © Crown Copyright 2021

	Claim No.	

Does, or will, your claim include any issues under the Human Rights Act 1998?   ☐ Yes   ☐ No

Particulars of Claim (attached)(to follow)

Statement of Truth

I understand that proceedings for contempt of court may be brought against anyone who makes, or causes to be made, a false statement in a document verified by a statement of truth without an honest belief in its truth.

☐ **I believe** that the facts stated in this particulars of claim are true.

☐ **The Claimant** believes that the facts stated this particulars of claim are true. **I am authorised** by the claimant to sign this statement.

Signature

☐ Claimant

☐ Litigation friend (where judgment creditor is a child or a patient)

☐ Claimant's legal representative (as defined by CPR 2.3(1))

Date

Day	Month	Year

Full name

Name of claimant's legal representative's firm

If signing on behalf of firm or company give position or office held

Claimant's or claimant's legal representative's address to which documents should be sent.

Building and street

Second line of address

Town or city

County (optional)

Postcode

If applicable

Phone number

Fax phone number

DX number

Your Ref.

Email

Notes for claimant on completing a claim form

Before you begin completing the claim form

- You must think about whether alternative dispute resolution (ADR) is a better way to reach an agreement before going to court. The leaflet 'I'm in a dispute - What can I do?' explains more about ADR and how you can attempt to settle your claim.

- Please read all the notes which follow the order in which information is required on the form.

- Before completing this form, consider whether you might prefer to issue online www.moneyclaim.gov.uk

- If you are filling in the claim form by hand, please use black ink and write in block capitals.

- Copy the completed claim form and the defendant's notes for guidance so that you have one copy for yourself, one copy for the court and one copy for each defendant.

- If the claim is for a sum of money then you must send it to the County Court Money Claims Centre, PO Box 527, Salford, M5 0BY.

- If it is a High Court claim or is a claim for anything other than money you should send the form and the fee to a court office.

- You can get additional help in completing this form from the Money Claim helpdesk - phone 0300 1231372. If you need legal advice you should contact a solicitor or a Citizens Advice Bureau.

Further information may be obtained from Direct.gov.uk or from the court in a series of free leaflets.

Notes on completing the claim form

Heading

You must fill in the heading of the form to indicate the name of the court where you want the claim to be issued. If you want the claim to proceed in the County Court and it is for money only, you must enter 'County Court Money Claims Centre'.

The claimant and defendant

As the person issuing the claim, you are called the 'claimant'. Please enter your name and address. The person you are suing is called the 'defendant'. Please enter their name.

You must provide the following information about yourself and the defendant according to the capacity in which you are suing and in which the defendant is being sued.

Providing information about yourself and the defendant

full address including postcode

You should provide the address including postcode for yourself and the defendant or its equivalent in any European Economic Area (EEA) state (if applicable).

If an address does not have a postcode you will need to ask the judge for permission to serve the claim with this information missing. There is no additional fee for this, but the court will not allow your claim to be served without the postcode, unless you have permission from the judge.

When suing or being sued as:-

an individual:

You must enter his or her full name where known, including the title (for example, Mr., Mrs., Ms., Dr.) and residential address postcode and telephone number. Where the defendant is a proprietor of a business, a partner in a firm or an individual sued in the name of a club or other unincorporated association, the address for service should be the usual or last known place of residence or principal place of business.

Where the individual is:

trading under another name

you must enter his or her full unabbreviated name where known, and the title by which he or she is known and the full name under which he or she is trading, for example, 'Mr. John Smith trading as Smith's Groceries'.

suing or being sued in a representative capacity you must say what that capacity is for example, 'Mr Joe Bloggs as the representative of Mrs Sharon Bloggs (deceased)'.

suing or being sued in the name of a club or other unincorporated association add the words 'suing/ sued on behalf of' followed by the name of the club or other unincorporated association.

an unincorporated business - a firm

In the case of a partnership (other than a limited liability partnership) you must enter the full name of the business followed by the suffix 'a firm' for example, 'Bandbox - a firm' and an address including postcode for service. This may either be one of the partners residential addresses or the principal or last known place of business of the firm.

a company registered in England and Wales or a Limited Liability Partnership

In the case of a registered company or limited liability partnership, enter the full name followed by the appropriate suffix (for example, 'Ltd.') and an address including postcode which is either the company's registered office or any place of business in the UK that has a connection with the claim e.g. where goods were bought.

a corporation (other than a company)
enter the full name of the corporation and any suffix and the address including postcode in the UK which is either its principal office or any other place where the corporation carries on activities and which has a connection with the claim.

an overseas company (defined by s744 of the Companies Act 1985)
enter the company's full name and any suffix if appropriate and address including postcode. The address must either be the registered address under s691 of the Act or the address of the place of business having a connection with the claim

under 18 write '(a child by Mr Joe Bloggs his litigation friend)' after the name. If the child is conducting proceedings on their own behalf write '(a child)' after the child's name.

a patient within the meaning of the Mental Health Act 1983 write '(by Mr Joe Bloggs his litigation friend)' after the patient's name.

Brief details of claim
You must set out under **this** heading:
- a concise statement of the nature of your claim
- the remedy you are seeking e.g. payment of money

Value
If you are claiming a **fixed amount of money** (a 'specified amount') write the amount in the box at the bottom right-hand corner of the claim form against 'amount claimed'.

If you are not claiming a fixed amount of money (an 'unspecified amount') under 'Value' write "I expect to recover" followed by whichever of the following applies to your claim:
- 'not more than £10,000' **or**
- 'more than £10,000 but not more than £25,000' **or**
- 'more than £25,000'

If you are **not able** to put a value on your claim, write 'I cannot say how much I expect to recover'.

Personal injuries
If your claim is for 'not more than £5,000' and includes a claim for personal injuries, you must also write 'My claim includes a claim for personal injuries and the amount I expect to recover as damages for pain, suffering and loss of amenity is' followed by either:
- 'not more than £1,000' **or**
- 'more than £1,000'

Housing disrepair
If your claim is for 'not more than £5,000' and includes a claim for housing disrepair relating to residential premises, you must also write 'My claim includes a claim against my landlord for housing disrepair relating to residential premises. The cost of the repairs or other work is estimated to be' followed by either:
- 'not more than £1,000' **or**
- 'more than £1,000'

If within this claim, you are making a claim for other damages, you must also write:

'I expect to recover as damages' followed by either:
- 'not more than £1,000' **or**
- 'more than £1,000'

Preferred Court
You may be asked to send this claim to a court centre that is not convenient for you to attend. If attendance is required the court will transfer the case to make it easier for one or all of the parties to attend. A list of County Courts hearing centre can be found at: hmctscourtfinder.justice.gov.uk State your preferred court where indicated. The court will take it into account if transfer is required.

Defendant's name and address
Enter in this box the title, full names, address and postcode of the defendant receiving the claim form (one claim form for each defendant). If the defendant is to be served outside the UK or any other state of the EEA, you may need to obtain the court's permission.

Legal representative's costs
These fixed sums may only be claimed where a legal representative has been instructed to make the claim on your behalf.

Particulars of claim
You must set out under this heading:
- a concise statement of the facts on which you rely
- a statement (if applicable) that you are seeking aggravated damages or exemplary damages
- details of any interest which you are claiming
- any other matters required for your type of claim as set out in the relevant practice direction

Statement of truth
This must be signed by you, your solicitor or your litigation friend.

Where the claimant is a registered company or a corporation the claim must be signed by either the director or other officer of the company or (in the case of a corporation) the mayor, chairman, president or town clerk.

Address for documents
Please note that the service regulation provides that cross-border service by any direct means including fax or email is not permitted within the EEA.

A(2)   Form N1C – Notes for Defendant on Replying to the Claim Form

Notes for defendant on replying to the claim form

Please read these notes carefully - they will help you decide what to do about this claim.
Further information may be obtained from the court in a series of free leaflets

- If this claim form was received with the particulars of claim completed or attached, you must reply within 14 days of the date it was served on you. If the words 'particulars of claim to follow' are written in the particulars of claim box, you should not reply until after you are served with the particulars of claim (which should be no more than 14 days after you received the claim form). If the claim was sent by post, the date of service is taken as the second business day after posting (see post mark). If the claim form was delivered or left at your address the date of deemed service will be the second business day (see CPR rule 6.14) after delivery.

- You may either:
  - pay the total amount i.e. the amount claimed, the court fee, and solicitor's costs (if any)
  - admit that you owe all or part of the claim and ask for time to pay, or
  - dispute the claim

- If you do not reply, judgment may be entered against you.

- The notes below tell you what to do.

- The response pack will tell you which forms to use for your reply. (The pack will accompany the particulars of claim if they are served after the claim form).

- Court staff can help you complete the forms of reply and tell you about court procedures. But they cannot give legal advice. If you need legal advice, for example about the likely success of disputing the claim, you should contact a solicitor or a Citizens Advice Bureau immediately.

Registration of Judgments: If this claim results in a judgment against you, details will be entered in a public register, the Register of Judgments, Orders and Fines. They will then be passed to credit reference agencies which will then supply them to credit grantors and others seeking information on your financial standing. **This will make it difficult for you to get credit.** A list of credit reference agencies is available from Registry Trust Ltd, 173/175 Cleveland Street, London W1T 6QR.

Costs and Interest: Additional costs and interest may be added to the amount claimed on the front of the claim form if judgment is entered against you. In a county court, if judgment is for £5,000 or more, or is in respect of a debt which attracts contractual or statutory interest for late payment, the claimant may be entitled to further interest.

Your response and what happens next

How to pay

Do not bring any payments to the court - they will not be accepted.

When making payments to the claimant, quote the claimant's reference (if any) and the claim number.

Make sure that you keep records and can account for any payments made. Proof may be required if there is any disagreement. It is not safe to send cash unless you use registered post.

Admitting the Claim

Claim for specified amount

If you admit all the claim, take or send the money, including the court fee, any interest and costs, to the claimant at the address given for payment on the claim form, within 14 days.

If you admit all the claim and you are asking for time to pay, complete Form N9A and send it to the claimant at the address given for payment on the claim form, within 14 days. The claimant will decide whether to accept your proposal for payment. If it is accepted, the claimant may request the court to enter judgment

against you and you will be sent an order to pay. If your offer is not accepted, the court will decide how you should pay.

If you admit only part of the claim, complete Form N9A and Form N9B (see 'Disputing the Claim' overleaf) and send them to the court within 14 days. The claimant will decide whether to accept your part admission. If it is accepted, the claimant may request the court to enter judgment against you and the court will send you an order to pay. If your part admission is not accepted, the case will proceed as a defended claim.

Claim for unspecified amount

If you admit liability for the whole claim but do not make an offer to satisfy the claim, complete Form N9C and send it to the court within 14 days. A copy will be sent to the claimant who may request the court to enter judgment against you for an amount to be decided by the court, and costs. The court will enter judgment and refer the court file to a judge for directions for management of the case. You and the claimant will be sent a copy of the court's order.

If you admit liability for the claim and offer an amount of money to satisfy the claim, complete Form N9C and send it to the court within 14 days. The claimant will be sent a copy and asked if the offer is acceptable. The claimant must reply to the court within 14 days and send you a copy. If a reply is not received, the claim will be stayed. If the amount you have offered is **accepted -**

- the claimant may request the court to enter judgment against you for that amount.
- if you have requested time to pay which is not accepted by the claimant, the rate of payment will be decided by the court.

If your offer in satisfaction is **not accepted -**

- the claimant may request the court to enter judgment against you for an amount to be decided by the court, and costs; and
- the court will enter judgment and refer the court file to a judge for directions for management of the case. You and the claimant will be sent a copy of the court's order.

Disputing the claim

If you are being sued as an individual for a specified amount of money and you dispute the claim, the claim may be transferred to a local court i.e. the one nearest to or where you live or carry on business if different from the court where the claim was issued.

If you need longer than 14 days to prepare your defence or to contest the court's jurisdiction to try the claim, complete the Acknowledgment of Service form and send it to the court within 14 days. This will allow you 28 days from the date of service of the particulars of claim to file your defence or make an application to contest the court's jurisdiction. The court will tell the claimant that your Acknowledgment of Service has been received.

If the case proceeds as a defended claim, you and the claimant will be sent a Directions Questionnaire. You will be told the date by which it must be returned to the court. The information you give on the form will help a judge decide whether your case should be dealt with in the small claims track, fast track or multi-track. After a judge has considered the completed questionnaires, you will be sent a notice of allocation setting out the judge's decision. The notice will tell you the track to which the claim has been allocated and what you have to do to prepare for the hearing or trial. **Leaflets telling you more about the tracks are available from the court office.**

Claim for specified amount
If you wish to dispute the full amount claimed or wish to claim against the claimant (a counterclaim), complete Form N9B and send it to the court within 14 days.

If you admit part of the claim, complete the Defence Form N9B <u>and</u> the Admission Form N9A and send them both to the court within 14 days. The claimant will decide whether to accept your part admission in satisfaction of the claim (see under 'Admitting the Claim - specified amount'). If the claimant does not accept the amount you have admitted, the case will proceed as a defended claim.

If you dispute the claim because you have already paid it, complete Form N9B and send it to the court within 14 days. The claimant will have to decide whether to proceed with the claim or withdraw it and notify the court and you within 28 days. If the claimant wishes to proceed, the case will proceed as a defended claim.

Claim for unspecified amount/return of goods/non-money claims

If you dispute the claim or wish to claim against the claimant (counterclaim), complete Form N9D and send it to the court within 14 days.

Personal injuries claims:
If the claim is for personal injuries and the claimant has attached a medical report to the particulars of claim, in your defence you should state whether you:

- agree with the report **or**
- dispute all or part of the report **and** give your reasons for doing so **or**
- neither agree nor dispute the report **or** have no knowledge of the report

Where you have obtained your own medical report, you should attach it to your defence.

If the claim is for personal injuries and the claimant has attached a schedule of past and future expenses and losses, in your defence you must state which of the items you:

- agree **or**
- dispute **and** supply alternative figures where appropriate **or**
- neither agree nor dispute or have no knowledge of.

Address where notices can be sent

This must be either the business address of your solicitor or European Lawyer or your own residential or business address within the UK or in any other European Economic Area state.

Statement of truth

This must be signed by you, by your solicitor or your litigation friend, as appropriate.

Where the defendant **is a registered company or a corporation** the response must be signed by either the director, treasurer, secretary, chief executive, manager or other officer of the company **or** (in the case of a corporation) the mayor, chairman, president or town clerk.

A(3)   Form N9, including Forms N9A–N9D – Response Pack

Response pack

You should read the 'notes for defendant' attached to the claim form which will tell you when and where to send the forms.

Included in this pack are:

- either **Admission Form N9A** (if the claim is for a specified amount)
- or **Admission Form N9C** (if the claim is for an unspecified amount or is not a claim for money)

- either **Defence and Counterclaim Form N9B** (if the claim is for a specified amount)
- or **Defence and Counterclaim Form N9D** (if the claim is for an unspecified amount or is not a claim for money)

- **Acknowledgment of service** (see below)

	Complete
If you admit the claim or the amount claimed and/or you want time to pay	the admission form
If you admit part of the claim	the admission form and the defence form
If you dispute the whole claim or wish to make a claim (a counterclaim) against the claimant	the defence form
If you need 28 days (rather than 14) from the date of service to prepare your defence, or wish to contest the court's jurisdiction	the acknowledgment of service
If you do nothing, judgment may be entered against you	

Acknowledgment of service

Defendant's full name if different from the name given on the claim form

In the	
Claim No.	
Claimant (including ref.)	
Defendant	

Address to which documents about this claim should be sent (including reference if appropriate)

	If applicable
Telephone no.	
Fax no.	
DX no.	
Your ref.	

Postcode ☐☐☐☐ ☐☐☐☐

E-mail

Tick the appropriate box

1. I intend to defend all of this claim ☐

2. I intend to defend part of this claim ☐

3. I intend to contest jurisdiction ☐

(My) (Defendant's) date of birth is

☐☐ / ☐☐ / ☐☐☐☐

If you file an acknowledgment of service but do not file a defence within 28 days of the date of service of the claim form, or particulars of claim if served separately, judgment may be entered against you.

If you do not file an application to dispute the jurisdiction of the court within 14 days of the date of filing this acknowledgment of service, it will be assumed that you accept the court's jurisdiction and judgment may be entered against you.

If served outside the jurisdiction see CPR rule 6.35 and 6.37(5).

Signed

(Defendant) (Defendant's legal representative) (Litigation friend)

Position or office held (if signing on behalf of firm or company)

Date ☐☐ / ☐☐ / ☐☐☐☐

For further details of the courts www.gov.uk/find-court-tribunal. When corresponding with the Court, please address forms or letters to the Manager and always quote the claim number.

Admission (specified amount)

- You have a limited number of days to complete and return this form
- Before completing this form, please read the notes for guidance attached to the claim form

When to fill in this form

- You are admitting all of the claim **and** you are asking for time to pay; **or**
- You are admitting part of the claim. (You should also complete form N9B).

How to fill in this form

Individual

- Tick the correct boxes and give as much information as you can. Then sign and date the form. If necessary provide details on a separate sheet add the claim number and attach it to this form.
- Make your offer of payment in box 11 on the back of this form. If you make no offer the claimant will decide how much and when you should pay.

Organisation

- If you are not an individual, you should ensure you attach a financial statement showing your companies profit, loss, assets and liabilities to support any offer of payment made in box 11. Ensure you tick the correct box and complete sections 1, 9 (if applicable) and 12. If you are a Limited Company, the claimant is under no obligation to accept your offer.
- You can get help to complete this form at any County Court or Citizen Advice Bureau.

Where to send this form

- **If you admit the claim in full**
  Send the completed form to the **claimants address** shown on the claim form as one to which documents should be sent.
- **If you admit only part of the claim**
  Send the form **to the issuing court** at the address given on the claim form, together with the defence form (N9B).

How much of the claim do you admit?

- ☐ I admit the full amount claimed as shown on the claim form **or**
- ☐ I admit the amount of £ [   ]

1 Personal/Organisation details

Surname/
Organisation [   ]

Forename [   ]

☐ Mr   ☐ Mrs   ☐ Miss   ☐ Ms

☐ Married   ☐ Single   ☐ Other (specify) [   ]

Date of birth [D D M M Y Y Y Y]

Address [   ]

Phone no. [   ]

Name of court	
Claim No.	
Claimant (including ref.)	
Defendant	

2 Dependants *(people you look after financially)*

Number of children in each age group

☐ under 11   ☐ 11-15   ☐ 16-17   ☐ 18 & over

Other dependants *(give details)* [   ]

3 Employment

☐ **I am employed as a** [   ]

My employer is [   ]

Jobs other than main job *(give details)* [   ]

☐ **I am self employed as a** [   ]

Annual turnover is £ [   ]

☐ **I am not** in arrears with my national insurance contributions, income tax and VAT

☐ **I am** in arrears and I owe £ [   ]

Give details of:

(a) contracts and other work in hand [   ]

(b) any sums due for work done [   ]

☐ **I have been unemployed for** [   ] years [   ] months

☐ **I am a pensioner**

4 Bank account and savings

☐ **I have a bank account**

☐ The account is **in credit** by £ [   ]

☐ The account is **overdrawn** by £ [   ]

☐ **I have a savings or building society account**

The amount in the account is £ [   ]

5 Residence

I live in   ☐ my own house   ☐ lodgings

☐ my jointly owned house   ☐ council accommodation

☐ rented accommodation

6 Income

My usual take home pay *(including overtime, commission, bonuses etc.)*	£	per
Income support	£	per
Child benefit(s)	£	per
Other state benefit(s)	£	per
My pension(s)	£	per
Others living in my home give me	£	per

Other income *(give details below)*

	£	per
	£	per
	£	per
Total income	**£**	**per**

7 Expenses

(Do not include any payments made by other members of the household out of their own income)

I have regular expenses as follows:

Mortgage *(including second mortgage)*	£	per
Rent	£	per
Council tax	£	per
Gas	£	per
Electricity	£	per
Water charges	£	per
TV rental and licence	£	per
HP repayments	£	per
Mail order	£	per
Housekeeping, food, school meals	£	per
Travelling expenses	£	per
Children's clothing	£	per
Maintenance payments	£	per

Others *(not court orders or credit debts listed in boxes 9 and 10)*

	£	per
	£	per
	£	per
Total expenses	**£**	**per**

8 Priority debts

(This section is for arrears only. Do not include regular expenses listed in box 7.)

Rent arrears	£	per
Mortgage arrears	£	per
Council tax/Community Charge arrears	£	per
Water charges arrears	£	per
Fuel debts: Gas	£	per
Electricity	£	per
Other	£	per
Maintenance arrears	£	per

Others *(give details below)*

	£	per
	£	per
Total priority debts	**£**	**per**

9 Court orders

Court	Claim No.	£	per
		£	per
		£	per
		£	per
Total court order instalments		**£**	**per**

Of the payments above, I am behind with payments to *(please list)*

10 Credit debts

Loans and credit card debts *(please list)*

	£	per
	£	per
	£	per

Of the payments above, I am behind with payments to *(please list)*

11 Offer of payment

☐ I can pay the amount admitted on [   ]

or

☐ I can pay by monthly instalments of **£** [   ]

If you cannot pay immediately, please give brief reasons below

12 Declaration   I declare that the details I have given above are true to the best of my knowledge

Signed [   ]

Position or office held
(if signing on behalf of firm or company) [   ]

Date [   ]

Defence and Counterclaim
(specified amount)

- Fill in this form if you wish to dispute all or part of the claim and/or make a claim against the claimant (counterclaim).
- You have a limited number of days to complete and return this form to the court.
- Before completing this form, please read the notes for guidance attached to the claim form.
- Please ensure that all boxes at the top right of this form are completed. You can obtain the correct names and number from the claim form. The court cannot trace your case without this information.

How to fill in this form

- Complete sections 1 and 2. Tick the correct boxes and give the other details asked for.
- Set out your defence in section 3. If necessary continue on a separate piece of paper making sure that the claim number is clearly shown on it. In your defence you must state which allegations in the particulars of claim you deny and your reasons for doing so. **If you fail to deny an allegation it may be taken that you admit it.**

Name of court	
Claim No.	
Claimant (including ref.)	
Defendant	

- If you dispute only some of the allegations you must
  - specify which you admit and which you deny; and
  - give your own version of events if different from the claimant's.
- If you wish to make a claim against the claimant (a counterclaim) complete section 4.
- Complete and sign section 5 before sending this form to the court. Keep a copy of the claim form and this form.

---

1. How much of the claim do you dispute?

☐ I dispute the full amount claimed as shown on the claim form.

or

☐ I admit the amount of £ _____

If you dispute only part of the claim you must **either**:

- pay the amount admitted to the person named at the address for payment on the claim form (see How to Pay in the notes on the back of, or attached to, the claim form). Then send this defence to the court

or

- complete the admission form **and** this defence form and send them to the court.

☐ I paid the amount admitted on

or ☐☐ / ☐☐ / ☐☐☐☐

☐ I enclose the completed form of admission
(go to section 2)

---

2. Do you dispute this claim because you have already paid it? *Tick whichever applies*

☐ **No** *(go to section 3)*

☐ **Yes** I paid £ _____ to the claimant

on ☐☐ / ☐☐ / ☐☐☐☐
(before the claim form was issued)

Give details of where and how you paid it in the box below *(then go to section 5)*

---

3. Defence (If you need to continue on a separate sheet put the claim number in the top right hand corner.)

(continue over the page)

Claim No.	

Defence (continued)

4. If you wish to make a claim against the claimant (a counterclaim)

- To start your counterclaim, you will have to pay a fee. Court staff can tell you how much you have to pay.
- You may not be able to make a counterclaim where the claimant is the Crown (e.g. a Government Department). Ask at your local county court office for further information.

If your claim is for a specific sum of money, how much are you claiming? £

I enclose the counterclaim fee of £

My claim is for *(please specify nature of claim)*

What are your reasons for making the counterclaim?
If you need to continue on a separate sheet put the claim number in the top right hand corner.

5. Signed - To be signed by you or by your solicitor or litigation friend.

*(I believe) (The defendant believes) that the facts stated in this form are true.
*I am duly authorised by the defendant to sign this statement.

delete as appropriate

Position or office held
(If signing on behalf of firm or company)

Date ☐☐/☐☐/☐☐☐☐

Defendant's date of birth, if an individual ☐☐/☐☐/☐☐☐☐

Give an address to which notices about this case can be sent to you

	If applicable
	Telephone no.
	Fax no.
Postcode	DX no.

E-mail

Find out how HM Courts and Tribunals Service uses personal information you give them when you fill in a form:
https://www.gov.uk/government/organisations/hm-courts-and-tribunals-service/about/personal-information-charter

Admission (unspecified amount, non-money and return of goods claims)

- Before completing this form please read the notes for guidance attached to the claim form. If necessary provide details on a separate sheet, add the claim number and attach it to this form.
- If you are not an individual, you should ensure that you provide sufficient details about the assets and liabilities of your firm, company or corporation to support any offer of payment made.

In the	
Claim No.	
Claimant (including ref.)	
Defendant	

In non-money claims only

☐ I admit liability for the whole claim
(Complete section 11)

In return of goods cases only

Are the goods still in your possession?
☐ Yes   ☐ No

Part A Response to claim *(tick one box only)*

☐ I admit liability for the whole claim but want the court to decide the amount I should pay / value of the goods

OR

☐ I admit liability for the claim and offer to pay [   ] in satisfaction of the claim
(Complete part B and sections 1 - 11)

Part B How are you going to pay the amount you have admitted? *(tick one box only)*

☐ I offer to pay on (date) [   ]

OR

☐ I cannot pay the amount immediately because *(state reason)*

[   ]

AND

I offer to pay by instalments of £ [   ]
per (week)(month)
starting *(date)* [   ]

1 Personal details

Surname [   ]

Forename [   ]

☐Mr   ☐Mrs   ☐Miss   ☐Ms

☐Married   ☐Single   ☐Other *(specify)* [   ]

Date of birth [D D M M Y Y Y Y]

Address [   ]

Postcode [   ]

Tel. no. [   ]

2 Dependants *(people you look after financially)*

Number of children in each age group

under 11 [   ]   11-15 [   ]   16-17 [   ]   18 & over [   ]

Other dependants *(give details)* [   ]

3 Employment

☐ **I am employed as a** [   ]
My employer is [   ]

Jobs other than main job *(give details)* [   ]

☐ **I am self employed as a** [   ]
Annual turnover is.......................... £ [   ]

☐ **I am not** in arrears with my national insurance contributions, income tax and VAT

☐ **I am** in arrears and I owe........... £ [   ]

Give details of:
(a) contracts and other work in hand
(b) any sums due for work done
[   ]

☐ **I have been unemployed for** [years   months]

☐ **I am a pensioner**

4 Bank account and savings

☐ **I have a bank account**

☐ The account is in credit by........ £ [   ]

☐ The account is overdrawn by.... £ [   ]

☐ **I have a savings or building society account**

The amount in the account is.......... £ [   ]

5 Residence

I live in   ☐ my own property   ☐ lodgings
☐ jointly owned house   ☐ rented property
☐ council accommodation

6 Income

My usual take home pay *(including overtime, commission, bonuses etc)*	£		per
Income support	£		per
Child benefit(s)	£		per
Other state benefit(s)	£		per
My pension(s)	£		per
Others living in my home give me	£		per
Other income *(give details below)*			
	£		per
	£		per
	£		per
Total income	**£**		**per**

8 Priority debts *(This section is for arrears only. Do not include regular expenses listed in section 7)*

Rent arrears	£		per
Mortgage arrears	£		per
Council tax/Community Charge arrears	£		per
Water charges arrears	£		per
Fuel debts: Gas	£		per
Electricity	£		per
Other	£		per
Maintenance arrears	£		per
Others *(give details below)*			
	£		per
	£		per
Total priority debts	**£**		**per**

7 Expenses

(Do not include any payments made by other members of the household out of their own income)

I have regular expenses as follows:

Mortgate *(including second mortgage)*	£		per
Rent	£		per
Council tax	£		per
Gas	£		per
Electricity	£		per
Water charges	£		per
TV rental and licence	£		per
HP repayments	£		per
Mail order	£		per
Housekeeping, food, school meals	£		per
Travelling expenses	£		per
Children's clothing	£		per
Maintenance payments	£		per
Others *(not court orders or credit debts listed in sections 9 and 10)*			
	£		per
	£		per
	£		per
Total expenses	**£**		**per**

9 Court orders

Court	Claim No.	£	per

Total court order instalments	**£**	**per**

Of the payments above, I am behind with payments to *(please list)*

10 Credit debts

Loans and credit card debts *(please list)*

	£		per
	£		per
	£		per

Of the payments above, I am behind with payments to *(please list)*

11 Declaration   I declare that the details I have given above are true to the best of my knowledge

Signed

Position or office held *(if signing on behalf of firm or company)*

Date

Defence and Counterclaim
(unspecified amount, non-money and return of goods claims)

Name of court	
Claim No.	
Claimant (including ref.)	
Defendant	

- Fill in this form if you wish to dispute all or part of the claim and/or make a claim against the claimant (a counterclaim)
- You have a limited number of days to complete and return this form to the court.
- Before completing this form, please read the notes for guidance attached to the claim form.
- Please ensure that all the boxes at the top right of this form are completed. You can obtain the correct names and number from the claim form. The court cannot trace your case without this information.

How to fill in this form
- Set out your defence in section 1. If necessary continue on a separate piece of paper making sure that the claim number is clearly shown on it. In your defence you must state which allegations in the particulars of claim you deny and your reasons for doing so. If you fail to deny an allegation it may be taken that you admit it.
- If you dispute only some of the allegations you must
  - specify which you admit and which you deny; and
  - give your own version of events if different from the claimant's.
- If the claim is for money and you dispute the claimant's statement of value, you must say why and if possible give your own statement of value.

- If you wish to make a claim against the claimant (a counterclaim) complete section 2.
- Complete and sign section 3 before returning this form.

Where to send this form
- send or take this form immediately to the court at the address given on the claim form.
- Keep a copy of the claim form and the defence form.

Need help with your legal problems?
Community legal advice is a free confidential service, funded by legal aid. They can help you find the information and advice you need by putting you in touch with relevant agencies, helplines or local advice services. And if you are eligible for legal aid, the service can offer specialist legal advice over the telephone in cases involving: debt; housing; employment; benefits; and education
Call **0845 345 4 345** or **www.communitylegaladvice.org.uk**

1. Defence

(continue over the page)

Claim No.	

Defence (continued)

2. If you wish to make a claim against the claimant (a counterclaim)

- To start your counterclaim, you will have to pay a fee. Court staff can tell you how much you have to pay.
- You may not be able to make a counterclaim where the claimant is the Crown (e.g. a Government Department). Ask at your local county court office for further information.

If your claim is for a specific sum of money, how much are you claiming?   £

I enclose the counterclaim fee of   £

My claim is for *(please specify nature of claim)*

What are your reasons for making the counterclaim?
If you need to continue on a separate sheet put the claim number in the top right hand corner.

3. Signed - To be signed by you or by your solicitor or litigation friend.

*(I believe) (The defendant believes) that the facts stated in this form are true.
*I am duly authorised by the defendant to sign this statement.

*delete as appropriate

Position or office held
(If signing on behalf of firm or company)

Date ☐☐ / ☐☐ / ☐☐☐☐

Defendant's date of birth, if an individual ☐☐ / ☐☐ / ☐☐☐☐

Give an address to which notices about this case can be sent to you

	If applicable	
	Telephone no.	
	Fax no.	
Postcode	DX no.	

E-mail

A(4)   Form N215 – Certificate of Service

Certificate of service

Name of court	Claim No.

Name of Claimant

Name of Defendant

On what day did you serve? ☐☐/☐☐/☐☐☐☐

The date of service is ☐☐/☐☐/☐☐☐☐

What documents did you serve?
Please attach copies of the documents you have not already filed with the court.

On whom did you serve?
(If appropriate include their position e.g. partner, director).

How did you serve the documents?
(please tick the appropriate box)

☐ by first class post or other service which provides for delivery on the next business day

☐ by delivering to or leaving at a permitted place

☐ by personally handing it to or leaving it with (.................time left, where document is other than a claim form) *(please specify)*

☐ by other means permitted by the court *(please specify)*

☐ by Document Exchange

☐ by fax machine (.................time sent, where document is other than a claim form) *(you may want to enclose a copy of the transmission sheet)*

☐ by other electronic means (.................time sent, where document is other than a claim form) *(please specify)*

Give the address where service effected, include fax or DX number, e-mail address or other electronic identification

Being the   ☐ claimant's   ☐ defendant's
    ☐ solicitor's   ☐ litigation friend

☐ usual residence

☐ last known residence

☐ place of business

☐ principal place of business

☐ last known place of business

☐ last known principal place of business

☐ principal office of the partnership

☐ principal office of the corporation

☐ principal office of the company

☐ place of business of the partnership/company/ corporation within the jurisdiction with a connection to claim

☐ other *(please specify)*

I believe that the facts stated in this certificate are true.

Full name	

Signed		Position or office held	
(Claimant) (Defendant) ('s solicitor) ('s friend)		*(If signing on behalf of firm or company)*	

Date ☐☐/☐☐/☐☐☐☐

Rules relating to the service of documents are contained in Part 6 of the Civil Procedure Rules (www.justice.gov.uk) and you should refer to the rules for information.

Calculation of deemed day of service of a claim

A claim form served within the UK in accordance with Part 6 of the Civil Procedure rules is deemed to be served on the second business day after the claimant has completed the steps required by CPR 7.5(1).

Calculation of the deemed day of service of documents other than the claim form (CPR 6.26)

Method of service	Deemed day of service
First class post or other service which provides for delivery on the next business day	The second day after it was posted, left with, delivered to or collected by the relevant service provider provided that day is a business day; or if not, the next business day after that day
Document exchange	The second day after it was left with, delivered to or collected by the relevant service provider provided that day is a business day; or if not, the next business day after that day
Delivering the document to or leaving it at a permitted address	If it is delivered to or left at the permitted address on a business day before 4.30pm, on that day; or in any other case, on the next business day after that day
Fax	If the transmission of the fax is completed on a business day before 4.30pm, on that day; or in any other case, on the next business day after the day on which it was transmitted
Other electronic method	If the email or other electronic transmission is sent on a business day before 4.30pm, on that day; or in any other case, on the next business day after the day on which it was sent
Personal service	If the document is served personally before 4.30pm on a business day, it is served on that day; or in any other case, on the next business day after that day

In this context 'business day' means any day except Saturday, Sunday or a bank holiday; (under the Banking and Financial Dealings Act 1971 in the part of the UK where service is to take place) includes Good Friday and Christmas Day.

A(5)   Form N218 – Notice of Service on Partner

Notice of service on partner

In the	
Claim No.	
Claimant (including ref.)	
Defendant	

The (claim form) (particulars of claim) served with this notice (is) (are) served on you

(tick only one box)

☐   as a partner of the business

☐   as a person having control or management of the partnership business

☐   as both a partner and as a person having control or management of the partnership business

named in the claim form (particulars of claim).

Signed [   ]   **Date** [   ]

Claimant ('s solicitor)

A(6)   Form N266 – Notice to Admit Facts

Notice to admit facts

In the	
Claim No.	
Claimant (include Ref.)	
Defendant (include Ref.)	

I (We) give notice that you are requested to admit the following facts or part of case in this claim:

I (We) confirm that any admission of fact(s) or part of case will only be used in this claim.

Signed

(Claimant)(Defendant)('s Solicitor)

Position or office held
(If signing on behalf of firm or company)

Date

Admission of facts

I (We) admit the facts or part of case (set out above)(in the attached schedule) for the purposes of this claim only and on the basis that the admission will not be used on any other occasion or by any other person.

Signed

(Claimant)(Defendant)('s Solicitor)

Position or office held
(If signing on behalf of firm or company)

Date

The court office at

is open between 10 am and 4 pm Monday to Friday. Address all communication to the Court Manager quoting the claim number

N266 - w3 Notice to admit facts (4.99)   *Printed on behalf of The Court Service*

A(7)   Form N181 – Directions Questionnaire

Directions questionnaire
(Fast track and Multi-track)

In the	Claim No.

To be completed by, or on behalf of,

who is [1st][2nd][3rd][   ][Claimant][Defendant][Part 20 claimant] in this claim

---

You should note the date by which this questionnaire must be returned and the name of the court it should be returned to since this may be different from the court where the proceedings were issued.

If you have settled this claim (or if you settle it on a future date) and do not need to have it heard or tried, you must let the court know immediately.

If the claim is not settled, a judge will allocate it to an appropriate case management track. To help the judge choose the most just and cost-effective track, you must now complete the directions questionnaire.

You should write the claim number on any other documents you send with your directions questionnaire. Please ensure they are firmly attached to it.

A   Settlement

Notes

Under the Civil Procedure Rules parties should make every effort to settle their case before the hearing. This could be by discussion or negotiation (such as a roundtable meeting or settlement conference) or by a more formal process such as mediation. The court will want to know what steps have been taken. Settling the case early can save costs, including court hearing fees.

For legal representatives only

I confirm that I have explained to my client the need to try to settle; the options available; and the possibility of costs sanctions if they refuse to try to settle.

☐ I confirm

For all

Your answers to these questions may be considered by the court when it deals with the questions of costs: see Civil Procedure Rules Part 44.

1. Given that the rules require you to try to settle the claim before the hearing, do you want to attempt to settle at this stage?

☐ Yes   ☐ No

2. If Yes, do you want a one month stay?

☐ Yes   ☐ No

3. If you answered 'No' to question 1, please state below the reasons why you consider it inappropriate to try to settle the claim at this stage.

Reasons:

The court may order a stay, whether or not all the other parties to the claim agree. Even if you are requesting a stay, you must still complete the rest of the questionnaire.

More information about mediation, the fees charged and a directory of mediation providers is available online from www.civilmediation.justice.gov.uk This service provides members of the public and businesses with contact details for national civil and commercial mediation providers, all of whom are accredited by the Civil Mediation Council.

B Court

B1. (High Court only)

The claim has been issued in the High Court. Do you consider it should remain there? ☐ Yes ☐ No

If Yes, in which Division/List?

If No, in which County Court hearing centre would you prefer the case to be heard?

High Court cases are usually heard at the Royal Courts of Justice or certain Civil Trial Centres. Fast or multi-track trials may be dealt with at a Civil Trial Centre or at the court where the claim is proceeding.

B2. Trial (all cases)

Is there any reason why your claim needs to be heard at a court or hearing centre? ☐ Yes ☐ No

If Yes, say which court and why?

C Pre-action protocols

You are expected to comply fully with the relevant pre-action protocol.

Have you done so? ☐ Yes ☐ No

If you have not complied, or have only partially complied, please explain why.

Before any claim is started, the court expects you to have complied with the relevant pre-action protocol, and to have exchanged information and documents relevant to the claim to assist in settling it. To find out which protocol is relevant to your claim see: www.justice.gov.uk/guidance/courts-and-tribunals/courts/procedure-rules/civil/menus/protocol.htm

D Case management information

D1. Applications

Have you made any application(s) in this claim? ☐ Yes ☐ No

If Yes, what for? (e.g. summary judgment, add another party).

For hearing on ☐☐ / ☐☐ / ☐☐☐☐

D1. Applications

It is important for the court to know if you have already made any applications in the claim (or are about to issue one), what they are for and when they will be heard. The outcome of the applications may affect the case management directions the court gives.

D2. Track

If you have indicated in the proposed directions a track attached which would not be the normal track for the claim, please give brief reasons below for your choice.

D2. Track

The basic guide by which claims are normally allocated to a track is the amount in dispute, although other factors such as the complexity of the case will also be considered. Leaflet *EX305 – The Fast Track and the Multi-track*, explains this in greater detail.

D Case management information (continued)

D3. Disclosure of electronic documents (multi-track cases only)

If you are proposing that the claim be allocated to the multi-track:

1. Have you reached agreement, either using the Electronic Documents Questionnaire in Practice Direction 31B or otherwise, about the scope and extent of disclosure of electronic documents on each side? ☐ Yes ☐ No

2. If No, is such agreement likely? ☐ Yes ☐ No

3. If there is no agreement and no agreement is likely, what are the issues about disclosure of electronic documents which the court needs to address, and should they be dealt with at the Case Management Conference or at a separate hearing?

D4. Disclosure of non-electronic documents (all cases)

What directions are proposed for disclosure?

For all multi-track cases, except personal injury.

Have you filed and served a disclosure report (Form N263) (see Civil Procedure Rules Part 31). ☐ Yes ☐ No

Have you agreed a proposal in relation to disclosure that meets the overriding objective? ☐ Yes ☐ No

If Yes, please ensure this is contained within the proposed directions attached and specify the draft order number.

E Experts

Do you wish to use expert evidence at the trial or final hearing? ☐ Yes ☐ No

Have you already copied any experts' report(s) to the other party(ies)? ☐ None yet obtained
☐ Yes ☐ No

Do you consider the case suitable for a single joint expert in any field? ☐ Yes ☐ No

E Experts (continued)

Please list any single joint experts you propose to use and any other experts you wish to rely on. Identify single joint experts with the initials 'SJ' after their name(s). Please provide justification of your proposal and an estimate of costs.

Expert's name	Field of expertise (e.g. orthopaedic surgeon, surveyor, engineer)	Justification for expert and estimate of costs

F Witnesses

Which witnesses of fact do you intend to call at the trial or final hearing including, if appropriate, yourself?

Witness name	Witness to which facts

G Trial or Final Hearing

How long do you estimate the trial or final hearing will take?

☐ **less than one day**

☐ **one day**

☐ **more than one day**

[ ] Hrs

[ ] State number of days

Give the best estimate you can of the time that the court will need to decide this case. If, later you have any reason to shorten or lengthen this estimate you should let the court know immediately.

Are there any days within the next 12 months when you, an expert or an essential witness will not be able to attend court for trial or final hearing?

You should only enter those dates when you, your expert(s) or essential witnesses will not be available to attend court because of holiday or other commitments.

If Yes, please give details

Name	Dates not available

You should notify the court immediately if any of these dates change.

4

H   Costs

Do not complete this section if:

1) you do not have a legal representative acting for you

2) the case is subject to fixed costs

If your claim is likely to be allocated to the Multi-Track form Precedent H must be filed at in accordance with CPR 3.13.

I confirm Precedent H is attached. ☐

I   Other information

Do you intend to make any applications in the future?   ☐ Yes   ☐ No

If Yes, what for?

In the space below, set out any other information you consider will help the judge to manage the claim.

J Directions

You must attempt to agree proposed directions with all other parties. **Whether agreed or not a draft of the order for directions which you seek must accompany this form.**

All proposed directions for multi-track cases must be based on the directions at www.justice.gov.uk/courts/procedure-rules/civil

All proposed directions for fast track cases must be based on CPR Part 28.

Signature

Date

[Legal Representative for the][1ˢᵗ][2ⁿᵈ][3ʳᵈ][   ]
[Claimant][Defendant][Part 20 claimant]

Please enter your name, reference number and full postal address including details of telephone, DX, fax or e-mail

		If applicable
	Telephone no.	
	Fax no.	
	DX no.	
Postcode	Your ref.	

E-mail	

A(8) Appendix to Part 28

Fast Track Standard Directions

Further Statements of Case

The   must file a   and serve a copy on   no later than   .

Requests for Further Information

Any request for clarification or further information based on another party's statement of case shall be served no later than

[Any such request shall be dealt with no later than   ].

Disclosure of Documents

[No disclosure of documents is required]

[[Each party] [The   ] shall give [to the   ] [to every other party] standard disclosure of documents [relating to   ] by serving copies together with a disclosure statement no later than   ]

[Disclosure shall take place as follows:

[Each party shall give standard discovery to every other party by list]

[Disclosure is limited to [standard] [disclosure by the   to the   ] [of documents relating to damage] [the following documents   ]

[The latest date for delivery of the lists is   ]

[The latest date for service of any request to inspect or for a copy of a document is   ]]

Witnesses of Fact

Each party shall serve on every other party the witness statements of all witnesses of fact on whom he intends to rely.

There shall be simultaneous exchange of such statements no later than   .

Expert Evidence

[No expert evidence being necessary, no party has permission to call or rely on expert evidence].

[On it appearing to the court that expert evidence is necessary on the issue of [   ] and that that evidence should be given by the report of a single expert instructed jointly by the parties, the   shall no later than   inform the court whether or not such an expert has been instructed].

[The expert evidence on the issue of   shall be limited to a single expert jointly instructed by the parties.

If the parties cannot agree by   who that expert is to be and about the payment of his fees either party may apply for further directions.

Unless the parties agree in writing or the court orders otherwise, the fees and expenses of such an expert shall be paid to him [by the parties equally] [   ] and be limited to £   .

[The report of the expert shall be filed at the court no later than   ].

[No party shall be entitled to recover by way of costs from any other party more than £   for the fees or   expenses of an expert].

The parties shall exchange reports setting out the substance of any expert evidence on which they intend to rely.

[The exchange shall take place simultaneously no later than   ].

[The   shall serve his report(s) no later than the   and the   shall serve his reports no later than the   ].

[The exchange of reports relating to [causation] [   ] shall take place simultaneously no later than   .
The   shall serve his report(s) relating to [damage] [   ] no later than   and the   shall
serve his reports relating to it no later than   ].

Reports shall be agreed if possible no later than [days after service] [   ].

[If the reports are not agreed within that time there shall be a without prejudice discussion between the
relevant experts no later than   to identify the issues between them and to reach agreement if possible.

The experts shall prepare for the court a statement of the issues on which they agree and on which they
disagree with a summary of their reasons, and that statement shall be filed with the court [no later than
     ] [with] [no later than the date for filing] [the pre-trial check list].

[Each party has permission to use [   ] as expert witness(es) to give [oral] evidence [in the form of a
report] at the trial in the field of   provided that the substance of the evidence to be given has been
disclosed as above and has not been agreed].

[Each party has permission to use in evidence   experts' report(s) [and the court will consider when the
claim is listed for trial whether expert oral evidence will be allowed].]

Questions to Experts

The time for service on another party of any question addressed to an expert instructed by that party is not
later than   days after service of that expert's report.

Any such question shall be answered within   days of service.

Requests for Information etc.

Each party shall serve any request for clarification or further information based on any document disclosed or
statement served by another party no later than   days after disclosure or service.

Any such request shall be dealt with within   days of service.

Documents to be filed with Pre-trial Check Lists

The parties must file with their pre-trial check lists copies of [their experts' reports] [witness statements]
[replies to requests for further information]

Dates for filing Pre-trial Checklists and the Trial

Each party must file a completed pre-trial check list no later than   .

The trial of this case will take place [on   ] [on a date to be fixed between   and   ].

Directions following filing of Pre-trial Check List

Expert Evidence

The parties have permission to rely at the trial on expert evidence as follows:

The claimant   Oral evidence

                      Written evidence

The defendant: Oral evidence

                      Written evidence

Trial Timetable

The time allowed for the trial is

[The timetable for the trial may be agreed by the parties, subject to the approval of the trial judge].

[The timetable for the trial (subject to the approval of the trial judge) will be that   ].

[The evidence in chief for each party will be contained in witness statements and reports, the time allowed for
cross-examination by the defendant is limited to   and the time allowed for cross-examination by the
claimant is limited to   ].

[The time allowed for the claimant's evidence is   . The time allowed for the defendant's evidence is   ].

The time allowed for the submissions on behalf of each party is   .

The remainder of the time allowed for the trial (being   ) is reserved for the judge to consider and give the judgment and to deal with costs].

Trial Bundle etc

The claimant shall lodge an indexed bundle of documents contained in a ring binder and with each page clearly numbered at the court not more than 7 days and not less than 3 days before the start of the trial.

[A case summary (which should not exceed 250 words) outlining the matters still in issue, and referring where appropriate to the relevant documents shall be included in the bundle for the assistance of the judge in reading the papers before the trial].

[The parties shall seek to agree the contents of the trial bundle and the case summary].

Settlement

Each party must inform the court immediately if the claim is settled whether or not it is then possible to file a draft consent order to give effect to their agreement.

A(9)   Precedent H – Costs Budget and Guidance Notes

	A	B	C	D	E	F
	Costs budget of [Claimant / Defendant] dated [ ]					page 1
		Incurred		Estimated		
	Work done / to be done	Disbs (£)	Time costs (£)	Disbs (£)	Time costs (£)	Total (£)
1						
2	In the:	xxx				
3	Parties:	yyy				
4	Claim number:	zzz				
7	Pre-action costs	£0.00	£0.00			£0.00
8	Issue /statements of case	£0.00	£0.00	£0.00	£0.00	£0.00
9	CMC	£0.00	£0.00	£0.00	£0.00	£0.00
10	Disclosure	£0.00	£0.00	£0.00	£0.00	£0.00
11	Witness statements	£0.00	£0.00	£0.00	£0.00	£0.00
12	Expert reports	£0.00	£0.00	£0.00	£0.00	£0.00
13	PTR			£0.00	£0.00	£0.00
14	Trial preparation			£0.00	£0.00	£0.00
15	Trial			£0.00	£0.00	£0.00
16	ADR / Settlement discussions	£0.00	£0.00	£0.00	£0.00	£0.00
17	Contingent cost A:			£0.00	£0.00	£0.00
18	Contingent cost B:			£0.00	£0.00	£0.00
19						
20						
21	incurred costs and estimated costs)	£0.00	£0.00	£0.00	£0.00	£0.00
22	This estimate <u>excludes</u> VAT (if applicable), success fees and ATE insurance premiums (if applicable), costs of detailed assessment, costs of any appeals, costs of enforcing any judgment and [complete as appropriate]					
23	Approved budget					£-
24	Budget drafting	1% of approved budget or £1,000				£-
25	Budget process	2%				£-
26	**Statement of Truth**					
27	*This budget is a fair and accurate statement of incurred and estimated costs which it would be reasonable and proportionate for my client to incur in this litigation.*					
28	Signed					
29	Position					
30	**version 24/02/2016 Appendix A**					

page 2

In the:		xxx
Parties:		yyy
Claim number:		zzz

			PRE-ACTION COSTS				ISSUE / STATEMENTS OF CASE				CMC			
		RATE (per hour)	Incurred costs £	Estimated costs Hours	Estimated costs £	TOTAL £	Incurred costs £	Estimated costs Hours	Estimated costs £	TOTAL £	Incurred costs £	Estimated costs Hours	Estimated costs £	TOTAL £
Fee earner time														
1	grade		£0.00			£0.00	£0.00	0.00	£0.00	£0.00	£0.00	0.00	£0.00	£0.00
2	grade		£0.00			£0.00	£0.00	0.00	£0.00	£0.00	£0.00	0.00	£0.00	£0.00
3	grade		£0.00			£0.00	£0.00	0.00	£0.00	£0.00	£0.00	0.00	£0.00	£0.00
4	grade		£0.00			£0.00	£0.00	0.00	£0.00	£0.00	£0.00	0.00	£0.00	£0.00
5	Time value (1 to 4)		£0.00			£0.00	£0.00	0.00	£0.00	£0.00	£0.00	0.00	£0.00	£0.00
	Expert's costs													
6	Fees		£0.00			£0.00	£0.00		£0.00	£0.00	£0.00		£0.00	£0.00
7	Disbursements		£0.00			£0.00	£0.00		£0.00	£0.00	£0.00		£0.00	£0.00
	Counsel fees													
8	Leading counsel		£0.00			£0.00	£0.00		£0.00	£0.00	£0.00		£0.00	£0.00
9	Junior counsel		£0.00			£0.00	£0.00		£0.00	£0.00	£0.00		£0.00	£0.00
10	Court fees		£0.00			£0.00	£0.00		£0.00	£0.00	£0.00		£0.00	£0.00
11	Other Disbursements		£0.00			£0.00	£0.00		£0.00	£0.00	£0.00		£0.00	£0.00
13	**Disbursements (6 to 11)**		£0.00			£0.00	£0.00		£0.00	£0.00	£0.00		£0.00	£0.00
14	Total		£0.00			£0.00	£0.00		£0.00	£0.00	£0.00		£0.00	£0.00

Assumptions: Issue / statements of case.

Assumptions: CMC:

page 3

				xxx
In the:				
Parties:				yyy
Claim number:				zzz

DISCLOSURE

WITNESS STATEMENTS

		RATE (per hour)	Incurred costs	Estimated costs		TOTAL	Incurred costs	Estimated costs		TOTAL
			£	Hours	£		£	Hours	£	
	Fee earner time									
1	grade	£0.00	£0.00	0.00	£0.00	£0.00	£0.00	0.00	£0.00	£0.00
2	grade	£0.00	£0.00	0.00	£0.00	£0.00	£0.00	0.00	£0.00	£0.00
3	grade	£0.00	£0.00	0.00	£0.00	£0.00	£0.00	0.00	£0.00	£0.00
4	grade	£0.00	£0.00	0.00	£0.00	£0.00	£0.00	0.00	£0.00	£0.00
5	Time value (1 to 4)		£0.00	0.00	£0.00	£0.00	£0.00	0.00	£0.00	£0.00
	Expert's costs									
6	Fees		£0.00		£0.00	£0.00	£0.00		£0.00	£0.00
7	Disbursements		£0.00		£0.00	£0.00	£0.00		£0.00	£0.00
	Counsel fees									
8	Leading counsel		£0.00		£0.00	£0.00	£0.00		£0.00	£0.00
9	Junior counsel		£0.00		£0.00	£0.00	£0.00		£0.00	£0.00
10	Court fees		£0.00		£0.00	£0.00	£0.00		£0.00	£0.00
11	Other Disbursements		£0.00		£0.00	£0.00	£0.00		£0.00	£0.00
13	Total Disbursements (6 to 11)		£0.00		£0.00	£0.00	£0.00		£0.00	£0.00
14	Total (5 + 13)		£0.00		£0.00	£0.00	£0.00		£0.00	£0.00

Assumptions: disclosure.

Assumptions: witness evidence.

	AM	AN	AO	AP	AQ	AR	AS	AT	AU	AV	AW	AX	AY
1													
2		In the:		xxx									
3		Parties:		yyy									
4		Claim number:		zzz									
5				EXPERT REPORTS (see separate breakdown for expert fees)				EXPERT FEE SUMMARY					
6			RATE (per hour)	Incurred costs	Estimated costs		TOTAL	Drafting note: Completing this summary will populate totals for fees in table on left.					
7				£	Hours	£			past	future	future	future	Total
8		Fee earner time						Type	incurred	report	conference	joint stms	Total future
9	1	grade	£0.00	£0.00	0.00	£0.00	£0.00 xx	£-	£-	£-	£-	£-	£-
10	2	grade	£0.00	£0.00	0.00	£0.00	£0.00 xx	£-	£-	£-	£-	£-	£-
11	3	grade	£0.00	£0.00	0.00	£0.00	£0.00 xx	£-	£-	£-	£-	£-	£-
12	4	grade	£0.00	£0.00	0.00	£0.00	£0.00 xx	£-	£-	£-	£-	£-	£-
13	5	Time value (1 to 4)		£0.00	0.00	£0.00	£0.00 xx	£-	£-	£-	£-	£-	£-
14		Expert's costs											
15	6	Fees		£0.00		£0.00	£0.00 xx	£-	£-	£-	£-	£-	£-
16	7	Disbursements		£0.00		£0.00	£0.00 xx	£-	£-	£-	£-	£-	£-
17		Counsel fees											
18	8	Leading counsel		£0.00		£0.00	£0.00 xx	£-	£-	£-	£-	£-	£-
19	9	Junior counsel		£0.00		£0.00	£0.00 xx	£-	£-	£-	£-	£-	£-
20	10	Court fees		£0.00		£0.00	£0.00 xx	£-	£-	£-	£-	£-	£-
21	11	Other Disbursements		£0.00		£0.00	£0.00 xx	£-	£-	£-	£-	£-	£-
22	13	Total Disbursements (6 to 11)		£0.00		£0.00	£0.00 Sub total	£-	£-	£-	£-	£-	£-
23	14	Total (5 + 13)		£0.00		£0.00	£0.00 Total expert fees (past and future)						£0.00
24				Assumptions: expert evidence.									
25													
26													
27													
28													
29													
30													

	AZ	BA	BB	BC	BD	BE	BF	BG	BH	BI	BJ	BK	BL	BM	BN	BO	BP
1																	page 5
2		In the:			xxx												
3		Parties:			yyy												
4		Claim number:			zzz												

PTR — Estimated costs / TOTAL

TRIAL PREPARATION — Estimated costs / TOTAL

		RATE (per hour)		PTR Hours	Estimated costs £	TOTAL £					Trial prep Hours	Estimated costs £	TOTAL £			
7	time															
8																
9	1 grade	£0.00		0.00	£0.00	£0.00					0.00	£0.00	£0.00			
10	2 grade	£0.00		0.00	£0.00	£0.00					0.00	£0.00	£0.00			
11	3 grade	£0.00		0.00	£0.00	£0.00					0.00	£0.00	£0.00			
12	4 grade	£0.00		0.00	£0.00	£0.00					0.00	£0.00	£0.00			
13	5 to 4)	£0.00		0.00	£0.00	£0.00					0.00	£0.00	£0.00			
14	Expert's costs															
15	6 Fees				£0.00	£0.00						£0.00	£0.00			
16	7 Disbursements				£0.00	£0.00						£0.00	£0.00			
17	Counsel fees															
18	8 Leading counsel				£0.00	£0.00						£0.00	£0.00			
19	9 Junior counsel				£0.00	£0.00						£0.00	£0.00			
20	10 Court fees				£0.00	£0.00						£0.00	£0.00			
21	11 Other Disbursements				£0.00	£0.00						£0.00	£0.00			
22	13 Total Disbursements (6 to 11)				£0.00	£0.00						£0.00	£0.00			
23	14 Total (5 + 13)				£0.00	£0.00						£0.00	£0.00			

Assumptions:PTR.

Assumptions:Trial prep.

	BQ	BR	BS	BT	BU	BV	BW	BX	BY	BZ	CA	CB	CC	CD	CE
1															page 6
2		In the:		xxx											
3		Parties:		yyy											
4		Claim number:		zzz											

TRIAL

SETTLEMENT / ADR

			RATE (per hour)	TRIAL — Estimated costs		TRIAL — TOTAL	SETTLEMENT / ADR — Incurred costs	SETTLEMENT / ADR — Estimated costs		SETTLEMENT / ADR — TOTAL
				Hours	£		£	Hours	£	
8		Fee earner time								
9	1		£0.00	0.00	£0.00	£0.00	£0.00	0.00	£0.00	£0.00
10	2		£0.00	0.00	£0.00	£0.00	£0.00	0.00	£0.00	£0.00
11	3		£0.00	0.00	£0.00	£0.00	£0.00	0.00	£0.00	£0.00
12	4		£0.00	0.00	£0.00	£0.00	£0.00	0.00	£0.00	£0.00
13	5	4)		0.00	£0.00	£0.00	£0.00	0.00	£0.00	£0.00
14		Expert's costs								
15	6	Fees			£0.00	£0.00			£0.00	£0.00
16	7	Disbursements			£0.00	£0.00			£0.00	£0.00
17		Counsel fees								
18	8	Leading counsel			£0.00	£0.00			£0.00	£0.00
19	9	Junior counsel			£0.00	£0.00			£0.00	£0.00
20	10	Court fees			£0.00	£0.00			£0.00	£0.00
21	11	Other Disbursements			£0.00	£0.00			£0.00	£0.00
22	13	Total Disbursements (6 to 11)			£0.00	£0.00	£0.00		£0.00	£0.00
23	14	Total (5 + 13)			£0.00	£0.00	£0.00		£0.00	£0.00

Assumptions: Trial.

Assumptions: Settlement / ADR.

	In the:	xxx
	Parties:	yyy
	Claim number:	zzz

		CONTINGENT COST A: [explain in assumptions box below]			CONTINGENT COST B: [explain in assumptions box below]		
	RATE (per hour)	Estimated costs		TOTAL	Estimated costs		TOTAL
		Hours	£		Hours	£	
Fee earner time							
1	£0.00	0.00	£0.00	£0.00	0.00	£0.00	£0.00
2	£0.00	0.00	£0.00	£0.00	0.00	£0.00	£0.00
3	£0.00	0.00	£0.00	£0.00	0.00	£0.00	£0.00
4	£0.00	0.00	£0.00	£0.00	0.00	£0.00	£0.00
5 4)		0.00	£0.00	£0.00	0.00	£0.00	£0.00
Expert's costs							
6 Fees			£0.00	£0.00		£0.00	£0.00
7 Disbursements			£0.00	£0.00		£0.00	£0.00
Counsel fees							
8 Leading counsel			£0.00	£0.00		£0.00	£0.00
9 Junior counsel			£0.00	£0.00		£0.00	£0.00
10 Court fees			£0.00	£0.00		£0.00	£0.00
11 Other Disbursements			£0.00	£0.00		£0.00	£0.00
13 Total Disbursements (6 to 11)			£0.00	£0.00		£0.00	£0.00
14 Total (5 + 13)			£0.00	£0.00		£0.00	£0.00

£0.00

Assumptions : CONTINGENT COST A.

Assumptions: CONTINGENT COST B

UPDATED:
pursuant to decisions of the Civil Procedure Rule Committee on 09-11-18
followed by the inclusion of a new paragraph 10 at its meeting on 05-04-19
to support the changes within the 109th PD Update which came into effect on 01-10-19

GUIDANCE NOTES ON PRECEDENT H

1. Where the monetary value of the case is less than £50,000 [or the costs claimed are less than £25,000] the parties must only use the first page of Precedent H.

2. Save in exceptional circumstances, the parties are not expected to lodge any documents other than Precedent H and the budget discussion report. Both are available in Excel format on the MOJ website with PD 3E. If the Excel format precedent on the MOJ website is used, the calculation on page one will calculate the totals automatically and the phase totals are linked to this page also.

3. This is the form on which you should set out your budget of budgeted costs in accordance with CPR Part 3 and Practice Direction 3E. In deciding the reasonable and proportionate costs of each phase of the budget the court will have regard to the factors set out at Civil Procedure Rules 44.3(5) and 44.4(3) including a consideration of where and the circumstances in which the work was done as opposed to where the case is heard.

4. This table identifies where within the budget form the various items of work, **in so far as they are required by the circumstances of your case**, should be included. The time estimated may have to be justified on the budget hearing along with the grade of fee earner doing the work.

5. Allowance must be made in each phase for advising the client, taking instructions and corresponding with the other party/parties and the court in respect of matters falling within that phase.

6. The 'contingent cost' sections of this form should be used for **anticipated costs** which do not fall within the main categories set out in this form. Examples might be the trial of preliminary issues, applications to amend, applications for disclosure against third parties or (in libel cases) applications re meaning. Only include costs which are more likely than not to be incurred. **Costs which are not anticipated** but which become necessary later are dealt with in paragraph 7.6 of PD3E.

7. Any party may apply to the court if it considers that another party is behaving oppressively in seeking to cause the applicant to spend money disproportionately on costs and the court will grant such relief as may be appropriate.

8. Assumptions:

   a. The assumptions that are reflected in this guidance document are **not** to be repeated. Include only those assumptions that **significantly** impact on the level of costs claimed such as the duration of the proceedings, the number of experts and witnesses or the number of interlocutory applications envisaged. Brief details only are required in the box beneath each phase. Additional documents are not encouraged and, where they are disregarded by the court, the cost of preparation may be disallowed, and additional documents should be included only where necessary.

1

UPDATED:
pursuant to decisions of the Civil Procedure Rule Committee on 09-11-18
followed by the inclusion of a new paragraph 10 at its meeting on 05-04-19
to support the changes within the 109th PD Update which came into effect on 01-10-19

b. Written assumptions are not normally required by the Court in cases where the parties are only required to lodge the first page.

9. Budget preparation: the time spent in preparing the budget and associated material must **not** be claimed in the draft budget under any phase. The permitted figure will be inserted once the final budget figure has been approved by the court.

10. Definition of budgeted and incurred costs: see CPR 3.15 and PD3E para 7.4.
    a. Incurred costs are all costs incurred up to and including the date of the first costs management order, unless otherwise ordered.
    b. Budgeted costs are all costs to be incurred after the date of the first costs management order.

Phase	Includes	Does NOT include
Pre-action	• Pre-Action Protocol correspondence • Investigating the merits of the claim and advising client • Settlement discussions, advising on settlement and Part 36 offers • All other steps taken and advice given pre action	• Any work already incurred in relation to any other phase of the budget
Issue/statements of case	• Preparation of Claim Form • Issue and service of proceedings • Preparation of Particulars of Claim, Defence, Reply, including taking instructions, instructing counsel and any necessary investigation • Considering opposing statements of case and advising client • Part 18 requests (request and answer) • Any conferences with counsel primarily relating to statements of case • Updating schedules and counter schedules of loss • Amendments to statements of case	
CMC	• Completion of DQs • Arranging a CMC • Reviewing opponent's budget • Correspondence with opponent to agree directions and budgets, where possible • Preparation for, and attendance at, the CMC	• Preparation of costs budget for first CMC (this will be inserted in the approved budget)

2

UPDATED:
pursuant to decisions of the Civil Procedure Rule Committee on 09-11-18
followed by the inclusion of a new paragraph 10 at its meeting on 05-04-19
to support the changes within the 109th PD Update which came into effect on 01-10-19

	• Finalising the order • Any further CMC that is built into the proposed directions order	
Disclosure	• Obtaining documents from client and advising on disclosure obligations • Reviewing documents for disclosure, preparing disclosure report or questionnaire response and list • Inspection • Reviewing opponent's list and documents, undertaking any appropriate investigations • Correspondence between parties about the scope of disclosure and queries arising • Consulting counsel, so far as appropriate, in relation to disclosure	• Applications for specific disclosure • Applications and requests for third party disclosure
Witness Statements	• Identifying witnesses • Obtaining statements • Preparing witness summaries Consulting counsel, so far as appropriate, about witness • statements • Reviewing opponent's statements and undertaking any appropriate • investigations • Applications for witness summaries	• Arranging for witnesses to attend trial (include in trial preparation)
Expert Reports	• Identifying and engaging suitable expert(s) • Reviewing draft and approving • report(s) • Dealing with follow-up questions of experts • Considering opposing experts' reports Any conferences with counsel primarily relating to expert evidence Meetings of experts (preparing agenda etc.)	• Obtaining permission to adduce expert evidence (include in CMC or a separate application) Arranging for experts to attend trial (include in trial preparation)
PTR	• Bundle • Preparation of updated costs budgets and reviewing opponent's budget Preparing and agreeing chronology, case summary and dramatis personae	• Assembling and/or copying the bundle (this is not fee earners' work).

UPDATED:
pursuant to decisions of the Civil Procedure Rule Committee on 09-11-18
followed by the inclusion of a new paragraph 10 at its meeting on 05-04-19
to support the changes within the 109th PD Update which came into effect on 01-10-19

	(if ordered and not already prepared earlier in case) • Completing and filing pre-trial checklists • Correspondence with opponent to agree directions and costs budgets, if possible • Preparation for and attendance at the PTR	
Trial Preparation	• Trial bundles • Witness summonses, and arranging • for witnesses to attend trial Any final factual investigations Supplemental disclosure and statements(if required) • Counsel's brief fee • Agreeing brief fee • Any pre-trial conferences and advice from counsel • Pre-trial liaison with witnesses	• Assembling and/or copying the trial bundle (this is not fee earners' work) • Counsel's refreshers
Trial	• Solicitors' attendance at trial • All conferences and other activity outside court hours during the trial Attendance on witnesses during the trial • Counsel's trial refreshers • Dealing with draft judgment and • related applications	• Preparation for trial • Counsel's brief fee for trial (include in trial preparation)
ADR/Settlement	• Any conferences and advice from counsel in relation to settlement • Work directed to settlement negotiations and meetings between the parties and any other ADR (including mediation), to include Part 36 and other offers and advising the client • Approval of settlement if needed • Drafting settlement agreement or • Tomlin order • Advice to the client on settlement (excluding advice included in the pre action phase)	

A(10)   Precedent R – Budget Discussion Report

Precedent R : Budget discussion report.

Party:	C/D etc
Court:	Name
Case Number	Number

Budgeted costs for: C/D/etc CCMC Date xx/xx/xxxx

X
Y
Z

Phase	Incurred costs	Budgeted costs : claimed			Budgeted costs : offered			Paying party comments on offers made	Order	Judge's comments / sums allowed	
	Incurred	Claimed	Time £	Disbs £	Offered	Time £	Disbs £		Budgeted costs	Judge Time (hours)	Judge Disbs
Pre action costs	£0.00	na	na	na	£0.00	na	na	na	£0.00		
Issue / stm of case	£0.00	£0.00			£0.00				£0.00		
CMC	£0.00	£0.00			£0.00				£0.00		
Disclosure	£0.00	£0.00			£0.00				£0.00		
Witness stms	£0.00	£0.00			£0.00				£0.00		
Experts reports	£0.00	£0.00			£0.00				£0.00		
PTR	na	£0.00			£0.00				£0.00		
Trial preparation	na	£0.00			£0.00				£0.00		
Trial	na	£0.00			£0.00				£0.00		
ADR		£0.00			£0.00				£0.00		
Contingent cost A:	na	£0.00			£0.00				£0.00		
Contingent cost B:	na	£0.00			£0.00				£0.00		
Total budgeted costs	£0.00	£0.00	£0.00	£0.00	£0.00	£0.00	£0.00		£0.00		

	Incurred	Claimed	Time £	Disbs £	Offered	Time £	Disbs £		Budgeted costs
Total budgeted costs	£0.00	£0.00	£0.00	£0.00	£0.00	£0.00	£0.00		£0.00

Total of budgeted and incurred costs

	Claimed	Offered
Incurred	£0.00	£0.00
Budgeted costs caimed	£0.00	£0.00
GT	£0.00	£0.00

Post CCMC costs summary

Incurred	£0.00
Budgeted sum ordered	£0.00
GT	£0.00

A(11)   Form N263 – Disclosure Report

Disclosure report

To be completed by, or on behalf of,

Name of court	Claim No.

who is [1st][2nd][3rd][   ][Claimant][Defendant]
[Part 20 claimant] in this claim

1. Please describe in the table below (or in a separate document filed with this report), using the number 1, 2 etc., all documents which exist or may exist and which may be relevant to the issues in the case and in respect of each such document, where and with whom it may be found, and in the case of electronic documents how the same are stored.

No.	Document description	Where it may be found	(if an electronic document) how it is stored

Note: If an Electronic documents questionnaire (Form N264) has been exchanged, it must be filed with this report.

2. Please state in the box below the broad range of costs that could be involved in giving standard disclosure in this case, including the costs of searching for and disclosing any electronically stored documents.

3. To the extent that this is not already dealt with in Section D4 of your Directions Questionnaire, please state in the boxes below your proposed directions for disclosure to include what particular scope and form of disclosure and related directions you propose for yourself and the other parties by reference to CPR 31.5 (6) and (7) and if not standard the broad range of costs for disclosure.

If not standard, broad range of costs	Form of disclosure (CPR 31.5 (6))

Other disclosure directions (CPR 31.5 (7))

I believe that the facts stated in this Disclosure Report are true.

Signature

[Legal Representative for the][1st][2nd][3rd][   ]
[Claimant][Defendant][Part 20 claimant]

Date

Your name and full postal address

Postcode

E-mail

	If applicable
Telephone no.	
Fax no.	
DX no.	
Your ref.	

A(12)   Form N244 – Application Notice

N244

Application notice

For help in completing this form please read
the notes for guidance form N244Notes.

Find out how HM Courts and Tribunals Service
uses personal information you give them
when you fill in a form: https://www.gov.uk/
government/organisations/hm-courts-and-
tribunals-service/about/personal-information-
charter

Name of court	Claim no.
Fee account no. (if applicable)	**Help with Fees – Ref. no.** (if applicable)
	H W F – ☐☐☐ – ☐☐☐
Warrant no. (if applicable)	
Claimant's name (including ref.)	
Defendant's name (including ref.)	
Date	

1. What is your name or, if you are a legal representative, the name of your firm?

2. Are you a   ☐ Claimant   ☐ Defendant   ☐ Legal Representative

    ☐ Other (please specify)

    If you are a legal representative whom do you represent?

3. What order are you asking the court to make and why?

4. Have you attached a draft of the order you are applying for?   ☐ Yes   ☐ No

5. How do you want to have this application dealt with?   ☐ at a hearing   ☐ without a hearing

    ☐ at a telephone hearing

6. How long do you think the hearing will last?   ☐ Hours   ☐ Minutes

    Is this time estimate agreed by all parties?   ☐ Yes   ☐ No

7. Give details of any fixed trial date or period

8. What level of Judge does your hearing need?

9. Who should be served with this application?

9a. Please give the service address, (other than details
    of the claimant or defendant) of any party named in
    question 9.

10. What information will you be relying on, in support of your application?

☐ the attached witness statement

☐ the statement of case

☐ the evidence set out in the box below

If necessary, please continue on a separate sheet.

Statement of Truth

I understand that proceedings for contempt of court may be brought against anyone who makes, or causes to be made, a false statement in a document verified by a statement of truth without an honest belief in its truth.

☐ **I believe** that the facts stated in section 10 (and any continuation sheets) are true.

☐ **The Applicant believes** that the facts stated in section 10 (and any continuation sheets) are true. **I am authorised** by the applicant to sign this statement.

Signature

☐ Applicant

☐ Litigation friend (where applicant is a child or a Protected Party)

☐ Applicant's legal representative (as defined by CPR 2.3(1))

Date

Day   Month   Year

Full name

Name of applicant's legal representative's firm

If signing on behalf of firm or company give position or office held

3

Applicant's address to which documents should be sent.

Building and street

Second line of address

Town or city

County (optional)

Postcode

If applicable

Phone number

Fax number

DX number

Your Ref.

Email

Application Notice (Form N244) – Notes for Guidance

Court Staff cannot give legal advice. You may qualify for legal aid. Visit www.gov.uk/legal-aid. Alternately you can contact your local Citizens Advice Bureau. Details of your local offices and contact numbers are available via their website www.citizensadvice.org.uk

Paying the court fee
A court fee is payable depending on the type of application you are making. For example:

- To apply for judgment to be set aside

- To apply to vary a judgment or suspend enforcement

- To apply for a summons or order for a witness to attend

- To apply by consent, or without service of the application notice, for a judgment or order.

No fee is payable for an application by consent for an adjournment of a hearing if it is received by the court at least 14 days before the date of the hearing.

What if I cannot afford the fee?
If you show that a payment of a court fee would involve undue hardship to you, you may be eligible for a fee remission.

For further information, or to apply for a fee remission, ask court staff for a copy of the combined booklet and form EX160A - Court and Tribunal fees - Do I have to pay them? This is also available from any county court office, or a copy of the leaflet can be downloaded from our website http://hmctsformfinder.justice.gov.uk

Completing the form

Question 3
Set out what order you are applying for and why; e.g. to adjourn the hearing because..., to set aside a judgment against me because... etc.

Question 5
Most applications will require a hearing and you will be expected to attend. The court will allocate a hearing date and time for the application. Please indicate in a covering letter any dates that you are unavailable within the next six weeks.

The court will only deal with the application 'without a hearing' in the following circumstances.

- Where all the parties agree to the terms of the order being asked for;

- Where all the parties agree that the court should deal with the application without a hearing, or

- Where the court does not consider that a hearing would be appropriate.

Telephone hearings are only available in applications where at least one of the parties involved in the case is legally represented. Not all applications will be suitable for a telephone hearing and the court may refuse your request.

Question 6
If you do not know how long the hearing will take do not guess but leave these boxes blank.

Question 7
If your case has already been allocated a hearing date or trial period please insert details of those dates in the box.

Question 8
If your case is being heard in the High Court or a District Registry please indicate whether it is to be dealt with by a Master, District Judge or Judge.

Question 9
Please indicate in the box provided who you want the court to send a copy of the application to, and their address for service.

Question 10
In this section please set out the information you want the court to take account of in support of the application you are making.
If you wish to rely on:

- **a witness statement,** tick the first box and attach the statement to the application notice.

- **a statement of case,** tick the second box if you intend to rely on your particulars of claim or defence in support of your application.

- **written evidence** on this form, tick the third box and enter details in the space provided. You must also complete the statement of truth. Proceedings for contempt of court may be brought against a person who signs a statement of truth without an honest belief in its truth.

Question 11
The application must be signed and include your current address and contact details. If you agree that the court and the other parties may communicate with you by Document Exchange, telephone, facsimile or email, complete the details

Before returning your form to the court
Have you:
- signed the form on page 2,
- enclosed the correct fee or an application for fee remission,
- made sufficient copies of your application and supporting documentation. You will need to submit one copy for each party to be served and one copy for the court.

A(13)   Form N260 – Statement of Costs for Summary Assessment

N260

Statement of Costs
(summary assessment)

(CPR PD44 9.5)

In the	
	Court
Case Reference	

Judge/Master

Case Title

[Party]'s

Statement of Costs for the hearing on Date   **(interim application/fast track trial)**

Description of fee earners*

(a) *(name) (grade) (hourly rate claimed)*	
(b) *(name) (grade) (hourly rate claimed)*	
(c) *(name) (grade) (hourly rate claimed)*	
(d) *(name) (grade) (hourly rate claimed)*	

Attendances on (party)

Personal attendances

(a) *(number)*		hours at £		£	0.00
(b) *(number)*		hours at £		£	0.00
(c) *(number)*		hours at £		£	0.00
(d) *(number)*		hours at £		£	0.00

Letters out/emails

(a) *(number)*		hours at £		£	0.00
(b) *(number)*		hours at £		£	0.00
(c) *(number)*		hours at £		£	0.00
(d) *(number)*		hours at £		£	0.00

Telephone

(a) *(number)*		hours at £		£	0.00
(b) *(number)*		hours at £		£	0.00
(c) *(number)*		hours at £		£	0.00
(d) *(number)*		hours at £		£	0.00

Attendances on opponents (including negotiations):

Personal attendances

	(a) *(number)*		hours at £		£	0.00
(b) *(number)*		hours at £		£	0.00
(c) *(number)*		hours at £		£	0.00
(d) *(number)*		hours at £		£	0.00

Letters out/emails

	(a) *(number)*		hours at £		£	0.00
(b) *(number)*		hours at £		£	0.00
(c) *(number)*		hours at £		£	0.00
(d) *(number)*		hours at £		£	0.00

Telephone

	(a) *(number)*		hours at £		£	0.00
(b) *(number)*		hours at £		£	0.00
(c) *(number)*		hours at £		£	0.00
(d) *(number)*		hours at £		£	0.00

Attendance on others:

Personal attendances

	(a) *(number)*		hours at £		£	0.00
(b) *(number)*		hours at £		£	0.00
(c) *(number)*		hours at £		£	0.00
(d) *(number)*		hours at £		£	0.00

Letters out/emails

	(a) *(number)*		hours at £		£	0.00
(b) *(number)*		hours at £		£	0.00
(c) *(number)*		hours at £		£	0.00
(d) *(number)*		hours at £		£	0.00

Telephone

	(a) *(number)*		hours at £		£	0.00
(b) *(number)*		hours at £		£	0.00
(c) *(number)*		hours at £		£	0.00
(d) *(number)*		hours at £		£	0.00

Site inspections etc.

(a) *(number)*		hours at £	£ 0.00
(b) *(number)*		hours at £	£ 0.00
(c) *(number)*		hours at £	£ 0.00
(d) *(number)*		hours at £	£ 0.00

Work done on documents, as set out in schedule: 0.00

Attendance at hearing:

(a) *(number)*		hours at £	£ 0.00
(b) *(number)*		hours at £	£ 0.00
(c) *(number)*		hours at £	£ 0.00
(d) *(number)*		hours at £	£ 0.00
(e) Fixed costs			£

(a) *(number)*		hours travel and waiting time £	£ 0.00
(b) *(number)*		hours travel and waiting time £	£ 0.00
(c) *(number)*		hours travel and waiting time £	£ 0.00
(d) *(number)*		hours travel and waiting time £	£ 0.00

Sub Total £   0.00

(A)   Solicitors and Chartered Legal Executives with over eight years post qualification experience including at least eight years litigation experience.

(B)   Solicitors and Chartered Legal Executives with over four years post qualification experience including at least four years litigation experience.

(C)   Other solicitors and Chartered Legal Executives and fee earners of equivalent experience.

(D)   Trainee solicitors, paralegals and other fee earners.

"Chartered Legal Executive" means a Fellow of the Chartered Institute of Legal Executives (CILEx). Those who are not Fellows of CILEx are not entitled to call themselves Chartered Legal Executives and in principle are therefore not entitled to the same hourly rate as a Chartered Legal Executive.

Brought forward £ | 0.00

Counsel's fees *(name) (year of call)*

[   ]

Fee for [advice/conference/documents]   £ [   ]

Fee for hearing   £ [   ]

Other expenses

Court fees   £ [   ]

Others *(give brief description)*   £ [   ]

[   ]

Total   £ | 0.00

Amount of VAT claimed

on solicitors and counsel's fees   £ [   ]

on other expenses   £ [   ]

Grand Total £ | 0.00

The costs stated above do not exceed the costs which the (party)   is liable to pay in respect of the work which this statement covers. Counsel's fees and other expenses have been incurred in the amounts stated above and will be paid to the persons stated.

(party)

[   ]   [   ]

Signed   Dated

[   ]

Name of Partner signing

[   ]

Name of firm of solicitors

Schedule of work done on documents

Item	Description of work (one line only)	(A) hours	(B) hours	(C) hours	(D) hours	Total £
1						
2						
3						
4						
5						
6						
7						
8						
9						
10						
11						
12						
13						
14						
15						
16						
17						
18						
19						
20						
21						
22						
23						
24						
25						
26						
27						
28						
29						
30						
Total						0.00

A(14)   Form N242A – Offer to Settle

Offer to settle

(Section I – Part 36)

This form may be used to settle the whole or part of, or any issue that arises in, a claim, counterclaim, other additional claim, appeal or cross-appeal. It may also be used to settle detailed costs assessment proceedings.

A **Notice of acceptance** form is attached to this form should the offeree wish to use it.

In the (If proceedings have started)
Claim No. (or other ref.)
Name of Claimant (including ref.)
Name of Defendant (including ref.)

**Before completing this form or responding to the offer
please read the notes on pages 4 and 5**

To the Offeree ('s legal representative) (Insert name and address)

Take notice that (insert name of party making the offer)

makes this offer to settle pursuant to Part 36 of the Civil Procedure Rules 1998.

This offer is intended to be a ☐ defendant's ☐ claimant's   Part 36 offer.

If the offer is accepted within _____ days of service of this notice,
the defendant will be liable for the claimant's costs in accordance with rule 36.13.

Note: Specify a period which, subject to rule 36.5(2), must be at least 21 days

The offer is to settle: *(tick as appropriate)*

☐ the whole of   ☐ part of   ☐ a certain issue or issues in
                           (give details over the page)   (give details over the page)

the

☐ claim   ☐ counterclaim   ☐ other additional claim

☐ appeal   ☐ cross-appeal   ☐ detailed costs assessment proceedings

Please give details below of the offer you are making (If necessary continue on a separate sheet ensuring the claim number, if proceedings have started, is shown clearly)

The offer   ☐ does ☐ does not   take into account   ☐ all ☐ part
of the following counterclaim (or other adverse claim):

Is this a personal injury claim?   ☐ Yes, please **complete section 2**,
                                              section 3 if applicable and **section 4**

                                          ☐ No, please go to **Section 4**

SECTION 2

PERSONAL INJURY CLAIMS

Is there a claim for provisional damages?   ☐ Yes, complete **either** part **A** or **B** below

Note: See rule 36.19

                                             ☐ No, please go to **Section 3**

A The offer is made in satisfaction of the claim on the assumption that the
claimant will not:

☐   develop
     (state the disease)
[   ]

OR

☐   suffer
     (state type of
     deterioration)
[   ]

But if this does occur, the claimant will be entitled to claim
further damages at any time before

[   ] [   ] [   ]
Day   Month   Year

B

☐   This offer does not include an offer in respect of the claim for provisional
     damages.

SECTION 3
To be completed only by DEFENDANTS in PERSONAL INJURY claims

Note: See rule 36.22

A ☐ This offer is made without regard to any liability for recoverable benefits under
         the Social Security (Recovery of Benefits Act) 1997.

      OR

B ☐ This offer is intended to include any relevant deductible benefits for which the
         defendant is liable under the Social Security (Recovery of Benefits Act) 1997.

The amount of £[   ] is offered by way of gross compensation.

If you have ticked **B**, complete this section

☐ The defendant has not yet received a certificate of recoverable benefits.

   OR

☐ The following amounts in respect of the following benefits are to be
   deducted. Please give details below.

Type of benefit	Amount

The net amount offered is therefore   £[   ]

SECTION 4

Complete in ALL cases

Details of the party making the offer

Full name	

Name of firm (if applicable)	

Signed		Position held (If signing on behalf of a firm or company)	

Offeror('s legal representative)

Date			
	Day	Month	Year

IMPORTANT NOTES:

1. This form may be used to settle the whole or part of, or any issue that arises in, a claim, counterclaim, other additional claim, appeal or cross-appeal. It may also be used to settle detailed costs assessment proceedings.

2. When used to make a Part 36 offer in respect of an appeal, an appellant seeking to settle their appeal should make a claimant's offer while a respondent should make a defendant's offer. [See rule 36.4.]

3. When used to make a Part 36 offer in respect of a counterclaim or other additional claim or a cross-appeal in certain appeal proceedings:

    -   the party bringing the counterclaim, additional claim or cross-appeal can make (a) a claimant's offer on such counterclaim, additional claim or cross-appeal; or (b) a defendant's offer on the claim or appeal; and

    -   the party bringing the original claim or appeal can make (a) a claimant's offer on such claim or appeal; or (b) a defendant's offer on the counterclaim or cross-appeal.

    In any case the offeror should make plain whether the offer takes into account any adverse claim. For example, when making an offer on a claim, state whether it takes into account the counterclaim. Equally when making an offer on a counterclaim, state whether it takes into account the claim. [See rules 36.2(3), 20.2 & 20.3 in respect of counterclaims and other additional claims. See rules 36.2(3) and 36.4 in respect of cross-appeals.]

4. When this form is used to make a Part 36 offer in detailed costs assessment proceedings, the receiving party in the assessment should make a claimant's offer while the paying party should make a defendant's offer. [See rule 47.20.]

5. In summary, Part 36 provides that:

    -   A party making a defendant's offer is offering something to settle their opponent's claim, counterclaim, additional claim, appeal, cross-appeal or costs assessment proceedings and to accept a liability to pay costs.

    -   A party making a claimant's offer is offering to accept something to settle their own claim, counterclaim, additional claim, appeal, cross-appeal or costs assessment proceedings on terms that their opponent pays their costs.

6. Part 6 of the Civil Procedure Rules makes detailed provision for the service of court documents.

NOTICE OF ACCEPTANCE

NOTES:

1. This form is suitable for the simple acceptance of the offer.

2. Where an offer relates only to part of the proceedings and the offeree wishes to abandon the balance of the claim then this should be made clear when accepting the offer. [See rule 36.13(2).]

3. See rule 36.15 where the offer was made by one or more but not all of the defendants.

In the (If proceedings have started)
Claim No. (or other ref.)
Name of Claimant (including ref.)
Name of Defendant (including ref.)

To the Offeror/legal representative

Take notice that (insert name of party accepting the offer)

accepts this offer to settle pursuant to rule 36.11 of the Civil Procedure Rules 1998.

Details of the party accepting the offer

Full name

Name of firm (if applicable)

Signed

Offeree('s legal representative)

Position held (If signing on behalf of a firm or company)

Date

Day   Month   Year

A(15)   Form N170 – Pre-trial Checklist

Listing questionnaire
(Pre-trial checklist)

Name of court

To be completed by, or on behalf of,

Claim No.	
Last date for filing with court office	
Date(s) fixed for trial or trial period	

who is [1st][2nd][3rd][   ][Claimant][Defendant]
[Part 20 claimant][Part 20 defendant] in this claim

This form must be **completed** and **returned** to the court no later than the date given above. If not, your statement of case may be struck out or some other sanction imposed.	If the claim has settled, or settles before the trial date, you must let the court know immediately.	**Legal representatives only:** If no costs management order has been made. You must **attach** estimates of costs incurred to date, and of your likely overall costs. In substantial cases, these should be provided in compliance with CPR.	For multi-track claims only, you must also **attach** a proposed timetable for the trial itself.

A Confirmation of compliance with directions

1. I confirm that I have complied with those directions already given which require action by me.   ☐ Yes ☐ No

   If you are unable to give confirmation, state which directions you have still to comply with and the date by which this will be done.

Directions	Date

2. I believe that additional directions are necessary before the trial takes place.   ☐ Yes ☐ No

   If Yes, you should attach an application and a draft order.

   *Include in your application all directions needed to enable the claim **to be tried on the date, or within the trial period, already fixed.** These should include any issues relating to experts and their evidence, and any orders needed in respect of directions still requiring action by any other party.*

3. Have you agreed the additional directions you are seeking with the other party(ies)?   ☐ Yes ☐ No

B Witnesses

1. How many witnesses (including yourself) will be giving evidence on your behalf at the trial? *(Do not include experts - see Section C)*   [   ]

Continued over ⇗

Witnesses continued

2. If the trial date is not yet fixed, are there any days within the trial period you or your witnesses would wish to avoid if possible? *(Do not include experts - see Section C)*

Please give details

Name of witness	Dates to be avoided, if posible	Reason

Please specify any special facilities or arrangements needed at court for the party or any witness (e.g. witness with a disability).

3. Will you be providing an interpreter for any of your witnesses?   ☐ Yes ☐ No

C Experts

You are reminded that you may not use an expert's report or have your expert give oral evidence unless the court has given permission. If you do not have permission, you must make an application (see section A2 above)

1. Please give the information requested for your expert(s)

Name	Field of expertise	Joint expert?	Is report agreed?	Has permission been given for oral evidence?
		☐ Yes ☐ No	☐ Yes ☐ No	☐ Yes ☐ No
		☐ Yes ☐ No	☐ Yes ☐ No	☐ Yes ☐ No
		☐ Yes ☐ No	☐ Yes ☐ No	☐ Yes ☐ No

2. Has there been discussion between experts?   ☐ Yes ☐ No

3. Have the experts signed a joint statement?   ☐ Yes ☐ No

4. If your expert is giving oral evidence and the trial date is not yet fixed, is there any day within the trial period which the expert would wish to avoid, if possible?   ☐ Yes ☐ No

If Yes, please give details

Name	Dates to be avoided, if possible	Reason

D Legal representation

1. Who will be presenting your case at the trial?   ☐ You   ☐ Solicitor   ☐ Counsel

2. If the trial date is not yet fixed, is there any day within the trial period that the person presenting your case would wish to avoid, if possible?   ☐ Yes   ☐ No

If Yes, please give details

Name	Dates to be avoided, if posible	Reason

E The trial

1. Has the estimate of the time needed for trial changed?   ☐ Yes   ☐ No

   If Yes, say how long you estimate the whole trial will take, including both parties' cross-examination and closing arguments   ☐ days   ☐ hours   ☐ minutes

2. If different from original estimate have you agreed with the other party(ies) that this is now the **total** time needed?   ☐ Yes   ☐ No

3. Is the timetable for trial you have attached agreed with the other party(ies)?   ☐ Yes   ☐ No

Fast track cases only
The court will normally give you 3 weeks notice of the date fixed for a fast track trial unless, in exceptional circumstances, the court directs that shorter notice will be given.

Would you be prepared to accept shorter notice of the date fixed for trial?   ☐ Yes   ☐ No

F Document and fee checklist
Tick as appropriate

I attach to this questionnaire -

☐ An application and fee for additional directions   ☐ A proposed timetable for trial

☐ A draft order   ☐ An estimate of costs

☐ Listing fee **or** quote your Fee Account no. _____

Signature	Your name and full postal address		
		If applicable	
		Telephone no.	
[Legal Representative for the] [1ˢᵗ][2ⁿᵈ][3ʳᵈ][ ] [Claimant][Defendant][Part 20 claimant]		Fax no.	
		DX no.	
	Postcode _____	Your ref.	
Date ___/___/_____	E-mail _____		

A(16)   Form N252 – Notice of Commencement of Assessment of Bill of Costs

Notice of commencement of assessment of bill of costs

Click here to clear all fields

In the	
Claim No.	
Claimant (include Ref.)	
Defendant (include Ref.)	

To the claimant(defendant)

Following an .... *(insert name of document eg. order, judgment)* dated ....
(copy attached) I have prepared my Bill of Costs for assessment. The Bill totals *£ .... If you choose to
dispute this bill and your objections are not upheld at the assessment hearing, the full amount payable (including the
assessment fee) will be £ .... *(together with interest (see note below))*. I shall also seek the costs of the
assessment hearing

Your points of dispute must include

- details of the items in the bill of costs which are disputed

- concise details of the nature and grounds of the dispute for each item and, if you seek a reduction in those items, suggest, where practicable, a reduced figure

You must serve your points of dispute by .... *(insert date 21 days from the date of service of this notice)* on me at:- *(give full name and address for service including any DX number or reference)*

You must also serve copies of your points of dispute on all other parties to the assessment identified below *(you do not need to serve your points of dispute on the court)*.

I certify that I have also served the following person(s) with a copy of this notice and my Bill of Costs:- *(give details of persons served)*

If I have not received your points of dispute by the above date, I will ask the court to issue a default costs certificate for the full amount of my bill *(see above*)* plus fixed costs and court fee in the total amount of £ ....

Signed .... **Date** ....
(Claimant)(Defendant)('s solicitor)

Note: Interest may be added to all High Court judgments and certain county court judgments of £5,000 or more under the Judgments Act 1838 and the County Courts Act 1984.

The court office at

is open between 10 am and 4 pm Monday to Friday. When corresponding with the court, please address forms or letters to the Court Manager and quote the claim number.

N252 Notice of commencement of assessment of bill of costs (12.99)   *The Court Service Publications Unit*

A(17)   Precedent S – Bill of Costs

IN THE HIGH COURT OF JUSTICE
QUEEN'S BENCH DIVISION

Claim No. 12345689

B E T W E E N:

Mr A   **Claimant**

-and-

Company B   **Defendant**

DEFENDANT'S BILL OF COSTS to be assessed on the standard basis and paid by the Claimant pursuant to orders dated xxxxxxxx

CERTIFICATES PAGE

I certify that this bill is both accurate and complete and

in respect of the bill the costs claimed herein do not exceed the costs which the receiving party is required to pay my firm.

CERTIFICATE AS TO INTEREST AND PAYMENTS

I certify that

No rulings have been made in this case which affects my/the receiving party's entitlement to interest on costs.

and

CERTIFICATE IN RESPECT OF DISBURSEMENTS NOT EXCEEDING £500

I hereby certify that all disbursements listed in this bill which individually do not exceed £500 (other than those relating to counsel's fees) have been duly discharged.

CERTIFICATE IN RESPECT OF VAT

With reference to the pending assessment of the [claimant's/defendant's] costs and disbursements herein which are payable by the [claimant/defendant] we the undersigned [solicitors to] [auditors of] the [claimant/defendant] hereby certify that the [claimant/defendant] on the basis of its last completed VAT return [would/would not be entitled to recover would/be entitled to recover only percent of the] Value Added Tax on such costs and disbursements , as input tax pursuant to the Value Added Tax Act 1994.

Signed...

ABC Firm
VAT NO:

INSTRUCTIONS

INTRODUCTION

The Issues

THE PROCEEDINGS

CONDUCT OF THE CLAIM/FUNDING

The claim was conducted throughout by……………………………

A full list of the legal team appears below. XYZ agreed to act on behalf of the Defendant on payment of disbursements and profit costs and the hourly rates claimed are set out below. The rates do not exceed the Defendant's solicitor/ client liability and are in accordance with the approved budget. Routine letters/ emails out and routine telephone calls are charged at one-tenth of the stated hourly rates.

STRUCTURE OF THE BILL

MASTER CHRONOLOGY

Date	Details

(This section would contain the chronological procedural steps during the litigation)

LEGAL TEAM, HOURLY RATES AND COUNSEL'S SUCCESS FEES

LTM	LTM Name	LTM Status	LTM Grade	Further Relevant Information	LTM Rate	LTM Rate Effective From	Counsel SF %
WT1	William Taylor	Partner	A		£240.00	to May 2012	
WT2	William Taylor	Partner	A		£300.00	from June 2012	
NLB		Medico-Legal Assistant	B		£180.00		
FD	Fiona Duggan	Legal Assistant	D		£160.00		
TI	Thomas Irwin	Costs Draftsman	D		£146.00		
NV	Nicholas Vine	Junior Counsel	JC				100%

FUNDING & PARTS TABLE

Part ID	Description	VAT Rate	Solicitors' Success Fee	Profit Costs incurred	Indemnity Principle Limit	Recoverable % of incurred profit costs	Profit Costs as Claimed
Part 1	Pre-CFA	20%		72.00		100.00%	72.00
Part 2	CFA	20%	95%	31,042.40		100.00%	31,042.40

TABLE OF COSTS AS SUMMARILY ASSESSED

Part ID	Date	Hearing Description	Counsel	Profit Costs Allowed	Counsel Fees Allowed	Disbursements Allowed	Solicitor's Success Fee %	Counsel Success Fee %	Solicitor's Success Fee	Counsel's Success Fee	VAT %	VAT on Solicitor's Success Fee	VAT on Counsel's Success Fee	Total Success Fees inc VAT
Part 2	09/11/12		NV	£3,000.00	£1,500.00		95.00%	100.00%	2,850.00	1,500.00	20.00%	£570.00	£300.00	£5,220.20
Total Base Costs Summarily Assessed				£3,000.00	£1,500.00	£0.00								
Total Success Fees including VAT									£2,850.00	£1,500.00		£570.00	£300.00	£5,220.00

MAIN SUMMARY BY PHASE

Total Bill 109,886.70
Success Fees on Summarily Assessed Costs 5,220.00

Phase Sort Order Number	Phase Name	Counsel's Base Fees	Other Disbursements	Base Profit Costs	Total Base Costs	Solicitor's Success Fees	Counsel's Success Fees	Total VAT	ATEI Premium	Total Costs
1	Initial and Pre-Action Protocol Work			1,236.00	1,236.00	1,105.80	0.00	468.36		2,810.16
2	Issue / Statements of Case	2,175.00	545.00	2,798.00	5,518.00	2,658.10	2,066.25	1,939.47		12,181.82
3	Case Management Conference			3,240.00	3,240.00	3,078.00	0.00	1,263.60		7,581.60
4	Disclosure		200.00	5,778.00	5,978.00	5,489.10	0.00	2,253.42		13,720.52
5	Witness statements		49.65	2,370.00	2,419.65	2,251.50	0.00	934.23		5,605.38
6	Expert reports		3,100.00	1,920.00	5,020.00	1,824.00	0.00	748.80		7,592.80
7	Pre-Trial Review			1,800.00	1,800.00	1,710.00	0.00	702.00		4,212.00
8	Trial preparation			5,100.00	5,100.00	4,845.00	0.00	1,989.00		11,934.00
9	Trial	5,000.00		2,100.00	7,100.00	1,995.00	4,750.00	2,769.00		16,614.00
10	ADR / Settlement	50.00		420.00	470.00	399.00	47.50	183.30		1,099.80
11	Interim Applications and Hearings (Interlocutory Applications)			930.00	930.00	883.50	0.00	362.70		2,176.20
12	Funding			0.00	0.00	0.00	0.00	0.00	11,130.00	11,130.00
13	Budgeting incl. costs estimates			2,276.40	2,276.40	2,162.58	0.00	887.80		5,326.78
15	Costs Assessment			1,146.00	1,146.00	1,088.70	0.00	446.94		2,681.64
	Grand Total	7,225.00	3,894.65	31,114.40	42,234.05	29,490.28	6,863.75	14,948.62	11,130.00	104,666.70

SUMMARY BY TASK, ACTIVITY AND EXPENSES

Total Bill 109,886.70
Success Fees on Summarily Assessed Costs 5,220.00

Task Name	Activity Name	Expense Name	LTM Grade	Time	Base Profit Costs	Counsel's Base Fees	Other Disbursements	Total Base Costs	Solicitor's Success Fees	Counsel's Success Fees	Total VAT	ATEI Premium	Total Costs
Factual investigation				2.10	528.00	0.00	0.00	528.00	433.20	0.00	192.24	0.00	1,153.44
Legal investigation				0.20	48.00	0.00	0.00	48.00	45.60	0.00	18.72	0.00	112.32
Pre-action protocol (or similar) work				2.70	660.00	0.00	0.00	660.00	627.00	0.00	257.40	0.00	1,544.40
Issue and Serve Proceedings and Preparation of Statement(s) of Case				9.30	2,528.00	2,175.00	545.00	5,248.00	2,401.60	2,066.25	1,834.17	0.00	11,550.02
Review of Other Party(s)' Statements of Case				0.90	270.00	0.00	0.00	270.00	256.50	0.00	105.30	0.00	631.80
Case Management Conference				10.80	3,240.00	0.00	0.00	3,240.00	3,078.00	0.00	1,263.60	0.00	7,581.60
Obtaining and reviewing documents				12.20	2,628.00	0.00	200.00	2,828.00	2,496.60	0.00	1,024.92	0.00	6,349.52
Preparing and serving disclosure lists				10.10	3,030.00	0.00	0.00	3,030.00	2,878.50	0.00	1,181.70	0.00	7,090.20
Inspection and review of the other side's disclosure for work undertaken after exchange of disclosure lists.				0.40	120.00	0.00	0.00	120.00	114.00	0.00	46.80	0.00	280.80
Taking, preparing and finalising witness statement(s)				7.90	2,370.00	0.00	49.65	2,419.65	2,251.50	0.00	934.23	0.00	5,605.38
Own expert evidence				7.30	1,920.00	0.00	3,100.00	5,020.00	1,824.00	0.00	748.80	0.00	7,592.80
Pre Trial Review				6.00	1,800.00	0.00	0.00	1,800.00	1,710.00	0.00	702.00	0.00	4,212.00
General work regarding preparation for trial				12.00	3,600.00	0.00	0.00	3,600.00	3,420.00	0.00	1,404.00	0.00	8,424.00
Advocacy				0.00	0.00	5,000.00	0.00	5,000.00	0.00	4,750.00	1,950.00	0.00	11,700.00
Other Settlement Matters	Communicate (Other Party(s)/other outside lawyers)		A	0.20	54.00	0.00	0.00	54.00	51.30	0.00	21.06	0.00	126.36
	Communicate (with client)		A	0.10	24.00	0.00	0.00	24.00	22.80	0.00	9.36	0.00	56.16
	Plan, Prepare, Draft, Review		A	1.00	252.00	0.00	0.00	252.00	239.40	0.00	98.28	0.00	589.68
		Counsel's Fees	JC	0.00	0.00	50.00	0.00	50.00	0.00	47.50	19.50	0.00	117.00
	Communicate (with Counsel)		A	0.30	90.00	0.00	0.00	90.00	85.50	0.00	35.10	0.00	210.60
Other Settlement Matters Total				1.60	420.00	50.00	0.00	470.00	399.00	47.50	183.30	0.00	1,099.80
Funding				0.00	0.00	0.00	0.00	0.00	0.00	0.00	0.00	11,130.00	11,130.00
Budgeting - between the parties				11.90	2,276.40	0.00	0.00	2,276.40	2,162.58	0.00	887.80	0.00	5,326.78

SUMMARY OF COSTS AS CLAIMED VS AMOUNTS IN LAST APPROVED / AGREED / SUBMITTED BUDGET

Precedent H Phase	Incurred Pre-Budget	Last Approved Budget / Agreed Budget Figure	Incurred Post-Budget	Departure from Last Approved / Agreed Budget
Pre-action	1,236.00	-	-	0.00
Issue/Pleadings	5,518.00	-	-	0.00
CMC	3,150.00	200.00	90.00	-110.00
Disclosure	3,218.00	2,000.00	2,760.00	760.00
Witness Statements	2,419.65	3,000.00	-	-3,000.00
Expert Reports	4,930.00	500.00	90.00	-410.00
PTR		2,000.00	1,800.00	-200.00
Trial Preparation		4,500.00	5,100.00	600.00
Trial		3,000.00	7,100.00	4,100.00
ADR/Settlement	440.00	1,000.00	30.00	-970.00
Contingent Cost A		2,500.00	900.00	-1,600.00
Contingent Cost B		3,000.00	30.00	-2,970.00
Contingent Cost C		-	-	0.00

MAIN SUMMARY - BY PART

Total Bill 109,886.70

Success Fees on Summarily Assessed Costs 5,220.00

Part Name	Part ID	Counsel's Fees	Other Disbursements	Base Profit Costs	Total Base Costs	Solicitor's Success Fees	Counsel's Success Fees	Total VAT	Sum of ATEI Premium	Total Costs
Pre-CFA	Part 1			72.00	72.00	0.00	0.00	14.40		86.40
CFA	Part 2	7,225.00	11.00	31,042.40	42,162.05	29,490.28	6,863.75	14,934.22	11,130.00	104,580.30
Grand Total		7,225.00	11.00	31,114.40	42,234.05	29,490.28	6,863.75	14,948.62	11,130.00	104,666.70

A(18)   Precedent G – Points of Dispute

SCHEDULE OF COSTS PRECEDENTS
PRECEDENT G: POINTS OF DISPUTE

IN THE HIGH COURT OF JUSTICE

QUEEN'S BENCH DIVISION   **Claim number: 2000 B 9999**

OXBRIDGE DISTRICT REGISTRY

B E T W E E N

WX	**Claimant**
- and -	
YZ	**Defendant**

POINTS OF DISPUTE SERVED BY THE DEFENDANT

Point 1 General point	Rates claimed for the assistant solicitor and other fee earners are excessive. Reduce to £158 and £116 respectively plus VAT.
	Receiving Party's Reply:
	Costs Officer's Decision:
Point 2 Point of principle	The claimant was at the time a child/protected person/insolvent and did not have the capacity to authorise the solicitors to bring these proceedings.
	Receiving Party's Reply:
	Costs Officer's Decision:
Point 3 (6), (12), (17), (23), (29), (32)	(i) The number of conferences with counsel is excessive and should be reduced to 3 in total (9 hours). (ii) There is no need for two fee earners to attend each conference. Limit to one assistant solicitor in each case.
	Receiving Party's Reply:
	Costs Officer's Decision:

Point 4 (42)	The claim for timed attendances on claimant (schedule 1) is excessive. Reduce to 4 hours.
	Receiving Party's Reply:
	Costs Officer's Decision:
Point 5 (47)	The total claim for work done on documents by the assistant solicitor is excessive. A reasonable allowance in respect of documents concerning court and counsel is 8 hours, for documents concerning witnesses and the expert witness 6.5 hours, for work done on arithmetic 2.25 hours and for other documents 5.5 hours. Reduce to 22.25 hours.
	Receiving Party's Reply:
	Costs Officer's Decision:
Point 6 (50)	The time claimed for preparing and checking the bill is excessive. Reduce solicitor's time to 0.5 hours and reduce the costs draftsman's time to three hours.
	Receiving Party's Reply:
	Costs Officer's Decision:

Served on .... [date] by ....[name] [legal representative of] the Defendant.

A(19)   Practice Direction – Pre-action Conduct and Protocols

Introduction

1. Pre-action protocols explain the conduct and set out the steps the court would normally expect parties to take before commencing proceedings for particular types of civil claims. They are approved by the Master of the Rolls and are annexed to the Civil Procedure Rules (CPR). (The current pre-action protocols are listed in paragraph 18.)

2. This Practice Direction applies to disputes where no pre-action protocol approved by the Master of the Rolls applies. A person who knowingly makes a false statement in a pre-action protocol letter or other document prepared in anticipation of legal proceedings may be subject to proceedings for contempt of court.

Objectives of pre-action conduct and protocols

3. Before commencing proceedings, the court will expect the parties to have exchanged sufficient information to—
    (a)   understand each other's position;
    (b)   make decisions about how to proceed;
    (c)   try to settle the issues without proceedings;
    (d)   consider a form of Alternative Dispute Resolution (ADR) to assist with settlement;
    (e)   support the efficient management of those proceedings; and
    (f)   reduce the costs of resolving the dispute.

Proportionality

4. A pre-action protocol or this Practice Direction must not be used by a party as a tactical device to secure an unfair advantage over another party. Only reasonable and proportionate steps should be taken by the parties to identify, narrow and resolve the legal, factual or expert issues.

5. The costs incurred in complying with a pre-action protocol or this Practice Direction should be proportionate (CPR 44.3(5)). Where parties incur disproportionate costs in complying with any pre-action protocol or this Practice Direction, those costs will not be recoverable as part of the costs of the proceedings.

Steps before issuing a claim at court

6. Where there is a relevant pre-action protocol, the parties should comply with that protocol before commencing proceedings. Where there is no relevant pre-action protocol, the parties should exchange correspondence and information to comply with the objectives in paragraph 3, bearing in mind that compliance should be proportionate. The steps will usually include—
    (a)   the claimant writing to the defendant with concise details of the claim. The letter should include the basis on which the claim is made, a summary of the facts, what the claimant wants from the defendant, and if money, how the amount is calculated;
    (b)   the defendant responding within a reasonable time - 14 days in a straight forward case and no more than 3 months in a very complex one. The reply should include confirmation as to whether the claim is accepted and, if it is not accepted, the reasons why, together with an explanation as to which facts and parts of the claim are disputed and whether the defendant is making a counterclaim as well as providing details of any counterclaim; and
    (c)   the parties disclosing key documents relevant to the issues in dispute.

Experts

7. Parties should be aware that the court must give permission before expert evidence can be relied upon (see CPR 35.4(1)) and that the court may limit the fees recoverable. Many disputes can be resolved without expert advice or evidence. If it is necessary to obtain expert evidence, particularly in low value claims, the parties should consider using a single expert, jointly instructed by the parties, with the costs shared equally.

Settlement and ADR

8. Litigation should be a last resort. As part of a relevant pre-action protocol or this Practice Direction, the parties should consider whether negotiation or some other form of ADR might enable them to settle their dispute without commencing proceedings.

9. Parties should continue to consider the possibility of reaching a settlement at all times, including after proceedings have been started. Part 36 offers may be made before proceedings are issued.

10. Parties may negotiate to settle a dispute or may use a form of ADR including—
    (a)   mediation, a third party facilitating a resolution;
    (b)   arbitration, a third party deciding the dispute;
    (c)   early neutral evaluation, a third party giving an informed opinion on the dispute; and

(d)   Ombudsmen schemes.

(Information on mediation and other forms of ADR is available in the Jackson ADR Handbook (available from Oxford University Press) or at—

https://www.gov.uk/guidance/a-guide-to-civil-mediation

11.   If proceedings are issued, the parties may be required by the court to provide evidence that ADR has been considered. A party's silence in response to an invitation to participate or a refusal to participate in ADR might be considered unreasonable by the court and could lead to the court ordering that party to pay additional court costs.

Stocktake and list of issues

12.   Where a dispute has not been resolved after the parties have followed a pre-action protocol or this Practice Direction, they should review their respective positions. They should consider the papers and the evidence to see if proceedings can be avoided and at least seek to narrow the issues in dispute before the claimant issues proceedings.

Compliance with this Practice Direction and the Protocols

13.   If a dispute proceeds to litigation, the court will expect the parties to have complied with a relevant pre-action protocol or this Practice Direction. The court will take into account non-compliance when giving directions for the management of proceedings (see CPR 3.1(4) to (6)) and when making orders for costs (see CPR 44.3(5)(a)). The court will consider whether all parties have complied in substance with the terms of the relevant pre-action protocol or this Practice Direction and is not likely to be concerned with minor or technical infringements, especially when the matter is urgent (for example an application for an injunction).

14.   The court may decide that there has been a failure of compliance when a party has—

(a)   not provided sufficient information to enable the objectives in paragraph 3 to be met;

(b)   not acted within a time limit set out in a relevant protocol, or within a reasonable period; or

(c)   unreasonably refused to use a form of ADR, or failed to respond at all to an invitation to do so.

15.   Where there has been non-compliance with a pre-action protocol or this Practice Direction, the court may order that:

(a)   the parties are relieved of the obligation to comply or further comply with the pre-action protocol or this Practice Direction;

(b)   the proceedings are stayed while particular steps are taken to comply with the pre-action protocol or this Practice Direction;

(c)   sanctions are to be applied.

16.   The court will consider the effect of any non-compliance when deciding whether to impose any sanctions which may include—

(a)   an order that the party at fault pays the costs of the proceedings, or part of the costs of the other party or parties;

(b)   an order that the party at fault pay those costs on an indemnity basis;

(c)   if the party at fault is a claimant who has been awarded a sum of money, an order depriving that party of interest on that sum for a specified period, and/or awarding interest at a lower rate than would otherwise have been awarded;

(d)   if the party at fault is a defendant, and the claimant has been awarded a sum of money, an order awarding interest on that sum for a specified period at a higher rate, (not exceeding 10% above base rate), than the rate which would otherwise have been awarded.

Limitation

17.   This Practice Direction and the pre-action protocols do not alter the statutory time limits for starting court proceedings. If a claim is issued after the relevant limitation period has expired, the defendant will be entitled to use that as a defence to the claim. If proceedings are started to comply with the statutory time limit before the parties have followed the procedures in this Practice Direction or the relevant pre-action protocol, the parties should apply to the court for a stay of the proceedings while they so comply.

Protocols in force

18.   The table sets out the protocols currently in force and from which date.

Protocol	Came into force
Personal Injury	6 April 2015
Resolution of Clinical Disputes	6 April 2015
Construction and Engineering	9 November 2016 2nd Edition
Defamation	02 October 2000
Professional Negligence	16 July 2000
Judicial Review	6 April 2015
Disease and Illness	8 December 2003

Protocol	Came into force
Housing Disrepair	6 April 2015
Possession Claims by Social Landlords	6 April 2015
Possession Claims for Mortgage Arrears	6 April 2015
Dilapidation of Commercial Property	1 January 2012
Low Value Personal Injury Road Traffic Accident Claims	30 April 2010 extended from 31 July 2013
Low Value Personal Injury Employers' and Public Liability Claims	31 July 2013

A(20)   Professional Negligence Pre-action Protocol

THIS PROTOCOL MERGES THE TWO PROTOCOLS PREVIOUSLY PRODUCED BY THE SOLICITORS INDEMNITY FUND (SIF) AND CLAIMS AGAINST PROFESSIONALS (CAP)

INTRODUCTION

1   Scope of the Protocol

1.1   This Protocol is designed to apply when a claimant wishes to claim against a professional (other than construction professionals and healthcare providers) as a result of that professional's alleged negligence or equivalent breach of contract or breach of fiduciary duty. Although these claims will be the usual situation in which the protocol will be used, there may be other claims for which the protocol could be appropriate.

1.2   'Professional' is deliberately left undefined in the protocol. If it becomes an issue as to whether a respondent to a claim is or is not a professional, parties are reminded of the overriding need to act reasonably (see paragraph 3.3 below). Rather than argue about the definition of 'professional', therefore, the parties are invited to use this Protocol, adapting it where appropriate.

1.3   Allegations of professional negligence are sometimes made in response to an attempt by the professional to recover outstanding fees. Where possible these allegations should be raised before court proceedings have commenced, in which case the parties should comply with the protocol before either party commences court proceedings.

1.4   The protocol is not intended to apply to claims:

   (a)   against architects, engineers and quantity surveyors – parties should use the Construction and Engineering Disputes (CED) protocol.

   (b)   against healthcare providers – parties should use the pre-action protocol for the Resolution of Clinical Disputes.

   (c)   concerning defamation – parties should use the pre-action protocol for defamation claims.

1.5   If at any time prior to the commencement of court proceedings the claimant decides not to proceed with the claim it should notify the professional as soon as reasonably practicable.

2   Aims of the Protocol

2.1   This Protocol sets out a code of good practice and contains the steps which parties should generally follow before commencing court proceedings in respect of a professional negligence claim.

2.2   The aims of the protocol are to enable parties to prospective claims to:

   (a)   understand and properly identify the issues in dispute in the proposed claim and share information and relevant documents;

   (b)   make informed decisions as to whether and how to proceed;

   (c)   try to settle the dispute without proceedings or reduce the issues in dispute;

   (d)   avoid unnecessary expense and keep down the costs of resolving the dispute; and

   (e)   support the efficient management of proceedings where court proceedings cannot be avoided.

2.3   This protocol is not intended to replace other forms of pre-action dispute resolution (such as those mentioned in paragraph 12 of this protocol). Where such procedures are available, parties are encouraged to consider whether they should be used. If, however, these other procedures are used and fail to resolve the dispute, the protocol should be used before court proceedings are started, adapting it where appropriate.

3   Compliance

3.1   The courts will treat the standards set out in this protocol as the normal reasonable approach for parties to a professional negligence claim. If court proceedings are started, it will be for the court to decide whether sanctions should be imposed as a result of substantial non-compliance with this protocol. Guidance on the courts' likely approach is given in the Practice Direction – Pre-Action Conduct and Protocols. The court is likely to disregard minor or technical departures from this protocol and so should the parties as between themselves.

3.2   Both in operating the timetable and in requesting and providing information during the protocol period, the parties are expected to act reasonably, in line with the court's expectations of them. Accordingly, in the event that the protocol does not specifically address a problem, the parties should comply with the spirit of the protocol by acting reasonably.

4   Limitation

4.1   The protocol does not alter the statutory time limits for commencing court proceedings. A claimant is required to start proceedings within those time limits. However, the claimant can request and the parties can agree a standstill agreement to extend the period in which a limitation defence will not be pursued. Alternatively, a claimant may commence court proceedings and invite the professional to agree to an immediate stay of the proceedings to enable the protocol procedures to be followed before the case is pursued.

THE PROTOCOL

5   Preliminary Notice

5.1   As soon as the claimant decides there is a reasonable chance that he will bring a claim against a professional, the claimant is encouraged to notify the professional in writing.

5.2   This letter (the "Preliminary Notice") should contain the following information:

(a)   the identity of the claimant and any other parties;

(b)   a brief outline of the claimant's grievance against the professional; and

(c)   if possible, a general indication of the financial value of the potential claim

5.3   The Preliminary Notice should be addressed to the professional and should ask the professional to inform his professional indemnity insurers, if any, immediately.

5.4   The Preliminary Notice should be acknowledged in writing within 21 days of receipt. Where the claimant is unrepresented the acknowledgment should enclose a copy of this protocol.

5.5   If, after 6 months from the date of the Preliminary Notice, the claimant has not sent any further correspondence to the professional regarding the claim, the claimant should notify the professional of its intentions with regard to the claim, i.e. whether the claimant is pursuing the claim, has decided not to pursue it or has yet to reach a decision and, if the latter, when the claimant envisages making a decision.

6   Letter of Claim

6.1   As soon as the claimant decides there are grounds for a claim against the professional, the claimant should write a detailed Letter of Claim to the professional.

6.2   The Letter of Claim will normally be an open letter (as opposed to being 'without prejudice') and should include the following –

(a)   The identity of any other parties involved in the dispute or a related dispute.

(b)   A clear chronological summary (including key dates) of the facts on which the claim is based. Key documents should be identified, copied and enclosed.

(c)   Any reasonable requests which the claimant needs to make for documents relevant to the dispute which are held by the professional.

(d)   The allegations against the professional. What has been done wrong or not been done? What should the professional have done acting correctly?

(e)   An explanation of how the alleged error has caused the loss claimed. This should include details of what happened as a result of the claimant relying upon what the professional did wrong or omitted to do, and what might have happened if the professional had acted correctly.

(f)   An estimate of the financial loss suffered by the claimant and how it is calculated. Supporting documents should be identified, copied and enclosed. If details of the financial loss cannot be supplied, the claimant should explain why and should state when he will be in a position to provide the details. This information should be sent to the professional as soon as reasonably possible. If the claimant is seeking some form of non-financial redress, this should be made clear.

(g)   Confirmation whether or not an expert has been appointed. If so, providing the identity and discipline of the expert, together with the date upon which the expert was appointed.

(h)   A request that a copy of the Letter of Claim be forwarded immediately to the professional's insurers, if any.

(i)   An indication of whether the claimant wishes to refer the dispute to adjudication. If they do, they should propose three adjudicators or seek a nomination from the nominating body. If they do not wish to refer the dispute to adjudication, they should give reasons.

6.3   The Letter of Claim is not intended to have the same formal status as a Statement of Case. If, however, the Letter of Claim differs materially from the Statement of Case in subsequent proceedings, the court may decide, in its discretion, to impose sanctions.

6.4   If the claimant has sent other Letters of Claim (or equivalent) to any other party in relation to the same dispute or a related dispute, those letters should be copied to the professional.

7   Letter of Acknowledgment

7.1   The Letter of Claim should be acknowledged in writing within 21 days of receipt.

7.2   Where the claimant is unrepresented, the Letter of Acknowledgment should enclose a copy of this protocol unless provided previously.

8   Investigations

8.1   If the professional considers that, for any reason, the Letter of Claim does not comply with section 6 above, the professional should as soon as reasonably practicable inform the claimant why and identify the further information which the professional reasonably requires.

8.2   The professional will have three months from the date of the Letter of Acknowledgment to investigate and respond to the Letter of Claim by the provision of a Letter of Response and/or a Letter of Settlement (as to which, see paragraph 9 below).

8.3   If the professional is in difficulty in complying with the three month time period, the problem should be explained to the claimant as soon as possible and, in any event, as long as possible before the end of the three month period. The professional should explain what is being done to resolve the problem and when the professional expects to be in a position to provide a Letter of Response and/or a Letter of Settlement. The claimant should agree to any reasonable requests for an extension of the three month period.

8.4   The parties should supply promptly, at this stage and throughout, whatever relevant information or documentation is reasonably requested.

8.5   If the professional intends to claim against someone who is not currently a party to the dispute, that third party should be identified to the claimant in writing as soon as possible.

9   Letter of Response and Letter of Settlement

9.1   As soon as the professional has completed his investigations (and in any event within 3 months of the Letter of Acknowledgment unless an extension has been agreed), the professional should send to the claimant:

(a)   a Letter of Response, or

(b)   a Letter of Settlement; or

(c)   both.

9.2   *The Letter of Response*

9.2.1   The Letter of Response should be an open letter (as opposed to being 'without prejudice') and should be a reasoned answer to the claimant's allegations:

(a)   if the claim is admitted the professional should say so in clear terms.

(b)   if only part of the claim is admitted the professional should make clear which parts of the claim are admitted and which are denied.

(c)   if the claim is denied in whole or in part, the Letter of Response should include specific comments on the allegations against the professional and, if the claimant's version of events is disputed, the professional should provide his version of events.

(d)   if the professional is unable to admit or deny the claim, the professional should explain why and identify any further information which is required.

(e)   if the professional disputes the estimate of the claimant's financial loss, the Letter of Response should set out the professional's estimate. If an estimate cannot be provided, the professional should explain why and when he will be in a position to provide an estimate. The professional's estimate should be sent to the claimant as soon as reasonably possible.

(f)   to the extent not already exchanged in the protocol process, key documents should be identified, copied and enclosed.

9.2.2   The Letter of Response is not intended to have the same formal status as a Defence. If, however, the Letter of Response differs materially from the Defence in subsequent court proceedings, the court may decide, in its discretion, to impose sanctions.

9.3   *The Letter of Settlement*

9.3.1   Any Letter of Settlement may be an open letter, a without prejudice letter, a without prejudice save as to costs letter or an offer made pursuant to Part 36 of the Civil Procedure Rules and should be sent if the professional intends to make proposals for settlement of all or part of the claim. It should:

(a)   set out the professional's views on the claim identifying those issues which the professional believes are likely to remain in dispute and those which are not. (The Letter of Settlement does not need to include this information if it is already included in a Letter of Response.)

(b)   make a settlement proposal or identify any further information which is required before the professional can formulate its proposal.

(c)   where additional documents are relied upon, copies should be provided.

9.4   *Effect of Letter of Response and/or Letter of Settlement*

9.4.1   If the Letter of Response denies the claim in its entirety and there is no Letter of Settlement, it is open to the claimant to commence court proceedings.

9.4.2   In any other circumstance, the professional and the claimant should commence negotiations with the aim of resolving the claim within 6 months of the date of the Letter of Acknowledgment (NOT from the date of the Letter of Response).

9.4.3   If the claim cannot be resolved within this period:

(a)   the parties should agree within 14 days of the end of the period whether the period should be extended and, if so, by how long.

(b)   the parties should seek to identify those issues which are still in dispute and those which can be agreed.

(c)   if an extension of time is not agreed it will then be open to the claimant to commence court proceedings.

10   Documents

10.1   This protocol is intended to encourage the early exchange of relevant information, so that issues in dispute can be clarified or resolved. The claimant should provide key documents with the Letter of Claim and (at any time) any other documents reasonably requested by the professional which are relevant to the issues in dispute. The professional should provide key documents with the Letter of Response, to the extent not provided by the claimant, and (at any time) any other documents reasonably requested by the claimant which are relevant to the issues in dispute.

10.2   Parties are encouraged to cooperate openly in the exchange of relevant information and documentation. However, the protocol should not be used to justify a 'fishing expedition' by either party. No party is obliged under the protocol to disclose any document which a court could not order them to disclose in the pre-action period under CPR 31.16.

10.3   This protocol does not alter the parties' duties to disclose documents under any professional regulation or under general law.

11 Experts

11.1   In professional negligence disputes, separate expert opinions may be needed on:

(a)   breach of duty;

(b)   causation; and/or

(c)   the quantification of the claimant's claim.

11.2   It is recognised that in professional negligence disputes the parties and their advisers will require flexibility in their approach to expert evidence. The parties should co-operate when making decisions on appropriate expert specialisms, whether experts might be instructed jointly and whether any reports obtained pre-action might be shared and should at all times have regard to the duty in CPR 35.1 to restrict expert evidence to that which is reasonably required to resolve the dispute.

11.3   When considering what expert evidence may be required during the protocol period, parties should be aware that any expert reports obtained pre-action will only be permitted in proceedings with the express permission of the court.

12   Alternative Dispute Resolution

12.1   Court proceedings should be a last resort. The parties should consider whether some form of alternative dispute resolution procedure might enable them to settle their dispute without commencing court proceedings, and if so, endeavour to agree which form to adopt.

12.2   Parties may negotiate to settle a dispute or may use a form of ADR including:

(a)   mediation – a third party facilitating a resolution;

(b)   arbitration – a third party deciding the dispute;

(c)   early neutral evaluation – a third party giving an informed opinion on the dispute;

(d)   adjudication – a process by which an independent adjudicator provides the parties with a decision that can resolve the dispute either permanently or on a temporary basis, pending subsequent court determination; and

(e)   Ombudsmen schemes.

         (Information on mediation and other forms of ADR is available in the Jackson ADR Handbook (available from Oxford University Press) or at—

         http://www.civilmediation.justice.gov.uk/

         http://www.adviceguide.org.uk/england/law_e/law_legal_system_e/law_taking_legal_action_e/alternatives_to_court.htm)

12.3   If court proceedings are issued, the parties may be required by the court to provide evidence that ADR has been considered. A party's refusal to engage or silence in response to an invitation to participate in ADR might be considered unreasonable by the court and could lead to the court ordering that party to pay additional costs.

13   Stocktake

13.1   Where the procedure set out in this protocol has not resolved the dispute between the parties, they should undertake a further review of their respective positions. The parties should consider the state of the papers and the evidence in order to see if proceedings can be avoided and, at the least, narrow the issues between them.

14   Court proceedings

14.1   Unless it is necessary (for example, to obtain protection against the expiry of a relevant limitation period (see paragraph 4 above)) the claimant should not start court proceedings until:

(a)   the Letter of Response denies the claim in its entirety and there is no Letter of Settlement (see paragraph 9.4.1 above); or

(b)   the end of the negotiation period (see paragraphs 9.4.2 and 9.4.3 above).

14.2   If proceedings are for any reason started before the parties have followed the procedures in this protocol, the parties are encouraged to agree to apply to the court for a stay whilst the protocol is followed.

14.3   Where possible 14 days written notice should be given to the professional before proceedings are started, indicating the court within which the claimant is intending to commence court proceedings.

14.4   If proceedings are commenced they should be served in accordance with Part 6 of the Civil Procedure Rules.

A(21)   Guidance for the Instruction of Experts in Civil Claims 2014

August 2014

Introduction

1. The purpose of this guidance is to assist litigants, those instructing experts and experts to understand best practice in complying with Part 35 of the Civil Procedure Rules (CPR) and court orders. Experts and those who instruct them should ensure they are familiar with CPR 35 and the Practice Direction (PD35). This guidance replaces the Protocol for the instruction of experts in civil claims (2005, amended 2009).

2. Those instructing experts, and the experts, must also have regard to the objectives underpinning the Pre-Action Protocols to:—

(a)   encourage the exchange of early and full information about the expert issues involved in the prospective claim;

(b)   enable the parties to avoid or reduce the scope of the litigation by agreeing the whole or part of an expert issue before proceedings are started; and

(c)   support the efficient management of proceedings where litigation cannot be avoided.

3. Additionally, experts and those instructing them should be aware that some cases will be governed by the specific pre-action protocols and some may be "specialist proceedings" (CPR 49) where specific rules may apply.

Selecting and Instructing experts

The need for experts

4. Those intending to instruct experts to give or prepare evidence for the purpose of civil proceedings should consider whether expert evidence is necessary, taking account of the principles set out in CPR Parts 1 and 35, and in particular whether "it is required to resolve the proceedings" (CPR 35.1).

5. Although the court's permission is not generally required to instruct an expert, the court's permission is required before an expert's report can be relied upon or an expert can be called to give oral evidence (CPR 35.4).

6. Advice from an expert before proceedings are started which the parties do not intend to rely upon in litigation is likely to be confidential; this guidance does not apply then. The same applies where, after the commencement of proceedings, experts are instructed only to advise (e.g. to comment upon a single joint expert's report) and not to prepare evidence for the proceedings. The expert's role then is that of an expert advisor.

7. However this guidance does apply if experts who were formerly instructed only to advise, are later instructed as an expert witness to prepare or give evidence in the proceedings.

8. In the remainder of this guidance, a reference to an expert means an expert witness to whom Part 35 applies.

Duties and obligations of experts

9. Experts always owe a duty to exercise reasonable skill and care to those instructing them, and to comply with any relevant professional code. However when they are instructed to give or prepare evidence for civil proceedings they have an overriding duty to help the court on matters within their expertise (CPR 35.3). This duty overrides any obligation to the person instructing or paying them. Experts must not serve the exclusive interest of those who retain them.

10. Experts should be aware of the overriding objective that courts deal with cases justly and that they are under an obligation to assist the court in this respect. This includes dealing with cases proportionately (keeping the work and costs in proportion to the value and importance of the case to the parties), expeditiously and fairly (CPR 1.1).

11. Experts must provide opinions that are independent, regardless of the pressures of litigation. A useful test of 'independence' is that the expert would express the same opinion if given the same instructions by another party. Experts should not take it upon themselves to promote the point of view of the party instructing them or engage in the role of advocates or mediators.

12. Experts should confine their opinions to matters which are material to the disputes and provide opinions only in relation to matters which lie within their expertise. Experts should indicate without delay where particular questions or issues fall outside their expertise.

13. Experts should take into account all material facts before them. Their reports should set out those facts and any literature or material on which they have relied in forming their opinions. They should indicate if an opinion is provisional, or qualified, or where they consider that further information is required or if, for any other reason, they are not satisfied that an opinion can be expressed finally and without qualification.

14. Experts should inform those instructing them without delay of any change in their opinions on any material matter and the reasons for this (see also paragraphs 64–66).

15. Experts should be aware that any failure to comply with the rules or court orders, or any excessive delay for which they are responsible, may result in the parties who instructed them being penalised in costs, or debarred from relying upon the expert evidence (see also paragraphs 89–92).

The appointment of experts

16. Before experts are instructed or the court's permission to appoint named experts is sought, it should be established whether the experts:

(a) have the appropriate expertise and experience for the particular instruction;

(b)   are familiar with the general duties of an expert;

(c)   can produce a report, deal with questions and have discussions with other experts within a reasonable time, and at a cost proportionate to the matters in issue;

(d)   are available to attend the trial, if attendance is required; and

(e)   have no potential conflict of interest.

17. Terms of appointment should be agreed at the outset and should normally include:

(a)   the capacity in which the expert is to be appointed (e.g. party appointed expert or single joint expert);

(b)   the services required of the expert (e.g. provision of an expert's report, answering questions in writing, attendance at meetings and attendance at court);

(c)   time for delivery of the report;

(d)   the basis of the expert's charges (e.g. daily or hourly rates and an estimate of the time likely to be required, or a fixed fee for the services). Parties must provide an estimate to the court of the costs of the proposed expert evidence and for each stage of the proceedings (CPR.35.4(2);

(e)   travelling expenses and disbursements;

(f)   cancellation charges;

(g)   any fees for attending court;

(h)   time for making the payment;

(i)   whether fees are to be paid by a third party;

(j)   if a party is publicly funded, whether the expert's charges will be subject to assessment; and

(k)   guidance that the expert's fees and expenses may be limited by the court (note expert's recoverable fees in the small claims track cannot exceed £750: see PD 27 paragraph 7).

18. When necessary, arrangements should be made for dealing with questions to experts and discussions between experts, including any directions given by the court.

19. Experts should be kept informed about deadlines for all matters concerning them. Those instructing experts should send them promptly copies of all court orders and directions that may affect the preparation of their reports or any other matters concerning their obligations.

Instructions

20. Those instructing experts should ensure that they give clear instructions (and attach relevant documents), including the following:

(a)   basic information, such as names, addresses, telephone numbers, dates of incidents and any relevant claim reference numbers;

(b)   the nature of the expertise required;

(c)   the purpose of the advice or report, a description of the matter(s) to be investigated, the issues to be addressed and the identity of all parties;

(d)   the statement(s) of case (if any), those documents which form part of disclosure and witness statements and expert reports that are relevant to the advice or report, making clear which have been served and which are drafts and when the latter are likely to be served;

(e)   where proceedings have not been started, whether they are contemplated and, if so, whether the expert is being asked only for advice;

(f)   an outline programme, consistent with good case management and the expert's availability, for the completion and delivery of each stage of the expert's work; and

(g)   where proceedings have been started, the dates of any hearings (including any case/costs management conferences and/or pre-trial reviews), the dates fixed by the court or agreed between the parties for the exchange of experts' reports and any other relevant deadlines to be adhered to, the name of the court, the claim number, the track to which the claim has been allocated and whether there is a specific budget for the experts' fees.

21. Those instructing experts should seek to agree, where practicable, the instructions for the experts, and that they receive the same factual material.

Acceptance of instructions

22. Experts should confirm without delay whether they accept their instructions.

23. They should also inform those instructing them (whether on initial instruction or at any later stage) without delay if:

(a)   instructions are not acceptable because, for example, they require work that falls outside their expertise, impose unrealistic deadlines, or are insufficiently clear. Experts who do not receive clear instructions should request clarification and may indicate that they are not prepared to act unless and until such clear instructions are received;

(b)   they consider that instructions are insufficient to complete the work;

(c)   they become aware that they may not be able to fulfil any of the terms of appointment;

(d)   the instructions and/or work have, for any reason, placed them in conflict with their duties as an expert. Where an expert advisor is approached to act as an expert witness they will need to consider carefully whether they can accept a role as expert witness; or

(e)   they are not satisfied that they can comply with any orders that have been made.

24. Experts must neither express an opinion outside the scope of their field of expertise, nor accept any instructions to do so.

25. Where an expert identifies that the basis of his instruction differs from that of another expert, he should inform those instructing him.

26. Experts should agree the terms on which they are to be paid with those instructing them. Experts should be aware that they will be required to provide estimates for the court and that the court may limit the amount to be paid as part of any order for budgeted costs (CPR 35.4(2) and (4) and 3.15).

Experts' Withdrawal

27. Where experts' instructions are incompatible with their duties, through incompleteness, a conflict between their duty to the court and their instructions, or for any other reason, the experts may consider withdrawing from the case. However, experts should not do so without first discussing the position with those who instruct them and considering whether it would be more appropriate to make a written request for directions from the court. If experts do withdraw, they must give formal written notice to those instructing them.

Experts' right to ask court for directions

28. Experts may request directions from the court to assist them in carrying out their functions (CPR 35.14), for example, if experts consider that they have not been provided with information they require. Experts should normally discuss this with those who instruct them before making a request. Unless the court otherwise orders, any proposed request for directions should be sent to the party instructing the expert at least seven days before filing any request with the court, and to all other parties at least four days before filing it.

29. Requests to the court for directions should be made by letter clearly marked "expert's request for directions" containing:

(a) the title of the claim;

(b) the claim number;

(c) the name of the expert;

(d) why directions are sought; and

(e) copies of any relevant documentation.

Experts' access to information held by the parties

30. Experts should try to ensure that they have access to all relevant information held by the parties, and that the same information has been disclosed to each expert in the same discipline. Experts should seek to confirm this soon after accepting instructions, notifying instructing solicitors of any omissions.

31. If a solicitor sends an expert additional documents before the report is finalised the solicitor must tell the expert whether any witness statements or expert reports are updated versions of those previously sent and whether they have been filed and served.

32. Experts should be specifically aware of CPR 35.9. This provides that, where one party has access to information that is not readily available to the other party, the court may direct the party who has access to the information to prepare, file and copy to the other party a document recording the information. If experts require such information which has not been disclosed, they should discuss the position with those instructing them without delay, so that a request for the information can be made, and, if not forthcoming, an application can be made to the court.

33. Any request for further information from the other party made by an expert should be in a letter to the expert's instructing party and should state why the information is necessary and the significance in relation to the expert issues in the case.

Single joint experts

34. CPR 35.7–8 and PD 35 paragraph 7 deal with the instruction and use of joint experts by the parties and the powers of the court to order their use. The CPR encourage the use of joint experts. Wherever possible a joint report should be obtained. Single joint experts are the norm in cases allocated to the small claims track and the fast track.

35. In the early stages of a dispute, when investigations, tests, site inspections, photographs, plans or other similar preliminary expert tasks are necessary, consideration should be given to the instruction of a single joint expert, especially where such matters are not expected to be contentious. The objective should be to agree or to narrow issues.

36. Experts who have previously advised a party (whether in the same case or otherwise) should only be proposed as single joint experts if the other parties are given all relevant information about the previous involvement.

37. The appointment of a single joint expert does not prevent parties from instructing their own experts to advise (but the cost of such expert advisors will not be recoverable from another party).

Joint instructions

38. The parties should try to agree joint instructions to single joint experts, but in default of agreement, each party may give instructions. In particular, all parties should try to agree what documents should be included with instructions and what assumptions single joint experts should make.

39. Where the parties fail to agree joint instructions, they should try to agree where the areas of disagreement lie and their instructions should make this clear. If separate instructions are given, they should be copied to the other instructing parties.

40. Where experts are instructed by two or more parties, the terms of appointment should, unless the court has directed otherwise, or the parties have agreed otherwise, include:

(a)   a statement that all the instructing parties are jointly and severally liable to pay the experts' fees and, accordingly, that experts' invoices should be sent simultaneously to all instructing parties or their solicitors (as appropriate); and

(b)   a copy of any order limiting experts' fees and expenses (CPR 35.8(4)(a)).

41. Where instructions have not been received by the expert from one or more of the instructing parties, the expert should give notice (normally at least 7 days) of a deadline for their receipt. Unless the instructions are received within the deadline the expert may begin work. If instructions are received after the deadline but before the completion of the report the expert should consider whether it is practicable to comply without adversely affecting the timetable for delivery of the report and without greatly increasing the costs and exceeding any court approved budget. An expert who decides to issue a report without taking into account instructions received after the deadline must inform the parties, who may apply to the court for directions. In either event the report must show clearly that the expert did not receive instructions within the deadline, or, as the case may be, at all.

Conduct of the single joint expert

42. Single joint experts should keep all instructing parties informed of any material steps that they may be taking by, for example, copying all correspondence to those instructing them.

43. Single joint experts are Part 35 experts and so have an overriding duty to the court. They are the parties' appointed experts and therefore owe an equal duty to all parties. They should maintain independence, impartiality and transparency at all times.

44. Single joint experts should not attend a meeting or conference that is not a joint one, unless all the parties have agreed in writing or the court has directed that such a meeting may be held. There also needs to be agreement about who is to pay the experts' fees for the meeting.

45. Single joint experts may request directions from the court (see paragraphs 28–29).

46. Single joint experts should serve their reports simultaneously on all instructing parties. They should provide a single report even though they may have received instructions that contain conflicts. If conflicting instructions lead to different opinions (for example, because the instructions require the expert to make different assumptions of fact), reports may need to contain more than one set of opinions on any issue. It is for the court to determine the facts.

Cross-examination of the single joint expert

47. Single joint experts do not normally give oral evidence at trial but if they do, all parties may ask questions. In general, written questions (CPR 35.6) should be put to single joint experts before requests are made for them to attend court for the purpose of cross-examination.

Experts' reports

48. The content of experts' reports should be governed by their instructions and general obligations, any court directions, CPR 35 and PD35, and the experts' overriding duty to the court.

49. In preparing reports, experts should maintain professional objectivity and impartiality at all times.

50. PD 35, paragraph 3.1 provides that experts' reports should be addressed to the court and gives detailed directions about their form and content. All experts and those who instruct them should ensure that they are familiar with these requirements.

51. Model forms of experts' reports are available from bodies such as the Academy of Experts and the Expert Witness Institute and a template for medical reports has been created by the Ministry of Justice.

52. Experts' reports must contain statements that they:

(a)   understand their duty to the court and have complied and will continue to comply with it; and

(b)   are aware of and have complied with the requirements of CPR 35 and PD 35 and this guidance.

53. Experts' reports must also be verified by a statement of truth. The form of the statement of truth is:

> "I confirm that I have made clear which facts and matters referred to in this report are within my own knowledge and which are not. Those that are within my own knowledge I confirm to be true. The opinions I have expressed represent my true and complete professional opinions on the matters to which they refer."

54. The details of experts' qualifications in reports should be commensurate with the nature and complexity of the case. It may be sufficient to state any academic and professional qualifications. However, where highly specialised expertise is called for, experts should include the detail of particular training and/or experience that qualifies them to provide that specialised evidence.

55. The mandatory statement of the substance of all material instructions should not be incomplete or otherwise tend to mislead. The imperative is transparency. The term "instructions" includes all material that solicitors send to experts. These should be listed, with dates, in the report or an appendix. The omission from the statement of 'off-the-record' oral instructions is not permitted. Courts may allow cross-examination about the instructions if there are reasonable grounds to consider that the statement may be inaccurate or incomplete.

56. Where tests of a scientific or technical nature have been carried out, experts should state:

(a)   the methodology used; and

(b)   by whom the tests were undertaken and under whose supervision, summarising their respective qualifications and experience.

57. When addressing questions of fact and opinion, experts should keep the two separate. Experts must state those facts (whether assumed or otherwise) upon which their opinions are based; experts should have primary regard to their instructions (paragraphs 20–25 above). Experts must distinguish clearly between those facts that they know to be true and those facts which they assume.

58. Where there are material facts in dispute experts should express separate opinions on each hypothesis put forward. They should not express a view in favour of one or other disputed version of the facts unless, as a result of particular expertise and experience, they consider one set of facts as being improbable or less probable, in which case they may express that view and should give reasons for holding it.

59. If the mandatory summary of the range of opinion is based on published sources, experts should explain those sources and, where appropriate, state the qualifications of the originator(s) of the opinions from which they differ, particularly if such opinions represent a well-established school of thought.

60. Where there is no available source for the range of opinion, experts may need to express opinions on what they believe to be the range that other experts would arrive at if asked. In those circumstances, experts should make it clear that the range that they summarise is based on their own judgement and explain the basis of that judgement.

Prior to service of reports

61. Before filing and serving an expert's report solicitors must check that any witness statements and other experts' reports relied upon by the expert are the final served versions.

Conclusions of reports

62. A summary of conclusions is mandatory. Generally the summary should be at the end of the report after the reasoning. There may be cases, however, where the court would find it helpful to have a short summary at the beginning, with the full conclusions at the end. For example, in cases involving highly complex matters which fall outside the general knowledge of the court the judge may be assisted in the comprehension of the facts and analysis if the report explains at the outset the basis of the reasoning.

Sequential exchange of experts' reports

63. Where there is to be sequential exchange of reports then the defendant's expert's report usually will be produced in response to the claimant's. The defendant's report should then:

(a)   confirm whether the background set out in the claimant's expert report is agreed, or identify those parts that in the defendant's expert's view require revision, setting out the necessary revisions. The defendant's expert need not repeat information that is adequately dealt with in the claimant's expert report;

(b)   focus only on those material areas of difference with the claimant's expert's opinion. The defendant's report should identify those assumptions of the claimant's expert that they consider reasonable (and agree with) and those that they do not; and

(c)   in particular where the experts are addressing the financial value of heads of claim (for example, the costs of a care regime or loss of profits), the defendant's report should contain a reconciliation between the claimant's expert's loss assessment and the defendant's, identifying for each assumption any different conclusion to the claimant's expert.

Amendment of reports

64. It may become necessary for experts to amend their reports:

(a) as a result of an exchange of questions and answers;

(b)   following agreements reached at meetings between experts; or

(c)   where further evidence or documentation is disclosed.

65. Experts should not be asked to amend, expand or alter any parts of reports in a manner which distorts their true opinion, but may be invited to do so to ensure accuracy, clarity, internal consistency, completeness and relevance to the issues. Although experts should generally follow the recommendations of solicitors with regard to the form of reports, they should form their own independent views on the opinions and contents of their reports and not include any suggestions that do not accord with their views.

66. Where experts change their opinion following a meeting of experts, a signed and dated note to that effect is generally sufficient. Where experts significantly alter their opinion, as a result of new evidence or for any other reason, they must inform those who instruct them and amend their reports explaining the reasons. Those instructing experts should inform other parties as soon as possible of any change of opinion.

Written questions to experts

67. Experts have a duty to provide answers to questions properly put. Where they fail to do so, the court may impose sanctions against the party instructing the expert, and, if there is continued non-compliance, debar a party from relying on the report. Experts should copy their answers to those instructing them.

68. Experts' answers to questions become part of their reports. They are covered by the statement of truth, and form part of the expert evidence.

69. Where experts believe that questions put are not properly directed to the clarification of the report, or have been asked out of time, they should discuss the questions with those instructing them and, if appropriate, those asking the questions. Attempts should be made to resolve such problems without the need for an application to the court for directions, but in the absence of agreement or application for directions by

the party or parties, experts may themselves file a written request to court for directions (see paragraphs 28–29).

Discussions between experts

70. The court has the power to direct discussions between experts for the purposes set out in the Rules (CPR 35.12). Parties may also agree that discussions take place between their experts at any stage. Discussions are not mandatory unless ordered by the court.

71. The purpose of discussions between experts should be, wherever possible, to:

(a)   identify and discuss the expert issues in the proceedings;

(b)   reach agreed opinions on those issues, and, if that is not possible, narrow the issues;

(c)   identify those issues on which they agree and disagree and summarise their reasons for disagreement on any issue; and

(d)   identify what action, if any, may be taken to resolve any of the outstanding issues between the parties.

They are not to seek to settle the proceedings.

72. Where single joint experts have been instructed but parties have, with the permission of the court, instructed their own additional Part 35 experts, there may, if the court so orders or the parties agree, be discussions between the single joint experts and the additional Part 35 experts. Such discussions should be confined to those matters within the remit of the additional Part 35 experts or as ordered by the court.

73. Where there is sequential exchange of expert reports, with the defendant's expert's report prepared in accordance with the guidance at paragraph 63 above, the joint statement should focus upon the areas of disagreement, save for the need for the claimant's expert to consider and respond to material, information and commentary included within the defendant's expert's report.

74. Arrangements for discussions between experts should be proportionate to the value of cases. In small claims and fast-tracks cases there should not normally be face to face meetings between experts: telephone discussion or an exchange of letters should usually suffice. In multi-track cases discussion may be face to face but the practicalities or the proportionality principle may require discussions to be by telephone or video-conference.

75. In multi-track cases the parties, their lawyers and experts should cooperate to produce an agenda for any discussion between experts, although primary responsibility for preparation of the agenda should normally lie with the parties' solicitors.

76. The agenda should indicate what has been agreed and summarise concisely matters that are in dispute. It is often helpful to include questions to be answered by the experts. If agreement cannot be reached promptly or a party is unrepresented, the court may give directions for the drawing up of the agenda. The agenda should be circulated to experts and those instructing them to allow sufficient time for the experts to prepare for the discussion.

77. Those instructing experts must not instruct experts to avoid reaching agreement (or to defer doing so) on any matter within the experts' competence. Experts are not permitted to accept such instructions.

78. The content of discussions between experts should not be referred to at trial unless the parties agree (CPR 35.12(4)). It is good practice for any such agreement to be in writing.

79. At the conclusion of any discussion between experts, a joint statement should be prepared setting out:

(a)   issues that have been agreed and the basis of that agreement;

(b)   issues that have not been agreed and the basis of the disagreement;

(c)   any further issues that have arisen that were not included in the original agenda for discussion; and

(d)   a record of further action, if any, to be taken or recommended, including if appropriate a further discussion between experts.

80. The joint statement should include a brief re-statement that the experts recognise their duties (or a cross-reference to the relevant statements in their respective reports). The joint statement should also include an

express statement that the experts have not been instructed to avoid reaching agreement (or otherwise defer from doing so) on any matter within the experts' competence.

81. The joint statement should be agreed and signed by all the parties to the discussion as soon as practicable.

82. Agreements between experts during discussions do not bind the parties unless the parties expressly agree to be bound (CPR 35.12(5)). However, parties should give careful consideration before refusing to be bound by such an agreement and be able to explain their refusal should it become relevant to the issue of costs.

83. Since April 2013 the court has had the power to order at any stage that experts of like disciplines give their evidence at trial concurrently, not sequentially with their party's evidence as has been the norm hitherto: PD 35 paragraphs 11.1–11.4 (this is often known as "hot–tubbing"). The experts will then be questioned together, firstly by the judge based upon disagreements in the joint statement, and then by the parties' advocates. Concurrent evidence can save time and costs, and assist the judge in assessing the difference of views between experts. Experts need to be told in advance of the trial if the court has made an order for concurrent evidence.

Attendance of experts at court

84. Those instructing experts should ascertain the availability of experts before trial dates are fixed; keep experts updated with timetables (including the dates and times experts are to attend), the location of the court and court orders; consider, where appropriate, whether experts might give evidence via video-link; and inform experts immediately if trial dates are vacated or adjourned.

85. Experts have an obligation to attend court and should ensure that those instructing them are aware of their dates to avoid and that they take all reasonable steps to be available.

86. Experts should normally attend court without the need for a witness summons, but on occasion they may be served to require their attendance (CPR 34). The use of witness summonses does not affect the contractual or other obligations of the parties to pay experts' fees.

87. When a case has been concluded either by a settlement or trial the solicitor should inform the experts they have instructed.

Experts and conditional and contingency fees

88. Payment of experts' fees contingent upon the nature of the expert evidence or upon the outcome of the case is strongly discouraged. In *ex parte Factortame* (no8) [2003] QB 381 at [73], the court said ' we consider that it will be a rare case indeed that the court will be prepared to consent to an expert being instructed under a contingency fee agreement'.

Sanctions

89. Solicitors and experts should be aware that sanctions might apply because of a failure to comply with CPR 35, the PD or court orders.

90. Whether or not court proceedings have been commenced a professional instructing an expert, or an expert, may be subject to sanction for misconduct by their professional body/regulator.

91. If proceedings have been started the court has the power under CPR 44 to impose sanctions:

(a)   cost penalties against those instructing the expert (including a wasted costs order) or the expert (such as disallowance or reduction of the expert'' fee) (CPR 35.4(4) and CPR 44).

(b)   that an expert's report/evidence be inadmissible.

92. Experts should also be aware of other possible sanctions

(a)   In more extreme cases, if the court has been misled it may invoke general powers for contempt in the face of the court. The court would then have the power to fine or imprison the wrongdoer.

(b)   If an expert commits perjury, criminal sanctions may follow.

(c)   If an expert has been negligent there may be a claim on their professional indemnity insurance.

Civil Justice Council
August 2014

A(22)   Guideline figures for the Summary Assessment of Costs

Solicitors' hourly rates

The guideline rates for solicitors provided here are broad approximations only.

Localities

The guideline figures have been grouped according to locality by way of general guidance only. Although many firms may be comparable with others in the same locality, some of them will not be.

In any particular case the hourly rate which it is reasonable to allow should be determined by reference to the rates charged by comparable firms. For this purpose the statement of costs supplied by the paying party may be of assistance. The rate to allow should not be determined by reference to locality or postcode alone.

Grades of fee earner

The categories of fee earners are as follows:

[A] Solicitors with over eight years post qualification experience including at least eight years litigation experience and Fellows of CILEX with 8 years' post-qualification experience.
[B] Solicitors and Fellows of CILEX with over four years post qualification experience including at least four years litigation experience.
[C] Other solicitors and Fellows of CILEX and fee earners of equivalent experience.
[D] Trainee solicitors, trainee legal executives, paralegals and other fee earners.

Qualified Costs Lawyers will be eligible for payment as grades B or C depending on the complexity of the work done.

Employed barristers' rates should be allowed at the grade which best reflects the length of their litigation experience.

"Legal executive" means a Fellow of the Chartered Institute of Legal Executives. Those who are not Fellows of the Institute are not entitled to call themselves legal executives and in principle are therefore not entitled to the same hourly rate as a legal executive.

Clerks without the equivalent experience of legal executives will be treated as being in the bottom grade of fee earner i.e. trainee solicitors, paralegals and fee earners of equivalent experience. Whether or not a fee earner has equivalent experience is ultimately a matter for the discretion of the court.

Rates to allow for senior fee earners and for substantial and complex work

Many High Court cases justify fee earners at a senior level. However the same may not be true of attendance at pre-trial hearings with counsel. The task of sitting behind counsel should be delegated to a more junior fee earner in all but the most important pre-trial hearings. The fact that the receiving party insisted upon the senior's attendance, or the fact that the fee earner is a sole practitioner who has no juniors to delegate to, should not be the determinative factors. As with hourly rates the statement of costs supplied by the paying party may be of assistance. What grade of fee earner did they use?

As stated in paragraph 29 of the Guide:
In substantial and complex litigation an hourly rate in excess of the guideline figures may be appropriate for grade A, B and C fee earners where other factors, for example the value of the litigation, the level of the complexity, the urgency or importance of the matter, as well as any international element, would justify a significantly higher rate. It is important to note (a) that these are only examples and (b) they are not restricted to high level commercial work, but may apply, for example, to large and complex personal injury work. Further, London 1 is defined in Appendix 2 as 'very heavy commercial and corporate work by centrally based London firms'. Within that pool of work there will be degrees of complexity and this paragraph will still be relevant.

Guideline hourly rates

Grade	Fee earner	London 1	London 2	London 3	National 1	National 2
A	Solicitors and legal executives with over 8 years' experience	£512	£373	£282	£261	£255
B	Solicitors and legal executives with over 4 years' experience	£348	£289	£232	£218	£218
C	Other solicitors or legal executives and fee earners of equivalent experience	£270	£244	£185	£178	£177
D	Trainee solicitors, paralegals and other fee earners	£186	£139	£129	£126	£126

London

Band	Area	Postcodes
London 1	(very heavy commercial and corporate work by centrally based London firms[3])	
London 2	City & Central London – other work	EC1-EC4, W1, WC1, WC2 and SW1
London 3	Outer London	All other London Boroughs, plus Dartford & Gravesend

National 1:

    i.   The counties of Berkshire, Buckinghamshire, Dorset, Essex, Hampshire (& Isle of Wight), Kent, Middlesex, Oxfordshire, East Sussex, West Sussex, Suffolk, Surrey and Wiltshire

    ii.   Birkenhead, Birmingham Inner, Bristol, Cambridge City, Cardiff Inner, Leeds Inner (within 2km of City Art Gallery), Liverpool, Manchester Central, Newcastle

---

[3] Not restricted to any particular London postcode

City Centre (within 2m of St Nicholas Cathedral), Norwich City, Nottingham City and Watford.

National 2:

All places not included in London 1-3 and National 1

A(23)   Precedent T – Variation of Costs Budget

A	B	C	D	E	F
		Precedent T Summary Sheet			Page
	Name			00/00/0000	
	Parties		Current Budget date:	00/00/0000	
	Number		Date Precedent T served:	00/00/0000	
	:		Cost budget for:	Party	
	Current Budget Costs (prior to variation)		Variations (+ or -)	Total estimated costs after variation (£)	Completion by the Court:
ne / to be done	Incurred (£)	Estimated (£)	Variation in estimate (see explanation sheet for details)		Estimated costs allowed or agreed after variationCompletion by the Court: Estimated costs allowed or agreed after variation
ts	£0.00				
ents of case	£0.00	£0.00	£0.00	£0.00	£0.00
	£0.00	£0.00	£0.00	£0.00	£0.00
	£0.00	£0.00	£0.00	£0.00	£0.00
ents	£0.00	£0.00	£0.00	£0.00	£0.00
	£0.00	£0.00	£0.00	£0.00	£0.00
	£0.00	£0.00	£0.00	£0.00	£0.00
on	£0.00	£0.00	£0.00	£0.00	£0.00
	£0.00	£0.00	£0.00	£0.00	£0.00
ent discussions	£0.00	£0.00	£0.00	£0.00	£0.00
st A:	£0.00	£0.00	£0.00	£0.00	£0.00
st B:	£0.00	£0.00	£0.00	£0.00	£0.00
	Total incurred	Total estimated	Variation	Total estimated costs after variation (£)	
	£0.00	£0.00	£0.00	£0.00	
ncluding both and estimated	£0.00			£0.00	£0.00
get after variation *(incurred and estimated)*					

cludes VAT (if applicable), success fees and ATE insurance premiums (if applicable), costs of detailed assessment, costs of any appeals, costs of enforcing any complete as appropriate]

ication pursuant to Part 3.15 (A) 3(c)

ne costs and disbursements included in this variation are not included in any previous budgeted costs or variation (including any contingency), d or approved by the court.

Signed	
ne (printed)	
osition	
Dated	00/00/0000

Precedent T Particulars

Name
Names
Number
Party

Phase	Time £ (A)	Disbs £ (B)	TOTAL (A+B)	Significant Development [General Explanation for Variation: significant development] Explanation for particular phase (where variation in any phase exceeds £10k complete xx)	Paying party's offer Comment if not agreed	Opposing party comm Brief explanation if not agreed by th
s of case	£0.00	£0.00	£0.00	xx	£0.00	
	£0.00	£0.00	£0.00	xx	£0.00	
	£0.00	£0.00	£0.00	xx	£0.00	
its	£0.00	£0.00	£0.00	xx	£0.00	
table below for disbs al)	£0.00	£0.00	£0.00	xx	£0.00	
	£0.00	£0.00	£0.00	xx	£0.00	
	£0.00	£0.00	£0.00	xx	£0.00	
	£0.00	£0.00	£0.00	xx	£0.00	
t discussions	£0.00	£0.00	£0.00	xx	£0.00	
t:	£0.00	£0.00	£0.00	xx	£0.00	
B:	£0.00	£0.00	£0.00	xx	£0.00	
	Total	Total £0.00	£0.00		Total £0.00	

VARIATION
Variation (+ or -)

A   B   C   D   E   F   G

A(24)   Precedent Q – Model form of breakdown of the costs claimed for each phase of the proceedings

SUMMARY OF COSTS AS CLAIMED VS AMOUNTS IN LAST APPROVED / AGREED BUDGET					
Precedent H Budget Phase	Phase Name	Pre Budget	Budgeted	Last Approved/ Agreed Budget	Departure from Last Approved/ Agreed Budget
		£	£	£	£
Pre-action	Initial and Pre-Action Protocol Work	3,440.23	0.00	0.00	0.00
ADR/ Settlement	ADR / Settlement	0.00	4,972.50	500.00	4,472.50
Issue/Pleadings	Issue / Statements of Case	2,208.50	0.00	2,750.00	-2,750.00
Disclosure	Disclosure	0.00	3,738.46	5,000.00	-1,261.54
Witness Statements	Witness statements	0.00	3,646.50	6,000.00	-2,353.50
Expert Reports	Expert reports	0.00	4,835.00	1,500.00	3,335.00
PTR	Case and Costs Management Hearings	0.00	2,159.00	4,500.00	-2,341.00
CMC	Interim Applications and Hearings (Interlocutory Applications)	960.54	0.00	2,500.00	-2,500.00
Trial Preparation	Trial preparation	0.00	17,635.00	15,000.00	2,635.00
Trial	Trial	0.00	23,187.50	35,000.00	-11,812.50

TEMPLATES FOR DRAFTING KEY DOCUMENTS

B(1)   Letter Before Claim under Practice Direction on Pre-action Conduct

B(2)   Letter of Claim under Professional Negligence Pre-action Protocol

B(3)   Particulars of Claim (Separate from Claim Form)

B(4)   Defence

B(5)   Defence and Counterclaim

B(6)   Case Summary for Use at a Multi-track Case Management Conference

B(7)   Directions Order: Drafting

B(8)   Directions Order: Key CPR Provisions

B(9)   List of Documents

B(10)   Witness Statement

B(11)   Hearsay Notice

B(12)   Expert's Report

B(13)   Part 36 Offer Letter

B(14)   Case Summary for Use at a Fast Track Trial

B(15)   Case Summary for Use at a Multi-track Trial ('Skeleton Argument')

B(1)   Letter Before Claim under Practice Direction on Pre-action Conduct

Dear

[Heading]

<u>Letter before Claim</u>

Introduction

['*We act for* [full names] *of* [full address]']

['Our instructions are to recover a debt/damages . . .']

The facts

[Set out the material background facts, eg relevant contract details.]

Legal basis of claim

[State relevant law such as misrepresentation, breach of contractual term(s), negligence, negligent misstatement, and give brief details.]

Factual basis of claim

[Set out material facts in chronological order, establishing the legal claim, eg the breach of contractual terms or tortious duty.]

Liability/Responsibility

['*We have advised our clients that your actions on [date] were in breach of clause 3 of the contract and/or negligent and that they are entitled to be compensated by you.*']

Debt/Damages/Compensation

[Set out details of amount(s) claimed, including any interest due on a debt under a contractual term.]

Documents enclosed

['*The following documents are relied on by our client in support of the claim and copies are enclosed*' (list relevant documents and state what issue each supports, eg receipts in respect of damages claimed).]

Your documents

[Ask for any relevant documents – list the documents required and explain why they are relevant.]

Alternative Dispute Resolution

[Set out any proposal for ADR that your client wishes to make at this stage, including the method(s) of ADR proposed.]

Practice Direction: Pre-action Conduct

[Enclose copy, if appropriate, and refer to para 16.]

Acknowledgement and response deadline

['*Please acknowledge safe receipt of this letter promptly and provide a full response by no later than* [give a specific date usually 14 days after receipt but up to three months in a complex case]'.]

Court proceedings

[Threat of court proceedings with associated claim for interest and costs if no acknowledgement or full response within [14] days.]

Copy of this letter

['A copy of this letter is enclosed and we suggest that you forward it to your insurers/solicitors immediately.']

Ending

B(2)   Letter of Claim under Professional Negligence Pre-action Protocol

Dear

[Heading]

Letter of Claim

Introduction

[Refer to preliminary notice and any subsequent correspondence.]

[Confirm full name and address of client.]

['*Our instructions are that you negligently . . . and our client is entitled to damages accordingly.*']

The facts

[Set out the material background facts, eg details of the professional services.]

Legal basis of claim

[State the allegations against the professional. As a matter of law, explain what has he done wrong/what has he failed to do.]

Factual basis of claim

[Set out material facts in chronological order, establishing the legal claim.]

[Confirm whether or not an expert has been appointed. If so, provide the identity and discipline of the expert, together with the date on which the expert was appointed.]

Liability/Responsibility

[Explain how the negligence has caused the loss claimed.]

Damages/Compensation

[Give an estimate of the financial loss suffered by the client and state how it is calculated. If details of the financial loss cannot be supplied, explain why and state when you will be in a position to provide the details. If the client is seeking some form of non-financial redress, this should be made clear.]

Documents enclosed

['*The following documents are relied on by our client in support of the claim and copies are enclosed*' (list relevant documents and state what issue each supports, eg receipts in respect of damages claimed).]

Your documents

[Ask for any relevant documents – list the documents required and explain why they are relevant.]

Alternative Dispute Resolution

[Set out any proposal for ADR that your client wishes to make at this stage, including the method(s) of ADR proposed.]

Acknowledgement deadline

['*Please acknowledge safe receipt of this letter promptly and by no later than* [give a specific date 21 days after receipt].']

Response deadline

['*Please provide a full response within 3 months of the date of your acknowledgement letter or let us know within that period how much longer you need to provide a full response and why.*']

Court proceedings

[Threat of court proceedings with associated claim for interest and costs if no acknowledgement (within 21 days) or full response within (3 months or otherwise as stated or agreed).]

Copy of this letter

['*A copy of this letter is enclosed and we suggest that you forward it to your insurers immediately.*']

Ending

B(3)　Particulars of Claim (Separate from Claim Form)

Heading

Name of court, claim number and title of the proceedings

PD 16, para 3.8(1)–(3)

Content

Must include a concise statement of the facts on which the claimant relies: **Rule 16.4(1)(a)**

Should be divided into numbered paragraphs: **PD 5A, para 2.2(5)**

So far as possible each paragraph or sub-paragraph should contain no more than one allegation: **QBD Guide, para 6.7.4(3)**

The facts and other matters alleged should be set out as far as reasonably possible in chronological order: **QBD Guide, para 6.7.4(4)**

Where particulars are given of an allegation (such as breach or loss and damage), the allegation should be stated first and followed by each particular listed in separate numbered sub-paragraphs: **QBD Guide, para 6.7.4(6)**

Have all numbers, including dates, expressed as figures: **PD 5A, para 2.2(6)**

Where a claim is based upon a written agreement, a copy of the contract or documents constituting the agreement should be attached: **PD 16, para 7.3(1)**

Where a claim is based upon an oral agreement, set out the contractual words used and state by whom, to whom, when and where they were spoken: **PD 16, para 7.4**

Where the claimant is seeking interest: **Rule 16.4(2)**

Ending

Statements of case drafted by a legal representative as a member or an employee of a firm should be signed in the name of the firm: **PD 5A, para 2.1**

Must be verified by a statement of truth, the form of which is as follows:
'[I believe] [the claimant believes] that the facts stated in these particulars of claim are true. I understand that proceedings for contempt of court may be brought against anyone who makes, or causes to be made, a false statement in a document verified by a statement of truth without an honest belief in its truth.' **PD 16, para 3.4** and **PD 22, para 2.1**

Failure to verify by a statement of truth: **Rule 22.2**

Must contain the claimant's address for service: **PD 16, para 3.8(4)**

B(4)   Defence

Heading

Name of court, claim number and title of the proceedings

PD 7A, para 4.1

Content

Must state (a) which of the allegations in the particulars of claim are denied; (b) which allegations are not admitted [because of lack of knowledge]; and (c) which allegations are admitted: **Rule 16.5(1)**

Must state for each allegation denied (a) the reasons for doing so; and (b) if putting forward a different version of events from that given by the claimant, must state that version: **Rule 16.5(2)**

Give details of the expiry of any relevant limitation period relied on: **PD 16, para 13.1**

Must be as brief and concise as possible and confined to setting out the bald facts and not the evidence: **QBD Guide, para 6.7.4(1)**

The facts and other matters alleged should be set out as far as reasonably possible in chronological order: **QBD Guide, para 6.7.4(4)**

Where particulars of claim make allegations on a point-by-point basis, answer each and every point: **QBD Guide, para 6.7.4(5)**

Where particulars of claim use definitions, continue with these: **QBD Guide, para 6.7.4(9)**

Should be divided into numbered paragraphs: **PD 5A, para 2.2(5)**

Have all numbers, including dates, expressed as figures: **PD 5A, para 2.2(6)**

Must contain the defendant's date of birth unless already stated in an acknowledgment of service: **PD 16, para 10.7**

Ending

Should be signed in the name of the solicitors' firm: **PD 5A, para 2.1**

Must be verified by a statement of truth, the form of which is as follows:

'[I believe] [the defendant believes] that the facts stated in this defence are true. I understand that proceedings for contempt of court may be brought against anyone who makes, or causes to be made, a false statement in a document verified by a statement of truth without an honest belief in its truth.': **PD 16, para 3.4** and **PD 22, para 2.1**

Failure to verify by a statement of truth: **Rule 22.2**

Must contain the defendant's address for service if no acknowledgment of service filed: **Rule 16.5(8)**

B(5)   Defence and Counterclaim

Heading

Name of court, claim number and title of the proceedings

PD 7A, para 4.1

Claimants and defendants in the original claim should always be referred to as such in the title to the proceedings, even if they subsequently acquire an additional procedural status

PD 20, para 7.3

Content

The defence should be drafted as in **Appendix B(4)**

The defence and counterclaim should normally form one document with the counterclaim following on from the defence (eg if the last numbered paragraph of the defence is paragraph 5, the first numbered paragraph of the counterclaim should be paragraph 6): **PD 20, para 6.1**

The Civil Procedure Rules apply generally to a counterclaim and it should be drafted as if it were a claim: **PD 20, para 3 and see Appendix B(3)**

Ending

Should be signed in the name of the solicitors' firm: **PD 5A, para 2.1**

Must be verified by a statement of truth, the form of which is as follows:

'[I believe] [the defendant believes] that the facts stated in this defence and counterclaim are true. I understand that proceedings for contempt of court may be brought against anyone who makes, or causes to be made, a false statement in a document verified by a statement of truth without an honest belief in its truth.': **PD 16, para 3.4** and **PD 22, para 2.1**

Failure to verify by a statement of truth: **Rule 22.2**

Must contain the defendant's address for service if no acknowledgment of service filed: **Rule 16.5(8)**

B(6)   Case Summary for Use at a Multi-track Case Management Conference

Heading/title of proceedings

Title of document: <u>Case Summary</u>

<u>Chronology of Proceedings</u>

<u>Agreed Issues of Fact</u>

<u>The Issues in Dispute</u>

Identify by suitable references, such as Liability and Quantum.

<u>The Evidence Required to Deal with the Disputed Issues</u>

Identify by suitable references, such as Liability and Quantum.

<u>The Claimant</u>

(i) Liability

Factual

Expert

(ii) Quantum

Factual

Expert

<u>The Defendant</u>

(i) Liability

Factual

Expert

(ii) Quantum

Factual

Expert

B(7)   Directions Order: Drafting

Alternative Dispute Resolution

At all stages the parties must consider settling this litigation by any means of Alternative Dispute Resolution (including Mediation); any party not engaging in any such means proposed by another must serve a witness statement giving reasons within 21 days of that proposal; such witness statement must not be shown to the trial judge until questions of costs arise.

Further Statements of Case

The   must file a   and serve a copy on   no later than   .

Amending Statements of Case

The   has permission to amend its

Requests for Further Information

Any request for clarification or further information based on another party's statement of case shall be served no later than

Any such request shall be dealt with no later than

Disclosure of Documents on Multi-track

Disclosure is hereby dispensed with.

Each party shall disclose by list the documents on which it relies and at the same time request any specific disclosure it requires from any other party.

Disclosure is to be given by each party on an issue by issue basis as follows.

Each party shall disclose by list all documents which it is reasonable to suppose may contain information which enables that party to advance its own case or to damage that of any other party, or which leads to an enquiry which has either of those consequences.

Each party shall give standard disclosure by list.

Standard Disclosure of Documents and Inspection

a)   by 4pm on xxxx the parties must give to each other standard disclosure of documents by list and category.

b)   by 4pm on xxxx any request must be made to inspect the original of, or to provide a copy of, a disclosable document.

c)   any such request unless objected to must be complied with within 14 days of the request.

d)   by 4pm on xxxx each party must serve and file with the Court a list of issues relevant to the search for and disclosure of electronically stored documents, or must confirm there are no such issues, following Practice Direction 31B.

Witnesses of Fact

a)   by 4pm on xxxx all parties must serve on each other copies of the signed statements of themselves and of all witnesses on whom they intend to rely and all notices relating to evidence.

b)   Oral evidence will not be permitted at trial from a witness whose statement has not been served in accordance with this order or has been served late, except with permission from the Court.

c)   Evidence of fact is limited to xx witnesses on behalf of each party.

d)   Witness statements must not exceed xx pages of A4 in length.

Expert Evidence

[No expert evidence being necessary, no party has permission to call or rely on expert evidence].

Single Joint Expert

The parties have permission to rely on the jointly instructed written evidence of an expert xxxx

a)   on the following issues: **or** The expert's report will be confined to the following issues:

i)   ....

ii)   ....

b)   By xxxx the expert should be agreed and instructed, and if no expert has been instructed by that date the Claimant must apply to court by 4pm the following day for further directions.

B(7)   continued

c)   By xxxx the expert will report to the instructing parties.

d)   By xxxx the parties may put written questions to the expert

e)   By xxxx the expert will reply to the questions.

f)   A copy of this order must be served on the expert by the Claimant with the expert's instructions.

g)   The expert may apply direct to the court for directions where necessary under Rule 35.14 Civil Procedure Rules.

h)   A party seeking to call the expert to give oral evidence at trial must apply for permission to do so before pre-trial check lists are filed.

i)   Unless the parties agree in writing or the Court orders otherwise, the fees and expenses of the expert shall be paid by the parties giving instructions for the report equally.

Each Party's Own Expert

The parties have permission to rely on the written evidence of an expert xxxx as follows

a)   on the following issues: **or** The expert's report will be confined to the following issues:

    i)   ....

    ii)   ....

b)   The parties have permission to use in evidence one such expert's report.

c)   By xxxx the expert must be identified to all parties.

And/or

d)   This permission relates to the following:

    i)   Mr Xxxx for the Claimant

    ii)   Mr Xxxx for the Defendant

e)   By 4pm on xxxx the parties must exchange reports.

f)   The parties may raise written questions of the authors of any reports served on them pursuant to this Order by 4pm on xxxx which must be answered by 4pm on xxxx.

g)   Unless the reports are agreed, there must be a without prejudice discussion between the experts by 4pm on xxxx in which the experts will identify the issues between them and reach agreement if possible. The experts will prepare for the court and sign a statement of the issues on which they agree and on which they disagree with a summary of their reasons in accordance with Rule 35.12 Civil Procedure Rules, and each statement must be sent to the parties to be received by 4pm on xxxx.

h)   A copy of this order must be served on the expert by the Claimant with the expert's instructions.

i)   The expert may apply direct to the court for directions where necessary under Rule 35.14 Civil Procedure Rules.

j)   The parties have permission to call oral evidence of these experts.

The parties each have permission to rely on the following written expert evidence:

a)   on the following issues: **or** The expert's report will be confined to the following issues:

    i)   ....

    ii)   ....

b)   The Claimant:

    i)   an expert xxxx, namely Mr A, whose report must be served by xxxx.

    ii)   an expert xxxx, namely Dr B, whose report must be served by xxxx.

    iii)   an expert xxxx, namely Ms C, whose report must be served by xxxx.

c)   The Defendant:

    i)   an expert xxxx, namely Mr AA, whose report must be served by xxxx.

    ii)   an expert xxxx, namely Mr BB, whose report must be served by xxxx.

    iii)   an expert xxxx, namely Ms CC, whose report must be served by xxxx.

d)   The parties may raise written questions of the authors of any reports served on them pursuant to this Order by 4pm on xxxx which must be answered by 4pm on xxxx.

B(7)   *continued*

e)   Unless the reports are agreed, there must be a without prejudice discussion between the experts of like discipline by 4pm on xxxx in which the experts will identify the issues between them and reach agreement if possible. The experts will prepare for the court and sign a statement of the issues on which they agree and on which they disagree with a summary of their reasons in accordance with Rule 35.12 Civil Procedure Rules, and each statement must be sent to the parties to be received by 4pm on xxxx.

f)   A copy of this order must be served on the expert by the Claimant with the expert's instructions.

g)   The expert may apply direct to the court for directions where necessary under Rule 35.14 Civil Procedure Rules.

h)   The parties have permission to call oral evidence of these experts.

Requests for Information etc

Each party shall serve any request for clarification or further information based on any document disclosed or statement served by another party no later than   days after disclosure or service. Any such request shall be dealt with within   days of service.

Trial Listing

The trial will be listed as follows.

a)   The trial window is between xxxx and xxxx inclusive.

b)   The estimated length of trial is xx days.

c)   By 4pm on xxxx the parties must file with the court their availability for trial, preferably agreed and with a nominated single point of contact. They will be notified of the time and place of trial.

d)   By 4pm on xxxx pre-trial check lists must be sent to the court.

Documents to be filed with Pre-trial Checklists

The parties must file with their pre-trial checklists copies of [their experts' reports] [witness statements] [replies to requests for further information].

Pre-trial directions

Pre-trial directions are as follows:

a)   There will be a pre-trial review 4 weeks before the trial window starts with a time estimate of 30 minutes.

b)   The pre-trial review will may be conducted by telephone if the parties so agree unless the court orders otherwise. The Claimant must make the relevant arrangements in accordance with Practice Direction 23A Civil Procedure Rules.

c)   At least 3 clear days before the pre-trial review the Claimant must file and send to the other party or parties preferably agreed and by email:

   i)   draft directions

   ii)   a chronology

   iii)   a case summary.

Trial Directions

The trial directions are as follows:

a)   Not more than 7 nor less than 3 clear days before the trial, the Claimant must file at court and serve an indexed and paginated bundle of documents, which complies with the requirements of Rule 39.5 Civil Procedure Rules and Practice Direction 32. The parties must endeavour to agree the contents of the bundle before it is filed. The bundle will include:

   i)   a case summary;

   ii)   a chronology.

   iii)   a trial timetable.

b)   the parties must file with the court and exchange skeleton arguments at least 3 days before the trial by email.

Costs management order

a)   The court approves the costs budgets of the parties as shown in the Table annexed hereto and initialled by the Master/District Judge.

B(7)   continued

b)	This costs management order by the Master/District Judge is without prejudice to any issue which a party wishes to take on detailed assessment save that the court will not depart from the receiving party's last approved or agreed budget unless there is good reason to do so.

Settlement

Each party must inform the court immediately if the claim is settled whether or not it is then possible to file a draft consent order to give effect to their agreement.

B(8)   Directions Order: Key CPR Provisions

Amending Statements of Case

PD 28, para 3.7(1) [fast track] and PD 29, para 4.8(1) [multi-track]

Directions agreed by the parties should also where appropriate contain provisions about the filing of any reply or amended statement of case that may be required.

Rule 17.1(2)

If his statement of case has been served, a party may amend it only –

(a)   with the written consent of all the other parties; or

(b)   with the permission of the court.

Requests for Further Information

Rule 18.1

(1)   The court may at any time order a party to –

    (a)   clarify any matter which is in dispute in the proceedings; or

    (b)   give additional information in relation to any such matter,

    whether or not the matter is contained or referred to in a statement of case.

(3)   Where the court makes an order under paragraph (1), the party against whom it is made must –

    (a)   file his response; and

    (b)   serve it on the other parties,

    within the time specified by the court.

Alternative Dispute Resolution

PD 29, para 4.10(9)

In such cases as the court thinks appropriate, the court may give directions requiring the parties to consider ADR.

Disclosure of Documents on Multi-track

Rule 31.5

(7)   At the first or any subsequent case management conference, the court will decide, having regard to the overriding objective and the need to limit disclosure to that which is necessary to deal with the case justly, which of the following orders to make in relation to disclosure:

    (a)   an order dispensing with disclosure;

    (b)   an order that a party disclose the documents on which it relies, and at the same time request any specific disclosure it requires from any other party;

    (c)   an order that directs, where practicable, the disclosure to be given by each party on an issue by issue basis;

    (d)   an order that each party disclose any documents which it is reasonable to suppose may contain information which enables that party to advance its own case or to damage that of any other party, or which leads to an enquiry which has either of those consequences;

    (e)   an order that a party give standard disclosure;

    (f)   any other order in relation to disclosure that the court considers appropriate.

Standard Disclosure of Documents and Inspection

Rule 31.5(1)

In all claims [apart from non-personal injury claims on the multi-track]:

    (a)   an order to give disclosure is an order to give standard disclosure unless the court directs otherwise;

    (b)   the court may dispense with or limit standard disclosure; and

    (c)   the parties may agree in writing to dispense with or to limit standard disclosure.

B(8)   *continued*

Rule 31.15

Where a party has a right to inspect a document –

(a)   that party must give the party who disclosed the document written notice of his wish to inspect it;

(b)   the party who disclosed the document must permit inspection not more than 7 days after the date on which he received the notice; and

(c)   that party may request a copy of the document and, if he also undertakes to pay reasonable copying costs, the party who disclosed the document must supply him with a copy not more than 7 days after the date on which he received the request.

Inadvertent Disclosure of Privileged Documents

Rule 31.20

Where a party inadvertently allows a privileged document to be inspected, the party who has inspected the document may use it or its contents only with the permission of the court.

Witnesses of Fact

Rule 32.2

(3)   The court may give directions –

(a)   identifying or limiting the issues to which factual evidence may be directed;

(b)   identifying the witnesses who may be called or whose evidence may be read; or

(c)   limiting the length or format of witness statements.

Rule 32.4

(2)   The court will order a party to serve on the other parties any witness statement of the oral evidence which the party serving the statement intends to rely on in relation to any issues of fact to be decided at the trial.

Rule 32.5

(1)   If –

(a)   a party has served a witness statement; and

(b)   he wishes to rely at trial on the evidence of the witness who made the statement,

he must call the witness to give oral evidence unless the court orders otherwise or he puts the statement in as hearsay evidence.

(2)   Where a witness is called to give oral evidence under paragraph (1), his witness statement shall stand as his evidence in chief unless the court orders otherwise.

Rule 32.10

If a witness statement or a witness summary for use at trial is not served in respect of an intended witness within the time specified by the court, then the witness may not be called to give oral evidence unless the court gives permission.

Expert Evidence

Rule 35.4

(1)   No party may call an expert or put in evidence an expert's report without the court's permission.

(2)   When parties apply for permission they must provide an estimate of the costs of the proposed expert evidence and identify –

(a)   the field in which expert evidence is required and the isues which the expert evidence will address; and

(b)   where practicable, the name of the proposed expert.

(3)   If permission is granted it shall be in relation only to the expert named or the field identified under paragraph (2). The order granting permission may specify the issues which the expert evidence should address.

B(8)   *continued*

(3A)   Where a claim has been allocated to the small claims track or the fast track, if permission is given for expert evidence, it will normally be given for evidence from only one expert on a particular issue.

Rule 35.5(1)

Expert evidence is to be given in a written report unless the court directs otherwise.

Rule 35.6

(1)   A party may put written questions about an expert's report (which must be proportionate) to –

(a)   an expert instructed by another party; or

(b)   a single joint expert appointed under rule 35.7.

(2)   Written questions under paragraph (1) –

(a)   may be put once only;

(b)   must be put within 28 days of service of the expert's report; and

(c)   must be for the purpose only of clarification of the report,

unless in any case –

(i)   the court gives permission; or

(ii)   the other party agrees.

Rule 35.7

(1)   Where two or more parties wish to submit expert evidence on a particular issue, the court may direct that the evidence on that issue is to be given by a single joint expert.

(2)   Where the parties who wish to submit the evidence ('the relevant parties') cannot agree who should be the single joint expert, the court may –

(a)   select the expert from a list prepared or identified by the relevant parties; or

(b)   direct that the expert be selected in such other manner as the court may direct.

Rule 35.8

(1)   Where the court gives a direction under rule 35.7 for a single joint expert to be used, any relevant party may give instructions to the expert.

(2)   When a party gives instructions to the expert that party must, at the same time, send a copy to the other relevant parties.

(3)   The court may give directions about –

(a)   the payment of the expert's fees and expenses; and

(b)   any inspection, examination or experiments which the expert wishes to carry out.

(4)   The court may, before an expert is instructed –

(a)   limit the amount that can be paid by way of fees and expenses to the expert; and

(b)   direct that some or all of the relevant parties pay that amount into court.

Rule 35.12

(1)   The court may, at any stage, direct a discussion between experts for the purpose of requiring the experts to –

(a)   identify and discuss the expert issues in the proceedings; and

(b)   where possible, reach an agreed opinion on those issues.

(2)   The court may specify the issues which the experts must discuss.

(3)   The court may direct that following a discussion between the experts they must prepare a statement for the court setting out those issues on which –

(a)   they agree; and

(b)   they disagree, with a summary of their reasons for disagreeing.

PD 35, para 9.2

The purpose of discussions between experts is not for experts to settle cases but to agree and narrow issues and in particular to identify –

B(8) *continued*

(i)   the extent of the agreement between them;

(ii)   the points of and short reasons for any disagreement;

(iii) action, if any, which may be taken to resolve any outstanding points of disagreement; and

(iv)   any further material issues not raised and the extent to which these issues are agreed.

PD 35, para 9.6

A statement must be prepared by the experts dealing with paragraphs 9.2(i)–(iv) above. Individual copies of the statements must be signed by the experts at the conclusion of the discussion, or as soon thereafter as practicable, and in any event within 7 days. Copies of the statements must be provided to the parties no later than 14 days after signing.

Rule 35.13

A party who fails to disclose an expert's report may not use the report at the trial or call the expert to give evidence orally unless the court gives permission.

PD 29, para 4.11

If it appears that expert evidence will be required both on issues of liability and on the amount of damages, the court may direct that the exchange of those reports that relate to liability will be exchanged simultaneously but that those relating to the amount of damages will be exchanged sequentially.

PD 29, para 5.5(1)

The court will not at this stage give permission to use expert evidence unless it can identify each expert by name or field in its order and say whether his evidence is to be given orally or by the use of his report.

Other Pre-trial Directions

Rule 28.2: Fast Track

(1)   When it allocates a case to the fast track, the court will give directions for the management of the case and set a timetable for the steps to be taken between the giving of the directions and the trial.

(2)   When it gives directions, the court will –

(a)   fix the trial date; or

(b)   fix a period, not exceeding 3 weeks, within which the trial is to take place.

(3)   The trial date or trial period will be specified in the notice of allocation.

(4)   The standard period between the giving of directions and the trial will be not more than 30 weeks.

Rule 29.2: Multi-track

(1)   When it allocates a case to the multi-track, the court will –

(a)   give directions for the management of the case and set a timetable for the steps to be taken between the giving of directions and the trial; or may

(b)   fix –

(i)   a case management conference; or

(ii)   a pre-trial review,

or both, and give such other directions relating to the management of the case as it sees fit.

(2)   The court will fix the trial date or the period in which the trial is to take place as soon as practicable.

(3)   When the court fixes the trial date or the trial period under paragraph (2), it will –

(a)   give notice to the parties of the date or period; and

(b)   specify the date by which the parties must file a pre-trial check list.

B(8)   *continued*

Costs management order

Rule 3.15

(2)   By a costs management order the court will—

    (a)   record the extent to which the budgets are agreed between the parties;

    (b)   in respect of budgets or parts of budgets which are not agreed, record the court's approval after making appropriate revisions.

Rule 3.15(A)

(1)   A party ('the revising party') must revise its budgeted costs upwards or downwards if significant developments in the litigation warrant such revisions.

(2)   Any budgets revised in accordance with paragraph (1) must be submitted promptly by the revising party to the other parties for agreement, and subsequently to the court, in accordance with paragraphs (3) to (5).

(3)   The revising party must—

    (a)   serve particulars of the variation proposed on every other party, using the form prescribed by Practice Direction 3E;

    (b)   confine the particulars to the additional costs occasioned by the significant development; and

    (c)   certify, in the form prescribed by Practice Direction 3E, that the additional costs are not included in any previous budgeted costs or variation.

(4)   The revising party must submit the particulars of variation promptly to the court, together with the last approved or agreed budget, and with an explanation of the points of difference if they have not been agreed.

(5)   The court may approve, vary or disallow the proposed variations, having regard to any significant developments which have occurred since the date when the previous budget was approved or agreed, or may list a further costs management hearing.

(6)   Where the court makes an order for variation, it may vary the budget for costs related to that variation which have been incurred prior to the order for variation but after the costs management order.

Settlement

Rule 1.1

(1)   These Rules are a new procedural code with the overriding objective of enabling the court to deal with cases justly.

(2)   Dealing with a case justly and at proportionate cost includes, so far as is practicable–

    (b)   saving expense;

    (e)   allotting to [a case] an appropriate share of the court's resources, while taking into account the need to allot resources to other cases.

PD 39A, para 4.1

Where –

(1)   an offer to settle a claim is accepted;

(2)   or a settlement is reached; or

(3)   a claim is discontinued, which disposes of the whole of a claim for which a date or 'window' has been fixed for the trial,

the parties must ensure that the listing officer for the trial court is notified immediately.

B(9)   Standard Disclosure List of Documents

Rule 31.6

Standard disclosure requires a party to disclose only –

(a)   the documents on which he relies; and

(b)   the documents which –

    (i)   adversely affect his own case;

    (ii)   adversely affect another party's case; or

    (iii)   support another party's case.

Rule 31.10

(2)   Each party must make and serve on every other party a list of documents in the relevant practice form [N265].

(5)   The list must include a disclosure statement.

(6)   A disclosure statement is a statement made by the party disclosing the documents –

    (a)   setting out the extent of the search that has been made to locate documents which he is required to disclose;

    (b)   certifying that he understands the duty to disclose documents; and

    (c)   certifying that to the best of his knowledge he has carried out that duty.

(7)   Where the party making the disclosure statement is a company, firm, association or other organisation, the statement must also –

    (a)   identify the person making the statement; and

    (b)   explain why he is considered an appropriate person to make the statement.

Part 1

Form N265 states: 'I have control of the documents numbered and listed here. I do not object to you inspecting them/producing copies.

(List and number here, in a convenient order, the documents (or bundles of documents if of the same nature, eg invoices) in your control, which you do not object to being inspected. Give a short description of each document or bundle so that it can be identified, and say if it is kept elsewhere, ie with a bank or solicitor.)'

PD 31A, para 3.2

It will normally be necessary to list the documents in date order, to number them consecutively and to give each a concise description (eg letter, claimant to defendant). Where there is a large number of documents all falling into a particular category, the disclosing party may list those documents as a category rather than individually, eg 50 bank statements relating to account number _ at _ Bank, _20_ to _20_; or, 35 letters passing between _ and _ between _20_ and _20_.

Summary – identify only the actual document, the maker, the recipient (if any) and its date, eg 'Letter from claimant's solicitors to defendant dated _/_/20_.'

Part 2

Form N265 states: 'I have control of the documents numbered and listed here, but I object to you inspecting them:

List and number here, as above, the documents in your control which you object to being inspected. (Rule 31.19).'

B(9)   *continued*

Rule 31.19(3)

A person who wishes to claim that he has a right or a duty to withhold inspection of a document, or part of a document, must state in writing –

(a)   that he has such a right or duty; and

(b)   the grounds on which he claims that right or duty.

Summary – identify the document generally and the privilege (legal professional advice privilege or legal professional litigation privilege) claimed, eg

'Correspondence between the claimant's solicitors and the claimant to give legal advice thereby attracting legal professional advice privilege from inspection.'

'An expert's report obtained by the claimant when this litigation was reasonably contemplated and for the sole purpose of having as evidence for this litigation thereby attracting legal professional litigation privilege from inspection.'

Part 3

Form N265 states: 'I have had the documents numbered and listed below, but they are no longer in my control.

List and number here the documents you once had in your control, but which you no longer have. For each document listed, say when it was last in your control and where it is now.'

Rule 31.10(4)(b)

The list must indicate (a) those documents [that are not privileged from inspection] which are no longer in the party's control; and (b) what has happened to those documents.

Summary – identify only the actual document, the maker, the recipient (if any), its date and, where known, what has happended to it, eg 'Laptop computer belonging to the claimant and stolen whilst the claimant was travelling on the London Underground on _/_/20_. The laptop has not been recovered and its whereabouts are unknown.'

B(10)   Witness Statement

On whose behalf made
Initials and surname of deponent
Number
Exhibit/s "   "
Date
The date of any translation
PD 32, para 17.2

Title to proceedings
PD 32, para 17.1, PD 7A, para 4.1

Full name, address, occupation/description of deponent and state if a party or an employee of a party.
PD 32, para 18.1(1)–(4)

Content

The statement must, if practicable, be in the intended witness's own words and must in any event be drafted in their own language: **PD 32, para 18.1**

The statement should be expressed in the first person: **PD 32, para 18.1**

A statement is the equivalent of the oral evidence which that witness would, if called, give in evidence: **PD 32, para 20.1**

The statement must indicate which of the statements in it are made from the witness's own knowledge and which are matters of information or belief, and the source for any matters of information or belief: **PD 32, para 18.2**

It is usually convenient for a statement to follow the chronological sequence of the events or matters dealt with; each paragraph of a witness statement should as far as possible be confined to a distinct portion of the subject: **PD 32, para 19.2**

The statement should be divided into numbered paragraphs: **PD 32, para 19.1(5)**

Numbers should be expressed as figures: **PD 32, para 19.1(6)**

Any document should be formally exhibited: **PD 32, para 18.3 (and para 18.4)**

The process by which the witness statement has been prepared, whether, for example, face-to-face, over the telephone, through an interpreter: **PD 32, para 18.1(5)**

Ending

Statement of truth: I believe that the facts stated in this witness statement are true. I understand that proceedings for contempt of court may be brought against anyone who makes, or causes to be made, a false statement in a document verified by a statement of truth without an honest belief in its truth: **PD 32, para 20.2 and PD 22, para 2.2**

The statement of truth must be dated with the date on which it was signed: **PD 22, para 2.5**

NOTE – Rule 22.3: if the maker of a witness statement fails to verify the witness statement by a statement of truth, the court may direct that it shall not be admissible as evidence.

B(11)   Hearsay Notice

Heading/title of proceedings

Title of document: <u>Hearsay Notice</u>

This notice is given pursuant to the Civil Procedure Rules 1998, Rule 33.2(1)(b) and (2) and s 2(1)(a) of the Civil Evidence Act 1995.

TAKE NOTICE that the [name of party] intends to rely on the following hearsay evidence at trial:

The witness statement of [name of witness]. A copy is served herewith pursuant to the court order of [date].

It is not proposed to call [name of witness] as [state any appropriate reason, eg witness dead].

[Date]

[Signed]

[Address for service]

B(12)   Expert's Report

Content

An expert's report should be addressed to the court and not to the party from whom the expert has received instructions: **PD 35, para 3.1**

By **PD 35, para 3.2** an expert's report must –

(1)   give details of the expert's qualifications;

(2)   give details of any literature or other material which has been relied on in making the report;

(3)   contain a statement setting out the substance of all facts and instructions which are material to the opinions expressed in the report or upon which those opinions are based;

(4)   make clear which of the facts stated in the report are within the expert's own knowledge;

(5)   say who carried out any examination, measurement, test or experiment which the expert has used for the report, give the qualifications of that person, and say whether or not the test or experiment has been carried out under the expert's supervision;

(6)   where there is a range of opinion on the matters dealt with in the report –

    (a)   summarise the range of opinions; and

    (b)   give reasons for the expert's own opinion;

(7)   contain a summary of the conclusions reached;

(8)   if the expert is not able to give an opinion without qualification, state the qualification;

(9)   contain a statement that the expert –

    (a)   understands their duty to the court, and has complied with that duty; and

    (b)   is aware of the requirements of Part 35, this practice direction and the Guidance for the Instruction of Experts in Civil Claims 2014.

The Civil Justice Council's Guidance for the Instruction of Experts in Civil Claims 2014 provides as follows:

54. The details of experts' qualifications in reports should be commensurate with the nature and complexity of the case. It may be sufficient to state any academic and professional qualifications. However, where highly specialised expertise is called for, experts should include the detail of particular training and/or experience that qualifies them to provide that specialised evidence.

55. The mandatory statement of the substance of all material instructions should not be incomplete or otherwise tend to mislead. The imperative is transparency. The term 'instructions' includes all material that solicitors send to experts. The omission from the statement of 'off-the-record' oral instructions is not permitted. Courts may allow cross-examination about the instructions if there are reasonable grounds to consider that the statement may be inaccurate or incomplete.

56. Where tests of a scientific or technical nature have been carried out, experts should state: a. the methodology used; and b. by whom the tests were undertaken and under whose supervision, summarising their respective qualifications and experience.

B(12)   *continued*

57. When addressing questions of fact and opinion, experts should keep the two separate. Experts must state those facts (whether assumed or otherwise) upon which their opinions are based; experts should have primary regard to their instructions (paragraphs 20–25 above). Experts must distinguish clearly between those facts that they know to be true and those facts which they assume.

58. Where there are material facts in dispute experts should express separate opinions on each hypothesis put forward. They should not express a view in favour of one or other disputed version of the facts unless, as a result of particular expertise and experience, they consider one set of facts as being improbable or less probable, in which case they may express that view and should give reasons for holding it.

59. If the mandatory summary of the range of opinion is based on published sources, experts should explain those sources and, where appropriate, state the qualifications of the originator(s) of the opinions from which they differ, particularly if such opinions represent a well-established school of thought.

60. Where there is no available source for the range of opinion, experts may need to express opinions on what they believe to be the range that other experts would arrive at if asked. In those circumstances, experts should make it clear that the range that they summarise is based on their own judgement and explain the basis of that judgement.

61. Before filing and serving an expert's report solicitors must check that any witness statements and other experts' reports relied upon by the expert are the final served versions.

62. A summary of conclusions is mandatory. Generally the summary should be at the end of the report after the reasoning. There may be cases, however, where the court would find it helpful to have a short summary at the beginning, with the full conclusions at the end. For example, in cases involving highly complex matters which fall outside the general knowledge of the court the judge may be assisted in the comprehension of the facts and analysis if the report explains at the outset the basis of the reasoning.

Formalities

At the end of an expert's report there must be a statement that the expert understands and has complied with his duty to the court: **Rule 35.10(2)**

The expert's report must state the substance of all material instructions, whether written or oral, on the basis of which the report was written: **Rule 35.10(3)**

By **PD 35, para 3.3** an expert's report must be verified by a statement of truth in the following form –

'I confirm that I have made clear which facts and matters referred to in this report are within my own knowledge and which are not. Those that are within my own knowledge I confirm to be true. The opinions I have expressed represent my true and complete professional opinions on the matters to which they refer.

I understand that proceedings for contempt of court may be brought against anyone who makes, or causes to be made, a false statement in a document verified by a statement of truth without an honest belief in its truth.'

B(13)   Part 36 Offer Letter

Dear ....

<u>Heading</u>

<u>PART 36 OFFER: WITHOUT PREJUDICE SAVE AS TO COSTS</u>

[Introduction; any relevant background explaining why offer being made/opponent should accept]

For the purposes of CPR, Rule 36.5(1)(b) we confirm that it is our intention that this offer is made pursuant to and should have the consequences set out in Part 36.

[For the purposes of CPR, Rule 36.5(1)(d) we confirm that this offer relates to the whole of the claim.]

[For the purposes of CPR, Rule 36.5(1)(e) we confirm that this offer takes into account the counterclaim.]

[Set out the proposals clearly and concisely, eg

1.   Your client returns the motor car to our client within seven days of acceptance of this offer.
2.   On receipt of the motor car we will send you £.........................
3.   For the sake of clarity we would confirm that the sum payable under clause 2 is inclusive of interest.]

In accordance with CPR, Rule 36.5(1)(c) the relevant period is 21 days from service of this offer on you. As we are faxing this letter to you before 4.30pm today, a business day, please acknowledge safe receipt and confirmation of service today.

[Closing]

Yours faithfully,

B(14)   Case Summary for Use at a Fast Track Trial

Heading/title of proceedings

Title of document: <u>Case Summary</u>

<u>The Issues in Dispute</u>

Where appropriate, cross-refer to the statements of case in the trial bundle, including reference to relevant paragraph numbers of the statement of case and page numbers in the trial bundle (eg 'PoC para 3 p 4 & Defence para 2 p 5').

<u>The Evidence Required to Deal with the Disputed Issues</u>

Sub-divided into legal and factual issues, if appropriate.

Where appropriate, cross-refer to the evidence in the trial bundle, including reference to relevant paragraphs in witness statements or experts' reports and page numbers in the trial bundle (eg 'Coulson's statement para 3 p 14').

<u>The Claimant</u>

[Legal issues]

Factual

Expert

[Factual issues]

<u>The Defendant</u>

[Legal issues]

Factual

Expert

[Factual issues]

NOTE: on the fast track the Appendix to PD 28 provides that a case summary (which should not exceed 250 words), outlining the matters still in issue and referring where appropriate to the relevant documents, shall be included in the trial bundle for the assistance of the judge in reading the papers before the trial. See also the case summary for use at a multi-track trial (skeleton argument) on the next page. The guidance for that document should be followed, where appropriate.

B(15)   Case Summary for Use at a Multi-track Trial ('Skeleton Argument')

Heading/title of proceedings

Title of document: <u>Case Summary/Skeleton Argument</u>

<u>The Agreed Issues</u>

Concisely set out the nature of the case generally and the background facts in so far as they are relevant to the matter before the court.

<u>The Issues in Dispute</u>

Sub-divided into legal and factual issues, if appropriate. Identify by suitable references, such as Liability and Quantum.

Where appropriate, cross-refer to the statements of case in the trial bundle, including reference to relevant paragraph numbers of the statement of case and page numbers in the trial bundle. Avoid formality and may make use of abbreviations, eg C for Claimant, A/100 for bundle A page 100, 1.1.10 for 1 January 2010 etc.

<u>The propositions of law relied on</u>

Cross-references should be made to relevant authorities.

<u>The Evidence Required to Deal with the Disputed Issues</u>

Where appropriate, cross-refer to the evidence in the trial bundle, including reference to relevant paragraphs in witness statements or experts reports and page numbers in the trial bundle (eg 'Report of C's Expert, Jones para 6 p 21').

<u>The Claimant</u>

[Legal issues]

Factual

Expert

[Factual issues]

<u>The Defendant</u>

[Legal issues]

Factual

Expert

[Factual issues]

OR

<u>The Claimant</u>

(i) *Liability*

Factual

Expert

(ii) *Quantum*

Factual

Expert

<u>The Defendant</u>

(i) Liability

Factual

Expert

(ii) Quantum

Factual

Expert

State the details of the advocate who prepared it.

FLOW DIAGRAMS

C(1)   Overview of the Five Stages of Litigation

C(2)   Steps under Practice Direction on Pre-action Conduct

C(3)   Steps under Professional Negligence Pre-action Protocol

C(4)   Interest

C(5)   Determining Jurisdiction under Regulation 1215/2012

C(6)   Possible Responses by Defendant to a Claim

C(7)   Table 1 – Admission of Claim in Whole but Request Time to Pay

C(8)   Table 2 – Admission of Part of Claim – Specified Amount

C(9)   Table 3 – File Acknowledgement of Service

C(10)   Table 4 – Default Judgment

C(11)   Possible Costs Orders on Setting Aside a Default Judgment

C(12)   Possible Costs Orders on Claimant's Application for Summary Judgment

C(13)   Consequences of Claimant Accepting Defendant's Part 36 Offer within Relevant Period

C(14)   Consequences of Defendant Accepting Claimant's Part 36 Offer within Relevant Period

C(15)   Consequences of Claimant Accepting Defendant's Part 36 Offer after Relevant Period has Expired

C(16)   Consequences of Defendant Accepting Claimant's Part 36 Offer after Relevant Period has Expired

C(17)   Consequences of Claimant Failing to Obtain Judgment More Advantageous Than Defendant's Part 36 Offer

C(18)   Consequences of Claimant Failing to Establish Liability at Trial and so not Obtaining Judgment More Advantageous Than Defendant's Part 36 Offer

C(19)   Consequences of Claimant Obtaining Judgment at Least as Advantageous as Own Part 36 Offer

C(20)   Consequences of Claimant Obtaining Judgment More Advantageous Than Defendant's Part 36 Offer but not as Advantageous as Own Part 36 Offer

C(21)   The Standard Basis of Assessment of Costs

C(1)   Overview of the Five Stages of Litigation

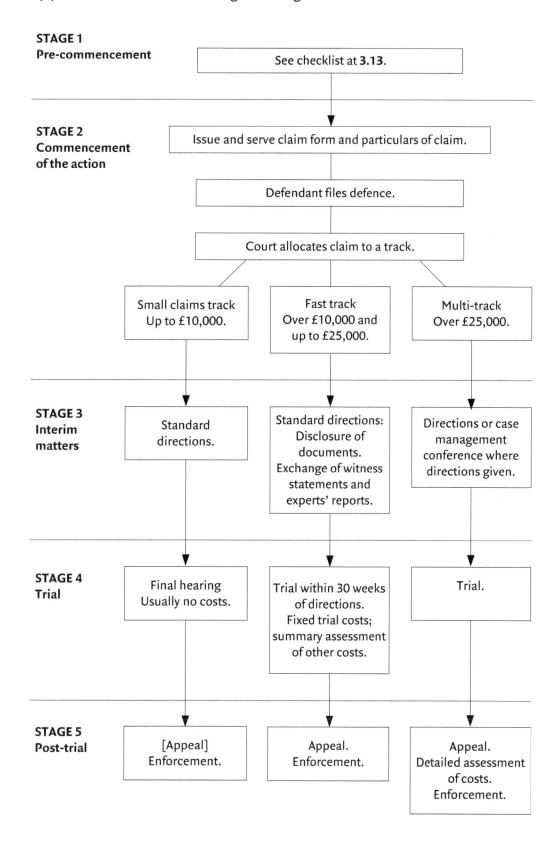

C(2)   Steps under Practice Direction on Pre-action Conduct

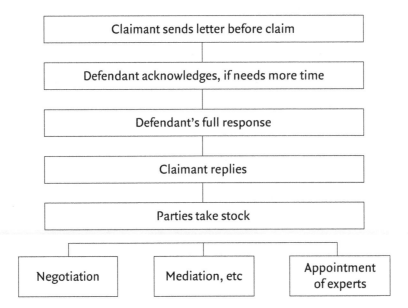

C(3) Steps under Professional Negligence Pre-action Protocol

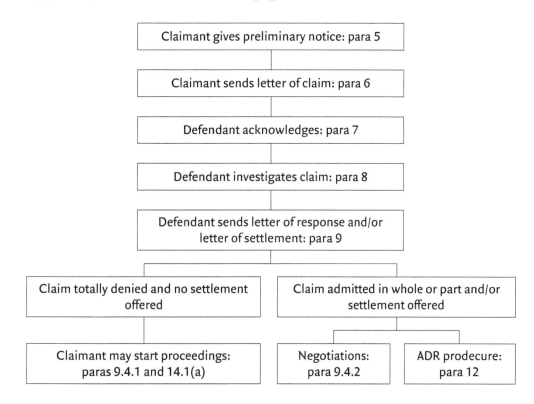

C(4)   Interest

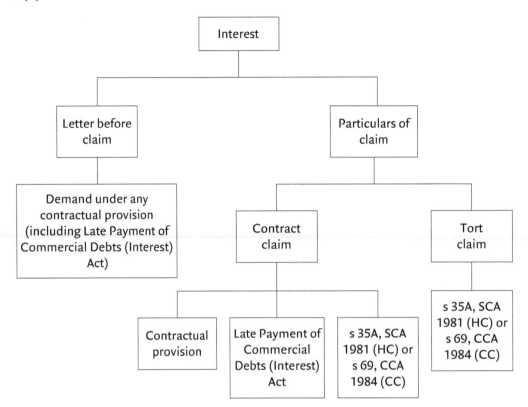

C(5)   Determining Jurisdiction under Regulation 1215/2012

The following questions can be used to determine if the court/s of a Member State of the EU has/have jurisdiction under Regulation 1215/2012 (no longer applicable in the UK).

Q1: Is exclusive jurisdiction conferred on the court/s of a Member State pursuant to Article 24? (a) Yes: proceedings must be taken in that court. (b) No: go to Q2.

Q2: Have the parties agreed for the purposes of Article 25 that the court/s of a Member State are to have exclusive jurisdiction to deal with the dispute? (a) Yes: proceedings must be taken in that court. (b) No: go to Q3.

Q3: Has the defendant entered an appearance in proceedings in the court/s of a Member State for the purposes of Article 26? (a) Yes: proceedings will continue in that court (unless the appearance was entered to contest the jurisdiction, or where another court has exclusive jurisdiction by virtue of Article 24). (b) No: go to Q4.

Q4: Is the defendant domiciled in a Member State for the purposes of Article 4? Yes: proceedings must be taken in that court unless any of the options listed below applies: (i) by Article 7(1), where the claim is in contract the proceedings may be taken in the Member State where the obligation in question was to be performed; (ii) by Article 7(2), where the claim is in tort the proceedings may be taken in the Member State where the harmful event occurred or may occur; (iii) by Article 7(5), where the claim arises out of the operations of a branch, an agency or another establishment, proceedings may be taken in the courts of the Member State where the branch, agency or other establishment is situated; (iv) as to co-defendants, third parties and counter-claimants, see Article 8(1), (2) and (3) respectively; (v) in matters relating to insurance, see Articles 10 to 16; (vi) for consumer contracts, see Articles 17 to 19; (vii) for employment contracts, see Articles 20 to 23.

C(6)   Possible Responses by Defendant to a Claim

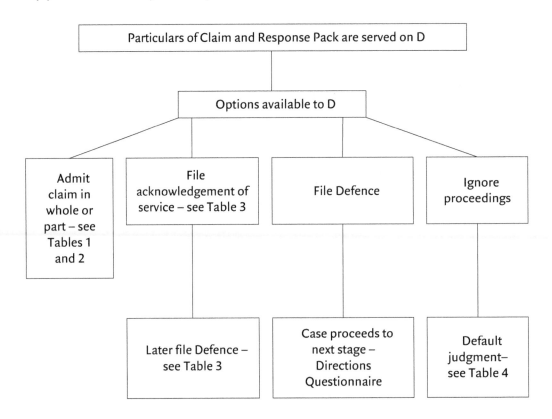

Table 1 – Admission of Claim in Whole but Request Time to Pay　　427

C(7)　Table 1 – Admission of Claim in Whole but Request Time to Pay

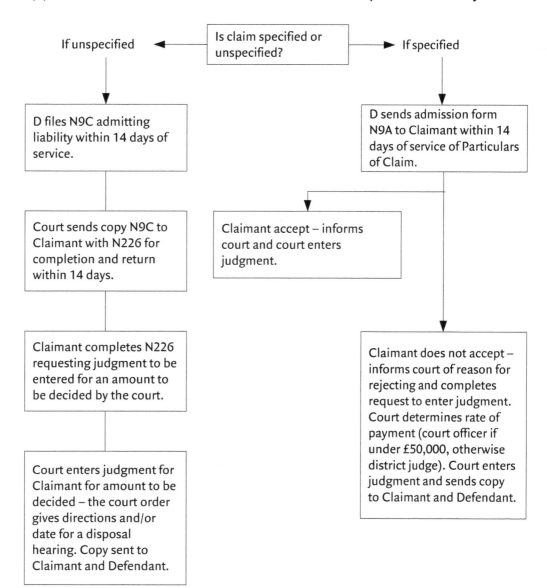

C(8)   Table 2 – Admission of Part of Claim – Specified Amount

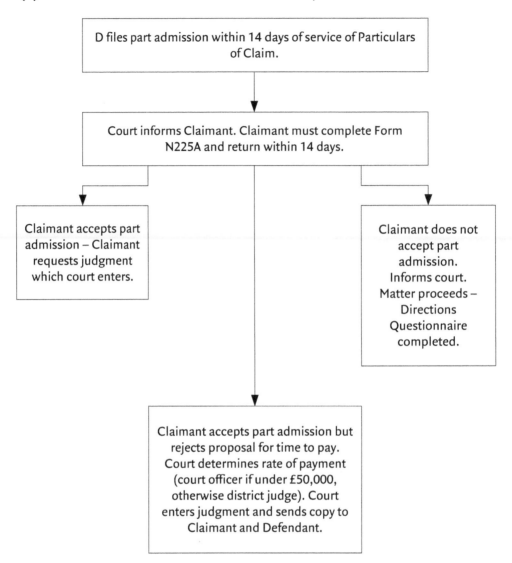

Table 3 – File Acknowledgement of Service   429

C(9)   Table 3 – File Acknowledgement of Service

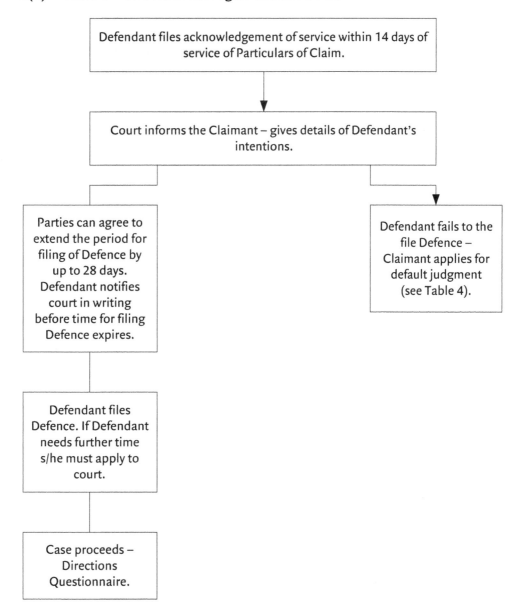

C(10)   Table 4 – Default Judgment

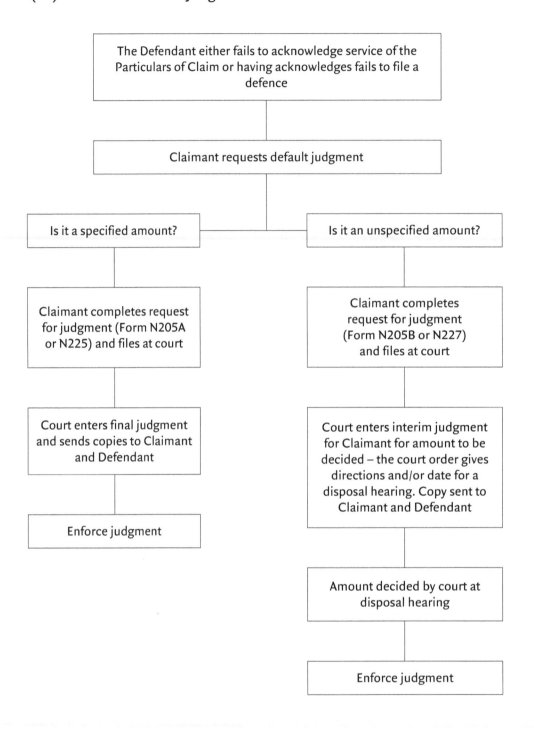

The Defendant either fails to acknowledge service of the Particulars of Claim or having acknowledges fails to file a defence

Claimant requests default judgment

Is it a specified amount?

Is it an unspecified amount?

Claimant completes request for judgment (Form N205A or N225) and files at court

Claimant completes request for judgment (Form N205B or N227) and files at court

Court enters final judgment and sends copies to Claimant and Defendant

Court enters interim judgment for Claimant for amount to be decided – the court order gives directions and/or date for a disposal hearing. Copy sent to Claimant and Defendant

Enforce judgment

Amount decided by court at disposal hearing

Enforce judgment

C(11)   Possible Costs Orders on Setting Aside a Default Judgment

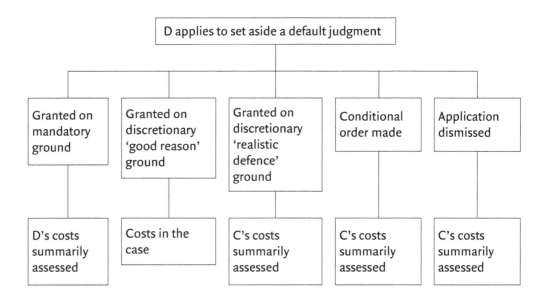

C(12)   Possible Costs Orders on Claimant's Application for Summary Judgment

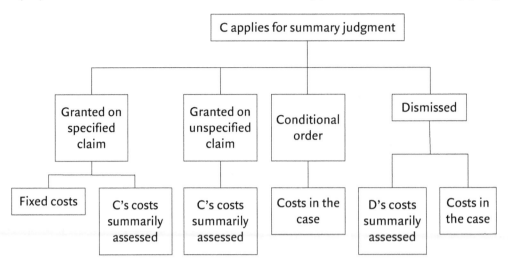

C(13)   Consequences of Claimant Accepting Defendant's Part 36 Offer within Relevant Period

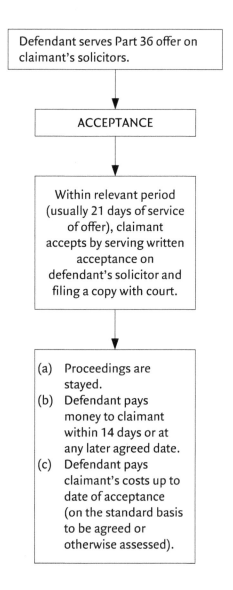

C(14)   Consequences of Defendant Accepting Claimant's Part 36 Offer within Relevant Period

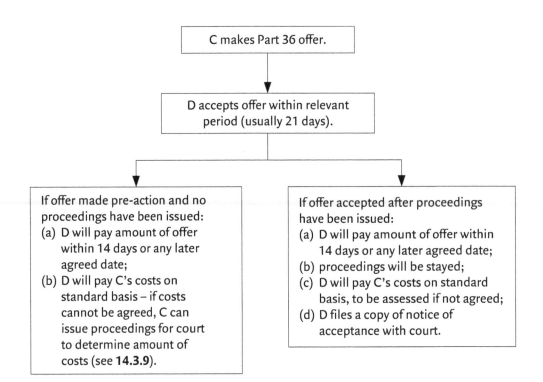

C(15)   Consequences of Claimant Accepting Defendant's Part 36 Offer after Relevant Period has Expired

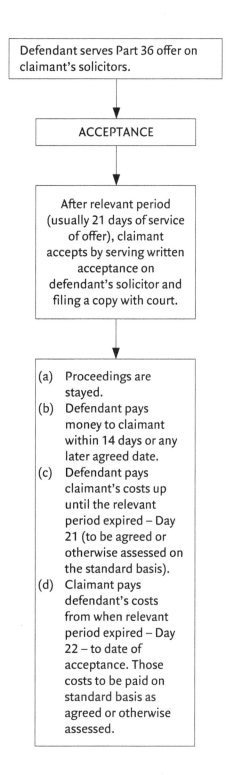

Note: to calculate actual dates, Day 1 = day after deemed service of Part 36 offer

C(16)   Consequences of Defendant Accepting Claimant's Part 36 Offer after Relevant Period has Expired

```
┌─────────────────────────────┐
│      C makes Part 36 offer   │
└─────────────────────────────┘
                ↓
┌───────────────────────────────────────────────────────┐
│ After relevant period expires, D accepts offer by filing written │
│        acceptance at court and serving copy on C.      │
└───────────────────────────────────────────────────────┘
```

If offer made pre-action and no proceedings have been issued:

(a) D will pay agreed sum within 14 days.

(b) If the parties cannot agree the liability for costs, C can issue proceedings for court to determine the issue of costs when the court must, unless it considers it unjust to do so, order that:

    (i) D pays C's costs up until the relevant period expired;

    (ii) D pays C's costs from when the relevant period expired to the date of acceptance;

    (iii) such costs to be paid on the standard basis, as agreed, or otherwise assessed by the court.

If offer accepted after proceedings have been issued:

(a) D will pay agreed sum within 14 days.

(b) Proceedings will come to an end.

(c) If the parties cannot agree the liability for costs, the court must, unless it considers it unjust to do so, order that:

    (i) D pays C's costs up until the relevant period expired;

    (ii) D pays C's costs from when the relevant period expired to the date of acceptance;

    (iii) such costs to be paid on the standard basis, as agreed, or otherwise assessed by the court.

C(17)   Consequences of Claimant Failing to Obtain Judgment More Advantageous than Defendant's Part 36 Offer

Rule 36.17(1) This rule applies where upon judgment being entered–

(a)   a claimant fails to obtain a judgment more advantageous than a defendant's Part 36 offer.

Rule 36.17(3) The court will, unless it considers it unjust to do so, order that the defendant is entitled to–

(a)   costs (including any recoverable pre-action costs) from the date on which the relevant period expired; and

(b)   interest on those costs.

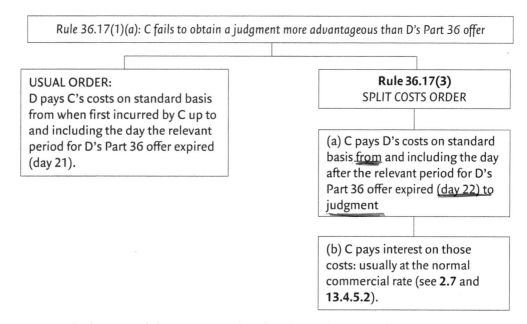

Note: to calculate actual dates, Day 1 = day after deemed service of Part 36 offer.

C(18)   Consequences of Claimant Failing to Establish Liability at Trial and so not Obtaining Judgment More Advantageous Than Defendant's Part 36 Offer

Order for Interest on Costs under Rule 36.17(3)(b)

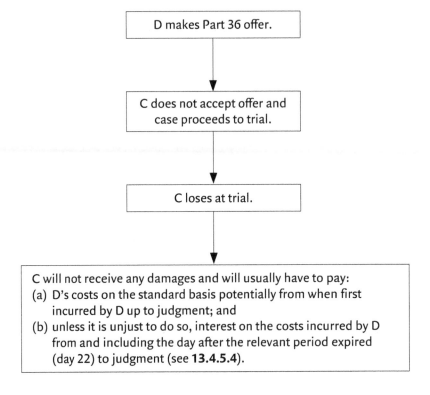

Note: to calculate actual dates, Day 1 = day after deemed service of Part 36 offer.

C(19)   Consequences of Claimant Obtaining Judgment at Least as Advantageous as Own Part 36 Offer

Rule 36.17(1) This rule applies where upon judgment being entered–

(b)   judgment against the defendant is at least as advantageous to the claimant as the proposals contained in a claimant's Part 36 offer.

Rule 36.17(4) The court will, unless it considers it unjust to do so, order that the claimant is entitled to–

(a)   interest on the whole or part of any sum of money (excluding interest) awarded at a rate not exceeding 10% above base rate for some or all of the period starting with the date on which the relevant period expired;

(b)   costs (including any recoverable pre-action costs) on the indemnity basis from the date on which the relevant period expired;

(c)   interest on those costs at a rate not exceeding 10% above base rate; and

(d)   an additional amount, which shall not exceed £75,000, calculated by a prescribed formula.

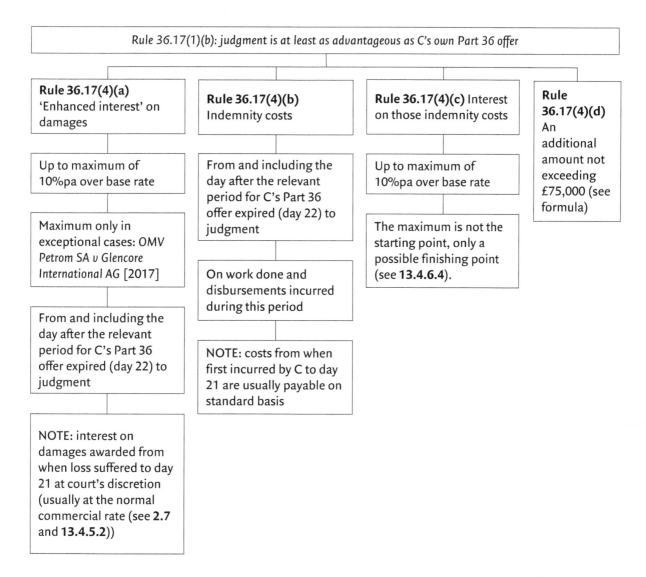

Note: to calculate actual dates, Day 1 = day after deemed service of Part 36 offer.

C(20)   Consequences of Claimant Obtaining Judgment More Advantageous Than Defendant's Part 36 Offer but not as Advantageous as Own Part 36 Offer

---

C wins and obtains a judgment more advantageous than D's Part 36 offer but not as advantageous as C's own Part 36 offer

---

C will receive:

(a)   the damages awarded by the court;

(b)   interest at the court's discretion on the damages awarded (see **2.7.2.3**) provided claimed in the particulars of claim;

(c)   costs on the standard basis potentially from when first incurred by C up to judgment.

Part 36 has no effect – C's offer was probably too high and D's offer probably too low.

C(21)   The Standard Basis of Assessment of Costs

Rule 44.4(1)

The court will have regard to all the circumstances when deciding whether costs were:

(a) proportionately and reasonably incurred

(b) proportionate and reasonable in amount

Rule 44.4(3)

Each factor listed will be applied to each item of cost

(a) the conduct of all the parties, including in particular –

    (i) conduct before, as well as during, the proceedings; and

    (ii) the efforts made, if any, before and during the proceedings in order to try to resolve the dispute;

(b) the amount or value of any money or property involved;

(c) the importance of the matter to all the parties;

(d) the particular complexity of the matter or the difficulty or novelty of the questions raised;

(e) the skill, effort, specialised knowledge and responsibility involved;

(f) the time spent on the case;

(g) the place where and the circumstances in which work or any part of it was done; and

(h) the receiving party's last approved or agreed budget.

Rule 44.3(2)

(a) costs allowable only if proportionate to the matters in issue even if reasonably and necessarily incurred

(b) any doubt resolved in favour of the paying party

Rule 44.3(5)

Costs are proportionate if they bear a reasonable relationship to:

(a) the sums in issue in the proceedings

(b) the value of any non-monetary relief in issue

(c) the complexity of the litigation

(d) any additional work as a result of the conduct of the paying party

(e) any wider factors, eg reputation or public importance

(Note: This rule applies where case commenced and costs incurred on or after 1 April 2013)

CASE STUDY DOCUMENTS

D(1)   Case Analysis

D(2)   Letter Before Claim

D(3)   Defendant's Letter of Response

D(4)   Particulars of Claim

D(5)   Defence and Counterclaim

D(6)   Reply and Defence to Counterclaim

D(7)   Defendant's Part 18 Request for Information

D(8)   Case Summary for Use at Case Management Conference

D(9)   Order for Directions

D(10) Claimant's List of Documents

D(11) Witness Statement of Marjorie Trudge

D(12) Experts' Without Prejudice Meeting Statement

D(13) Claimant's Part 36 Offer Letter

D(14) Defendant's Brief to Counsel

D(15) Consent Order

D(1)   Case Analysis

When carrying out an initial case analysis (see **2.5**) and periodically reviewing the case thereafter, ensure that you answer the following questions:

1.   Have all possible causes of action and potential defendants been identified?
2.   What as a matter of law must the client establish?
3.   What facts will the client have to establish ('the material facts')?
4.   What evidence is currently available to establish the material facts?
5.   What evidence needs to be obtained in order to establish any particular material fact?
6.   How strong is the client's case? What material facts are favourable and unfavourable?

Consider the case study that follows. Assume that you act for Mr and Mrs Simpson. They own a large house locally and had agreed to let out part of it for a couple of months to a Mr Templar. Apparently, when he arrived to take up his tenancy at 11 pm that night, he lost control of his car when driving up the clients' driveway and crashed into their recently completed extension. The clients' garden, the extension and some of their furnishings and fittings were all damaged.

The first step is to establish whether the clients have any basis for making a claim against Mr Templar. This is known as the cause of action. The most obvious claim is in negligence.

What, as a matter of law, must the clients prove to make a claim in negligence successfully against Mr Templar?

(a)   That Mr Templar owed them a duty of care.
(b)   The material facts that establish a breach of that duty.
(c)   The material facts that establish that the damage to the client's property was caused by the breach of that duty, ie the link between Mr Templar's car leaving the driveway and crashing into their extension.
(d)   That as a consequence of the crash the clients suffered damage and loss.

This might be presented in a simple case analysis grid chart, as shown below.

Client: Mr and Mrs Simpson.		
Opponent: Mr Templar.		
Cause of action: Negligence.		
Elements to establish	**Facts to establish**	**Available evidence**
Duty of care	That the clients occupy the property and Mr Templar (a road user) entered onto the driveway.	Clients own the property and saw Mr Templar enter the driveway in his car.
Breach of duty	By driving too fast and erratically, Mr Templar lost control, left the drive and did not avoid crashing into the extension.	Clients who saw Mr Templar do this.
Causation	That by crashing into the extension the clients thereby suffered loss.	Clients who saw Mr Templar do this.
Loss and damage	Damage to garden, the extension, some furnishings and fittings.	Clients.

Where does this case analysis take us next?

We need to consider the strengths and weaknesses of the known case, as follows:

(a) *Duty of care.* This is unlikely to be an issue unless Mr Templar is going to deny that he was the driver. It is well established law that a driver owes a duty to drive to the standard of a reasonable competent driver. By entering the driveway in his car, Mr Templar owed them a duty to drive with reasonable care.

(b) *Breach of duty.* This will probably be a key disputed issue. Why did the car leave the drive and crash into the house? Any evidence needs to be preserved. It may be appropriate to obtain an expert's opinion at this stage.

(c) *Causation.* This is unlikely to be an issue unless Mr Templar denies that the crash took place. If breach can be proved, it will not be disputed that his vehicle caused damage to the clients' property.

(d) *Loss and damage.* However, even if the clients can establish breach of duty (liability), they will still have to prove the amount (quantum) of their claim. Do they have any receipts for repair works already done, or estimates for works that need to be done? These may well be disputed, and the evidence available to prove each item claimed must be considered. At the first interview you will need to itemise each item of loss and analyse the evidence you have or may be able to obtain to prove the amount claimed. This is usually not so problematic where property is damaged as (subject to the duty to mitigate) the cost of replacement/repair is a guide to the amount of the loss. However, where the loss does not have a readily ascertainable financial value, eg loss of profits, more thought must be given to the evidence which can be obtained and relied upon to support the amount claimed.

In the case analysis table above, we have some evidence to support each of the legal elements which must be proved. This will not always be the case – you may have no evidence in respect of a particular element, and that column in your case analysis table will be blank.

So, what should we do, and how might we develop the chart as the case progresses?

Clearly, we could add a column at this stage, setting out the evidence that should be obtained, for example:

Client: Mr and Mrs Simpson.			
Opponent: Mr Templar.			
Cause of action: Negligence.			
Elements to establish	**Facts to establish**	**Available evidence**	**Evidence to obtain**
Duty of care	That the clients occupy the property and Mr Templar (a road user) entered onto the driveway.	Clients own the property and saw Mr Templar enter the driveway in his car.	
Breach of duty	By driving too fast and erratically, Mr Templar lost control, left the drive and did not avoid crashing into the extension.	Clients who saw Mr Templar do this.	Expert evidence: an examination of the vehicle/ driveway may produce evidence which supports the clients' evidence as to the speed of the vehicle/ loss of control.
Causation	That by crashing into the extension the clients thereby suffered loss.	Clients who saw Mr Templar do this.	

Elements to establish	Facts to establish	Available evidence	Evidence to obtain
Loss and damage	Damage to garden, the extension, some furnishings and fittings.	Clients.	An expert will need to produce a report detailing the damage to the extension and the cost of repair.

As the litigation progresses you will need to ensure all necessary procedural steps are taken for the evidence to be used at trial. You may find it helpful to classify each piece of evidence as documentary, witness of fact, expert or real.

You must always remember that the process of case analysis is one of evaluation – will the evidence enable the client to succeed on the balance of probabilities. Throughout a case, in order to assess and advise on its merits, we are looking for favourable facts and unfavourable facts (often called 'good' facts and 'bad' facts). For example, it would be a favourable ('good') fact if, say, Mr Templar had previous convictions or points on his driving licence for speeding. That would point towards liability on this occasion. It would not prove liability, but it would be circumstantial evidence implying that he may have been speeding up Mr and Mrs Simpson's drive. Equally it would be an unfavourable ('bad') fact if, say, Mr and Mrs Simpson's builders had left nails or sharp objects on or near the driveway when completing the extension works. If such items caused the tyres on Mr Templar's car to burst and he lost control of the car as a result, he could argue that he was not to blame, in whole or part, for the accident.

At the end of Stage 1 of Civil Litigation, once we know the prospective defendant's response to the claim, we can then record what legal and factual issues are agreed, and those that are disputed. Whilst it will still be necessary for the statements of case to refer to the facts relating to all issues – whether disputed or not – the procedural and evidential focus will be on the issues in dispute between the parties.

D(2)   Letter Before Claim

SOLICITORS LLP
1 Avenue Road
Nowhere
Mythshire
MC1V 2AA

Our reference: 1234/PO

Mr G Templar
1 The Cottage
Grassy Knowle
Nowhere
Mythshire MY76 9T   24 August 2021

Dear Sir,

Incident at Bliss Lodge, Steep Lane, Nowhere on 2 August 2021
Letter Before Claim

We are instructed by Mr W Simpson and Mrs R Simpson of Bliss Lodge, Steep Lane, Nowhere in connection with a claim for damages following an incident which occurred at their home on 2 August 2021.

The facts

Our clients advise us that at approximately 11 pm on 2 August 2021 you drove your motor car, a Land Cruiser 4x4, 4.5 litre turbo model, registration GIT 13 ('the Car'), on their drive. We understand you were about to take up a short-term let in part of the premises. The Car crashed into the recently completed extension of our clients' property causing serious damage to the garden, building, furnishings and fittings.

Legal basis of claim

By entering our clients' premises, it became your responsibility to ensure that you drove with the degree of care and skill that would be expected from a competent driver.

Factual basis of claim

We are instructed that you drove up the drive at excessive speed and without properly controlling the Car.

You were seen to swerve repeatedly on and off the driveway. The tyre tracks at the property confirm this. It is clear that you failed to apply your Car's brakes sufficiently or at all and that you failed to steer, manage, control or stop the Car so as to avoid the collision. You thereby breached your obligation to drive on our clients' driveway with the degree of care and skill that would be expected from a competent driver. As a result, you drove into our client's extension and this will now have to be demolished, rebuilt and refitted.

Responsibility

We have advised our clients that your actions on 2 August 2021 were negligent and that they are entitled to be compensated by you.

Calculation of damage to the extension at 'Bliss Lodge'

	£
Putting right damage to garden & drive	8,000
Demolishing and rebuilding extension	96,000
Kitchen refit	57,000
Bedroom refit	10,000
TOTAL	**171,000**

Documents relied on

The above figures are based on current available estimates copies of which are enclosed.

In addition to the above losses our clients have been put to considerable expense in making safe the extension.

Calculation of loss in making safe the extension at 'Bliss Lodge'

	£
Weather-proofing the extension	8,000
Installing a temporary alarm system for the parts of 'Bliss Lodge' accessible from the extension	5,000
Making safe the electrical supply to and in the extension	1,000
Sealing off the plumbing supply to the extension	500
TOTAL	**14,500**

Documents relied on

We enclose copies of receipted invoices for the above matters.

Acknowledgment and response

As we are arranging for this letter to be hand delivered to you today, please acknowledge safe receipt of this letter promptly and by no later than 7 September 2021.

Please provide a full written response by 21 September 2021 or such later time as we may agree with you.

Practice Direction on Pre-Action Conduct

We advise you to notify your insurers of this claim, if you have not already done so and take independent legal advice. Should you choose not to instruct solicitors, we enclose a copy of a Practice Direction issued by the courts and we draw your attention to the power of the courts to impose sanctions under paragraph 16.

Alternative Dispute Resolution

At this stage we are not aware that you have any grounds to dispute this claim. If we receive a full written response as requested, then our clients will then be in a better position to consider if any alternative dispute resolution method is appropriate to any issue you raise.

Court proceedings

Please note that if you fail to acknowledge and/or respond as requested above we are instructed to start court proceedings against you without further notification. The court proceedings will include a claim for damages as detailed in this letter, interest on those damages and legal costs incurred by our client.

Raven Lunar Insurance Plc

Following the incident, you informed our clients that you were insured with this company. We enclose a copy of a letter that we have sent to that company giving formal notification of the possible commencement of court proceedings.

Yours faithfully,

D(3)   Defendant's Letter of Response

Advocates & Co
30 Cheapway
Nowhere
Mythshire
MB2X 5PP
DX Never2020
Telephone: 0307 637-2222
Fax: 0307 637-7321

28 September 2021

Our Ref: CF/GIT/13
Your Ref: 1234/PO

Solicitors LLP
1 Avenue Road
Nowhere
Mythshire
MC1V 2AA

Dear Sirs

Incident at Bliss Lodge, Steep Lane, Nowhere

Your clients: Mr and Mrs Simpson

Our client: Mr G Templar

We acknowledged your letter before claim on 27 August and you subsequently agreed that we had until 30 September to make this full response. We have had an opportunity to investigate this claim on behalf of our client and his insurers. Please note that we are instructed as follows.

Denial of liability

Our client denies liability for the damage to your clients' property.

He did not lose control of his car through any fault of his own but because broken shards of glass were present on your clients' driveway. This glass caused two of the tyres on our client's car to burst. For that reason alone he lost control of the car.

In these circumstances our client did not drive negligently.

Counterclaim

Further, your clients' failure to clear away the glass amounts to a breach of their duty of care to our client as a visitor to their property under the Occupiers' Liability Act 1957.

Contributory negligence

Please note that should your clients pursue their claim our client will allege contributory negligence in the alternative on these facts.

Calculation of loss

As a result of your clients' breach of duty our client has suffered the following losses.

1. His car, a 4x4 Land Cruiser, has been damaged beyond economic repair. It has been confirmed as a write-off due to a twisted chassis and other damage. We enclose a letter from We-Haul Recovery & Repair Service confirming this to be the case. Our client's loss on this item is equivalent to the value of the vehicle which was purchased new for £58,995 only the week before this incident.

2. His Diasan PC notebook was also irreparably damaged. This machine's specification is 450mhz, 200Gb hard disk with 128 Mb RAM 32 speed CD Rom notebook with ISDN card and built-in printer. This was only 1 month old and a replacement is valued at £6,500.

3. His Mercuriam satellite mobile phone was also irreparably damaged. Again, this was relatively new and a replacement would cost about £2,000.

4. As his vehicle could not be driven away after this incident, your clients arranged for a local towing service, We-Haul, to tow this away at our client's expense. He has paid their invoice of £440.63 which loss he now seeks from your clients.

5. Our client has had to hire a car while he awaits delivery of the vehicle to replace his Land Cruiser. He has been quite modest in the car he has hired (a Ford Focus). Car hire is £150 per week excluding insurance. He is not due to take delivery of his replacement Land Cruiser until the end of October and our client intends to continue with the hire contract for the Ford Focus.

6. As your clients know, our client had 2 months in which he required accommodation in between selling his London property and completing the purchase of his new home. He has therefore had to obtain alternative accommodation. He spent the first week at The Cherub Inn in Wye-on-Wey at a cost of £175 per night excluding meals, totalling £1,225. Thereafter he has found rooms to rent at £600 a week. Our client claims the difference between this amount spent and what he would have paid to your clients in rental of the stable block, namely £450 a week.

7. Our client has also had to pay for the storage of the Land Cruiser at We-Haul's premises. This costs £50 per week and will continue until the parties can agree that the car is no longer required.

Documents relied on

We enclose:

1. A letter from We-Haul Recovery & Repair Service about the car and a copy of the purchase note.

2. A copy receipt for the Diasan PC notebook.

3. A copy receipt for the Mercuriam satellite mobile phone.

4. A copy receipted invoice from We-Haul for the towing charge.

5. A copy of the hire agreement for the Ford Focus.

6. A copy receipted invoice from The Cherub Inn and for the rooms our client rented.

7. A copy of the storage agreement with We-Haul.

ADR

It is clear that on the issue of liability we have differing expert views. In these circumstances we consider that ADR is inappropriate. However, it may well be that certain items of quantum can be agreed between us subject to the issue of liability. Perhaps you would telephone the writer to discuss? Thereafter we can better consider the question of expert evidence and ADR as to quantum.

<u>Acknowledgement and response</u>

Please acknowledge receipt of this letter by 12 October or in the alternative please telephone the writer by then. Subject to any telephone conversation we may have, please let us have a full response by 26 October 2021.

Please note that we do have instructions to issue proceedings against your client for damages, interest and costs should we not hear from you as requested.

Yours faithfully,

D(4)   Particulars of Claim

IN THE HIGH COURT OF JUSTICE   WF-22-1234
QUEEN'S BENCH DIVISION
WEYFORD DISTRICT REGISTRY

BETWEEN   MR WILLIAM ULYSSES SIMPSON (1)   Claimants
                          MRS RUPINDER SIMPSON (2)

                                    and

                          MR GEOFFREY IAN TEMPLAR   Defendant

PARTICULARS OF CLAIM

1. At all material times the Claimants owned the property known as 'Bliss Lodge', Steep Lane, Nowhere, Mythshire GU15 6AB ('the Property').

2. On 2 August 2021 at about 11.00 pm, the Defendant drove a Land Cruiser 4x4, 4.5 litre turbo model registration number GIT 13 ('the Car') down the driveway leading to the Property. In the circumstances, the Defendant was under a duty of care that he would exercise reasonable care and skill when using the driveway.

3. In breach of that duty and owing to the negligent driving of the Defendant, the Car left the driveway and collided with the Property, partially destroying a recently constructed two-storey extension.

PARTICULARS OF NEGLIGENCE

The Defendant drove negligently in that he:

    (a)   drove at excessive speed;
    (b)   lost control of the Car;
    (c)   swerved repeatedly on and off the driveway;
    (d)   failed to apply the Car's brakes sufficiently or at all;
    (e)   failed to steer, manage, control or stop the Car so as to avoid the collision.

4. Owing to the Defendant's negligence, the Claimants have suffered loss and damage.

PARTICULARS OF LOSS AND DAMAGE

	£
(a) Costs incurred rendering the extension safe following the collision:	
– Weather-proofing the extension	8,000.00
– Installation of temporary alarm system for parts of Bliss Lodge accessible from the extension	5,000.00
– Making safe electrical supply to and in the extension	1,000.00
– Sealing off plumbing supply to the extension	500.00
	14,500.00

(b) Particulars of the estimated costs that follow are given in the attached Schedule.

Estimated costs to be incurred repairing damage to the extension:–

– demolishing and rebuilding the extension	96,000.00
– refitting custom-made kitchen	57,000.00
– refitting bedroom	10,000.00
– remedial and reinstatement works to garden and driveway	8,000.00
	171,000.00
TOTAL	185,500.00

5.   In respect of damages awarded to them the Claimants claim interest under section 35A of the Senior Courts Act 1981 at such rate and for such period as the court thinks fit.

AND THE CLAIMANTS CLAIM:

(1)   Damages as stated in paragraph 4 above;

(2)   Interest as stated in paragraph 5 above.

Dated 4 March 2022   Signed: *Solicitors LLP*
                                                  SOLICITORS LLP

STATEMENT OF TRUTH

I believe that the facts stated in these Particulars of Claim are true. I understand that proceedings for contempt of court may be brought against anyone who makes, or causes to be made, a false statement in a document verified by a statement of truth without an honest belief in its truth.

Signed: *William Ulysses Simpson*
....
WILLIAM ULYSSES SIMPSON
FIRST CLAIMANT

Dated: 4 March 2022

Signed: *Rupinder Simpson*
....
RUPINDER SIMPSON
SECOND CLAIMANT

Dated: 4 March 2022

The Claimants' solicitors are Solicitors LLP, 1 Avenue Road, Nowhere, Mythshire, MC1V 2AA where they will accept service of proceedings on behalf of the Claimants.

To: the Defendant and the Court Manager

D(5)   Defence and Counterclaim

IN THE HIGH COURT OF JUSTICE   WF-22-1234
QUEEN'S BENCH DIVISION
WEYFORD DISTRICT REGISTRY

BETWEEN   MR WILLIAM ULYSSES SIMPSON (1)   Claimants
                           MRS RUPINDER SIMPSON (2)

                                   and

                        MR GEOFFREY IAN TEMPLAR   Defendant

DEFENCE AND COUNTERCLAIM

DEFENCE

1. The Defendant admits paragraph 1 of the Particulars of Claim. The Claimants were the occupiers of the Property and the Defendant was a visitor within the meaning of the Occupiers' Liability Act 1957 ('the Act'). The Defendant visited the Property at the Claimants' invitation on 2 August 2021 to use accommodation in a converted stable block there under an agreement made on 18 July 2021.

2. The Defendant admits paragraph 2.

3. Save that the Defendant admits that he lost control of the Car and that it collided with the Property, the Defendant denies for the reasons that follow that he drove negligently as alleged in paragraph 3 or at all or that the matters complained of were caused as alleged or at all.

4. Further or alternatively, the collision was caused or contributed to by the breach of statutory duty of the Claimants.

PARTICULARS OF BREACH OF STATUTORY DUTY

The Claimants acted in breach of statutory duty in that they:

(a) unknown to the Defendant caused or allowed shards of broken glass to be present on the driveway of the Property which caused the front and rear offside tyres of the Car to suddenly burst, thus resulting in him losing control of the Car;

(b) failed by means of notices or otherwise to warn the Defendant of the presence and position of the glass referred to in (a);

(c) required or allowed the Defendant to use the driveway when it was unsafe;

(d) exposed the Defendant to danger and a foreseeable risk of damage to his property;

(e) failed to take proper care for the Defendant's safety.

5. As to paragraph 4, the Defendant admits that the Property was damaged by the collision but denies for the reasons set out above that he caused any damage. The Defendant otherwise makes no admissions as to the loss or damage alleged by the Claimants in paragraph 4 of the Particulars of Claim as he has no knowledge of such.

6. In the circumstances, the Defendant denies that the Claimants are entitled to the relief claimed in paragraph 4 or any relief.

COUNTERCLAIM

7. The Defendant repeats paragraphs 1 to 5 of the Defence.

8. Owing to the above matters, the Defendant has suffered loss and damage.

PARTICULARS OF LOSS AND DAMAGE

	£
(a) Value of Defendant's Car irreparably damaged	58,995.00
(b) Value of other items in the Car irreparably damaged:	
– Diasan PC notebook computer	6,500.00
– Mercuriam satellite mobile phone	2,000.00
(c) Towing charges paid to We-Haul in removing the Car	440.63
(d) Cost of storing the Car at We-Haul's premises for 9 weeks at £50.00 per week	450.00
(e) Alternative car hire charges for 13 weeks at £150.00 per week	1,950.00
(f) Additional cost of alternative accommodation in Nowhere	1,825.00
TOTAL	**72,160.63**

9.   The Defendant therefore counterclaims from the Claimants damages in respect of the above.

10.   The Defendant claims interest under section 35A of the Senior Courts Act 1981 on damages awarded to him at such rate and for such period as the court thinks fit.

AND THE DEFENDANT COUNTERCLAIMS:

(1)   Damages as stated in paragraph 9 above;

(2)   Interest as stated in paragraph 10 above.

Dated 18 March 2022

Signed: *Advocates & Co*
....
ADVOCATES & CO

STATEMENT OF TRUTH

I believe that the facts stated in this Defence and Counterclaim are true. I understand that proceedings for contempt of court may be brought against anyone who makes, or causes to be made, a false statement in a document verified by a statement of truth without an honest belief in its truth.

Signed: *G I Templar*
....
GEOFFREY IAN TEMPLAR
DEFENDANT

Dated: 18 March 2022

The Defendant's solicitors are Advocates & Co, 30 Cheapway, Nowhere, Mythshire, MB2X 5PP where they accept service of proceedings in behalf of the Defendant.

To: the Claimants

To: the Court Manager

D(6)   Reply and Defence to Counterclaim

IN THE HIGH COURT OF JUSTICE   WF-22-1234
QUEEN'S BENCH DIVISION
WEYFORD DISTRICT REGISTRY

BETWEEN   MR WILLIAM ULYSSES SIMPSON (1)   Claimants
                          MRS RUPINDER SIMPSON (2)

                                    and

                          MR GEOFFREY IAN TEMPLAR   Defendant

---

REPLY AND DEFENCE TO COUNTERCLAIM

REPLY

1. The Claimants admit paragraph 1 of the Defence.

2. The Claimants deny that they were in breach of statutory duty as alleged in paragraph 4 of the Defence or at all. The Claimants also deny that the collision was caused or contributed to by their breach of statutory duty. The Claimants contend that:

    (a) There was no broken glass and/or debris on the driveway. Alternatively, if there was broken glass and/or debris on the driveway, it was placed there by the actions of the Defendant, referred to in paragraph (b) below, whereby the Defendant swerved onto broken glass and/or debris on the grass and thereby caused it to scatter;

    (b) There was a small amount of builders' debris on the grass bordering the right hand side of the driveway. The debris was well away from the normal passage of any vehicle and did not constitute a hazard. It was solely due to the Defendant's excessive speed that he lost control of the Car, veered off the driveway onto the grass and drove onto the debris;

    (c) If the Defendant had been driving at an appropriate speed, he should have been able to control the Car, after the front and rear offside tyres burst, so as to avoid colliding with the Property.

3. Except where the Defendant has made admissions and except as appears in this statement of case, the Claimants join issue with the Defendant upon his Defence.

DEFENCE TO COUNTERCLAIM

4. The Claimants repeat paragraphs 1, 2 and 3 above.

5. As to paragraph 8 of the Counterclaim, the Claimants admit that the Defendant's Car suffered damage but deny for the reasons given above that they caused such loss and damage. The Claimants otherwise do not admit the loss and damage alleged in paragraph 8 of the Counterclaim as they have no knowledge of such.

6. In the circumstances the Claimants deny that the Defendant is entitled to any damages whatsoever.

Dated: 4 April 2022.

Signed: *Solicitors LLP*
         SOLICITORS LLP

STATEMENT OF TRUTH

I believe that the facts stated in this Reply and Defence to Counterclaim are true. I understand that proceedings for contempt of court may be brought against anyone who makes, or causes to be made, a false statement in a document verified by a statement of truth without an honest belief in its truth.

Signed: *William Ulysses Simpson*
....
WILLIAM ULYSSES SIMPSON
FIRST CLAIMANT

Signed: *Rupinder Simpson*
....
RUPINDER SIMPSON
SECOND CLAIMANT

Dated: 4 April 2022

The Claimants' solicitors are Solicitors LLP, 1 Avenue Road, Nowhere, Mythshire, MC1V 2AA where they will accept service of proceedings on behalf of the Claimants.

To: the Defendant and the Court Manager

D(7)   Defendant's Part 18 Request for Information

IN THE HIGH COURT OF JUSTICE   WF-22-1234
QUEEN'S BENCH DIVISION
WEYFORD DISTRICT REGISTRY

BETWEEN   MR WILLIAM ULYSSES SIMPSON (1)   Claimants
                              MRS RUPINDER SIMPSON (2)

                                      and

                          MR GEOFFREY IAN TEMPLAR   Defendant

DEFENDANT'S PART 18 REQUEST FOR FURTHER INFORMATION

This Request is made on 8 April 2022 and the Defendant expects a response to it no later than 22 April 2022.

1. Under paragraph 4 of the Particulars of Claim, please provide a detailed description and financial breakdown of all work undertaken and each and every item of cost incurred in respect of:
    (a) weather-proofing the extension;
    (b) installing a temporary alarm system at Bliss Lodge;
    (c) making safe the electrical supply to and in the extension;
    (d) sealing off plumbing supply to the extension.

2. Under the same paragraph, please provide a detailed description and financial breakdown of all work which it is proposed be undertaken and each and every item of cost it is proposed to incur in respect of:
    (a) demolishing and rebuilding the extension;
    (b) refitting custom-made kitchen;
    (c) refitting bedroom;
    (d) remedial and reinstatement works to garden and driveway.

Advocates & Co
ADVOCATES & CO

30 Cheapway, Nowhere, Mythshire MB2X 5PP
Solicitors for the Defendant

To the Claimants

D(8)   Case Summary for Use at Case Management Conference

IN THE HIGH COURT OF JUSTICE   WF-22-1234
QUEEN'S BENCH DIVISION
WEYFORD DISTRICT REGISTRY

BETWEEN   MR WILLIAM ULYSSES SIMPSON (1)   Claimants
                         MRS RUPINDER SIMPSON (2)

                                   and

                      MR GEOFFREY IAN TEMPLAR   Defendant

Case Summary agreed by the parties for the purpose of the case management conference to be held on 27 June 2022

Chronology of Proceedings

Claim form	4 March 2022
Particulars of claim	4 March 2022
Acknowledgment of service	11 March 2022
Defence and Counterclaim	18 March 2022
Reply and defence to Counterclaim	4 April 2022
Directions questionnaires	19 April 2022

Agreed Issues of Fact

1. On 18 July 2021 the Defendant agreed with the Claimants to rent the stable block of Bliss Lodge, Steep Lane, Nowhere, Mythshire, the Claimants' property and home known as 'Bliss Lodge' for the period of two months commencing on 2 August 2021.

2. The Defendant drove onto the driveway leading to 'Bliss Lodge' on 2 August 2021 at about 11.00 pm.

3. The Defendant's car crashed into Bliss Lodge.

4. The car was a Land Cruiser registration no. GIT 13. The car is a write-off.

5. There was substantial damage done to Bliss Lodge.

6. The quantum of the Defendant's Counterclaim is agreed, subject to liability, as follows:

	£
Land Cruiser	58,995.00
Diasan Notebook	6,500.00
Mercuriam mobile telephone	2,000.00
We-Haul Ltd towage charges	440.63
We-Haul Ltd storage charges	450.00
Excess accommodation costs for 2 months	1,825.00
Car hire 13 weeks	1,950.00
	72,160.63

Issues in Dispute – Claim

Liability

1. Was the Defendant driving negligently by going too fast and/or without due care and attention down the Claimants' drive?

2. Was there glass on or near the drive?

3. If so, should the Defendant have been in a position to take appropriate avoiding action?

4.　　Did the Defendant's negligence cause the damage to the Claimants' property?

5.　　Were the Claimants contributorily negligent in leaving glass on or near the drive?

Quantum

6.　　What are the Claimants' losses and can these be recovered in full from the Defendant?

Issues in Dispute – Counterclaim

Liability

1.　　Were the Claimants in breach of their duties under the Occupiers' Liability Act 1957 in leaving or allowing their builders to leave glass on the drive?

2.　　Did the Claimants' breach of statutory duties cause the damage to the Defendant's car and possessions?

3.　　Was the Defendant contributorily negligent in any way?

Quantum

4.　　Can the Defendant's losses be recovered in full from the Claimants?

The Evidence Required to Deal with the Disputed Issues

The Claimants

The First Claimant will give evidence as to the Defendant's driving, the accident and consequent damage.

The Second Claimant will give evidence about the location of the glass, the accident and consequent damage.

As to expert evidence, the Claimant wishes to rely on:

(a)　　Anthony Bacon: accident reconstruction expert: as to the cause of the accident

(b)　　Fiona McFadden: structural engineer: in respect of structural damage to the Claimant's property

(c)　　John Eaves: quantity surveyor: as to quantum of the Claimants' claim in respect of structural damage to their property.

The Defendant

The Defendant will give evidence as to his driving, the accident and consequent damage.

Colonel Trudge, the Claimants' neighbour, will give evidence as to the Defendant's driving and consequent damage.

Mrs Marjory Trudge will give evidence as to the location of the glass.

As to expert evidence, the Defendant wishes to rely on:

(a)　　Raymond Crow: an accident reconstruction expert: as to the cause of the accident

(b)　　Kieran O'Donnell: building surveyor: in respect of structural damage to the Claimant's property and its quantum.

Areas of Disagreement

The Defendant does not agree with the Claimants that evidence from a structural engineer is required.

Signed:

Solicitors LLP　　　　　　　　　　　　　Advocates & Co

Solicitors LLP　　　　　　　　　　　　*Advocates & Co*
------------------------------　　　　------------------------------

Dated 10 June 2022　　　　　　　　　　Dated 10 June 2022

D(9)　Order for Directions

IN THE HIGH COURT OF JUSTICE   WF-22-1234
QUEEN'S BENCH DIVISION
WEYFORD DISTRICT REGISTRY
DISTRICT JUDGE HARDCASTLE

BETWEEN   MR WILLIAM SIMPSON (1)   Claimants
                         MRS RUPINDER SIMPSON (2)

                                  and

                         MR GEOFFREY IAN TEMPLAR   Defendant

                         <u>ORDER FOR DIRECTIONS</u>

Upon hearing the solicitors for the parties and upon reading the agreed Case Summary dated 10 June 2022

IT IS ORDERED as follows:

ALTERNATIVE DISPUTE RESOLUTION

1.　At all stages the parties must consider settling this litigation by any means of Alternative Dispute Resolution (including Mediation); any party not engaging in any such means proposed by another must serve a witness statement giving reasons within 21 days of that proposal; such witness statement must not be shown to the trial judge until questions of costs arise.

DISCLOSURE OF DOCUMENTS

2.　Disclosure of documents will be dealt with as follows:

　(a)　By 4pm on 11 July 2022 the parties must give to each other standard disclosure of documents by list and category.

　(b)　By 4pm on 18 July 2022 any request must be made to inspect the original of, or to provide a copy of, a disclosable document.

　(c)　Any such request unless objected to must be complied with within 14 days of the request.

WITNESSES OF FACT

3.　Evidence of fact will be dealt with as follows:

　(a)　By 4pm on 22 August 2022 all parties must serve on each other copies of the signed statements of themselves and of all witnesses on whom they intend to rely and all notices relating to evidence.

　(b)　Oral evidence will not be permitted at trial from a witness whose statement has not been served in accordance with this order or has been served late, except with permission from the Court.

EXPERT EVIDENCE

4.　Expert evidence is directed as follows.

　(a)　The parties have permission to rely on the written evidence of one expert on each of the following issues:

　　(i)　the cause of the accident on 2 August 2021; and

　　(ii)　the amount of losses sustained by each party.

(b) By 31 August 2022 each expert must be identified to all parties.

(c) By 4pm on 14 September 2022 the parties must exchange reports.

(d) The parties may raise written questions of the authors of any reports served on them pursuant to this Order by 4pm on 28 September 2022 which must be answered by 4pm on 12 October 2022.

(e) Unless the reports are agreed, there must be a without prejudice discussion between the experts of like discipline by 4pm on 9 November 2022 in which the experts will identify the issues between them and reach agreement if possible. The experts will prepare for the court and sign a statement of the issues on which they agree and on which they disagree with a summary of their reasons in accordance with Rule 35.12 Civil Procedure Rules, and each statement must be sent to the parties to be received by 4pm on 7 December 2022.

(f) A copy of this order must be served on each expert by the party instructing that expert along with the expert's instructions.

(g) Any expert may apply direct to the court for directions where necessary under Rule 35.14 Civil Procedure Rules.

(h) The parties have permission to call oral evidence of these experts.

PRE-TRIAL AND TRIAL

5. The trial will be listed as follows:

(a) The trial window is between 5 April 2023 and 5 May 2023 inclusive.

(b) The estimated length of trial is 2 days.

(c) By 4pm on 4 January 2023 the parties must file with the court their availability for trial, preferably agreed and with a nominated single point of contact. They will be notified of the time and place of trial.

(d) By 4pm on 25 January 2023 pre-trial check lists must be sent to the court.

6. Pre-trial directions are as follows:

(a) There will be a pre-trial review 4 weeks before the trial window starts with a time estimate of 30 minutes.

(b) The pre-trial review may be conducted by telephone if the parties so agree, unless the court orders otherwise. The Claimant must make the relevant arrangements in accordance with Practice Direction 23A Civil Procedure Rules.

(c) At least 3 clear days before the pre-trial review the Claimant must file and send to the other party or parties preferably agreed and by email:

(i) draft directions

(ii) a case summary.

7. The trial directions are as follows:

(a) Not more than 7 nor less than 3 clear days before the trial, the Claimant must file at court and serve an indexed and paginated bundle of documents, which complies with the requirements of Rule 39.5 Civil Procedure Rules and Practice Direction 32. The parties must endeavour to agree the contents of the bundle before it is filed. The bundle will include:

(i) a case summary;

(ii) a chronology.

(iii) a trial timetable.

(b) The parties must file with the court and exchange skeleton arguments at least 3 days before the trial by email.

COSTS MANAGEMENT ORDER

8.   The court approves the costs budgets of the parties as shown in the Table annexed hereto and initialled by the District Judge.

9.   This costs management order by the District Judge is without prejudice to any issue which a party wishes to take on detailed assessment save that the court will not depart from the receiving party's last approved or agreed budget unless there is good reason to do so.

SETTLEMENT

10.   Each party must inform the court immediately if the claim is settled whether or not it is then possible to file a draft consent order to give effect to their agreement.

COSTS

11.   The costs of the case management conference be costs in the case.

Dated 27 June 2022.

D(10) Claimant's List of Documents

List of documents: standard disclosure

Notes

- The rules relating to standard disclosure are contained in Part 31 of the Civil Procedure Rules.
- Documents to be included under standard disclosure are contained in Rule 31.6
- A document has or will have been in your control if you have or have had possession, or a right of possession, of it **or** a right to inspect or take copies of it.

In the	High Court of Justice Queens Bench Division Weyford District Registry
Claim No.	WF-22-1234
Claimant (including ref)	SIMPSON (Ref: 1234/PO)
Defendant (including ref)	TEMPLAR (Ref: CF/GIT/13)
Date	04/07/22

Disclosure Statement

I, the above named

☑ Claimant ☐ Defendant

☐ Party (if party making disclosure is a company, firm or other organisation identify here who the person making the disclosure statement is and why he is the appropriate person to make it)

state that I have carried out a reasonable and proportionate search to locate all the documents which I am

required to disclose under the order made by the court on (date of order) 27/06/22

☑ I did not search for documents:-

☑ pre-dating 01/01/21

☐ located elsewhere than
N/A

☐ in categories other than
N/A

☐ for electronic documents

☑ I carried out a search for electronic documents contained on or created by the following:
(list what was searched and extent of search)

Our home PC files and e-mails.
Our mobile phones.
The files on the first claimant's laptop.
Neither claimant owns or has owned any other electronic storage device.

☐ I did not search for the following:-

☐ documents created before [   ]

documents contained on or created by the ☐ Claimant ☐ Defendant

☐ PCs ☐ portable data storage media
☐ databases ☐ servers
☐ back-up tapes ☐ off-site storage
☐ mobile phones ☐ laptops
☐ notebooks ☐ handheld devices
☐ PDA devices

documents contained on or created by the ☐ Claimant ☐ Defendant

☐ mail files ☐ document files
☐ calendar files ☐ web-based applications
☐ spreadsheet files ☐ graphic and presentation files

documents other than by reference to the following keyword(s)/concepts
(delete if your search was not confined to specific keywords or concepts)

[   ]

I certify that I understand the duty of disclosure and to the best of my knowledge I have carried out that duty. I further certify that the list of documents set out in or attached to this form, is a complete list of all documents which are or have been in my control and which I am obliged under the order to disclose.

I understand that I must inform the court and the other parties immediately if any further document required to be disclosed by Rule 31.6 comes into my control at any time before the conclusion of the case.

☐ I have not permitted inspection of documents within the category or class of documents (as set out below) required to be disclosed under Rule 31(6) (b) or (c) on the grounds that to do so would be disproportionate to the issues in the case.

[   ]

Signed | *W. Simpson* R. Simpson | **Date** | *4 July 2022*

(Claimant)(~~Defendant~~)(~~'s litigation friend~~)

List and number here, in a convenient order, the documents (or bundles of documents if of the same nature, e.g. invoices) in your control, which you do not object to being inspected. Give a short description of each document or bundle so that it can be identified, and say if it is kept elsewhere i.e. with a bank or solicitor

I have control of the documents numbered and listed here. I do not object to you inspecting them/producing copies.

1. Correspondence between the Claimants' solicitors and the Defendant or the Defendant's solicitors from 24/08/21 to date.
2. Copy letter from Claimants' solicitors to Defendant's insurers dated 24 August 2021.
3. Bundle of plans, estimates and receipts for the construction of the Claimants' extension - various dates in 2020 and 2021.
4. Bundle of receipts and estimates in respect of the costs referred to in paragraph 4 of the Claimants' particulars of claim - various dates in 2021.
5. Statements of case in these proceedings - various dates in 2022.

List and number here, as above, the documents in your control which you object to being inspected. (Rule 31.19)

I have control of the documents numbered and listed here, but I object to you inspecting them:

1. Correspondence, attendance notes, memoranda, instructions to counsel and counsel's advice and similar documentation between the Claimants' solicitor and the Claimants.
2. An expert's report.
3. Correspondence between the Claimants' solicitor and witnesses, both expert and factual, including proofs, statements, reports, drafts and similar documentation.

Say what your objections are

I object to you inspecting these documents because:

As to the documents referred to in section 1 above, these were created for the sole purpose of giving or receiving legal advice and so are covered by legal professional, advice privilege.
As to the document referred to in section 2 above, this was obtained by the Claimants when this litigation was reasonably contemplated for the sole purpose of taking legal advice in regard to this litigation and so is covered by legal professional, litigation privilege.
As to the documents referred to in section 3 above, these were created by the Claimant's solicitors from when this litigation was reasonably contemplated to date for the sole purpose of obtaining or collecting evidence to be used in this litigation and so are covered by legal professional, litigation privilege.

List and number here, the documents you once had in your control, but which you no longer have. For each document listed, say when it was last in your control and where it is now.

I have had the documents numbered and listed below, but they are no longer in my control.

The original of the copy letters referred to in the first list above. These were last in the Claimants' control on the day that the originals were posted or otherwise sent.

D(11)   Witness Statement of Marjorie Trudge

On behalf of the Defendant
M Trudge
1st
Exhibit: MT 1
5 August 2022

IN THE HIGH COURT OF JUSTICE   WF-22-1234
QUEEN'S BENCH DIVISION
WEYFORD DISTRICT REGISTRY

BETWEEN   MR WILLIAM ULYSSES SIMPSON (1)   Claimants
                   MRS RUPINDER SIMPSON (2)

and

MR GEOFFREY IAN TEMPLAR   Defendant

_____

WITNESS STATEMENT OF MARJORIE TRUDGE
_____

Marjorie Trudge, retired pharmacist of Paradise Manor, Steep Lane, Nowhere, Mythshire, MB22 7TB will say as follows.

1. I have lived at Paradise Manor with my husband, Harold for the past 35 years. Paradise Manor is next door to Bliss Lodge and I have known the Simpson family since they moved there in 1993.

2. During the early evening of 2 August 2021 whilst I was dusting in a bedroom which overlooks Bliss Lodge, I saw a builders' van stop approximately half-way down the driveway. A couple of men got out and ran back to the house. Within a minute I saw them come out holding a pane of glass. I thought they must have forgotten it. They were walking quite fast but I was rather surprised when I saw them drop it just before they reached the van. They had started to clear it up and had swept it into a pile at the side of the drive when Mr Simpson came out. He looked at his watch and waved them away, seeming to indicate that he was happy for them to go, which they did. He then went back into the house. I did not see him come back out again during the next 30 or so minutes which I spent cleaning the room.

3. I refer to the sketch plan marked "**MT1**". I was asked by Mr Templar's solicitors to prepare this. I have indicated with a cross as best as I can where the plane of glass was dropped. As far as I can recall it was very close to the third light away from the house on the right-hand side of the drive as you go up it towards the house.

4. Unfortunately, I am unlikely to be able to give evidence in this case. I am about to go to Australia to care for my sister who is very ill. I don't expect to return during the next 12 months.

5. I would confirm that this witness statement has been taken from me by the Defendant's solicitor, Chris Taylor, at a face-to-face meeting and via subsequent telephone calls that I had with him.

I believe that the facts stated in this witness statement are true. I understand that proceedings for contempt of court may be brought against anyone who makes, or causes to be made, a false statement in a document verified by a statement of truth without an honest belief in its truth.

Signed: *Marjorie Trudge*

MARJORIE TRUDGE

Dated   5 August 2022

'MT1'

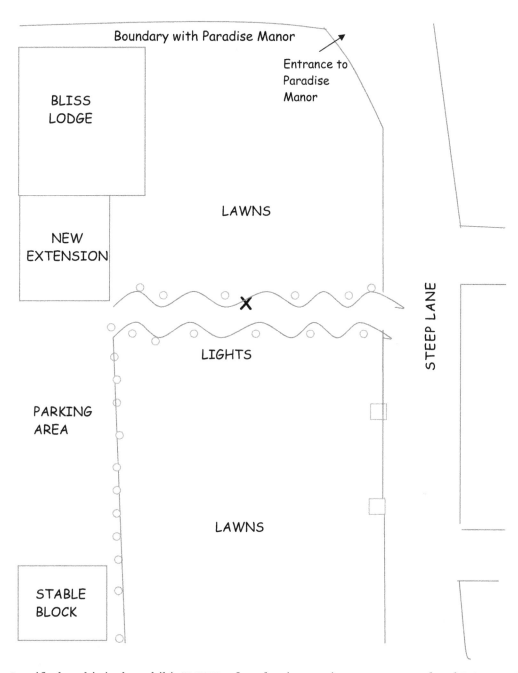

I verify that this is the exhibit "MT1" referred to in my witness statement dated 5 August 2022

Signed: *Marjorie Trudge*

D(12)   Experts' Without Prejudice Meeting Statement

<u>SIMPSON AND SIMPSON -v- TEMPLAR</u>

<u>CASE No. WF-22-1234</u>

<u>NOTE OF 'WITHOUT PREJUDICE' MEETING BETWEEN MR JOHN EAVES AND MR KIERAN O'DONNELL ON 7 NOVEMBER 2022 IN ACCORDANCE WITH THE ORDER FOR DIRECTIONS DATED 27 JUNE 2022</u>

To: the Court

Date: 7 November 2022

The meeting took place at the offices of O'Donnell & Co, at 64 High Street, Nowhere at 9.30 am. It was followed by a short site visit to the Claimants' property at Bliss Lodge, Steep Lane, Nowhere.

Agreed Issues

We agreed that:

1. The sum of £8,000 claimed in respect of emergency weatherproofing work following the accident was reasonable in all the circumstances given the inclement weather in August 2021.

2. A sum of £2,275 is agreed in respect of the installation of a temporary security system at the property pending full repairs.

3. £1,500 is reasonable for the associated electrical and plumbing work.

4. There was no structural damage to the main fabric of Bliss Lodge arising from the accident. We agreed that the evidence of slight subsidence in the back of the playroom where the extension abuts the house pre-dates the accident and is in any event not a cause for concern.

5. There is structural damage to the extension's joists. These will need to be stripped out and re-fixed. As a result, the extension's roof will need to be removed and rebuilt.

6. The extension's foundations are only marginally damaged and can be made good with minor repairs.

7. The cost of refitting the kitchen is agreed at £38,775. It is agreed that the majority of the units will need to be replaced because of water damage.

Disputed Issues

1. Mr Eaves for the Claimants maintains that the load-bearing walls of the extension are fundamentally damaged and need to be demolished and rebuilt. This effectively means that the whole extension has to be demolished.

    Mr O'Donnell for the Defendant maintains that only part of one load-bearing wall must be rebuilt. There is no requirement to demolish the whole extension and the extent of any rebuilding work can be limited to the removal and repair of the roof and joists referred to in paragraph 5 above and the repair *in situ* of the one damaged wall.

In terms of cost (all figures exclude VAT), the figures are as follows:

	Mr Eaves	Mr O'Donnell
Demolition work	£25,600	Nil
Clear site	£8,645	Nil
Rebuild walls	£36,600	£12,460
Make good interior plastering and tiling	£6,700	£5,000

2. The cost of removing the roof, repairing the joists and replacing the roof is disputed:

Mr Eaves   £18,550

Mr O'Donnell   £14,750

3. The extent of repairs required to the bedroom and the associated costs are not agreed:

Mr Eaves	Strip out, replaster and rewallpaper and make good windows and paintwork	£6,560
	Make good floor joists and boards and re-carpet	£4,200
Mr O'Donnell	Minor repairs to lower half of walls in bedroom including re-wallpaper where necessary	£1,300
	Make good floor joists, boards and re-carpet	£2,300

John Eaves

....

John Eaves

(for the Claimants)

Kieran O'Donnell

....

Kieran O'Donnell

(for the Defendant)

D(13)   Claimant's Part 36 Offer Letter

SOLICITORS LLP
1 Avenue Road
Nowhere
Mythshire
MC1V 2AA

Our reference: 1234/PO
Your Ref: CF/GIT/13

Advocates & Co
30 Cheapway
Nowhere
Mythshire
MB2X 5PP   14 November 2022

Dear Sirs,

Simpson v Templar

PART 36 OFFER: WITHOUT PREJUDICE SAVE AS TO COSTS

We refer to previous correspondence in this matter.

Our clients are confident that should this matter proceed to trial they will be successful in establishing liability and recovering the full amount claimed from your client. However, in a final attempt to settle the matter we have our clients' instruction to make your client an offer of settlement. For the purposes of CPR, Rule 36.5(1)(b) we confirm that it is our intention that this offer is made pursuant to and should have the consequences set out in Part 36.

In accordance with CPR, Rule 36.5(1)(d) and (e), the offer on the part of our clients is to accept the sum of £175,000 in relation to the whole of their claim for damages, after taking into account your client's counterclaim. For clarity we would confirm that the offer is inclusive of interest.

In accordance with CPR, Rule 36.5(1)(c) the relevant period is 21 days from the date of service. As we are sending this to you today by first-class post we calculate that the offer will be deemed to be served on 16 November 2022. Please acknowledge and confirm.

Yours faithfully,

D(14)   Defendant's Brief to Counsel

IN THE HIGH COURT OF JUSTICE   WF-22-1234
QUEEN'S BENCH DIVISION
WEYFORD DISTRICT REGISTRY

BETWEEN   MR WILLIAM ULYSSES SIMPSON (1)   Claimants
                              MRS RUPINDER SIMPSON (2)

                                      and

                          MR GEOFFREY IAN TEMPLAR   Defendant

---

**BRIEF TO COUNSEL TO APPEAR ON BEHALF OF THE DEFENDANT AT
THE TRIAL OF THE ACTION ON 19 APRIL 2023**

Counsel has the following copy documents:

(1)   Bundle of correspondence between the parties and solicitors;

(2)   Statements of case;

(3)   Directions questionnaires and pre-trial checklists;

(4)   Orders made during the action;

(5)   Claimants' Part 36 offer letter;

(6)   Case summary from case management conference;

(7)   Documents obtained from the Claimant on inspection;

(8)   The Defendant's documents in Part 1 of his list;

(9)   Exchanged witness statements;

(10)   Civil Evidence Act Hearsay Notice;

(11)   Exchanged expert reports;

(12)   Replies from experts to parties' questions;

(13)   Experts' 'without prejudice' statement filed at court;

(14)   Case summary from pre-trial review hearing;

(15)   Directions for trial;

(16)   Proposed index for trial bundle;

(17)   Proposed index for core bundle;

(18)   Previous instructions to counsel and advice.

BACKGROUND

1.   We act for the Defendant in this action. Counsel will be familiar with the main issues having advised on evidence after disclosure. The action is fixed for trial on 19 April 2023 at 10 am at Weyford District Registry.

FACTS

2.   Counsel is referred to the case summaries prepared in advance of the case management conference and pre-trial review. The facts are briefly as follows.

3.   On 2 August 2021 the Defendant drove his brand-new car, a 4x4 Land Cruiser to the Claimants' property Bliss Lodge, where he was due to take up a two-month tenancy in that property's converted stable block. The Claimants had given him directions. He arrived at about 11 pm. This was observed by the Claimants' neighbour, Colonel Trudge. According to his wife, Mrs Marjory Trudge, the Claimants' builders had earlier that day dropped a pane of glass on the Claimants' driveway. It is the Defendant's case that some broken glass was left on the drive. The Defendant drove over the glass which

caused his two offside tyres to burst. The car went out of his control. The drive was relatively steep and the Defendant's car careered into Bliss Lodge itself, severely damaging the Claimants' newly built extension.

Issues – liability

4.   The issues in the action turn mainly on whether:
   (a)   the Defendant can be shown to have driven negligently; and
   (b)   the Claimants breached their duty, as occupiers, to the Defendant under the Occupiers' Liability Act 1957, in failing to clear away the broken glass and debris and/or warn the Defendant adequately of its presence. It is clear from Mrs Trudge's statement for the Defendant that the Claimants were aware of the glass on and around the drive and there are no issues arising about the liability of the builders.

5.   There is a dispute on the facts about the precise location of the pile of glass and debris. The Claimants maintain that it was to the side of the drive and that the Defendant, in driving too fast down the drive, drove slightly off the drive and over the glass. Their position is that if he had not been driving negligently, he would not have strayed off the drive and would not have hit the glass. This is supported by their expert, Mr Bacon.

6.   Clearly if the Claimants succeed on these points, the counterclaim on the Occupiers' Liability Act is likely to fail at least in part. The Defendant will then face at least partial liability for the damage to Bliss Lodge. The evidence on these points is dealt with in more detail below.

Evidence on liability

7.   Counsel is referred to the reports of the accident reconstruction experts, Mr Bacon for the Claimants and Mr Crow for the Defendant and to the witness statements of Mr Simpson, Colonel and Mrs Trudge. The witness statements are self-explanatory.

8.   Neither expert's report is favourable to the Defendant in terms of the speed at which he was allegedly driving before the accident.

9.   The experts' reports are inconclusive on the question of whether the broken glass was originally on or beside the drive. Therefore, this remains a disputed fact and will have to be resolved by non-expert evidence only (see above). Mr Bacon says that there is evidence of tyre tracks on the grass and he thinks it likely that they were made before the car hit the glass. This opinion is based on the car's subsequent erratic route. However, Mr Crow says he is unable to tell whether the car went over the grass or glass first. He may well be vulnerable in cross-examination. Both experts are of the view that the car hit the house at something approaching 35 to 40 mph. It appears from the reports that there was glass both on and next to the drive at the time of the inspections, possibly as a result of the accident.

10.   Subject to the above comments we have advised the Defendant that there is a risk that the Judge may find in favour of the Claimants. We have discussed settlement and the possibility of a Part 36 offer in order to try to protect his position as to costs. Nevertheless, he is determined to defend the action and pursue his counterclaim. Please would Counsel telephone upon receipt of these instructions to discuss. A pre-trial conference can be arranged should counsel consider it necessary.

Claimant's Part 36 Offer

11.   Counsel will note that the Claimants made a Part 36 offer where the relevant period expired on 7 December 2022 to settle the claim for £175,000 inclusive of interest and taking the Defendant's counterclaim into account. We have advised the Defendant of the potential additional interest, additional costs and additional sum payable under CPR Rule 36.17(4)(a)–(d) should the Claimants obtain a judgment at least as favourable as that at trial.

Issues – quantum

12. The quantum of the counterclaim is agreed, subject to liability, at £72,160.63 (see the case summary).

13. The Claimants' quantum is not agreed. Full details of the issues which are still disputed appear in the without prejudice meeting statement filed by the parties' respective experts on 7 November 2022.

14. There are no issues of remoteness of damage arising and the dispute on quantum relates almost wholly to the scope of demolition and repair work required to the Claimants' extension. The difference amounts to approximately £72,000.

Trial

15. Duncan Murray of Instructing Solicitors will be attending the trial. We will make the necessary arrangements to ensure that Colonel Trudge attends. Mrs Trudge will not be attending trial. Mrs Trudge is in Australia caring for her ailing sister. A Civil Evidence Act Hearsay Notice was served when her witness statement was exchanged and the Claimants' solicitors have not objected to her absence.

16. Counsel is asked to liaise with Duncan Murray as to the final content of the Trial and Core Bundles.

17. Please let us know if Counsel requires any further information.

Counsel is briefed to appear at the trial of the action on 19 April 2023 at Weyford District Registry at 10 am.

Advocates & Co
20 March 2023

D(15)   Consent Order

IN THE HIGH COURT OF JUSTICE   WF-22-1234
QUEEN'S BENCH DIVISION
WEYFORD DISTRICT REGISTRY

BETWEEN   MR WILLIAM ULYSSES SIMPSON (1)   Claimants
                          MRS RUPINDER SIMPSON (2)

                                  and

                        MR GEOFFREY IAN TEMPLAR   Defendant

CONSENT ORDER

Upon the parties agreeing to settle this matter

AND BY CONSENT

IT IS ORDERED THAT

1.   The Defendant shall pay the Claimants the sum of £150,000 by 2.30 p.m. on Friday, 21 April 2023;

2.   Upon payment, the claim and counterclaim are stayed;

3.   No order as to costs.

We consent to the terms of this order.	We consent to the terms of this order.
Solicitors LLP	Advocates & Co
Solicitors LLP	*Advocates & Co*
------------------------------	--------------------------------------
Dated 14 April 2023	Dated 14 April 2023

Index

Academy of Experts 61
Access to Justice (Woolf Report) 1–5
acknowledgement of service 87, 88–90
  companies 89
  flow diagram 429
  form 89
  partnerships 89
  time limits 88–9
addition of parties 76–7
additional proceedings 125–30
  application for permission to make 127
  contribution or indemnity between co-defendants 126–7
  directions 128
  judgment in default 128
  procedure 126–8
  service 128
  third parties 126, 127
  title of proceedings 128
admissibility
  expert evidence 230–1
  hearsay evidence 214–16
admissions
  challenging court's decision 92–3
  form 91–3, 304–5, 308–9
  interest 93
  notice to admit documents 222
  notice to admit facts 222, 315
  specified amount 91–2, 304–5
    part admission 92, 428
  time to pay request 427
  unspecified amount 92, 308–9
  variation of payment rate 93
ADR Group 61
affidavits 213
  oath 213
after-the-event insurance 20
  other side's costs 22
allocation to track 7–8
  automatic transfer of money claims 141–2
  directions questionnaire
    case management information 140
    completion 139–41
    costs 141
    experts 140
    failure to file 142
    Form N181 138, 139–41, 316–21
    pre-action protocols 140
    scrutinising opponent's 142
    trial 141
    witnesses 140–1
  dissatisfaction with allocation 143
  factors considered 142–3
  fast track 145–7
  financial value of claim 142–3
  multi-track 147–52
  notice of proposed allocation 138–9
  small claims track 143–5

alternative dispute resolution (ADR) 7, 28, 33–4
  Academy of Experts 61
  ADR Group 61
  advantages 56–7
  agreement 62
  arbitration 33, 55
  cases where not appropriate 58–9
  Centre for Effective Dispute Resolution 61
  Chartered Institute of Arbitrators 61
  choice of 62–3
  commercial reality 57
  compulsory 63
  conciliation 59
  confidentiality 56, 62
  costs 56–7, 272–3
  criminal compensation order 35
  Criminal Injuries Compensation Authority 34
  disadvantages 57–9
  disclosure obligations 58, 62
  early neutral evaluation 60–1
  enforcement 58
  expert appraisal 33, 60
  expert determination 33, 60
  final offer arbitration 60
  flexibility 57
  independent third party 56
  insurance 34
  judicial appraisal 60
  'Med-arb' 59
  mediation 33, 59
  Mediation UK 61
  mini-trial 59
  Motor Insurers Bureau 34
  nature of 55–6
  negotiation 34, 56
  non-binding nature 57–8
  non-cooperation 62
  non-disclosure 58, 62
  organisations providing 61
  preserving business relationship 57
  privacy 56
  professional bodies 61
  Royal Institution of Chartered Surveyors 61
  speed 56–7, 58
  structured settlement procedure 59
  third parties 56
  trade schemes 34
  use 62
  voluntary nature 55–6
appeals
  assessment of costs 279
  interim order 166–7
applications to court
  appeals against interim order 166–7
  choice of court 160
  consent order 160
    sample 476

applications to court – *continued*
  content 160
  draft order 160
  evidence in support
    attached to notice 160
    preparation 161–2
  form N244 159, 338–42
  freezing injunction 174
  further information 174
  interim costs 163–6
  interim order appeals 166–7
  interim payments 175–8
    consequences of order 177
    discretion of court 177
    grounds 176–7
    poverty and 177
    procedure 176
  interim remedies 174–5
    evidence in support 176
  public or private hearings 162
  search order 174
  security for costs 178–82
  service 160
  setting aside default judgment 167–70
  specific disclosure 198–9
  summary judgment
    conditional orders 172–3
    costs 173
    directions 173
    grounds 170–1
    orders 172–3
    procedure 171–2
  telephone hearings 161
  video conferencing 161
  without notice orders 161
appraisal
  expert 33, 60
  judicial 60
arbitration 33, 55
  see also **alternative dispute resolution (ADR)**
  enforcement of award 58
  final offer arbitration 60
assessment of costs
  agreeing costs 279
  bases compared 271–2
  bill of costs 275, 357–62
  Case Management Orders 268–9
  costs budgets 268–9
  damages-based agreements 278
  detailed 8
    appeals 279
    challenging the bill 276–7
    interim orders 279
    late commencement of assessment 276
    offer to settle 279
    provisional assessment 277
  factors considered 267, 270
  fast track 274
  guideline figures 273–4, 382–4
  indemnity basis 266, 271
  multi-track 275–9
  notice of commencement (form N252) 275, 356
  points of dispute service 276–7, 363–4

assessment of costs – *continued*
  procedure 274
  standard basis 270–1, 272
    flow diagram 441
  statement of costs 275, 343–7
  summary 8, 382–4
    conditional fee agreements 166
    statement of costs 164, 275, 343–7
assessors 231–2
attachment of earnings 289–90

balance of probabilities 29
bankruptcy 290–1
before-the-event insurance 22
bill of costs
  challenging 276–7
  notice of commencement of assessment 275, 356
  opponent's 280
  points of dispute service 276–7, 363–4
  Precedent S 275, 357–62
breach of contract 9–11
briefing counsel 43–4, 257–8
  sample brief 473–5
burden of proof
  balance of probabilities 29
  legal 28–9
Business and Property Courts 66–7
  Capped Costs pilot scheme 278–9
  disclosure pilot scheme 201–3

Capped Costs Pilot Scheme 278–9
case analysis 9–11, 24–7, 445–7
case management
  allocation to tracks *see* **track allocation**
  by court 4
  case summary for conference 150–1, 398, 460–1
  conditions 134
  conference *see* **case management conference**
  directions 8
  disclosure 8
  inadequate statements of case 134–5
  judicial 4
  non-compliance sanctions
    costs 136
    interest 136
    limiting issues 136
    relief 137–8
    striking out 135–6
  powers of court 133–4
  striking out sanction 134–7
  timetables 4, 7, 145
  track allocation *see* **track allocation**
  unless order 136–7
case management conference 8
  attendees 149–50
  case summary for 150–1, 398, 460–1
  multi-track 149–50
  overview 157
  preparation 149–50
Case Management Orders
  costs assessment 268–9
case summary 259–60
  fast track trial 260, 415

case summary – *continued*
    multi-track
        case management conference 150–1, 398, 460–1
        trial 416–17
    templates 151, 398, 415–17
cause of action 9
Centre for Effective Dispute Resolution 61
certificate of service (N215) 82, 312–13
charging order
    on land
        choice of court 287
        notice 287
        order for sale 287
        procedure 287–8
        registration 286–7
        restrictions on making 286
    on securities 288
Chartered Institute of Arbitrators 61
children
    see also litigation friend
    limitation 25
    oath 265
    party to proceedings 73–4
    settlements 74, 255–6
    as witnesses 265
choice of court
    applications to court 160
    charging order on land 287
    commencement of proceedings 65–7
    taking control of goods 284–5
    third party debt orders 288
    value of claim 65
chronology of claim 150
Civil Procedure Rules
    overriding objective 1–4
    scope 5
    Woolf reforms 1–5
claim form
    amount claimed 69
    claimant details 68–9
    completion 7, 68–70
    court fees 70
    defendant details 68–9
    details of claim 69
    form N1 295–8
    form N1A notes for claimant 29
    High Court cases 69–70
    human rights issues 70
    notes for claimant 299–300
    particulars of claim 70
    service 77–83
        time for 81
    solicitor's costs 70
    statement of truth 70–3, 297–8
claim, letter before *see* letter before claim
closing speeches 265
co-defendants
    default judgment 94–5
commencement of proceedings
    choice of court 65–7
    claim form 68–70, 295–8
    costs, assessment *see* assessment of costs
    issuing proceedings 68–73

commencement of proceedings – *continued*
    overview 7–8, 421
    particulars of claim *see* particulars of claim
    parties *see* parties to proceedings
    professional conduct 77
    service *see* service
commercial debts, late payment 30
    particulars of claim 103
competence
    hearsay evidence 219
compromise 256
computation of time 88
conciliation 59
conditional fee agreements 18–19
    disbursements 20
    drafting 19
    interim application costs assessment 166
    opponent's costs 20
    Part 36 offer and 255
    paying party funded 166
    receiving party funded 166
    success fee 19
confidentiality 14
    ADR 56, 62
    Part 36 offer 255
conflict of interest 14–15
consent orders 160, 235
    sample 476
contract
    claims based on 102
    contractual limitation 25
    damages 26
    interest claims 29–30
    limitation 24–5
        contractual 25
    particulars of claim 102
contribution
    additional proceedings 126–7
copies
    disclosure 187–8
cost-benefit analysis 52
costs
    alternative dispute resolution 56–7, 272–3
    amended statements of case 119
    in any event 163
    in the application 163
    applications to court 163–6
    assessment *see* assessment of costs
    before-the-event insurance 22
    between parties 17
    bill of costs 275, 357–62
        challenging 276–7
        opponent's 280
    Capped Costs pilot scheme 278–9
    in the case 163
    of and caused by 163, 164
    CFAs and 166
    claimant's 163
    conditional fee agreements 18–19
    conduct of parties 268
    contingency fees 17–18
        see also conditional fee agreements; damages-based
            agreements

costs – *continued*
  cost-benefit analysis 52
  costs-capping order 155, 165–6
  damages-based agreements 20–2
  defendant's 163
  discontinuance of claim 256
  discretion of court 267
  explained to client 16–17
  fast track
    summary assessment of other costs 275
    trial costs 274
    valuing claim 274–5
  fixed 164
  indemnity basis 271
  indemnity principle 266
  information at first interview 16–17
  interest 234, 266
    after judgment 266
    up to date of judgment 266
  meaning 267
  multi-track 275–9
    agreeing costs 279
    bill of costs, challenging 276–7
    interim orders 279
    late commencement of assessment 276
    notice of commencement (form N252) 275, 356
    offer to settle 279
  no order as to 164
  non-acceptance of Part 36 offer 252, 253
  non-compliance sanction 136
  offer to settle 279
  orders 269
    setting aside default judgment 170, 431
    summary judgment 432
  own costs 164
  'pay as you go' litigation 163
  payment 8
  points of dispute service 276–7, 363–4
  pre-action settlement 234
  regional hourly guideline figure 273
  security for, application 178–82
  solicitor and client costs 17
  split costs order 245–8, 437
  standard basis 270–1, 272
    flow diagram 441
  statement of costs 164, 275, 343–7
  success fee 19
  summary judgment applications 173
  third party debt orders 289
  thrown away 164
  unjust orders 253–5
costs budget 152–5
  amendment 153–4
  assessment of costs 268–9
  budget discussion report 153, 336
  contents 153
  date for filing 153
  failure to file 154
  Precedent H 153, 325–35
  Precedent Q 275, 387
  Precedent R 153, 336
  Precedent T 154, 385–6
  preparation costs 155

costs budget – *continued*
  re-filing and re-serving 156
  reliance on 157
  scope 152
  subsequent changes 153–4
  timing 153
  variation 153–4, 385–6
costs judge 8
costs management 152–7
  budgets 152–5
  judicial approach 155–6
  orders 156–7
costs only proceedings 279–80
costs-capping order
  application 165
  circumstances for 165
  effect 155, 166
  grounds 165–6
counsel
  briefing 43–4, 257–8, 473–5
  conference 43–4
  method of instructing 43–4
  professional conduct 44
  sample brief 473–5
  use 43
counterclaims
  additional proceedings 126, 455–8
  drafting 129
  form 306–7, 310–11
  paragraph numbering 129
  procedure 115, 126
  reply and defence to 457–8
  structure 129
  template 115, 129, 397
county courts 66
  interest on judgment debts 282
  money claims 66, 142
  particulars of claim 104–7
  specified claims 66
  taking control of goods 284–5
  unspecified claims 66
courts
  choice
    applications to court 160
    charging order on land 287
    commencement of proceedings 65–7
    taking control of goods 284–5
    third party debt orders 288
    value of claim 65
  county courts *see* **county courts**
  High Court *see* **High Court**
  personnel 68
  transfers 67
credibility
  hearsay evidence 219
  proof of evidence 39–40
criminal compensation order 35
Criminal Injuries Compensation Authority 34
cross-examination 263–4

damages 26
  contract 26
  duty to mitigate loss 26

damages – *continued*
  failure to mitigate loss 113
  quantum 27
  tort 26
damages-based agreements 20–2
  assessment of costs 278
debt action 26–7
  interest claims 29–30
default judgment
  additional proceedings 128
  co-defendants 94–5
  failure of defendant to respond 93
  flow diagram 430
  interest 94
  procedure 93–4
  request form N227 93
  setting aside 95
    application 167–70
    costs orders 170, 431
    discretionary grounds 167–9
    mandatory grounds 167
  specified amounts 94
  unspecified amounts 94
  where not available 93
defence 98
  see also **statements of case**
  address for service 113
  admissions, non-admissions, denials and assertions 112–13
  causation 113
  comprehensive response 112–13
  contents 112
  drafting 91, 122–3
  example, High Court 114
  expiry of limitation period 113
  failure to mitigate loss 113
  filing 91
  form 310–11
  limitation 113
  point-by-point response 113
  reply to 115
  service 91
  template 115, 396
  time limits 90
    extensions 90
  to each allegation 112–13
defence and counterclaim
  drafting 129
  form N9 306–7, 310–11
  procedure 115, 126
  sample 455–6
  structure 129
  template 397
defendants
  acknowledgement of service 87, 88–90
  admissions
    challenging court's decision 92–3
    form 91–3, 304–5, 308–9
    part claim 428
    specified amount 91–2, 304–5, 428
    time to pay request 427
    unspecified amount 92, 308–9
    variation of payment rate 93

defendants – *continued*
  capacity 27–8
  counterclaim 306–7, 310–11
  default judgment 94–5
  defence 90–1, 306–7, 310–11
  details in claim form 68–9
  disputing jurisdiction 89–90
  identification 27–8
  notes for defendants (N1C) 87, 301–2
  response flow diagram 426
  response pack (N9) 87, 303–11
  solvency 28
  status 27–8
  whereabouts 28
directions 8
  additional proceedings 128
  fast track 322–4
    exchange of expert reports 146
    exchange of witness statements 146
    failure to comply 146
    listing directions 147
    timetable 145
    variation 145–6
    variation by consent 146
  multi-track 147–8
    case management conference 149
    non-compliance 151
    variation 151
  order for 462–4
    key CPR provisions 403–7
    template 399–402
  summary judgment applications 173
disclosure 8, 40
  see also **inspection of documents**
  Business and Property Court pilot scheme 201–3
  continuing obligation 191
  control of documents 187
  copies 188
  definition 184
  Disclosure Guidance Hearing 203
  documents defined 184–5
  duty to search 188–9
  electronic documents 184, 188–9
  extended 202–3
  failure to disclose 198
  fast track 185
  form N265 189, 198
  inadvertent 195–6
  initial 202
  issues in dispute 186–7
  list of documents 189, 197–8, 201, 465–7
  multi-track 185–6
  N263 disclosure report 185, 337
  non-party 199–200
  obvious mistake 195
  order 49–50
  pre-action 49–50, 199
  privilege *see* **privilege**
  purpose 183–4
  searches 188–9
  small claims track 185
  solicitors' duties 200–1
  specific 198–9

disclosure – *continued*
  standard 186–7, 201
    list of documents 408–9
    procedure 189–90
  statement 190
    contempt of court 190
    signature 190
    solicitor's duties 191
  subsequent use of documents 198
  third parties 199–200
  'without prejudice' documents 196
discontinuance of claim
  costs 256
  general provisions 256
  procedure 256
district judges 68
documents
  control 187
  definition 184–5
  disclosure *see* **disclosure**
  electronic 184, 188–9
  as hearsay evidence 220–1
  information recorded in 184–5
  inspection *see* **inspection of documents**
  meaning 41
  notice to admit 222
  notice to prove 222
  photocopies 201
  preservation 40–1
  proof of evidence 39
  service *see* **service**
  statements contained in 220–1
  'without prejudice' 50–1, 196

early neutral evaluation 60–1
electronic documents 188–9
  disclosure 184
enforcement 9
  alternative dispute resolution awards 58
  attachment of earnings 289–90
  bankruptcy 290–1
  charging order on land
    choice of court 287
    notice 287
    order for sale 287
    procedure 287–8
    registration 286–7
    restrictions on making 286
  charging order on securities 288
  controlled goods agreement 286
  enquiry agents 282, 283
  interest on judgment debts
    county courts 282
    High Court 282
  investigation of means 283–4
  judgment against partnership 281–2
  methods 284–91
  money judgments 281
  taking control of goods
    choice of court 284–5
    controlled goods agreement 286
    county courts 284–5
    High Court 284, 285

enforcement – *continued*
    items exempt from seizure 285–6
  third party debt orders
    choice of court 288
    costs 289
    deposit taking institution 289
    procedure 289
  tracing 282
  winding up 291
enquiry agents 282, 283
evidence
  affidavits 213
  assessors 231–2
  at trial 262–4
  exchange before trial 8
  exhibits 209–10
  experts *see* **expert evidence**
  first interview 6
  hearsay *see* **hearsay evidence**
  judicial approach 206–7
  judicial control 205–6
  models 221–2
  notice to admit documents 222
  notice to admit facts 222
  notice to prove documents 222
  opinion 213–14
  oral 206–7, 210
    experts 143, 146, 149, 224
    hearsay 214–21
  photographs 221–2
  plans 221–2
  previous inconsistent statement 219–20, 264
  relevance 205
  Rules 205–6
  in support of application
    attached to notice 160
    interim remedies 176
    preparation 161–2
  trial bundle 259–60
  witness evidence 207–8
  witness statements 207
  witness summaries 39, 211–12
expert appraisal 33, 60
expert determination 33, 60
expert evidence
  admissibility 230–1
  assessors 231–2
  attendance at trial 258–9
  challenging admissibility 230–1
  changing experts 228
  court power to restrict 223–4
  directions 223–4, 227, 229–30
    failure of expert to comply 227–8
  discussion between experts 227–8
  duty of expert 223
  fees 41–2, 224
  form of 225
  guidance 222–3, 373–81
  instructions 41, 49, 224–5
  opinion 42, 214
  oral 143, 146, 149, 224, 230
  privilege 224
  professional negligence claims 231

expert evidence – *continued*
   questions to expert 226–7
   report 42, 100, 412–13
      content 225–6
      exchange 146
      statement of truth 226
   restrictions on use 42
   single joint expert 42, 49, 229–30
   'without prejudice' meeting statement 227, 470–1
   written joint statement 227

fast track 7–8
   allocation to 145–7
   case summary 260, 415
   costs
      management 152
      summary assessment of other costs 275
      trial costs 274
      valuing claim 274–5
   directions
      exchange of expert reports 146
      exchange of witness statements 146
      failure to comply 146
      listing 147
      standard 145, 322–4
      timetable 145
      variation 145–6
   disclosure 185
   listing directions 147
   listing questionnaire 145, 146–7, 353–5
   pre-trial checklist 145, 146–7, 353–5
   timetable 261
   trial 8
   trial bundle 147
final offer arbitration 60
first interview 6
   alternative remedies 28
   burden of proof 28–9
   capacity of defendant 27–8
   confirmation of instructions 37–8
   costs information 16–17
     see also **funding**
   damages 26
   debt actions 26–7
   evidence 6
   identification of defendants 27–8
   interest 29–32
   liability 24
   limitation 6, 24–5
   merits of claim 28
   money claims 29
   professional conduct 14–16
   public funding 23
   purpose 14
   remedy sought 25–6
   solvency of defendant 28
   standard of proof 29
   viability of claim 27
   whereabouts of defendant 28
fixed costs 164
foreign elements
   see also **jurisdiction**
   choice of forum 32–3

forms
   admissions 91–3, 304–5, 308–9
   defence and counterclaim 306–7, 310–11
   N1 295–8
   N1A notes for claimant 29, 299–300
   N1C notes for defendants 87, 301–2
   N9 response pack 87, 303–11
   N170 pre-trial checklist, listing questionnaire 145, 146–7, 353–5
   N181 directions questionnaire 138, 139–41, 316–21
   N205A 94
   N205B 94
   N208 Part 8 claim form 130
   N215 certificate of service 82, 312–13
   N218 service on partner 78, 314
   N225 request for judgment 94
   N227 request for judgment in default 94
   N242A notice of offer to settle 239, 348–52
   N244 application notice 159, 338–42
   N252 notice of commencement of assessment 275, 356
   N260 statement of costs 164, 274, 343–7
   N263 disclosure report 185, 337
   N265 standard disclosure documents 189, 198
   N266 notice to admit facts 315
freezing injunctions
   affidavit evidence 213
   applications 174
funding
   after-the-event insurance 20, 22
   before-the-event insurance 22
   conditional fee agreements 18–19
   costs information 16–17
   damages-based agreements 20–2
   insurance 22
   public 23
   success fee 19
   third party 22
   trade unions 22
further information
   applications to court 174
   requests for 119–21

hearsay evidence
   admissibility 214–16
   competence 219
   credibility 219
   cross-examination on 219
   definition 214–16
   first-hand 215–16
   judicial approach 217–18
   multiple 215–16
   notice 216, 411
   previous inconsistent statements 219–20
   'second best' evidence 217
   statements contained in documents 220–1
   statutory guidelines 218
   use 216–17
   weight attached 218
   witness statements as 211, 216–17
High Court 66–7
   appeals 279
   claim form 69–70
   example defence 114

High Court – *continued*
  interest on judgment debts 282
  particulars of claim 108–9
  taking control of goods 284, 285
HM Courts and Tribunals Service website 11
hostile witness 264

indemnity
  additional proceeding 126–7
  costs basis 271
  principle 266
inspection of documents
  see also **disclosure**
  failure to allow 198
  photocopies 201
  purpose 183–4
  right 189
  withholding 191–6
    see also **privilege**
instructions
  counsel 43–4, 257–8
  expert witness 41, 49, 224–5
  writing to confirm 38
insurance 22
  after-the-event 20, 22
  alternative dispute resolution (ADR) 34
  before-the-event 22
interest
  admissions 93
  after judgment 266
  amount 31–2
  before judgment 266
  breach of contract 29–30
  debt action 29–30
  default judgment 94
  entitlement to 29–32
  flow diagram 424
  on judgment debts
    county courts 282
    High Court 282
  non-compliance sanction 136
  Part 36 offer 239, 244, 249–50
  particulars of claim 29, 103
  pre-action settlement 234
  tort actions 31
  up to date of judgment 266
  when payable 31–2
interim costs
  applications to court 163–6
interim matters
  overview 8, 421
interim payments
  applications to court 175–8
  consequences of order 177
  discretion of court 177
  grounds 176–7
  poverty and 177
  procedure 176
interim remedies
  applications to court 174–5
  evidence in support 176
interview with solicitor
  first *see* **first interview**

interviewing witnesses 38–40
investigation of means
  defendant 28
  judgment debtor 283–4
issuing proceedings *see* **commencement of proceedings**

Jackson report 1
judgment
  in default *see* **enforcement**
  delivery of 265
  Register of Judgments Orders and Fines 266
  request for 94
  summary *see* **summary judgment applications**
judgment debtor
  investigation of means 283–4
  obtaining information
    application 283
    hearing 283–4
judgment debts
  enforcement *see* **enforcement**
judicial appraisal 60
jurisdiction
  defendant served in England and Wales 32–3
  determination for EU domicile 425
  disputed 89–90
  domicile 425
  foreign elements 32–3
  service
    in England and Wales 32–3
    outside jurisdiction 83

latent damage
  limitation 25
legal burden 28–9
legal professional privilege
  advice privilege 191–2
  expert evidence 224
  litigation privilege 192–4
  purpose 194
  third parties 192–4
  waiver 194
letter before claim 7
  acknowledgement 48
  claimant's reply 49
  content 46–7
  professional conduct 46
  response of defendant 7, 48–9
  sample 448–9
  sending out 46
  taking stock after correspondence 49
  templates 47, 391–4
letter of response 7, 48–9
  claimant's reply 49
  sample 450–2
limitation 6
  contract actions 24–5
  contractual 25
  latent damage 25
  persons under disability 25
  solicitor's role 24
  tort actions 24–5
limited companies
  parties to action 75

limited companies – *continued*
  service on 79
list of documents
  disclosure 189, 197–8, 201, 465–7
  inspection of opponent's 201
  standard disclosure 408–9
  template 198
listing questionnaire
  fast track 145, 146–7, 353–5
litigation
  last resort 6, 45
  overview flow diagram 421
litigation friend
  actions by 73–4
  cessation of appointment 74
  requirement for 73
live text
  use from trial 262

masters 68
'Med-arb' 59
mediation 33, 59, 272–3
Mediation UK 61
mini-trial 59
Ministry of Justice
  website 11
minors *see* **children**
mitigation of loss
  duty 26
  failure to mitigate 113
models 221–2
money claims
  county court 66, 142
  failure to file directions questionnaire 142
  online issue 66
  specified 29
  transfer 66, 141–2
  unspecified 29
money judgments
  enforcement *see* **enforcement**
money laundering 15
Motor Insurers Bureau 34
multi-track 8
  case management conference 8
    case summary 150–1, 398, 460–1
    chronology of claim 150
    directions
      sanctions for improper preparation 149
      template 152
    preparation 149–50
    topics considered 149
  case summary 150–1, 398, 416–17, 460–1
  chronology of claim 150
  costs
    agreeing costs 279
    areas challenged 277–8
    bill of costs 275, 357–62
      challenging 276–7
    categories of work 275–6
    detailed assessment 276
    interim orders 279
    late commencement of assessment 276
    management 152–7

multi-track – *continued*
    notice of commencement (N252) 275, 356
    offer to settle 279
  directions 147–8
    non-compliance 151
    order for 148
    variation 151
  disclosure
    directions 185–6
    disclosure report 185
    overriding objective 185
  Part 8 claims 131
  pre-trial checklist 151–2, 353–5
  timetable 261
  trial 8
    case summary 260, 416–17

negotiation 56
  authority of solicitor 233–4
  basis on which to conduct 234
notice of commencement of assessment 275, 356
notice of offer to settle (N242A) 239, 348–52
notice of service on partner (N218) 78, 314
notice to admit facts 222, 315

oaths
  affidavits 213
  children 265
obtaining information
  application 283
  hearing 283–4
offer to settle
  see also **Part 36 offer**
  detailed assessment of costs 279
  'without prejudice' 237–8
ombudsmen schemes 61
opinion evidence 213–14
order for directions
  sample 462–4
overriding objective 1–2
  parties' duty to further 2–4
overview
  commencement of action 7–8
  flowchart 421
  interim matters 8
  post-trial 8–9
  pre-commencement procedure 5–7
  trial 8

Part 8 claims
  claim form N208 130
  multi-track 131
  procedure 130–1
  types of claim 130
Part 36 offer
  acceptance 241
    costs consequences 242–4
    practical consequences 241–2
  'advantageous' meaning 252–3
  application 265
  change in terms 240–1
  children 255–6
  claimant's 238, 248–52

Part 36 offer – *continued*
>additional amount 251–2
>failure to beat offer 248
>indemnity costs 250
>interest 249–50
>'like with like' comparison 249
>succeeding in beating offer 248–9
>tactical considerations 252
>clarification 241
>close to trial 240
>conditional fee arrangements and 255
>consequences flow diagram 433–40
>content 238–40
>defendant's 238
>>claimant's loss at trial 248
>>interest 244
>>late acceptance 243–4
>>'like with like' comparison 244–5
>>split costs order 245–8
>>tactical considerations 248
>flow diagrams 433–40
>form 238–40
>formalities 238–9
>interest 239
>late acceptance 243–4
>more than one offer 239–40
>non-acceptance 252, 253
>notice of acceptance 241
>notice of offer to settle 348–52
>partial award 252
>patients 255–6
>pre-action offers 51–2
>in respect of counterclaim 255
>sample 472
>secrecy 255
>split costs order 245–8, 437
>template 414
>unjust orders 253–5
>when made 240
>withdrawal 240–1

particulars of claim 7, 70, 98–9
>*see also* **statements of case**
>breach and damage 109
>chronology of material facts 110
>contents 102–10
>drafting 110, 121–2
>example
>>county court 104–7
>>High Court 108–9
>interest 103
>oral contract 102
>purpose 102
>sample 453–4
>service 85–6
>statement of truth 106–7, 110
>summary for relief 109
>template 110–12, 395
>written contract 102

parties to proceedings
>addition 76–7
>children 73–4
>limited companies 75
>litigation friend 73–4

parties to proceedings – *continued*
>names 73
>partnerships 75
>persons under disability 73–4
>>limitation 25
>sole traders 75
>substitution 76–7
>unnamed 75–6
>vulnerable witnesses 4–5

partnerships
>acknowledgement of service 89
>enforcement of judgment 281–2
>notice of service on 78, 314
>party to proceedings 75
>service on 78
>statement of truth, signature 71

patients
>parties to proceedings 73–4
>settlements 255–6

'pay as you go' litigation 163

personal injury actions
>pre-action disclosure 50

persons under disability
>limitation 25
>parties to proceedings 73–4
>settlements 255–6

photographs
>as evidence 221–2
>site visits 42–3

plans 221–2
>site visits 42–3

post-trial procedure
>overview 8–9, 421

postal service 77, 78

Practice Directions 5
>Pre-action Conduct and Protocols 6, 44–5, 365–7
>>aims 44
>>claimant's reply 49
>>failure to comply 45–6
>>flowchart 422
>>instruction of experts 49
>>letter of acknowledgement 48
>>letter before claim 46–8, 391–2
>>letter of response 48–9
>>summary 53–4

practitioner works 52

pre-action disclosure 49–50, 199

pre-action offers 51–2

pre-action protocols 6
>aims 44
>failure to comply 45–6
>false statements 49
>flowcharts 47, 422–3
>instruction of experts 49
>non-compliance costs 45–6
>Practice Directions 5
>>Pre-Action Conduct *see* **Practice Directions**, Pre-action Conduct and Protocols
>professional negligence 44, 368–72
>>flowchart 47, 423
>>letter before claim 393–4

pre-action settlement
>costs 234

pre-action settlement – *continued*
  interest 234
  recording 234
pre-commencement procedure
  ADR 7, 28
  client's objectives 5–6
  costs 6
  costs information *see* **funding**
  dispute resolution 6
  evidence 6
  first interview 6
    limitation 6, 24–5
    purpose 14
  jurisdiction 6
  letter before claim 7
  letter of response 7
  limitation 6, 24–5
  parties 6
  pre-action protocols 6
  summary 52–3
pre-trial checklist
  fast track 145, 146–7, 353–5
  multi-track 151–2, 353–5
preparations for trial
  attendance of witnesses
    experts 258–9
    general 258
  briefing counsel 43–4, 257–8, 473–5
  case summary 259–60
  'core' bundle 260
  skeleton arguments 259–60
  time estimates 260
  trial bundle 259–60
preservation of documents 40–1
previous inconsistent statements 219–20, 264
privilege
  challenging claim for 194–5
  claim in list of documents 197
  inadvertent disclosure 195–6
  legal professional
    advice privilege 191–2
    expert evidence 224
    litigation privilege 192–4
    third parties 192–4
    waiver 194
  public policy 194
  self-incrimination 194
  'without prejudice' documents 196
professional conduct
  Code of Conduct principles 16
  counsel 44
  letter before claim 46
  statements of case 101
professional negligence pre-action protocol 44, 368–72
  flowchart 47, 423
  letter before claim 393–4
proof of evidence 38
  credibility 39–40
  documents 39
  open and closed questions 39
  personal questions 39
  'picture painting' 39
  structure 39

proof of evidence – *continued*
  taking 39–40
public funding 23
  see also **funding**
  statutory charge 23
public policy privilege 194

quantum of damages 27

re-examination 264
recognised practitioner works 52
Register of Judgments Orders and Fines 266
remedies
  damages 26
  debt action 26–7
  interest 29–32
  interim *see* **interim payments; interim remedies**
  money claims 29
reply and defence to counterclaim 457–8
reply to defence 115
request for further information
  application for court order 121
  no response 121
  request 119–20
  response to request 120–1
  sample 459
request for judgment
  form N225 94
request for judgment in default
  form N227 94
response
  defendant's response pack 87, 303–11
  flow diagram 426
  to letter before claim 48–9
Royal Institution of Chartered Surveyors 61

search
  limits 189
  potential problems 189
  reasonable 188
search orders
  affidavit evidence 213
  application 174
security for costs
  application to court 178–82
  claimant making enforcement difficult 179
  claimant outside Hague Convention State 178–9
  claimant's ability to provide 180
  discretion of court 178
  effect 181–2
  failure to comply with rule 182
  form 181–2
  grounds 178–9
  impecuniosity 179, 180
  procedure 181
  property within jurisdiction 181
  relevant factors 179–81
  statutory provisions 179
  strength of claim 180
  timing 181
seizure
  exempt items 285–6
self-incrimination privilege 194

service
    acknowledgement of 87, 88–90, 429
    additional proceedings 128
    address for 80–1
    application notice 160
    by court 82
    by party 82
    certificate of service (N215) 82, 312–13
    claim form 77–83
        time for 81
    court documents 84–5
    deemed date calculation 81–2, 84–5
    dispensing with 81
    document exchange 77, 78
    e-mail 78–9
    electronic means 78–9, 80
    extension of time 83–4
    fax 77, 78
    foreign elements 32–3
    leaving at address 77, 78
    limited companies 79
    next working day 78
    notice of service on partner 78, 314
    out of jurisdiction
        contract cases 83
        Hague Convention countries 83
    particulars of claim 85–6
    partnerships 78
    personal 77, 78
    persons served 79–80
    place for service 80–1
    postal 77, 78
    solicitor's authority to accept 79–80
setting aside default judgment 95
    application 167–70
    costs orders 170, 431
    discretionary grounds 167–9
    mandatory grounds 167
settlements
    after issue of proceedings 234–7
    children's claims 74, 255–6
    compromise 256
    consent orders 235
    discontinuance 256
    judgments 235
    negotiations 50–1
        authority of solicitor 233–4
        basis on which to conduct 234
    offer to settle
        see also **Part 36 offer**
        'without prejudice' 237–8
    Part 36 offers see **Part 36 offer**
    patients 255–6
    persons under disability 255–6
    pre-action
        costs 234
        interest 234
        recording 234
    Tomlin orders 235–7
    'without prejudice' correspondence 50–1
single joint expert 42, 49, 229–30
site visits 42–3
skeleton arguments 259–60, 416–17

small claims track 8
    allocation to 143–5
    costs management 152
    disclosure 185
    trial 8
sole traders 75
solicitors
    authority 15
    Code of Conduct principles 16
    confidentiality duty 14
    confirmation of instructions 37–8
    conflict of interest 14–15
    core duties 16
    disclosure duties 191, 200–1
    duty as advocate 15
    duty to court 4, 15
    instructing counsel 43–4, 257–8
    instructing expert witnesses 41, 49, 224–5
    interviewing witnesses 38–40
    preservation of documents 40–1
    researching the law 52
    service of claim on 79–80
    site visits 42–3
    statement of truth, signature 71–2
    writing to client after first interview 38
split costs order 245–8, 437
standard of proof 29
statement of costs
    summary assessment 164, 343–7
statement of truth
    amended statements of case 119
    claim form 70–3, 297–8
    evidence in support of application 160
    expert report 226
    omitted 72
    particulars of claim 106–7, 110
    signature
        client 71
        companies 71
        partnerships 71
        solicitor 71–2
    witness statements 210
statements of case
    amendments 117–19
        before service 117
        costs 119
        directions following 119
        outside limitation period 119
        with permission 117–18
        statement of truth 119
        without permission 119
    defence see **defence**
    defining issues 115–17
    disclosed documents 100
    effect of stay on time limits 95
    formalities 100–1
    further information see **request for further information**
    particulars of claim see **particulars of claim**
    professional conduct 101
    reference to law 99–100
    reply to defence 115
    role 97–8
    statement of truth 71

statements of case – *continued*
  witnesses 98, 99–100
statutory charge 23
striking out
  case management power 134–7
  inadequate statements of case 134–5
  non-compliance sanction 135–6
structured settlement procedure 59
substitution of parties 76–7
success fee 19
summary judgment applications
  costs 173, 432
  directions 173
  grounds 170–1
  orders 172–3
  procedure 171–2

taking control of goods
  controlled goods agreement 286
  county courts 284–5
  High Court 284, 285
  items exempt from seizure 285–6
telephone hearings 161
third parties
  additional proceedings 126, 127
  disclosure 199–200
  funding 22
third party debt orders
  choice of court 288
  costs 289
  deposit taking institutions 289
  procedure 289
timetables
  case management 4, 7, 145
  for trial 261
***Tomlin* orders 235–7**
tort
  damages 26
  interest claims 31
  limitation 24–5
tracing 282
track allocation 7–8
  automatic transfer of money claims 141–2
  directions questionnaire
    case management information 140
    completion 139–41
    costs 141
    experts 140
    failure to file 142
    Form N181 138, 139–41, 316–21
    pre-action protocols 140
    scrutinising opponent's 142
    trial 141
    witnesses 140–1
  dissatisfaction with allocation 143
  factors considered 142–3
  fast track 145–7
  financial value of claim 142–3
  multi-track 147–52
  notice of proposed allocation 138–9
  small claims track 143–5
trade unions
  funding litigation 22

trial
  briefing counsel 43–4, 257–8, 473–5
  bundles 147, 259–60
  child witnesses 265
  claimant's case
    cross-examination 263–4
    evidence 263–4
    examination in chief 263
    opening speech 263
    re-examination 264
  closing speeches 265
  costs *see* **costs**
  cross-examination 263–4
  defendant's case 264
  examination in chief 263
  final preparations 257–60
  hostile witness 264
  judgment 265
  live text use 262
  order of proceedings 262–4
  overview 8, 421
  Part 36 application 265
  preliminary issues 262
  previous inconsistent statement 264
  professional conduct 261–2
  re-examination 264
  small claims track 8
  timetable 261
  venue 261
  witnesses
    attendance 258
    experts 258–9
trial bundle 147, 259–60

unless order 136–7

video conferencing 161
vulnerable witnesses 4–5

winding up
  enforcement by 291
'without prejudice' documents 196
  settlement negotiations 50–1
'without prejudice' meeting of experts
  sample statement 470–1
witness statements 38–40, 98, 99
  contents 208–9
  drafting 210–11
  as evidence in chief 211
  exchange 207
    fast track 146
  exhibits in connection with 209–10
  form 208–11
  hearsay evidence 211, 216–17
  late service 212–13
  new evidence 208, 209
  non-service sanctions 212–13
  objections 208
  opinion evidence 213
  own words 209
  sample 468–9
  source of information and belief 209
  statement of truth 210

witness statements – *continued*
    structure 208–9
    in support of application 181
    sworn *see* **affidavits**
    template 210, 410
    use at trial 211
    use by opponent 211
witness summary 39, 211–12
witnesses
    attendance at trial 258
    children 265
    compulsory attendance 39
    experts *see* **expert evidence**

witnesses – *continued*
    hostile 264
    interview by solicitor 38–40
    oral evidence 206–7, 211, 214–21
        experts 143, 146, 149, 224, 230
    professional conduct 38–9
    proof of evidence 39–40
    reluctant 39
    statements *see* **witness statements**
    in statements of case 98, 99–100
    summaries 211–12
    vulnerable 4–5
Woolf reforms 1–5